A HISTORY OF ENGLISH CRITICISM

A HISTORY

OF

ENGLISH CRITICISM

BEING THE ENGLISH CHAPTERS OF

A HISTORY OF CRITICISM AND LITERARY TASTE IN EUROPE

REVISED, ADAPTED, AND SUPPLEMENTED

BY

GEORGE SAINTSBURY

M.A. Oxon.; Hon. LL.D. Aberd.; Hon. D.Litt. Durh.

HONORARY FELLOW OF MERTON COLLEGE, OXFORD
LATE PROFESSOR OF RHETORIC AND ENGLISH LITERATURE
IN THE UNIVERSITY OF EDINBURGH

WILLIAM BLACKWOOD & SONS LTD.
EDINBURGH AND LONDON
MCMLV

PREFACE.

My publishers having requested me to prepare a separate edition
of the English part of my *History of Criticism*, which appeared
in three volumes between 1900 and 1904, I saw no objection
to complying. One of my subordinate (and not so very subordinate) objects in writing the larger book was to vindicate
our literature from the charge of being second-hand and second-
rate in this matter: and while some reviewers had received
the old prejudice too obediently, and with too little knowledge
of the subject, to discard it, others were good enough to admit
that I had made out no bad case. There can be no doubt
that, in the present drift of public opinion, an ever-dwindling
minority of students obtains the full liberal education of
Classics first, with English and Modern Languages to follow
in the natural order; but that is no reason why the majority
should be deprived of the meat they are prepared to digest.

At the same time, a reader who has no knowledge of ancient
criticism cannot understand the history of English; and one
who does not know something of the state of Italian criticism at the beginning of ours—of that of French, German, and
French again later—will find himself constantly at a loss. He
requires, therefore, a new Introduction, to put him in a position
to comprehend the standpoint of Ascham and Gascoigne, as

well as much that follows; while there should be, in place of the old Interchapters, shorter links of the same kind, giving a brief view of the new influences as they came in. Those who desire more light still on these subjects can, and should, consult the larger *History*.

The bulk of the matter may remain unaltered except for careful revision and correction of slips, obscurities, and the like. If some such things have escaped notice I can only ask for pardon.[1]

EDINBURGH, *October* 1911.

[1] Since this book was in type, I have received, by the great kindness of Professor Bouton of New York University, a full abstract of the rare pamphlet on Fielding and Novel-writing (see *Hist. Crit.*, ii. 497, note, or *inf.*, p. 230, note). It is highly laudatory of Fielding himself (with some gentle strictures on morality, digressions, &c.), but severe on his imitators and followers, including Smollett. On some general points of novel-writing, and of criticism at large, the writer is sound and almost original. The piece is worth reprinting.

CONTENTS.

CHAPTER I.

INTRODUCTORY.

	PAGE
The documents of criticism when English practice in it began	1
Earliest Greek criticism to Plato	3
Aristotle—his great importance	4
Drawbacks to it	5
Later Greek Criticism : The *De Interpretatione*	7
Dionysius of Halicarnassus	8
The Rhetoricians	9
Plutarch	9
Lucian	10
Longinus	10
His principles and message	11
The Gospel of Transport and the rejection of Faultlessness	12
Photius	13
Latin Criticism	13
Cicero	14
Horace—The *Epistle to the Pisos*—its consummate expression	14

	PAGE
Its plausibility	15
Its superficial, desultory, and arbitrary character	16
Others—Petronius	17
Quintilian	17
Great merits of his work generally	17
Interesting shortcomings in his judgment of authors	18
Later Latin critics of the Empire and the "Dark" Ages	20
Barrenness of the Middle Ages	21
Except Dante	21
The *De Vulgari Eloquio*	22
Criticism revived in Italy at the Renaissance : The strict Neo-Classics : Vida	23
The innovators : Patrizzi	23
French criticism : The *Pléiade*	24
Earliest glimmerings of English	25

CHAPTER II.

ELIZABETHAN CRITICISM.

	PAGE
Backwardness of English Criticism not implying inferiority	27
Its cause	28
The influence of Rhetoric and other matters	29

	PAGE
Hawes	29
The first Tudor critics	30
Wilson : his *Art of Rhetoric*	32
His attack on "Inkhorn" terms	32
His dealing with Figures	33

Cheke: his resolute Anglicism and anti-preciosity 34
His criticism of Sallust . . . 35
Ascham 36
His patriotism 37
His horror of Romance . . . 37
And of the *Morte d'Arthur* . . 38
His general critical attitude to Prose 39
And to Poetry 39
The craze for Classical Metres . 40
Special wants of English Prosody . 40
Its kinds: (1) Chaucerian . . 41
(2) Alliterative 41
(3) Italianated 42
Deficiencies of all three . . . 42
The temptations of Criticism in this respect 43
Its adventurers: Ascham himself . 43
Watson and Drant 44
Gascoigne 45
His *Notes of Instruction* . . 46
Their capital value 47
Spenser and Harvey . . . 48
The Puritan attack on Poetry . 52
Gosson 52
The School of Abuse . . . 53
Lodge's *Reply* 53
Sidney's *Apology for Poetry* . 54
Abstract of it 55
Its minor shortcomings . . . 57
And major heresies . . . 57
The excuses of both . . . 58
And their ample compensation . 59
King James's *Reulis and Cautelis* . 59

Webbe's *Discourse* 61
Slight in knowledge . . . 62
But enthusiastic 63
If uncritical 63
In appreciation 65
Puttenham's (?) *Art of English Poesie* 65
Its erudition 66
Systematic arrangement . . . 67
And exuberant indulgence in Figures 68
Minors: Harington, Meres, Webster, Bolton, &c. 69
Campion and his *Observations* . 70
Daniel and his *Defence of Rhyme* . 72
Bacon 74
The *Essays* 75
The *Advancement of Learning* . 75
Its denunciation of mere word-study 76
Its view of Poetry 77
Some *obiter dicta* 77
The whole of very slight importance 78
Stirling's *Anacrisis* . . . 79
Ben Jonson: his equipment . . 80
His *Prefaces*, &c. 81
The Drummond Conversations . 82
The *Discoveries* 83
Form of the book 86
Its date 87
Mosaic of old and new . . . 87
The fling at Montaigne . . . 88
At *Tamerlane* 89
The Shakespeare passage . . 89
And that on Bacon . . . 89
General character of the book . 91

INTERCHAPTER I. 93

CHAPTER III.

DRYDEN AND HIS CONTEMPORARIES.

Dead water in English Criticism . 105
Milton 105
Cowley 106
The Prefatory matter of *Gondibert*. 107
The "Heroic Poem" . . . 108
Davenant's *Examen* . . . 109
Hobbes's Answer 110
Dryden 111
His advantages 112
The Early Prefaces 113
The *Essay of Dramatic Poesy* . 116

Its setting and overture . . . 116
Crites for the Ancients . . . 117
Eugenius for the "last age" . . 118
Lisideius for the French . . . 118
Dryden for England and Liberty . 119
Coda on rhymed plays, and conclusion 120
Conspicuous merits of the piece . 121
The Middle Prefaces . . . 122
The *Essay on Satire* and the *Dedication of the Æneis* . . . 125

The Parallel of Poetry and Painting 126
The *Preface to the Fables* . . 126
Dryden's general critical position . 126
His special critical method . . 127
Dryden and Boileau . . . 129
Rymer 131
The *Preface to Rapin* . . 132
The *Tragedies of the Last Age* . 134
The *Short View of Tragedy* . . 135
The Rule of Tom the Second . . 137

Sprat 138
Edward Phillips . . . 138
His *Theatrum Poetarum* . . 139
Winstanley's *Lives*. . . 140
Langbaine's *Dramatic Poets* . 140
Temple 141
Bentley 141
Collier's *Short View* . . 142
Sir T. P. Blount . . . 144
Periodicals: *The Athenian Mercury*, &c. 146

INTERCHAPTER II. 147

CHAPTER IV.

FROM ADDISON TO JOHNSON.

Criticism at Dryden's death . 159
Bysshe's *Art of English Poetry* . 159
Gildon 162
Welsted 163
Dennis 164
On Rymer 165
On Shakespeare . . . 167
On "Machines" . . . 168
His general theory of Poetry . . 168
Addison 170
The *Account of the Best known English Poets* . . . 171
The *Spectator* criticisms . . 173
On True and False Wit . . 174
On Tragedy 174
On Milton 176
The "Pleasures of the Imagination" 177
His general critical value . . 180
Steele 181
Atterbury 182
Swift 183
The Battle of the Books . . 183
The Tale of a Tub . . . 184
Minor works 184
Pope 185
The *Letters* 186
The Shakespeare Preface . . 187
Spence's *Anecdotes* . . . 187
The *Essay on Criticism* . . 188
The *Epistle to Augustus* . . 190
Remarks on Pope as a critic . 190
And the critical attitude of his group 193
Philosophical and Professional Critics 194

Trapp 195
Blair 195
The *Lectures on Rhetoric* . . 196
The *Dissertation on Ossian* . 197
Kames 198
The *Elements of Criticism* . 199
Campbell 203
The *Philosophy of Rhetoric* . 203
Harris 206
The *Philological Enquiries* . 207
"Estimate" Brown: his *History of Poetry* 209
Johnson: his preparation for criticism 210
The Rambler on Milton . . 213
On Spenser 215
On History and Letter-writing . 216
On Tragi-comedy . . . 216
"Dick Minim" . . . 217
Rasselas 217
The Shakespeare Preface . . 218
The *Lives of the Poets* . . 219
Their general merits . . . 220
The *Cowley* 222
The *Milton* 222
The *Dryden* and *Pope* . . 223
The *Collins* and *Gray* . . 224
The critical greatness of the *Lives* and of Johnson . . . 226
Minor Criticism: Periodical and other 229
Goldsmith 231
Vicesimus Knox 232
Scott of Amwell 233

INTERCHAPTER III. 235

CHAPTER V.

THE ENGLISH PRECURSORS OF ROMANTICISM.

The first group 246	Studies in Prosody 273
Mediæval reaction 246	John Mason : his *Power of Num-*
Gray 247	*bers* in Prose and Poetry . . 274
Peculiarity of his critical position . 248	Mitford—his *Harmony of Language* 276
The Letters 249	Importance of prosodic inquiry . 279
The *Observations* on Aristophanes	Sterne and the stop-watch . . 279
and Plato 252	Shaftesbury 281
The *Metrum* 253	Hume 283
The Lydgate Notes . . . 254	Examples of his critical opinions . 284
Shenstone 256	His inconsistency 286
Percy 257	Burke on the Sublime and Beautiful 287
The Wartons 259	The Scottish æsthetic - empirics :
Joseph's *Essay on Pope* . . 259	Alison 288
The *Adventurer* Essays . . 260	The *Essay on Taste* . . . 289
Thomas Warton on Spenser . 261	Its confusions 290
His *History of English Poetry* . 263	And arbitrary absurdities . . 291
Hurd : his Commentary on Addison 265	An interim conclusion on the æs-
The Horace 266	thetic matter 292
The Dissertations . . . 267	The study of Literature . . 294
Other Works 268	The study of Shakespeare . . 295
The *Letters on Chivalry and Ro-*	Spenser 296
mance 268	Chaucer 297
Their doctrine . . . 269	The Elizabethan minors . . 297
His real importance . . . 271	*Note :* T. Hayward . . . 298
Alleged imperfections of the group 272	Middle and Old English . . 298

INTERCHAPTER IV. 301

CHAPTER VI.

WORDSWORTH AND COLERIDGE : THEIR COMPANIONS AND ADVERSARIES.

Wordsworth and Coleridge . . 310	Coleridge's examination of Words-
The former's Prefaces . . 311	worth's views . . . 315
That to *Lyrical Ballads,* 1800 . 312	His critical qualifications . 316
Its history 312	Unusual integrity of his critique . 317
The argument against poetic diction,	Analysis of it 317
and even against metre . 313	The "suspension of disbelief" . 318
The appendix : Poetic Diction again 314	Attitude to metre 318
The Minor Critical Papers . . 314	Excursus on Shakespeare's *Poems* . 320

Challenges Wordsworth on "real" and "rustic" life . . . 320
"Prose" diction and metre again . 321
Condemnation in form of Wordsworth's theory 322
The *Argumentum ad Gulielmum* . 322
The study of his poetry . . . 323
High merits of the examination . 323
Wordsworth a rebel to Longinus and Dante 324
The *Preface* compared more specially with the *De Vulgari* . . 325
And Dante's practice . . . 325
With Wordsworth's . . . 326
The comparison fatal to Wordsworth as a critic . . . 327
Other critical places in Coleridge . 328
The rest of the *Biographia* . . 328
The Friend 329
Aids to Reflection, &c. . . . 330
The *Lectures on Shakespeare,* &c. . 330
Their chaotic character . . . 331
And preciousness 332
Some noteworthy things in them: general 333
And particular 334
Coleridge on other dramatists . 334
The *Table Talk* 334
The *Miscellanies* 335
The Lecture *On Style* . . . 336
The *Anima Poetæ* 337
The *Letters* 339
The Coleridgean position and quality 340
He introduces once for all the criterion of Imagination, realising and disrealising . . . 341
The "Companions" . . . 342
Southey 343
General characteristics of his Criticism 344
Reviews 345
The Doctor 345
Altogether somewhat *impar sibi* . 346
Lamb 347
His "occultism" 348
And alleged inconstancy . . 348
The early *Letters* 349
The *Specimens* 350
The Garrick Play Notes . . . 351
Miscellaneous Essays . . . 352
Elia 352
The later *Letters* 353
Uniqueness of Lamb's critical style 354
And thought 355

Leigh Hunt : his somewhat inferior position 356
Reasons for it 356
His attitude to Dante . . . 357
Examples from *Imagination and Fancy* 358
Hazlitt 361
Method of dealing with him . . 361
His surface and occasional faults : Imperfect knowledge and method 362
Extra-literary prejudice . . . 363
His radical and usual excellence . 364
The English Poets 365
The *Comic Writers* 366
The Age of Elizabeth . . . 367
Characters of Shakespeare . . 368
The Plain Speaker 369
The Round Table, &c. . . . 371
The Spirit of the Age . . . 372
Sketches and Essays . . . 373
Winterslow 373
Hazlitt's critical virtue . . . 373
In set pieces 374
And universally 375
Blake 376
His critical position and dicta . 377
The "Notes on Reynolds" . . 378
And Wordsworth 378
Commanding position of these . 378
Sir Walter Scott commonly undervalued as a critic . . . 380
Injustice of this 381
Campbell : his *Lectures on Poetry* . 382
His *Specimens* 382
Shelley : his *Defence of Poetry* . 384
Landor 386
His lack of judicial quality . . 386
In regular Criticism . . . 386
The Conversations 387
Loculus Aureolus 388
But again disappointing . . . 388
The revival of the Pope quarrels . 389
Bowles 389
Byron 391
The *Letter to Murray,* &c. . . 391
Others : Isaac Disraeli . . . 392
Sir Egerton Brydges . . . 393
The Retrospective Review . . 393
The *Baviad* and *Anti-Jacobin* . 396
With Wolcot and Mathias . . 396
The influence of the new *Reviews,* &c. 398
Jeffrey 399
His loss of place and its cause . 399
His inconsistency 400

His criticism on Madame de Staël	401
Its lesson	403
Hallam	403
His achievement	404
Its merits	404
And defects	404
In general distribution and treatment	405
In some particular instances	406
His central weakness	407
And the value left by it	408

INTERCHAPTER V. 409

CHAPTER VII.

BETWEEN COLERIDGE AND ARNOLD.

The English Critics of 1830-60	425
Wilson	425
Strange medley of his criticism	426
The *Homer* and the other larger critical collections	426
The *Spenser*	427
The *Specimens of British Critics*	428
Dies Boreales	429
Faults in all	429
And in the republished work	430
De Quincey: his anomalies	431
And perversities as a critic	432
In regard to all literatures	433
Their causes	433
The *Rhetoric* and the *Style*	434
His compensations	435
Lockhart	436
Difficulty with his criticism	436
The *Tennyson* review not his	436
On Coleridge, Burns, Scott, and Hook	437
His general critical character	438
Hartley Coleridge	438
Forlorn condition of his criticism	438
Its quality	439
Defects	439
And examples	440
Maginn	440
His parody-criticisms	441
And more serious efforts	441
Macaulay	443
His exceptional competence in some ways	443
The early articles	443
His drawbacks	443
The practical choking of the good seed	444
His literary surveys in the *Letters*	445
His confession	446
The *Essays*	446
Similar dwindling in Carlyle	448
The earlier *Essays*	450
The later	450
The attitude of the *Latter-day Pamphlets*	451
The conclusion of this matter	452
Thackeray	453
His one critical weakness	453
And his excellence	454
Blackwood in 1849 on Tennyson	455
George Brimley	457
His Essay on Tennyson	458
His other work	460
His intrinsic and chronological importance	461
"Gyas and Cloanthus"	461
Milman, Croker, Hayward	462
Sydney Smith, Senior, Helps	462
Elwin, Lancaster, Hannay	463
Dallas	464
The *Poetics*	464
The Gay Science	465
Others: J. S. Mill	467

CHAPTER VIII.

ENGLISH CRITICISM FROM 1860-1900.

Matthew Arnold: one of the greater critics	468
His position defined early	469
The *Preface* of 1853	470
Analysis of it	470
And interim summary of its gist	473

Contrast with Dryden	473
Chair-work at Oxford, and contributions to periodicals	474
On Translating Homer	475
"The grand style".	475
Discussion of it	476
The Study of Celtic Literature	479
Its assumptions	480
The *Essays :* their case for Criticism	480
Their examples thereof	482
The latest work	483
The Introduction to Ward's *English Poets*	484
"Criticism of Life"	484
Poetic Subject or Poetic Moment	485
Arnold's accomplishment and position as a critic	487
The Carlylians	490
Kingsley.	491
Froude	492
Ruskin	492
G. H. Lewes	493
His *Principles of Success in Literature*	493
His *Inner Life of Art*	495
Bagehot	495
R. H. Hutton	496
His evasions of literary criticism	497

Pater	497
His frank Hedonism	498
His *polytechny* and his style	498
His formulation of the new critical attitude	499
The Renaissance	499
Objections to its process	500
Importance of *Marius the Epicurean*	500
Appreciations and the *Guardian Essays*	501
Universality of his method	504
J. A. Symonds	504
Thomson ("B. V.")	505
William Minto	506
His books on English Prose and Poetry	507
H. D. Traill	507
His critical strength	508
On Sterne and Coleridge	508
Essays on Fiction	509
"The Future of Humour"	509
Others : Mansel, Venables, Stephen, Lord Houghton, Pattison, Church, &c.	510
Patmore	511
Edmund Gurney	512
The Power of Sound	512
Tertium Quid	513

CONCLUSION

CONCLUSION	515

APPENDIX.

THE OXFORD CHAIR OF POETRY.

The holders	525
Eighteenth-century minors	526
Lowth	527
Hurdis	527
The rally : Copleston	528
Conybeare	530
Milman	530
Keble	531

The *Occasional* [English] *Papers*	532
The *Prælections*	532
Garbett	535
Claughton	536
Doyle	536
Shairp	537
Palgrave	538
Salutantur vivi	539

BIBLIOGRAPHICAL NOTE.

Besides the books on special authors, periods, and subjects which will be found mentioned in the footnotes, the following general works of reference may be tabulated here :—

(By the present writer.) *A History of Criticism and Literary Taste in Europe.* 3 vols. Edinburgh and London, 1900-1904. The matrix of this present volume.

(By the same.) *Loci Critici.* Boston, U.S.A., and London, 1903.

Gayley and Scott. *Introduction to the Methods and Materials of Literary Criticism.* Boston, U.S.A., 1899.

Théry. *Histoire des Opinions Littéraires.* Paris, ed. 2, 1849.

Egger. *Essai sur l'Histoire de la Critique chez les Grecs.* Paris., ed. 3, 1887.

Spingarn. *History of Literary Criticism in the Renaissance.* New York, 1899.

A HISTORY OF ENGLISH CRITICISM.

CHAPTER I.

INTRODUCTORY.

THE DOCUMENTS OF CRITICISM WHEN ENGLISH PRACTICE IN IT BEGAN — EARLIEST
GREEK CRITICISM TO PLATO—ARISTOTLE : HIS GREAT IMPORTANCE—DRAWBACKS
TO IT — LATER GREEK CRITICISM : THE 'DE INTERPRETATIONE'—DIONYSIUS OF
HALICARNASSUS — THE RHETORICIANS — PLUTARCH — LUCIAN — LONGINUS — HIS
PRINCIPLES AND MESSAGE — THE GOSPEL OF TRANSPORT AND THE REJECTION
OF FAULTLESSNESS — PHOTIUS — LATIN CRITICISM — CICERO — HORACE : THE
'EPISTLE TO THE PISOS': ITS CONSUMMATE EXPRESSION — ITS PLAUSIBILITY —
ITS SUPERFICIAL, DESULTORY, AND ARBITRARY CHARACTER — OTHERS : PETRO-
NIUS — QUINTILIAN — GREAT MERITS OF HIS WORK GENERALLY — INTERESTING
SHORTCOMINGS IN HIS JUDGMENT OF AUTHORS — LATER LATIN CRITICS OF THE
EMPIRE AND THE "DARK" AGES—BARRENNESS OF THE MIDDLE AGES—EXCEPT
DANTE — THE 'DE VULGARI ELOQUIO'— CRITICISM REVIVED IN ITALY AT THE
RENAISSANCE : THE STRICT NEO-CLASSICS : VIDA — THE INNOVATORS : PATRIZZI
—FRENCH CRITICISM—THE 'PLÉIADE'—EARLIEST GLIMMERINGS OF ENGLISH.

WHEN English literary criticism came (under the conditions
and circumstances to be stated in the next chapter) into an
The docu- existence, tardy indeed, but not so very much
ments of crit- tardier than criticism in other modern languages,
icism when the subject itself was, of course, a very old one.
English prac-
tice in it But though the documents of it, as a critic of the
began. mid-sixteenth century might know them, covered
something like two thousand years in dates of composition,
they were by no means evenly spread over that period. For
about half of it, indeed—say, roughly, the space covered by the
'Dark" and "Middle" Ages only, from a little after 500 A.D.
to a little before 1500—they were almost non-existent; the
few important exceptions will be noted later. But for seven

or eight hundred continuous years, at least, in Greek and Latin literature, they were abundant and various, while for some forty or fifty years, at least, before the time of our English beginning, they had been and were being produced in Italy. Now classical literature was, in the opinion of every scholar of the sixteenth century, the absolute canon of literature generally; and Italian was the modern literature which was chiefly attracting subordinate study. Had not the labours of Renaissance scholars and the printing-press together made study of the classics not merely fashionable and almost imperative but comparatively easy, English criticism might still have lingered. Had not the Italians taken the subject up so vigorously, it is certain that some—though it may be matter of question how much—stimulus would have been lacking to the prosecution of the new art.

But the Italians themselves, though they deviated more widely than they knew or intended from classical principles in some respects, never, at first, failed to start from the classics. The "Ancient and Modern Quarrel"[1] did not arise till the close of the sixteenth century or the beginning of the next; and though men of intelligence (see the latter part of this chapter) might be pretty early forced to acknowledge that there were kinds of modern literature to which, inasmuch as they had not existed in ancient times, ancient rules did not apply, they themselves did not for some generations proceed to question the authority of these ancient rules in themselves. And in hardly any respect did the classical researches and classical discoveries of the Renaissance provide so much new matter, and treat it in so novel a fashion, as in regard to the critical department of Greek and Latin letters. Idolised as Aristotle had been in the Middle Ages, the *Poetics* had been less studied than any other of his works, and the *Rhetoric* had been obscured by later compilations. Plato had been little read, and lay under suspicion of heresy. The great critic who is usually called (and quite possibly was) Longinus, seems to have been known to Greek contemporaries of Dante: but he exercised no influence in the West till Robortelli printed him in

---

[1] *V. inf.*, in the chapters concerning these centuries.

mid-sixteenth century. The Greek rhetoricians were first made accessible by Aldus. Horace had never been a very popular author in the Middle Ages, and, with their knowledge of classical literature, it was hardly possible to perceive the drift of the *Epistle to the Pisos.* Quintilian was not completely known till the beginning of the fifteenth century. But now all these and others were eagerly studied, and a department of intellectual exercise, which had before been absolutely unknown, or casually glimpsed only by men of the highest genius like Dante and Chaucer, lay open. It was promptly occupied as far as its ancient subjects went; and the exercise was almost as promptly turned in application to the new literatures themselves.

The work so long neglected, and at last so greedily studied, had certain general characteristics, not all of which were *Earliest* equally applicable to the criticism of the newer *Greek criti-* literatures. From a very early time it would seem *cism to* that the restless intellect of the Greeks had de- *Plato.* voted itself to the subject, especially in reference to the great national treasure of the Homeric poems. But— very mainly owing, no doubt, to the absence of any other literature for comparison—this study directed itself, as far as the few and fragmentary remains of it that we possess go, to questions of matter chiefly, and especially to the rather dangerous division of allegorical interpretation. The growth of oratory, however, and its political importance in the small Greek communities, made technical analysis of "Rhetoric," and instruction in it, a necessity. Rhetoric as necessarily involves, and sometimes becomes almost identical with, Criticism, and as the body of creative literature itself increased, it was impossible that the Greek mind should not busy itself with that literature's forms and general phenomena. But neither the Socrates of Plato nor the Socrates of Xenophon gives us the idea of a man who would pay much attention to literary criticism proper: all the more so because "the enemy"—the Sophist—was, as a rule, a professional teacher of something like it. And Plato himself, though one of the very greatest men of letters of all time, and possessed of an intensely subtle and powerful mind as well as of the keenest appreciation of beauty, either caught from his master or developed for himself a positive aversion to poetry—then practically the only original part of literature—as deceptive to the individual and disastrous to the State. He in fact expresses, for the first time, the curious mental attitude of distrust towards the productions of great human art. And this has always held sway over a large part of mankind since, though it has been expressed by persons holding points of view so different from Plato's and from each other's as those of all the Fathers of the Church and some later orthodox theologians on the one side, and as the Lollard and Puritan sectaries, with their English descendants, on the other.

But if the greatest pupil of Socrates followed his master in a direction antipathetic to criticism, the greatest pupil of Plato *Aristotle— his great im- portance.* did not pursue a similar course. Despite his ethical preoccupations, there is in Aristotle—if we except, perhaps, his attitude to Comedy and to mere style—no sign of contempt or distrust in respect of literature. The object of Poetry is to please by "imitating" nature ; the object of Oratory (hardly any other division of prose was yet really recognised) is to "persuade," but persuasion is largely affected by the appropriate selection and arrangement of words. In the *Poetics* and the *Rhetoric* we get these general principles elaborated and applied after a fashion which laid down once for all some of the greatest doctrines of criticism. The adequacy, if not the accuracy, of his famous definition of tragedy, to be found below,[1] is still, and always must be, matter of controversy ; and so also must be his assignment of overpowering preponderance to the "fable" or "action," his comparative depreciation of character, and the like. But, on the other hand, the widest changes of style in drama have only established more solidly

---

[1] "Tragedy is an imitation of some action that is serious, entire, and of some magnitude, by language embellished and rendered pleasurable, but by different means in different parts—in the way, not of narration, but of action, effecting through pity and terror the purgation of such [*al.* 'these'] passions." On the difficulties of the word "purgation," and indeed on the whole subject, see Butcher, *Aristotle's Theory of Poetry and Fine Art*, 3rd ed. London, 1902.

his doctrine that the essence of tragic situation consists, not so much in crime or in mere misfortune as in a certain "failing" or "frailty,"[1] perhaps not very bad in itself, but leading in some cases to crime, in all to misfortune. Such, again, is his recognition—constantly forgotten but essential to real criticism —that each literary kind, if not each literary production, has its "peculiar pleasure,"[2] which, and which only, you are entitled to demand from it. While in prose criticism, among many other notable *dicta*, he has, in the same way, once for all established the distinction between "staple"[3] words, which provide clearness and perspicuity, "foreign" or "strange" words, which strike, affect, and elevate. Already we find in him that irreconcilable objection to "frigidity," bombast, &c., which distinguishes all ancient criticism; while sometimes he flies higher and achieves a great philosophical as well as critical truth, in opposition to Plato, by declaring that poetry is more really "philosophical" than history, and that a probable impossibility can be more artistic and satisfactory than a possibility which is not made probable.

But great as the advance apparently made by Aristotle was; fundamental as (in a manner) his work must always be; almost imperative as it is that some direct knowledge of that work should precede any inquiries into the later criticism which sometimes directly rests on him and always touches questions first, as far as is known, by him mooted—there are two grave drawbacks, each of which has done harm almost to the present day. The first arises from the fact that, careful and philosophical as was Aristotle's induction, it was almost inevitably based upon existing Greek literature only, and is in fact based, in so far as we have it, not even on the whole of that. When Dryden (*v. inf.*) said that "if Aristotle had seen ours [*i.e.*, our form of tragedy] he might have changed his mind," he not only hit a fatal blow against part, but made a damaging innuendo against the whole of the great Stagirite's criticism. When Aristotle wrote he had before him abundant supplies of a certain kind of Tragedy and of a certain kind of Comedy; but the kind of the tragedy was unnecessarily

Drawbacks to it.

---

[1] ἁμαρτία.　　　[2] οἰκεία ἡδονή.　　　[3] κύρια and ξένα.

strict in one way and that of the comedy unnecessarily loose in
another. He had plenty of Epic, which unfortunately we have
not got, though we have the most important pieces; but most
of this epic again appears to have been of one type only. He
had great lyric—some of the greatest in the world's literature ;
but he says little about it, and one somehow gathers that he would
not have set it very high. He had again some, if not much, of
the very greatest history in the world: you can hardly go
beyond Thucydides in one direction; beyond Herodotus, and
perhaps even Xenophon, in another. But he deals with it,
directly, not at all. Worst of all, he probably had nothing that
can properly be called prose fiction—a few short tales, "mimes,"
&c., being the only possible exceptions. From this came the
disproportionate importance that he ascribes in poetry to the
mere fiction, the *mere* "imitation," as if it and nothing else were
poetry. He is, in fact, dealing with a literature magnificent
in partial accomplishment, but not (to use an excellent phrase
of De Quincey's) "fully equipped," and he is not dealing even
with the whole of what that literature gives him. Hence at
least a risk of error as to things that he sees, and almost
certainly of deception when his dealings are applied to other
things which he had not seen.

The other drawback—one which may not at first seem to
have much connection with the first, but which really works
together with it, disadvantageously, on nearly all ancient
criticism—is that Aristotle never, as a matter of fact, gives us
what in modern terms may be called an "appreciation" of a
single book, much less of a single author. We may find references to books and authors, but they are always incidental and
illustrative, never thorough-going and all-embracing. It is
"the kind" in poetry, the several devices of the craft in
rhetoric, wherein he is interested. It is true that he never—he
was both too much of a philosopher and too much of a critic
to do so, even if he had not, by date and circumstance,
been spared such temptation — pushes this system, of
criticism by kinds or title-labels, to the damnatory extreme
of the *neo*-classics, who falsely alleged his principles in the
seventeenth and eighteenth centuries. But he goes near to it

sometimes, and the negative fault of nowhere giving a real critical estimate of play or poem, of poet or prose - writer, attaches itself to him throughout. And this drawback pursues ancient criticism: with some exceptions, it is never entirely removed. Dionysius of Halicarnassus to some extent, Quintilian (perhaps relying on Dionysius), and Longinus most of all, *are* exceptions, but they are almost the only ones of importance. Now even Johnson, no Romantic or rebel to the Classics, added to the title of his projected but never written *History of Criticism* the words, *as it relates to Judging of Authours;* and there can be little doubt that this judging of " authours " and of books, sometimes as preliminary to such judgment, sometimes as sufficient in itself, is the most profitable and the most pleasant part of the whole matter, if it is not even that matter's whole end and aim.

The order of descent by pupilship is said to have been further illustrated in the case of Theophrastus, the chief disciple of Aristotle, in regard to criticism; but the few and well-known remains which we have of his work do not touch the subject. He has, however, been credited with the useful but tolerably obvious division of styles into ornate, plain, and middle. Nor have we much representing the later Greek age before Christ.[1] There are, however, two exceptions of note— the book usually called *De Interpretatione*,[2] but more boldly re - christened by its latest and best editor and translator, Professor Roberts, *On Style.*[3] Perhaps this is going a little too far, and "Of Expression" would be the best rendering. It is practically a rhetorical treatise on " Composition," now busying itself about very simple points of an almost schoolboy kind, now ascending higher. But it seldom touches on really critical questions, and still more seldom on criticism of particular books and authors. It used to be attributed to Demetrius the Phalerean, a man famous both in letters and politics, and it would so have come not much later than Aristotle himself.

Later Greek criticism : The De Interpretatione.

---

[1] All, or at least most, of what there is will be duly found discussed in the larger *History of Criticism.*

[2] Περὶ ἑρμηνείας.

[3] Cambridge, 1902.

But it is pretty certainly Alexandrian, though the practically " common " name " Demetrius " has been kept for its author. The busy literary courtiers of the Ptolemies must have dealt largely with critical matters : it seems certain that the original suggester of the doctrines of Horace's *Epistle to the Pisos* was a certain Neoptolemus of Parium, also Alexandrian ; but we have no solid remains even of the grammarians and textual critics who made Alexandria so famous.[1]

On the other hand, the works by or ascribed to Dionysius of Halicarnassus, a teacher of rhetoric and historian who lived *Dionysius* at Rome from 50 B.C. to 7 B.C., are of the greatest *of Halicar-* interest and importance, and rank with those of *nassus.* Aristotle and Longinus as furnishing the chief storehouse of Greek criticism proper.[2] The remarks of Dionysius on style and composition generally show much originality, and we have from him the first distinct acknow- ledgment of the immense importance of actual *words*, even of actual *letters*. But he is almost of more value as giving us detailed examinations of critical writers, some at length, as of Plato, Thucydides, and Demosthenes, others more frag- mentary but precious, inasmuch as some of them are on authors now lost.[3]

It does not matter that these estimates are sometimes injured by the tendency of all times to regard, and be guided by, sympathy with substance rather than appreciation of form, and by the special *parochialism* of the Greeks. This leads Dionysius, as a Halicarnassian, to exalt Herodotus, his towns- man, at the expense of Thucydides ; just as it later led Plutarch, a Bœotian, to depreciate Herodotus as too little favourable to his countrymen. We cannot be too grateful to Dionysius for such observations—truisms in a way, like all observations worth making, but constantly ignored to the present day—as that " beautiful words are the cause of beauti- ful phrase "; that " no rhythm whatsoever is banished from

---

[1] In fact, the whole body of ancient *Scholia* on Greek, and Commentaries on Latin, literature is singularly bare of criticism proper.

[2] His *Three Literary Letters* have been edited, with annotations, by Prof. Roberts (Cambridge, 1901).

[3] Extracts from Dionysius will be found in *Loci Critici.*

unmetred composition "; that Plato's style combines pellucid freshness with peculiar charm of archaism ; that the noblest style is that which has the greatest variety. We owe him the actual quotation of Sappho's hymn to Aphrodite, and of the only considerable passage we possess of Pindar's Dithyrambic. And if we agree with him less here, we can learn almost as much, and be almost as grateful for the learning, from his repeated expression—in regard to Plato— of that horror of gorgeousness in prose style which is so characteristic of the ancients.

His successors in Greek criticism must be despatched briefly,[1] for we are here only concerned with the more important influences and supplies of matter which they could furnish to English criticism when it started, or had furnished to that Italian criticism which was to be so powerful on all modern successors.

Of these, the whole mass of the strictly "rhetorical" writers must be briefly set aside. They had, it has been said, no small influence, by their publication at the Aldine press,

The Rheto-ricians. in determining the general resurrection of criticism : but they could give little assistance in detail, and the chief special subject to which they helped to draw attention—that of Figures—had much more bane than antidote in it.[2] Plutarch has, in his miscellaneous writings, a

Plutarch. great deal of ostensibly critical or semi - critical matter, and has been put forward by some as a possible author of the great little book attributed (*v. inf.*) to Longinus. But, except in the way of general exhortation to the study of literature, made even then from a wrong point of view, it is almost impossible to discover any real critical stuff in him. The moral prepossession dominates everywhere. It is dif-

[1] They will be found fully treated in the original *History*.

[2] In one, half rhetorician, half bellettrist, Philostratus (*c.* 200), occurs a remarkable definition of φαντασία, Imagination, as "fashioning what one has not seen, supposing and conceiving it on the analogy of the Real." There

is nothing in any other ancient—not even in Plato, not even in Longinus— so like the Imagination of Shakespeare in the famous "of Imagination all compact," and of Coleridge, *v. inf.* (For Addison and *his* Imagination, *v. inf.* likewise.)

ferent with Lucian. One of the shrewdest of men, possessed
himself of an admirable gift of writing; a trained rhetorician, though a deserter (not without good reason,

Lucian.   as things went) from Rhetoric's service ; a born
miscellanist too, and a magazine-writer and reviewer a
millennium and a half before magazines and reviews
existed, — it would have been amazing if Lucian had not
touched the subject. He did: and the *Vera Historia* is partly
criticism of " wonder " voyages and travels; the *Lexiphanes*
a satire on accepted and outlandish phraseology ; the " How
History should be Written " a half sober, half ironic tractate of
advice. " The Master of the Orators " and " The Twice-accused
Man " are skits on his old profession ; and the very curious
little piece entitled " To one who said ' You are the Prometheus of Prose,' " a tantalising but entirely baffling discussion of the writer's own attitude in Dialogue and literature
generally. In no author is this critical attitude more omni-
present than in Lucian; and from hardly any can a reader,
whom gods have made critical himself, learn more. But as a
direct teacher of the subject he can hardly be said to exist.

The greatest of late Greek critics — a critic as great as
Aristotle, though in a slightly different kind — was the

Longinus.   author of the treatise commonly called *On the
Sublime*,[1] and long identified with Longinus, the
Minister of Zenobia. Of the doubts (sometimes too peremptorily turned into positive denials) of this identification, it is
not necessary to say any more here than that the evidence
for it is very weak, but that the evidence against it, of a
kind really to be called evidence, is non-existent. And the
contingent question whether the date is the first century
after Christ as some think, or that of Longinus (*fl. c.* 250 A.D.)
himself, is of still less importance. The book, from its
references, cannot be earlier than the period of the Roman

---

[1] Περὶ Ὕψους. The best edition of
the Greek (*with* translation) is that of
Prof. Rhys Roberts, uniform with
other books recently mentioned (Cambridge, 1899). There are also valuable
English versions by Mr H. R. Havell, with
an Introduction by Mr A. Lang (London, 1890) and by Mr A. O. Prickard
(Oxford, 1906). The present writer
has selected and translated the most
important passages in *Loci Critici*.

Empire; how late it may be in that period is, from internal evidence, quite uncertain. The only fact of importance for us is that here — in Greek of a curious and rather difficult but not barbarous type, and showing on the one hand a knowledge of all classical Greek literature, on the other a state of society such as only existed in the first three centuries of the Christian era — is a critical treatise which adopts a remarkably different standpoint from that of almost all its predecessors, and contains some of the most admirable critical utterances to be found in all literature.

The great and distinguishing note of Longinus is that his main critical object is "appreciation" — the quest after the

His principles and message. great principle or quality of "Sublimity" and the enjoyment of the "transport" which it causes. It is on this quality that he lays his finger from the first. It had been admitted, though by no means universally, that Art should delight, but almost always with a *caveat* that it must at the same time instruct or profit. Longinus cuts off this *caveat*, and insists wholly and solely on the transport—the ecstasy—caused by great literary art. He is not, indeed, wholly and unintelligibly "modern,"—he would not be half so interesting or a tithe as important if he were,—but he is surprisingly so. He still lays, and could hardly but lay, if he was (as the historical Longinus certainly was) a rhetorical teacher, stress—too much stress— on the "Figures," not only as useful tickets of nomenclature, but as positive self-existing agents in the production of Sublimity. He still has the excessive terror of gorgeous style—of language poetically figurative in the other sense, and the like. And, most noteworthy of all, though his usual judgments are startlingly like our own, he is uncompromisingly "ancient" in his dislike to the "Romantic" elements—the adventures, the marvels, and so forth—of the *Odyssey*. Hence he is no portent or sport, dissociated from his time and kind by irreconcilable differences. He is simply one who has "gone up higher,"—has transcended (like his own Sublime) the lower rules, and roamed beyond the narrow inductions of his predecessors; who has, above all, discovered that it is only the

intermediate business, if even that, of the critic to frame
rules and kinds for the production of great literature,—that
it is his highest and main business to enjoy and examine
the great literature that has been produced, and so to aid the
enjoyment of it by others.

Of this exaltation of view-point and alteration of attitude
his little book — it is, unfortunately, not only truncated at

The gospel of Transport and the rejection of Faultlessness. the end, but presents numerous large and lamentable gaps in its actual continuity—provides con-
stant examples. The substitution of "transport" for
the old rhetorical shibboleth of "persuasion" comes
at the very beginning, and would almost suffice of
itself. The decreased insistence on mere story or subject—
he does, of course, admit and insist that great thoughts will
make for great expression, but does not take it as matter of
course that they will effect it—is another. His heightening
of the expressions of Dionysius[1] into the final doctrines that
"beautiful words are the very light of thought," and that
critical judgment is "the last acquired fruit of long endeavour," put, finally, important and, up to his time (whatever
it was), mostly neglected truths. Although all the best
critics had laid some proper stress on rhythmical harmony
in prose as well as verse, no one had been quite so emphatic
on the subject as he is. But the most important thing,
perhaps, to be noticed in his treatise, from the point of view
of critical progress, is its rejection—its positive treading
under foot — of "faultlessness" as a criterion of perfection.
For though it is not to be supposed for a moment that the
greater ancient critics — that such a man as Aristotle, for
instance—would have definitely inculcated *mere* faultlessness
as constituting perfection, yet it cannot be denied that the
whole tendency of classical criticism—including, perhaps, some
of Longinus's own in the instance noted above—is in this
direction. The provision of large numbers of positive rules
inevitably suggests—to the feebler minds, at any rate—that if

---

[1] One of the conjectural attributions
in the MSS. is to "Dionysius" the
Halicarnassian being not so named,
though probably intended. But it is
a mere guess, with "Longinus" or
"Anon." for suggested alternatives.

you do not break these rules it will be all right with you. The nervous terror of excess has an even stronger influence in the same direction.

But Longinus, though he may have shared this last to some extent, did not allow himself to be influenced by it here; and more or less elaborately prefers the "faulty" Homer, Sophocles, Demosthenes, Plato, to the "faultless" Apollonius, Ion, Hypereides, Lysias. Now, as the reader will see at once, this of itself involves judging of the books in themselves and by the effect they produce, not by reference to previously constructed rules of fault and beauty.

Of later Greek criticism little need be said. The late rhetoricians—Libanius, Themistius, Julian the Apostate, and others—give not much in amount and still less in positive

Photius. value; and from Byzantine times the really remarkable *Bibliotheca* of the Patriarch Photius (late ninth century) is almost the only book that need be mentioned. From the special point of view of influence, indeed, these writers hardly require notice here.[1] Even Longinus, though published in mid-sixteenth century, did not exercise much till late in the seventeenth, when, by one of the oddest *coups* of Fortune, he was taken up, translated, and treated as an authority by the critic of the world (among persons not dunces), who was probably most alien from him in spirit, purpose, and creed—by Boileau.

The intrinsic importance of the Latin criticism which the men of the English Renaissance had, or might have had, before

Latin Criticism. them is very much smaller than that of the Greek; and what it has is, as in other cases, almost wholly, and not always intelligently, borrowed from Greek itself. But it was handier of application, and so it happened that, while Quintilian and Seneca and others almost dominated the stubborn intelligence of Ben Jonson, Horace's medley of secondhand and arbitrary dogma in the *Epistle to the Pisos* took

[1] The reason why Photius appears is that he gives us a large amount of interesting *estimate* of books—especially valuable considering his date.

early effect, and became pure gospel to the late seventeenth and most of the eighteenth century.

Latin criticism itself began as late as might be expected, and even later. There seems to have been hardly anything

Cicero. deserving the name before Varro, of whose work in the kind we have practically nothing left, and Cicero, from whom we have a great deal, naturally enough devoted mainly to his own division of oratory, but amounting to very little in substance. Most of it is—again naturally enough—concerned with actual technical rhetoric, and we have seen that while this might promise something, it performed very little for real literary criticism. Of his most famous and interesting critical dictum of the proper kind, in reference to his own contemporary, Lucretius, the text is uncertain and the interpretations of that text hopelessly contradictory.[1] And the most interesting thing that can be extracted from him is a list (which has been actually drawn up) of Latin technical critical terms corresponding to those which had been previously evolved into something like a regular critical vocabulary by the Greeks.

When, however, we pass from Cicero to Horace, the case is not a little altered. There are numerous passages of criticism

Horace— in the Satires and Epistles, but they all yield in
The Epistle interest, and may even be said to be subsumed in
to the Pisos substance, when we turn from them to the above-
—its con- mentioned *Epistle to the Pisos*,[2] commonly, unjusti-
summate ex- fiably, and in almost every sense unfortunately
pression. termed the *Ars Poetica*. Unjustifiably, for there is no evidence that Horace ever called it so, and very little likelihood that so shrewd a person, so well versed in the ways of the world,

---

[1] *Ep. ad Quintum*, ii. 11 (*or* 9): *Lucretii poemata, ut scribis, ita sunt: multis luminibus ingenii multæ tamen artis.* This is said to be the MS. reading, and but for the stumbling-block of *tamen* would be wholly laudatory. But in that case *tamen* is almost impossible to admit with its usual meaning of "adversative quali-

fication": and most editors, till recently, have supposed that a *non* must have slipped out either before *multis* or before *multæ.*

[2] The present writer has inserted a translated cento of this in *Loci Critici.* The verse translations of Jonson and of Lord Roscommon are in a manner classics, and prose ones abound.

would have attached such an *ampulla* of a title to a slight
tissue of hints on Dramatic Composition, thrown together in
what his own adorers in the eighteenth century might have
called an elegant dishabille, as by a gentleman of parts and
spirit speaking to gentlemen of the like. But its singular
clarity and felicity of expression—the very triumph, on the
less poetical side, of its author's gifts in that way,—and the
manner in which it puts, with that confident and unhesitating
though urbane dogmatism which has such an effect on the
common run of readers, the opinions on the subject, and the
typical method of arriving at those opinions, common during
the whole classical period—these things naturally made it all-
powerful with the neo-classics. You wanted "rules," and you
had them here, in a form giving no trouble to the memory and
attractive to the taste, put forth, not by a mere "preceptist"
but by a craftsman of unsurpassed competence in more than
one branch of poetry itself, with no insolent dictation or irritating pedantry, but in an easy take-for-granted manner, which
it might seem at once insolent and pedantic to resist.

The little piece is, indeed, full of plausible generalities, put
(as must again be noted) with the most unsurpassable and

*Its plausi-
bility.*
hardly imitable literary neatness. Who can deny
that "inconsistent things must not be joined"; that
excess of any quality is dangerous, and attempts at
constant variation teasing; that you should choose subjects
suitable to your strength; not endeavour to say everything you
can think of; stick (not without a little gentle attempt at
originality) to accepted diction and metre; abstain from disgusting subjects; try to instruct or delight, or both? It is
true that all this is exceedingly obvious,—obvious (sometimes,
at any rate) not with the true and great obviousness noticed
above, but with a kind of superficiality which, when stripped of
Horace's exquisite expression, looks half puerile and half anile.
But, with that expression especially, it sounds exactly fitted to
provoke the sentiment which Tennyson has so excellently
formulated—

" I thowt 'a said whot 'a owt to 'a said,"

and to encourage a mild intellectual satisfaction.

Yet when other passages—or even some of these same passages with context and second consideration — are studied, *Its superficial, desultory,* perhaps the effect is not quite so satisfactory. In the first place, the whole is seen to be extremely desultory. There is not, as in Aristotle, any theory of drama presented; and though there is, as in Aristotle and on larger basis, a sort of induction from existing dramas as to what will and will not "do," it is in the highest degree fragmentary and casual. But the greatest and most pervading drawback is the extraordinary arbitrariness of many, indeed of most, of the special precepts.

For instance, why lay down (without reason given except as to usage) that certain metres have been irrevocably and *and arbitrary character.* finally assigned to certain kinds of poetry? Why declare that the personages of mythology—Achilles, Medea, &c.—are always to be presented in the same way? Still worse (for some fight might be made, in the cases just mentioned, for preserving types already famous in art), why assign a slavish uniformity to ages, classes, &c., and insist that boys shall always be boys, old men always testy and avaricious, &c. For it is this which leads directly to such ineffable absurdities as Rymer's contention that Iago ought not to have been represented as a crafty traitor, because he is a soldier, and soldiers are always frank and open.

And the habit hardens on him. Why must plays always have five acts, no more and no less? Why may there not be a "tetragonist"? The experience of ages has shown that, though it must be carefully managed, a murder on the stage need not excite disgust; and that so far from "keeping out of sight what can be presently narrated," you will be much better advised in keeping in sight whatever you can, and curtailing mere narration as much as possible.

In short, Horace shows, with every possible advantage of form but to considerable disadvantage of substance when carefully studied, the strictest classic, nay, neo-classic, creed of order, restraint, positive rule.

There is, in proportion, far more critical matter, both of an indirect and a direct purtenance, in post-Augustan than in earlier Latin; and the satiric poets—Juvenal to some extent, Persius and Martial still more—are full of it. There is also a good deal in the elder Seneca, some in Pliny, and *Others—* at least two passages in the *Satyricon* of Petronius *Petronius.* which attracted attention from the critics of the seventeenth century. But most of the references which would bear out this statement are so fragmentary, scattered, and in their individual value minute, that it would be impossible to give them in detail, and rather useless to summarise them here.[1] It may, however, be said generally that while they indicate the general tone of tendency mentioned above, they give us evidence of a strong bent in the Roman taste, when it took to literature at all, towards a semi-barbaric gorgeousness which was the reverse of Attic.

But the most important Latin document of this period—the most important document, indeed, of the whole of Latin *Quintilian.* criticism—is furnished by the *Oratorical Institutions* or *Institutes of Oratory* of Quintilian. It may indeed be said that a man's competence in criticism itself may almost be measured by the estimate he holds of this remarkable book. It is not precisely a work of genius : its intentions were too strictly practical for that. But it is the work of a master in his own craft, who to professional knowledge and practical experience added unusual common-sense, a sufficient dose of originality, a saving sense of humour, acuteness, freedom from any blinding or paralysing partiality, with at the same time a sensible though not extravagant patriotism in regard to the literature of his own country.

To those who have not read the book the oratorical pre-*Great merits* occupation may seem likely to do harm,—indeed, *of his work* it has been said already more than once that *generally.* Oratory and Rhetoric, while encouraging the existence, did somewhat damage the quality and range, of ancient

---

[1] They will be found cited and discussed in the larger *History.* The passages from the *Satyricon* are translated in full in *Loci Critici.* These latter condemn the practice of declamations on imaginary subjects (a very favourite one at Rome), but inculcate the doctrine of *furor poeticus,* which was much taken up by the earlier neo-classics to give licence to the restriction of their "rules," but discountenanced by the later.

criticism. But Rhetoric had long acquired the nearly complete sense of "literary education," and Quintilian's identification of good writing and good speaking, though it may or may not be excessive from the oratorical side, is wholly advantageous from the literary. His description of a good Professor of Oratory is applicable, with hardly a word changed, to a good reviewer or critic; his judgments of Greek or Latin writers, whether original or not, whether wholly sound or not, are almost purely literary; his remarks on the linguistic peculiarities of Greek and Latin, as contrasted with each other, are wholly connected with literary effect; and while, of course, portions (and large portions) of his work are of professional and technical bearing only, almost the whole of the last five books might be separated and (with nothing but verbal changes) made into a Treatise of Criticism. On Figures Quintilian, though he may pay disproportionate attention to them, still is perfectly aware of the danger of the actually and constantly committed fault of separating off some quite ordinary fashion of speech, ticketing it with a long Greek name, and thenceforward regarding the ticket as something real, the attaching of which to similar phrases is an illuminative and profitable exercise of the critical faculty.[1] His remarks on the old divisions of style are sensible ; his criticism of Seneca the Younger—who represented the very opposite school of writing to his own—is one of the fairest of such things that we have from any ancient ; and, in fact, his whole voluminous work is full of enlightenment, judgment, and intellectual instruction generally.

The chief point in which Quintilian comes short is the point in which nearly all ancient critics except Longinus do come short, the "judging of authors," especially poets, from the appreciative point of view. That he to *Interesting shortcomings in his judgment of authors.* some extent subordinates his criticism to the *rhetorical* value of the author concerned is no great matter. It was natural, it was constantly done ; and, odd as it seems to us, it was pushed to the most extravagant extent by both Greeks (especially with regard to

[1] His earlier observation that " it is often difficult to distinguish Faults from Figures of Speech," is also a far-reaching one, and worth meditating.

Homer) and Latins (especially by Macrobius in regard to Virgil). But we are somewhat disappointed, though not exactly surprised, especially if we remember Longinus's selection of this poet as a "faultless" foil to Homer, when we find that Apollonius Rhodius has only "an evenly sustained mediocrity." For the charm of the Rhodian is a distinctly Romantic charm, and to this (since even Longinus could be insensible to it in the greater instance of the *Odyssey*) we could not expect Quintilian to be open. The point of view is again obvious, again disappointing, again instructive, when we find Theocritus allowed to be admirable as far as he goes, but patronisingly dismissed as "rustic and pastoral." Alcæus "descends to amorous subjects," Æschylus is bombastic and extravagant.

But the Greek judgments may be—to some extent they certainly are—traditional: the Latin must be awaited with more interest, as likely to be more at first hand. Disappointment, it is to be feared, will come here too. Virgil is not over-praised—in fact, not merely the Virgiliomaniacs of the Renaissance, but some more modern adorers of the Mantuan, might think Quintilian half-hearted. If he is, as some might expect, nearer to Renaissance monomania on the prose side in his Ciceronianism, it is very pardonable. He is far from being as enthusiastic as he might be about Ovid on the one hand, or about Plautus on the other. But the sharpest, though very far indeed from the most unexpected, contrast with modern ideas is to be found in reference to Catullus and to Lucretius. That Horace should be praised, and praised highly, is inevitable and well deserved; but when we find that he is almost the only Roman lyric poet worth reading, and that Catullus is only mentioned for his "bitter iambics"—*i.e.*, satires—then the difference of the point of view does come before us unmistakably. And, on the other hand, that Lucretius—that the *furor arduus Lucreti* which Statius, a contemporary of Quintilian's and a poet, had covered himself with glory and almost deserved his Middle-Age popularity by defending—should be dismissed with the mere ticket "difficult" pinned to him,—this is the most eloquent item in the whole catalogue of judgments. It is pretty certain that Quintilian disapproved of the poet's philosophical and religious ideas; it is pretty certain also, from his remarks about Ennius and Plautus himself, that he did not like his archaisms of language. The matter of even the *De Rerum Natura*, putting these things aside, is certainly not always "easy." And the poetry, as poetry, does not strike Quintilian at all.

After Quintilian, the importance and interest of Latin critical writing diminishes, if it does not actually come to an end. Aulus Gellius and Macrobius provide *Later Latin critics of the Empire and the "Dark" Ages.* us with a good deal of critical matter, not of much value; and we continue to get indirect supplies from the poets, such as Ausonius. Moreover, there is a certain bulk, but not nearly so large as that in Greek, of directly rhetorical writing, including a treatise (pretty certainly spurious) assigned to St Augustine, who was actually a teacher of the subject. On the verge of the so-called "Dark" Ages, or over it, we have documents of a certain attraction, because they show us the way in which literary appreciation died off into the almost absolute trance which we find in the "Middle" Ages. Such are the numerous critical observations of the poet-bishop, Sidonius Apollinaris, and the allegorical treatise on the Seven Liberal Arts (among them very particularly Rhetoric) of Martianus Capella, which retained a certain vogue for a good thousand years. Both are of the fifth century. Later still (sixth century), we find curious but substantially valueless examples of indulgence in criticism based upon false etymology, and mythology hopelessly muddled, from a group of writers bearing, with various additions, the name of "Fulgentius"; and a little from the theologian-encyclopædist Isidore of Seville and the poet Venantius Fortunatus, both of whom lived into the seventh century; while there is something of the sort in the "Venerable" Bede, who did not die till the eighth had seen its first generation. We find, as the various barbarian or at least provincial elements begin to leaven the lump of the decaying Roman Empire, an increasing taste for not very well chosen gorgeousness of language, an increasing attention to the mere technical details of Rhetoric, and an increasing fancy for chasing the will-o'-the-wisps of ethical - allegorical interpretation; but at the same time an ever - decreasing grasp of anything that can be called real criticism.[1]

In the Middle Ages proper this grasp has relaxed itself to such an extent that for the most part it hardly even attempts to touch its object. A few technical *Barren-ness of the Middle Ages.* treatises exist, and we meet, now and then, a more or less banal expression of approval of a writer. Even the earliest dawn of the Renaissance in Italy and the renewed study (from at any rate textual and subject points of view) of the classical authors, give us little, if anything, of the kind; and from the year 1000 A.D. —the rather imaginary line between "Dark" and "Middle"— to the beginning of the sixteenth century, we meet practically nothing[2] that can be called a critical treatise of substantive importance, except the solitary and in some respects rather puzzling, but extraordinarily valuable, document of the *De Vulgari Eloquio* by Dante.[3]

The puzzles of this—or most of them—do not concern us. The document itself does. In it we have—beyond all reasonable doubt, from the pen of the greatest man of *Except Dante.* letters between Homer and Shakespeare—a treatise of astonishing precision on the nature and conditions of a standard literary language; and on the formal (and something more than the formal) characteristics of Italian poetry, extending incidentally to poetry at large. Dante knows, with sufficient and almost scientific exactness, the actual distribution of European speech. He recognises and deplores the excessively *dialectic* character of Italian, and recommends—

[1] Those who are curious about these matters will find them fully treated in vol. i., bk. ii., chap. iv., and bk. iii., chap. i., of the larger *History*.

[2] For what there is see *Hist. Crit.*, the rest of the chapter just cited, and chap. iii. of the same bk. and vol.

[3] The original Latin can best be read in Dr Moore's *Opere di Dante* (Oxford, 1897); but there is a good annotated English translation by Mr Ferrers - Howell (London, 1890). A catena of the most striking passages is in *Loci Critici*. An interesting article on Dante's critical attitude, from a point of view different from that taken here, appeared in the *Quarterly Review* for October 1910, by Professor Herford.

what he was, in fact, himself to accomplish — the selection
and construction, out of these dialects, of a standard form. And
then he goes on to the consideration of the special requirements and characteristics of poetry itself.

The critical interests of Dante's work are numerous, and
deserve thorough examination. In fact, every one who attacks
The De   this subject seriously should read, in original or
Vulgari   translation, the tractate, which is very short, as
Eloquio.   a companion to Aristotle's two books, the *Epistle
to the Pisos*, Longinus, and some at least of Quintilian. As
a whole, its importance lies in the way in which this almost
greatest of poets—a poet of intense quality as regards choice
of subject as well as religious and philosophical attitude,—a
poet as different as even fancy can conceive from a mere
"idle singer of an empty day" or a mere versifier—insists
upon *form*, upon language. It is impossible to lay more stress
than Dante does on the necessity of specially selected and
"sifted" poetic diction, in which the finest words only shall
be permitted,—no childish talk or rustic phrase, no weak or
trivial term. It is impossible, again, to insist more peremptorily and perseveringly than he does on the importance of
the mere "numbers"—on the fact that the poet must not
expect harmony of versification to come to him of its own
accord, and as a sort of necessary accident inseparable from
his other gifts, but must choose the best example and follow
the best modes in order to attain it. It is not easy to think
of a greater contrast to the usual attitude of the ancients or
to that of some of the moderns, as in the cases especially of
Wordsworth and Mr Matthew Arnold.[1] Attempts have indeed been made to disprove this opposition, and the student
should form his own opinion after consulting them; but if
the comparison be made without preliminary prejudice, there
is no doubt in the mind of the present writer what the
result will be.

The book, though there are early references to its existence,
seems to have remained long unknown as an actual composition; and it was only when Italian was beginning to devote

----

[1] See the sections on them *post*.

itself largely to criticism that it at last (1529) appeared translated into the vernacular, and issued with rather ambiguous

Criticism revived in Italy at the Renaissance : The strict Neo-Class- ics : Vida. attribution by the poet Trissino. But it was published in the original form fifty years later (1577),
and between the two dates a great critical efflor-
escence had taken place. Still in Latin, but in verse,
was written the remarkable treatise of Girolamo
Vida (1527). In this the neo-classic system—of
not merely worshipping and imitating the ancients, but of
actually "stealing"[1] from them to the utmost possible extent,
of adoration of Virgil, of dislike of conceit and of Romance—
is formulated in a fashion which extracted from Pope,[2] as a
sympathiser, two centuries later, the epithet "Immortal," and
which now remains the *ne plus ultra* of purely arbitrary
criticism. But the vernacular soon asserted its rights; and
from Daniello (1536) onwards a great herd of dissertators and
commentators[3] devoted themselves for more than two full
generations to the subject. Most of these took a more or less
classical line, and to one of the two greatest of them (which
actually deserves the doubtful honour is uncertain), Castelvetro
(1570) and Scaliger (1561), is assigned the establishment of
those three Unities — Action, Time, and Place — of which
Aristotle had not so much as mentioned the third, and had
passed the second over as lightly as possible. Yet another,
Minturno (1559), spent great labour and considerable ability
on the subject, and has been supposed by some to have exercised
special influence on Sir Philip Sidney.

Some, however, of these critics, observing the difficulty of
accommodating Aristotle's rules—especially as tightened and

The innovators : Patrizzi. extended by his new interpreters—to the recent work
especially in Romance, of which Italy was justly
proud, began to hint, or even boldly to assert,
doctrines or positions which, though they hardly made many
disciples at the moment, were destined to inspire the great

---

[1] Vida's own word.

[2] In the *Essay on Criticism*. Vida's
Poetics were actually translated by
Pitt, one of the Pope school, and
figure in Chalmers's and other collections of "British Poets."

[3] The names of nearly all of them
will be found, and the work of nearly
all of any importance is analysed, in
the larger *History*.

Romantic revolt of the latest eighteenth century. They [1] asked why times in which manners, morals, religion were so totally different, should prescribe to comedy its lines and scenes and atmosphere. They [2] pointed out that while classical Epic might be a fine and legitimate kind, that supplied no reason why modern Romance, with its different plan, should not be equally fine and equally legitimate. They began, almost or quite for the first time, to take a directly historical view of literature,—a view which almost inevitably suggests to those who take it that one part of the history cannot lay down the law to another. And one of the most remarkable of them, the Platonist philosopher Patrizzi (perhaps not in full consciousness of the meaning of his words, but practically), anticipated [3] the whole modern Romantic doctrine on the matter by declaring that "any subject *that can be poetically treated* is a fit subject for poetry," thereby at once transferring the criterion and constructive essence of poetry from the subject to the treatment. But these innovators, who were followed up remarkably in Spain on the special subject of the Drama, were on the whole in a minority, and the general bent of Italian criticism was towards the classical side, or rather the neo-classic—that is to say, the strengthening and hardening of "classical" rules. [4]

Considering the relations of France and Italy at the time, it was inevitable that this Italian criticism should affect the *French critic-* "Middle Kingdom" of the West before it came to *ism: The* us; and it did, but not to so great an extent as might *'Pléiade.'* perhaps have been thought. The great Pléiade school was indeed critical or nothing, and its two chief poets each produced critical treatises [5] of note, the latter of which undoubtedly had something to do with early prosodic criticism, both in Southern and Northern English. But the effect was not very strong or lasting, and it never amounted to anything like that produced later, when Malherbe and Boileau had sup-

---

[1] For instance, the comic writer and tale-teller, Grazzini ("Il Lasca").

[2] Especially the famous novel-writer Cinthio and his pupil Pigna.

[3] In his *Della Poetica* (1586).

[4] *V. inf.*, Interchapter I.

[5] The *Défense et Illustration de la Langue Française* of Du Bellay (1549), and the *Abrégé de l'Art Poétique* of Ronsard (1565).

planted Ronsard and Du Bellay, with infinite loss to poetry and not much gain to criticism.

From our own older writers the Elizabethans, when at last they took to criticism, had very little to borrow or to criticise.[1]

Earliest glimmerings of English. There never was a poet with much more of the critical spirit in him than Chaucer; and he shows it not merely in *Sir Thopas*, which is mainly a parody-criticism of the sillier forms of Romance, but in a hundred remarks, serious and comic, scattered about his work. Yet he never dreamt of providing any regular critical work, though a parallel to Dante's *De Vulgari Eloquio* from him is not actually unthinkable, and would have been priceless. More immediately before the Elizabethans themselves, Wyatt and Surrey had gone about the work of Ronsard and Du Bellay, but without manifesto or dogmatic utterance. It was all to come : and at last it came.

[1] The chief exceptions are some interesting but very novice-like observations of Caxton's, in the Prefaces to some of his translations and editions.

CHAPTER II

ELIZABETHAN CRITICISM.

BACKWARDNESS OF ENGLISH CRITICISM NOT IMPLYING INFERIORITY—ITS
CAUSE—THE INFLUENCE OF RHETORIC AND OTHER MATTERS—HAWES—
THE FIRST TUDOR CRITICS—WILSON : HIS 'ART OF RHETORIC'; HIS AT-
TACK ON "INKHORN TERMS"—HIS DEALING WITH FIGURES—CHEKE : HIS
RESOLUTE ANGLICISM AND ANTI-PRECIOSITY—HIS CRITICISM OF SALLUST
—ASCHAM—HIS PATRIOTISM—HIS HORROR OF ROMANCE, AND OF THE
'MORTE D'ARTHUR'—HIS GENERAL CRITICAL ATTITUDE TO PROSE,
AND TO POETRY—THE CRAZE FOR CLASSICAL METRES—SPECIAL WANTS
OF ENGLISH PROSODY—ITS KINDS : (1) CHAUCERIAN—(2) ALLITERATIVE
—(3) ITALIANATED—DEFICIENCIES OF ALL THREE—THE TEMPTATIONS
OF CRITICISM IN THIS RESPECT—ITS ADVENTURERS : ASCHAM HIMSELF
—WATSON AND DRANT—GASCOIGNE—HIS 'NOTES OF INSTRUCTION'—
THEIR CAPITAL VALUE—SPENSER AND HARVEY—THE PURITAN ATTACK
ON POETRY—GOSSON—'THE SCHOOL OF ABUSE'—LODGE'S 'REPLY'—
SIDNEY'S 'APOLOGY FOR POETRY'—ABSTRACT OF IT—ITS MINOR SHORT-
COMINGS AND MAJOR HERESIES—THE EXCUSES OF BOTH, AND THEIR
AMPLE COMPENSATION — KING JAMES'S 'REULIS AND CAUTELIS'—
WEBBE'S 'DISCOURSE'—SLIGHT IN KNOWLEDGE, BUT ENTHUSIASTIC,
IF UNCRITICAL, IN APPRECIATION—PUTTENHAM'S (?) 'ART OF ENGLISH
POESIE'—ITS ERUDITION—SYSTEMATIC ARRANGEMENT AND EXUBERANT
INDULGENCE IN FIGURES — MINORS : HARINGTON, MERES, WEBSTER,
BOLTON, ETC.—CAMPION AND HIS 'OBSERVATIONS'—DANIEL AND HIS
'DEFENCE OF RHYME'—BACON—THE 'ESSAYS'—THE 'ADVANCEMENT
OF LEARNING'—ITS DENUNCIATION OF MERE WORD-STUDY—ITS VIEW
OF POETRY—SOME "OBITER DICTA"—THE WHOLE OF VERY SLIGHT
IMPORTANCE—STIRLING'S "ANACRISIS"—BEN JONSON : HIS EQUIPMENT
—HIS 'PREFACES,' ETC.—THE DRUMMOND CONVERSATIONS—THE 'DIS-
COVERIES'—FORM OF THE BOOK—ITS DATE—MOSAIC OF OLD AND NEW
—THE FLING AT MONTAIGNE—AT 'TAMERLANE'—THE SHAKESPEARE
PASSAGE—AND THAT ON BACON—GENERAL CHARACTER OF THE BOOK.

THE fortune of England in matters political has often been
noticed; and it has at least deserved to be noticed, hardly less

often, in matters literary. One of the luckiest of these chances came at the time of the Renaissance; when the necessary changes were effected with the minimum of direct foreign influence, and so slowly that the natural force of the nation and the language was able completely, or almost completely, to assimilate the influences, both foreign and classical, that rained upon it.

Nor was this least the case in respect of criticism.[1] The history of this part of English literary evolution has been, *Backward-* until recently, much neglected; and it can hardly *ness of* be said even yet to have received comprehensive *English* attention. It is all the more necessary to bestow *Criticism* *not implying* some time and pains on it here, with at least some *inferiority.* fair hope of correcting an unfair depreciation. The Baron of Bradwardine (displaying that shrewd appreciation of contrast between English and Scottish characteristics which belonged, if not to himself, to his creator) remarked to Colonel Talbot that it was the Colonel's "humour, as he [the Baron] had seen in other gentlemen of birth and honour" in the Colonel's country, "to derogate from the honour of his burgonet." Gentlemen of the most undoubted birth and honour (as such things go in literature), from Dryden to Matthew Arnold, have displayed this humour in regard to English criticism. But there has been something too much of it; and it has been taken far too literally by the ignorant. M. Brunetière has expressed his opinion that Frenchmen would make *un véritable marché de dupe* if they exchanged Boileau, Marmontel, La Harpe, and Co. for Lessing and some others. I shall not in this place express any opinion on that question directly. But, if this book does what I shall endeavour to make it do, it will at least show that to exchange, for any foreign company, our own critics, from Sidney and Ben Jonson, through Dryden and Addison,

[1] The two chief monographs on this are J. E. Spingarn, *Literary Criticism in the Renaissance,* New York, 1899 (pp. 253-310), and Professor F. E. Schelling, *Poetic and Verse Criticism of the Reign of Elizabeth,* Philadelphia, 1891. Haslewood reprinted most of the texts in *Ancient Critical Essays,* 2 vols., London, 1811-15, and Mr Arber the most important in his *English Reprints.* Professor Gregory Smith has more lately edited the fullest collection yet issued (2 vols., Oxford, 1904).

Samuel Johnson and Coleridge, Lamb and Hazlitt, to Mr Arnold himself, would be "*un véritable marché de*"—Moses Primrose.

It will have been sufficiently seen in the last chapter that the backwardness of English—a backwardness long exaggerated, but to some extent real, and to no small extent healthy—was nowhere exhibited more distinctly than in the department which supplies the materials of this history. Until the close of the fifteenth century, and for some decades afterwards, not a single critical treatise on English existed in the English language, or even in Latin; the nearest approach, even in fragment, to any utterance of the kind being the *naïf* and interesting, but only infantinely critical, remarks of Caxton in his prefaces.[1]

The fact is that, not only until a nation is in command of a single form of "curial" speech for literary purposes, but *Its cause.* until sufficient experiments have been made in at least a majority of the branches of literature, criticism is impossible, and would, if possible, be rather mischievous than beneficial. Now England, though it possessed at least one very great author, and more than a fair number of respectable seconds to him, was, up to 1500 at least, in neither case. Till the end of the fourteenth century it had been practically trilingual; it was bilingual till past the end of the fifteenth, if not till far into the seventeenth, so far as literature was concerned. Nor, till the towering eminence of Chaucer had helped to bring the vernacular into prominence, was there any one settled dialect of primacy in the vernacular itself. Further, the fourteenth century was nearly at its end before any bulk of prose, save on religious subjects, was written; and for another century the proportion of translation over original work in prose was very large indeed.

At the same time the scholastic Rhetoric—which had always played to criticism the part of a half-faithless guardian, who keeps his pupil out of the full enjoyment of his property,

---

[1] Such as those on the "fair language of France," and the strictures passed by Margaret of England and Burgundy on the "default in mine English" (*History of Troy*); on the "right good and fair English" of Lord Rivers (*Dicts and Sayings of the Philosophers*), and the prefatory observations on Chaucer.

yet preserves that property in good condition to hand over

The influ- to him perforce at some future time — was still
ence of faithfully taught.[1] The enlarged and more accurate
Rhetoric
and other study of the classics at the Revival of Learning
matters. set classical criticism once more before students in
the originals; the eager study of those originals by Continental
scholars was sure to reflect itself upon England; and, lastly,
religious zeal and other motives combined, here as elsewhere,
to make men determined to get the vernacular into as complete
and useful a condition as possible. Nowhere does the intense
national spirit, which is the glory of the Tudor period, appear
more strongly than in this our scholastic and "umbratile"
division of the national life.

Long, indeed, before this scholastic and regular criticism made
its appearance, and during the whole course of the fifteenth

Hawes. century, critical appreciation, stereotyped and un-
methodised it may be, but genuine for all that, and
stimulating, had made its appearance. The extraordinary
quality of Chaucer, the amiable pastime-making of Gower,
and, a little later, the busy polygraphy and painful rhetoric
of Lydgate, had, almost from the moment of Chaucer's death,
attracted and inspired students. The pretty phrase about
Chaucer's "gold dew-drops of speech," which justly drew the
approval of a critic so often unjustly severe on ante-Renais-
sance work as Mr Arnold, was, as is known even by tyros in
the study of English literature, repeated, expanded, varied by
almost every prominent writer for a century and a quarter at
least, till it reached, not exactly final, but most definite and
noteworthy, expression in the work of Stephen Hawes, that
curious swan-singer of English mediæval poetry. In the to us
eccentric, if not positively absurd, exposition of the *Trivium*
and *Quadrivium* which diversifies the account of the courtship

---

[1] There has been some disposition
to deny this, and to argue that despite the constant use of the *word*
Rhetoric in the fifteenth century,
the teaching of the *thing* had declined.
I do not think there is much evidence
of this as regards England; and the
long and curious passage of Hawes,
to be presently discussed, is strong
evidence against it. Rhetoric has no
less than *eight* chapters of the *Pastime
of Pleasure*, as against *one* apiece for
Grammar and Logic.

of Grandamour and La Bell Pucell,[1] the praise of the Three is
led up to by a discussion of Rhetoric and Poetics so elaborate
and minute that it occupies more space than is given to all the
other Arts together, and nearly double that which is given to all
the rest, except a largely extended Astronomy. Rhetoric herself, after being greeted by and greeting her pupil in the most
" aureate " style, divides herself into five parts, each of which
has its chapter, with a " Replication against ignorant Persons"
intervening, and many curious digressions, such as the description of a sort of Earthly Paradise of Literature with four rivers,
" Understanding," " Closely-Concluding," " Novelty," and " Car-
buncles,"[2] and a " Tower of Virgil" in their midst. Lydgate
has been already praised for " versifying the depured[3] rhetoric
in English language," but he comes up once more for eulogy as
" *my* master" in the peroration, and has in fact considerably
more space than either Gower or Chaucer. Nor, confused and
out of focus as such things must necessarily appear to us, should
we forget that Hawes and his generation were not altogether
uncritically endeavouring at what was " important to *them*"—
the strengthening and enriching, namely, of English vocabulary,
the extension of English literary practice and stock.

Yet their criticism could but be uncritical: and the luck
above referred to appears first in the peculiar scholastic character of the criticism of the first English school of
critics deserving the name. No one of its members
was exactly a man of genius, and this was perhaps
lucky; for men of genius have rarely been observed to make
the best schoolmasters. All were fully penetrated with the
Renaissance adoration of the classics; and this was lucky again,
because the classics alone could supply the training and the
models just then required by English prose, and even to some
extent by English poetry. All were very definitely set against
Gallicising and Italianising; and yet again this was lucky,
because England had been overdosed with French influence

The first Tudor critics.

---

[1] *The Pastime of Pleasure,* ed.
Wright (Percy Society, London, 1845),
pp. 27-56.
[2] This Fourth River will appear a

less startling "novelty" when the
illuminating power attributed to the
stone is remembered.
[3] = "purified."

for centuries, while their opposition to Italian did perhaps some good, and certainly little harm. But all were thoroughly possessed by the idea that English, adjusted to classical models as far as possible, but not denationalised or denaturalised, ought to be raised into a sufficient medium of literary, as of familiar, communication for Englishmen. And—with that intense Renaissance belief in education, and a high and noble kind of education too, which puts to shame the chattering and pottering of certain later periods on this unlucky subject —all were determined, as far as in them lay, to bring English up to this point. The tendency was spread over a great number of persons, and a considerable period of time. Its representatives ranged from healthy and large-souled, if not quite heroic or inspired, scholars like Ascham to "acrid-quack" pedants like Gabriel Harvey. But the chief of these representatives were the well-known trio, of whom one has just been mentioned—Sir [1] Thomas Wilson, Sir John Cheke, and Roger Ascham. They were all friends, they were all contemporary members (to her glory be it ungrudgingly said) of one University, the University of Cambridge, and though the moral character of all, and especially of the first two, had something of the taints of self-seeking and of sycophancy, which were the blemishes of the Tudor type of writers, all had the merits of that type as exhibited in the man of the study rather than of the field—intense curiosity and industry, a real patriotism, a half-instinctive eagerness to action, a consciousness how best to adorn the Sparta that had fallen to their lot, and a business-like faculty of carrying their conceptions out. From various indications, positive and indirect, it would seem that Cheke, who was the eldest, was also the most "magnetic," the most Socratically suggestive and germinal of the three: but his actual literary work is of much inferior importance to that of Ascham and Wilson.

Wilson's *Art of Rhetoric* [2] is, as the other dates given in the

---

[1] Wilson has usually been dignified in this way: but some authorities, including the *Dict. Nat. Biog.*, deny him knighthood.

[2] It was not actually the first in English, Leonard Coxe having preceded him "about 1524" with an English adaptation, apparently, of Melanchthon. But this is of no critical importance.

text and notes will show sufficiently, by no means the first
Wilson: his book of the school; nor is it that which has, on the
Art of whole, the most interest for us. But it deserves
Rhetoric; precedence historically because, as no other does, it
keys, or gears, the new critical tendency on to the old technical
rhetoric. The first edition appeared in 1553, dedicated to
Edward VI. Wilson dates his prologue to the second[1] on the
7th December 1560; but it does not seem to have been published till 1563. Between the date of the first edition and the
writing of this Prologue, Wilson, an exile at Rome, had fallen
into the claws of the Inquisition as author of the book and of
another on Logic; and, as he recounts with natural palpitation,
escaped literally "so as by fire," his prison-house being in
flames.

His two first Books Wilson faithfully devotes to all the old
technicalities—Invention, Disposition, Amplification, "States,"
his attack on and the rest. But his third Book, "Of Elocution,"[2]
"Inkhorn announces from the first an interest in the matter
terms." very different from the jejune rehashings of the
ancients (and chiefly of those ancients least worth rehashing)
which the mediæval Rhetorics mostly give us. In fact, Wilson
had shown himself alive to the importance of the subject in
the very opening of the work itself[3] by recounting, with much
gusto, how "Phavorinus the Philosopher (as Gellius telleth the
tale) did hit a young man over the thumbs very handsomely
for using over-old and over-strange words." And as soon as
he has divided the requirements of Elocution under the four
heads of Plainness, Aptness, Composition, and Exornation, he
opens the stop which has been recognised as his characteristic
one, by denouncing "strange inkhorn terms." He inveighs
against the "far-journeyed gentlemen" who, on their return
home, as they love to go in foreign apparel, so they "powder
their talk with oversea language," one talking French-English,
another "chopping in" with English-Italianated. Professional
men, lawyers and auditors, have their turn of censure, and a real
literary "document" follows in the censure of the "fine cour-

---

[1] My copy is of this, which is the
fuller.

[2] Fol. 82.

[3] Fol. 1, *verso*, at bottom.

tier who will talk nothing but Chaucer." Most copious is he
against undue "Latining" of the tongue, in illustration of
which he gives a letter, from a Lincolnshire gentleman, which
may owe royalty either to the Limousin Scholar of Rabelais, or
even to Master Francis' own original, Geoffroy Tory himself.
And he points the same moral (very much after the manner of
Latimer, for whom, as elsewhere appears, he had a great
admiration) by divers facetious stories from his experience,
"when I was in Cambridge, and student in the King's College,"
and from other sources. After which he falls in with Cicero
as to the qualifications of words allowable.

"Aptness" follows: and here Sir Thomas, without knowing
it, has cut at a folly of language revived three hundred years
His dealing and more later than his own time. For he laughs
with Figures. at one who, "seeing a house fair-builded," said to
his fellow, " Good Lord, what a handsome *phrase* of building is
this!" Wilson's butt would have been no little thought of by
certain persons at the end of the nineteenth century and the
beginning of the twentieth. Indeed, one may seem to remember a sentence about the merits of a "passage" in a
marble chimney-piece, which is a mere echo, conscious or unconscious, of his "phrase." The same temper appears in the
longer remarks on Composition; but when we come to Exornation, "a gorgeous beautifying of the tongue with borrowed
words and change of sentence," Wilson's lease of originality
has run out. He is still in the bondage of the Figures, which
he describes ambitiously as a kind "not equally sparpled [1]
about the whole oration, but so dissevered and parted as stars
stand in the firmament, or flowers in a garden, or pretty-
devised antiques in a cloth of Arras." The enumeration is
full of character and Elizabethan piquancy; but it still has
the old fault of beginning at the wrong end. When a man
writes even a good oration, much more that far higher thing
a good piece of prose (which may be an oration, if need serves,
or anything else), he does not say to himself, "Now I shall

---

[1] One may regret "sparple" and
"disparple," which are good and picturesque Englishings of *e(s)parpiller.*

The forms "spar*k*le" and "dispar*k*le,"
which seem to have been commoner,
are no loss, as being equivocal.

throw in some hyperbaton; now we will exhibit a little ana-
diplosis; this is the occasion, surely, for a passage of zeugma."
He writes as the spirit moves him, and as the way of art leads.
One could wish, in reading Wilson, for another Sir Thomas,
to deal with the Figurants as he has dealt with the Chaucerists
and the Lincolnshire Latinisers. But we must not expect too
much at once: and lucky are we if we often, or even sometimes, get so bold a striking out into new paths for a true end
as we find in this *Art of Rhetoric*.

Cheke has left no considerable English work, and he seems
—as it is perhaps inevitable that at least some of the leaders
in every period of innovation should seem—to have
*Cheke: his
resolute An-
glicism
and anti-
preciosity.* pushed innovation itself to and over the verge of
crotchet. He was a spelling and pronouncing reformer both in Greek and English; and, classical
scholar and teacher as he was, he seems to have
fallen in with that curious survival of "Saxon" rendering of
words not of Saxon origin, the great storehouse of which is
the work of Reginald Pecock a century earlier. But he appears to have been one of the main and most influential
sources of the double stream of tendency observable in Wilson
himself, and still more in Ascham—the tendency on the one
hand to use the classics as models and trainers in the formation of a generally useful and practicable English style, and
on the other to insist that neither from classical nor from
any other sources should English be adulterated by "inkhorn
terms," as Wilson calls them,[1] of any kind—that is to say, by
archaisms, technicalities, preciousnesses, fished up as it were
from the bottom of the ink-pot, instead of simply and naturally
taken as they came from its surface to the pen. What Ascham
tells us that he said of Sallust is the spirit, the centre, the
kernel, of the criticism of the whole school—a dread that is
to say, and a dislike and a censure of what he calls the "un-
contented care to write better than he could."[2] And it must

---

[1] Not that the phrase is of his invention. It seems to have been a
catchword of the time, and occurs in
Bale (1543), in Peter Ashton's version

of Jovius (1546), &c.
[2] Of course Cheke had in his mind
the passage of Quintilian concerning
Julius Florus (see *Hist. Crit.*, i. 313).

be obvious that this sharply formulated censure is itself a
critical *point de repère* of the greatest value. It is well that
it was not too much listened to—for the greatest results of
English prose and verse in the great period, beginning a few
years after Cheke's death and continuing for an old man's
lifetime, were the result of this "never contented care," which
still reached something better than content. But if, at this
early period, it had had too much way given to it, if the vigorous but somewhat sprawling infancy of Elizabethan English
had been bid and let sprawl simply at its pleasure, the consequences could not but have been disastrous.

This criticism of Sallust, which may be found at length in
Ascham's *Schoolmaster*,[1] is quite a *locus* in its kind. It is not
His criticism of the justest, for the prepossession of the sentence
of Sallust. quoted above (which stands in the forefront of it)
colours it all through. It has funny little scholastic lapses in
logic, such as the attempt to apply the old brocard *Orator est
vir bonus dicendi peritus* to the disadvantage of Sallust, as compared not only with Cicero but with Cæsar, on the score of
morality. It would have been pleasant to observe the coun-
tenances of Fausta and Servilia if this had been argued in their
joint presence. And the dislike of Thucydides, to which a
disliker of Sallust is almost necessarily driven, argues a literary
palate not of the most refined. But the disposition of the
supposed causes of the faults of Sallust's style, when, having
sown his wild oats, he took to literature, and borrowed his
vocabulary from Cato and Varro, and his method from Thucydides himself, is an exceedingly ingenious piece of critical
pleading. Even if it will not hold water, it shows us a stage
of criticism advanced, in some directions, beyond anything that
classical or mediæval times can show. The other great "place"
of Cheke's writing occurs in his letter[2] to Hoby on that learned
knight's translation of Castiglione, with its solemn judgment
(the author, though but in middle age, was ill, and in fact
almost dying), "I am of this opinion, that our own tongue

---

[1] Ed. Arber, pp. 154-159.
[2] This may be found in Arber's Introduction to the book just cited, p.

5 ; or in Professor Raleigh's ed. of
Hoby (London, 1900), pp. 12, 13.

should be written clean and pure, unmixed and unmangled
with borrowing of other tongues, wherein if we take no heed
betimes, ever borrowing and never paying, she shall be fain to
keep house as a bankrupt." The analogy, of course, is a false
one :—there is no need to pay, nor possibility of payment, any
more than a conquering monarchy needs to fear the repayment
of the tribute it draws from others, or than a sturdy plant
need dread bankruptcy because it owes nourishment to earth,
and air, and the rain of heaven. But once more the position
is a definite, and not a wholly untenable, critical position : and
Cheke shows himself here as at once engineer and captain of it.

The chief representative of this school is, however, beyond
question, the always agreeable, and but seldom other than

Ascham.   admirable, author of *Toxophilus* and *The Schoolmaster* himself.[1] His positive achievements in English literature do not here directly concern us ; nor does the
debate between those who regard him as a Euphuist before
Euphuism, and those who will have him to be the chief example of the plain style in early Elizabethan literature. I
confess myself to be on the side of the latter ; though I know
what the former mean. But it is with what Ascham thought
as a critic, not with what he did as a writer, that we are here
busy ; and on this there is no reasonable opening for serious
difference of opinion. Ascham's critical position and opinions
are clear, not only from his two famous and pleasant little
books, but from the constant literary references in his letters,
ranging from elaborate lucubrations on the study of the classics
to an amusing little Cambridge fling at the older university,
where, as we learn from a letter of exactly the middle of the
century, taste was in so shocking a condition that Oxford men
actually paid more attention to Lucian and Apuleius than to
Cicero and Xenophon.[2]

[1] For these two books Mr Arber's
excellent reprints can hardly be bettered. But for our purposes the *Letters*
are also needed ; and these, with other
things, will be found in Giles's edition of
the *Works,* 3 vols. in 4, London, 1864-65.

[2] *Quid omnes Oxonienses sequuntur
plane nescio, sed ante aliquot menses*
*in Aula incidi in quendam illius Aca-
demiæ, qui nimium præferendo Luci-
anum, Plutarchum et Herodianum, Sene-
cam, A. Gellium, et Apuleium, utramque
linguam in nimis senescentem et effœtam
ætatem compingere mihi videbatur—*
Giles, i. 190. The whole letter (to
Sturm) is worth reading.

The *Toxophilus* itself is a critical document in parts, both for the initial manifesto of his desire "to write this English matter *His patriotism.* in the English tongue for English men," and for the more elaborate defence of the proceeding (a defence repeated in the numerous Latin letters accompanying the copies of the book he sent to his friends), as well as for one of those hits at Romance which were characteristic of Renaissance scholars too generally, and were particularly to be expected in very moral and rather prosaic persons like Ascham. But we necessarily turn to the *Schoolmaster* for a full exposition of Ascham's critical *ethos,* and we find it.

A tendency rather to slight poetry, one great heresy concerning it (of which more presently), and the above - mentioned *His horror of* contempt or even horror of romance — these are *Romance,* the worst things to be noted here. All these are connected with a wider critical heresy, which is prevalent in England to this day, and which emerges most interestingly in this infancy of English criticism. This heresy is the valuing of examples, and even of whole kinds, of literary art, not according to their perfection on their own artistic standards, not according to the quantity or quality of artistic pleasure which they are fitted to give; but according to certain principles—patriotic, political, ethical, or theological—which the critic holds or does not hold, as the case may be. This fallacy being one of those proper—or, at least, inseparably accidental—to the human intellect, is of course perceptible enough in antiquity itself. It is, as we have seen, rife in Plato, and more rife in Plutarch; and there is no doubt that the devotion of the Renaissance to the greatest of Greek philosophers and prosemen, to the most entertaining of Greek biographers and moralists, had not a little to do with its reappearance, though the struggle of the Reformation, and the national jealousies which this struggle bred or helped, had more. But no one has given more notable examples of it than Ascham by his attack on "books of feigned chivalry," in *Toxophilus,*[1] and his well-known censure of the *Morte d'Arthur* in *The Schoolmaster.*[2]

[1] P. 19, ed. Arber. The passage contains a stroke at monasticism.

[2] P. 80, ed. Arber.

Than this book there was, at Ascham's date, no more exquisite example of English prose in existence. There is not to this day *and of the Morte d'Arthur.* a book, either in prose or in verse, which has more of the true Romantic charm. There are few better instances anywhere of subtly combined construction of story than are to be found in some of its parts; and, to a catholic judgment, which busies itself with the matter and spirit of a book, there are few books which teach a nobler temper of mind, which inculcate with a more wonderful blending of sternness and sympathy the great moral that "the doer shall suffer," that "for all these things God shall bring us into judgment," or which display more accomplished patterns of man and sweeter examples of woman. Yet Ascham (and he had read the book) saw in, it nothing but "open manslaughter and bold bawdry."

Apart from this somewhat Philistine prudery—which occupies itself more reasonably with Italian *novelle*, and the translations of them into English—Ascham's criticism is of a piece with that of the whole school in all but a very few points. He differed with Wilson, and with most of the scholars of his time, on the subject of translation, which he rightly enough regarded as a useful engine of education, but as quite incapable of giving any literary equivalent for the original. He agreed both with Wilson and with Cheke as to the impropriety of adulterating English with any foreign tongue, ancient or modern. He was, none the less, an exceedingly fervent Ciceronian and devotee of the golden age of Latin. And when we come in one[1] of his letters to Sturm on the name of Giovanbattista Pigna, the rival of Cinthio Giraldi, there seems to be established a contact, of the most interesting, between English and Italian criticism. But (as indeed we might have expected) no allusion to Pigna's view of the despised romances is even hinted: it is his dealing with the *aureolum libellum* of Horace that Ascham has read, his dealings with Aristotle and Sophocles that he wishes to read.

Putting his theory and his practice together, and neglecting

---

[1] Thought to be his last, and written in Dec. 1568; ed. Giles, ii. 189. The correspondence with Sturm is, as we should expect, particularly literary.

for the moment his moral "craze," we can perceive in him a
His general   tolerably distinct ideal of English prose, which he
critical atti-   has only not illustrated by actual criticism of the
tude to Prose, reviewing sort, because the material was so scanty.
This prose is to be fashioned with what may be excusably called
a kind of squint—looking partly at Latin and Greek construction and partly at English vernacular usage. It does not seem
that, great as was his reverence for Cheke, he was bitten by
Cheke's mania for absolute Teutonism; nor does he appear to
have gone to the extreme of Latimer and Latimer's admirer,
Wilson, in caring to mingle merely familiar speech with his
ordered vernacular. But he went some way in this direction: he
was by no means proof against that Delilah of alliteration which,
like a sort of fetch or ghost of the older alliterative prosody,
bewitched the mid-sixteenth-century verse and prose of England, and had not lost hold on Spenser himself. And he had
belief in certain simple Figures of the antithetic and parallel
kind. But he was, above all, a schoolmaster — as even being
dead he spoke—to English literature; and his example and his
precepts together tended to establish a chastened, moderately
classical, pattern of writing, which in the next generation produced the admirable English prose of Hooker, and was not
without influence on the less accomplished, but more germinal
and protreptic, style of Jonson.

We must praise him less when we come to poetry. The
history of the craze for classical metre and against rhyme in
and to   England, which practically supplies our earliest sub-
Poetry.   ject of purely critical debate, is a very curious one,
and may—perhaps must—be considered from more points of
view than one, before it is rightly and completely understood.
At first sight it looks like mere mid-summer madness—the
work of some Puck of literature—if not even as the incursion
into the calm domains of scholarship and criticism of that
popular *delirium tremens*, which has been often illustrated in
politics. Shifting of the standpoint, and more careful consideration, will discover some excuses for it, as well as much
method in it. But it must be regarded long, and examined
carefully, before the real fact is discovered — the fact that,

mischievous and absurd as it was in itself, unpardonable as
are the attempts to revive it, or something like it, at this time
of day, it was in its own day a kind of beneficent "distemper"
—a necessary, if morbid, stage in the development of English
prosody and English criticism.

Inasmuch as the most obvious and indubitable, as well as
universal, cause of the craze was the profound Renaissance
The craze admiration for the classics, it was inevitable that
for Classical something of the kind should make its appearance
Metres. in most European countries. But other and coun-
teracting causes prevented it from assuming, in any of them,
anything like the importance that it attained in England.
Unrhymed classical metres, like almost every literary innovation of the time, had been first attempted in Italy; but
the established and impregnable supremacy of forms like the
Sonnet, the Canzone, the *ottava* and *terza rima*, put rhyme out
of real danger there. They were attempted in France. But
French had for centuries possessed a perfectly well-defined
system of prosody, adapted and adequate to the needs and
nature of the language. And, moreover, the singularly *atonic*
quality of this language, its want not only of the remotest
approach to quantity but even of any decided accent, made
the experiment not merely ridiculous, as indeed it mostly was
in English, but all but impossible. Spanish was following
Italian, and did not want to follow anything else: and German
was not in case to compete.

With English the patient was very much more predisposed
to the disease. Not only two, but practically three, different
Special systems of prosody, which were really to some extent
wants of opposed to each other, and might well seem more op-
English posed than they actually were, disputed, in practice,
Prosody. the not too fertile or flourishing field of English
poetry. There was the true Chaucerian system of blended English prosody, the legitimate representative of the same composite
influences which have moulded English language throughout.
These influences had continued, and their results had been
slowly developed through the half-chaotic beginnings of
Middle English verse, and then, with almost premature sud-

denness, perfected up to a certain stage by Chaucer himself.
This system combined—though not yet in perfect freedom—
Its kinds : the strict syllabic foot-division of the French with
(1) *Chau-* the syllabic licence of Anglo-Saxon, so as to produce
cerian. a system of syllabic equivalence similar in nature
to, if not yet fully in practice freer than, that of the Greek
Iambic trimeter. It admitted a considerable variety of metres,
the base-integers of which were the octosyllable and decasyllable, with lines of six, twelve, and others occasionally, combined in pairs or arranged in stanzas of more or less intricate
forms. But—by a historic accident which has even yet to be
rather taken as found than fully explained—nobody for more
than a hundred years had been able to produce really good
regular [1] poetry in Southern English by this metre, and certain
changes in pronunciation and vocabulary—especially the disuse
of the final vocalised *e* — were putting greater and greater
difficulties in the way of its practice.

Secondly, there was the revived alliterative metre, either
genuine—that is to say, only roughly syllabic and not rhymed,
(2) *Alliter-* but rhythmed nearer to the anapæstic form than to
ative. any other — or allied with rhyme, and sometimes
formed into stanzas of very considerable intricacy. This,
which had arisen during the fourteenth century, no one
quite knows how or where, apparently in the North, and
which had maintained a vigorous though rather artificial
life during the fifteenth, had not wholly died out, being represented partly by the ballad metre, by doggerel twelves,
fourteeners, and other long shambling lines, and by a still
lively tendency towards alliteration itself, both in metred
verse and in prose. Latterly, during Ascham's own youth,
a sort of *rapprochement* between these two had made the
fourteeners and Alexandrines, rather less doggerelised, very
general favourites; but had only managed to communicate to
them a sort of lolloping amble, very grievous and sickening to
the delicate ear.

Thirdly, and in close connection with this combination,

---

[1] There had, of course, been some charming jets of folk-song in ballad, carol,
and what not.

Wyatt, Surrey, and other poets had, by imitating Italian
(3) *Italian-* models, especially in the sonnet, striven to raise, to
ated. bind together, to infuse with energy and stiffen with
backbone, the ungainly shambling body of English verse: and
Surrey, again following the Italians, had tried, with some success, the unrhymed decasyllable, soon to be so famous as blank
verse.

Now critical observation at the time might survey this field
with view as extensive and intensive as it could apply, and be
Deficiencies far from satisfied with the crops produced. To re-
of all three. present the first system there was nobody but
Chaucer, who, great and greatly admired as he was, was
separated from the men of 1550 by a period of time almost
as long as that which separates us from Pope, and by a much
greater gulf of pronunciation and accent. Nobody could write
like Chaucer—unless the Chaucerian *Chorizontes* are right in
attributing *The Court of Love* to this time, in which case there
was some one who could write very much like Chaucer indeed.
There was no Langland, and nobody who could write in the
least like Langland. In sheer despair, men of talent like
Skelton, when they were not Chaucerising heavily, were
indulging (of course with more dulcet intervals now and then)
in mere wild gambades of doggerel.

But it will be said, Was there not the new Italianated style
of poets of such promise as Wyatt and Surrey? There was.
Yet it must be remembered that Wyatt and Surrey themselves
are, after all, poets of more promise than performance; that
their promise itself looks much more promising to us, seeing
as we do its fulfilment in Spenser and onward, than it need
have done, or indeed could do, to contemporaries; that stalwart
Protestants and stout Englishmen feared and loathed the
Italianation of anything English; and lastly, that even the
prosody of Wyatt and Surrey is, in a very high degree, experimental, tentative, incomplete. We laugh, or are disgusted, at
the twists and tortures applied by the hexametrists to our poor
mother tongue; but Wyatt at least puts almost as awkward
constraints on her.

It is not surprising that, in the presence of these unsatisfying

things, and in the nonage of catholic literary criticism, men
should have turned for help to those classics which
The temptations of Criticism in this respect. were the general teachers and helpers of the time.
There was indeed—already published just as Ascham
had attained his year of discretion—a treatise, by
the greatest man of letters for some fifteen hundred years
at least, which contained the germ of a warning. But it is
not likely that Ascham or any of his good Cambridge friends
had seen Trissino's translation of the *De Vulgari Eloquio ;* and, if
any had, it would have been a stroke of genius to carry Dante's
generalisation from the Romance tongues further. To almost any
man of the Renaissance it would have seemed half sacrilege and
half madness to examine ancient and modern literatures on the
same plane, and decide what was germane to each and what
common to all. Greek Prosody had been good enough, with
very minor alterations, for Latin ; how should any of these
upstart modern tongues refuse what had been good enough for
both ? And let it be remembered, too, that they were only half
wrong Greek and Latin *did* provide up to a certain point—
that of the foot as distinguished from the metre—examples
which, duly guarded, could be quite safely followed, which
indeed could not and cannot be neglected without loss and
danger for English. It was when they went further, and
endeavoured to impose the classical combinations of feet on
English, that they fell.

Yet even from the first they had glimpses and glimmerings
of truth which might have warned them ; while in
Its adventurers: Ascham himself. their very errors they often display that combination
of independence and practical spirit which is the
too often undervalued glory of English criticism.
Ascham himself—besotted as he is with wrath [1] against " our

---

[1] It is curious that, in this very *début* of English criticism, the incivility with which critics are constantly and too justly charged makes its appearance. Ascham would seem to have been a good-natured soul enough. Yet he abuses rhyme and its partisans in the true " Père Duchêne " style which some critics still affect. " To follow the Goths in rhyming instead of the Greeks in versifying" is " to eat acorns with swine, when we may eat wheat bread among men." Rhymers are " a rude multitude," " rash, ignorant heads," " wandering blindly in their foul wrong way," &c.

rude beggarly rhyming," confident as he is that the doggerel of his old friend Bishop Watson of Lincoln—

> " All travellers do gladly report great praise of Ulysses,
>   For that he knew many men's manners, and saw many cities,"—

exhibits[1] as " right quantitie" of syllables and true order of versifying as either Greek or Latin—yet saw[2] that " our English tongue doth not well receive the nature of *Carmen Heroicum*, because *dactylus*, the aptest foot for that verse, is seldom found in English." Truly it is not; your dactyl is apt to play the " Waler "—to buck under an English rider, and either throw him altogether, or force the alteration of the pace to anapæsts. The best apparent dactylics in English—the verses of Kingsley's *Andromeda*—are not really dactylic-hexameters at all, they are five-foot anapæstics, with a very strong *anacrusis* at the beginning, and a weak hypercatalectic syllable at the end. And with this fatal confession of Ascham (who had not a very poetical head), that of Campion, an exquisite poet and a keen though warped critic, coincides, as we shall see, a generation later. But the thing had to be done; and it was done, or at least attempted.

When the craze first took form in England we do not exactly know. Ascham observes vaguely that " this misliking of rhyming beginneth not now of any newfangle singularity, *Watson and* *Drant.* but hath been long been misliked, and that of men of greatest learning and deepest judgment."[3] We all think that the persons who agree with us are men of great learning and deep judgment, so that matter may be passed over. But apparently the thing was one, and not the best, of the fruits of that study of the classics, and specially of Greek, which, beginning at Oxford, passed thence to Cambridge, and was taken up so busily in Ascham's own college, St John's. Thomas Watson,[4]

---

[1] *Schoolmaster, ed. cit.,* p. 73. Ascham actually *quotes* the Greek and the Latin of Homer and Horace, and declares Watson's stuff to be made as "naturally" as the one and as "aptly" as the other!

[2] Ibid., p. 145.

[3] P. 147. The extraordinary confusion of mind of the time is illustrated by Ascham's sheltering himself behind Quintilian !

[4] Not to be confounded with Thomas Watson, the author of the *Hecatompathia*, who came later, and was an Oxford man.

the Bishop of Lincoln, above referred to, was Master of the College; Ascham himself, it is hardly necessary to say, was a fellow of it. And still descending in the collegiate hierarchy, it was an undergraduate of St John's, Thomas Drant, who somewhat later drew up rules for Anglo-Classic versifying—rules that occupied Spenser and Harvey, producing some interesting letters and some very deplorable doggerel. Drant seems to have been the "legislator of Parnassus" to the innovators; but his "rules" are not known to exist, and what we have of his does not bear on the special subject.

Mischievous craze as it was, however,[1] it had the merit of turning the attention of Englishmen to really critical study of poetry, and it appears, more or less, as the *motif* of most of the group of critical writings, from Gascoigne's *Notes of Instruction* to Daniel's *Defence of Rhyme*, which we shall now discuss.

In the most interesting little treatise [2] which heads or initials [3] the now goodly roll of books in English criticism, George Gascoigne, though he was himself a Cambridge man, does not make any reference to the craze. The tract was written at the request of an Italian friend, Eduardo Donati. It is exceedingly short; but as full of matter, and very good matter, as need be. In duty bound Gascoigne begins with insistence on fine invention, without which neither "thundering in rym ram ruff, quoth my master Chaucer," nor "rolling in pleasant words," nor "abounding in apt vocables," will suffice. But he passes over this very swiftly, as over trite and obvious expressions,[4] suitableness of phrase, &c., and attacks the great literary question of the time, Prosody.

Gascoigne.

---

[1] Some authorities have been much too mild towards it. For instance, the late Mr Henry Morley, who says, "Thomas Drant, of course, did not suppose that his rules were sufficient." This is charitable, but outside, or rather against, the evidence.

[2] *Certain Notes of Instruction concerning the making of verse or rhyme in English,* ed. Arber (with *The Steel Glass,* &c.), pp. 31-41, London, 1868

Originally in the 4to edition of Gascoigne's *Poems* (London, 1575). Mr Spingarn sees indebtedness in it to Ronsard.

[3] The observations of Ascham, Wilson, and the others being incidental merely.

[4] "If I should undertake to write in praise of a gentlewoman, I would neither praise her crystal eye nor her cherry lip."

He begins his attack by the modest and half - apologetic request, "This may seem a presumptuous order," that, what-His Notes of ever the verse chosen be, it be regular, and not Instruction. wobbling backwards and forwards between twelve and fourteen syllables on no principle. Then he enjoins the maintenance of regular and usual accent or quantity; and in so doing insists on a standard in regard to which not merely Wyatt and Surrey earlier, but even Spenser later, were much less scrupulous. "Treasure," he says, you must use with the first syllable long and the second short: you must not make it "treasùre." And then he makes a very curious observation :—

"Commonly nowadays in English rhymes, for I dare not call them English verses, we use none other order but a foot of two syllables," to wit, the Iamb. "We have," he says, "in other times used other kinds of metres," as

"No wight | in the world | that wealth | can attain," [1]

(*i.e.*, anapæsts), while "our Father Chaucer had used the same liberty in feet and measures that the Latinists do use," that is to say, syllabic equivalence of two shorts to a long. And he laments the tyranny of the Iamb; but says, "we must take the ford as we find it."

Then, after some particular cautions,—a renewed one as to quantifying words aright—"understànd," not "undérstand," &c., as to using as many monosyllables as possible (it is amusing to read this and remember the opposite caution of Pope),—he comes to rhyme, and warns his scholar against rhyme without reason. Alliteration is to be moderate: you must not "hunt a letter to death." Unusual words are to be employed carefully and with a definite purpose to "draw attentive reading." Be clear and sensible.[2] Keep English order, and invert substantive and adjective seldom and cautiously. Be moderate in the use

---

[1] Gascoigne does not use this division, or — and ᵛ, but ´ and ` for long and short, ◠ (circumflex) for common, and indented lines (ᴧᴧᴧ and ᴧᴧ ᴡ) for dissyllabic and trisyllabic foot arrangements.

[2] "For the haughty obscure verse doth not much delight, and the verse that is too easy is like a tale of a roasted horse."

also of that "shrewd fellow, poetical licence," who actually reads "hea|ven" for "heavn"![1]

As for the pause or Cæsura, Gascoigne is not injudicious. "The pause," he says, "will stand best in the middle" of an octosyllable, at the fourth syllable in a "verse of ten," at the sixth (or middle again) of an Alexandrine, and at the eighth in a fourteener. But it is at the discretion of the writer in Rhythm royal: "it forceth not where the pause be till the end of the line"—and this liberty will assuredly draw to more.

Next he enumerates stanzas:—Rhyme royal itself, ballades, sonnets, Dizains, and Sixains, Virelays, and the "Poulter's measure," of twelve and fourteen alternately, to which his own contemporaries were so unfortunately addicted. You must "finish the sentence and meaning at the end of every staff": and (by the way) he has "forgotten a notable kind of rhyme called riding rhyme, which is what our father Chaucer used in his Canterbury tales, and in divers other delectable and light enterprises." It is good for "a merry tale," Rhyme royal for a "grave discourse," Ballads and Sonnets for love-poems, &c., and it would be best, in his judgment, to keep Poulter's measure for Psalms and hymns. And so he makes an end, "doubting his own ignorance."

The chief points about this really capital booklet are as follows:—Gascoigne's recognition of the importance of overhaul-*Their cap-* ing English Prosody; his good sense on the matter of *ital value.* the cæsura, and of Chaucer's adoption of the principles of equivalenced scansion; his acknowledgment, with regret, of the impoverishment which, in the sterility of the mid-sixteenth century before Spenser, was a fact, as resulting from the tyranny of the iamb; the shrewdness of his general remarks; and, last but not least, his entire silence about the new versifying, the "Dranting of Verses." It is possible (for though he was at Cambridge he seems to admit that he did not acquire

---

[1] See Mitford, *Harmony of Language*, p. 105, who thinks the licence just the other way, and indeed roundly pronounces the pronunciation in one syllable "impossible." A little later, again, Guest thinks the *dis*-syllable "uncouth and vulgar." A most documentary disagreement!

any great scholarship there) that he had not come into contact with any one who took interest in this: but it is improbable that it would have appealed to his robust sense of poetry, unsicklied by Harvey's pedantry, and not misled by Spenser's classical enthusiasm.

At this time, however, or not long after—the *Notes* must have been written between 1572 and 1575, and the correspondence of Spenser and Harvey actually appeared in 1579—these other persons were thinking a great deal about the classical metres. The *Five Letters* ("Three" and "Two"[1]—not to be confused with the *Four Letters* which Harvey issued long afterwards about Greene) are full of the subject, and of poetical criticism generally. They, together with the controversy which arose over Gosson's *School of Abuse*, and which indirectly produced Sidney's *Apology for Poetry*, make the years 1579-1580 as notable in the history of English criticism as the appearances of *Euphues* and *The Shepherd's Calendar* make them in that of creative literature.

Spenser's first letter informs Harvey that "they [Sidney and Dyer] have proclaimed in their ἀρειωπάγῳ[2] [the literary *Spenser and* cénacle of Leicester House] a general surceasing and *Harvey.* silence of bald rhymers, and also of the very best too: instead whereof they have, by the authority of their whole Senate, prescribed certain laws and rules of quantities of English syllables for English verse, having had thereof already great practice, and drawn me to their faction." And later, "I am more in love with English versifying than with rhyming, which I should have done long since if I would have followed your counsel." He hints, however, gently, that Harvey's own verses (these coterie writers always keep the name "verses" for their hybrid abortions) once or twice "make a breach in Master Drant's rules." Which was, of course, a very dreadful thing, only to be "condoned *tanto poetæ.*" He requites Harvey with a few Iambics, which he "dare warrant precisely perfect for the feet, and varying not one

---

[1] See Grosart's *Works of Gabriel Harvey*, vol. i. pp. 6-150. Parts will be found in the Globe edition of Spenser, pp. 706-710.

[2] I am not responsible for the eccentricities of this form.

inch from the Rule." And then follows the well-known piece
beginning—

> "Unhappy verse, the witness of my unhappy state,"

where certainly the state must have been bad if it was as
infelicitous as the verse.

Not such was Gabriel Harvey that he might take even a
polite correction; and his reply is a proper donnish setting-
down of a clever but presumptuous youth. He respects the
Areopagus—indeed they were persons of worship, and Harvey
was a *roturier*—more than Spenser can or will suppose, and he
likes the trimeters (indeed, though poor things, they were
Spenser's own after all, and such as no man but Spenser could
have written in their foolish kind) more than Spenser "can or
will easily believe." But—and then follows much reviewing
in the now stale hole-picking kind, which has long been abandoned, save by the descendants of Milbourne and Kenrick, and
a lofty protestation that "myself never saw your gorbellied
master's rules, nor heard of them before."

The Three Letters which follow [1] are distributed in subject
between an Earthquake (which has long since ceased to quake
for us) and the hexameters. They open with a letter from
Spenser, in which he broaches the main question, "Whether
our English accent will endure the Hexameter?" and doubts.
Yet he has a hankering after it, encloses his own—

> "See ye the blindfoldèd pretty god, that feathered archer," &c.,

and prays that Harvey would either follow the rules of the
great Drant, indorsed by Sidney, or else send his own. Harvey
replies in double. The first part is some very tragical mirth
about the earthquake; the second, "A Gallant Familiar Letter,"
tackles the question of versification.

This gallant familiarity might possibly receive from harsh
critics the name of uneasy coxcombry; but it is at any rate
clear that the author has set about the matter very seriously.
He expresses delight that Sidney and Dyer, "the two very
diamonds of her Majesty's Court," have begun to help forward

---

[1] In order of composition, not of publication.

"the exchange of barbarous and balductum[1] rhymes with artificial verses"; thinks their "lively example" will be much better than Ascham's "dead advertisement" in the *Schoolmaster*. He would like (as should we) to have Drant's prosody. His own Rules and Precepts will probably not be very different; but he will take time before drafting them finally. He thinks (reasonably enough) that before framing a standard English Grammar or Rhetoric (therein including Prosody), a standard orthography must first be agreed upon. And he suggests that "we beginners" (this from the author of these truly "barbarous and balductum" antics to the author of the *Faerie Queene* is distinctly precious) have the advantage, like Homer and Ennius, of setting examples. "A New Year's Gift to M. George Bilchaunger," in very doleful hexameters, follows, and after a little gird at Spenser's "See ye the Blindfoldèd," another sprout of Harvey's brain in the same kind, which has been, perhaps, more, and more deservedly, laughed at than any of these absurdities, except the scarcely sane jargon-doggerel of Stanyhurst—

"What might I call this tree? a Laurell? o bonny Laurell!
Needs to thy boughs will I bow this knee, and veil my bonetto;"

with yet another—

"Since *Galateo*[2] came in, and Tuscanism gan usurp."

He thinks that the author of this last "wanted but some delicate choice elegant poesy" of Sidney's or Dyer's for a good pattern. After some further experiments of his own, or his brother's, in hexametring some of Spenser's own "emblems" in the *Calendar*, he turns to Spenser himself, whom, it seems, he ranks next the same "incomparable and miraculous genius in the catalogue of our very principal English Aristarchi." He

[1] This word, which is certainly a cousin of "balderdash," is a good example of the slang and jargon so often mixed with their preciousness by the Elizabethans. Nash borrowed it from Harvey to use against him; and the eccentric Stanyhurst even employs it in his *Virgil*. Stanyhurst's hexameters, by the way (*vide* Mr Arber's Reprint in the *English Scholars Library*, No. 10, London, 1880), are, thanks partly to their astounding lingo, among the maddest things in English literature; but his prose prefatory matter, equally odd in phrase, has some method in its madness.

[2] La Casa's book of etiquette and behaviour.

proceeds to speak of some of that earlier work which, as in *The Dying Pelican,* is certainly, or in the *Dreams,* possibly, lost. After which he writes himself down for all time in the famous passage about the *Faerie Queene,* which he had "once again nigh forgotten," but which he now sends home "in neither better nor worse case than he found her." "As for his judgment," he is "void of all judgment if Spenser's *Nine Comedies* [also lost] are not nearer Ariosto's than that Elvish Queene is to the *Orlando,* which" Spenser "seems to emulate, and hopes to overgo." And so he ends his paragraph with the yet more famous words, "If so be the *Faery Queene* be fairer in your eye than the Nine Muses, and Hobgoblin run away with the garland from Apollo, mark what I say, and yet I will not say what I thought, but there an end for this once, and fare you well till God or some good Angel put you in a better mind!" Which words let all who practise criticism grave in their memories, and recite them daily, adding, "Here, but for the grace of God——!" if they be modest and fear Nemesis.

After an interval, however, Harvey returns to actual criticism, and shows himself in rather better figure by protesting, in spite of "five hundred Drants," against the alteration of the quantity of English words by accenting "Majesty" and "Manfully," and "Carpenter" on the second syllable. And he falls in with Gascoigne on the subject of such words as "Heaven." Nor could he, even if he had been far less of a pedant and coxcomb, have given better or sounder doctrine than that with which he winds up. "It is the vulgar and natural mother Prosody, that alone worketh the feat, as the only supreme foundress and reformer of Position, Diphthong, Orthography, or whatsoever else; whose affirmatives are nothing worth if she once conclude the negative." And for this sound doctrine, not unsoundly enlarged upon, and tipped with a pleasant Latin farewell to "*mea domina Immerita, mea bellissima Collina Clouta,*" let us leave Gabriel in charity.[1]

---

[1] The further letters to Spenser, which Dr Grosart has borrowed from the Camden Society's *Letter-book of Gabriel Harvey,* touch literary matters not seldom, but with no new important deliverances. In the later (1592) *Four Letters,* the embroidery of railing at the dead Greene and the living Nash has almost entirely hidden the literary canvas.

Meanwhile the strong critical set of the time—so interesting, if not so satisfying, after the absolute silence of criticism in English earlier—was being shown in another direction by a different controversy, to which, as we have seen, Spenser makes allusion. The points which chiefly interested him at the moment were formal; those to which we now come were partly of the same class though of another species, partly transcending form.

The Puritan attack on Poetry.

Stephen Gosson is one of the persons of whom, as is by no means always the case, it would really be useful to know more than we do know about their private history and character. What disgust, what disappointment, what tardy development of certain strains of temper and disposition he underwent, we do not know; but something of the kind there must have been to make a young man of four-and-twenty, a fair scholar, already of some note for both dramatic and poetical writing, and obviously of no mean intellectual powers, swing violently round, and denounce plays, and poems, and almost literature generally, as the works of the Devil. It is quite insufficient to ejaculate " Puritanism!" or " Platonism!" for neither of these was a new thing, and the question is why Gosson was not affected by them earlier or later.

Gosson.

Let us, however, now as always, abstain from speculation when we have fact; and here we have at least three very notable facts — Gosson's *School of Abuse*,[1] with its satellite tractates, Lodge's untitled *Reply*,[2] and the famous *Defence of Poesy* or *Apology for Poetry*[3] which Sidney (to whom Gosson had rashly dedicated his book) almost certainly intended as a counterblast, though either out of scorn, as Spenser hints, or (more probably from what we know of him) out of amiable

---

[1] Reprinted by Mr Arber, with its almost immediately subsequent *Apology*. I wish he had added the *Ephemerides of Phialo* which accompanied the *Apology*, and the *Plays Confuted* of three years later; for these books—very small and very difficult of access—add something to the controversy.

[2] Several times reprinted : as for instance by the present writer in *Elizabethan and Jacobean Pamphlets* (London, 1892).

[3] Also frequently (indeed oftener) reprinted, as by Arber, London, 1868 ; Shuckburgh, Cambridge, 1891 ; Cook, Boston (U.S.A.), 1890.

and courteous dislike to requite a compliment with an insult, he takes no direct notice of Gosson at any time.

The School of Abuse (which is written in such a style as almost to out-Euphuise the contemporary *Euphues* itself) is The School critical wholly from the moral side, and with refer-of Abuse. ence to the actual, not the necessary or possible, state of poetry. There are even, the author says, some good plays, including at least one of his own; but the whole of ancient poetry (he says little or nothing of modern) is infected by the blasphemy and immorality of Paganism, and nearly the whole of the modern stage is infected by the abuses of the theatre—of which Gosson speaks in terms pretty well identical with those which Puritan teachers had for some years past been using in sermon and treatise. But outside of the moral and religious line he does not step: he is solely occupied with the lies and the licence of poets and players.

Lodge's reply (the title - page of it has been lost, but it *may* be the *Honest Excuses* to which Gosson refers as Lodge's having been published against him) is almost en-Reply. tirely an appeal to authority, seasoned with a little personal invective. Lodge strings together all the classical names he can think of, with a few mediæval, to show that Poetry, Music (which Gosson had also attacked), and even the theatre, are not bad things. But he hardly attempts any independent justification of them as good ones, especially from the purely literary point of view. In fact, his pamphlet—though interesting as critical work from the associate of great creators in drama, himself a delightful minor poet and no contemptible pioneer of English prose fiction—is merely one of the earliest adaptations in English of an unreal defence to an attack, logically as unreal, though actually dangerous. The charlatan-geniuses of the Renaissance, with Cornelius Agrippa[1] at their head, had refurbished the Platonic arguments for the sincere but pestilent reformers of the Puritan type. Lodge and his likes, in all countries from Italy outward and from Boccaccio downward, accept the measure of the shadowy daggers of their opponents, and attempt to meet them with weapons

[1] In his *De Vanitate Scientiarum* (1527).

of similar temper. The only reality of the debate is in its accidents, not in its main purport. But the assailants, in England at least, had for the time an unfair advantage, because the defence could point to no great poet but Chaucer. The real answer was being provided by one of themselves in the shape of *The Faerie Queene.*

Sidney's book, though pervaded by the same delusion, is one of far more importance. It is not free from faults—in fact, it *Sidney's* has often been pointed out that some of Sidney's doc-Apology for trines, if they had been accepted, would have made Poetry. the best efforts of Elizabethan literature abortive. But the defects of detail, of which more presently, are mixed with admirable merits; the critic shows himself able, as Gosson had not been able, to take a wide and catholic, instead of a peddling and pettifogging, view of morality. Instead of merely stringing authorities together like Lodge, he uses authority indeed, but abuses it not; and while not neglecting form he does not give exclusive attention to it.

His main object, indeed (though he does not know it), is the defence, not so much of Poetry as of Romance. He follows the ancients in extending the former term to any prose fiction : but it is quite evident that he would have, in his *mimesis,* a quality of imagination which Aristotle nowhere insists upon, and which is in the best sense Romantic. And of this poetry, or romance, he makes one of the loftiest conceptions possible. All the hyperboles of philosophers or of poets, on order, justice, harmony, and the like, are heaped upon Poetry herself, and all the Platonic objections to her are retorted or denied.[1]

It has been said that there is no direct reference to Gosson

[1] Our two chief English - writing authorities, Mr Symonds and Mr Spingarn, are at odds as to Sidney's indebtedness to the Italians. He quotes them but sparingly — Petrarch, Boccaccio, Landino, among the older writers, Fracastoro and Scaliger alone, I think, of the moderns—and Mr Symonds thought that he owed them little or nothing. Mr Spingarn, on the other hand, represents him as following them all in general, and Minturno in particular. As usual, it is a case of the gold and silver shield. My own reading of the Italian writers of 1530-80 leaves me in no doubt that Sidney knew them, or some of them, pretty well. But his *attitude* is very different from theirs as a whole, and already significant of some specially English characteristics in criticism.

in the *Apology*, though the indirect references are fairly clear.

Abstract of it. Sidney begins (in the orthodox Platonic or Ciceronian manner) somewhat off his subject, by telling how the right virtuous Edward Wotton, and he himself, once at the Emperor's Court learnt horsemanship of John Pietro Pugliano, the Imperial Equerry, and recounting with pleasant irony some magnifying of his office by that officer. Whence, by an equally pleasant rhetorical turn, he slips into a defence of *his* office—his "unelected vocation" of poet. Were not the earliest and greatest authors of all countries, Musæus, Homer, Hesiod, in Greece (not to mention Orpheus and Linus), Livius Andronicus and Ennius among the Romans, Dante, Boccaccio, and Petrarch in Italy, Chaucer and Gower for " our English "— were they not all poets ? Even the philosophers in Greece used poetry, and Plato himself is a poet almost against his will. Herodotus called his nine books after the Muses; and he and all historians have stolen or usurped things of poetry. Wales, Ireland, " the most barbarous and simple Indians," are cited. Nay, further, did not the Romans call a poet *vates*, a " prophet " ? and, by presumption, may we not call David's psalms a divine poem ? Whatever some may think,[1] it is no profanation to do so. For what is a poet ? What do we mean by adopting that Greek title for him ? We mean that he is a *maker*. All other arts and sciences limit themselves to nature; the poet alone transcends nature, improves it, nay, brings himself (" let it not be deemed too saucy a comparison ") in some sort into competition with the Creator Himself whom he imitates.

The kinds of this imitation are then surveyed—" Divine," " Philosophical," and that of the third or right sort, who only imitate to invent and improve, which neither divine nor philosophic poets can do. These classes are subdivided according to their matter—heroic, tragic, comic, &c.—or according to the sorts of verses they liked best to write in, " for, indeed, the greatest part of poets have apparelled their poetical inventions in that numerous kind of writing which is called verse—indeed but apparelled, verse being but an ornament and no cause to poetry." And again, " it is not rhyming and versing that

[1] Savonarola, probably.

maketh a poet." Xenophon and Heliodorus were both poets in prose.

Now let us "weigh this latter part of poetry first by works and then by parts," having regard always to the "Architectonice or mistress-knowledge," the knowledge of a man's self, ethically and politically. Philosophy, history, law, &c., are then "weighed" against poetry at some length: and the judgment of Aristotle that Poetry is *philosophoteron* and *spoudaioteron* than history, is affirmed chiefly on the odd ground of poetical justice,—the right always triumphing in poetry though not in fact. Instances of the moral and political uses of poetry follow. Then for the parts. Pastoral, comedy, tragedy, &c., are by turns surveyed and defended; and it is in the eulogy of lyric that the famous sentence about *Chevy Chase*[1] occurs. After this, and after a stately vindication of Poetry's right to the laurel, he turns to the objections of the objectors. Although repeating the declaration that "rhyming and versing make not poetry," he argues that if they *were* inseparable,[2] verse is the most excellent kind of writing, far better than prose. As to the abuses of poetry, they are but abuses, and do not take away the use, as is proved by a great number of stock examples.

Why, then, has England grown so hard a stepmother to poets? They are bad enough as a rule, no doubt; though Chaucer did excellently considering his time. The *Mirror for Magistrates* is good; so is Surrey; and *The Shepherd's Calendar* "hath much poetry," though "the old rustic language" is bad, since neither Theocritus, nor Virgil, nor Sannazar has it. And what is the reason of our inferiority? The neglect of rule. From this point onwards Sidney certainly "exposes his legs to the arrows" of those who ignore the just historic estimate. He pours ridicule on all our tragedies except *Gorboduc*, and still more on our mongrel tragi-comedies. We must follow the Unities, which, as it is, are neglected even in *Gorboduc*, "how much more in all the rest?" Whence he proceeds (uncon-

---

[1] "I must confess my own barbarousness: I never heard the old song of Percy and Douglas that I found not my heart moved more than with a trumpet."

[2] "As indeed it seemeth Scaliger judgeth."

scious how cool the *reductio ad absurdum* will leave us) to the famous ridicule of "Asia on the one side and Africa on the other," of "three ladies walking to gather flowers," and how the same place which was a garden becomes a rock, and then a cave with a monster, and then a battlefield with two armies—of the course of two lives in two hours' space, &c. And he concludes with some remarks on versification, which we should gladly have seen worked out. For he does not now seem to be in that antagonistic mood towards rhyme which Spenser's letters to Harvey discover in him. On the contrary, he admits *two* styles, ancient and modern, the former depending on quantity, the latter depending on "number," accent, and rhyme. He indeed thinks English fit for both sorts, and denies "neither sweetness nor majesty" to rhyme, but is, like almost all his contemporaries and followers (except Gascoigne partially), in a fog as to "numbers" and cæsura. The actual end comes a very little abruptly by an exhortation of some length, half humorous, half serious, to all and sundry, to be "no more to jest at the reverent title of a rhymer."

The importance of this manifesto, both symptomatically and typically, can hardly be exaggerated. It exhibits the temper *Its minor* of the generation which actually produced the first-*shortcomings* fruits of the greatest Elizabethan poetry; it served as a stimulant and encouragement to all the successive generations of the great age. That Sidney makes mistakes both in gross and detail—that he even makes some rather serious mistakes from the mere "point of view of the examiner"—is of course undeniable. He has a good deal of the merely traditional mode of Renaissance respect for classical—and for some modern—authority. That, for instance, there is a good deal to be said, and that not only from the point of view of Ben Jonson, against Spenser's half-archaic half-rustic dialect in the *Calendar*, few would refuse to grant. But Theocritus *did* use dialect: it would not in the least matter whether either he or Virgil did not; and if it did, what has the modern and purely vernacular name of Sannazar to do with the matter? It can only be replied that Spenser, by permitting " E. K.'s " annotation, did much to invite this sort of criticism ; and that Englishmen's reluctance to rely on the inherent powers of the English language was partly justified (for hardly any dead poet but Chaucer and no dead prose-writers but Malory and perhaps Berners deserved the title of "great"), partly came from very pardonable ignorance.

It has been already observed that Sidney is by no means peremptory about the "new versifying"; and in particular has absolutely none of the craze against rhyme as rhyme which animated persons of every degree of ability, from Stanyhurst to Milton, during more than a century. His remarks on versification are, however, too scanty to need much comment.

There remain his two major heresies, the declaration that verse is not inseparable from poetry, and the denunciation of *and major* tragi-comedy. In both the authority of the ancients *heresies.* must again bear good part of the blame, but in both he has additional excuses. As to the "pestilent heresy of prose poetry," he is at least not unwilling to argue on the hypothesis that verse *were* necessary to poetry, though he does not think it is. He is quite sure that verse is anyhow a nobler medium than prose. As for the plays, there is still more excuse for him. His classical authorities were quite clear on the point; and as yet there was nothing to be quoted on the other side— at least in English. Spanish had indeed already made the experiment of tragi-comic and anti-unitarian treatment; but I do not think any of the best Spanish examples had yet appeared, and there is great difference between the two theatres. In English itself not one single great or even good play certainly existed on the model at Sidney's death; and, from what we have of what did exist, we can judge how the rough verse, the clumsy construction, or rather absence of construction, the entire absence of clear character-projection, and the higgledy-piggledy of huddled horrors and horseplay, must have shocked a taste delicate in itself and nursed upon classical and Italian litera- *The excuses* ture. And it is noteworthy that even *Gorboduc*, *of both,* with all its regularity and "Senecation," does not bribe Sidney to overlook at least some of its defects. He is here, as elsewhere,—as indeed throughout,—neither blind nor bigoted. He is only in the position of a man very imperfectly supplied with actual experiments and observations, confronted with a stage of creative production but just improving from a very bad state, and relying on old and approved methods as against new ones which had as yet had no success.

And had his mistakes been thrice what they are, the tone and temper of his tractate would make us forgive them three *and their* times over. That "moving of his heart as with a *ample com-* trumpet" communicates itself to his reader even *pensation.* now, and shows us the motion in the heart of the nation at large that was giving us the *Faerie Queene,* that was to give us *Hamlet* and *As You Like It.* What though the illustrations sometimes make us smile ? that the praise of the moral and political effects of poetry may sometimes turn the smile into a laugh or a sigh ? Poetry after all, like all other human things, has a body and a soul. The body must be fashioned by art—perhaps the body *is* art ; but the soul is something else. The best poetry will not come without careful consideration of form and subject, of kind and style ; but it will not necessarily come with this consideration. There must be the inspiration, the enthusiasm, the *afflatus,* the glow ; and they are here in Sidney's tractate. Nor must we fail to draw attention, once more, to the difference of the English critical spirit here shown as regards both Italian and French.

In the decade which followed,[1] three notable books of English criticism appeared, none of them exhibiting Sidney's *afflatus,* but *King James's* all showing the interest felt in the subject, and one *Reulis and* exceeding in method, and at least attempted range, *Cautelis.* anything that English had known, or was to know, for more than a century. These were King James the First's (as yet only "the Sixth's") *Reulis and Cautelis to be observit and eschewit in Scottis Poesie,* 1585 ; William Webbe's *Discourse of English Poesie,* next year ; and the anonymous *Arte of English Poesie,* which appeared in 1589, and which (on rather weak evidence, but with no counter-claimant) is usually attributed to George or to Richard Puttenham.

---

[1] It may be desirable to note that Sidney's book, though very well known, as was the wont then, in MS., to all who cared to know, was never printed till 1595, nearly ten years after the author's death.

[2] All three are included in Mr Arber's *Reprints* and Prof. Gregory Smith's collection, with due biographical and bibliographical apparatus.

The first is the slightest; but it is interesting for more than its authorship. It was attached to James's *Essays of a Prentice in the Divine Art*, of which it gives some rules: it shows that Buchanan had taken pains with his pupil; and it also exhibits that slightly scholastic and "peddling," but by no means unreal, shrewdness and acumen which distinguished the British Solomon in his happier moments. It is characteristic that James is not in the least afraid of the charge of attending to mint, anise, and cumin. He plunges without any rhetorical exordium into what he calls "just colours"—do not rhyme on the same syllable, see that your rhyme is on accented syllables only, do not let your first or last word exceed two or three syllables at most. This dread of polysyllables, so curious to us, was very common at the time: it was one of the things from which Shakespeare's silent sovereignty delivered us by such touches of spell-dissolving mastery as

"The multitudinous seas incarnadine."

Then he passes to feet, of which he practically allows only the iamb; while he very oddly gives the *word* "foot" to the syllable, not the combination of syllables; and lays down the entirely arbitrary rule that the number of "feet"—*i.e.*, syllables—must be even, not odd. There is to be a sharp section ("cæsura") in the middle of every line, long or short; and the difference of long, short, and "indifferent" (common) feet or syllables is dwelt upon, with its influence of "flowing," as the King calls rhythm. Cautions on diction follow, and some against commonplaces, which look as if the royal prentice had read Gascoigne, a suggestion confirmed elsewhere.[1] Invention is briefly touched; and the tract finishes with a short account of the kinds of verse: "rhyme" —*i.e.*, the heroic couplet, "quhilk servis onely for lang historieis"; a heroical stanza of nine lines, rhymed *aabaabbab; ottava rima*, which he calls "ballat royal"; rhyme royal, which he calls "Troilus verse"; "rouncifals," or "tumbling verse" (doggerel alliterative, with bob and wheel); sonnets; "common" verse (octosyllable couplets); "all kinds of broken or cuttit verse," &c.

The tract is, as has been said, interesting, because it is an

---

[1] It is, however, excessive to represent James as a mere copyist of Gascoigne.

honest, and by no means unintelligent, attempt to make an English prosody, with special reference to a dialect which had done great things in its short day, but which had been specially affected—not to say specially disorganised—by the revived and bastard alliteration of the fifteenth century. Probably it was the study of French (where the iamb had long been the only foot) which, quite as much as mere following of Gascoigne, induced James to extend that crippling limitation to English; and the same influence may be seen in his insistence on the hard-and-fast section. These things (the latter of which at least rather endeared him to Dr Guest)[1] are, of course, quite wrong; but they express the genuine and creditable desire of the time to impose some order on the shambling doggerel of the generation or two immediately preceding. We find the same tendency even in Spenser, as far as rigid dissyllabic feet and sections are concerned; and it is certainly no shame for the Royal prentice to follow, though unknowing, the master and king of English poetry at the time when he wrote.

One would not, however, in any case have expected from James evidence of the root of the matter in poetry. There is *Webbe's* more of this root, though less scholarship and also *Discourse.* more "craze," in the obscure William Webbe, of whom we know practically nothing except that he was a Cambridge man, a friend of Robert Wilmot (the author of *Tancred and Gismund*) and private tutor to the sons of Edward Sulyard of Flemyngs, an Essex squire. The young Sulyards must have received some rather dubious instruction in the classics, for Webbe, in his inevitable classical exordium, thinks that Pindar was older than Homer, and that Horace came after—apparently a good while after—Ovid, and about the same time as Juvenal and Persius. He was, however, really and deeply interested in English verse; and his enthusiasm for Spenser — "the new poet," "our late famous poet," "the mightiest English poet that ever lived," is, if not in every case quite according to knowledge, absolutely right on the whole, and very pleasant and

---

[1] Who also caught at James's "tumbling verse" as a convenient stigmatisation for the true English equivalenced liberty.

refreshing to read. It is, indeed, the first thing of the kind
that we meet with in English; for the frequent earlier praises
of Chaucer are almost always long after date, always uncritical,
and for the most part [1] much rather expressions of a conventional tradition than of the writer's deliberate preference.

It was Webbe's misfortune, rather than his fault, that, like
his idol (but without that idol's resipiscence), and, like most
loyal Cambridge men, with the examples of Watson, Ascham,
and Drant before them, he was bitten with "the new versifying." It was rather his fault than his misfortune that he seems
to have taken very little pains to acquaint himself with the
actual performance of English poetry. Even of Gower he
speaks as though he only knew him through the references of
Chaucer and others: though three editions of the *Confessio*—
Caxton's one and Berthelette's two—were in print in his time.
His notice of Chaucer himself is curiously vague, and almost
limited to his powers as a satirist; while he has, what must
seem to most judges,[2] the astonishing idea of discovering "good
proportion of verse and meetly current style" in Lydgate,
though he reproves him for dealing with "superstitious and odd
matters." That he thinks *Piers Plowman* later than Lydgate
is unlucky, but not quite criminal. He had evidently read it
—indeed the book, from its kinship in parts to the Protestant,
not to say the Puritan, spirit, appealed to Elizabethan tastes,
and Crowley had already printed two editions of it, Rogers a
third. But he makes upon it the extraordinary remark, "The first
I have seen that observed the quantity of our verse without the
Slight in   curiosity of rhyme." What Webbe here means by
knowledge,   "quantity," or whether he had any clear deliberate
meaning at all, it is impossible to see: it is needless to say that
Langland is absolutely non-quantitative in the ordinary sense,
that if "quantity" means number of syllables he observes none,

---

[1] Occleve—no genius, but a true
man enough—deserves exception perhaps best.

[2] Some Germans—in this, as in other
matters, more hopelessly to seek in English now than, *teste* Porson, they were a
century ago in Greek—have followed

Webbe, as indeed Warton had strangely
done; and of course some Englishmen
have followed the Germans. Lydgate
himself knew better, though some of
the shorter poems attributed to him
are metrically, as well as in other ways,
not contemptible.

and that he can be scanned only on the alliterative-accentual system. For Gascoigne Webbe relies on "E. K."; brackets "the divers works of the old Earl of Surrey" with a dozen others; is copious on Phaer, Golding, &c., and mentions George Whetstone and Anthony Munday in words which would be adequate for Sackville (who is not named), and hardly too low for Spenser; while Gabriel Harvey is deliberately ranked with Spenser himself. Yet these things, rightly valued, are not great shame to Webbe. If he borrows from "E. K." some scorn of the "ragged rout of rakehell rhymers," and adds more of his own, he specifies nobody; and his depreciation is only the defect which almost necessarily accompanies the quality of his enthusiasm.

His piece, though not long, is longer than those of Gascoigne, Sidney, and King James. After a dedication (not more *but enthusi-* than excusably laudatory) to his patron Sulyard, *astic,* there is a curious preface to "The Noble Poets of England," who, if they had been inclined to be censorious, might have replied that Master Webbe, while complimenting them, went about to show that the objects of his compliment did not exist. "It is," he says, "to be wondered of all, and is lamented of many, that, while all other studies are used eagerly, only Poetry has found fewest friends to amend it." We have "as sharp and quick wits" in England as ever were Greeks and Romans: our tongue is neither coarse nor harsh, as she has already shown. All that is wanted is "some perfect platform or Prosodia of versifying: either in imitation of Greeks and Latins, or with necessary alterations. So, if the Noble Poets would "look so low from their divine cogitations, and "run over the simple censure" of Master Webbe's "weak brain," something might, perhaps, be done.

The treatise itself begins with the usual etymological definition of poetry, as "making," and the usual comments on *if uncritical,* the word "Vates"; but almost immediately digresses into praise of our late famous English poet who wrote the *Shepherd's Calendar* and a wish to see his "English Poet" (mentioned by "E. K."), which, alas! none of us have ever seen. This is succeeded, first by the classical and then by the English historical sketches, which have been commented upon. It ends with fresh laudation of Spenser.

Webbe then turns to the general consideration of poetry (especially from the allegoric-didactic point of view), of subjects, kinds, &c.; and it is to be observed that, though he several times cites Aristotle, he leans much more on Horace, and on Elyot's translations from him and other Latins. He then proceeds to a rather unnecessarily elaborate study of the *Æneid*, with large citations both from the original and from Phaer's translation, after which he returns once more to Spenser, and holds him up as at least the equal of Virgil and Theocritus. Indeed the *Calendar* is practically his theme all through, though he diverges from and embroiders upon it. Then, after glancing amiably enough at Tusser, and mentioning a translation of his own of the *Georgics*, which has got into the hands of some piratical publisher, he attacks the great rhyme-question, to which he has, from the Preface onwards, more than once alluded. Much of what he says is borrowed, or a little advanced, from Ascham; but Webbe is less certain about the matter than his master, and again diverges into a consideration of divers English metres, always illustrated, where possible, from the *Calendar*. Still harking back again, he decides that "the true kind of versifying" might have been effected in English: though (as Campion, with better wits, did after him) he questions whether some alteration of the actual Greek and Latin forms is not required. He gives a list of classical feet (fairly correct, except that he makes the odd confusion of a trochee and a tribrach), and discusses the liberties which must be taken with English to adjust it to some of them. Elegiacs, he thinks, will not do: Hexameters and Sapphics go best. And, to prove this, he is rash enough to give versions of his own, in the former metre, of Virgil's first and second eclogues, in the latter, **of** Spenser's beautiful

"Ye dainty nymphs that in this blessed brook."

It is enough to say that he succeeds in stripping all three of **every rag** of poetry. A translation of Fabricius'[1] prose sylla-

---

[1] *V. Hist. Crit.*, ii. 354.

bus of Horace's rules, gathered not merely out of the *Ep. ad Pisones* but elsewhere, and an " epilogue," modest as to himself, sanguine as to what will happen when " the rabble of bald rhymes is turned to famous works," concludes the piece.

On the whole, to use the hackneyed old phrase once more, we could have better spared a better critic than Webbe, who *in appreci-* gives us—in a fashion invaluable to map-makers of *ation.* the early exploration of English criticism — the workings of a mind furnished with no original genius for poetry, and not much for literature, not very extensively or accurately erudite, but intensely *interested* in matters literary, and especially in matters poetical, generously enthusiastic for such good things as were presented to it, not without some mother-wit even in its crazes, and encouraged in those crazes not, as in Harvey's case, by vanity, pedantry, and bad taste, but by its very love of letters. Average dispositions of this kind were, as a rule, diverted either into active life—very much for the good of the nation—or—not at all for its good—into the acrid disputes of hot-gospelling and Puritanism. Webbe, to the best of his modest powers, was a devotee of literature: for which let him have due honour.

Puttenham—or whosoever else it was, if it was not Puttenham [1]—has some points of advantage, and one great one *Putten-* of disadvantage, in comparison with Webbe. In *ham's (?)* poetical faculty there is very little to choose be-*Art of Eng-* tween them—the abundant specimens of his own *lish Poesie.* powers, which the author of *The Art of English Poesie* gives (and which are eked out by a late copy of one of the works referred to, *Partheniades*), deserve the gibes they receive in one of our scanty early notices of the book, that by Sir John Harington (*v. infra*). On the other hand, Puttenham has very little of that engaging enthusiasm which atones for

---

[1] The whole of the documents in the case will be found, clearly put, in Arber and Gregory Smith: also in Mr Herbert Croft's edition of *The Governor* of Sir Thomas Elyot, the Puttenhams' uncle. The first attribution is in Bolton (*v. infra*) some fifteen years later than the date of the book, and not quite positive ("as the Fame is "). Whether it was George or whether it was Richard, *non liquet.*

so much in his contemporary. But this very want of enthusiasm somewhat prepares us for, though it need not necessarily
accompany, merits which we do not find in Webbe, considered
as a critic. *The Art of English Poesy*, which, as has been said,
appeared in 1589, three years later than Webbe's, but which,
from some allusions, may have been written, or at least begun,
before it, and which, from other allusions, must have been the
work of a man well advanced in middle life, is methodically
composed, very capable in range and plan, and supported with
a by no means contemptible erudition, and no inconsiderable
supply of judgment and common - sense. It was unfortunate
for Puttenham that he was just a little too old: that having
been—as from a fairly precise statement of his he must have
been—born *cir.* 1530-35, he belonged to the early and uncertain
generation of Elizabethan men of letters, the Googes and
Turbervilles, and Gascoignes, not to the generation of Sidney
and Spenser, much less to that of Shakespeare and Jonson.
But what he had he gave: and it is far from valueless.

The book is "to-deled" (as the author of the *Ancren Riwle*
would say) into three books—"Of Poets and Poesie," "Of Proportion," and "Of Ornament." It begins, as usual,
Its erudition. with observations on the words poet and maker,
references to the ancients, &c.; but this exordium, which is
fitly written in a plain but useful and agreeable style, is com-
mendably short. The writer lays it down, with reasons, that
there may be an Art of English as of Latin and Greek poetry;
but cannot refrain from the same sort of "writing at large" as to
poets being the first philosophers, &c., which we have so often
seen.[1] Indeed we must lay our account with the almost
certain fact that all writers of this period had seen Sidney's
Defence at least in MS. or had heard of it. He comes closer to
business with his remarks on the irreption of rhyme into Greek
and Latin poetry; and shows a better knowledge of leonine and
other mediæval Latin verse, not merely than Webbe, but even
than Ascham. A very long section then deals with the
question—all-interesting to a man of the Renaissance—in what

---

[1] Harington, a person of humour, and a typical Englishman, perstringes this as well as other things in his fling at the *Art*.

reputation poets were with princes of old, and how they be now contemptible (wherein Puttenham shows a rather remarkable acquaintance with modern European literature), and then turns to the subject or matter of poesy and the forms thereof, handling the latter at great length, and with a fair sprinkle of literary anecdote. At last he comes to *English* poetry; and though, as we might expect, he does not go behind the late fourteenth century, he shows rather more knowledge than Webbe and (not without slips here and elsewhere) far more comparative judgment. It must, however, be admitted that, engaging as is his description of Sir Walter Raleigh's "vein most lofty, insolent, and passionate," he does not show to advantage in the patronising glance in passing at "that other gentleman who wrote the late *Shepherd's Calendar*," contrasted with the description of the Queen our Sovereign lady, "whose Muse easily surmounteth all the rest in any kind on which it may please her Majesty to employ her pen." But here the allowance comes in: the stoutest Tory of later days can never wholly share, though he may remotely comprehend, the curious mixture of religious, romantic, patriotic, amatory, and interested feelings with which the men of the sixteenth century wrote about Gloriana.

The second book deals with Proportion, in which word Puttenham includes almost everything belonging to Prosody *Systematic* in its widest sense—staff, stanza, measure, metres, *arrangement* and feet, "cæsure," rhyme, accent, cadence, situation (by which he means the arrangement of the rhymes), and proportion in figure. On most of these heads he speaks more or less in accordance with his fellows (though he very noticeably abstains from extreme commendation or condemnation of rhyme), save that, for the moment, he seems to neglect the "new versifying." It is, however, but for a moment. After his chapters on "proportion" in figure (the fanciful egg, wheel, lozenge, &c., which he himself argues for, and which were to make critics of the Addisonian type half-angry and half-sad), he deals with the subject.

About this "new versifying" he is evidently in two minds. He had glanced at it before (and refers to the glance now)[1] as "a nice and scholastic curiosity." However, "for the information of our young makers, and pleasure to those who be delighted in novelty, *and to the intent that we may not seem by ignorance or oversight to omit,*"[2] he "will now deal with it." Which he does at great length; and, at any rate sometimes, with a clearer perception of the prosodic values than any other, even Spenser, had yet shown. But he does not seem quite at home in the matter, and glides off to a discussion of feet—classical feet—in the usual rhymed English verse.

The third book is longer than the first and second put together, and is evidently that in which the author himself *and ex-* took most pleasure. It is called "Of Ornament," *uberant* but practically deals with the whole question of *indulgence* *lexis* or style, so that it is at least common to *in Figures.* Rhetoric and Poetics. In one respect, too, it belongs more specially to the former, in that it contains the most elaborate treatment of rhetorical figures to be found, up to its time, in English literature. Full eighty pages are occupied with the catalogue of these "Figures Auricular" wherein Puttenham (sometimes rather badly served by his pen or his printer) ransacks the Greek rhetoricians, and compiles a list (with explanations and examples) of over one hundred and twenty. It is preceded and followed by more general remarks, of which some account must be given.

Beginning with an exordial defence of ornament in general, Puttenham proceeds to argue that set speeches, as in Parliament, not merely may but ought to be couched in something more than a conversational style. This added grace must be given by (1) Language, (2) Style, (3) Figures. On diction he has remarks both shrewd and interesting, strongly commending the language of the Court and of the best citizens, not pro-

---

[1] Here as elsewhere we may note evidences of possible revision in the book. That there was some such revision is certain; for instance, Ben Jonson's copy (the existence of which is not uninteresting) contains a large cancel of four leaves, not found in other copies known. For this and other points of the same kind, see the editions cited.

[2] "Reviewing" was as yet in its infancy—a curiously lively one though, with Nash and others coming on. Puttenham seems to have understood its little ways rather well.

vincial speech, or that of seaports, or of universities, or in other ways merely technical. "The usual speech of the court, and that of London and the shires lying about London, within ten miles and not much above" is his norm. There is also a noteworthy and very early reference to English dictionaries, and a cautious section on neologisms introduced from other tongues to fill wants. Style he will have reached by "a constant and continual tenor of writing," and gives the usual subdivision of high, low, and middle. And so to his Figures.

The details and illustrations of the long catalogue of these invite comment, but we must abstain therefrom. When the list is finished, Puttenham returns to his generalities with a discussion of the main principle of ornament, which he calls *Decorum* or "Decency," dividing and illustrating the kinds of it into choice of subject, diction, delivery, and other things, not without good craftsmanship, and with a profusion of anecdotes chiefly of the Helotry kind. He then (rather oddly, but not out of keeping with his classical models) has a chapter of decorum in behaviour, turns to the necessity of concealing art, and ends with a highly flattering conclusion to the Queen.

We have yet to mention some minorities; less briefly, the two champions—Campion and Daniel, who brought the question of "Rhyme *v.* 'Verse'" to final arbitrament of battle; the great name (not so great here as elsewhere) of Francis Bacon; and lastly, Ben Jonson, who, if he long survived Elizabeth, is far the greatest of Elizabethan critics, and perhaps the only English critic who deserves the adjective "great" before Dryden.

The earliest (1591) of these is Sir John Harington, in the *Minors:* prefatory matter [1] of his translation of the *Orlando*, *Harington,* which contains the gibe at Puttenham above re-*Meres,* *Webster,* ferred to. It is otherwise much indebted to Sidney, *Bolton, &c.* from whom, however, Harington differs in allowing more scope to allegorical interpretation. Then comes Francis

---

[1] Reprinted by Haslewood. Whetstone's Preface to *Promos and Cassandra* (1578) and A. Fraunce's *Arcadian Rhetoric* (1588) are earlier still. The former anticipates Sidney in objecting to the irregularity of English plays: the latter is a strong partisan of classical metres, his practice in which is sufficiently roughly treated by Ben Jonson in his *Conversations, v. infra,* p. 82.

Meres, whose *Palladis Tamia*[1] (1598) is to be eternally mentioned with gratitude, because it gives us our one real document about the order of Shakespeare's plays, but is quite childish in the critical characterisation which it not uninterestingly attempts. Webster's equally famous, and universally known, epitheting of the work of Shakespeare and others in the Preface to *The White Devil* (1612) adds yet another instance of the short sight of contemporaries; but tempting as it may be to comment on these, it would not become a Historian of Criticism to do so in this context. William Vaughan in *The Golden Grove* (1600) had earlier dealt, and Bolton[2] in his *Hypercritica* (1616), and Peacham in his *Complete Gentleman* (1622), were later to deal, with Poetry, but in terms adding nothing to, and probably borrowed from, the utterances of Sidney, Webbe, and Puttenham. Their contributions are "sma' sums," as Bailie Nicol Jarvie says, and we must neglect them.

The most interesting literary result of the "new versifying" craze is to be found, without doubt, in the *Observations in the Art of English Poesy* of Thomas Campion[3] and the subsequent *Defence of Rhyme* of Samuel Daniel. The former was issued in 1602, and the latter still later ; —that is to say more than twenty years after Spenser's and Harvey's letters, and more than thirty after the appearance—let alone the writing—of Ascham's *Schoolmaster*. In the interval the true system of English prosody had put itself practically beyond all real danger; but the critical craze had never received its quietus. Nay, it survived to animate Milton : and there are persons whom we could only name for the sake of honour, who would not appear to see that it is dead even yet. Both the writers mentioned were true poets: and

Campion and his Observations.

---

[1] Reprinted (in its critical section) by Mr Arber, *English Garner*, ii. 94 *sq.*, and in Gregory Smith.

[2] Bolton's criticism of his contemporaries is extracted in Warton (iv. 204 *sq.*, ed. Hazlitt). The writer, who is dealing with History, and speaking directly of language, disallows most of Spenser (excepting the *Hymns*) and all Chaucer, Lydgate, Langland, and Skelton, can "endure" Gascoigne, praises Elizabeth and James (of course), Chapman, Daniel, Drayton, Constable, Southwell, Sackville, Surrey, Wyatt, Raleigh, Donne, and Greville, but gives the palm for "vital, judicious, and practicable" language to Jonson.

[3] Ed. Bullen, *Works of Campion*, London, 1889, and in Gregory Smith.

the curious thing is that the more exquisitely romantic poet of
the two was the partisan of classical prosody. But Campion—
who dedicated his book to Lord Buckhurst, the *doyen* (except
poor old Churchyard) of English poetry at the time, and one
whose few but noble exercises in it need hardly vail their crest
to any contemporary poetry but Spenser's and Shakespeare's
—was far too wise a man, as well as far too good a poet, to
champion any longer the break-neck and break-jaw hexameters
of Harvey and Stanyhurst. We have seen that, almost from
the first, there had been questions of heart among the partisans
of the New Versifying. That English is not tolerant of dactyls
—that dactyls, do what you will, in English, will tilt themselves
up into anapæsts with anacrusis—is a truth which no impartial
student of metre with an ear, and with an eye to cover the
history of English poetry, can deny. Some even of these
pioneers had seen this: Campion has the boldness to declare it
in the words, "It [the dactylic hexameter] is an attempt altogether against the nature of our language." But though he was
bold so far, he was not quite bold enough. He could not sur-
mount the queer Renaissance objection to rhyme. That all the
arguments against the "barbarism" of this tell equally against
Christianity, chivalry, the English constitution, the existence
of America, gunpowder, glass-windows, coal-fires, and a very
large number of other institutions of some usefulness, never
seems to have occurred to any of these good folk. But no man
can escape his time. Campion, not noticing, or not choosing
to notice, the intensely English quality of the anapæst, limits,
or almost limits, our verse to iambs and trochees. It was possible for him—though it still appears to be difficult for some—
to recognise the tribrach, the mere suggestion of which in English verse threw Dr Guest into a paroxysm of "! ! ! !'s," but
which exists as certainly as does the iamb itself. On the contrary he shows himself in advance of Guest, and of most behind Guest to his own time, by admitting tribrachs in the third
and fifth places. Nay, he even sees that a trochee may take
the place of an iamb (Milton's probably borrowed secret) in
the first place, though his unerring ear (I think there is no
verse of Campion's that is unmusical) insists on some other foot

than an iamb following — otherwise, he says, "it would too much *drink up* the verse." But, on the whole, he sets himself to work, a self-condemned drudge, to make iambic and trochaic verses without rhyme. And on these two, with certain licences, he arranges schemes of English elegiacs, anacreontics, and the rest. Some of the examples of these are charming poems, notably the famous "Rose-Cheeked Laura," and the beautiful "Constant to None," while Campion's subsequent remark on English quantity are among the acutest on the subject. But the whole thing has on it the curse of "flying in the face of nature." You have only to take one of Campion's own poems (written mostly *after* the *Observations*) in natural rhyme, and the difference will be seen at once. It simply comes to this—that the good rhymeless poems would be infinitely better with rhyme, and that the bad ones, while they might sometimes be absolutely saved by the despised invention of Huns and Vandals, are always made worse by its absence.

In the preface of Daniel's answering *Defence of Rhyme to all the worthy lovers and learned professors* [*thereof*] *within His Majesty's dominions*,[1] he says that he wrote it "about a year since," upon the "great reproach" given by Campion, and some give it the date of 1603 or even 1602; but Dr Grosart's reprint is dated five years later. The learned gentleman to whom it was specially written was no less a person than William Herbert, Earl of Pembroke, whom some of us (acknowledging that the matter is no matter) do not yet give up as "Mr W. H." The advocate affects, with fair rhetorical excuse (though of course he must have known that the craze was nearly half a century old, and had at least not been discouraged by his patron's uncle nearly a generation before), to regard the attack on rhyming as something new, as merely concerned with the "measures" of Campion. Daniel, always a gentleman, deals handsomely with his antagonist, whom he does not name, but describes as "this detractor whose commendable rhymes, albeit now an enemy to rhyme, have given heretofore to the world the best notice of his worth," and as a man "of fair parts and good reputation." And having put

Daniel and his Defence *of Rhyme.*

---

[1] In Chalmers's *Poets*, Grosart's *Works of Samuel Daniel*, and Gregory Smith.

himself on the best ground, in this way, from the point of view
of morals and courtesy, he does the same in matter of argument
by refusing to attack Campion's "numbers" in themselves (" We
could," he says, " well have allowed of his numbers, had he not
disgraced our rhymes "), and by seizing the unassailable position
given by custom and nature—" Custom that is before all law;
Nature that is above all art." In fact, not Jonson himself, and
certainly none else before Jonson, has comprehended, or at least
put, the truth of the matter as Daniel puts it, that arbitrary
laws imposed on the poetry of any nation are absurd—that the
verse of a language is such as best consorts with the nature of
that language. This seems a truism enough perhaps; but it
may be very much doubted whether all critics recognise it, and
its consequences, even at the present day. And it is certain
that we may search other early English critics in vain for a
frank recognition of it. With an equally bold and sure foot he
strides over the silly stuff about "invention of barbarous ages"
and the like. Whatever its origin (and about this he shows a
wise carelessness), it is "an excellence added to this work of
measure and harmony, far happier than any proportion quantity
could ever show." It "gives to the ear an echo of a delightful
report," and to the memory "a deeper impression of what is
delivered." He is less original (as well as, some may think, less
happy) in distinguishing the accent of English from the quantity
of the classical tongues; but the classicisers before Campion, if
not Campion himself, had made such a mess of quantity, and
had played such havoc with accent, that he may well be
excused. The universality of rhyme is urged, and once more
says Daniel (with that happy audacity in the contemning of
vain things which belongs to the born exploders of crazes),
"If the barbarian likes it, it is because it sways the affections of
the barbarian; if civil nations practise it, it works upon their
hearts; if all, then it has a power in nature upon all." But it
will be said, "Ill customs are to be left." No doubt: but the
question is begged. Who made *this* custom "ill"? Rhyme
aims at pleasing—and it pleases. Suffer then the world to enjoy
that which it knows and what it likes, for all the tyrannical
rules of rhetoric cannot make it otherwise. Why are we to be

a mere *servum pecus*, only to imitate the Greeks and Latins?
Their way was natural to them: let ours be so to us. "Why
should laboursome curiosity still lay affliction on our best
delights?" Moreover, "to a spirit whom nature hath fitted
for that mystery," rhyme is no impediment, "but rather giveth
wings to mount." The necessary historical survey follows, with
a surprising and very welcome justification of the Middle Ages
against both Classics and Renaissance. "Let us," says this true
Daniel come to judgment, "go not further, but look upon the
wonderful architecture of the State of England, and see whether
they were unlearned times that could give it such a form?"
And if politically, why not poetically? Some acute and, in the
other sense, rather sharp criticism of Campion's details follows,
with a few apologetic remarks for mixture of masculine and
feminine rhymes on his own part: and the whole concludes in
an admirable peroration with a great end-note to it. Not easily
shall we find, either in Elizabethan times or in any other, a
happier combination of solid good sense with eager poetic sentiment, of sound scholarship with wide-glancing intelligence, than
in this little tractate of some thirty or forty ordinary pages,
which dispelled the delusions of two generations, and made the
poetical fortune of England sure.

The contributions of "large-browed Verulam" to criticism
have sometimes been spoken of with reverence: and it is not uncommon to find, amid the scanty classics of the subject,

Bacon.

which until recently have been recommended to the
notice of inquirers, not merely a place, but a place of very high
honour, assigned to *The Advancement of Learning*. Actual,
unprejudiced, and to some extent expert, reference to the works,
however, will not find very much to justify this estimate : and,
indeed, a little thought, assisted by very moderate knowledge,
would suffice to make it rather surprising that Bacon should give
us so much, than disappointing that he should give us little or
nothing. A producer of literature who at his best has few
superiors, and a user of it for purposes of quotation, who would
deserve the name of genius for this use alone if he had no other
title thereto—Bacon was yet by no means inclined by his main
interests and objects, or by his temperament, either towards

great exaltation of letters, or towards accurate and painstaking examination of them. Indeed, it is in him—almost first of all men, certainly first of all great modern men—that we find that partisan opposition between literature and science which has constantly developed since. It is true that his favourite method of examination into "forms" might seem tempting as applied to literature; and that it would, incidentally if not directly, have yielded more solid results than his Will-o'-the-wisp chase of the Form of Heat. But this very craze of his may suggest that if he had undertaken literary criticism it would have been on the old road of Kinds and Figures and Qualities, in which we could expect little but glowing rhetorical generalisation from him.

Nor is the nature of such small critical matter as we actually have from him very different. The Essays practically give us *The Essays.* nothing but the contents of that *Of Studies*, a piece too well known to need quotation; too much in the early pregnant style of the author to bear compression or analysis; and too general to repay it. For the critic and the man of letters generally it is, in its own phrase, to be not merely tasted, nor even swallowed, but chewed and digested; yet its teachings have nothing more to do with the critical function of "study" than with all others.

The *Advancement* [1] at least excuses the greatness thrust upon it in the estimates above referred to, not merely by the *The* Advance- apparent necessity that the author should deal with ment of Criticism, but by a certain appearance of his Learning. actually doing so. Comparatively early in the First Book he tackles the attention to style which sprang up at the Renaissance, opening his discussion by the ingenious but slightly unhistorical attribution of it to Martin Luther, who was forced to awake all antiquity, and call former times to his succour, against the Bishop of Rome. Not a few names, for the best part of two centuries before the great cause of *Martinus* v.

---

[1] It ought to be, but from certain signs perhaps is not, unnecessary to say that the *De Augmentis* is itself no mere Latin version of the *Advancement*, but a large expansion of it. There seems, however, no necessity here to deal with both.

Papam was launched, from Petrarch and Boccaccio to Erasmus and Reuchlin, will put in evidence before the tribunal of chronology against this singular assertion; and though the Italian Humanists of the fifteenth century might not (at least in thought) care anything for the Pope except as a source of donatives and benefices, it is certain that most of them were as constitutionally disinclined to abet Luther as they were chronologically disabled from in any way abetting him. Bacon's argument and further survey are, however, better than this beginning. To understand the ancients (he says justly enough) it was necessary to make a careful study of their language. Further, the opposition of thought to the School-men naturally brought about a recoil from the barbarisms of Scholastic style, and the anxiety to win over the general imprinted care and elegance and vigour on preaching and writing. All this, he adds as justly, turned to excess. Men *Its denunci-* began to "hunt more after words than matter; *ation of mere* more after the choiceness of the phrase and the *word-study.* round and clean composition of the sentence, and the sweet falling of the clauses, and the varying and illustra-tion of their words with tropes and figures, than after the weight of matter, worth of subject, soundness of argument, life of invention, or depth of judgment." The Ciceronianism of Osorius, Sturm, "Car of Cambridge," and even Ascham, receives more or less condemnation; and Erasmus is, of course, cited for gibes at it. On this text Bacon proceeds to enlarge in his own stately rhetoric, coolly admitting that it "is a thing not hastily to be condemned, to clothe and adorn the obscurity even of philosophy itself with sensible and plausible elocution." But he very quickly glides off into his usual denunciations of the schoolmen. Nor have I found anything else in this First Book really germane to our purpose; for one cannot cite as such the desultory observations on patronage of literature (among other branches of learning) which fill a good part of it.

The Second Book is somewhat more fruitful in quantity, if not very much; but the quality remains not very different. The opening "Address to the King" contains, in an interesting first draft (as we may call it), the everlasting grumble of the scientific man, that science is not sufficiently endowed, the further grumble at mere book-learning, the cry for the promotion—by putting money in its purse—of research. The Second and Third Chapters contain some plans of books drawn up in Bacon's warm imaginative way, especially a great series of Histories, with the *History of England* for their centre. And then we come, in the Fourth Chapter, to Poesy.

But except for Bacon's majestic style (which, however, by accident or intention, is rather below itself here) there is *Its view of* absolutely nothing novel. The view (which, as we *Poetry.* have seen, all the Elizabethan critics adopted, probably from the Italians)—the view is that poetry is just a part of learning licensed in imagination; a fanciful history intended to give satisfaction to the mind of man in things where history is not; something particularly prevalent and useful in barbarous ages; divisible into narrative, representative and allusive; useful now and then, but (as Aristotle would say) not a thing to take very seriously. Yet poetry, a *vinum dæmonum* at the worst, a mere illusion anyhow, is still, even as such, a refuge from, and remedy for, sorrow and toil. Of its form, as distinguished from its matter, he says,[1] " Poetry is but a character of style, and belongeth to arts of speech, and is not pertinent for the present." He attempts no defence of it as of other parts of learning, because " being as a plant that cometh of the lust of the earth without a formal seed, it hath sprung up and spread abroad more than any other kind." And he turns from it to philosophy, with the more than half-disdainful adieu, " It is not good to stay too long in the theatre."

We might almost quit him here with a somewhat similar leave-taking; but for his great reputation some other places *Some* obiter shall be handled. At XIV. 11 there are some *dicta.* remarks on the delusive powers of words; at XVI. 4, 5 some on grammar and rhetoric, including a rather interesting observation, not sufficiently expanded or worked out, that " in modern languages it seemeth to me as free to make new measures of verses as of dances "; in XVIII. a handling of strictly oratorical rhetoric, with a digression to these " Colours

---

[1] *Advancement of Learning*, Bk. II. iv.

of Good and Evil" which interested Bacon so much; in XX.
another descant on the same art; in XXI. a puff of the
Basilikon Doron; in XXXII. observations on the moral
influence of books; in XXXV. some general observations on
literature; and, just before the close, a well-known and often-
quoted eulogy, certainly not undeserved, of the eloquence of the
English pulpit for forty years past.

If it were not for the singular want of a clear conception
of literary Criticism, which has prevailed so long and so widely,
The whole of it would hardly be necessary to take, with any
very slight seriousness at all, a man who has no more than this
importance. to say on the subject.[1]   It is most assuredly no
slight to Bacon to deny him a place in a regiment where he
never had the least ambition to serve.   That he was himself
a great practitioner of literature, and so, necessarily if indirectly, a critic of it in his own case, is perfectly true; the
remarks which have been quoted above on the Ciceronians
show that, when he took the trouble, and found the opportunity, he could make them justly and soundly.   But his
purpose, his interests, his province, his vein, lay far elsewhere.
To him, it is pretty clear, literary expression was, in relation
to his favourite studies and dreams, but a higher kind of pen-
and-ink or printing - press.   He distrusted the stability of
modern languages, and feared that studies couched in them
might some day or other come to be unintelligible and lost to
the world.   This famous fear explains the nature and the
limits of his interest in literature.   It was a vehicle or a
treasury, a distributing agent or a guard.   Its functions and
qualities accorded: it was to be clear, not disagreeable, solidly
constructed, intelligible to as large a number of readers as
possible.   The psychological character and morphological def-

---

[1] Those who wish to see what has
been said for Bacon will find references
in Gayley and Scott.   The panegyrists
—from Professor Masson to Mr Worsfold—chiefly rely on the description of
poetry above referred to, as "Feigned
History," with what follows on its
advantages and on poetical justice, &c.

All this seems to me, however admirably expressed, to be very obvious and
rudimentary.   Recently Mr Spingarn,
in *Cambridge History of Eng. Lit.,* vol.
vii., has claimed for Bacon an appreciation of literary history which I also
cannot fully grant.

inition of poetry interested him philosophically. But in the art and the beauty of poetry and literature generally, for their own sakes, he seems to have taken no more interest than he did in the coloured pattern-plots in gardens, which he compared to "tarts." To a man so minded, as to those more ancient ones of similar mind whom we have discussed in the first volume, Criticism proper could, at the best, be a pastime to be half ashamed of—a "theatre" in which to while away the hours; it could not possibly be a matter of serious as well as enthusiastic study.

Between Bacon and Ben may be best noticed the short *Anacrisis or Censure of Poets, Ancient and Modern*,[1] by Sir William Alexander, Earl of Stirling. It has re-

Stirling's Anacrisis.

ceived high praise;[2] but even those who think by no means ill of *Aurora*, may find some difficulty in indorsing this. It is simply a sort of "Note," written, as the author says, to record his impressions during a reading of the poets, which he had undertaken as refreshment after great travail both of body and mind. He thinks Language "but the apparel of poesy," thereby going even further than those who would assign that position to verse, and suggesting a system of "Inarticulate Poetics," which he would have been rather put to it to body forth. He only means, however, that he judges in the orthodox Aristotelian way, by "the fable and contexture." A subsequent comparison of a poem to a garden suggests the French critic Vauquelin de la Fresnaye, whom he may have read. Alexander is a sort of general lover in poetry; he likes this in Virgil, that in Ovid, that other in Horace; defends Lucan against Scaliger, even to the point of blaming the conclusion of the *Æneid;* finds "no man that doth satisfy him more than the notable Italian, Torquato Tasso"; admits the

---

[1] To be most readily found in Rogers's *Memorials of the Earl of Stirling* (vol. ii. pp. 205-210; Edinburgh, 1877), where, however, it appears merely as one of the Appendices to a book of more or less pure genealogy, without the slightest editorial information as to date or *provenance*. It seems to be taken from the 1711 folio of Drum-

mond's *Works;* and to have been written in 1634, between Bacon's death and Ben's. (It has since been given in Mr O. Smeaton's *Scots Essayists*.)

[2] From Park, and from Messrs Gayley and Scott. I did not always agree with my late friend Dr Grosart: but I think he was better advised when he called it "disappointing."

historical as well as the fictitious poetic subject; but thinks that "the treasures of poetry cannot be better bestowed than upon the apparelling of Truth; and Truth cannot be better apparelled to please young lovers than with the excellences of poetry." Disrespectful language neither need nor should be used of so slight a thing, which is, and pretends to be, nothing more than a sort of table-book entry by a gentleman of learning as well as quality. But, if it has any "importance" at all, it is surely that of being yet another proof of the rapid diffusion of critical taste and practice, not of stating "theory and methods considerably in advance of the age." If we could take extensively his protest against those who "would bound the boundless liberty of the poet," such language might indeed be justified; but the context strictly limits it to the very minor, though then, and for long before and after, commonly debated, question of Fiction v. History in subject.

Save perhaps in one single respect (where the defect was not wholly his fault), Ben Jonson might be described as a critic *Ben Jonson: his equipment.* armed at all points. His knowledge of literature was extremely wide, being at the same time solid and thorough. While he had an understanding above all things strong and masculine, he was particularly addicted, though in no dilettante fashion, to points of form. His whole energies, and they were little short of Titanic, were given to literature. And, lastly, if he had not the supremest poetic genius, he had such a talent that only the neighbourhood of supremacy dwarfs it. Where he came short was not in a certain hardness of temper and scholasticism of attitude: for these, if kept within bounds, and tempered by that enthusiasm for letters which he possessed, are not bad equipments for the critic. It was rather in the fact that he still came too early for it to be possible for him, except by the help of a miracle, to understand the achievements and value of the vernaculars. By his latest days, indeed,[1] the positive per-

[1] These days carried him far beyond the 16th century. His solidarity with the Elizabethans proper, however, makes his inclusion here imperative. It may be added that since this book was first written, the classical strain of the *Discoveries* has been indicated with much learning, but with excessive stress of unfavourable reference, by a French critic, M. Castellain.

formance of these was already very great. Spain has hardly added anything since, and Italy not very much, to her share of European literature; France was already in the first flush of her "classical" period, after a long and glorious earlier history: and what Ben's own contemporaries in England had done, all men know. But mediæval literature was shut from him, as from all, till far later; he does not seem to have been much drawn to Continental letters, and, perhaps in their case, as certainly in English, he was too near—too much a part of the movement—to get it into firm perspective.

In a sense the critical temper in Jonson is all-pervading. It breaks out side by side with, and sometimes even within, his *His* sweetest lyrics; it interposes what may be called *Prefaces,* *parabases* in the most unexpected passages [1] of his *&c.* plays. *The Poetaster* is almost as much criticism dramatised as *The Frogs.* But there are three "places," or groups of places, which it inspires, not in mere suggestion, but with propriety—the occasional Prefaces, or observations, to and on the plays themselves, the *Conversations with Drummond,* and, above all, the at last fairly (though not yet sufficiently) known *Discoveries* or *Timber.*

To piece together, with any elaboration, the more scattered critical passages would be fitter for a monograph on Jonson than for a History of Criticism. The "Address to the Readers" of *Sejanus,* which contains a reference to the author's lost *Observations on Horace, his Art of Poetry* (not the least of such

---

[1] Take this interesting passage in the masque of *The New World Discovered in the Moon*—

Chro. Is he a man's poet or a woman's poet, I pray you?

2nd Her. Is there any such difference?

Fact. Many, as betwixt your man's tailor and your woman's tailor.

1st Her. How, may we beseech you?

Fact. I'll show you: your man's poet may break out strong and deep i' the mouth, . . . but your woman's poet must flow, and stroke the ear, and as one of them said of himself sweetly—

"Must write a verse as smooth and calm as cream,

In which there is no torrent, nor scarce stream."

On this Gifford discovered in Theobald's copy the note: "*Woman's Poet, his soft versification—Mr P——.*"

The Induction to *Every Man out of His Humour,* a very large part of *Cynthia's Revels,* not a little of *The Silent Woman,* and scores of other places, might be added. (Since this was written Dr David Klein has made a good collection, *Literary Criticism from the Elizabethan Dramatists* (New York, 1910), including Ben and drawing on others.)

losses) is a fair specimen of them: the dedication of *Volpone*
to "the most noble and most equal sisters, Oxford and Cambridge," a better.   In both, and in numerous other passages of
prose and verse, we find the real and solid, though somewhat
partial, knowledge, the strong sense, the methodic scholarship
of Ben, side by side with his stately, not Euphuistic, but
rather too close-packed style, his not ill-founded, but slightly
excessive, self-confidence, and that rough knock-down manner
of assertion and characterisation which reappeared in its most
unguarded form in the *Conversations* with Drummond.

The critical utterances of these *Conversations* are far too
interesting to be passed over here, though we cannot discuss

The Drum- them in full.   They tell us that Ben thought all
mond Con- (other) rhymes inferior to couplets, and had written
versations. a treatise (which, again, would we had!) against both
Campion and Daniel (see *ante*).   His objection to "stanzas and
cross rhymes" was that "as the purpose might lead beyond them,
they were all forced."   Sidney "made every one speak as well as
himself," and so did not keep "decorum" (cf. Puttenham above).
Spenser's stanzas and language did not please him.   Daniel
was no poet.   He did not like Drayton's "long verses," nor Sylvester's and Fairfax's translations.   He thought the translations
of Homer (Chapman's) and Virgil (Phaer's) into "long Alexandrines" (*i.e.*, fourteeners) were but prose: yet elsewhere we hear
that he "had some of Chapman by heart."   Harington's *Ariosto*
was the worst of all translations.   Donne was sometimes
"profane," and "for not keeping of accent deserved hanging";
but elsewhere he was "the first poet of the world in some
things," though, "through not being understood, he would
perish." [1]   Shakespeare "wanted art": and "Abram Francis
(Abraham Fraunce) in his English Hexameters was a fool."
"Bartas was not a poet, but a verser, because he wrote not
fiction."   He cursed Petrarch for reducing verses to sonnets,
"which were like Procrustes' bed."   Guarini incurred the

---

[1] These dicta, thus juxtaposed, should make all argument about apparently one-sided judgments superfluous.   If Drummond had omitted almost any single one, we should have been utterly wrong in arguing from the remainder.

same blame as Sir Philip: and Lucan was good in parts only. "The best pieces of Ronsard were his Odes." Drummond's own verses "were all good, but smelled too much of the schools." The "silver" Latins, as we should expect, pleased him best. "To have written Southwell's 'Burning Babe,' he would have been content to destroy many of his."

These are the chief really critical items, though there are others (putting personal gossip aside) of interest; but it may be added, as a curiosity, that he told Drummond that he himself "writ all first in prose" at Camden's suggestion, and held that "verses stood all by sense, without colours or accent" (poetic diction or metre), "which yet at other times he denied," says the reporter, a sentence ever to be remembered in connection with these jottings. Remembering it, there is nothing shocking in any of these observations, nor anything really inconsistent. A true critic never holds the neat, positive, "reduced-to-its-lowest-terms" estimate of authors, in which a criticaster delights. His view is always facetted, conditioned. But he may, in a friendly chat, or a conversation for victory, exaggerate this facet or condition, while altogether suppressing others; and this clearly is what Ben did.

For gloss on the *Conversations*, for reduction to something like system of the critical remarks scattered through the works, and for the nearest approach we can have to a formal presentment of Ben's critical views, we must go to the *Discoveries*.[1]

The fact that we find no less than four titles for the book— *Timber, Explorata, Discoveries*, and *Sylva* — with others of its

The Discoveries. peculiarities, is explained by the second fact that Jonson never published it. It never appeared in print till the folio of 1641, years after its author's death. The *Discoveries* are described as being made "upon men and matter as they have flowed out of his daily reading, or had their reflux to his peculiar notions of the times." They are, in fact, notes

[1] The best separate edition is that of Prof. Schelling of Philadelphia (Boston, U.S.A., 1892). I give the pp. of this, as well as the Latin Headings of sections, which will enable any one to trace the passage in complete editions of the Works such as Cunningham's Gifford. It is strange that no one has numbered these sections for convenience of reference.

unnumbered and unclassified (though batches of more or fewer sometimes run on the same subject), each with its Latin heading, and varying in length from a few lines to that of his friend (and partly master) Bacon's shorter *Essays*. The influence of those "silver" Latins whom he loved so much is prominent: large passages are simply translated from Quintilian, and for some time [1] the tenor is ethical rather than literary. A note on *Perspicuitas—elegantia* (p. 7) breaks these, but has nothing noteworthy about it, and *Bellum scribentium* (p. 10) is only a satiric exclamation on the folly of "writers committed together by the ears for ceremonies, syllables, points," &c. The longer *Nil gratius protervo libro* (pp. 11, 12) seems a retort for some personal injury, combined with the old complaint of the decadence and degradation of poetry.[2] There is just but rather general stricture in *Eloquentia* (p. 16) on the difference between the arguments of the study and of the world. "I would no more choose a rhetorician for reigning in a school," says Ben, "than I would choose a pilot for rowing in a pond." [3] *Memoria* (p. 18) includes a gird at Euphuism. At last we come to business. *Censura de poetis* (p. 21), introduced by a fresh fling at Euphuism, in *De vere argutis*, opens with a tolerably confident note, "Nothing in our age is more preposterous than the running judgments upon poetry and poets," with much more to the same effect, the whole being pointed by the fling, "If it were a question of the water-rhymer's [4] works against Spenser's, I doubt not but they would find more suffrages." The famous passage on Shakespeare follows : and the development of Ben's view, "would he had blotted a thousand," leads to a more general disquisition on the differences of wits, which includes the sentence already referred to. "Such [*i.e.*, haphazard and inconsistent] are all the Essayists, even their master Mon-

---

[1] It may be observed that the shorter aphorisms rise to the top—at least the beginning.

[2] "He is upbraidingly called a poet. . . . The professors, indeed, have made the learning cheap."

[3] It is here that Ben borrows from Petronius not merely the sentiment but the phrase, "umbratical doctor" (see *Hist. Crit.*, i. 244 note).

[4] "Taylor the Water - Poet," certainly bad enough as a poet—though not as a man. But the selection of Spenser as the other pole is an invaluable correction to the sweeping attack in the *Conversations*.

taigne." The notes now keep close to literature throughout in substance, though their titles (*e.g.*, *Ignorantia animœ*), and so forth, may seem wider. A heading, *De Claris Oratoribus* (p. 26), leads to yet another of the purple passages of the book —that on Bacon, in which is intercalated a curious *Scriptorum catalogus*, limited, for the most part, though Surrey and Wyatt are mentioned, to prose writers. And then for some time ethics, politics, and other subjects, again have Ben's chief attention.[1]

We return to literature, after some interval (but with a parenthetic glance at the *poesis et pictura* notion at p. 49), on p. 52, in a curious unheaded letter to an unnamed Lordship on Education, much of which is translated directly from Ben Jonson's favourite Quintilian; and then directly accost it again with a tractatule *De stilo et optimo scribendi genere*, p. 54, hardly parting company thereafter. Ben's prescription is threefold: read the best authors, observe the best speakers, and exercise your own style much. But he is well aware that no "precepts will profit a fool," and he adapts old advice to English ingeniously, in bidding men read, not only Livy before Sallust, but also Sidney before Donne, and to beware of Chaucer or Gower at first. Here occurs the well-known *dictum*, that Spenser "in affecting the ancients writ no language; yet I would have him read for his matter." A fine general head opens with the excellent version of Quintilian, "We should not protect our sloth with the patronage of Difficulty," and this is followed by some shrewd remarks on diction—the shrewdest being that, after all, the best custom makes, and ever will continue to make, the best speech—with a sharp stroke at Lucretius for "scabrousness," and at Chaucerisms. Brevity of style, Tacitean and other, is cautiously commended. In the phrase (*Oratio imago animi*), p. 64, "language most shows a man," Ben seems to anticipate Buffon, as he later does Wordsworth and Coleridge, by insisting that style is not merely the dress, but the body of thought.[2] All this dis-

---

[1] Perhaps, indeed, an exception should be made in favour of the section *De malignitate Studentium*, p. 84, which reiterates the necessity of "the exact knowledge of all virtues and their contraries" on the part of the poet.

[2] He may have taken this from the Italians.

cussion, which enters into considerable detail, is of the first importance, and it occupies nearly a quarter of the whole book. It is continued, the continuation reaching till the end, by a separate discussion of poetry.

It is interesting, but less so than what comes before. A somewhat acid, though personally guarded, description of the present state of the Art introduces the stock definition of "making," and its corollary that a poet is not one who writes in measure, but one who feigns—all as we have found it before, but (as we should expect of Ben) in succincter and more scholarly form. Yet the first requisite of the poet is *ingenium* —goodness of natural wit; the next exercise of his parts— "bringing all to the forge and file" (*sculpte, lime, cisèle!*); the third Imitation—to which Ben gives a turn (not exactly new, for we have met it from Vida downwards), which is not an improvement, by keeping its modern meaning, and understanding by it the following of the classics. "But that which we especially require in him is an exactness of study and multiplicity of reading." Yet his liberty is not to be so narrowly circumscribed as some would have it. This leads to some interesting remarks on the ancient critics, which the author had evidently meant to extend: as it is, they break off short.[1] We turn to the Parts of comedy and tragedy, where Ben is strictly regular—the fable is the imitation of one entire and perfect action, &c. But this also breaks off, after a discussion of fable itself and episode, with an evidently quite disconnected fling at "hobbling poems which run like a brewer's cart on the stones."

These *Discoveries* have to be considered with a little general care before we examine them more particularly. They were, it *Form of the book.* has been said, never issued by the author himself, and we do not know whether he ever would have issued them in their present form. On the one hand, they are very carefully written, and not mere jottings. In form (though more modern in style) they resemble the earlier essays of that Bacon whom they so magnificently celebrate, in their

[1] This is one of the most lacrimable of the gaps. Ben must have known other authorities besides Quintilian well: he even quotes, though only in part, the great passage of Simylus (see *Hist. Crit.*, i. 25 note).

deliberate conciseness and pregnancy. On the other hand, it is almost impossible to doubt that some at least were intended for expansion; it is difficult not to think that there was plenty more stuff of the same kind in the solidly constructed and well-stored treasuries of Ben's intelligence and erudition. It is most difficult of all not to see that, in some cases, the thoughts are co-ordinated into regular tractates, in others left loose, as if for future treatment of the same kind.

Secondly, we should like to know rather more than we do of the *time* of their composition. Some of them—such as the

Its date. retrospect of Bacon, and to a less degree that of Shakespeare—*must* be late; there is a strong probability that all date from the period between the fire in Ben's study, which destroyed so much, and his death—say between 1620 and 1637. But at the same time there is nothing to prevent his having remembered and recopied observations of earlier date.

Thirdly, it is most important that we rightly understand the composition of the book. It has sometimes been discovered[1] in

Mosaic of these *Discoveries*, with pride, or surprise, or even *old and new.* scorn, that Ben borrowed in them very largely from the ancients. Of course he did, as well as something, though less, from the Italian critics of the age immediately before his own.[2] But in neither case could he have hoped for a moment —and in neither is there the slightest reason to suppose that he would have wished if he could have hoped—to disguise his borrowings from a learned age. When a man—such as, for

---

[1] Not by Dr Schelling, whose own indagations of Ben's debts are most interesting, and always made in the right spirit, while, like a good farmer and sportsman, he has left plenty for those who come after him to glean and bag. For instance, the very curious passage, taken verbatim from the elder Seneca, about the Platonic *Apology* (cf. *Hist. Crit.*, i. 237). As for M. Castellain, he does, I think, exaggerate the want of originality.

[2] Yet in re-reading Jonson, just after a pretty elaborate overhauling of the Italians, I find very little certain indebtedness of detail. Mr Spingarn seems to me to go too far in tracing, p. 88, "small Latin and less Greek" to Minturno's "small Latin and *very* small Greek," and the distinction of *poeta, poema, poesis* to Scaliger or Maggi. Fifty people might have independently thought of the first; and the second is an application of a "common form" nearly as old as rhetoric. Ben, however, owes a good deal to Heinsius.

instance, Sterne—wishes to steal and escape, he goes to what nobody reads, not to what everybody is reading. And the Latins of the Silver Age, the two Senecas, Petronius, Quintilian, Pliny, were specially favourites with the Jacobean time. In what is going to be said no difference will be made between Ben's borrowings and his original remarks: nor will the fact of the borrowing be referred to unless there is some special critical reason. Even the literal translations, which are not uncommon, are made his own by the nervous idiosyncrasy of the phrase, and its thorough adjustment to the context and to his own vigorous and massive temperament.

Of real "book-criticism" there are four chief passages, the brief flings at Montaigne and at "*Tamerlanes* and *Tamerchams*," and the longer notices of Shakespeare and Bacon.

The flirt at "all the Essayists, even their master Montaigne," is especially interesting, because of the high opinion which *The fling at* Jonson elsewhere expresses of Bacon, the chief, if *Montaigne;* not the first, English Essayist of his time, and because of the fact that not a few of these very *Discoveries* are "Essays," if any things ever were. Nor would it be very easy to make out a clear distinction, in anything but name, between some of Ben's most favourite ancient writers and these despised persons. It is, however, somewhat easier to understand the reason of the condemnation. Jonson's classically ordered mind probably disliked the ostentatious desultoriness and incompleteness of the Essay, the refusal, as it were out of mere insolence, to undertake an orderly treatise. Nor is it quite impossible that he failed fully to understand Montaigne, and was to some extent the dupe of that great writer's fanfaronade of promiscuousness.

The "*Tamerlane* and *Tamercham*"[1] fling is not even at first sight surprising. It was quite certain that Ben would seriously despise what Shakespeare only laughed at—the con-

---

[1] P. 27. "The *Tamerlanes* and *Tamerchams* of the late age, which had nothing in them but the scenical strutting and furious vociferation to warrant them." It is just worth noting that Jonson thought there was more than this in Marlowe; and that the early edd. of *Tamburlaine* are anonymous.

fusion, the bombast, the want of order and scheme in the
at Tamer-lane, "University Wits"—and it is not probable that he
was well enough acquainted with the even now
obscure development of the earliest Elizabethan drama to
appreciate the enormous improvement which they wrought.
Nay, the nearer approach even of such a dull thing as
Gorboduc to "the height of Seneca his style," might have a
little bribed him as it bribed Sidney. He is true to his side
—to his division of the critical creed—in this also.

The train of thought—censure of the vulgar preference—
runs clear from this to the best known passage of the whole,
the Shake-speare Passage, the section *De Shakespeare Nostrat.* It cannot be
necessary to quote it, or to point out that Ben's
eulogy, splendid as it is, acquires tenfold force from
the fact that it is avowedly given by a man whose general literary
theory is different from that of the subject, while the censure
accompanying it loses force in exactly the same proportion.
What Ben here blames, any ancient critic (perhaps even
Longinus) would have blamed too: what Ben praises, it is not
certain that any ancient critic, except Longinus, would have
seen. Nor is the captious censure of "Cæsar did never wrong
but with just cause" the least interesting part of the whole.
The paradox is not in our present texts: and there have, of
course, not been wanting commentators to accuse Jonson of
garbling or of forgetfulness. This is quite commentatorially
gratuitous and puerile. It is very like Shakespeare to have
written what Ben says: very like Ben to object to the paradox
(which, *pace tanti viri*, is not "ridiculous" at all, but a deliberate and effective hyperbole); very like the players to have
changed the text; and most of all like the commentators to
make a fuss about the matter.

What may seem the more unstinted eulogy of Bacon is not
less interesting. For here it is obvious that Ben is speaking
and that on Bacon. with fullest sympathy, and with all but a full acknowledgment of having met an ideal. Except the
slight stroke, "when he could spare or pass by a jest," and the
gentle insinuation that *Strength*, the gift of God, was what

Bacon's friends had to implore for him, there is no admixture whatever in the eulogy of "him who hath filled up all numbers,[1] and performed that in our tongue which may be compared or preferred to insolent Greece or haughty Rome." Indeed it could not have been—even if Ben Jonson had not been a friend, and, in a way, follower of Bacon—but that he should regard the Chancellor as his chief of literary men. Bacon, unluckily for himself, lacked the "unwedgeable and gnarled" strength of the dramatist, and also was without his poetic fire, just as Ben could never have soared to the vast, if vague, conceptions of Bacon's materialist-Idealism. But they were both soaked in "literature," as then understood; they were the two greatest masters of the closely packed style that says twenty things in ten words: and yet both could, on occasion, be almost as rhetorically imaginative as Donne or Greville. It is doubtful whether Bacon's own scientific scorn for words without matter surpassed Jonson's more literary contempt of the same phenomenon. Everywhere, or almost everywhere, there was between them the *idem velle et idem nolle.*

A limited précis, however, and a few remarks on special points, cannot do the *Discoveries* justice. The fragmentary character of the notes that compose it, the pregnant and deliberately "astringed" style in which these notes are written, so that they are themselves the bones, as it were, of a much larger treatise, defy such treatment. Yet it is full of value, as it gives us more than glimpses

"Of what a critic was in Jonson lost,"

or but piecemeal shown. We shall return, in the next chapter, to his relative position; but something should be said here of his intrinsic character.

---

[1] One cannot but remember—with pity or glee, according to mood and temperament — how the Bacon-Shakespeare-maniacs have actually taken this in the sense of *poetic* "numbers." But in truth their study is not likely to be much in haughty Rome and its language, or to have led them either to Petronius and his *omnium nume[ro]rum,* or to Seneca and his *insolenti Græciæ.*

He does not, as must have been clearly seen, escape the "classical" limitation. With some ignorance, doubtless, and *General* doubtless also some contempt, of the actual achieve-*character of* ments of prose romance, and with that stubborn *the book.* distrust of the modern tongues for miscellaneous prose purposes, which lasted till far into the seventeenth century, if it did not actually survive into the eighteenth, he still clings to the old mistakes about the identity of poetry and "fiction," about the supremacy of oratory in prose. We hear nothing about the "new versifying," though no doubt this would have been fully treated in his handling of Campion and Daniel: but had he had any approval for it, that approval must have been glanced at. His preference for the (stopped) couplet[1] foreshadowed that which, with beneficial effects in some ways, if by no means in all, was to influence the whole of English poetry, with the rarest exceptions, for nearly two centuries. The personal arrogance which, as in Wordsworth's case, affected all Ben's judgment of contemporaries, and which is almost too fully reflected in the Drummond Conversations, would probably have made even his more deliberate judgments of these—his judgments "for publication"—inadequate. But it is fair to remember that Ben's theory (if not entirely his practice, especially in his exquisite lyrics and almost equally exquisite masques) constrained him to be severe to those con-temporaries, from Spenser, Shakespeare, and Donne down-wards. The mission of the generation may be summed up in the three words, Liberty, Variety, Romance. Jonson's tastes were for Order, Uniformity, Classicism.

He is thus doubly interesting—interesting as putting both with sounder scholarship and more original wit what men from Ascham to Puttenham, and later, had been trying to say before him, in the sense of adapting classical precepts to English : and far more interesting as adumbrating, beforehand, the creed of Dryden, and Pope, and Samuel Johnson. Many of his in-dividual judgments are as shrewd as they are one-sided ; they are always well, and sometimes admirably, expressed, in a

---

[1] Daniel had frankly defended *enjambement.*

style which unites something of Elizabethan colour, and much of Jacobean weight, with not a little of Augustan simplicity and proportion. He does not head the line of English critics; but he heads, and worthily, that of English critics who have been great both in criticism and in creation.[1]

[1] It seemed unnecessary to enlarge the space given to the men of Eliza and our James, by including the merer grammarians and pedagogues, from Mulcaster to that fervid Scot, Mr Hume, who, in 1617, extolled the "Orthography and Congruity" of his native speech (ed. Wheatley, E.E.T.S., 1865). Of Mulcaster, however, it deserves to be mentioned that, not so much in his *Positions* (1581 : ed. Quick, London, 1887), which have been, as in his *Elementarie*, which should be, reprinted, he displays a more than Pléiade enthusiasm for the vernacular. Unluckily this last is not easy of access, even the B.M. copy being a "Grenville" book, and hedged round with forms and fears. As to Ben himself, it is perhaps desirable to repeat that, in the opinion of the present writer, far too much stress has been laid (even by Mr Spingarn in *Camb. Hist. of Eng. Lit.* as above) on the recent exhibition by a French critic (also named *supra*) of his indebtedness to the ancients, Heinsius, &c. This indebtedness ought always to have been known to all and was known to some : nor does it in any material degree interfere with Jonson's position. His selection and arrangement is something : his application to Shakespeare, Bacon, Spenser, more : and after all, in the vulgar sense of "originality," how much original criticism is there in the world?

INTERCHAPTER I.

THE proper appreciation of Renaissance criticism is hardly second in importance to that of the criticism of pure Antiquity. And without it, in regard to English criticism more particularly, the appreciation of what follows in our own language — of our "Augustan" criticism — is practically impossible. It is true that, except as regards Jonson, and perhaps even in his case to all but a small extent, our critics, from Dryden onwards, knew little of, and cared less for, their English predecessors. It is true also that the work of those predecessors, as exhibited in the last chapter, does not come to very much. But the total critical advance in Europe, though it had strayed into doubtful roads, had been considerable, indeed immense; and it had substituted an abundant literature of the subject for a practically entire neglect and ignoring of it. This literature began in Italy. But Italian criticism, active and voluminous as it was, settled very early into certain well-marked limits and channels, and almost wholly confined itself within them, though these channels underwent no infrequent intersection or confluence.

The main texts and patterns of the critics of the Italian Renaissance were three—the *Ars Poetica* of Horace, the *Poetics* of Aristotle, and the various Platonic places dealing with poetry. These latter had begun to affect Italian thought, directly or by transmission through this or that medium, before the close of the fourteenth century; and the maintenance of the Platonic ban, the refutation of it, or the more or less ingenious acceptance and evasion of it, with the help of the Platonic blessing, had been a tolerably familiar exer-

cise from the time of Boccaccio to the time of Savonarola.
But Horace and Aristotle gave rules and patterns of much
more definiteness.   Of the writers of the abundant critical
literature which has been partly surveyed, some directly comment these texts; others follow them with more or less selection or combination; many take up separate questions suggested by them; very few, if any, face the subject without
some prepossession derived from them.   There is the almost
abject "Ancient-worship" and exhortation to "steal" of Vida;
there are the doubts as to Romance being subject, or not,
to the rules of Epic; there is the attempt at historic estimate.

But between all the schools, and from among the welter of
the individuals, there arises, in the mysterious way in which
such things do arise, and which defies all but shallow and
superficial explanation, a sort of general critical creed, every
particular article of which would probably have been signed
by no two particular persons—perhaps by no one—but which
is ready to become, and in the next century does become,
orthodox and accepted as a whole.   And this creed runs
somewhat as follows:—

On the higher and more abstract questions of poetry
(which are by no means to be neglected) Aristotle is the
guide; but the meaning of Aristotle is not always self-
evident even so far as it goes, and it sometimes requires
supplementing.   Poetry is the imitation of nature: but
this imitation may be carried on either by copying nature
as it is or by inventing things which do not actually
exist, and have never actually existed, but which conduct
themselves according to the laws of nature and reason.
The poet is *not* a public nuisance, but quite the contrary.
He must, however, both delight *and* instruct.

As for the Kinds of poetry, they are not mere working
classifications of the practice of poets, but have technically
constituting definitions from which they might be independently developed, and according to which they ought
to be composed.   The general laws of Tragedy are given
by Aristotle; but it is necessary to extend his prescription of Unity so as to enjoin three species—of Action,

Time, and Place. Tragedy must be written in verse, which, though not exactly the constituting form of poetry generally, is almost or quite inseparable from it. The illegitimacy of prose in Comedy is less positive. Certain extensions of the rules of the older Epic may be admitted, so as to constitute a new Epic or Heroic Poem ; but it is questionable whether this may have the full liberty of Romance, and it is subject to Unity, though not to the dramatic Unity. Other Kinds are inferior to these.

In practising them, and in practising all, the poet is to look first, midmost, and last to the practice of the ancients. " The ancients " may even occasionally be contracted to little more than Virgil ; they may be extended to take in Homer, or may be construed much more widely. But taking things on the whole, " the ancients " have anticipated almost everything, and in everything that they have anticipated have done so well that the best chance of success is simply to imitate them. The detailed precepts of Horace are never to be neglected ; if supplemented, they must be supplemented in the same sense.

It is less the business of the historian, after drawing up this creed, to criticise it favourably or unfavourably, than to point out that it had actually, by the year 1600, come very near to formulated existence. We shall find it in actual formulation in the ensuing chapter ; we have already seen it in more than adumbration, governing the pronouncements of a scholar and a man of genius like Ben Jonson, thirty years later than the close of the sixteenth century. A full estimate of its merits and demerits would not be in place at this juncture. But it may be observed at once that it is, *prima facie,* not a perfect creed by any means. It has (and this, I think, has been too seldom noticed) a fault, almost, if not quite, as great on the *a priori* side as that which it confessedly has on the *a posteriori.* It does not face the facts ; it blinks all mediæval and a great deal of existing modern literature. But, then, to do it justice, it does not pretend to do other than blink them. The fault in its own more special province is much more glaring, though, as has been said, it has, by a sort of sympathy, been much more ignored. There is no real connection between the higher and the lower principles of Neo-Classicism. There is not merely one crevasse, not easily to be crossed, in this glacier of Correctness; there are two or three.

Yet it would be an act of the grossest injustice and ingratitude to refuse or to stint recognition of the immense services that the Italians rendered to criticism at this time. It was, in their own stately word, a veritable case of *risorgimento ;* and of resurrection in a body far better organised, far more gifted, than that which had gone to sleep a thousand years before.

It is something—nay, it is very much—to have created a Kind. Up to their time Criticism had been a mere Cinderella in the literary household. Aristotle had taken her up as he had taken all Arts and Sciences. The Rhetoricians had found her a useful handmaid to Rhetoric. Roman *dilettanti* had dallied with her. The solid good sense and good feeling of Quintilian had decided that she must be "no casual mistress but a wife" (perhaps on rather polygamic principles) to the student of oratory. Longinus had suddenly fixed her colours on his helmet, and had ridden in her honour the most astonishing little *chevauchée* in the annals of adventurous literature. The second greatest poet of the world—Dante—had done her at once yeoman's service and stately courtesy. And yet she was, in the general literary view, not so much *déclassée* as not classed at all—not "out," not accorded the *entrées.*

This was now all over. The country which gave the literary tone and set the literary fashions of Europe had adopted Criticism in the most unmistakable manner—whether in the manner wisest or most perfect is not for the present essential. Rank thus given is never lost; at any rate, there is no recorded instance of a literary attainder for Kinds, whatever there may be for persons.

When this criticism passes the Alps, a curious difference is to be perceived. French criticism, soon to be the most important of all, is at first by much the least important. Not only does it begin late ; not only does it fail to be very fertile ; but its individual documents require a certain kindness to speak very highly of their virtues, and a good deal of blindness to conceal their shortcomings. The criticism of Du Bellay and Ronsard is, indeed, extremely *germinal*. Those who contend that the classical French criticism of the seventeenth century was only the Pléiade criticism of the sixteenth, denying its masters, omitting some, if not always the worst, parts of their creed, narrowed in range, and perfected in apparent system, have a great deal to say for themselves. But this criticism is exceedingly limited; and it tends almost exclusively to the promotion, not the grouping, of literature.

Again, in such work as Vauquelin de la Fresnaye's[1] we have the whole of the Italian teaching that had commended itself to the French mind up to this time, with such additions and corrections as the vernacular needed. We see in it the obsession of the "long poem," which France was not to outgrow for two centuries, and which weighed not a little on England. We see the tendency to burden criticism with innumerable petty "rules" and "licences," which was also to beset the nation. But once more, there is little real criticism in it.

Crossing the Channel, as we just now crossed the Alps, we do not find a simple transmission of indebtedness. It would have been surprising, considering the strong intellectual interests of the Colet group, and the early presence in England of such a critical force as Erasmus, if this country had waited to receive a current merely transmitted through France from Italy. It is possible that, later, Gascoigne may have derived something from Ronsard, and it is quite certain that "E. K.'s" notes on the *Calendar* show symptoms of Pléiade influence, even in the bad point of contempt, or at least want of respect, for Marot. But it is exceedingly improbable that Ascham derived any impulsion from Du Bellay: it is certain, as we have seen, that he knew Italian critics like Pigna directly; and it is equally

[1] It may be noted here, once for all, that further and generally full information, on all foreign critics mentioned, will be found in the larger *History* if the student cares to seek it. Only *necessary* matter as to foreign drifts and influences is given here.

certain that, either by his own studies or through Cheke, his critical impulses must have been excited humanistically long before the French had got beyond the merely *rhétoriqueur* standard.

Hence, as well as for other reasons, English criticism develops itself, if not with entire independence, yet with sufficient conformity to its own needs. That practical bent which we have noticed in the French shows itself here also; but it is conditioned differently. We had, as they had in France, to fashion a new poetic diction; but it cannot be said that the critics did much for this: Spenser, as much as Coriolanus, might have said, "Alone I did it." They did more *in re metrica*, and it so happened that they had, quite in their own sphere, to fight an all-important battle, the battle of the classical metres, which was of nothing like the same importance in French or in Italian. In dealing with these and other matters they fall into certain generations or successive groups.

In Ascham and his contemporaries the critical attitude was induced, but not altogether favourably conditioned, by certain forces, partly common to them with their Continental contemporaries, partly not. They all felt, in a degree most creditable to themselves (and contrasting most favourably with the rather opposite feeling of men so much greater and so much later as Bacon and Hobbes), that they must adorn their Sparta, that it was their business to get the vernacular into as good working order, both for prose and verse, as they possibly could. And what is more, they had some shrewd notions about the best way of doing this. The exaggerated rhetoric and "aureateness" of the fifteenth century had inspired them, to a man, with a horror of "inkhorn terms," and, if mainly wrong, they were also partly right in feeling that the just and deserved popularity of the early printed editions of the whole of Chaucer threatened English with an undue dose of archaism.

Further, they were provided by the New Learning, not merely with a very large stock of finished examples of literature, but also with a not inconsiderable library of regular criticism. They did their best to utilise these; but, in thus endeavouring, they fell into two opposite, yet in a manner complementary, errors. In the first place, they failed altogether to recognise the continuity, and in a certain sense the *equipollence*, of literature—the fact that to blot out a thousand years of literary history, as they tried to do, is unnatural and destructive. In the second place, though their instinct told them rightly that Greek and Latin had invaluable lessons and models for English, their reason failed to tell them that these lessons must be applied, these models used, with special reference to the nature, the history, the development of English itself. Hence they fell, as regards verse, into the egregious and fortunately self-correcting error of the classical metres, as regards prose, into a fashion of style, by no means insalutary as a corrective and reaction from the rhetorical bombast and clumsiness of the Transition, but inadequate of itself, and needing to be counterdosed by the fustian and the familiarity which are the worst sides of Euphuism, in order to bring about the next stage. Lastly, these men looked too much to the future, and not enough to the past: they did not so much as condescend to examine the literary manner and nature even of Chaucer himself, still less of others.

In the next generation, which gives us Gascoigne, Webbe, Puttenham, and Sidney, the same tendencies are perceived; but the Euphuist movement comes in to differentiate them on one side, and the influence of Italian criticism on the other. The classical metre craze has not yet been blown to pieces by the failure of even such a poet as Spenser to do any good with it, the fortunate recalcitrance of the healthy English spirit, and at last the crushing broadside of Daniel's *Defence of Rhyme.* But it does no very great practical harm: and prose style is sensibly beautified and heightened. Some attempts are made, from Gascoigne downwards, to examine the actual wealth of English, to appraise writers, to analyse methods—attempts, however, not very well sustained, and still conditioned by the apparent ignorance of the writers that there was anything behind Chaucer, though Anglo-Saxon was actually studied at the time under Archbishop Parker's influence. Further, the example of the Italian critics deflects the energy of our writers from the right way, and sends them off into pretty Platonisings about the proud place due to poetry, the stately status of the singer, and other agreeable but unpractical aberrations. This tendency is much strengthened by the Puritan onslaught on poetry generally and dramatic poetry in particular. In all this there is a great deal of interest, and many scattered *aperçus* of much value. Gascoigne's little treatise is almost priceless, as showing us how English prosody was drifting on the shallows of a hard-and-fast syllabic arrangement, when the dramatists came to its rescue. Sidney, wrong as he is about the drama, catches hold of one of the very lifebuoys of English poetry in his praise of the ballad. Daniel's *Defence* puts the root of the rhyme-matter in the most admirable fashion. But we see that the classics are exercising on all the men of the time influences both bad and good, and in criticism, perhaps, rather bad than good; that the obsession of Latin in particular is heavy on them; and that the practice, both Latin and Greek, of what we have called beginning at the wrong end lies heaviest of all.

Nothing will show this more curiously than the words in which Sidney anticipated (and perhaps suggested) Ben's censure of Spenser's diction as to the *Shepherd's Calendar*, especially if we remember that they proceeded from a personal friend and by an ardent lover of poetry. That there is something to be said against the dialect of the *Calendar* all reasonable critics will allow. As a poetic language it is, at its best, but a preliminary exercise for the glorious medium of *The Faerie Queene;* it is awkwardly and in some cases incorrectly blended; and, above all, the *mere* rusticity — the "hey-ho" and the rest — is a dangerous and doubtful expedient. But observe that Sidney says nothing of this kind. He "looks merely at the stop-watch." Theocritus did not do it; Virgil did not do it; Sannazar did not do it; therefore Spenser must not do it. That his own elevation of a mere modern like Sannazar to this position of a lawgiver of the most tyrannic kind — of an authority not merely whose will is law, not merely whose prohibition is final, but whose bare abstention from something taboos that something from the use of all mankind for ever and ever,—that this did not strike Sidney as preposterous in itself, and as throwing doubt on the whole method, is wonderful. But even if he had stopped at Theocritus and Virgil, he would have been wrong enough. Here once more is the false Mimesis, the *prava imitatio*. Not only is the good poet to be followed in what he does, but what he does not do serves as a bar to posterity in all time from doing it.

There is another point in which Sidney and Ben are alike, and in which they may even seem to anticipate that general adoption of "Reason," of "Good Sense" as the criterion, which the late seventeenth and eighteenth centuries claimed as their own, and which some recent critics have rather kindly allowed them. Sidney's raillery of the Romantic life-drama, Ben's reported strictures on the sea-coast of Bohemia, and his certain ones on "Cæsar did never wrong," &c., express the very spirit of this cheap rationalism, which was later to defray a little even of Dryden's criticism, almost the whole of Boileau's, and far too much of Pope's. The ancients, to do them justice, are not entirely to be blamed for this. There is very little of it in Aristotle, who quite understands that the laws of poetry are not the laws of history or of science.[1] But there is a great deal of it in Horace: and, as we shall see, the authority of the great Greek was, during the three centuries which form the subject of this volume, more and more used as a mere cloak for the opinions of the clever Roman. Meanwhile, such books as those of Webbe and Puttenham, such an ordeal by battle as that fought out by Campion and Daniel, even such critical *jaculata* as those of Meres and Bolton,[2] were all in different ways doing

---

[1] Yet even he does condescend to it too much in his notices of "objections" towards the end of the *Poetics*.

[2] These judgments might of course be reinforced enormously by extracts from letters and poems commendatory, as well as from substantive examples, of Elizabethan literature, prose or verse. But this is just one of the points in which the constantly increasing pressure of material makes abstinence, or at least rigid temperance, necessary as we come downwards. Some very notable passages in creative works — Shakespeare's remarks on drama among the more, and Ben's on "men's and women's poets" among the less — are glanced at elsewhere: Webster's famous "catalogue *déraisonné*" (yet not wholly so) of his great companions, and his odd confession of inability to manage "the passionate and weighty *nuntius*," tempts fuller notice. But one must refrain.

work, mistaken sometimes in kind, but always useful in general effect.

On the general Elizabethan position, as we have seen, Jonson himself made no great advance : in fact, he threw fresh intrenchments around it and fresh forces into its garrison. We may even, contrary to our wont in such cases, be rather glad that he did not enter upon a more extensive examination of his own contemporaries, because it is quite clear that he was not at the right point of view for making it. But it does not follow from this that he was not a critic, and a great critic. No one who was not this could have written the Shakespeare and the Bacon passages—in fact, in the former case, only a great magnanimity and a true sense of critical truth could have mixed so generous an acknowledgment with the candid avowal of so much disapproval. And, as we have said above, even where Ben was wrong, or at least insufficient, his critical gospel was the thing needed for the time to come, if not for the actual time. By a few years after his own death—by the middle of the century, that is to say—seventy years and more of such a harvest as no other country has ever had, had filled the barns of English to bursting with the ripest crops of romantic luxuriance — its treasure-houses with the gold and the ivory and the spices—if sometimes also with the apes and the peacocks—of Romantic exploration and discovery. There was no need to invite further acquisition — the national genius, in Ben's own quotation, *sufflaminandus erat*. It was his task to begin the sufflamination : and he did it, not perhaps with a full apprehension of the circumstances, and certainly with nothing like a full appreciation of what the age, from its "*Tamerlanes* and *Tamerchams*" onwards, had done; but still did it. In his most remarkable book we see the last word of Elizabethan criticism, not merely in point of time, but in the other sense. Ben is beyond even Sidney, much more Webbe and Puttenham, not to mention Ascham and Wilson, in grasp; while, if we compare him with the Continental critics of his own time, he shows a greater sense of real literature than almost any of them. But, at the same time, he has not occupied the true standing-ground of the critic ; he has not even set his foot on it,

as Dryden, born before his death, was to do.   In him, as in all
these Renaissance critics, we find, not so much positive errors
as an inability to perceive clearly where they are and what
their work is.

But between Ben and Dryden, though the actual interval
of time was small, a great change of influence took place,
and the position of European countries, in regard to its exercise, changed even more remarkably.   Although there is
still a large body of Italian criticism belonging to the seventeenth century, it includes among its authors no single name
of great authority; and its contents are for the most part
negligible.   The "Ancient and Modern" quarrel is indeed
started in Italy; but it does not acquire European position
till it has been restarted in France.   And in France, much
earlier and to much greater purpose, the "Neo-classic" creed,
formulated above, reinforces, concentrates, and entrenches itself in the most remarkable fashion.   The establishment of
the French Academy embodies this critical tendency in a
world-noticeable fashion; the quarrel over the *Cid* illustrates
it; and after the strictures of Malherbe (as condemning the
Romantic element that lurked in the Pléiade), the half
recalcitrant, half Unitarian utterances of Corneille himself;
the obscurantist neo-classicism (in drama, if not elsewhere)
of Chapelain and the lesser names of La Mesnardière, Mambrun,
the Abbé d'Aubignac, and others,—the neo-classic attitude
found its greatest expression in Boileau, with his deification
of "Nature" and "Good Sense" in general, and his thousand
arbitrary prescriptions and prohibitions in particular.   This
movement partly preceded, partly coincided with, the earlier
English writers to be noticed in the next chapter; but it
undoubtedly exercised influence in England, and Dryden
may be taken as partly expressing, partly resisting and
revolting from, the ideas of Boileau (1669) himself and of
his contemporaries or successors, Rapin (1674) and Le Bossu
(1680).

France, however, had not been won for Neo-Classicism without something of a struggle; and in the earlier seventeenth
century a few persons (such as the little known Jean de

Schélandre, author of *Tyr et Sidon*) made endeavours at the
English-Spanish tragi-comic or romantic-tragic pattern of drama.
While in Spain itself, partly under the influence of the
national theatre, partly in pursuance of the protests of some
Italians earlier, a remarkable series of expressions adverse
to the Neo-classic theories can be gleaned from Alfonso
Sanchez (1618), Tirso de Mollina (1624), and Gonzales de
Salas (1633), all arguing for liberty in drama; rules adjusted
to, not *a priori* controlling, work; and a "nature" which
is not the Bolæan convention.   But despite an unconfirmed
and late assertion (quite contrary to all likelihood) that
Dryden was acquainted with Spanish criticism, these views
seem to have attracted no notice, and exerted no influence,
outside of Spain itself.[1]

[1] Characteristic examples of the French and Spanish criticisms referred to will be found in *Loci Critici*.

CHAPTER III.

DRYDEN AND HIS CONTEMPORARIES.

DEAD WATER IN ENGLISH CRITICISM—MILTON—COWLEY—THE PREFATORY
MATTER OF 'GONDIBERT'—THE "HEROIC POEM"—DAVENANT'S 'EX-
AMEN'—HOBBES'S ANSWER—DRYDEN—HIS ADVANTAGES—THE EARLY
PREFACES—THE 'ESSAY OF DRAMATIC POESY'—ITS SETTING AND
OVERTURE—CRITES FOR THE ANCIENTS—EUGENIUS FOR THE "LAST
AGE"—LISIDEIUS FOR THE FRENCH—DRYDEN FOR ENGLAND AND
LIBERTY—'CODA' ON RHYMED PLAYS, AND CONCLUSION—CONSPICUOUS
MERITS OF THE PIECE—THE MIDDLE PREFACES—THE 'ESSAY ON
SATIRE' AND THE 'DEDICATION OF THE ÆNEIS'—THE PARALLEL OF
POETRY AND PAINTING—THE 'PREFACE TO THE FABLES'—DRYDEN'S
GENERAL CRITICAL POSITION—HIS SPECIAL CRITICAL METHOD—DRYDEN
AND BOILEAU—RYMER—THE 'PREFACE TO RAPIN'—THE 'TRAGEDIES
OF THE LAST AGE'—THE 'SHORT VIEW OF TRAGEDY'—THE RULE OF TOM
THE SECOND—SPRAT—EDWARD PHILLIPS—HIS 'THEATRUM POETARUM'
—WINSTANLEY'S 'LIVES'—LANGBAINE'S 'DRAMATIC POETS'—TEMPLE—
BENTLEY—COLLIER'S 'SHORT VIEW'—SIR T. P. BLOUNT—PERIODICALS :
THE 'ATHENIAN MERCURY,' ETC.

THE middle third, if not the whole first half, of the seventeenth
century in England was too much occupied with civil and re-
Dead water ligious broils to devote attention to such a subject
in English as literary criticism. Between the probable date of
Criticism. Jonson's *Timber* (1625-37) and the certain one of
Dryden's *Essay of Dramatic Poesy* (1668) we have practically
nothing substantive save the interesting prefatory matter to
Milton. *Gondibert* (1650). Milton, the greatest man of letters
wholly of the time, must indeed during this time
have conceived, or at least matured, that cross-grained prejudice
against rhyme, which is more surprising in him than even in Cam-

pion, and which was itself even more open to Daniel's strictures.
For not only is Milton himself in his own practice a greater
and more triumphant vindicator of rhyme than Campion, but
Daniel's strongest and soundest argument, "Why condemn this
thing in order to establish that?" applies far more strongly to
blank verse than to Campion's artificial metres. Custom and
Nature, those greater Cæsars to whom Daniel so triumphantly
appealed, had already settled it, as they were to confirm it later,
that rhymed and unrhymed verse, each obeying the natural
evolution of English prosody, should be the twin horses to
draw its car. But Milton never developed his antipathy to
rhyme (which in all probability arose, mainly if not merely,
from the fact that nearly all the most exquisite rhymers
of his time, except himself, were Cavaliers) in any critical
fashion, contenting himself with occasional flings and *obiter
dicta*.[1]

Another poet of the time, Cowley, ought to have given us
criticism of real importance. He had the paramount, if not
exclusive, literary interests which are necessary to
Cowley.   a great critic; he had the knowledge; and he
was perhaps the first man in England to possess the best
kind of critical style—lighter than Daniel's, and less pregnant,
involved, and scholastic than Jonson's—the style of well-bred

---

[1] The chief critical *loci* in Milton are
all among the best known passages of
his work. They are the peremptory
anathema on rhyme in the prose note
added to *Paradise Lost*, in what Professor Masson has settled to be the
"Fifth Form of the First Edition";
the short Defence of Tragedy (wholly
on Italian principles but adapted to
Puritan understandings) prefixed to
Samson Agonistes; the first description
of his own studies in *The Reason of
Church Government;* the more elaborate
return upon that subject—a singular
mixture of exquisite phrasing and literary appreciation with insolent abuse
—in the *Apology for Smectymnuus*
(which is not, as some have thought,
the same thing as *The* [Platonic]

Apology) and divers clauses in the
Tractate of Education, especially the
reference to "Castelvetro, Tasso, and
Mazzoni," whom he credits with "sublime art," and puts on a level with
Aristotle and Horace. We might add
a few casual girds, such as that at the
supposed cacophony of Hall's "Teach
each" in the *Apology for Smectymnuus,*
which has been compared to Malherbe's
vellications of Desportes (*Hist. Crit.*, ii.
245). A complete critical treatise from
him (if only he could have been prevailed upon to write in a good temper)
would have been of supreme interest:
it is not so certain that it would have
been of supreme value, even if he had
been in that temper.

conversational argument.[1] But he was a little bitten with the
scientific as opposed to the literary mania, and, in his own
person, he was perhaps too much of a Janus as regards
literary tastes to be able to give—or indeed to take—a clear
and single view. There were, as in Lope, two poets in Cowley,
and each of these was wont to get in the way of the other.
The one was a "metaphysical" of the high flight, who at
least would, if he could, have been as intensely fantastic as
Donne, and as gracefully fantastic as Suckling. The other
was a classical, "sensible," couplet-poet, who was working
out Ben Jonson's theories with even less admixture of
Romanticism than that which tinged Ben Jonson's practice.
The entanglement of these was sufficiently detrimental to his
poetry; but it would have been absolutely fatal to his criticism, which must either have perpetually contradicted itself
or else have wandered in a maze, perplexing as perplexed.

It is with Davenant's Preface to *Gondibert*, in the form of
a Letter to Hobbes, and with Hobbes's answer to it,[2] that
The Prefatory matter of Gondibert. England strikes once more into the main path of
European critical development. And it is of capital
importance that, both the writers being exiled
royalists, these documents were written at Paris
in the year 1650. There was much interest there in English
affairs, while, as we have seen, the habit of literary discussion

---

[1] He has practically given us nothing
but a slight apology for sacred verse
(common in his time and natural
from the author of the *Davideis*);
with a slighter seasoning of the also
familiar defence of poetry from being
mere "lying," in the Preface to the
folio edition of his Poems ; some still
slighter remarks on Comedy in that to
Cutter of Coleman Street ; and hardly
more than a glance at literary education
in his *Proposition for the Advancement
of Experimental Philosophy.* In this
last we may feel a sort of gust of the
same spirit which appears in his disciple Sprat's *History of the Royal Society*
(*v. infra*).

[2] Both these will be found in Chalmers' *Poets*, vi. 349 - 372. Hobbes's
Answer is also in Molesworth's ed. of
the *Works*, iv. 443-458. It is there
followed by a short literary letter to
Edward Howard of the *British Princes*,
the most egregious of Dryden's egregious leash of brothers-in-law. To these
may be added the brief literary passage in the chapter of "Intellectual
Virtues" in the First Part of *Leviathan*
(ibid., iii. 58) and the "Brief" of the
Rhetoric (compare *Hist. Crit.*, i. 40);
ibid., vi. 416-510. I have a copy of
the first edition of this, anonymous
and undated, but assigned to 1655-57
by bibliographers. It does not contain
the shorter *Art of Rhetoric*, which follows in Molesworth.

had, for more than a generation, become ingrained in Frenchmen. When Davenant set himself to write *Gondibert*, he was
doing exactly what Chapelain and Desmarets and the rest were
doing; and when he and his greater friend exchanged their
epistles, they were doing exactly what all the French literary
world had been doing, not merely, as is commonly thought,
from the time of the *Cid* dispute, but from one much earlier.
Taking all things together, it was natural that the subject
should be the *Heroic Poem*, which had been a favourite of
Italian and French critics for some seventy years and more
but had been little touched in England, though the conclusion
of Ben's *Discoveries* shapes a course for it. It was at the
moment interesting France immensely, and producing those
curious epics or quasi-epics of Chapelain, Scudéry, St Amant,
the Père Le Moyne, and others, which were before very long
to incur the bitter, not entirely just, but partly justified and
almost destructive answer of Boileau.

The "Heroic Poem" was to be neither pure Romance nor
pure Epic, but a sort of medley between the two. Or, rather, it
The "Heroic   was to be a thing of shreds and patches, strictly epic
Poem."   (or at least Virgilian-epical) in theory and rules, but
borrowing from Romance whatever it could, as our Elizabethans
would say, " convey cleanly " enough in the way of additional
attractions.   The shreds and patches, too, were not purely
poetical : they were not taken simply from Homer and Virgil,
nor even from Horace, Virgil, Lucan, Statius, and the rest down
to that Musæus whom Scaliger thought so superior to the Chian.
A great deal of ancient critical dictum was brought in, and as
Aristotle and Horace had said less about Epic than about
Drama, they were to be supplemented from others, especially
by that treacherous and somewhat obscure passage of Petronius
which has been referred to above (chap. i.) In fact the whole
of this Heroic-Poem matter is a sort of satire on criticism by
Kinds, in its attempt—and failure—to discover a Kind. If the
founders of the novel (who, indeed, in some notable cases were
by no means free from the obsession) had persisted in construct-
ing it on the lines of the Heroic Poem, it would indeed have

been all up with Fiction. To read Tasso (who, as we might expect, is not the least reasonable) and others, from Ronsard and Du Bellay down to Desmarets and Le Bossu (both of whom, let it be remembered, wrote some time after Davenant) —to find even Dryden a Martha of "machinery," and comforting himself with a bright new idea of getting the *deorum ministeria* out of the limited intelligences of angels, so that you might not know at once which side was going to win, as you do in the ordinary Christian Epic [1]—is curious. Nay, it is more—humorous, with that touch of "the pity of it" which humour nearly always has.

The ingenious knight, in explaining his performance and its principles to his friend the philosopher, takes a very high tone. *Davenant's Examen.* Homer, Virgil, Lucan, and Statius are passed successively in review, and receive each his appropriate compliment, put with dignified reserves, especially in the two latter cases. Only two moderns are admitted—Tasso of the Italians —" for I will yield to their opinion who permit not Ariosto—no, not Du Bartas—in this eminent rank of the heroicks, rather than to make way by their admission for Dante, Marino, and others" [2]—and Spenser of our own men. But Tasso is roundly taken to task for his fairy-tale element, Spenser for his allegory and his archaism. And the faults of all from Homer downwards are charged against "the natural humour of imitation." [3]

After a by no means despicable, but somewhat rhapsodical,

[1] See the *Discourse on Satire*—Scott (in the edition revised by the present writer) (London, 1882-93), xiii. 24 *sq.*, or Ker (*ed. cit. post*), ii. 33 *sq.*

[2] I do not smile so much as some may over "no, not Du Bartas." But though oases are far from rare in what may seem, to those who know it not, this thirsty land of criticism, I hardly know a more delightful "diamond of the desert" than the refusal to admit somebody else lest you should have to admit Dante, and the subsequent "Dante, Marino, *and others.*" When the eye is weary of italic print, or of a too closely packed quarto page, or of François Hédelin, Abbé d'Aubignac, in any type or *format*, it is pleasant half to shut it, and let the dream of these "others" wave before one. I see that they must have written in Italian; but other common measure, other link to bind them both to the *Commedia* and to the *Adone*, is yet to seek for me.

[3] Lest the last note should lead any one to think that I wish to make inept and ignoble game of Davenant, let me observe that he can write ad-

digression on this—it is to be observed that Davenant uses
"Imitation" in the frank modern sense—and an apology for it
as "the dangerous fit of a hot writer," he gives reasons, partly
no doubt drawn from Italian and French sources, why he has
made his subject (1) Christian, (2) antique but not historical,
(3) foreign, (4) courtly and martial, (5) displaying the distem-
pers of love and ambition.   Then he expounds in turn his
arrangement of five books (to correspond to acts), with cantos
to answer to scenes,[1] his arguments, his quatrain-stanza.   He
asserts that "the substance is Wit,' and discusses that matter at
some length, and with a noteworthy hit at conceits, which reminds us that Davenant was *à cheval* between the First and
the Second Caroline period. He indulges in not unpardonable loquacity about his poetic aspirations, with a fresh
glance at the great poets of old, and brings in thereby, with
some ingenuity but at too great length as a finale, the old
prefatory matter of the *Arts Poetic* about the importance
and dignity of poetry in the world, concluding exactly where
most begin, with Plato and that "divine anger" of his
which some have turned to the "unjust scandal of Poesie."
And so a pleasant echo of Sir Philip blends agreeably
with the more prosaic tone, and time, and temper of Sir
William.

Hobbes, as we should expect, is much briefer; and those
bronze sentences of his (though he had not at this time quite
Hobbes's   brought them to their full ring and perfect circum-
Answer.   scription) give no uncertain sound. He is not, he
says, a poet (which is true), and when he assigns to *Gondibert*
"various experience, ready memory, clear judgment, swift and
well-governed fancy," it is obvious enough that all these might
be there and yet poetry be absent. He divides the kinds of

---

mirable things, worthy a son, in double
sense, of Oxford. Could anything be
happier than this of Spenser : "His
noble and most artful hands" ?   The
mere selection of the epithets is good,
the combination of them famously so.

[1] This attempt to get Epic as close
as possible to Drama—to work all the

kinds of Imitation back into one arch-
kind—appears more or less fitfully in
the whole Neo-Classic school. And we
shall never quite understand the much
discussed "Heroic Play," till we take
it in conjunction with the "Heroic
Poem" (see the present writer's *Caroline Poets* (Oxford, 1905-6)).

poetry "swiftly" enough, and ranges himself with his customary decision against those who "take for poesy whatsoever is writ in verse," cutting out not merely didactic poetry, but sonnets, epigrams, and eclogues, and laying it down that "the subject of a poem is the manners of men." "They that give entrance to fictions writ in prose err not so much," but they err. And accordingly he begins the discussion of verse. He does not quarrel with Davenant, as Vida would have done, for deliberately eschewing Invocation; and rapidly comments on the plot, characters, description, &c., of the poem. On the head of diction he would not be Hobbes if he could or did spare a sneer at words of no sense, words "contunded by the schools," and so forth. And since he *is* Hobbes, there is piquancy in finding him at one with Walton in the objection to "strong lines." He is rather striking on a subject which has been much dwelt on of late, the blunting of poetic phrase by use. And when he says that he "never yet saw poem that had so much shape of art, health of morality, and vigour of beauty and expression" as *Gondibert*—when, in the odd timorousness he had caught from Bacon, he adds, that it is only the perishableness of the modern tongues which will prevent it from lasting as long as the *Æneid* or the *Iliad*—let us remember that, though criticism is one thing and compliment another, they sometimes live in a rather illicit *contubernium*. At any rate, there *is* criticism, and real criticism, in the two pieces; and they are about the first substantial documents of it in English of which as much can be said for many years.[1]

Thus, although two of these four were of the greatest of our writers, the third an interesting failure of greatness, and the fourth far from contemptible, they were in all cases prevented, by this or that disqualification, from doing much in criticism.

Dryden, on the contrary, started with every advantage, ex-

Dryden. cept those of a body of English criticism behind him, and of a thorough knowledge of the whole of English literature. He was a poet nearly, if not quite, of the first

---

[1] There is, of course, critical matter in Howell's *Letters,* and in a score or scores of other places; but it is of the kind that we must *now* neglect, or select from with the most jealous hand.

class: and though his poetry had a strong Romantic spirit in virtue of its perennial quality, it took the form and pressure of the time so thoroughly and so kindly that there was no internal conflict. Further, he had what by no means all poets of the first class have had, a strong, clear, common-sense judgment, and a very remarkable faculty of arguing the point. And, finally, if he had few predecessors in English, and perhaps did not know much of those few except of Jonson, he was fairly, if not exactly as a scholar, acquainted with the ancients, and he had profited, and was to profit, by the best doctrine of the moderns.

Moreover, from a certain not unimportant point of view, he occupies a position which is only shared in the history of *His advantages.* criticism by Dante and (in some estimations, though not in all) by Goethe,—the position of the greatest man of letters in his own country, if not also in Europe, who is at the same time the greatest critic, and who is favoured by Fortune with a concentration of advantages as to time and circumstance. His critical excellence has indeed been never wholly overlooked, and, except by the unjuster partisanship of the early Romantic movement in England, generally admitted with cheerfulness.[1] The want, however, of that synoptic study of the subject, which it is the humble purpose of this book to facilitate, has too often prevented his full pre-eminence from being recognised. It may even be said that it is in criticism that Dryden best shows that original faculty which has often been denied him elsewhere. He borrows, indeed, as freely as everywhere: he copies, with a half ludicrous deference, the stock opinions of the critics and the criticasters in vogue; he gives us pages on pages of their pedantic trivialities instead of his own shrewd and racy judgments. But, despite of all this, there is in him (and with good luck we may perhaps not fail to disengage

[1] Of the great critical men of letters of 1800-1850 only Leigh Hunt — the least of them — was just to Dryden; even Hazlitt is inadequate on him. Among our *preceptistas* of the same or a little later date, Keble (*Præl.* v.) mildly perstringes Dryden's inconsistency ("*male sibi constat D.*"), but rather as poet than as critic. Garbett, his successor and opponent, a great admirer of Dryden's style, and one who expresses just regret at the want of common knowledge of it, is very severe (*Præl.* x.) on his want of philosophical profundity and sincerity. But the reverend Professor had found nearly as much fault on this score with Longinus.

it) a vein and style in "judging of Authours" which goes straight back to Longinus, if it is not even independent of that great ancestry.[1]

This vein is perceptible[2] even in the slight critical essays which precede the *Essay of Dramatic Poesy*, though of course it *The Early* is much more evident in the *Essay* itself. In the *Prefaces.* preface to the *Rival Ladies* (written, not indeed when Dryden was a very young man, but when, except for *Juvenilia*, he had produced extremely little) we find his critical path clearly traced, and still more in the three years later Preface to *Annus Mirabilis.* The principles of this path-making are as follows : Dryden takes—without perhaps a very laborious study of them, but, as has been said already, with an almost touching docility in appearance—the current theories and verdicts of the French, Italian (and Spanish?) critics (sufficient survey of whom may be sought in the larger *History*). He does not—he never did to the date of the glorious Preface to the *Fables* itself—dispute the general doctrines of the sages from Aristotle downwards. But (and this is where the Longinian resemblance comes in) he never can help considering the individual works of literature almost without regard to these principles, and simply on the broad, the sound, the unshakable ground of the impression they make on him. Secondly (and this is where the resemblance to Dante comes in), he is perfectly well aware that questions of diction, metre, and the like are not mere catchpenny or claptrap after-thoughts, as ancient criticism was too apt to think them, but at the root of the pleasure which literature gives. Thirdly (and

---

[1] Dryden made no mistake about Longinus. He calls him, in the *Apology* prefixed to *The State of Innocence*, "the greatest critic among the Greeks after Aristotle," cites him often, and parades and uses a long passage of the Περὶ Ὕψους in the Preface to *Troilus and Cressida*. The references are conveniently collected in Mr Ker's index (*v. inf.*)

[2] Dryden's critical work, which until recently was accessible with ease only in Scott's elaborate edition of his works, or in Malone's less bulky, but still bulky and not excessively common, edition of the Prose, has recently been given, with quite admirable editorial matter, by Professor Ker (2 vols., Oxford, 1900). I wish he had included the *Heads of an answer to Rymer ;* but the authenticity of these is not absolutely certain, and the correct text still less so. See note on Rymer *infra*, and my edition of Scott, xv. 378 *sq.*, for text and history. (There is a fair selection from Dryden in *Loci Critici.*)

this is where, though Aristotle did not deny the fact, the whole criticism of antiquity, except that of Longinus, and most of that of modern times, swerves timorously from the truth), he knows that this delight, this transport, counts first as a criterion. Literature in general, poetry in particular, should, of course, instruct: but it *must* delight.[1]

The "blundering, half-witted people," as in one of his rare bursts of not absolutely cool contempt [2] he calls his own critics, who charged him with plagiarising from foreign authors, entirely missed these differences, which distinguish him from every foreign critic of his day, and of most days for long afterwards. He may quote—partly out of that genuine humility and generosity combined which make his literary character so agreeable; partly from an innocent parade of learning. But he never pays for what he borrows the slavish rent, or royalty, of surrendering his actual and private judgment.

In the Preface to the *Rival Ladies* the poet-critic takes (as indeed he afterwards himself fully acknowledged) a wrong line —the defence of what he calls "verse" (that is to say, rhymed heroic couplets, not blank verse) for play-writing. This was his mistress of the time; he rejoiced in her caresses, he wore her colours, he fought for her beauty—the enjoyment authorising the argument. But as he has nothing to say that has not been better said in the *Essay*, we may postpone the consideration of this. There is one of the slips of fact which can be readily excused to (and by) all but bad critics,—and which bad critics are chiefly bound to avoid, because accuracy of fact is their only title to existence—in his mention of "Queen" *Gorboduc* and his addition that the dialogue in that play is rhymed; there is an interesting sigh for an Academy (Dryden, let it be remembered,

---

[1] *Defence of an Essay of Dramatic Poesy.* Scott, *ed. cit.*, xi. 295: Ker, i. 113.

[2] Preface to *Miscellanies*, ii.; Scott, *ed. cit.*, xii. 295; Ker, i. 263. I wish that Dryden were alive for many reasons: not least because he would certainly pay the debt that he owes to my friend Mr Ker *magnificentissime.* No one has vindicated him better against the half-witted blunderers. But I am not quite so much inclined as even Mr Ker is to father his critical *style* on Chapelain and La Mesnardière, Sarrasin and Scudéry, or on Corneille himself. It is not till Saint-Evremond, perhaps even till Fénelon, that I can find in French the indescribable *omne tulit punctum* as in him. And both are his inferiors.

was one of the earliest members of the Royal Society); and there is the well-known and very amiable, though rather dangerous, delusion that the excellence and dignity of rhyme were never known till Mr Waller taught it, and that John Denham's *Cooper's Hill* not only is, but ever will be, the exact standard of good writing. But he knows Sidney and he knows Scaliger, and he knows already that Shakespeare "had a larger soul of poesy than any of our nation." And a man who knows these three things in 1664 will go far.

The Preface to *Annus Mirabilis*[1] is again submissive in form, independent in spirit. Dryden obediently accepts the prescription for epic or "Heroic" poetry, and though he makes another slip of fact (or at least of term) by saying that Chapman's *Homer* is written in "Alexandrines or verses of six feet" instead of (as far as the *Iliad* is concerned) in the fourteener, he is beautifully scholastic on the differences between Virgil and Ovid, the Heroic and the Burlesque, "Wit Writing" and "Wit Written." But he does it with unconquerable originality, the utterance of his own impression, his own judgment, breaking through all this school-stuff at every moment; and also with a valuable (though still inadequate) account of "the Poet's imagination."[2]

Yet another point of interest is the avowed intention (carried out in the poem, to the disgust or at least distaste of Dr Johnson) of using technical terms. This, one of the neo-classic devices for attaining propriety, was, as we have seen, excogitated in Italy, and warmly championed by the Pléiade; but it had been by this time mostly abandoned, as it was later by Dryden himself.

[1] I have not thought it necessary to encumber the page with references in the case of the shorter Essays, where any one can discover the passages cited, whether he uses Scott, Malone, the originals, or Mr Ker's special collection, with no more labour than is good for him and deserved by them. In the case of the longer pieces the references will be given at least sufficiently often to make the locating of the others easy, without turning the lower part of the page into a kind of arithmetical table.

[2] As including Invention, Fancy, and Elocution, but in itself merely considered as synonymous with "Wit." It was probably from this that Addison (see below) started that Imagination theory of his which has been so much overrated.

The *Essay of Dramatic Poesy* is much better known than it was only two or three decades ago,[1] and it is perhaps super-
The Essay of fluous to say that it is a dialogue in form, and that
Dramatic the interlocutors are Dryden himself (Neander), his
Poesy. brother - in - law Sir Robert Howard (Crites), Sir Charles Sedley (Lisideius), and Lord Buckhurst (Eugenius). The two last, though at the time the wildest of scapegraces, were men of distinct poetic gift and varied literary faculty. And Howard, though no great poet, and possessing something of the prig, the coxcomb, and the pedant in his composition, was a man of some ability, of real learning of a kind, and of very distinct devotion to literature.

The *Essay* was first published in 1668, but had been written, according to Dryden's statement in his Preface to Lord Buck-
Its setting hurst, "in the country" (at his father-in-law Lord
and overture. Berkshire's seat of Charlton near Malmesbury), when the author was driven out of London by the Great Plague three years before. He had, he says, altered some of his opinions; but it did not much matter in an Essay "where all I have said is problematical." The "Address to the Reader" promises a second part dealing with Epic and Lyric, which never appeared, and of which only the Epic part is represented by later works. This is a pity, for while we have treatises on Drama and Epic *ad nauseam*, their elder and lovelier sister has been, "poor girl! neglected." It begins with a picturesque setting, which represents the four inter-locutors as having taken boat and shot the bridge, attracted by the reverberation of the great battle with the Dutch in the early part of June 1665, when Admiral Opdam's flag-ship was

---

[1] When the present writer began his revision of Scott's *Dryden* in the year 1881 there were no separate editions of the *Essay* since the originals. There are now, of annotated issues of it, either by itself or with more or less of its author's related work, no less than five known to me,— those of Mr Thomas Arnold (Oxford, 1886), Mr Strunk (New York, 1898), Mr Low (London, n. d.), Mr Nichol Smith (Glasgow, 1900), and Professor Ker's. The study of English literature in schools and colleges has been much abused, very foolishly talked about by some of its advocates, and no doubt not always wisely directed. But it is at least something to be said for it that it has made such a masterpiece as this known to probably a hundred persons for every one who knew it thirty years ago.

blown up. Eugenius augurs victory from the gradual dying away of the noise; and Crites observes (in character) that he should like this victory better if he did not know how many bad verses he should have to read on it. Lisideius adds that he knows some poets who have got *epinikia* and funeral elegies all ready for either event, and the dialogue proceeds for some time in the same way of literary banter, especial set being made at two poets (one of whom is certainly Wild, while the other *may* be Flecknoe) with incidental sneers at Wither(s) and Cleveland. At last Crites brings it to something like the quarrel of Ancient *v.* Modern. Eugenius picks up the glove, but consents, at Crites' suggestion, to limit the discussion to dramatic poetry,[1] and so the "dependence" is settled.

Eugenius thinks that though modern plays are better than Greek or Roman, yet those of "the last age" (1600-1660) are *Crites for* better than "ours." As for epic and lyric, the last *the Ancients.* age must yield. And all the quartette agree that "the sweetness of English verse was never understood or practised" by our fathers, and that some writers yet living first taught us to mould our thoughts into easy and significant words, to retrench the superfluities of expression, and to make our rhyme so properly a part of the verse that it should never mislead the sense. Lisideius having (with the consent of the company, subject to a slight scholastic objection from Crites) defined or described a play as "A just and lively image of human nature, representing its passions and humours, and the changes of fortune to which it is subject, for the delight and instruction of mankind," Crites takes up his brief for the ancients. His speech is a set one, extolling the classical conception of drama, and especially the modern-classical Unities,

[1] One of the very earliest evidences of the interest in dramatic criticism felt in England, immediately after the Restoration, must be Pepys' note that on September 1, 1660, when he was dining at the Bullhead, there "rose . . . a dispute between Mr Moore and Dr Clerke—the former affirming that it was essential to a tragedy to have the argument of it true, which the Doctor denied." The question, on the very English terms of another dinner and a bet, was to be settled by Pepys himself three days later. He does not tell us whether he read up for it; but on the 4th he decided for the Doctor (*Diary*, ed. Wheatley, i. 233).

but rather a panegyric than an argument, and particularly weak
in this—that it takes no critical account of the modern drama
at all.   Except Ben Jonson, "the greatest man of the last age,"
not a single modern dramatic writer of any country is so much
as named.

Eugenius, though his discourse is livelier, falls into something the same fault, or at least the counterpart of it.   He
Eugenius rallies the ancients unmercifully, and has very good
for the game of the stock plots and characters in Terence;
"last age." but his commendation of the moderns has a disappointing generality, and he lays himself rather open to the
good-humoured but forcible interruption of Crites that he and
Eugenius are never likely to come to an agreement, because
the one regards change as in itself an improvement, and the
other does not.

Still, Lisideius gives a new turn to the discussion by asking
Eugenius why he puts English plays above those of other
Lisideius for nations, and whether we ought not to submit our
the French. stage to the exactness of our next neighbours.
Eugenius in reply commits the further and especial defence of
the English to Neander, and Lisideius begins his part as
eulogist of the French.   For some forty years, he says, we have
not had leisure to be good poets.   The French have: and, by
Richelieu's patronage and Corneille's example, have raised their
theatre till it now surpasses ours, and the rest of Europe.
Who have kept the Unities so well?   Who have avoided "that
absurd thing," the English tragi-comedy, so completely?   In
tragedy they take well-known stories, and only manageable
parts of them, while Shakespeare crams the business of thirty
or forty years into two hours and a half.   They make only one
person prominent, they do as much as possible behind the
scenes, keep dying off the stage altogether, and never end their
plays with a conversion, or simple change of will.   Nobody,
with them, appears on the stage, unless he has some business
there: and as for the beauty of their rhyme, why, that is
"already partly received by us," and it will, no doubt, when we
write better plays, "exceedingly beautify them."

To him, Neander—that is to say—Dryden himself.

There is a reminder (though the matter is quite different) of Daniel, and a comforting augury for English criticism, in the _Dryden for_ swift directness with which "the new critic" (as a _England and_ Webbe of his own day might have called him) _Liberty._ strikes at the heart of the question. The French are more regular, he grants, and our irregularities are, in some cases, justly taxed. But, nevertheless, he is of opinion that neither our faults nor their virtues are sufficient to place them above us. For Lisideius himself has defined a play as a lively imitation _of nature._ And these beauties of the French stage are beauties, not natural, but thoroughly artificial. Before Molière, where are the humours of French comedy, save, perhaps, in _Le Menteur_ and a few others? Elsewhere they work in comedy only by the old way of quarrels and reconciliations, or by the conventions of Spanish intrigue-drama. "On which lines there is not above one play to be writ: they are too much alike to please often."

Then, as to tragi-comedy. What is the harm of this? why should Lisideius "imagine the soul of man more heavy than his senses?" The eye can pass, and pass with relief, from an unpleasant to a pleasant object, in far less time than is required on the stage. He must have stronger arguments before he concludes that compassion and mirth destroy each other: and in the meantime he will hold that tragi-comedy is a more pleasant way than was known to the ancients, or any moderns who have eschewed it.

Next, and closely connected, as to single-plot _v._ plot+underplot. Why is the former to be preferred to the latter? Because it gives a greater advantage to the expression of passion? Dryden can only say that he thinks "their" verse the "coldest" he has ever read, and he supports this by a close and pleasant beating-up-the-quarters of _Cinna_ and _Pompey_, "not so properly to be called plays as long discourses on reason of state"; of _Polyeucte_, "as solemn as the long stops on an organ," of their mighty tirades and _récits._ "Whereas in tragedy it is unnatural for any one either to speak or listen long, and in comedy quick repartee is the chiefest grace." Yet again "they" are praised for making only one person considerable. Why? If variety is not mere confusion, is it not always pleasing?[1]

The question of narrative against represented action is treated with less boldness, and, therefore, with less success: but he comes to the sound, if not very improving, conclusion that, if we show too much action, the French show too little. He has an interesting rebuke, however, here to Ben Jonson, for reprehending "the incomparable Shakespeare."[2] And he rises again, and makes a capital point, by citing Corneille's own confession of the cramping effect of the Unities, enlarging whereon himself, he has an admirable exposure of the utterly unnatural conditions which observance of these Unities brings about. Then, after some remarks on prosody and the earlier use of rhyme in English—remarks partly true, partly vitiated by imperfect knowledge—he undertakes to produce plays as regular as theirs and with more variety, instancing *The Silent Woman*. Of this he is proceeding to a regular *examen* when Eugenius requests a character of the author: and Neander, after a little mannerly excuse, not only complies with this request, but prefixes similar characters of Shakespeare and Fletcher.

The first of these is universally, the second and third should be pretty well known. It must be sufficient to say here that

Coda *on rhymed plays, and conclusion.*

nothing like even the worst of the three (that of Beaumont and Fletcher, which wants the adequacy and close grip of the other two) had previously been seen in English, and not many things in any other language, while to this day, with all faults, the character of Shakespeare is one of the *apices* of universal criticism. The characters are followed by the *examen*—also admirable and quite new in English, though with more pattern elsewhere. And he ends with a short peroration, the keynote of which is, "I ask no favour from the French." Lisideius is going to reply; but Crites interrupting, diverts the discussion to a particular point already glanced at—the use of rhyme in plays. He (sen-

---

[1] Here, to glance at the matter of Dryden and the Spaniards (*v. Hist. Crit.*, ii. 331, 332, and *inf.*, on Spence), is a *possible* reminiscence of Lope's *Arte Nuevo*, 178-180—

Que aquesta variedad deleyta mucho :
Buen exemplo nos da naturaleza,
Que por tal variedad tiene belleza.

[2] Scott, xv. 337 ; Ker, i. 75.

sibly enough) declines to investigate very carefully whether this was a revival of the old English custom or an imitation of the French, but attacks its legitimacy with the usual, obvious, and fairly sound argument that since no man without premeditation speaks in rhyme, he ought not to do it on the stage, anticipating the retort, "neither does he speak blank verse" by urging that this at any rate is "nearest nature" or less *un*natural. Neander, taking up the glove for "his *new*-loved mistress," practically admits the weakness of his case by first advancing the very argument as to blank verse which Crites has disallowed by anticipation. The rest of his answer is a mixture of true and not so true, of imperfect knowledge and ingenious argument, constantly open to reply, but always interesting as a specimen of critical advocacy. He represents himself as pursuing the discourse so eagerly that Eugenius had to remind him that "the boat stood still," and that they had come to their destination at Somerset stairs. And with a pleasant final patch of description the dialogue closes.

In reading it we should keep in mind what he says a quarter of a century later to the same correspondent,[1] that he was at this *Conspicuous merits of the piece.* time seeking his way "in a vast ocean" of criticism, without other help than the pole-star of the ancients, and the rules of the French stage amongst the moderns. He has given the readings of the pole-star to Crites, and has pointed out the dangers of reckoning solely by it. He has put into the mouth of Sedley (with a touch of malice which that ingenious good-for-nothing must have noticed, and which it is to his credit that he did not resent) a similar reading of the bearings of the different French lights, and has shown how little they assisted the English mariner—indeed, how some of them actually led to rocks and quicksands, instead of warning off from them. In the mouth of Buckhurst, and in his own, he has put the patriotic apology, inclining it in the former case towards laudation of the past, and in the latter to defence of the present: and he has allowed divers excursions from the immediate subject—especially that on "verse," or rhymed heroics, as a dramatic medium. One of the chief of

---

[1] In the *Discourse on Satire.* Scott, xiii. 3 ; Ker, ii. 17.

the many merits of the piece is precisely this, that at the time
Dryden had read less than at a later, and was less tempted to
add quotations or comments. He was following chiefly a very
safe guide—Corneille—and he bettered his guide's instruction.
It may be said boldly that, up to the date, nothing in the way of
set appreciation—no, not in Longinus himself—had appeared
equal to the three characters of Shakespeare, Jonson, and
Fletcher; while almost greater still is the constant application
of the "leaden rule," the taking of book, author, kind, *as it is*,
and judging it accordingly, instead of attempting to force everything into agreement or disagreement with a prearranged
schedule of rules.

After the publication of the *Essay of Dramatic Poesy*, Dryden
(English literature can hardly give too many thanks for it) had
The Middle more than thirty well-filled years of life allowed
Prefaces. him; and to the very last, and at the very last,
criticism had its full share of his labours. The "Prefaces of
Dryden" never fail to give valuable matter; and we shall have
to notice most, if not all of them, though the notices may be of
varying length. The immediate successor and, in fact, appendix
to the *Essay*, the *Defence* thereof, was only printed in one edition,
the second, of *The Indian Emperor*, and is very far from being
of the best. Sir Robert Howard was, as has been said, a
man conceited and testy, as Shadwell's nickname for him in
The Sullen Lovers, Sir Positive Atall, hints. He seems to
have been nettled by his part of Crites, and replied with
some heat in a Preface to his own play, *The Duke of Lerma.*
Dryden, who never quite learned the wisdom of Bacon's
dictum, "Qui replicat multiplicat," and who at this time
had not yet reached the easy disdain of his later manner,
riposted (1668) with more sense but with not much more temper.
The piece (which was practically withdrawn later) contained,
besides not too liberal asperities on Sir Robert's own work, a
further "defence of Rhyme," not like Daniel's, where it should
be, but where it should not. It is redeemed by an occasional
admission, in Dryden's usual and invaluable manner, that he is
quite aware of the other side, and by an unhesitating assertion
of the primacy of Delight among the Objects of Poetry.

In none of the next three or four of the pieces do we find
him quite at his best. For some few years, indeed, the popularity of his splendid, if sometimes a little fustianish, heroics,
the profits of his connection with the theatre (which, added to
other sources of revenue, made him almost a rich man in his
way), and his association with the best society, seem to have
slightly intoxicated him. He saw his error, like other wise
men, all in good time, and even the error itself was not more
than human and pardonable.

The Preface to *An Evening's Love* promises, but for the time
postpones, an extension of the criticism of "the last age,"
and intersperses some valuable remarks on the difference
between Comedy and Farce, between Wit and Humour, with
a good deal of egotism and some downright arrogance.[1]
The *Essay of Heroic Plays* prefixed to *The Conquest of
Granada* (1672) is as yet unconverted as to rhyme on the
stage; but contains some interesting criticism of Davenant's
essays in the kind, and a curious defence (recurred to later)
of supernatural "machinery." The main gist of the Preface,
besides its excuse of the extravagances of Almanzor, is an
elaborate adjustment of the Heroic Play to the rules of the
much-talked-of Heroic Poem. But though there is a good
deal of self-sufficiency here, it is as nothing to the drift of the
Epilogue to the second part of the play, and of an elaborate
Prose "Defence" of this Epilogue. Here Dryden takes up the
position that in "the last age," when men were dull and conversation low, Shakespeare and Fletcher had not, while Jonson
did not avail himself of, access to that higher society which delighted to honour him, Dryden. Divers flings at the "solecisms,"
"flaws in sense," "mean writing," "lame plots," "carelessness,"
"luxuriance," "pedantry" of these poor creatures lead up to a
statement that "*Gentlemen* will now be entertained with the
foibles *of each other*." Never again do we find Dryden writing
like this; and for his having done it at all Rochester's "Black

---

[1] "I have further to add that I
seldom use the wit and language of
any romance or play which I undertake to alter; because my own invention, as bad as it is, can furnish me
with nothing so dull as what is there."
But he makes ample amends by a bold
challenge to the advocates of "the
subject." "*The story is the least
part.*"

Will with a cudgel" exacted sufficient, as suitable, atonement
in the Rose Alley ambuscade, even from the lowest point of
view. From a higher, he himself made an ample apology to
Shakespeare in the Prologue to *Aurungzebe*, and practically
never repeated the offence.

The curious *State of Innocence* (1677) (a much better thing
than rigid Miltonists admit) is preceded by an equally curious
Apology of Heroic Poetry, in which, yet once more, we find the
insufficient sense in which Imagination (here expressly limited
to "Imaging") was used; while the Preface to *All for Love* (1678)
is a very little ill-tempered towards an anonymous lampooner,
who was, in fact, Rochester. *Troilus and Cressida* (1679) was
ushered by a set preliminary *Discourse on the Grounds of Criticism in Tragedy*. No piece illustrates more remarkably that
mixed mode of criticism in Dryden, to bring out which is our
chief design. On a canvas, not it must be confessed of much
interest, woven out of critical commonplaces from Aristotle and
Longinus down to Rymer and Le Bossu, he has embroidered a
great number of most valuable observations of his own, chiefly
on Shakespeare and Fletcher, which culminate in a set description of Fletcher as "a limb of Shakespeare"—a thing happy in
itself and productive of happy imitations since. The Preface to
the translation of Ovid's *Epistles* (1680) chiefly consists of a
fresh defence of that ingenious writer (for whom Dryden had no
small fancy), and the Dedication to Lord Haughton of *The
Spanish Friar* (1681) is mainly notable for an interesting confession of Dryden's changes of opinion about Chapman and Du
Bartas (Sylvester rather), and a sort of apology for his own
dallying with these Delilahs of the theatre in the rants of
Almanzor and Maximin.

But that to the *Second Miscellany*, five years later, after a
period chiefly occupied with the great political satires, ranges
with the *Essay*, and not far below the *Fables* Preface, among
Dryden's critical masterpieces. The thing is not long—less
than twenty pages. But it gives a coherent and defensible, if
also disputable, theory of translation, a singularly acute, and, it
would appear, original contrast of the *faire* of Ovid and of Claudian, more detailed studies of Virgil, Lucretius (singularly good)

Horace, and Theocritus, and the best critical stricture in
English on "Pindaric" verse. After it the note of the
same year on Opera, which ushered *Albion and Albanius*, is of
slight importance.

The Dedication of the Third Miscellany (specially named
Examen Poeticum, as the second had been sub-titled *Sylvæ*)
contains some interesting protests against indiscriminate critical
abuse, the final formulation of a saying sketched before ("the
corruption of a poet is the generation of a critic"), illustrated
from Scaliger in the past and (not obscurely though not *nominatim*) from Rymer in the present; and, among other things,
some remarks on prosody which might well have been fuller.

Between this and the Fables, besides some lesser things,[1]
there appeared two of the longest and most ambitious in
The Essay   appearance of Dryden's critical writings, the *Essay*
on Satire   [strictly *Discourse*] *on Satire* prefixed to the *Juvenal*,
and the   and the *Dedication of the Æneis*, with, between them,
Dedication
of the   the first writing at any length by a very distinguished
Æneis.   Englishman of letters, on the subject of pictorial art,
in the shape of the *Parallel of Poetry and Painting* prefixed to
the translation of Du Fresnoy *De Arte Graphica*. All, being
Dryden's, are, and could not but be, admirably written and full
of interest. But the *Juvenal* and *Virgil* Prefaces are, in respect
of permanent value, both intrinsically and representively injured
by an excess of critical erudition. The time was perhaps not
yet ripe for an honest and candid address straight to the English
reader. The translator was bound to recommend himself to
classical scholars by attention to the paraphernalia of what
then regarded itself as scholarship ("other brides, other paraphernalia" no doubt), and to propitiate wits, and Templars, and
the gentlemen of the Universities, with original or borrowed
discourses on literary history and principle. Dryden fell in
with the practice, and obliged his readers with large decoctions
of Rigaltius and Casaubon, Dacier and Segrais, which are at
any rate more palatable than the learned originals, but which

---

[1] Lesser, but far from negligible ; for
the *Character of Saint-Evremond* is both
personally and critically interesting,
and the critical biographies of Lucian
and Plutarch lead straight to Johnson.

make us feel, rather ruefully, that boiling down such things was not the work for which the author of *Absalom and Achitophel* and of *The Essay on Dramatic Poesy* was born.

As for the *Parallel*, it is of course interesting as being nearly our first Essay, and that by a master hand, in a kind of criticism

The Parallel of Poetry and Painting. which has later given excellent results. But Dryden, as he most frankly admits, did not know very much about the matter, and his work resolves itself very mainly into a discussion of the principles of Imitation in general, applied in an idealist manner to the two arts in particular. Again we may say, "Not here, O Apollo!"

We have nothing left but the *Preface to the Fables*, the extraordinary merit of which has been missed by no competent critic

The Preface to the Fables. from Johnson to Mr Ker. The wonderful ease and urbanity of it, the artfully varied forms of reply to the onslaughts of Collier and others, are not more generally agreeable than are, in a special division, the enthusiastic eulogy of Chaucer (all the more entertaining because of its lack of mere pedantic accuracy in places), and the interesting, if again not always rigidly accurate, scraps of literary history. It winds up, as the *Essay* had practically begun, a volume of critical writing which, if not for pure, yet for applied, mixed, and sweetened criticism, deserves to be put on the shelf—no capacious one —reserved for the best criticism of the world.

We have seen, over and over again, in individual example; have already partially summed more than once; and shall have to re-sum with more extensive view later, the character and the faults of the critical method which had been forming itself for some hundred and fifty years when Dryden began his critical work. It would be absurd to pretend that he was entirely superior to this "Spirit of the Age"—which was also that of the age

Dryden's general critical position. behind him, and (with rare exceptions) of the age to come for nearly a hundred years. But, although it may be paradoxical, it is not absurd at all, to express satisfaction that he was not so entirely superior. He was enabled by his partial—and, in so far as his consciousness went, quite sincere — orthodoxy, to obtain an access to the general hearing in England, and even to influence,

long after his death, important literary authorities, as he never
could have done if he had set up for an iconoclast. Further-
more, it was not yet time to break these idols. Apollo winked
at the neo-classical ignorance and heresy because it was useful.
We are so apt—so generously and excusably apt—to look at the
Miltons without considering the Clevelands, that we forget how
absolutely ungoverned, and in some cases how near to puerility,
the latest Elizabethan school was. We forget the slough of
shambling verse in which true poets, men like Suckling in
drama, men like Lovelace in lyric, complacently wallowed.
The strait waistcoat was almost necessary, even after the fine
madness, much more after the madness not so fine, of mid-
seventeenth-century verse, and, in a less degree, prose. And so,
when we find Dryden belittling the rhymes of *Comus* and
Lycidas,[1] shaking his head over Shakespeare's carelessness, unable with Chapman, as Ben had been with Marlowe, to see the
fire for the smoke, we need not in the least excite ourselves, any
more than when we find him dallying with the Dowsabels of
Renaissance school-criticism. In the first place, the thing had
to be done; and in the second place, his manner of doing it
went very far to supply antidote to all the bane, as well as to
administer the "corsives," as they said then, in the mildest
and most innocuous way possible.

Dryden's moly, an herb so powerful that—herein excelling
its original—it not only prevented men like Addison from becoming beasts like Rymer, but had the virtue of turning beasts
into men,—of replacing the neo-classic jargon by the pure language of criticism,—was that plan of actual comparison and
examination of actual literature which is not merely the *via
prima* but the *via sola* of safety for the critic. By his time
there was assembled a really magnificent body of modern
His special letters, in addition to classical and mediæval. But
critical nobody in the late seventeenth century, except
method. Dryden, really utilised it. Italy and Spain were
sinking into premature senility. The French[2] despised or

---

[1] "In his *Juvenilia* . . . his rhyme
is *always* constrained or forced."—*Discourse on Satire.*

[2] Chapelain might like the early romances (*Hist. Crit.*, ii. 260). But here
Boileau was the spokesman of France.

ignored all modern literatures but their own, and despised and ignored almost equally their own rich and splendid mediæval stores.

Dryden's freedom from this worst and most hopeless vice is all the more interesting because, from some of his utterances, we might have expected him not to be free from it.[1]   That theory of his as to Mr Waller; that disastrous idea that Shakespeare and Fletcher were low people who had not the felicity to associate with gentlemen,—might seem likely to produce the most fatal results.   But not so.   He accepts Chaucer at once, rejoices in him, extols him, just as if Chaucer had taken lessons from Mr Waller, and had been familiar with my Lord Dorset. Back his own side as he may in the duel of the theatres, he speaks of the great lights of the last age in such a fashion that no one has outgone him since.   He cannot really take an author in hand, be he Greek or Latin, Italian or French or English, without his superiority to rules and systems and classifications appearing at once, however he may, to please fashion and fools, drag these in as an afterthought, or rather (for Dryden never "drags" in anything save the indecency in his comedies) draw them into the conversation with his usual adroitness. And he is constantly taking authors in hand in this way,—we are as certain that this, and not twaddling about unities and machines, was what he liked doing, as we are that he wrote comedies for money, and satires and criticism itself for love. Now this,—the critical reading without theory, or with theory postponed, of masses of different literatures, and the formation and expression of genuine judgment as to what the critic liked and disliked in them, not what he thought he ought to like and dislike,—this was what was wanted, and what nobody had yet done.   Dryden did it—did it with such mastery of expression as would almost have commended a Rymer, but with such genuine critical power and sympathy as would almost have

[1] They have deceived the very elect, e.g., M. Rigault, who in not altogether unnatural amazement at the dictum, "Spenser wanted only to have read the rules of Bossu," classes (*Q. des A. et des M.*, p. 311) Dryden as an *ancien* enragé.   But M. Rigault is at a wrong angle in most of the English part of his book,—so much so as to strike a chill into any one who has to criticise a foreign literature, lest, lacking the grace of the Muses, he too go astray

carried off the absence of merits of expression altogether. He established (let us hope for all time) the English fashion of criticising, as Shakespeare did the English fashion of dramatising,—the fashion of aiming at delight, at truth, at justice, at nature, at poetry, and letting the rules take care of themselves.

Perhaps in no single instance of critical authorship and authority does the great method of comparison assist us so *Dryden and* well as in the case of Dryden and Boileau. This *Boileau.* comparison is absolutely fair. The two were almost exact contemporaries; they represented—so far at least as their expressed and, in both cases, no doubt conscientious, literary creed went—the same sect. *Enfin Malherbe vint* is an exact parallel, whether as a wonderful discovery or a partly mischievous delusion, to the exploits on our numbers by Mr Waller. Both were extremely powerful satirists. Both, though not comparable in intrinsic merit, were among the chief men of letters of their respective countries. Both had a real, and not merely a professional or affected, devotion to literature. Both applied, with whatever difference of exclusiveness and *animus,* a peculiar literary discipline, new to the country of each. And in the case of both—it has been decided by a consensus of the best judges, with all the facts before them up to the present time—there was an insufficient looking before and after, a pretension to limit literature to certain special developments.

The defects of Boileau in carrying out the scheme are worth contrasting with the merits of Dryden.[1]

That, though he makes mistakes enough in literary history, these mistakes are slight in comparison with Boileau's, matters not very much; that, though his satiric touch was more withering even than the Frenchman's, he has no love of lashing merely for the sport, and never indulges in insolent flings at harmless dulness, suffering poverty, or irregular genius; that, though quite prone enough to flatter, he declined to bow the knee to William of Orange, while Boileau persistently grovelled at the feet of William's enemy,—these things matter even less to

[1] For a very full account of Boileau see *Hist. Crit.*, ii. 280-300.

us. The fact, the critical fact, remains that the faults of his
time and his theory did the least harm to Dryden of all men
whom we know, while they did the most to Boileau. And the
reason of the fact is more valuable than the fact itself. Boileau,
beyond controversy, has left us not a single impartial and appreciative criticism of a single author, ancient or modern. Dryden
simply cannot find himself in presence of a man of real genius,
whether he belongs to his own school or another, without
having his critical lips at once touched by Apollo and Pallas.
He was sadly ignorant about Chaucer,—a board-school child
might take him to task; but he has written about Chaucer with
far more real light and sympathy than some at least of the
authors of the books from which the board-school child derives
its knowledge have shown. His theory about Shakespeare,
Fletcher, and Jonson was defective; but he has left us criticisms
of all three than which we have, and are likely to have, no
better. About the ancients he borrows from both ancients and
moderns; but it is remarkable that while Boileau's borrowings
are his best, Dryden's are infinitely his worst part. So the
consequence is that while Boileau is merely a *point de repère*, a
historical document which men simply strive to bring to some
relation with the present and the future, Dryden is and will
remain at once a source and a model for ever. And he is these
because he had the wisdom to ask himself the question, " Do I
think this good or bad ? " and the wit to answer it, instead of
asking and answering the other, " Is it good or bad according
to this or that scheme and schedule ? "

We have, in short, in Dryden the first very considerable
example in England, if not anywhere, of the critic who, while
possessing fairly wide knowledge of literature, attributes no
arbitrary or conventional eminence to certain parts of it, but at
least endeavours to consider it as a whole; of the critic who is
never afraid to say " Why ? "; of the critic who asks, not whether
he ought to like such and such a thing, but whether he does
like it, and why he likes it, and whether there is any real reason
why he should not like it; of the critic, finally, who tries, without prepossession or convention, to get a general grasp of the
book or author, and then to set forth that grasp in luminous

language, and with a fair display of supporting analysis and argument. Dryden, of course, is far—very far—from being a faultless monster of criticism. The application of his own process to his own theory will discover in it many mistakes, independent of the imperfect knowledge which has been already admitted, of the inconsistencies which are more of a virtue than of a defect, and of the concessions to tradition and fashion which are almost wholly unfortunate. Nay, more, it may be granted that Dryden did not escape the dangers of the process itself, the dangers of vagueness, of desultoriness, of dilettantism. But he has the root of the matter in him. He knows that art exists to give pleasure, and when he says "I am pleased with this," he insists on strong reasons being given to show that he ought not to be so. He admits also—nay, insists on—nature, variety, individuality. He will " connoisseur no man out of his senses," [1] and refuses to be so connoisseured by any, while he will give good reasons for his own and others' pleasure. These are the marks of the true and catholic criticism; and Dryden has them.

Let us pass from him directly to one who has them not. There are few English critics who require to be dealt with at once more carefully and more faithfully than does Thomas Rymer. He has become a name, and to become a name is to be at least on the way to becoming a legend, if not a myth. Moreover, as his legend is (for good reasons) far from a favourable one, it has been made more legendary by those generous or wayward revolts against it which are not uncommon. It has even been held proper, for some time, to shake the head of deprecation over Macaulay's " the worst critic that ever lived." Moreover, Rymer is by no means very accessible—in his critical works, of course, for we speak not here of the *Fœdera*. Whether these were originally published in very small numbers; whether the common-sense of mankind rose against them and subjected them in unusual proportions to the " martyrdom of pies "; or whether (by one of Time's humorous revenges) the copies have been absorbed into special collections relating to that *altissimo poeta* whom Rymer

Rymer.

---

[1] A phrase of Blake's.

blasphemed, I cannot say. But it is certain that very good
libraries often possess either none or only a part of them, and
that on the rare occasions on which they appear in catalogues
they are priced at about as many pounds as they are intrinsically worth farthings.[1] I think I have seen notices of Rymer
which evidently confused *The Tragedies of the Last Age* (1678)
with *A Short View of Tragedy* (1693).   Besides these two,
Rymer, independently of smaller things and reissues, had produced, earlier than the earlier, in 1674, a preface to his own
translation of Rapin's *Reflections*, which completes the trinity
of his important criticism.   No one of the three is long ; in fact,
The Tragedies of the Last Age is a very tiny book, which, short
as it is, seems to have exhausted the author before he could
carry out half his scheme.

A careful and comparative reading of all three has given me
a settled, and I think a just, conception of Rymer as of a man
of remarkable learning for his age and country, but intensely
stupid to begin with, and Puck - led by the *Zeitgeist* into a
charcoal-burner's faith in "the rules."   In the *Preface*[2] he is
less crabbed than in the two booklets ; and, though he already
The Preface uses the would-be humorous hail-fellow-well-met
to Rapin. colloquialism characteristic of the lower Restoration
style, and employed even by such a man of letters as L'Estrange
and such scholars as Collier and Bentley, he does not push it to
the same lengths of clumsy ass-play as later.   He thinks that
" poets would grow negligent if Critics had not a strict eye

[1] Parts, but parts only, are given
in Mr Spingarn's extremely useful
Critical Essays of the 17th Century (3
vols. : Oxford, 1908-9), which takes up
the ball from Professor Gregory Smith's
collection, and will illustrate this and
part of the last and next chapters
with texts. I do not think Mr Spingarn very happy in his attempts to
"whitewash" Rymer and others ; but
the student can easily judge for himself.

[2] Vol. ii. pp. 107-130 of the 1706
edition of Rapin in English.   At p.
113 Rymer says that he will not here
examine the various qualities which
make English fit above all other
languages for Heroic Poesy, "the
world expecting these matters learn-
edly and largely discussed in a particular treatise on the subject." This
apparently important announcement is
marginally annotated "Sheringham."
I presume this was Robert S., a Nor-
folk man (as his name imports), of
Caius College, and Proctor at Cambridge just before the Commonwealth
ejection.   I suppose the world was
disappointed of this work by his sudden death in May 1678, four years
after Rymer wrote.

on their miscarriages," yet he admits that this **eye** sometimes
squints, and compares some critics to " Wasps that rather annoy
the Bees than terrify the drones." Then he skims the past,
noticing Castelvetro, Malherbe, and others, but thinks that till
lately "England was as free from Critics as from Wolves," Ben
Jonson having all the critical learning to himself. After praise
of Aristotle and a short notice of his actual author, he then proceeds to consider the history of English poetry independently.
As for Chaucer, " our language was not then capable of any heroic
character," nor indeed was the most polite wit of Europe "sufficient for a great design." Spenser had " a large spirit, a sharp
judgment, and a genius for Heroic poetry perhaps above any
that ever wrote since Virgil," but " wanted a true idea," and
was misled by Ariosto. " They who can love Ariosto will be
ravished with Spenser, but men of juster thoughts," &c. His
stanza is " nowise proper for our language."

Davenant and Cowley are criticised with politeness, but not
very favourably; the faults of both, as well as their designs,
were what Rymer was capable of understanding, and neither
provokes him to any rudeness on the one hand or stupidity on
the other, though there is an occasional ripple betraying an
undercurrent of asperity. Then, after some more general remarks, he takes the accepted test of the Description of Night,
and applies it with mixed commendation to Apollonius Rhodius,
with rather independent criticism to Virgil, slightingly to Ariosto, and rather cavillingly to Tasso, with a good deal of censure
to Marino, and with more to Chapelain, with about as much to
Père Le Moyne, and then with very considerable praise to that
passage of Dryden's in the *Conquest of Mexico* to which Wordsworth was afterwards nearly as unjust as Rymer himself to far
greater things.[1] And with this rather patronising " Well done
our side !" he stops.

Had Rymer done nothing more than this in criticism it would
indeed be absurd to call him our best critic, but it would be
still more absurd to call him our worst. There is fair know-

---

[1] I do not think that Rymer ever
intended to be rude to Dryden, though
his clumsy allusions to " Bays " in
the *Short View* naturally rubbed the
discrowned Laureate the wrong way for
a time.

ledge, there is fair common-sense judgment; the remarks on Chaucer are merely what might be expected, and on Spenser rather better than might be expected; the detailed censure is correct enough; and though there cannot be said to be any great appreciation of poetry, there is interest in it. Above all, if the piece stood alone, we should hardly think of detecting in it even a murmur of the pedantic snarl which is the one unpardonable sin of a critic.

In *The Tragedies of the Last Age* Rymer *ruit in pejus*. He had, in the interval, received some praise, which is always bad for an ill-conditioned man and dangerous for a stupid one; he had conceived the idea of being bee as well as wasp; and he undertook to show Beaumont and Fletcher, Shakespeare and Jonson, their errors, though as matter of fact he lost his wind in belabouring the twins, and had to leave the others till he had taken fifteen years' breath. He shows himself at once in a mood of facetious truculence and self-importance. *He* is not going to emulate "the *Remarks* and eternal triflings of French Grammaticasters." But he is going to set the "quibble-catching" of his countrymen right, and to put an end to "the Stage-quacks and Empirics in poetry" who despise the rules. "Fancy leaps and frisks, and away she's gone; while Reason rattles the chain, and follows after," in which flight Rymer, as often, does not seem to perceive that he is not exactly giving Reason and himself the *beau rôle*. Then he sets to work on three plays of Beaumont and Fletcher. In *Rollo* there is nothing to move pity and terror, nothing to delight, nothing to instruct.[1] In *A King and No King* Panthea actually suggests kissing![2] Arbaces is so bad that he really made Rymer think of Cassius—a withering observation which foretells what the critic was going to say about Shakespeare, though on this occasion he was too exhausted to say it.

The Tragedies of the Last Age.

---

[1] Rymer's elaborate directions for removing the Romantic offence of this play, and adjusting it to Classical correctness and decorum, are among the most involuntarily funny things in criticism (pp. 19-24).

[2] Rymer knew something of Old French. How horrified he would have been if he had come across the lines in *Floriant et Florete* (2904, 2905)—

"Si samble qu' enfès voit disant
'Baise, baise, je voil baisier!'"

He said it fifteen years later with no uncertain voice. The one redeeming feature of the *Short View* is its remarkable, if

The Short View of Tragedy.

not quite impeccable, learning. Rymer really knows something about "Provencial" poetry, though he confuses it (and thereby made Dryden confuse it) with old French, and actually regards Philippe Mouskès—not even a Frenchman but a Fleming—as a "troubadour." Still, his knowledge is to be praised, and his ignorance forgiven. Less forgivable, but still not fatal, are the singular want of method with which he flings the result of his learning, pell-mell with his own remarks, on the reader, and (in a yet further degree of culpability) the vulgar jeering of his style. But all this might still pass. His mistakes are much less, and his knowledge much greater, than those of any critic of his age. Others have lacked method; and Bentley was quite, Collier very nearly, as coarsely rude. On some general points, such as the utility of the chorus in keeping playwrights to the rules, he is not unintelligent. He is a great admirer of dumb-show, and thinks that many of the tragical scenes, not merely in Shakespeare, but in Jonson, would go better without words.

More than half the little book[1] is occupied with a display of his learning—first in some general remarks on the drama, and then in a history of it which is, with all its mistakes, better informed than anything of the kind earlier. And then Rymer falls on *Othello*. He grants it "a phantom of a fable." But it is a very bad phantom. Ridiculous that Desdemona should love a blackamoor at all; more ridiculous that she should be attracted by his stories of adventure; most that Othello should be made a Venetian general—and so on throughout. But the characters are worse. Rymer simply cannot away with Iago; and this on grounds exquisitely characteristic, not merely of him but of the whole system, of which he is the *reductio ad absurdum*. It is not nearly so much Iago's *theriotes* by which Rymer is shocked, as his violation of the type and the general

---

[1] It has (excluding an appended extract from the Registers of the Parliament of Paris about Mysteries) only 168 pages of perhaps 200 words each; and much of it is quotation. But it is far longer than *The Tragedies of the Last Age*.

law. "He would pass upon us a close, dissembling, false, in-
sinuating rascal instead of an open-hearted, frank, plain-dealing
soldier—a character constantly worn by them for some thousand
years in the world."[1]   Again, "Philosophy tells us it is a
principle in the nature of Man to be grateful. . . . Philosophy
must be [the poet's] guide,"[2] therefore Iago is a poetical impossibility.   Rymer knows that historically all men are *not* grateful: but never mind.   The Type! the Type! the Type![3]   One
need hardly go farther, but in going we cannot, in one sense,
fare worse.[4]   "Godlike Romans" (as Mr Dryden had already
called them) are, in *Julius Cæsar*, "put in fools' coats and made
jack-puddings of," which, says Tom justly, "is a sacriledge."
Brutus and Cassius "play a prize, a tryal of skill in huffing and
swaggering like two drunken Hectors."   In Tragedy Shakespeare "appears quite out of his element; his brains are
turned; he raves and rambles without any coherence, any
spark of reason, or any rule to control him, and set bounds to
his frenzy."   Nor does Ben fare much better.   He indeed
"knew to distinguish men and manners at another rate."   In
Catiline "we find ourselves in Europe, we are no longer in the
land of Savages," sighs Rymer with relief.   Still Ben, too,
"gropes in the dark, and jumbles things together without
head and tail;" he, though not "in the gang of the strolling
fraternity," like Shakespeare, "must lie a miserable heap of
ruins for want of architecture;" he "sins against the clearest
light and conviction" by "interlarding fiddle-faddle comedy
and apocryphal matters."   And so forth.

That Rymer was utterly deaf to the poetry of *Othello*

---

[1] *Short View*, p. **94.**

[2] Ibid., p. 144.

[3] Rymer has been defended as an
apostle of "Common Sense." But
this is sheer nonsense.

[4] It may be not unamusing to give
an instance or two of the way in which
Nemesis has made poor Tom speak
truth unconsciously,—

"They who like this author's writing
will not be offended to find so much

repeated from him" [Shakespeare].—
P. 108.

"Never in the world had any pagan
Poet his brains turned at this monstrous rate."—P. 111.

"No Pagan poet but would have
found some machine for her deliverance."—P. 134.

"Portia is . . . scarce one remove
from a *Natural*. She is the own
cousin - german . . . with Desdemona."—P. 156.

and of *Julius Cæsar*, that he thinks "the neighing of a horse

The Rule of Tom the Second. or the howling of a mastiff possesses more meaning" than Shakespeare's verse, merely demonstrates that he understood the language of the beasts and did not understand that of the man. It disqualifies him for his business, no doubt, hopelessly and of itself. But in the nature of the case we cannot quarrel with him for this Judgment of God; and, on his own theory, mere poetry is of so little consequence that it does not much matter. But where he is cast hopelessly on his own pleadings, where he shows himself (as he has been called) utterly stupid, is in his inability to understand the fable, the characters themselves. He cannot see that the very points which he blunderingly picks out are the *adunata pithana* of his own law - giver — the improbabilities or impossibilities made plausible by the poet's art; and that the excess of this or that quality in Iago, in Desdemona, in Othello, is utterly lost in, or is unerringly adjusted to, their perfect humanity. He is not bound to feel "the pity of it"—which he quotes, much as the pig might grunt at the pearl. But he *is* bound, on Aristotelian, no less than on the most extreme Romantic, principles, to feel that universality which Dryden had ascribed a quarter of a century before, and for all time to come. Therefore, for once, though no Macaulayan, I venture to indorse my unimportant name on a dictum of Macaulay's. I have read several critics — I trust this book may show sufficiently that this is no idle boast. I have known several bad critics from Fulgentius to the Abbé d'Aubignac, and from Zoilus to persons of our own day, whom it is unnecessary to mention. But I never came across a worse critic than Thomas Rymer.[1]

Between its King and its Helot, our Sparta of the last forty years of the seventeenth century does not offer many persons for exornation, with crown or with stripe, as the case may be.

---

[1] His best deed was to elicit from Dryden, in *Heads of an Answer to Rymer* (*Works*, xv. 390), the memorable observation that "if Aristotle had seen ours [*i.e.*, "our plays"] he might have changed his mind." One may add that, if Dryden had worked these "Heads" out, he might have solved the whole mystery of criticism as far as in all probability it ever can be solved, or at the very least as far as it could be solved with the knowledge of literature at his disposal. (The most notable of them are in *Loci Critici*.)

Sprat in the famous passage of his *History of the Royal Society*;
Phillips and Winstanley and Langbaine in their attempts at
literary history; Sir Thomas Pope Blount in his other attempt
at a critical summary of literature; Collier in his moral *chev-
auchées* against the ethical corruption of the Drama,—these we
may legitimately notice, but at no great length. Dennis, Gildon,
and Bysshe will come better in the next Book; and it is hoped
that no reader will be so insatiable as to demand the inclusion
of Milbourn or of Hickeringill.

The Sprat passage[1] is of the very first importance in the
History of English Literature, and has at last been recognised

Sprat.

as being so. In it the gorgeous, floriated, conceited
style of the earlier century is solemnly denounced,
and a " naked natural style of writing" enjoined. But Sprat is
careful to point out that this was for the purposes of the Society
—for the improvement not of literature but of science; and he
does not attempt to argue it out at all from the literary side.
The pronouncement expresses the whole sense of the time; it
is epoch-making in the history of literary taste; but it does
not give itself out as literary criticism, though the spirit of it
may be seen in half the literary criticism that follows for nearly
a hundred and fifty years.

The infant historians[2] also may be pretty briefly despatched.
Edward Phillips, Milton's nephew, was by all accounts a most

*Edward
Phillips.*

respectable person; and considering the prevalence
of Royalist opinions (especially as he shared them),
he says quite as much about his uncle as could be expected.
Besides, it is just possible that Milton was no more engaging as
an uncle and schoolmaster than he was as a husband and father.
He was not alive when *Theatrum Poetarum*[3] appeared in the
winter of 1674-75, but the dignity of the opening " Discourse of

[1] History of the Royal Society, 4to,
London, 1667, p. 111 *sq*. It may be
found conveniently extracted at vol.
iii. pp. 271, 272 of Sir Henry Craik's
English Prose Selections (London,
1894).

[2] It is well known that Thomas
Heywood, the dramatist, had planned,
if he did not actually execute, a *Lives*

of the Poets very much earlier, and
some sanguine souls have hoped that
it may yet turn up. But the famous
passage about poets' nicknames, as well
as the whole cast of Heywood's work,
suggests that, though biography may
have lost something, criticism has not
lost much.

[3] London, 12mo.

the Poets and Poetry in general" has made some think that he
had had a hand in it. I am not so sure of this. That it is
addressed to Thomas Stanley and Sir Edward Sherburne (each,
for all the learning of the former and the literary merits of
both, among those "rhyming amorists" and Cavaliers whom
Milton certainly disliked, and at least affected to disdain) need
not much matter. But the style, though often ambitious, does
not seem to me above the reach of a man of some learning and
moderate ability, who had been about Milton in his youth for
years, and at intervals afterwards. Such a man would naturally
take the noble-sentiment view of Poetry, talk of the *melior
natura* and "that noble thing education," and the like; nor
would he be at a loss for Miltonic precedents of another kind
when he felt inclined to speak of "every single-sheeted pie-
corner poet who comes squirting out an Elegy." The
*His
Theatrum
Poetarum.* piece is creditable as a whole, and ends with a hesitating attribution of poetic merit to Spenser and
Shakespeare, in spite of the "rustic obsolete words," the "rough-
hewn clowterly verse" of the one, and the "unfiled expressions,
the rambling and undigested fancies" of the other. The body
of the book—an alphabetical dictionary, first of ancient then of
modern poets, and lastly of poetesses, alphabetically arranged in
a singularly awkward fashion by their *prænomina* or Christian
names when Phillips knows these, and by others when he does
not—is much less important. Here again the nephew has been
robbed to give to the uncle the notices of Marlowe and Shakespeare, in both of which the most noticeable expressions, "Clean
and unsophisticated wit" and "unvulgar style," apply to Shakespeare himself. Phillips has undoubted credit for appreciation
of Drummond (whom he had partially edited from the papers
of Scot of Scotstarvit many years earlier) and for singling out
from the work of Wither (which was then a by-word with
Cavalier critics) *The Shepherd's Hunting* for admiration. But
he is much more of a list-maker than of a critic.

William Winstanley (who brought out his *Lives of the Most
Famous English Poets*[1] some dozen years later, and levied contributions on Phillips himself in the most nonchalant manner)

[1] 8vo, London, 1686.

was a mere bookmaker, to whom is assigned the post of
Winstanley's manufacturer for years of "Poor Robin's Almanack,"
Lives. and who did other hack-work. His book is chiefly
an unmethodical compilation of anecdotes ; and as the lives
of men of letters have always had more attraction than their
works, Winstanley has been found readable. His place here
is simply due to the fact that, putting archaics like Bale and
Pits aside, he is the second English Historian of Poets, if not
of Poetry.

In connection with Phillips and Winstanley (whom he
avowedly follows and acridly comments, accusing them at the
Langbaine's same time of having stolen his thunder from a pre-
Dramatic viously published *Catalogue*) it may be well to notice
Poets. Gerard Langbaine, the somewhat famous author of
the *Account of the English Dramatic Poets.*[1] Of real criticism
there is hardly even as much in Langbaine as in his two Esaus
or Jacobs, taking it which way you please. But he is the
spiritual ancestor of too many later critics ; and there are still
too many people who confuse his method with that of criticism
for him to be quite left out. That he had a particular animosity
to Dryden[2] is less to his discredit than to that of the class to
which he belongs. This kind of parasite usually fastens on the
fattest and fairest bodies presented to it. Langbaine is first of
all a *Quellenforscher*. Having some reading and a good memory,
he discovers that poets do not as a rule invent their matter, and
it seems to him a kind of victory over them to point out where
they got it. As a mere point of literary history there is of course
nothing to object to in this : it is sometimes interesting, and need
never be offensive. But, as a matter of fact, it too often is made so,
and is always made so in Langbaine. "I must take the freedom
to tell our author that most part of the language is stolen."
"Had Mr W. put on his spectacles he would have found it
printed thus," &c., &c. This hole-picking generally turns to
hole-forging ; and one is not surprised to find Langbaine, after

---

[1] 1691 : but pirated earlier.

[2] I do not know whether this was
cause or consequence of his being a
friend of Shadwell. But I am bound
to note, though with much surprise,
that my friend Sir Sidney Lee finds
(*D. N. B.*) "no malice" in Langbaine.

quoting at great length Dryden's cavillings at the men **of**
the last age, huddling off as "some praises" the magnificent
and immortal eulogies [1] which atone for them. I am afraid that
Dante, if he had known Langbaine, would have arranged a
special *bolgia* for him; and it would not have lacked later
inhabitants.

The only too notorious quarrel of the Ancients and Moderns
produced some deservedly famous literature of the critical kind

Temple. in England, but its greatest result in that way, *The
Battle of the Books*, will be best noticed, together
with its author's other works, and in the order rather of its own
publication than of its composition.   Nor need the earlier prot-
agonists, Temple and Bentley, occupy us much; though the
latter will give an opportunity of paying at least respects to a
kind of Criticism of which we have perforce said little.   Temple,
a charming writer, and the author, at the close of his critical
Essay on Poetry, of one of the most exquisite sentences in
English, is simply a critic *pour rire*.   The hundred pages of
his *Works*,[2] which are devoted to literature, invited the exercise
of Macaulay's favourite methods by the enormity of their ignorance, the complacency of their dogmatism, and the blandness
of their superficiality.   Temple has glimmerings—he intimates
pretty plainly some contempt of at least the French "rules";
but he will still be talking of what he has given himself hardly
the slightest pains to know.

This could not be said of Bentley, and the *Phalaris* Dissertation has been not undeservedly ranked as one of the repre-

Bentley. sentative pieces of critical literature.   It is only
unfortunate that Bentley has meddled so little with
the purely literary side of the matter; and the sense of this misfortune may be tempered by remembrance of his dealings with

---

[1] This is the odder, and the more
discreditable, because one of the few
things to be counted to Langbaine for
righteousness is a distinct admiration
of Shakespeare.

[2] Ed. 1757, vol. iii., pp. 394-501,
containing the *Poetry*, the *Ancient and
Modern Learning*, and the *Thoughts
upon Reviewing that Essay*.   Some
have charitably found in Temple
better knowledge of the Moderns,
whom he scorned, than of the Ancients, whom he championed, on
the strength of his references to
"Runes" and "Gothic Dithyrambics."
I cannot be so amiable.   It is all a
mere parade of pretentious sciolism
varnished by style.

Milton.   He is, however, perfectly right in at least hinting[1] that the Pseudo-Phalaris might have been convicted on literary counts, as well as on linguistic and chronological, and that, on grounds of style, the theory of those half-sceptics who attributed the *Letters* to Lucian was almost worse than the error of the true believers.   That Lucian could have written a line of this skimble-skamble stuff is simply impossible; and it must always remain an instance of the slight sense of style possessed by the Humanists that a really great man of letters, like Politian, should have given countenance to the absurdity.

From any point of critical consideration Collier's famous book[2] must be a most important document in the History of

Collier's Short View.

Criticism; and though from some such points it may be of even greater importance than it is to us, we can in no wise omit it.   For it is probably the earliest instance in our history where a piece of criticism has apparently changed, to a very great extent, the face of an important department of literature, and has really had no small part in bringing about this change.   It is, however, indirectly rather than directly that it concerns us; for it is only here and there that Collier takes the literary way of attack, and in that way he is not always, though he is sometimes, happy.   Curiously enough, one of his felicities in this kind has been imputed to him for foolishness by his great panegyrist.   It is not necessary to feel that sympathy with his opinions on ecclesiastical and political affairs which Macaulay naturally disclaimed, and which some others may cheerfully avow, in order to see that the Tory critic was quite right, and the Whig critic quite wrong, in regard to the dissertations on the Greek and Latin Drama.   What may be thought of their technical scholarship does not matter.   But Macaulay's undoubted familiarity with

---

[1] *Diss.*, § xvi.   My copy is the London ed. of 1817.

[2] *A Short View of the Profaneness and Immorality of the English Stage.* London, 1698.   The great popularity of the book caused it to be quickly reprinted: my copy, though of the first year, is the third edition.   Collier's rejoinder to his victims next year contains good things, but is of less importance.   And it does not matter much to us whether he originally drew anything from the Prince de Conti's pietist *Traité sur la Comédie* (1667).   The Ancients, and the Fathers, and the Puritans were in any case quite sufficient sources.

the classics must have had a gap in it, and his wide knowledge of modern literature several much greater gaps, if he did not know—first, that Collier *had* ancient criticism on his side, and secondly, that the allegation of ancient authority and practice where favourable, the arguing-off of it where inconvenient, were exactly the things to influence his generation. When everybody was looking back on the Vossian precept, "Imitate the Ancients, but imitate them only in what is good," and drawing forward to the Popian axiom,

"To copy Nature is to copy *them*,"

"dissertations on the Greek and Latin Drama" were not otiose at all, they were absolutely necessary.

But for the most part, as is notorious, Collier is as ethical as Plutarch or Plato. It was desirable that he should be so, and nobody but a paradoxer will ever defend the style of play-writing which produced such things as *Limberham*, and *The Old Bachelor*, and even *The Relapse*—though the first be Dryden's, and contain some good things in the characters of Prudence and Brainsick, though the second show us the dawn of Congreve's wit, and though the third contain handfuls of the sprightliest things in the English language. It is in reference to this last, by the way, that Collier chiefly quits the path of ethical criticism, and takes to that of literary, or at least dramatic. There is hardly a sharper and more well-deserved beating-up of the quarters of a ragged dramatic regiment anywhere than that (at p. 212 *sq.*) on the glaring improbabilities of Vanbrugh's plot, the absolute want of connection between the title part of it and the real fable—Tom Fashion's cheating his brother of Hoyden—and the way in which the characters are constantly out of character in order that the author may say clever things. But Collier has serious matters on his mind too much to give us a great deal of this; and the other definitely literary points which I have noted, in a very careful re-reading of the piece for this book, are not numerous. I wish he had not called *Love's Labour's Lost* (p. 125) "a very silly play"; but how many people were there then living who would have thought differently? I wish he had worked out his statement (rather rash from his own point

of view) at p. 148, "Poets are not always exactly in rule." He
might have developed his views on the Chorus (p. 150) interestingly. I have some other places; but they are not important.
The sum is, that though Collier evidently knew most critical
authorities, from Aristotle and Horace, through Heinsius and
Jonson, to Rapin, and Rymer, and Dryden himself, very well;
though he could (pp. 228, 229) state the Unities, and even argue
for them—this was not his present purpose, which was simply
to cleanse the stage. His interest in other matters in fact
blunted what might have been a keen interest in literature
proper. And this is thoroughly confirmed by study of his
interesting and characteristic *Essays*,[1] where, out of more than
five hundred pages, exactly four are devoted to literature, and
these give us nothing but generalities.

That Collier's victory was very mainly due to the fact that
he struck in at the right moment, as spokesman of an already

Sir T. P. Blount.   formed popular opinion, would be a matter of reasonable certainty in any case; but the certainty is here
historical. One of many proofs at hand is in the curious lighter-
full of critical lumber which Sir Thomas Pope Blount launched
four (or eight ?) years before Collier let his fireship drive into
the fleet of the naughty playwrights. In this book,[2] dedicated
to Mulgrave, that noble poet himself, Roscommon, Cowley, and
the lately published and immensely influential *Whole Duty of
Man*, are quoted to support the argument that "A poet may
write upon the subject of Love, but he must avoid obscenity."[3]

Sir Thomas, however, comes within the inner, and not merely
the outer, circle of criticism for his aims and his collections,
though certainly not for any critical genius that he displays.

---

[1] *Essays upon Several Moral Subjects*
(3rd ed., 2 vols., London, 1698). Nor
can one make out an entirely good
case (though something may be done)
for Collier in the matter of that description of Shakespeare, which Mr
Browning has maliciously chosen, as a
motto for *Ferishtah's Fancies*, from the
Historical Dictionary : "His genius
was jocular, but, when disposed, he
could be very serious."

[2] *De Re Poetica*, or *Remarks upon
Poetry*, &c., 4to, London, 1694. It is
even said to have first appeared in 1690.

[3] Both Roscommon and Mulgrave
were critics in their way, and the
former's *Essay on Translated Verse* is
one of those numerous documents
which would have been of the utmost
service to us if directly preceptist
criticism in prose had not now been
plentiful.

His "Remarks upon Poetry," no less than the "Characters and Censures" which make up the other part of his work, are the purest compilation: and though we are certainly not without compilers in these days (what indeed can a Historian of Criticism do but compile to a great extent?), there are very few of us who are at once honest enough and artless enough to follow the method of Blount. Whether he is arguing that good humour is essentially necessary to a poet (how about the *genus irritabile?*) or that a poet should not be addicted to flattery, or discussing the "Eglogue, Bucholic [*sic*], or Pastoral," whether he is following Phillips and Winstanley and borrowing from both, in compiling a dictionary of poets, he simply empties out his common-place book. "Dryden remarks," "Rapin observes," "Mr Cowley tells us," "Mr Rymer can nowise allow" (this is happy, for it was habitual with Mr Rymer "nowise to allow"), such are the usherings of his paragraphs. He is not uninteresting when he is original (*cf.* his remarks on Waller); but one is almost more grateful to him for his collections, which put briefly, and together, the critical dicta of a vast number of people. Here we may read, with minimum of trouble, how Julius Scaliger could not see anything in Catullus but what is common and ordinary; how Dr Sprat said that till the time of Henry the Eighth there was nothing wrote in the English language except Chaucer that a man would care to read twice; how Scaliger once more, and Petrus Crinitus, and Johannes Ludovicus Vives, and Eustatius Swartius, thought Claudian quite in the first rank of poets; how Tanneguy le Fèvre shook his head over Pindar as having "something too much the air of the Dithyrambick"; and how Cœlius Rhodiginus was good enough to find that same Dantes Aligerus, who displeased others, a "poet not contemptible."[1] These things are infinitely pleasant to read, and give one a positive affection for Sir Thomas Pope Blount as one turns them in the big black print of his handy quarto; yet perhaps it would be excessive to call him a great critic. What he does, besides providing this *gazophylacium*

---

[1] The remark may with more proportion be made of Cœlius himself, a very worthy Humanist, whom Lilius Giraldus pronounces to be *multifariam eruditus, parum tamen in pangendis versibus versatus.*

for the connoisseur, is to show how wide the interest in criticism was.

A further turn, and the last in this walk, may be furnished to us by one of his own quotations (p. 137 of the *Characters and Censures*) of an answer to the question, "Whether Milton and Waller were not the best English poets, and which was the better of the two?" from *The Athenian Mercury*, vol. v., No. 4. For this curious and interesting medley of Dunton's, and Samuel Wesley's, and others', was almost the first to provide something in English answering, or that might have answered, to the *Journal des Savants* and the *Mercure Galant*. Actually, the *Mercury* was not very literary. I do not pretend to have examined the original volumes with any very great care. But in the three copious books which were either directly compiled out of it, or composed in imitation — *the Athenian Oracle*,[1] *Athenian Sport*, and *The British Apollo* — literature holds no very large place. The *Oracle* does indeed give at p. 438 a very elaborate answer to the question, " Whether the Dramatic Poets of the Last Age exceeded those of this? " and the *Apollo*, besides a versification of the identical query and answer which Blount had quoted, contains a long descant on the Origin of Poetry, and a remarkably shrewd answer to the question, " Which is the best poet—Boileau, Molière, or La Fontaine?" But the time of literary periodicals in England was not yet, though this was the very eve of it: and they must therefore be postponed.[2]

Periodicals: The Athenian Mercury, &c.

---

[1] The *Athenian Mercury* (1690-97) ran to twenty volumes. The *Oracle*, from which the late Mr Underhill made his interesting selection (London, n. d.), was issued in *four*. I have *one* (London, 1703), which calls itself an "Entire Collection," as well as *Athenian Sport* (London, 1707), and *The British Apollo* (3rd ed., London, 1718).

[2] Excepting perhaps J. [Cornand] de La Croze's *Works of the Learned*, which, translated mainly from the French, began to appear monthly in August 1691, and was collected before long.

Its contents are real reviews, and though the books reviewed are of no great interest, the summaries of their contents are generally good, and the views advanced are fairly argued. (Texts, complete or extracted, of most of the critics discussed in the latter part of this chapter will be found in Spingarn, *op. cit. sup.* The same author's also cited chapter in *Camb. Hist. Eng. Lit.*, vol. vii. (1911), may be consulted again as to the earlier part of this.)

INTERCHAPTER II.

In the present Interchapter we come to a sort of Omphalos of the whole of critical history. Here and here only, up to the present day, do we find a Catholic Faith [1] of criticism, not merely at last constituted, but practically accepted over the whole literary world. In ancient times, though it is not difficult to discern a creed of a not wholly dissimilar character, yet that creed was arrived at in roundabout fashion, and was never applied universally to poetry and prose as literature. In the Middle Ages there was no such creed at all. In the eighteenth century, which—or rather a certain aspect of it—continues the seventeenth in England as elsewhere with little break, the catholic faith still maintains, and even, as is the wont of such things, rather tightens, its hold as received orthodoxy; but there are grumblings, and threatenings, and upheavals on the one hand, and on the other the tendency to a dangerous latitudinarianism. In the Dissidents of the Eighteenth, and in the whole Nineteenth, with so much of the Twentieth as can be seen or foreseen, there is no parallel consensus even of a prevailing party. Take a dozen critics of any distinction, at different times and in different countries of the seventeenth century in Europe, and ask them to enunciate some general laws and principles of literary criticism. The results, if not slavishly identical, would be practically the same, putting aside particular and half unreal squabbles of Ancient and Modern and the like. Do the same at any time for the last hundred—certainly for the last eighty or ninety—years, and the result would be a Babel. If any two of the utterances did not betray direct

---

[1] For a draft "Confession" of it, *v. sup.*, Interchapter I., pp. 94, 95.

contradiction, it would probably be because the speakers began at entirely different facets of the subject.

We have seen in the last Interchapter how something like this orthodoxy had been achieved—not without a good deal of opposition, and hardly, in any case, with the result of authoritative and complete statement—in Italy, and to some extent borrowed thence, in other countries, before the end of the sixteenth century itself. The seventeenth did little more than crystallise it, lay stress on particular points, fill up some gaps, arrange, codify, illustrate. The absence of dissidence, except on the minor points, is most remarkable. In regard to Aristotle, in particular, there are no Patrizzis and hardly any Castelvetros. Men tack on a considerable body of Apocrypha to the canonical books of the Stagirite, and misinterpret not a little that he actually said. But they never take his general authority in question, seldom the authority of any ancient, and that of Horace least of all. The two great artificial conceptions of the elaborate "Unities" drama, with Acts and Scenes taking the place of the choric divisions, and of the still more artificial "Heroic Poem," with its Fable, its Epic Unity, its Machines, and so forth, acquire in theory — though, luckily, as far as England goes, by no means in practice—greater and greater dignity. It becomes a sort of truism that the drama is the most beautiful and ingenious, the heroic poem the noblest, thing on which the human mind can exercise itself. But they are difficult things, sir! very difficult things. Each is sharply isolated as a Kind: and the other Kinds are ranged around and below them. You never criticise any thing first in itself, but with immediate reference to its Kind. If it does not fulfil the specifications of that Kind, it is either cast out at once or regarded with the deepest suspicion.

Further, all the Kinds in particular, as well as poetry itself in general, possess, and are distinguished by, Qualities which are, in the same way, rigidly demanded and inquired into. It is generally, if not quite universally, admitted that a poem must please: though critics are not quite agreed whether you are bound to please only so as to instruct. But you must please in the Kind, by the Quality, according to the Rule.

There is no room for nondescripts; or, if they are admitted at all, they must cease to be nondescripts, and become Heroi-comic, Heroi-satiric, " Tragical-comical-historical-pastoral," [1] or what not.

This general view may seem unorthodox to those who put faith in the notion—to be found in some books of worth, as well as of worship—that there was a " Romantic revolt " in the beginning of the seventeenth century—that there was even a kind of irruption or recrudescence of mediæval barbarism, and that the pronounced and hardened classicism of the later century was a fresh reaction—a case of *Boileau à la rescousse!* The texts, and the facts, and the dates, do not, to my thinking, justify this view of history, in so far, at least, as criticism is concerned.   The crystallising of the classical creed goes on regardless of Euphuism, earlier and later, in England, of Marinism in Italy, of Culteranism and Conceptism in Spain, of the irregular outburst of similar tastes in France, which marks the reign of Louis XIII.   In England, Sidney, at the beginning of the great Elizabethan period, holds out hands to Jonson at the end.

At the same time, this accepted faith of Criticism, when we come to examine it, is a very peculiar Catholicity.   Uncom-promisingly Aristotelian in profession, its Aristotelianism, as has been recognised by an increasing number of experts from the time of Lessing downwards, is hopelessly adulterated. Many of the insertions and accretions are purely arbitrary ; others come from a combination of inability to forget, and obstinate refusal frankly to recognise, the fact that the case is quite a different case from that which Aristotle was dia-gnosing.   But, by the time at least when the creed became triumphant, a new Pope, a new Court of Appeal, has been foisted in, styling itself Good Sense, Reason, or even (though quite Antiphysic) Nature.   That this anti-Pope, this Antiphysis, was partly created by the excesses of the Euphuist-Gongorist

---

[1] It may be doubted whether there is anything more wonderful in Shake-speare than the way in which this Polonian speech, at one slight side-blow, impales sixteenth-seventeenth-century criticism, with the due pin, on the due piece of cork, for ever.

movements, need not be denied; but this is comparatively
irrelevant. The most interesting by-product of the processes
going on is the curious, and sometimes very ludicrous, attempt
to conciliate that *furor poeticus* which the ancients had never
denied, with those dictates of good sense which the ancients
were presumed to have accepted and embodied.

By degrees critical supremacy passed from Italy to France.[1]
This passing is an accepted truth, and like most, though not all,
accepted truths, this has so much of the real quality that it
is idle to cavil at it. That it has been abused there can be
little doubt—or could be little if people would take the small
trouble necessary to ascertain the facts. I do not know who
first invented the term "Gallo-Classic," which, to judge by
those Röntgen rays which the reader of examination-papers
can apply, has sunk deep into the youthful mind of this
country. It is a bad word. I have taken leave to call it
"question-begging, clumsy, and incomplete," before now; and
I repeat those epithets with a fresh emphasis here. It begs
the question whether "Italo-Classic" would not, in its own
kind, be the properer term: it is clumsy because the two parts
of it are not used in the same sense; and it is incomplete
because it does not intimate that much beside French influence, and that a very peculiar and sophisticated kind of
Classical influence, went to the making of the thing. But
there *was* French influence: and for some three-quarters of
a century France was the head manufactory in which Italian,
Classical, and other ideas were torn up and remade into a
sort of critical shoddy with which (as with other French
shoddy in that and other times) Europe was rather too eager
to clothe itself.

The Quarrel of the Ancients and Moderns—Italian in origin
and English by borrowing from France, but in the main
French—might look like revolt against Neo-Classicism,[2] and

---

[1] The attitude of Milton and Dryden
respectively illustrates this well. There
was scarcely more than twenty years
between the two poets. But Milton
looks to the Italians first, if not also
last, among the moderns, for criticism.

Dryden, though he knows and cites
them, does not.

[2] "Neo-classic" itself is not a very
"blessed" word; but it has been long
recognised, and the objections to it are
mainly formal.

it undoubtedly spread seeds of the more successful revolution which followed; but the more one studies it, the more one sees that the revolt was in the main unconscious. The Moderns were, as a rule, just as "classical" in their ideas as the Ancients. They were as incapable of catholic judgment; they were even more ignorant of literature as a whole; they were at least as apt to introduce non-literary criteria; they were as much under the obsession of the Kind, the Rule (cast-iron, not leaden), the sweeping generalisation. Too commonly the thing comes to this— that the man who can conjugate *tupto* will not hear of anything which lessens the importance of that gift, and that the man who cannot conjugate *tupto* will not hear of any virtue attaching to it.

But though France may usurp and apparently possess the hegemony, England is of almost the greatest importance, though this importance belongs entirely to one man. This one man in his time played many parts: and as the main aim of literature is to give pleasure, and to produce original sources thereof, we cannot perhaps say that his critical part was the greatest. But we may almost say that it was the most important. We can imagine English literature without the poetry of Dryden: it would be wofully impoverished, but somebody would take up the burden, probably before Pope. Certainly Pope would take it up, though with much more to do. But English criticism, and, what is more, European criticism of the best and most fruitful kind, would have had, if Dryden had been absent, to seek some totally new source: and it is impossible to tell where that source would have been found. There is no precedent anywhere for Dryden's peculiar way of shaking different literatures and different examples of literature together, of indicating the things that please him in all, and of at least attempting to find out why they please him. It is this, not his parade of Rules, and his gleanings from the books, that makes his critical glory: and it is this in which, among critics up to his own time, he is alone.

Yet even he does parade "rules"; even he does belaud

Rapin, and Le Bossu, and even Rymer; even he would have been, no doubt, quite as ready to take the oath to Boileau as he was nobly determined not to take it to William. His genius is recalcitrant to the orthodoxy of the time; but something else in him accepts it. It is not for nothing that he never *published* that word of power which dissolves all the spells of Duessa—"Had Aristotle seen our plays, he might have changed his mind."

As one result of the establishment of Neo-Classicism, there was evolved, towards the end of the seventeenth century, a sort of false Florimel or Duessa, who was called Taste. She was rather a Protean Goddess, and reflected the knowledge or the want of it, the real taste or the want of it, possessed by her priests and worshippers. The Taste of Dryden and the Taste of Rymer are totally different things. But in all save the very happiest minds, Taste, as far as Poetry is concerned almost wholly, and to a great extent as regards prose, is vitiated by all manner of mistaken assumptions, polluted by all manner of foolish and hurtful idolatries. There is the Idol of the Kind which has been noticed; the Idol of the Quality; the Idol of Good Sense, the most devouring of all.[1] It is agreed, and agreed very pardonably, that it is not well to write

> "And periwig with snow the baldpate woods."

But the baser folk go on from this—and all but the very noblest have some difficulty in preventing themselves from going on—to think that a man should not write

> "The multitudinous seas incarnadine."

There is a sense, and a very proper sense, that, in a certain general way, style must suit subjects: that you ought not to write to a Child of Quality, aged five, as you would do to Queen Anne, aged fifty.[2] But this topples over into the most absurd

---

[1] Perhaps there is not a more unhappy gibe in literature (which has many such) than that in *The Rehearsal* on Bayes, who is made to say that "Spirits must not be confined to talk sense." They certainly must not; even Addison (*Sp.*, 419) admits that "their sense ought to be a little *discoloured.*" There is much virtue in this "discolour."

[2] It may be said that this was later. But Prior was a man of thirty-six in 1700.

limitations, so that, a little later than our actual time, we shall find Pope taking modest credit to himself with Spence for that, though Virgil in his Pastorals "has sometimes six or eight lines together *that are epic*," he had been so scrupulous as "scarce ever to have two together, even in the *Messiah*." Indeed it is hardly possible to find a better *reductio ad absurdum* of Neo-Classicism than this. You lay down (as in late classic times Servius did lay it down), from a general induction of the practice of a particular poet, such and such a rule about Virgil's styles in his various works. Then you turn this individual observation into a general rule. And then you go near to find fault with the very poet from whom you have derived it because he does not always observe it—as if his unquestionable exceptions had not as much authority as his supposed rules. Nor is there any doubt that this fallacy derives colour and support from the false Good Sense, the Pseudo-Reason. The induction from practice is hitched on to Reason so as to become a deduction and a demonstration, and once established as that, you deduce from it anything you like. Meanwhile Good Sense, as complaisant to the critic as stern to the victim of his criticism, will approve or disapprove anything that you choose to approve or disapprove, will set her seal to any arbitrary decision, any unjust or purblind whim, and can only be trusted with certainty to set her face invariably against the highest poetry, and often against certain kinds not so high.[1]

The result of all this is that, with the exception of Dryden, no critic of the time achieves, with any success, the highest function of the true critic of literature, the discovery and celebration of beautiful literary things. It is not their business, or their wish, to set free the "lovely prisoned soul of Eucharis." If Eucharis will get a ticket from the patronesses of the contemporary Almack's, and dress herself in the prescribed uniform, and come up for judgment with the

---

[1] Yet it is not for the twentieth century to throw stones at the seventeenth, till we leave off laying down rules of our own manufacture for still earlier ages, and reproving Marlowe and the youthful Shakespeare for being "too lyrical" in tragedy.

proper courtesy, they will do her such justice as Minerva has enabled them to do; but if not, not. Sometimes (as in the case of the immortal Person of Quality who took the trouble to get Spenser into order[1]) they will good-naturedly endeavour to give her a better chance, poor thing! But they will never kiss the daughter of Hippocrates on the mouth, and receive the reward thereto appropriated.

That, on the other hand, there is observable, throughout the century, a certain interpenetration of the older and more Romantic spirit—in the creative work chiefly, but even there dying down, in the critical overmastered from the first, and less and less perceptible,—this opinion will meet with no contradiction here, but, on the contrary, with the strongest support. All the eccentric phenomena, as they may be called, which have been noticed from Euphuism to Gongorism, are symptoms of this. Yet even this was, as has been said, steadily dying down; and by the end of the century the old Phœnix was nearly in ashes, though the new bird was to take slow rebirth from them. I am myself inclined to think that the signs of Romantic leaning in Dryden belong to the new, not to the old, chapter of symptoms; and that in this way England, the last, save perhaps Spain, to give up, was the first to feel again for, the standard of Romanticism. But in this Dryden was in advance, not merely of all his countrymen, but of all Europe; and he did not himself definitely raise any flag of revolt. On the contrary, he always supposed himself to be, and sometimes was, arguing for a reasonable and liberal Classicism.

The Italian poet, satirist, and critic, Tassoni,[2] once wrote an interesting paradox on the admitted lovesomeness, body and soul, of *le donne brutte*, and on the tricks which *bruttezza* and *bellezza* play to each other. If that ingenious poet and polemic had but pushed his inquiries a little further, and extended

---

[1] See *Spenser Redivivus*. London, 1686-87. The Person of Quality "delivers" Spenser "in Heroick numbers," as per sample—

' Then to the lady gallant Arthur said,
All grief repeated is more grievous made."

This is "what Spenser ought to have been, instead of what is to be found in himself."

[2] *Hist. Crit.*, ii. 326.

them in purview as well as lineally, he might have come to
great things in criticism. It might, for instance, have struck
him whether the accepted notions of literary beauty were not
peculiarly like those of physical beauty, which were also those
of his century. These laws laid it down that "from the chin to
the pit betwixt the collar-bones there must be two lengths of
the nose," that the whole figure must be "ten faces high," and
that "the inside of the arm, from the place where the muscle
disappears to the middle, is four noses"; while the careful
calculators noted all the while with dismay that both the
Apollo Belvidere and the Medicean Venus set these proportions
at the most god-like defiance.[1] He would (or he might) have
observed that, just as when you have settled exactly what a
bella donna must not have, there is apt to sail, or slip, into the
room somebody with that particular characteristic to whom
you become a hopeless slave, so, when you have settled the
qualifications of the drama and those of the epic with all the
infallible finality of Stome's stop-watch critic, there comes you
out some impudent production which is an admirable poem,
while the obedient begettings of your rules are worthless
rubbish. Tassoni, I say, might have done this; he seems to
have had quite the temper to do it; but he did it not. It was
doubtless with him, as with others, a case of *Di terrent et
Jupiter hostis*—the gods of their world and their time forbade
them.

A summary of the whole merits and defects of Neo-Classicism must again be postponed; while as for the special defects
of this special period we have said enough. Its special
merits are partly of a negative kind, but they certainly exist.
In the Middle Ages, as we have seen, there was no code of
criticism at all; in the sixteenth century only a growing
approach to one, though the approach had become very near at
the last. Some outbreaks of heterodoxy—the last stand of
Romance for the time—had, as usually happens, drawn the
orthodox together, had made them sign a definite, or almost
definite, instrument or confession. Just or unjust, adequate or

[1] See the whole absurd scheme in
the appendix - matter to Dryden's
Translation of Du Fresnoy (*ed. cit.
sup.*, xvii. 429).

inadequate, even consistent or inconsistent, as it may be, from the point of view of a very searching and all-inspecting logic, the Neo-Classicism of the late seventeenth century was a thing about which there could be no mistake. It knew its own mind about everything which it chose to consider, and valiantly shut its eyes to everything which it chose to ignore. For a time— a short time only, of course, for the triumph of a religion is always the signal for the appearance of a heresy—the majority of people had not much more doubt about what was the proper thing to believe in and admire in literature, than they had about the multiplication table. It became possible to write real literary histories: it became still more easily possible to criticise new books on a definite basis of accepted postulates. And it is by no means certain that this provisional orthodoxy was not a necessary condition of the growth of the new study of Æsthetic, which, though it has done criticism harm as well as good, has certainly done it good as well as harm.

Nor is it possible to deny that there was something to admire in the creed itself. It was weakest—it was in fact exceedingly weak—on the poetical side; but the world happened to have accumulated a remarkably good stock of poetry in the last two centuries or so, and a fallow, or a cessation of manufacture, was not undesirable. Prose, on the other hand, had never been got into proper order in the vernaculars; and it was urgently desirable that it should be so got. The very precepts of the classical creed which were most mischievous in poetry were sovereign for prose. Here also they might hinder the development of eccentric excellence; but it was not eccentric excellence that was wanted. Unjust things have been said about the poetry of the Augustan ages; just things may be said against the criticism which mainly controlled that poetry. But it is hardly excessive to say that every precept—not purely metrical —contained in the *Arts* of Boileau and of Pope, is just and true for Prose. You may fly in the face of almost every one of these precepts and be all the better poet; fly in the face of almost any one of them in prose, and you must have extraordinary genius if you do not rue it.

Even as to poetry itself some defence may be made. This

poetry needed these rules; or rather, to speak more critically, these rules expressed the spirit of this poetry. The later and weaker metaphysicals in England, and fantasts in France, the Marinists and Gongorists in Spain and Italy, had shown what happens when *Furor* [*vere*] *Poeticus* ceases to ply the oars, and Good Sense has not come to take the helm. It is pretty certain that if this criticism had not ruled, its absence would not have brought about good or great Romantic poetry; we should at best have had a few more Dyers and Lady Winchelseas. But if it had not ruled we should have had a less perfect Pope and less presentable minorities of this kind, and have been by no means consoled by a supply of eighteenth-century Clevelands. Once more, the period has the criticism that it wants, the criticism that will enable it to give us its own good things at their own best, and to keep off things which must almost certainly have been bad.

CHAPTER IV.

FROM ADDISON TO JOHNSON.

CRITICISM AT DRYDEN'S DEATH—BYSSHE'S 'ART OF ENGLISH POETRY'—GILDON
—WELSTED—DENNIS—ON RYMER—ON SHAKESPEARE—ON "MACHINES"
—HIS GENERAL THEORY OF POETRY—ADDISON—THE 'ACCOUNT OF THE
BEST KNOWN ENGLISH POETS'—THE 'SPECTATOR' CRITICISMS—ON TRUE
AND FALSE WIT—ON TRAGEDY—ON MILTON—THE "PLEASURES OF THE
IMAGINATION"—HIS GENERAL CRITICAL VALUE—STEELE—ATTERBURY
—SWIFT—'THE BATTLE OF THE BOOKS'—THE 'TALE OF A TUB'—MINOR
WORKS—POPE—THE 'LETTERS'—THE SHAKESPEARE PREFACE—SPENCE'S
'ANECDOTES'—THE 'ESSAY ON CRITICISM'—THE 'EPISTLE TO AUGUSTUS'
—REMARKS ON POPE AS A CRITIC, AND THE CRITICAL ATTITUDE OF HIS
GROUP—PHILOSOPHICAL AND PROFESSIONAL CRITICS—TRAPP—BLAIR—
THE 'LECTURES ON RHETORIC'—THE 'DISSERTATION ON OSSIAN'—KAMES
—THE 'ELEMENTS OF CRITICISM'—CAMPBELL—THE 'PHILOSOPHY OF
RHETORIC'—HARRIS—THE 'PHILOLOGICAL ENQUIRIES'—"ESTIMATE"
BROWN : HIS 'HISTORY OF POETRY'—JOHNSON : HIS PREPARATION FOR
CRITICISM—'THE RAMBLER' ON MILTON—ON SPENSER—ON HISTORY AND
LETTER-WRITING — ON TRAGI-COMEDY — "DICK MINIM"—'RASSELAS'
—THE SHAKESPEARE PREFACE — THE 'LIVES OF THE POETS'—THEIR
GENERAL MERITS—THE 'COWLEY'—THE 'MILTON'—THE 'DRYDEN' AND
'POPE'—THE 'COLLINS' AND 'GRAY'—THE CRITICAL GREATNESS OF
THE 'LIVES' AND OF JOHNSON—MINOR CRITICISM : PERIODICAL AND
OTHER—GOLDSMITH—VICESIMUS KNOX—SCOTT OF AMWELL.

THE death of Dryden punctuates, with an exactness not often
attainable in literary history, the division between seventeenth-
and eighteenth-century literature in England.[1] In general letters

[1] An interesting monograph on our
subject, before and after 1700, is Herr
Paul Hamelius's *Die Kritik in der
Engl. Literatur des* 17 *und* 18 *Jahr-
hunderts* (Leipsic, 1897). Herr Hamelius agrees with me on the romantic
element in Dryden (though not as to
that in Dennis), and as to reducing
the importance of French influence in
England. To the collections of texts
previously mentioned should be added
Mr Nichol Smith's most useful 18*th
Century Essays on Shakespeare* (Glasgow, 1903).

it is succeeded—not at all immediately—by the great school of
Criticism at Dryden's death. Queen Anne men. In criticism [1] one of the greatest of these, a special pupil of Dryden, takes up the running at this interval, and others a little later; but the succession is steadily maintained. Dennis, an unhappily belated person, continues his exercitations; but has very much the worse fortune, critical as well as pecuniary, in his later days. And in the very year of the death there appears an egregious work—extremely popular, maleficently powerful beyond all doubt throughout the eighteenth century, and now chiefly known to non-experts in our days by the humorous contradiction which gave its author's name to Shelley, and by the chance which made a literary connection, towards the very end of its period of influence, between three such extraordinarily assorted persons as Afra Behn, Bysshe himself, and William Blake. [2]

Edward Bysshe's *Art of English Poetry* [3] puts the eighteenth-century theory of this art with a rigour and completeness which
Bysshe's Art of English Poetry. can only be attributed either to something like genius, or to a wonderful and complete absence of it. His *Rules for Making English Verse* are the first part of the book in order, but much the least in bulk. Then follow, first a collection of " the most natural and sublime thoughts of the best English poets," or, in other words, an anthology, reasoned under headings, from poets of the seven-

---

[1] The excessively rare *Parliament of Critics* (London, 1702), a copy of which has been kindly lent me by Mr Gregory Smith, is more of what it calls itself, a " banter," than of a serious composition. But it connects itself not obscurely with the Collier quarrel.

[2] See Mr Swinburne's *William Blake*, p. 130 note, for the *sortes Bysshianæ* of Blake and his wife.

[3] My copy is the Third Edition, " with large improvements," London, 1708. Some put the first at 1702, not 1700. Before Bysshe, Joshua Poole, a schoolmaster, had given posthumously (1657 : I have ed. 2, London, 1677),

—with a short dedication and a curious verse proem of his own, and an *Institution* signed J. D.,—*The English Parnassus*. This contains a double gradus of epithets and passages, an " Alphabet of [Rhyming] Monosyllables," and some " Forms of Compliment," &c. The *Institution* stoutly defends " Rhythm " [*i.e.*, rhyme], notices Sidney, Daniel, Puttenham, &c., shortly defines Kinds, objects to excessive enjambment (note the time, 1657) and to polysyllables, but is sensible. (See, for more on it, the present writer's *History of English Prosody* (London, 1906-10), ii. 345-8.)

teenth century, extending to about four hundred and fifty pages; and last a Dictionary of Rhymes. The "best English poets" may be useful to give in a note.[1] The Dictionary is preceded by a few prefatory remarks, including one important historically, "Rhyme is *by all* allowed to be the chief ornament of versification in the modern languages." The killing frost which had fallen on the flowers of Elizabethan poetry had killed one weed at any rate—the craze against rhyme.

The Rules are preceded by a partly apologetic Preface, which disclaims any wish to furnish tools to poetasters, and puts the work "under the awful guard of the immortal Shakespeare, Milton [note that this was before Addison's critique], Dryden, &c." The keynote is struck, in the very first sentence of the text, with that uncompromisingness which makes one rather admire Bysshe. "The Structure of our verses, whether blank or in rhyme, consists *in a certain number of syllables; not* in feet composed of long and short syllables, as the verse of the Greeks and Romans." And he adds that, though some ingenious persons formerly puzzled themselves in prescribing rules for the quantity of English syllables, and composed verses by the measure of dactyls and spondees, yet that design is now wholly exploded. In other words, he cannot conceive classical feet without classical arrangement of feet.

"Our poetry admits, for the most part, of but three sorts of verses, those of 10, 8, and 7 syllables. Those of 4, 6, 9, 11, 12, and 14 are generally employed in masks and operas." But 12 and 14 may be used in Heroic verse with grace. Accent must be observed; and the Pause *must be* at or near the middle, though in Heroics it may be at the 3rd, 4th, 5th, 6th, or 7th syllable, determined by the seat of the accent. Still, pauses at the 3rd and 7th must be used sparingly. The 2nd and 8th "can produce no true harmony"; and he seems to have refused

[1] Addison, Atterbury, Beaumont and Fletcher, Afra Behn, Blackmore, Tom Brown, Buckingham, Cleveland, Congreve, Cowley, Creech, Davenant (2), Denham, Dennis, Dorset, Dryden, Duke, Garth, Halifax, Harvey, Sir R. Howard, *Hudibras*, Jonson, Lee. Milton, Mulgrave, Oldham, Otway, Prior, Ratcliff, Rochester, Roscommon, Rowe, Sedley, Shakespeare, Southern, Sprat, Stafford, Stepney, Suckling, Tate, Walsh, Waller, Wycherley, and Yalden. Observe that no non-dramatic poet earlier than Cowley is admitted.

to contemplate anything so awful as a pause at the 1st or 9th.
After decasyllables, octosyllables are commonest. As for lines
of 9 and 11 syllables, "with the accent on the last [*i.e.*, anapæstic measures], the disagreeableness of their measure has
wholly excluded them from serious subjects." The refining
effected since the days of Chaucer, Spenser, and other ancient
poets consists especially in the avoidance of the concourse of
vowels and in the rigid elision of the article, the contraction of
preterperfect tenses (" amaz'd," not " amazed "), the rejection of
alliteration (an instance in Dryden is apologised for), of split-
ting words closely connected at the end of a verse, and of
polysyllables.

And a very large number of minute rules follow, the one
guiding principle of which is to reduce every line to its
syllabic minimum, never allowing trisyllabic substitution.

The book, base and mechanical as it may seem, is of the
first historical importance. It will be seen, even from these
few extracts, that the excellent Bysshe has no doubts, no half-
lights. The idea, which we have seen crystallising for a
century and a half, that English poetry is as strictly and
inexorably syllabic as French, and much more so than Greek
or Latin, is here put in its baldest crudity. Bysshe will have
no feet at all : and no other division within the line but at the
pause, which is to be as centripetal as possible, like the French
cæsura. It follows from this that, except the feminine or double
ending, which is allowed ostensibly as a grace to rhymes, though
also in blank verse, nothing extra to the ten, the eight, or
whatever the line-norm may be, is permitted on any account.
Articles, prepositions that will stand it, pronouns, are to be
rigidly elided; weak or short syllables in the interior of words
must be slurred out. There is (only that Bysshe will not have
even the name of foot) no room for a trisyllabic foot anywhere,
in what he equally refuses to call iambic or trochaic verse.

But what is more startling still is that trisyllabic feet disappear, not merely from the octosyllable and the heroic, but
from English prosody, or are admitted only to " Compositions
for Musick and the lowest sort of burlesque." Dryden might
have written, "After the pangs of a desperate lover"; Prior

might be writing "Dear Chloe, how blubbered is that pretty face": but Bysshe sternly averts *his* face from them.

Now, if this astonishing impoverishment of English poetry had been the isolated crotchet of a pedant or a poetaster, it would at most deserve notice in a note. But it was nothing of the kind. "He," this insignificant person, "said it": they went and did it. It expressed the actual poetic practice of serious poets from Pope to Goldsmith: and it expressed the deliberate theoretic creed of such a critic as Johnson. The contrary practice of the great old poets was at best a "licence," at worst a "fault." What had actually happened to French—that it had been reduced to the iamb—what Gascoigne had lamented and protested against, long before, was here threatened —or rather, with bland ignoring, even of threat, laid down—as the unquestioned and unquestionable law of English. The whole eighteenth century did not, indeed, go the entire length of Bysshe. Prior—it is his everlasting glory in English poetical history—took care of that, and not only saved anapæstic cadence for us, but made it more popular than ever. But the eighteenth century continued, charmingly as it wrote them, to be a little ashamed of its anapæsts, to write them affectedly as a relaxation, if not even a derogation—to indulge in them (just as it might indulge in leap-frog with wig and long-skirted coat laid aside) avowedly for a frolic. And about the decasyllable — not quite so rigidly about the octosyllable— it accepted Bysshe almost without a protest. All the infinite variety of true English prosody, all the gliding or melting trochees, all the passion and throb which trisyllabic feet give to iambic verse, were sacrificed, all freedom of pause was relinquished, and the decasyllable tramped, the octosyllable tripped, as regularly and as monotonously as a High Dutch grenadier or a Low Dutch clock.

Bysshe had been frankly formal; it is not a small merit in him that he knew what he had to do and did it: but persons

Gildon. who were little if at all above him in taste or in intellect affected to despise him for this, and Mr Charles Gildon in his *Complete Art of Poetry*,[1] published a few

[1] London, 1718.

years later, is very high and mighty with Bysshe. As for himself he does not think that Poetry consists even in "colouring," but in Design: and he hashes up his French originals into some would - be modish dialogues, in which ladies of fashion attack and defend poetry on the old lines, before he comes to minuter recommendations. These differ chiefly from Bysshe's in that they are wordier, less peremptory, and given to substitute the vagueness of the journalist for the precision of the schoolmaster. Nor was this by any means Gildon's only contribution to criticism. Among the others perhaps the most interesting is an anonymous and undated, but apparently not doubtful, *rifacimento* of Langbaine,[1] which is curious as an example of *peine du talion.* Gildon (who has employed his own or some other "careful hand" to give himself an ingeniously, because not extravagantly, complimentary notice in the Appendix) serves Langbaine in Langbaine's own fashion; and, not contented with reversing his judgments, indulges freely in such phrases as "Mr Langbain mistakes," "those scurrilous and digressory remarks with which Mr Langbain has bespattered him [Dryden]," &c. The book is in the main bibliographic and biographic rather than critical.

A name which has something to do with criticism, and which associates itself naturally with those of Dennis and *Welsted.* Gildon in the regiment of Pope's victims, is that of Leonard Welsted, who in 1712 published a translation of Longinus, "with some remarks on the English Poets." Welsted's translation, whether made directly from the Greek or not,[2] is readable enough, and his alternative title, "A treatise on *the Sovereign Perfection of Writing,*" is not unhappy. Neither are his Preface and his appended "Remarks" contemptible. He can appreciate not merely Milton but Spenser; is (how unlike Rymer!) transported with *Othello,* and

---

[1] *Lives . . . improved and continued down to this time by a Careful Hand.* (No date in my copy, but the *Dict. Nat. Biog.* gives 1699.) Since this was written Gildon has found some defenders or apologists. He needs them.

[2] I hope the passing suspicion is not illiberal. But why should he call the Palmyrene "Zenobie" in English? *Cela sent furieusement son Français.* (For the critical work of yet another who felt the lash of Pope—James Ralph—see *Hist. Crit.,* ii. 554.

especially with its conclusion; and if he is not superior to others in scorning "Latin rhymes," at least has sufficient independence to be very irreverent to Buchanan.

But there was a contemporary of Bysshe's, more famous than either Gildon or Welsted, whose soul was equally above mere prosodic precept, and to whom, as it happens, Gildon himself pays a compliment, as to a denizen of Grub Street, of whom Grub Street could not but feel that he did it some honour by herding with its more native and genuine population. Of him we must say something — not, as we might almost have said it, in juxtaposition with the great poet and critic whom he had earlier admired, but before dealing with the lesser, but still great, successors of Dryden, with whom he came into collision in his evil days.

If John Dennis had been acquainted with the poetry of Tennyson (at which he would probably have railed in his best

Dennis. manner, in which he would certainly have detected plagiarisms from the classics), he too might have applied to himself the words of Ulysses, "I am become a name." Everybody who has the very slightest knowledge of English literature knows, if only in connection with Dryden, Addison, and Pope, the surly, narrow, but not quite ignorant or incompetent critic, who in his younger and more genial days admired the first, and in his soured old age attacked the second and third. But it may be doubted whether very many persons have an acquaintance, at all extensive, with his works. They were never collected; the *Select Works of John Dennis*[1] mainly consist of his utterly worthless verse. Much of the criticism is hidden away in prefaces which were seldom reprinted, and the original editions of which have become very rare. Even good libraries frequently contain only two or three out of more than a dozen or a score of separate documents: and though the British Museum itself is well furnished, it is necessary to range through a large number of publications to obtain a complete view of Dennis as a critic.

That view, when obtained, may perhaps differ not a little from those which have, in a certain general way, succeeded each

[1] 2 vols., London, 1718.

other in current literary judgment. During the reign of Pope and Addison, the scurrilous assailant of the first, and the more courteous but in part severe censor of the second, was naturally regarded as at best a grumbling pedant, at worst a worthless Zoilus. The critics of the Romantic school were not likely to be much attracted by Dennis. More recently, something of a reaction has taken place in his favour; and it has become not unusual to discover in him, if not exactly a Longinus or a Coleridge, yet a serious and well-equipped critic, who actually anticipated not a little that after-criticism has had to say.[1]

That this more charitable view is not entirely without founda-
tion may be at once admitted. As compared with Rymer, in
On Rymer.   whose company he too often finds himself in modern appreciation, Dennis shows, indeed, pretty well. He very seldom—perhaps nowhere—exhibits that crass insensibility to poetry which distinguishes " the worst critic who ever lived." One of his earliest and not his worst pieces, *The Im-partial Critic* of 1693, an answer to Rymer himself, points out with acuteness and vigour that "Tom the Second" would ruin the English stage if he had his way, and even approaches the sole causeway of criticism across the deep by advancing the argument that the circumstances of the Greek drama were per-fectly different from those of the English.[2] Yet already there are danger-signals. That the piece (which includes a Letter to a Friend and some dialogues) contains a great deal of clumsy jocularity, does not much matter. But when we find Dennis devoting some of this jocularity to Antigone's lamentation over her death unwedded, we feel sadly that the man who can write thus is scarcely to be trusted on the spirit of poetry. And the admission that Rymer's censures of Shakespeare are " in most of the particulars very sensible and just " is practically ruinous.[3]

---

[1] See, among others, Herr Hamelius, *op. cit.* Yet it is interesting to find that the passage of Dennis to which his panegyrist gives the single and signal honour of extract in an appen-dix is purely ethical : it is all on " the previous question."

[2] Had Dryden let his Cambridge admirer see the *Heads* ? (*v. supra,* pp. 113, 137 notes.)

[3] Although Dennis's fun is heavy enough, there are some interesting touches, as this : " Port [then a novelty in England, remember] is not so well tasted as Claret : and intoxicates sooner." (See note at end of chapter.)

Dennis's answer to Collier is a little later,[1] but still earlier than most of his better known work; and it is very characteristic of his manner, which has not often, I think, been exactly described. As elsewhere, so in this tract, which is entitled *The Usefulness of the Stage to the Happiness of Mankind, to Government and to Religion*, Dennis is uncompromisingly ethical; but he had here the excuse that Collier, to whom he was replying, had taken the same line. There is less excuse here or elsewhere for his method. This is to make a loud clatter of assertions, arranged in a kind of pseudological order, which seems to have really deceived the author, and may possibly have deceived some of his readers, into believing it syllogistic and conclusive. Dennis is very great at the word "must." "As Poetry is an Art it *must* be an imitation of nature"[2] and so forth; seldom shall you find so many "musts" anywhere as in Dennis, save perhaps in some of his modern analogues. Like all who argue in this fashion, he becomes unable to distinguish fact and his own opinion. Collier, for instance, had quoted (quite correctly) Seneca's denunciation of the Stage. To which Dennis replies, "It is not likely that Seneca should condemn the drama, . . . since . . . he wrote plays himself." That the identity of the philosopher and the dramatist is not certain does not matter: the characteristic thing is the setting of probability against fact. But with Dennis hectoring assertion is everything. "It cannot possibly be conceived that so reasonable a diversion as the drama can encourage or incline men to so unreasonable a one as gaming or so brutal a one as drunkenness." With a man who thinks this an argument, argument is impossible.

The fact is that, though he has, as has been admitted, a certain advantage over Rymer, Lord Derby's observation that "He

---

[1] It appeared in the very year of the *Short View* (1698). I have a reprint of it, issued many years later (1725), but long before Dennis's death, together with *The Advancement and Reformation of Modern Poetry* and the tragedy of *Rinaldo and Armida*, all separately titled, but continuously paged.

[2] This is from the *Advancement and Reformation*, which contains its author's full definition of Poetry itself—not the worst of such definitions. "Poetry is an Imitation of Nature by a pathetic and numerous speech."

never knew whether it was John or Thomas who answered
On Shake-
speare. the bell" will too often apply here. Rymer himself
was not ignorant; Dennis, especially in regard to
ancient criticism, was still better instructed: and though both
were bad dramatists, with, in consequence, a conscious or unconscious bias on dramatic matters, Dennis was not so bad as
Rymer. His devotion to Dryden does him credit, though we
may suspect that it was not the best part of Dryden that he
liked: and, amid the almost frantic spite and scurrility of his
later attacks on Pope, he not unfrequently hits a weak place in
the "young squab short gentleman's" bright but not invulnerable armour. Yet Dennis displays, as no really good critic
could do, the weaknesses of his time and school both in generals
and particulars. It is perfectly fair to compare him (giving
weight for genius of course) with Johnson, a critic whose general
views (except on port and claret) did not materially differ from
his own. And, if we do so, we shall find that while Johnson is
generally, if not invariably, "too good for such a breed," Dennis
almost as constantly shows its worst features. He altered *The
Merry Wives of Windsor* into *The Comical Gallant* [1]—a most
illaudable action certainly, yet great Dryden's self had done
such things before. But he aggravated the crime by a preface,
in which he finds fault with the original as having "no less than
three actions" [would there were thirty-three!] by remarking
that, in the second part of *Henry the Fourth*, Falstaff "does
nothing but talk" [would he had talked so for five hundred
acts instead of five!] and by laying down *ex cathedra* such
generalities as that "Humour, not wit, is the business of
comedy," a statement as false as would be its converse. In his
Essay on the Genius of Shakespeare [2] he is not so very far
from Rymer himself in the drivelling arbitrariness of his
criticism. Shakespeare has actually made Aufidius, the general
of the Volscians, a base and profligate villain! Even Coriolanus
himself is allowed to be called a traitor by Aufidius, and nobody contradicts! The rabble in *Julius Cæsar* and other such
things "show want of Art," and there is a painful disregard of
Poetical Justice. The same hopeless wrong-headedness and (if

[1] London, 1702.   [2] London, 1712.

I may so say) wrong-mindedness appear in a very different work, the *Remarks on the Rape of the Lock*.[1] I do not refer to Dennis's mere scurrilities about "AP—E" and the like. But *On "Machines."* part of the piece is quite serious criticism. Few of us in modern times care much for the "machinery" of this brilliantly artificial poem; but fewer would think of objecting to it on Dennis's grounds. Machines, it seems, must be—

    i. Taken from the religion of the Poet's country.

    ii. Allegorical in their application.

    iii. Corresponding though opposed to each other.

    iv. Justly subordinated and proportioned.

And Pope's machines, we are told, fail in all these respects.

Now, putting the fourth ground aside as being a mere matter of opinion (and some who are not fervent Papists think the machines of the *Rape* very prettily and cleverly arranged in their puppet-show way), one may ask Dennis " Who on earth told you so ? " in respect of all the others. And if he alleged (as he might) this or that sixteenth or seventeenth century authority, " And who on earth told *him* so ? and what authority had the authority ?   Why should machines be taken only from the religion of the country ?   Why should they be allegorical ? Why should Machine Dick on the one side invariably nod to Machine Harry on the other ? "   And even if some sort of answer be forthcoming, " Why should the poet not do as he please if he succeeds thereby in giving the poetic pleasure ? " To which last query of course neither Dennis nor any of his school could return any answer, except of the kind that requires bell, book, and candle.

Nor would he have hesitated to use this, for he is a rule-critic of the very straitest kind, a " Tantivy " of poetic Divine *His general theory of Poetry.* Right. In his three chief books of abstract criticism [2] he endeavours to elaborate, with Longinus in part for code, and with Milton for example, a noble indeed, and creditable, but utterly arbitrary and hopelessly

---

[1] London, 1728.

[2] *The Advancement and Reformation of Poetry*, 1701 ; *A Large Account of the Taste in Poetry*, next year ; and *Grounds of Criticism in Poetry*, 1704.

narrow theory of poetry as *necessarily* religious, and as having for its sole real end the reformation of the mind, by a sort of enlarged Aristotelian *katharsis* as to spirit, and by attention to the strict laws of the art in form. Poetical Justice was a kind of mediate divinity to Dennis: as we have seen, he upbraided Shakespeare for the want of it; he remonstrated, in the *Spectator*, No. 548, and elsewhere, with Addison for taking too little account of it; part at least of his enthusiasm for Milton comes from Milton's avowed intention to make his poem a theodicy.

A noble error! let it be repeated, with no hint or shadow of sarcasm or of irreverence; but a fatal error as well. That Poetry, like all things human, lives and moves and has its being in God, the present writer believes as fervently and unhesitatingly as any Platonic philosopher or any Patristic theologian; and he would cheerfully incur the wrath of Savonarola by applying the epithet "divine," in its fullest meaning, not merely to tragedy and epic and hymn, but to song of wine and of love. But this is not what Dennis meant at all. He meant that Poetry is to have a definitely religious, definitely moral *purpose*—not that it is and tends of itself necessarily *ad majorem Dei gloriam*, but that we are to shape it according to what our theological and ethical ideas of the glory of God are. This way easily comes bad poetry, not at all easily good; and it excludes poetic varieties which may be as good as the best written in obedience to it, and better. Moreover, putting Dennis's notion of the end of Poetry together with his notion of its method or art (which latter is to be adjusted to some at least of the straitest classical precepts), we can easily comprehend, and could easily have anticipated, the narrow intolerance and the hectoring pedantry which he shows towards all who follow not him. In a new sense—not so very different from the old mediæval one, though put with no mediæval glamour, and by an exponent full of eighteenth-century prosaism, yet destitute of eighteenth-century neatness and concinnity—Poetry becomes a part of theology; and the mere irritableness of the man of letters is aggravated into the *odium theologicum*. Bad poets (that is to say, bad according to

Dennis) are not merely faulty artists but wicked men; of this Dennis is sure. "And when a man is sure," as he himself somewhere naïvely observes, "'tis his duty to speak with a modest assurance." We know, from examples more recent than poor Dennis, that, when a man is thus minded, his assurance is very apt to eat up his modesty, taking his charity, his good manners, and some other things, as condiments to the meal.

Dennis and Addison, though the latter did not escape the absolute impartiality of the former's carping, were on terms of *Addison.* mutual respect which, considering all things, were creditable to both. During the latter part of his rather short lifetime Addison, it is hardly necessary to say, enjoyed a sort of mild dictatorship in Criticism as in other departments of literature; and his right to it was scarcely disputed till near the close of the century, though Johnson knew that he was not deep, and tells us that, in his own last days, it was almost a fashion to look down on Addisonian criticism. If, like others, he was displaced by the Romantic revival, he received more lenient treatment than some, in virtue partly of his own general moderation, partly of his championship of Milton. Yet while his original literary gifts recovered high place during the nineteenth century, his criticism has often been considered to possess scarcely more than historic interest, and has sometimes been rather roughly handled—for instance, by Mr Matthew Arnold. But a recent writer,[1] by arguing that Addison's treatment of the Imagination, as a separate faculty, introduced a new principle into criticism, has at any rate claimed for him a position which, if it could be granted, would seat him among the very greatest masters of the art, with Aristotle and Longinus among his own forerunners. As usual let us, before discussing these various estimates, see what Addison actually did as a critic.[2]

His *début* as such was not fortunate. He was, it is true, only

[1] Mr W. Basil Worsfold in his *Principles of Criticism* (London, 1897). I hope that nothing which, in a politely controversial tone, I may have to say here, will be taken as disparagement of a very interesting and valuable essay.

[2] The most convenient edition of Addison's *Works* is that of Bohn, with Hurd's editorial matter and a good deal more (London, 6 vols., 1862).

three-and-twenty when at "dearest Harry's" request (that is to say Mr Harry Sacheverell's) he undertook an *Account of the greatest English Poets*.[1] In 1694 nobody, except Dryden, could be expected to write very good verse, so that the poetical qualities of this verse-essay need not be hardly dwelt upon, or indeed considered at all. We may take it, as if it were prose, for the matter only. And thus considered, it must surely be thought one of the worst examples of the pert and tasteless ignorance of its school. Before Cowley nobody but Chaucer and Spenser is mentioned at all, and the mentions of these are simply grotesque. The lines convict Addison, almost beyond appeal, of being at the time utterly ignorant of English literary history up to 1600, and of having read Chaucer and Spenser themselves, if he had read them at all, with his eyes shut. The Chaucer section reads as if it were describing *A C. Merry Tales* or the *Jests of George Peele*. Where Dryden, if he did not understand Chaucer's versification, and missed some of his poetry, could see much even of that, and almost all the humour, the grace, the sweetness, the "God's plenty" of life and character that Chaucer has, Addison sees nothing but a merry-andrew of the day before yesterday.[2] So, too, the consummate art of Spenser, his exquisite versification, his great ethical purpose, and yet his voluptuous beauty, are quite hidden from Addison. He sees nothing but a tedious allegory of improbable adventures, and objects to the "dull moral" which "lies too plain below," much as Temple had done before him.[3] Cowley, Milton, and Waller are mentioned next, in at least asserted chronological order. Cowley is "a mighty genius" full of beauties and faults,

"Who more had pleased us had he pleased us less,"

[1] It is fair to say that he never published this, and that, as Pope told Spence, he used himself to call it "a poor thing," and admitted that he spoke of some of the poets only "on hearsay." Now when Pope speaks to Addison's credit it is not as "what the soldier said." It *is* evidence, and of the strongest.

[2] "In vain he jests in his unpolished strain,
And tries to make his readers laugh in vain."

[3] "His moral lay so bare that it lost the effect" (*Ess. on Po.*, iii. 420, *ed. cit. sup.*) Indeed it has been suggested that Addison's debt to Temple here is not confined to this.

but who is a perfect "milky way" of brilliancy, and has made
Pindar himself "take a nobler flight." Milton alternately strikes
Addison with awe, rapture, and shock at his politics. He

> "Betrays a bottom odious to the sight."

So we turn to Waller, who is not only "courtly" but "moves
our passion," (what a pity that he died too soon to "rehearse
Maria's charms"!) to Roscommon, who "makes even Rules a
noble poetry," and Denham, whose Cooper's Hill "we must,"
of course, not "forget." "Great Dryden" is then, not unhappily, though not quite adequately, celebrated, and the line
on his Muse—

> "She wears all dresses, and she charms in all,"

is not only neat, but very largely true. When Dryden shall
decay, luckily there is harmonious Congreve: and, if Addison
were not tired with rhyming, he would praise (he does so at
some length) noble Montague, who directs his artful muse to
Dorset,

> "In numbers such as Dorset's self might use,"—

as to which all that can be said is that, if so, either the verses
of Montague or the verses of Dorset referred to are not those
that have come down to us under the names of the respective
authors.

To dwell at all severely on this luckless production of a
young University wit would be not only unkind but uncritical.
It shows that at this time Addison knew next to nothing[1]
about the English literature not of his own day, and judged
very badly of what he pretended to know.

The prose works of his middle period, the *Discourse on
Medals* and the *Remarks on Italy*, are very fully illustrated
from the Latin poets—the division of literature that Addison
knew best—but indulge hardly at all in literary criticism. It
was not till the launching of the *Tatler*, by Steele and Swift,
provided him with his natural medium of utterance, that

---

[1] He proposes to give an account of
"*all* the Muse possessed" between
Chaucer and Dryden; and, as a matter
of fact, mentions nobody but Spenser
between Chaucer and Cowley.

Addison became critical. This periodical itself, and the less known ones that followed the *Spectator*, all contain exercises in this character: but it is to the *Spectator* that men look, and look rightly, for Addison's credentials in the character of a critic. The *Tatler* Essays, such as the rather well known papers on Tom Folio and Ned Softly, those in the *Guardian*, the good-natured puff of Tom D'Urfey, &c., are not so much serious and deliberate literary criticisms, as applications, to subjects more or less literary, of the peculiar method of gently malicious censorship, of laughing castigation in manners and morals, which Addison carried to such perfection in all the middle relations of life. Not only are the *Spectator* articles far more numerous and far more weighty, but we have his own authority for regarding them as, in some measure at least, written on a deliberate system, and divisible into three groups. The first of these groups consists of the early papers on True and False Wit, and of essays on the stage. The second contains the famous and elaborate criticism of Milton with other things; and the third, the still later, still more serious, and still more ambitious, series on the Pleasures of the Imagination. Addison is looking back from the beginning of this last when he gives the general description,[1] and it is quite possible that the complete trilogy was not in his mind when he began the first group. But there is regular development in it, and whether we agree or not with Mr Worsfold's extremely high estimate of the third division, it is quite certain that the whole collection—of some thirty or forty essays—does clearly exhibit that increasing sense of what criticism means, which is to be observed in almost all good critics. For criticism is, on the one hand, an art in which there are so few manuals or trustworthy short summaries —it is one which depends so much more on reading and knowledge than any creative art—and, above all, it is necessary to make so many mistakes in it before one comes right, that,

The Spectator criticisms.

---

[1] In the last paragraph of *Sp.* 409. The whole paper has been occupied by thoughts on Taste and Criticism: it contains the excellent comparison of a critic to a tea-taster, and it ends with this retrospect, and the promise of the "Imagination" Essays (*v. ed. cit.,* iii. 393).

probably, not one single example can be found of a critic of importance who was not a much better critic when he left off than when he began.

In Group One[1] Addison is still animated by the slightly desultory spirit of moral satire, which has been referred to *On True and* above; and, though fifteen or sixteen years have *False Wit.* passed since the *Account,* he does not seem to be so entirely free as we might wish from the crude sciolism, if not the sheer ignorance, of the earliest period.　He is often admirable: his own humour, his taste, almost perfect within its own narrow limits, and his good sense, made that certain beforehand.　But he has somewhat overloaded it with unduly artificial allegory, the ethical temper rather overpowers the literary, and there is not a little of that arbitrary "blackmarking" of certain literary things which is one of the worst faults of neo-classic criticism.　The Temple of Dulness is built (of course) "after the Gothic manner," and the image of the god is dressed "after the habit of a monk."　Among the idolatrous rites and implements are not merely rebuses, anagrams, verses arranged in artificial forms, and other things a little childish, though perfectly harmless, but acrostics—trifles, perhaps, yet trifles which can be made exquisitely graceful, and satisfying that desire for mixing passion with playfulness which is not the worst affection of the human heart.

He had led up to this batch, a few weeks earlier, by some cursory remarks on Comedy, which form the tail of a more *On Tragedy.* elaborate examination of Tragedy, filling four or five numbers.[2]　Readers who have already mastered the general drift of the criticism of the time before him, will scarcely need any long *précis* of his views, which, moreover, are in everybody's reach, and could not possibly be put more readably.　Modern tragedies, he thinks, excel those of Greece and Rome in the intricacy and disposition of the fable, but fall short in the moral.　He objects to rhyme (except an end-couplet or two), and, though he thinks the style of our tragedies superior to the sentiment, finds the former, especially in Shakespeare, defaced by "sounding phrases, hard metaphors,

---

[1] *Sp.* 58-63.　　　　　[2] *Sp.* 39, 40, 42, 44, 45.

and forced expressions." This is still more the case in Lee.
Otway is very "tender": but it is a sad thing that the
characters in *Venice Preserved* should be traitors and rebels.
Poetic justice (this was what shocked Dennis), as generally
understood, is rather absurd, and quite unnecessary. And the
tragi-comedy, which is the product of the English theatre, is
"one of the most monstrous inventions that ever entered into a
poet's thought." You "might as well weave the adventures of
Æneas and Hudibras into one poem" [and, indeed, one might
find some relief in this, as far as the adventures of Æneas are
concerned]. Tragedies are not even to have a double plot.
Rants, and especially impious rants, are bad. Darkened stages,
elaborate scenery and dresses, troops of supers, &c., are as bad:
bells, ghosts, thunder, and lightning still worse. "Of all our
methods of moving pity and terror, there is none so absurd and
barbarous as the dreadful butchering of one another," though
all deaths on the stage are not to be forbidden.

Now, it is not difficult to characterise the criticism which
appears in this first group, strengthened, if anybody cares, by a
few isolated examples. It contains a great deal of common
sense and good ordinary taste; many of the things that it
reprehends are really wrong, and most of what it praises is
good in a way. But the critic has as yet no guiding theory,
except what he thinks he has gathered from Aristotle, and has
certainly gathered from Horace, *plus* Common Sense itself,
with, as is the case with all English critics of this age, a good
deal from his French predecessors, especially Le Bossu and
Bouhours. Which borrowing, while it leads him into numerous
minor errors, leads him into two great ones—his denunciations
of tragi-comedy, and of the double plot. He is, moreover,
essentially arbitrary : his criticism will seldom stand the application of the "Why?" the "*Après?*" and a harsh judge might,
in some places, say that it is not more arbitrary than ignorant.

The Second Group,[1] or Miltonic batch, with which may be

---

[1] These began in *Sp.* 267, and were
the regular Saturday feature of the
paper for many weeks. References to
Milton outside of them will be found
in the excellent index of the ed. cit. or
in that of Mr Gregory Smith's exact
and elegant reproduction of the *Spectator* (8 vols., London, 1897).

taken its "moon," the partly playful but more largely serious

On Milton.   examen of *Chevy Chase*, is much the best known, and
has been generally ranked as the most important
exhibition of Addison's critical powers. It is not, however, out
of paradox or desire to be singular that it will be somewhat
briefly discussed here. By the student of Addison it cannot be
too carefully studied; for the historian of criticism it has indeed
high importance, but importance which can be very briefly
summed up, and which requires no extensive analysis of the
eighteen distinct essays that compose the Miltonic group, or
the two on *Chevy Chase*. The critic here takes for granted—
and knows or assumes that his readers will grant—two general
positions :—

1. The Aristotelian-Horatian view of poetry, with a few of
the more commonplace utterances of Longinus, supplies the
orthodox theory of Poetics.

2. The ancients, especially Homer and Virgil, supply the most
perfect examples of the orthodox practice of poetry.

These things posed, he proceeds to examine *Chevy Chase* at
some, *Paradise Lost* at great, length by their aid; and discovers in the ballad not a few, and in the epic very great and
very numerous, excellences. As Homer does this, so Milton
does that: such a passage in Virgil is a more or less exact
analogue to such another in *Paradise Lost*. Aristotle says this,
Horace that, Longinus the third thing; and you will find the
dicta capitally exemplified in such and such a place of Milton's
works. To men who accepted the principle—as most, if not all,
men did—the demonstration was no doubt both interesting and
satisfactory; and though it certainly did not start general admiration of Milton, it stamped that admiration with a comfortable seal of official orthodoxy. But it is actually more anti-
quated than Dryden, in assuming that the question whether
Milton wrote according to Aristotle is coextensive with the
question whether he wrote good poetry.

The next batch is far more important.

What *are* the Pleasures of the Imagination ? It is of the
first moment to observe Addison's exact definition.[1] Sight is

---

[1] *Sp.* 411, ed. cit., iii. 394.

the " sense which furnishes the imagination with its ideas; so

The "Pleasures of the Imagination." that by the ' Pleasures of the Imagination ' or Fancy, which I shall use promiscuously, I here mean such as arise from visible objects, either when we have them actually in our view, or when we call up their ideas into our minds by paintings, statues, descriptions, or any the like occasion." We can have no images not thus furnished, though they may be altered and compounded by imagination itself. To make this quite sure, he repeats that he means *only* such pleasures as thus arise. He then proceeds, at some length, to argue for the innocence and refinement of such pleasures, their usefulness, and so on ; and further, to discuss the causes or origins of pleasure in sight, which he finds to be three—greatness, uncommonness, and beauty. The pleasantness of these is assigned to such and such wise and good purposes of the Creator, with a reference to the great modern discoveries of Mr Locke's Essay.

Addison then goes on to consider the sources of entertainment to the imagination, and decides that, for the purpose, art is very inferior to nature, though both rise in value as each borrows from the other. He adduces, in illustration, an odd rococo mixture of scene-painting and reflection of actual objects which he once saw (p. 404). Italian and French gardens are next praised, in opposition to the old formal English style, and naturally trained trees to the productions of the *ars topiaria ;* while a very long digression is made to greatness in Architecture, illustrated by this remark (p. 409), " Let any one reflect on the disposition of mind in which he finds himself at his first entrance into the Pantheon at Rome, . . . and consider how little in proportion he is affected with the inside of a Gothic cathedral, though it be five times larger than the other," the reason being " the greatness of the manner in the one, and the meanness in the other."

So the " secondary " pleasures of the imagination—*i.e.*, those compounded and manufactured by memory—are illustrated by the arts of sculpture and painting, with a good passage on description generally, whence he turns to the Cartesian doctrine of the association of ideas, and shows very ingeniously how the

poet may avail himself of this. Next comes a curious and often
just analysis of the reasons of pleasure in description—how, for
instance, he likes Milton's Paradise better than his Hell, because brimstone and sulphur are not so refreshing to the
imagination as beds of flowers and wildernesses of sweets.
Or we may like things because they "raise a secret ferment
in the mind," either directly, or so as to arouse a feeling of relief
by comparison, as when we read of tortures, wounds, and deaths.
Moreover, the poet may improve Nature. Let oranges grow
wild, and roses, woodbines, and jessamines flower at the same
time. As for "the fairy way of writing"[1]—that is to say, the
supernatural—it requires a very odd turn of mind. We do it
better than most other nations, because of our gloominess and
melancholy of temper. Shakespeare excels everybody else in
touching "this weak superstitious part" of his reader's imagination. The glorifying of the imagination, however, is by no means
confined to the poet. In good historians we "see" everything.
None more gratify the imagination than the authors of the
new philosophy, astronomers, microscopists. This (No. 420) is
one of Addison's most ambitious passages of writing, and the
whole ends (421) with a peroration excellently hit off.

It is upon these papers mainly that Mr Worsfold[2] bases
his high eulogium of Addison as "the first genuine critic," the
first "who added something to the last word of Hellenism,"
the bringer of criticism "into line with modern thought," the
establisher of "a new principle of poetic appeal." Let us, as
uncontroversially as possible, and without laying any undue
stress on the fact that Mr Worsfold practically omits Longinus
altogether,[3] stick, in our humdrum way, to the facts.

In the first place, supposing for the moment that Addison
uses "imagination" in our full modern sense, and supposing,
secondly, for the moment also, that he assigns the appeal to the
imagination as the special engine of the poet, is this an original
discovery of his ? By no means: there are many *loci* of former

---

[1] This phrase is originally Dryden's
(dedication to *King Arthur*, viii. 136,
ed. cit.), who, however, has "kind"
for "way."

[2] *Op. cit.*, pp. 93-107, and more largely

pp. 55-93.

[3] Students of the Stagirite may be
almost equally surprised to find Aristotle regarded as mainly, if not wholly,
a critic of Form as opposed to Thought.

writers to negative this—there is one that is fatal. And this is no more recondite a thing than the famous Shakespearian description of

> " The lunatic, the lover, and the poet,"

as

> " Of *imagination* all compact,"

with what follows. But this is a mere question of property, plagiarism, suggestion ; and such questions are at best the exercises of literary holiday-makers, at the worst the business of pedants and of fools.

A more important as well as a more dangerous question is this. *Does* Addison make " the appeal to the imagination " the test of poetry ? It can only be answered that, by his own explicit words, he does nothing of the kind. If he advances anything, it is that the appeal to the imagination is the appeal of art generally—of prose (even of scientific) literary art as well as of poetry, of painting, sculpture, architecture, as well as of literature. In doing this he does a good thing : he does something notable in the history of general æsthetics ; but in so far as literature, and especially poetry, is concerned, he scarcely goes as far as Longinus in the well-known passage,[1] though he works out his doctrine at much greater length, and with assistance from Descartes and Locke.

But the most important and the most damaging question of all is this, " Are not Addison and his panegyrist using words in equivocal senses ? *Does* Imagination in Addison's mouth bear the meaning which we, chiefly since Coleridge's day, attach to the word ? Does it even mean what it meant to Longinus, much more what it meant to Shakespeare ? "

I have no hesitation in answering the two latter questions with an absolute and unhesitating " No ! "

It seems indeed extraordinary that, in face of Addison's most careful and explicit limitations, any one should delude himself into thinking that even the Shakespearian and Addisonian Imaginations are identical—much more that Addison's Imagination is the supreme faculty, creative, transcending

---

[1] *De Sublimitate*, cap. xv.

Fancy,[1] superior to fact, not merely compounding and refining upon, but altogether superseding and almost scorning, ideas of sensation, which we mean by the word, and which Philostratus or Apollonius[2] partly glimpsed. Addison tells us—tells us over and over again—that *all* the ideas and pleasures of the imagination are pleasures of sense, and, what is more, that they are all pleasures of one sense—Sight. Why he should have limited himself in this singular manner it is hard to say; except that he was evidently full of Locke when he wrote, and, indeed, almost entirely under the influence of the *Essay*. That he had a contempt for music is elsewhere pretty evident; and this probably explains his otherwise inexplicable omission of the supplies and assistance given to Imagination by Hearing. His morality, as well as old convention, excluded Touch, Taste, and Smell as low and gross, though no candid philosophy could help acknowledging the immense influence exercised upon Imagination by at least the first and the last—Taste, because the most definite, being perhaps the least imaginative of all. But the fact that he does exclude even these senses, and still more rigidly excludes everything but Sense, is insuperable, irremovable, ruthless. Addison may have been the first modern critic to work out the appeal of art to the pleasures and ideas furnished by the sense of sight. He is certainly nothing more.

But is he therefore to be ignored, or treated lightly, because of this strange overvaluation of him? Certainly not. Though *His general critical value.* by no means a very great critic, he is a useful, an interesting, and a representative one. He represents the classical attitude tempered, not merely by good sense almost in quintessence, but by a large share of tolerance and positive good taste, by freedom from the more utterly ridiculous pseudo-Aristotelianisms, and by a wish to extend a *concordat* to everything good even if it be not "faultless." In his *Account* he is evidently too crude to be very censurable: in his first group of essays much of his censure is just. The elaborate vindication of Milton, though now and for a long

---

[1] It would be unfair to lay too much stress on his identification of Imagination and Fancy; but there is some-thing tell-tale in it.

[2] See *Hist. Crit.*, i. 118 *sq.*, and the present volume, p. 9, note 2.

time past merely a curiosity, is again full of good sense, displays (if not altogether according to knowledge) a real liking for real poetic goodness, and had an inestimable effect in keeping at least one poet of the better time privileged and popular with readers throughout the Eighteenth Century. As for the essay on the Pleasures of the Imagination, the fact that it has been wrongly praised need not in the least interfere with a cordial estimate of its real merits. It is not an epoch-making contribution to literary criticism; it is rather one-sided, and strangely limited in range. But it is about the first attempt at a general theory of æsthetics in English; it is a most interesting, and a very early, example of that application of common - sense philosophy to abstract subjects which Locke taught to the English eighteenth century; and many of its remarks are valuable and correct. Moreover, it did actually serve, for those who could not, or who did not, read Longinus, as a corrective to pure form-criticism, to Bysshe with his rigid ten syllables, to bare good sense and conventional rule. Its Imagination was still only that which supplies Images, and was strangely cramped besides; but it was better than mere correctness, mere decency, mere stop-watch.

Between Addison and Pope, Steele, Atterbury, and Swift call for notice. Steele has little for us.[1] There are few things *Steele.* more curious than the almost entire abstinence from any expression, in the slightest degree really critical, to be found in the eulogy of Spenser, which he generously enough inserted in *Sp.* 540 to express "his passion for that charming author." The numerous friends whom he has so justly won for himself may perhaps insist that there is criticism of the best in this very phrase; and that the rather rash encomium on the poet's "old words" as being "all truly English" is balanced by the justice of the reference to his "exquisite numbers." But the fact is that Steele had neither the knowledge, nor the patience, nor the coolness for critical work.

---

[1] Herr Hamelius, *op. cit. sup.*, p. 103, and elsewhere, thinks much more highly of Steele than I do, and even makes him a "Romantic before Romanticism." Steele's temperament was undoubtedly Romantic, and both in essays and plays he displayed it; but he was not really critical.

Atterbury gives rather more.   He was himself a man of
great intellectual power, a scholar, an eloquent and delicate
Atterbury.   writer, and possessed independent taste enough to
admire Milton fervently at a time when Addison
had not yet made it wholly orthodox to admire that poet at all,
and when most Tories detested him.   But his observations on
Waller[1] are the very quintessence of pseudodoxy, as to that respectable person ; and, by a curious combination, though Waller
is a rhymer confirmed and complete, Atterbury joins with his
admiration for him an antipathy to rhyme — " this jingling
kind of poetry," " this troublesome bondage, as Mr Milton well
calls it."   As for this we need say little ; the danger lay not
there.   But it lay in the direction of such remarks as that
" English came into Waller's hands like a rough diamond ; he
polished it first," that, " for aught I know, he stands last as well
as first in the list of refiners " [imagine the excellent Waller as
be-all and end-all of English !], that " verse before Waller was
" downright prose tagged with rhyme," &c., &c.   Once more let
our impatience of this talk not be ignorant—as is the impatience
of those who nowadays cannot see music in Dryden, poetry
in Pope, " cry " and clangour now and then even in persons
like Langhorne and Mickle.   He expressed an opinion ; but in
expressing it he showed this same ignorance from which we
should abstain.   Instead of pointing out that Waller introduced a *different* kind of music, he insisted that Waller substituted music for discord : instead of saying that he introduced a
new fashion of cutting the diamond, he would have it that the
diamond was merely rough before.   This was the *culpa*, the
maxima culpa of eighteenth-century criticism, and Atterbury
illustrates and shares it.[2]

The critical work of Swift[3] is much more important, and

---

[1] In his Preface to the Second Part
of the *Poems* (1690).

[2] Of course he might, to some extent, have sheltered himself under
Dryden's own authority for all this.

[3] I have thought it useless to give
references to particular editions of the
better known writings of Swift and

Pope, as they are so numerous.   As to
Works, Scott's *Swift* is much inferior
to his *Dryden ;* but in Pope's case the
edition of the late Mr Elwin and Mr
Courthope is not likely soon to be
superseded.   The very useful " Bohn "
ed. of Swift's Prose in 12 vols. was
completed in 1908.

though a good deal of it is inextricably mixed up with the
Swift. writings of Pope and of Arbuthnot, the lion's claw is
generally perceptible enough. The famous *Tatler*
of September 28, 1710, on the corruptions of English style and
writing, ought to hold place in every history and course of
lectures on the subject, next to Sprat's passage in the *History
of the Royal Society* forty years before, as the manifesto of
a fresh stage in English style-criticism; and it practically
precedes everything that Addison, Steele, and Pope published
on, or in connection with, the subject. But long before this,
in the wonderful volume which first (1704) revealed his genius
to the world, Swift had shown how critical the Gods had made
him.

The Battle of the Books is one of the most eccentric documents in the whole History of our subject. Directly, and on
The Battle its face, it may be said to be of the first critical im-
of the portance; because it shows how very little subject,
Books. intention, accuracy of fact, verisimilitude, and half-
a-dozen other indispensables according to certain theories, have
to do with the goodness of a book. The general characteristics
of *The Battle of the Books,* in all these named respects and some
of the unnamed ones, are deplorable. In a tedious and idle
quarrel which, at least as it was actually debated, need never
have been debated at all, Swift takes the side which, if not the
intrinsically wrong one, is the wrong one as he takes it. To
represent Bentley, or even Wotton, as enemies of the Ancients
might seem preposterous, if it were not outdone by the prepos-
terousness of selecting Temple as their champion. The details are often absurd—from that ranking of "Despréaux" side
by side with Cowley as a Modern brigadier (which is probably
a slip, perhaps for "Desportes," of pen or press)—to the spiteful
injustices on Dryden. The idea of the piece was probably taken
from Callières.[1] Its composition, from the rigid "Ancient"
point of view, is sadly lax; and the two most brilliant episodes
—the "Sweetness and Light" quarrel of the Spider and the Bee,
and the "machine" of the Goddess of Criticism—have little or
nothing to do with the action. But yet it is—and one knows
it is—a masterpiece; and it is pretty certain from it that in

[1] A French writer a little earlier. See *Hist. Crit.,* ii. 553 note.

certain kinds of destructive criticism, and even in certain kinds
of what may be called destructive-constructive, the author will
be able to accomplish almost anything that he is likely to try.

Though the *Tale of a Tub* is less ostensibly bookish, it shows
even greater purely critical power : for the power of the *Battle*

The Tale is mainly that of a consummate craftsman, who can
of a Tub. accomplish by sheer craftsmanship whatsoever his
hand findeth to do.　In the *Tale* the crusade against bad
writing and bad writers, which Swift carried on more or less for
the whole of his middle and later years, and in which he enlisted
Addison and Pope, Arbuthnot and Gay, is all but formally proclaimed, and is most vigorously waged with or without pro-
clamation.　In the "Dedication to Somers" the sword is being
something more than loosened in the sheath ; it flashes out in
"The Bookseller to the Reader" ; it is doing sanguinary work in
the great "Epistle to Prince Posterity" ; and it has only momen-
tary rests in the "Preface" and the "Induction" : while there
is hardly a section of the main text in which the quarters of
Grub Street are not beaten up, and the Conclusion is even as
the preludes and the main body.

A shrewd judge could hardly fail to perceive, from these
famous twin-books, that a new genius of thoroughly critical

Minor works. character had arisen : but such a judge might well
have doubted how far its exercise could be anything
but negative.　His doubts, as we have already hinted, were
to be justified.　Indirectly, indeed, not merely in the *Tatler*
paper above referred to and elsewhere, but by that almost uncanny influence which he seems to have exerted in so many
ways on men only less than himself, Swift had very much to
do with the rescuing of Style, by the hands of Addison and the
rest, from the vulgarisation which it was undergoing at the
close of the seventeenth century, not merely in common writers,
not merely in the hands of an eccentric like L'Estrange, but in
those of scholars like Collier and Bentley.　But even this was
a task of destruction rather than of positive construction, and
he was always most at home in such tasks.　The *Meditation on
a Broomstick* and the *Tritical Essay*, though every good reviewer should know them by heart, and will have but too many
opportunities of using his knowledge, are delivered with the

backward, not the forward, speech of the critic ; the *Proposal for correcting the English Tongue,* which falls in with the *Tatler* paper, aims at a sort of stationary state of language and literature alike, at proscriptions and ostracisings ; the *Letter to a Young Clergyman* and the *Essay on Modern Education,* though both touch on literature, are exceedingly general in their precepts ; and though all persons with a true English appreciation of shameless puns and utter nonsense must delight in *The Antiquity of the English Tongue,* it cannot be called serious criticism. There is more in the *Advice to a Young Poet :* but even here Swift is rather "running humours" on his subject than discussing it in the grave and chaste manner.

We shall therefore hardly be wrong if, after excepting the literary directions of the universal satiric *douche* in the *Tale of a Tub,* and the useful but somewhat rudimentary warnings of the *Tatler* paper, we see the most characteristic critical work of Swift in *Martinus Scriblerus* and the *Peri Bathous,* especially in the latter, which, though it be principally attributed to Arbuthnot and Pope, is as surely Swiftian in suggestion as if the Dean had written and published it alone. Often as it has been imitated, and largely as its methods have been drawn upon, it has never been surpassed as an Art of General and Particular " Slating " : and the sections on the Figures, with the immortal receipt for making an epic poem (the full beauty of which is lost on those who do not know how appallingly close it is to the approved prescriptions of the best neo-classic critics), cannot be too highly praised. But, once more, the critic is here at hangman's work only : he allows himself neither to admire nor to love.

These principles, put in various ways by writers of more or less genius for half a century, found what seemed to more than

Pope. two generations (always with a few dissidents) something like consummate expression in certain well-known utterances of Pope. As expression these utterances may still receive a very high degree of admiration : as anything else it is difficult to believe that any turn of fashion, unless it brings with it oblivion for large districts of noble literature, can restore them to much authority. Pope, though better read than he seems in his poems, was by no means a learned man ; and it is now pretty generally admitted that his intellect was acute rather than powerful. The obstinate superficiality—the reduction of everything, even the most recondite problems of philosophy, even the most far-ranging questions of erudition, to a jury of "common-sense" persons, decorated with a little of the fashion of the town—which had set in, found in him an exponent as competent to give it exquisite expression as he was indisposed, and probably incompetent, to deepen or extend its scope. He attained early to nearly his full powers, and it does not much matter whether the *Essay on Criticism* was written at the age of twenty or at that of twenty-two. He could have improved it a little in form, but would hardly have altered it at all in matter, if he had written it thirty years later. The *Imitation of the Epistle of Horace to Augustus*, which was actually written about that time, is, though superior as verse, almost inferior as criticism, and more " out " in fact. The two together give a sufficient view of Pope as he wished to be taken critically. But to be perfectly fair we must add the

The Letters.

critical utterances in his *Letters*,[1] his Preface to Shakespeare, and (with caution of course) the remarks attributed to him by Spence. The Preface has received much praise; and has deserved some even from those who follow not Pope generally. It would be unfair to blame him for adopting the mixed " beauty and fault " system which had the patronage of great names in antiquity, and found hardly even questioners in his own time. And it is something that he recognises Shakespeare's power over the passions, the individuality of his characters, his intuitive knowledge of the world and of nature. He is moderate and sensible on the relations of Shakespeare and Jonson ; he has practically said all that is to be said, in an

[1] The most important of these is the sentence on Crashaw (with whom Pope has some points of sympathy), that he is wanting in "design, form, fable, which is the soul of poetry," and " exactness or consent of parts, which is the body," while he grants him " pretty conceptions, fine metaphors, glittering expressions, and something of a neat cast of verse, which are properly the dress, gems, or loose ornaments" of it. See my friend Mr Courthope (in his *Life*, ed. cit. of the *Works*, v. 63), with whom, for once, I am in irreconcilable disagreement.

endless and tiresome controversy, by writing, " To judge Shake-

The speare by Aristotle's rules is like trying a man by
Shakespeare the laws of one country who acted under those of
Preface. another." And for such utterances we may excuse,
or at least pass over with little or no comment, the remarks that
Shakespeare kept bad company, that he wrote to please the
populace, that he resembles " an ancient majestic piece of Gothic
architecture [so far, so good], where many of the details are
childish, ill-placed, and unequal to its grandeur." The little-
ness of this patchy, yea-nay criticism beside the great and everlasting appreciation of his master Dryden speaks for itself ; it
is only fair to remember that the very existence of Dryden's for
once really marmoreal inscription almost inevitably belittled and
hampered Pope. He was obliged to be different ; and internal
as well as external influences made it certain that if he were
different he would be less.

The *Popiana* of Spence[1] add more to our idea of Pope's
critical faculty, or at least of its exercises ; in fact, it is possible
Spence's to take a much better estimate of Pope's "litera-
Anecdotes. ture " from the *Anecdotes* than from the *Works.*
Although the Boswellian spirit was, fortunately enough for
posterity, very strong in the eighteenth century, there was no
particular reason why Spence should toady Pope—especially
as he published nothing to obtain pence or popularity from
the toadying. That rather remarkable collection, or re-collec-
tion, of Italian-Latin poetry of the Renaissance,[2] of which not

---

[1] Spence (whose *Anecdotes* were
printed partly by Malone, and completely by Singer in 1820, reprinted
from the latter edition in 1858, and re-
selected by Mr Underhill (London,
n. d.) in the last decade of the nineteenth century, has sometimes received
praise as a critic himself. His *Poly-
metis* usefully brought together classical
art and letters, and the *Anecdotes* themselves are not without taste. But his
elaborate criticism of Pope's *Odyssey,*
published in 1726, is of little value,
neither praising nor blaming its subject
for the right things, and characterised

as a whole by a pottering and peddling
kind of censorship.

[2] *Selecta Poemata Italorum qui Latine
Scripserunt. Cura cujusdam Anonymi
anno* 1684 *congesta, iterum in lucem data,
una cum aliorum Italorum operibus.
Accurante A. Pope.* 2 vols., London,
1740. The title-page contains absolutely all the ostensible editorial matter,
and, as I have not got hold of the work
of the Anonymus, I do not know how
much Pope added. But his collection,
as I can testify from some little knowledge of the subject, is good.

much notice has been taken by Pope's biographers, would, of itself, show critical interest in a part, and no unnoteworthy part, of literature: and a few of the Spencean salvages bear directly upon this. He need not have been ashamed of his special liking for Politian's *Ambra:* and he was right in thinking Bembo "stiff and unpoetical," though hardly in joining Sadolet with him in this condemnation. We know perfectly well why he did not like Rabelais, for which Swift very properly scolded him: indeed, he tells us himself, twice over, that "there were so many things" in Master Francis, "in which he could not see any manner of meaning driven at," that he could not read him with any patience. This is really more tale-telling than the constantly quoted passage about Walsh and correctness. For, after all, everybody aspires to be correct: only everybody has his own notions of what is correctness. It is not everybody—and, as we see, it was not the great Mr Pope—who could, or can, appreciate nonsense, and see how much more sensible than sense the best of it is. It would skill but little to go through his isolated judgments: but there are one or two which are eloquent.

Still, it is to the *Essay* and the *Epistle* that we must turn for his deliberate theory of criticism, announced in youth, indorsed *The* Essay and emphasised in age. And we meet at once with on Criticism. a difficulty. The possessor of such a theory ought, at least, to have something like a connected knowledge, at least a connected view, of literature as a whole, and to be able to square the two. All Pope seems to have done is to take the *Arts* of Horace, Vida, and Boileau, to adopt as many of their principles as he understood, and as would go into his sharp antithetic couplet, to drag their historical illustrations head and shoulders into his scheme without caring for the facts, and to fill in and embroider with criticisms, observations, and precepts, sometimes very shrewd, almost always perfectly expressed, but far too often arbitrary, conventional, and limited. He is most unfortunate of all in the historical part, where Boileau had been sufficiently unfortunate before him. The Frenchman's observations on Villon and Ronsard had been ignorant enough, and forced enough: but Pope managed to go a little beyond them in the *Essay*, and a great distance further still in the *Epistle*. The history of the famous passage,

"We conquered France, but felt our captive's charms," [1]

is like nothing on earth but the history-poetry of the despised monkish ages, in which Alexander has twelve peers, and Arthur, early in the sixth century, overruns Europe with a British force, and fights with a Roman Emperor named Lucius. And the sketch of European literature in the *Essay*, if it contains no single statement so glaringly absurd, is as much a "tissue of gaps" as the Irishman's coat.

Attempts have been made (including some by persons deserving all respect, and thoroughly acquainted with the subject) to give Pope a high place, on the score of his charges to "follow nature." Unfortunately this is mere translation of Boileau, of Vida, and of Horace, in the first place: and, still more unfortunately, the poet's own arguments on his doctrine show that what *he* meant by "following nature," and what *we* mean by it, are two quite different things. He, usually at least, means "stick to the usual, the ordinary, the commonplace." Just so the legendary King of Siam, had he written an *Art of Poetry*, would have said "Follow nature, and do not talk about such unnatural things as ice and snow."

Regarded merely as a manual of the art of Pope's own poetry, without prejudice to any other, and as a satire on the faults of other kinds, without prejudice to the weaknesses of his own, the *Essay* is not merely an interesting document, but a really valuable one. Its cautions against desertion of nature in the directions of excess, of the unduly fantastic, are sound to this day: and its eulogies of ancient writers, though perhaps neither based on very extensive and accurate first-hand knowledge, nor specially appropriate to the matter in hand, contain much that is just in itself. One of the weakest parts, as might have been expected, is the treatment of rules, licences, and faults. The poet-critic practically confesses the otiosity of the whole system by admitting that a lucky licence is a rule, and

[1] *Ep. to Aug.*, l. 263.

that it is possible, as one of his own most famous and happiest lines says,

> "To snatch a grace beyond the reach of art."

And when he paraphrases Quintilian to the effect that you must criticise

> "With the same spirit that the author writ,"

and judge the whole, not the parts, he again goes perilously near to jettison his whole system.

In the same way consistency is the last thing that can be claimed for his chapters, as they may be called, on conceit, on language, "numbers" (the most famous and the most ingenious passage of the *Essay*), extremes, "turns," the Ancient and Modern quarrel, &c. The passage on Critics is among the best—for here sheer good sense (even in the temporary, much more in the universal, meaning) tells—and the historical sketch of them, though not too accurate, is vigorous.

The much later *Epistle* is far more desultory, and inevitably tinged by those personal feelings which many years of literary *The* Epistle squabble had helped ill-health and natural disposi- *to Augustus.* tion to arouse in Pope. But its general critical attitude is not different. He is angry with the revival of old literature which Watson and Allan Ramsay in Scotland, Oldys and others in England, were beginning, hints sneers even at Milton and the "weeds on Avon's bank," is at least as hackneyed as he is neat in his individual criticisms on poets nearer his own day, and defends poetry and literature generally in a patronising and half-apologetic strain. In fact, what he has really at heart is to be politely rude to George II.; not to give any critical account of English literature.

But the *Essay on Criticism* is too important a thing not to require a little more notice here. It is extremely desultory; *Remarks* but so is the *Epistola ad Pisones*, and it is by no *on Pope as* means certain that Pope was not wise in falling *a critic,* back upon the Roman method, instead of emulating the appearance of system in the *Art Poétique.* This latter emphasises faults; Pope's *causerie* veils promiscuousness in the elegant chit-chat of conversation. A bad critic is a more dangerous person than a bad poet; and true taste is as uncommon as true genius. Bad education is responsible for bad taste, and we must be very careful about our own. Nature is the guide; the "rules" are but methodised nature. We derive them, however, not from nature but from the ancient poets, whom we must study. Even in licences we must follow them. Bad critics are made by various causes, from ignorance and party spirit to personal animus. A good critic is candid, modest, well-bred, and sincere. The sort of history of criticism which concludes the piece makes it specially surprising that Johnson should have been so much kinder to Pope's learning than he was to Dryden's; but the author of the actual *Essay on Criticism*, and the author of the unhappily but projected *History* of it, were too thoroughly in agreement about poetry, and even about criticism itself, to make the latter quite an impartial judge of the former.

When we pass from generals to particulars Pope's cleverness at least appears more than ever. The sharply separated, neatly flying, and neatly ringing couplets deliver "one, two" in the most fascinating cut-and-thrust style, not without a brilliant parry now and then to presumed (and never very formidable) objections. The man's perfect skill in the execution of his own special style of poetry raises, and in this case not delusively, the expectation that he will know his theory as well as his practice. The "good sense," the "reason," are really and not merely nominally present. A great deal of what is said is quite undoubtedly true and very useful, not merely for reproof and correction in point of critical and poetical sin, but actually for instruction in critical and poetical righteousness.

But on further examination there is too often something wanting; nay, there is too often no real root of the matter present. The preliminary flourishes are well enough. And certainly no school will quarrel—though each school may take the privilege of understanding the words in its own way—with the doctrine "Follow Nature." But

"One science only will one genius fit"

is notoriously false to nature, and if intended as a hint to the critic, can only result in too common mistakes and injustices. So, too, when we pass from the glowing eulogy of Nature, and of her union with Art, to the Rules, there is a most deplorable gap. Those Rules, "discovered not devised," are "nature methodised." Very good. This means, if it means anything, a very true thing—that the Rules are extracted from observed works of genius. But how, a most fervent admirer of the Greeks may ask, did it happen that the Greeks discovered *all* these rules? How, especially, did it happen that they did so, when some kinds of literature itself were notoriously neither discovered nor devised? And when we get a little further, and are bidden to

> "Know well each Ancient's proper character,"

we may, or rather must, reply, "It is most necessary; but you will neglect the Moderns at your peril."

In short, here as elsewhere, Pope's dazzling elocution, winged with a distinct if narrow conception of his general purpose, flies right enough in the inane, but makes painfully little progress when it lights on the prosaic ground. The picture of "young Maro," with a sort of ciphering book before him, "totting up" Homer, Nature, and the Stagirite, and finding them all exactly equivalent, is really far more ludicrous than those flights of metaphysical fancy at which critics of Pope's school delight to gird; while the very climax of another kind of absurdity is reached by the accordance to the Ancients, not merely of the prerogative of laying down the rule always to be followed, but of the privilege of making the not-to-be-imitated exception. So again, fine as is the Alps passage, the famous doctrine of a "little learning" is an ingenious fallacy. It is not the little learning acquired, but the vast amount of ignorance left, that is dangerous. The admirable couplet,

> "True Wit is nature to advantage drest;
> What oft was thought, but ne'er so well expressed,"

though in itself the best thing in the whole poem, is unluckily placed, because this sensation of familiarity beneath novelty is constantly given by those very "conceits" which Pope is denouncing. On "Language" and "Numbers" he is too notoriously speaking to a particular brief. And as for his more general cautions throughout, they are excellent sense for the most part, but have very little more to do with criticism than with any other function of life. A banker or a fishmonger, an architect, artist, or plain man, will no doubt be the better for avoiding extremes, partisanship, singularity, fashion, mere jealousy (personal or other), ignorance, pedantry, vice. And if he turns critic he will find these avoidances still useful to him, but not more specially useful than in his former profession.

What then was the critical attitude which was expressed so brilliantly, and which gave Pope a prerogative influence over *and the* all the orthodox criticism of his own century in *critical* England and even elsewhere? It can be sketched *attitude* *of his* very fairly as being a sort of compromise between *group.* a supposed following of the ancients, and a real application, to literature in general and to poetry in particular, of the general taste and cast of thought of the time. The following of the Ancients—it has been often pointed out already—was, as the Articles of the Church of England have it, a "corrupt following": those who said Aristotle meant now nobody more ancient than Boileau, now no one more ancient than Vida, scarcely ever any one more ancient than Horace. The classics as a whole were very little studied, at least by those who busied themselves most with modern literature; and it had entered into the heads of few that, after all, the standards of one literature might, or rather must, require very considerable alteration before they could apply to another.[1] But Greek and Roman literature presented a body of poetry and of most other kinds, considerable, admittedly excellent, and mostly composed under the influence of distinct and identical critical principles. Very few men had a complete knowledge of even a single modern literature; hardly a man in France knew Old French as a whole, hardly a man in England, except mere antiquaries, knew Old English even as a part. There was

---

[1] Pope, *v. supra*, p. 187, actually admitted this as regards Aristotle and Shakespeare; yet the admission practically revokes most of the *Essay*.

probably not a man in Europe till Gray (and Gray was still young at Pope's death) who had any wide reading at once in classical literature and in the mediæval and modern literatures of different countries. Accordingly the principles of ancient criticism, not even in their purity fully adequate to modern works, and usually presented, not in their purity but in garbled and bastardised form, were all that they had to stand by.

This classical, or pseudo-classical, doctrine was further affected, in the case of literature generally, by the *ethos* of the time, and, in the case of poetry, by the curious delusion as to hard and fast syllabic prosody which has been noticed in connection with Bysshe. Classicism, in any pure sense, was certainly not to blame for this, for everybody with the slightest tinge of education knew that the chief Latin metre admitted the substitution of trisyllabic for dissyllabic feet in every place but one, and most knew that this substitution was almost as widely permitted by Greek in a standard metre, approaching the English still nearer. But it had, as we have seen, been a gradually growing delusion, for a hundred and fifty years, in almost every kind of non-dramatic poetry.

As for the general tendency, the lines of that are clear— though the arbitrary extension and stiffening of them remain a little incomprehensible. Nature was to be the test; but an artificialised Nature, arranged according to the fashion of a town-haunting society—a Nature which submitted herself to a system of convention and generalisation. In so far as there was any real general principle it was that you were to be like everybody else—that singularity, except in doing the usual thing best, was to be carefully avoided. Pope, being a man of genius, could not help transcending this general conception constantly by his execution, not seldom by his thought, and sometimes in his critical precepts. But it remains the conception of his time and of himself.

The writers whom we have been discussing, since we parted *Philosophical* with Dennis, have all been considerable men of letters, *and Profes-* who in more or less degree busied themselves with *sional Critics.* criticism. We must now pass to those who, without exactly deserving the former description, undertook the subject either as part of those "philosophical" inquiries which, however loosely understood, were so eagerly and usefully pursued by the eighteenth century, or as direct matter of professional duty. The first division supplies Lord Kames in Scotland and "Hermes" Harris in England. Whether we are right in reserving Shaftesbury, Hume, Adam Smith, &c., from it, so as to deal with them from the Æsthetic side in another chapter, may be matter of opinion.

To the second belong Trapp, Blair, and Campbell. Trapp need not detain us very long; but as first occupant of the first

Trapp.
literary chair in England, and so the author of a volume of *Prælections* respectable in themselves, and starting a line of similar work which, to the present day, has contributed admirable critical documents, he cannot be omitted. He was the author of one of the wittiest epigrams[1] on record, but he did not allow himself much sparkle in his lectures.[2] Perhaps, indeed, he was right not to do so.

Hugh Blair, half a century later than Trapp, in 1759, started, like him, the teaching of modern literature in his own country.

Blair.
He had the advantage, as far as securing a popular audience goes, of lecturing in English, and he was undoubtedly a man of talent. The *Lectures on Rhetoric and Belles Lettres*,[3] which were delivered with great *éclat* for nearly a quarter of a century from the Chair of their subject, are very far, indeed, from being devoid of merit. They provide a very solid, if a somewhat mannered and artificial instruction, both by precept and example, in what may be called the "full-dress plain style" which was popular in the eighteenth century. They are

[1] Individual preference, in the case of the famous pair of epigrams on the books and the troop of horse sent by George I. to Cambridge and to Oxford respectively, may be biassed by academical and by political partisanship. But while it is matter of opinion whether "Tories own no argument but force," and whether, in certain circumstances, a University may not justifiably "want loyalty," no one can ever maintain that it is not disgraceful to a university to "want learning."

This it is which gives the superior wing and sting to Trapp's javelin.

[2] *Prælectiones Poeticæ*, London, 3rd ed., 1736. The first of the first batch was printed as early as 1711, and an English translation (not by the author) was published in 1742. See *Appendix* for a complete account, detailed in all important instances, of Trapp and his successors in the Oxford Chair.

[3] The first ed. is that of Edinburgh, 1783 : mine is that of London, 1823.

as original as could be expected. The critical examination of Addison's style, if somewhat meticulous, is mostly sound, and has, like Johnson's criticisms of Dryden and Pope, the advantage of thorough sympathy, of freedom from the drawback—so common in such examinations—that author and critic are standing on different platforms, looking in different directions, speaking, one may almost say, in mutually incomprehensible tongues. The survey of Belles Lettres is, on its own scheme, ingenious and correct: there are everywhere evidences of love of Literature (as the lover understands her), of good education and reading, of sound sense. Blair is to be very particularly commended for accepting to the full the important truth that "Rhetoric" in modern times really means "Criticism"; and for doing all he can to destroy the notion, authorised too far by ancient critics, and encouraged by those of the Renaissance, that Tropes and Figures are not possibly useful classifications and names, but fill a real arsenal of weapons, a real cabinet of reagents, by the employment of which the practitioner can refute, or convince, or delight, as the case may be.

But with this, and with the further praise due to judicious borrowings from the ancients, the encomium must cease. *The* Lectures In Blair's general critical view of literature the on Rhetoric. eighteenth-century blinkers are drawn as close as possible. From no writer, even in French, can more "awful examples" be extracted, not merely of perverse critical assumption, but of positive historical ignorance. Quite early in the second Lecture, and after some remarks (a little arbitrary, but not valueless) on delicacy and correctness in taste, we find, within a short distance of each other, the statements that "in the reign of Charles II. such writers as *Suckling and Etheridge* were held in esteem for dramatic composition," and later, "If a man shall assert that Homer has no beauties whatever, that he holds him to be a dull and spiritless writer, and that he *would as soon peruse any legend of old knight-errantry* as the *Iliad*, then I exclaim that my antagonist is either void of all taste," &c. Here, on the one hand, the lumping of Suckling and Etherege together, and the implied assumption that not merely Suckling, but Etherege, is a worthless dramatist, gives us one "light," just as the similar implication that "an old legend of knight-errantry" is necessarily an example of dulness, spiritlessness, and absence of beauty, gives us another. That Blair lays down, even more peremptorily than Johnson, and as peremptorily as Bysshe, that the pause in an English line may fall after the 4th, 5th, 6th, or 7th syllable, and no other, is not surprising; and his observations on Shakespeare are too much in the usual "faults-saved-by-beauties" style to need quotation. But that he cites, with approval, a classification of the great literary periods of the world which excludes the Elizabethan Age altogether, is not to be omitted. It stamps the attitude.

These same qualities appear in the once famous but now little read *Dissertation on Ossian*.[1] That, in the sense of the word on *The Dissertation on Ossian.* which least stress is laid in these volumes, this "Critical Dissertation" is absolutely *un*critical does not much matter. Blair does not even attempt to examine the evidence for and against the genuineness of the work he is discussing. He does not himself know Gaelic; friends (like Hector M'Intyre) have told him that they heard Gaelic songs very like *Ossian* sung in their youth; there are said to be manuscripts; that is enough for him. Even when he cites and compares parallel passages—the ghost-passage and that from the book of Job, Fingal's "I have no son" and *Othello* —which derive their whole beauty from exact coincidence with the Bible or Shakespeare, he will allow no kind of suspicion to cross his mind. But this we might let pass. It is in the manner in which he seeks to explain the "amazing degree of regularity and art," which he amazingly ascribes to Macpherson's redaction, the "rapid and animated style," the "strong colouring of imagination," the "glowing sensibility of heart," that the most surprising thing appears. His citations are as copious as his praises of them are hard to indorse. But his critical argument rests almost (not quite) wholly on showing that *Fingal* and *Temora* are worked out quite properly on Aristotelian principles by way of central action and episode, and that there are

---

[1] I have it with *The Poems of Ossian*, 2 vols., London, 1796. Blair had taken Macpherson under his wing as early as 1760.

constant parallels to Homer, the only poet whom he will allow
to be Ossian's superior. In short, he simply applies to *Ossian*
Addison's procedure with *Paradise Lost*. The critical piquancy
of this is double. For we know that *Ossian* was powerful—
almost incredibly powerful—all over Europe in a sense quite
opposite to Blair's; and we suspect, if we do not know, that Mr
James Macpherson was quite clever enough purposely to give it
something of the turn which Blair discovers.

The charge which may justly be brought against Blair—that
he is both too exclusively and too purblindly " belletristic "—

Kames. cannot be extended to Henry Home, Lord Kames.
Johnson, whom Kames disliked violently, and who
returned the dislike with rather good-natured if slightly contemptuous patronage, dismissed the *Elements of Criticism*, 1761,[1]
as " a pretty Essay, which deserves to be held in some estima-
tion, though much of it is chimerical." [2] The sting of this lies,
as usual, in the fact that it is substantially true, though by no
means all the truth. The *Elements of Criticism* is a pretty
book, and an estimable one, and, what is more, one of very
considerable originality. Its subtlety and ingenuity are often
beyond Johnson's own reach; it shows a really wide knowledge
of literature, modern as well as ancient; and it is surprisingly,
though not uniformly, free from the special " classical " purblindness of which Johnson and Blair are opposed, but in their
different ways equal, examples. Yet a very great deal of it *is*
" chimerical," and, what is worse, a very great deal more is,
whether chimerical or not in itself, irrelevant. It presents a
philosophical treatise, vaguely and tentatively æsthetic rather
than critical, yoked in the loosest possible manner to a bundle of
quasi-professorial exercises in Lower and Higher Rhetoric. The
second part might not improperly be termed " Critical Illustrations of Rhetoric." The first could only be properly entitled
" Literary Illustrations of Morals."

Of course this excellent Scots lawyer and ingenious

---

[1] It had reached its eighth edition in
1807, the date of my copy. Perhaps
some may think that Kames, as being
mainly an æsthetician, ought to be
postponed with Shaftesbury, Hume, &c.

My reason for not postponing is the
large amount of *positive* literary criticism in his book.

[2] Boswell, Globe ed., p. 132. He
was elsewhere more, and less, kind.

"Scotch metaphysician" had strong precedents to urge for
The making a muddle of Moral Philosophy and Literary
Elements of Criticism. It has been pointed out that Aristotle
Criticism. himself is not a little exposed to the same imputa-
tion. But Kames embroils matters to an extent never surpassed, except by those, to be found in every day, who are incapable of taking the literary point of view at all, and who simply
treat literature as something expressing agreement or disagreement with their moral, political, religious, or other views. He
seems himself to have had, at least once, a slight qualm. "A
treatise of ethics is not my province: I carry my view no
farther than to the elements of criticism, in order to show that
the fine arts are a subject of reasoning as well as of taste."[1] If
this was his rule he certainly gives himself the most liberal
indulgence in applying it. His First Chapter is devoted to
"Perceptions and Ideas in a Train"; the second (an immensely
long one, containing a good third of the first volume) to "Emotions and Passions"; while the whole of the rest till the end
of the seventeenth chapter is really occupied by the same class of
subject. Kames excels in that constantly ingenious, and often
acute, dissection of human nature which was the pride and
pleasure of his century and his country, but which is a little
apt to pay itself with clever generalisations as if they were
veræ causæ. In one place we find a distribution of all the
pleasures of the senses into pain of want, desire, and satisfaction. In another[2] the philosopher solemnly informs us, "I
love my daughter less after she is married, and my mother less
after a second marriage; the marriage of my son or my father
diminishes not my affection so remarkably." An almost burlesque illustration of the procedure of the school is given in the
dictum,[3] "Where the course of nature is joined with Elevation
the effect must be delightful; and hence the singular beauty of
smoke ascending in a calm morning." When one remembers
this, and comes later[4] to the admirable remark, "Thus, to

---

[1] Vol. i. chap. iii., on "Beauty"; i. 195 ed. cit.

[2] i. 77.

[3] i. 26.

[4] i. 288, *note*. Kames had just before, in his chapter on "Motion and Force" (i. 250-255), referred complacently to his own indulgence in this foible, and had accumulated others of the same kind.

account for an effect of which there is no doubt, any cause,
however foolish, is made welcome," it is impossible not to say
"Thou sayest it"; as also in another case, where he lays it
down that "Were corporeal pleasures dignified over and above
[*i.e.*, beside the natural propensity which incites us to them]
with a place in a high class, they would infallibly disturb the
balance of the mind by outweighing the social affections. This
is a satisfactory final cause for refusing to these pleasures any
degree of dignity."[1] I am tempted to quote Kames's philosophy
of the use of tobacco[2] also, but the stuff and method of his first
volume must be sufficiently intelligible already.

The second, much more to the purpose, is considerably less
interesting. A very long chapter deals with Beauty of Language
with respect to Sound, Signification, Resemblance between Sound
and Signification, and Metre. It is abundantly stocked with
well-chosen examples from a wide range of literature, and full
of remarks, generally ingenious and sometimes both new and
bold, as where at the outset Kames has the audacity to contradict Aristotle, by implication at least, and lay it down that "of
all the fine arts, painting and sculpture only are in their nature
imitative."[3] But it is not free from the influence of the idols
of its time. Of such, in one kind, may be cited the attribution
to Milton of "many careless lines";[4] for if there is one thing
certain in the risky and speculative range of literary dogmatism, it is that Milton never wrote a "careless" line in his
life. If his lines are ever bad (and perhaps they are sometimes), they are bad deliberately and of malice. In another
and more serious kind may be ranged the predominating determination to confuse the sensual with the intellectual side of
poetry. This, of course, is Kames's root-idea; but that it is a
root of evil may be shown sufficiently by the following passage
in his discussion of the pause—in relation to which subject he
is as wrong as nearly all his contemporaries. He is talking of
a pause between adjective and substantive.[5] What occurs to
him is that "a quality cannot exist independent of a subject,
nor are they separable even in imagination, because they make

---

[1] i. 359.   [2] i. 405, 410, 411, 416, 417.   [3] ii. 3.

[4] ii. 163.   [5] ii. 129.

part of the same idea, and for that reason, with respect to melody as well as to sense, it must be disagreeable to bestow upon the adjective a sort of independent existence by interjecting a pause between it and its substantive." His examples are no doubt vitiated by the obsession of the obligatory "middle" pause, which makes him imagine one between adjective and substantive in

> "The rest, his many-coloured robe concealed,"

where the only real pause, poetic as well as grammatical, is at "rest." But his principle is clear, and it is as clearly a wrong principle. It ignores the great fact glanced at above, that the pleasure of poetry is double—intellectual *and* sensual—and that the two parts are in a manner independent of each other. And in the second place, even on its own theory, it credits the mere intellect with too sluggish faculties. In the first line which Kames suggests as "harsh and unpleasant" for this reason,

> "Of thousand bright inhabitants of air,"

the pause at "bright" is so slight a one that some might deny its existence. But if it be held necessary, can we refuse to the *subtilitas intellectus* the power of halting, for the second of a second, to conceive the joint idea of number and brightness, before it moves further to enrich this by the notion of "inhabitants of air"? The mere and literal Lockist may do so; but no other will. The Figures enjoy a space which, without being surprised at it, one grudges; and the Unities are handled rather oddly, while a digression of some fifty pages on Gardening and Architecture speaks for itself. The conclusion on the Standard of Taste is singularly inconclusive; and an interesting appendix on "terms defined and explained" presents the singularity that not, I think, one of the terms so dealt with has anything specially to do with literature or art at all.

Nevertheless, though it is easy to be smart upon Kames, and not very difficult to expose serious inadequacies and errors both in the general scheme and the particular execution, the *Elements of Criticism* is a book of very great interest and importance, and worthy of much more attention than it has for a long

time past received. To begin with, his presentation, at the
very outset of his book, of Criticism as "the most agreeabie
of all amusements"[1] was one of those apparently new and
pleasant shocks to the general which are, in reality, only the
expression of an idea for some time germinating and maturing
in the public mind. Even Addison, even Pope, while praising
and preaching Criticism, had half-flouted and half-apologised for
it. Swift, a great critic on his own day, had flouted it almost
or altogether in others. The general idea of the critic had
been at worst of a malignant, at best of a harmless, pedant.
Kames presented him as something quite different,—as a man
no doubt of learning, but also of position and of the world,
"amusing," as well as exercising himself, and bringing the fashionable philosophy to the support of his amusement.

But he did more than this. His appreciation of Shakespeare
is, taking it together (and his references to the subject are
numerous and important), the best of his age. His citations
show a remarkable relish for the Shakespearian humour, and
though he cannot clear his mind entirely from the "blemish-
and-beauty" cant, which is ingrained in the Classical theory,
and which, as we saw, infected even such a critic as Longinus, he
is far freer from it than either Johnson or Blair. In his chapter
on the Unities he comes very near to Hurd[2] (to whom, as the
Elements of Criticism preceded the *Letters on Chivalry* in time,
he may have given a hint) in recognising the true Romantic
Unity of Action which admits plurality so far as the different
interests work together, or contrast advantageously. He has a
most lucid and sensible exposure of the difference between the
conditions of the Greek theatre and ours. In short, he would
stand very high if he were not possessed with the pseudological mania which makes him calmly and gravely write[3]—
"Though a cube is more agreeable in itself than a parallelopipedon,[4] yet a large parallelopipedon set on its smaller base is by
its elevation more agreeable, and hence the beauty of a Gothic

[1] i. 33.

[2] Hurd is reserved for the next
chapter.

[3] ii. 457.

[4] Kames has this spelling, which is
indeed so universal that any other
may seem pedantic. Yet it is needless to say that the word so spelt is a
vox nihili, and should be "parallele
pipedon."

tower." But this *amabilis insania* is in itself more amiable than insane. He wants to admit the Gothic tower, and that is the principal thing. Magdalen, and Merton, and Mechlin may well, in consideration of his slighting in their favour the more intrinsic charms of a cube, afford to let a smile flicker round their venerable skylines at his methodical insistence on justifying admiration of them by calling them large parallelopipeda set on their smaller ends. And the cube can console herself with his admission of her superior intrinsic loveliness.

The faults of Blair and of Kames are both, for the most part, absent, while much more than the merit of either, in method and closeness to the aim, is present, in the very re-
Campbell. markable *Philosophy of Rhetoric*[1] which Dr George Campbell began, and, to some extent, composed, as early as 1750; though he did not finish and publish it till nearly thirty years later (1777). It may indeed be admitted that this piecemeal composition is not without its effect on the book, which contains some digressions (especially one on Wit, Humour, and Ridicule, and another on the cause of the pleasure received from the exhibition of painful objects) more excrescent than properly episodic. It is, moreover, somewhat weighted by the author's strictly professional and educational design, in retaining as much of the mere business part of the ancient Rhetoric as would or might be useful to future preachers, advocates, or members of Parliament. Campbell, too, is a less "elegant" writer than Blair; and his acuteness has a less vivacious play than that of Kames. But here concessions are exhausted; and the book, however much we may disagree with occasional expressions in it, remains the most important treatise on the New Rhetoric that the eighteenth century produced. Indeed, strange as it may seem, Whately's, its principal formal successor in the nineteenth, is distinctly retrograde in comparison.

The New Rhetoric—the Art of Criticism—this is what Campbell really attempts. He is rather chary of acknow-
The Philosophy of Rhetoric. ledging his own position, and, in fact, save in his title, seldom employs the term Rhetoric, no doubt partly from that unlucky contempt of scholastic appellations

---

[1] I use the Tegg edition, London, 1850.

which shows itself in his well-known attack on Logic. But his
definition of "Eloquence"—the term which he employs as a
preferred synonym of Rhetoric itself—is very important, and
practically novel. The word "Eloquence, in its greatest lati-
tude, denotes that art or talent by which the discourse is adapted
to its end." Now this, though he modestly shelters it under
Quintilian's *scientia bene dicendi* and *dicere secundum virtutem
orationis*, asserting also its exact correspondence with Cicero's
description of the best orator as he who *dicendo animos de-
lectat audientium et docet et permovet*, is manifestly far more
extensive than the latter of these, and much less vague than the
former. In fact Rhetoric, new dubbed as Eloquence, becomes
the Art of Literature, or in other words Criticism.

It has been allowed that this bold and admirable challenge of
the whole province—for "discourse" is soon seen to include
"writing"—is not always so well supported. After an interesting introduction (vindicating the challenge, and noting Kames
more especially as one who, though in a different way, had
made it before him), Campbell for a time, either because he is
rather afraid of his own boldness, or to conciliate received
opinions on the matter (or, it has been suggested, because the
book was written at different times, and with perhaps slightly
different ends), proceeds to discuss various matters which have
very little to do with his general subject. Sometimes, as in
the Chapter, before referred to, on "The Nature and Use of the
Scholastic Art of Syllogising," he wrecks himself in a galley
which he had not the slightest need to enter. The longer discourse on Evidence which precedes this is, of course, fully justified on the old conception of Rhetoric, but digressory, or at
least excursory, on his own. The above-mentioned sections on
Ridicule, and on the æsthetic pleasure derivable from painful
subjects, are excursions into the debatable kinds between
literature and Ethics, though much less extravagant than those
of Kames, and perhaps, as excursions, not absolutely to be
barred or banned; while chapters vii.-x., which deal with the
"Consideration of Hearers," &c., &c., are once more Aristotelian
relapses, pardonable if not strictly necessary. But not quite a
third part of the whole treatise is occupied by this First Book of

the three into which it is divided; and not a little of this third is, strictly or by a little allowance, to the point. The remaining two-thirds are to that point without exception or digression of any kind, so that the Aristotelian distribution is exactly reversed.

The titles of the two Books, " The Foundations and Essential Properties of Elocution," and " The Discriminating Properties of Elocution," must be taken with due regard to Campbell's use of the last word.[1] But they require hardly any other proviso or allowance. He first, with that mixture of boldness and straight-hitting which is his great merit, attacks the general principles of the use of Language, and proceeds to lay down nine Canons of Verbal Criticism, which are in the main so sound and so acute that they are not obsolete to the present day. There is more that is arbitrary elsewhere, and Campbell seems sometimes to retrograde over the line which separates Rhetoric and Composition. But it must be remembered that this line has never been very exactly drawn, and has, both in Scotland and in America, if not also in England, been often treated as almost non-existent up to the present day. In his subsequent distinction of five rhetorical Qualities of Style—Perspicuity, Vivacity, Elegance, Animation, and Music—Campbell may be thought to be not wholly happy. For the three middle qualities are practically one, and it is even questionable whether Music would not be best included with them in some general term, designating whatever is added by style proper to Perspicuity, or the sufficient but unadorned conveyance of meaning. As, however, is very common, if not universal, with him, his treatment is in advance of his nomenclature, for the rest of the book—nearly a full half of it—is in fact devoted to the *two* heads of Perspicuity and Vivacity, the latter tacitly subsuming all the three minor qualities. And there is new and good method in the treatment of Vivacity, as shown first by the choice of words, secondly by their number, and thirdly by their arrangement, while a section

---

[1] He had, of course, good authority for it, including that of Dryden; but it is obviously better to limit it in the modern sense than to use it equivocally. Mason (not Gray's friend, but an in-teresting and little-known person to whom we shall recur in the next chapter) had already seen this, and expressly referred to it.

under the first head on "words considered as sounds" comes
very near to the truth. That there should be a considerable
section on Tropes was to be expected, and, as Campbell treats
it, it is in no way objectionable. His iconoclasm as to logical
Forms becomes much more in place, and much more effective, in
regard to rhetorical Figures.

One, however, of the best features of the work has hardly yet
been noticed; and that is the abundance of examples, and the
thorough way in which they are discussed. To a reader turning
the book over without much care it may seem inferior as a
thesaurus to Kames, because the passages quoted are as a rule
embedded in the text, and not given separately, in the fashion
which makes of large parts of the *Elements of Criticism* a sort
of anthology, a collection of beauties or deformities, as the
case may be. But this is in accordance with the singularly
businesslike character of Campbell's work throughout. And if
it also seem that he does not launch out enough in appreciation
of books or authors as wholes, let it be remembered that English
criticism was still in a rather rudimentary condition, and that the
state of taste in academic circles was not very satisfactory. It
would not, of course, be impossible to produce from him examples
of those obsessions of the time which we have noticed in his two
compatriots, as we shall notice them in the far greater Johnson.
But he could not well escape these obsessions, and he suffers
from them in a very mild form.

James Harris,[1] author of *Hermes* (and of the house of Malmesbury, which was ennobled in the next generation), is perhaps

Harris.   the chief writer whom England, in the narrower sense,
       has to set against Blair, Kames, and Campbell in
mid-eighteenth century. But he is disappointing. It would
not be reasonable to quarrel with the *Hermes* itself for not
being literary, because it does not pretend to be anything but
grammatical; and the *Philosophical Arrangements*, though they
do sometimes approach literature, may plead benefit of title for
not doing so oftener. But the *Discourse on Music, Painting, and
Poetry*, and the *Philological Enquiries*—in which Philology is
expressly intimated to mean "love of letters" in the higher

[1] *Works*, Oxford, 1841.

sense—hold out some prospects. The performance is but little.
Readers of Boswell will remember that Johnson, though the
author of *Hermes* was very polite to him, both personally and
with the pen, used, to his henchman's surprise and grief, to
speak very roughly of Harris, applying to him on one occasion
the famous and damning phrase, "a prig, and a bad prig," and
elsewhere hinting doubts as to his competency in Greek. That
the reproach of priggishness was deserved (whether with the
aggravation or not) nobody can read half-a-dozen pages of
Harris without allowing,—his would-be complimentary observation on Fielding [1] would determine by itself. But the principal
note of Harris, as a critic, is not so much priggishness as confused superficiality. These qualities are less visible in the
Dialogue (which is an extremely short, not contemptible, but
also not unimportant, exercitation in the direction of Æsthetic
proper) than in the *Enquiries*, which were written late in life, and
which, no doubt, owe something of their extraordinary garrulity
to "the irreparable outrage."

This book begins, with almost the highest possible promise for
us, in a Discussion of the Rise of Criticism, its various species,
The Philosophical, Historical, and Corrective, &c. It goes
Philological on hardly less promisingly, if the mere chapter-head-
Enquiries. ings are taken, with discourses on Numbers, Composition, Quantity, Alliteration, &c.; the Drama, its Fable and
its Manners, Diction, and, at the end of the second part, an im-
passioned defence of Rules. But the Third, which promises a
discussion of "the taste and literature of the Middle Age," raises
the expectation almost to agony-point. Here is what we have
been waiting for so long: here is the great gap going to be
filled. At last a critic not merely takes a philosophic-historic
view of criticism, but actually proposes to supplement it with
an inquiry into those regions of literature on which his predecessors have turned an obstinately blind eye. As is the
exaltation of the promise, so is the aggravation of the disappointment. Harris's first part, though by no means ill-
planned, is very insufficiently carried out, and the hope of
goodness in the third is cruelly dashed beforehand by the

---

[1] Note to Pt. II. chap. vii. of the *Enquiries*, p. 433, ed. cit.

sentence, "At length, after a long and barbarous period, when the shades of monkery began to retire," &c. The writer's mere enumeration of Renaissance critics is very haphazard, and his remarks, both on them and their successors, perfunctory in the extreme. He hardly dilates on anybody or anything except— following the tradition from Pope and Swift—on Bentley and his mania for correction and conjecture.

In the second part he gives himself more room, and is better worth reading, but the sense of disappointment continues. In fact, Harris is positively irritating. He lays it down, for instance, that "nothing excellent in a literary way happens merely by chance," a thesis from the discussion of which much might come. But he simply goes off into a loose discussion of the effects and causes of literary pleasure, with a good many examples in which the excellence of his precept, "seek the cause," is more apparent than the success of his own researches. The rest is extremely discursive, and seldom very satisfactory, being occupied in great part with such tenth-rate stuff as Lillo's *Fatal Curiosity*. As for Harris's defence of the Rules, he does not, in fact, defend them at all; but, as is so common with controversialists, frames an indictment, which no sensible antagonist would ever bring, in order to refute it. He says that "he never knew any genius cramped by rules, and had known great geniuses miserably err by neglecting them." A single example of this last would have been worth the whole treatise. But Harris does not give it. Finally, "the Taste and Literature of the Middle Age" seem to him to be satisfactorily discussed by ridiculing the Judgment of God, talking at some length about Byzantine writers, giving a rather long account of Greek philosophy in its ancient stages, quoting freely from travellers to Athens and Constantinople, introducing "the Arabians," with anecdotes of divers caliphs, saying something of the Schoolmen, a little about the Provençal poets, something (to do him justice) of the rise of accentual prosody,[1] and a very, very little about Chaucer, Petrarch, Mandeville, Marco Polo, Sir John Fortescue, and—Sannazar! "And now having done with the

---

[1] Harris deserves a good word for his prosodic studies, which may entitle him to reappear.

Middle Age," he concludes—having, that is to say, shown that, except a *pot-pourri* of mainly historical anecdote, he knew nothing whatever about it; or, if this seem harsh, that his knowledge was not of any kind that could possibly condition his judgment of literature favourably. In fact, no one shows that curious eighteenth-century confusion of mind, which may be noticed frequently in other countries, better than Harris. He is, as we have seen, a fervent devotee of the Rules—he believes [1] that, before any examples of poetry, there was an abstract schedule of Epic, Tragedy, and everything else down to Epigram, which you cannot follow but to your good, and cannot neglect but to your peril. Yet, on the one hand, he feels the philosophic impulse, and on the other, the literary and historical curiosity, before which these rules were bound to vanish.

A few allusions,[2] in contemporaries of abiding fame, have kept half alive the name—though very few, save specialists, are likely

"Estimate" Brown: his History of Poetry.
to be otherwise than accidentally acquainted with the work—of John Brown of Newcastle, author of the once famous *Estimate of the Manners and Principles of the Times,*[3] and afterwards, when he had gained reputation by this, of a *Dissertation on the Rise of Poetry and Music,*[4] later still slightly altered, and re-christened *History of the Rise and Progress of Poetry.*[5] The *Estimate* itself is one of those possibly half-unconscious pieces of quackery which from time to time put (in a manner which somehow or other tickles the longer ears among their contemporaries) the old cry that *every*thing is rotten in the state of Denmark. There is not much in it that is directly literary; the chief point of the kind is an attack on the Universities: it may be noted that quacks generally do attack Universities. The *Dissertation-History* is a much less

---

[1] "There never was a time when rules did not exist ; they always made a part of that immutable truth," &c. —P. 450.

[2] The best known is Cowper's, in *Table Talk,* ll. 384, 385—

"The inestimable Estimate of Brown
Rose like a paper-kite and charmed the town."

See also Chesterfield, to the Bishop of Waterford, April 14, 1758. Chesterfield was no Bottom, but, being melancholy at the time, he was tickled.

[3] London, 1757, 8vo.

[4] London, 1763, 4to.

[5] Newcastle, 1764, 8vo.

claptrap piece, but far more amusing to read. Brown is one
of those rash but frank persons who attempt creation as well
as criticism ; and those who will may hear how

> " Peace on Nature's lap reposes [why not *vice versa ?*]
>   Pleasure strews her guiltless roses,"

and so forth. The difference of the two forms is not important.
In the second, Brown simply left out Music, so far as he could,
as appealing to a special public only. He believes in *Ossian*,
then quite new. He thinks it contains " Pictures which no
civilised modern could ever *imbibe* in their strength, nor con-
sequently could ever *throw out*" — an image so excessively
Georgian (putting aside the difficulty of imbibing a picture)
that one has to abbreviate comment on it. For the rest, Brown
rejoices, and wallows, in the naturalistic generalisation of his
century. He begins, of course, with the Savage State, lays it
down that, at religious and other festivals, men danced and sang,
that then organised professional effort supplemented unorgan-
ised, and so poets arose. Then comes about a sort of Established Choir, whence the various kinds are developed. And we
have the Chinese—the inevitable Chinese—Fow-hi, and Chao-
hao, and all their trumpery. Negligible as an authority, Brown
perhaps deserves to rank as a symptom.

But we must leave minorities, and come to him who is here
ὁ μέγας.

There is no reason to doubt that Johnson's critical opinions
were formed quite early in life, and by that mixture of natural

Johnson : his bent and influence of environment which, as a rule,
preparation forms all such opinions. There has been a tendency
for criticism. to regard, as the highest mental attitude, that of considering everything as an open question, of being ready to
reverse any opinion at a moment's notice. As a matter of fact,
we have record of not many men who have proceeded in this
way ; and it may be doubted whether among them is a single
person of first-rate genius, or even talent. Generally speaking,
the men whose genius or talent has a " stalk of carle hemp" in
it find, in certain of the great primeval creeds of the world,
political, ecclesiastical, literary, or other, something which suits

their bent. The bent of their time may assist them in fasten-
ing on to this by attraction or repulsion—it really does not
much matter which it is. In either case they will insensibly,
from an early period, choose their line and shape their course
accordingly. They will give a certain independence to it; they
will rarely be found merely "swallowing formulas." It is the
other class which does this, with leave reserved to get rid of
the said formulas by a mental emetic and swallow another set,
which will very likely be subjected to the same fate. But the
hero will be in the main *Qualis ab incepto*.

Johnson was in most things a Tory by nature, his Toryism
being conditioned, first by that very strong bent towards a sort
of transcendental scepticism which many great Tories have
shown; secondly, by the usual peculiarities of social circumstance and mental constitution; and lastly, by the state of
England in his time—a state to discuss which were here im-
pertinent, but which, it may be humbly suggested, will not be
quite appreciated by accepting any, or all, of the more ordinary
views of the eighteenth century.

His view of literature was in part determined by these
general influences, in part—perhaps chiefly—by special imping-
ing currents. His mere birth-time had not very much to do
with it—Thomson, Dyer, Lady Winchelsea, who consciously or
unconsciously worked against it, were older, in the lady's case
much older, than he was; Gray and Shenstone, who consciously
worked against it in different degrees, were not much younger.[1]
The view was determined in his case, mainly no doubt by that
natural bent which is quite inexplicable, but also by other
things explicable enough. Johnson, partly though probably not
wholly in consequence of his near sight, was entirely insensible to the beauties of nature; he made fun of "prospects";
he held that "one blade of grass is like another" (which it most
certainly is not, even in itself, let alone its surroundings);
he liked human society in its most artificial form—that provided
by towns, clubs, parties. In the second place, his ear was only

[1] His birth-year was 1709; Thomson's 1700; Dyer's perhaps the
same; Shenstone's 1714; Gray's
1716. Lady Winchelsea had been born
as far back as 1660.

less deficient than his eye. That he did not care for music, in
the scientific sense, is not of much importance; but it is quite
clear that, in poetry, only an extremely regular and almost mathematical beat of verse had any chance with him. Thirdly, he
was widely read in the Latin Classics, less widely in Greek,
still more widely in the artificial revived Latin of the Renaissance and the seventeenth century.[1] Fourthly, he was, for a
man so much given to reading—for one who ranged from Macrobius in youth to *Parismus and Parismenus* in age, and from
Travels in Abyssinia to *Prince Titi*—not very widely read either
in mediæval Latin or in the earlier divisions of the modern languages; indeed, of these last he probably knew little or nothing.
Fifthly, the greatest poet in English immediately before his
time, and the greatest poet in English during his youth and
early manhood, had been exponents, the one mainly, the other
wholly, of a certain limited theory of English verse. Sixthly,
the critical school in which he had been brought up was strictly
neo-classic. Seventhly, and to conclude, such rebels to convention as appeared in his time were chiefly men whom he
regarded with unfriendly dislike, or with friendly contempt.
Nor can it be said that any one of the contemporary partisans of
"the Gothick" was likely to convince a sturdy adversary. Walpole was a spiteful fribble with a thin vein of genius;[2] Gray a
sort of Mr Facing-Both-Ways in literature, who had "classical"
mannerisms worse than any of Johnson's own, and whose
dilettante shyness and scanty production invited ridicule.
Both were Cambridge men (and Johnson did not love Cambridge men, nor they him), and both were Whigs. Percy and
Warton were certainly not very strong as originals, and had
foibles enough even as scholars. But whether these reasons
go far enough, or do not so go, Johnson's general critical attitude never varies in the least.[2] It was, as has been said, prob-

---

[1] He was perhaps the last man of
very great power who entertained the
Renaissance superstition of Latin. He
was horrified at the notion of an English epitaph; and in the first agony of
his stroke in 1783 he rallied and
racked his half-paralysed brains to
make Latin verses as the best test
of his sanity.

[2] This judgment is a little severe
perhaps: but not wholly unjust.

[3] However, in Johnson, as in most
strong men, there were certain leanings
to the other side. His sense of mys-

ably formed quite early; it no doubt appeared in those but dimly known contributions to periodical literature which defrayed so ill the expense of his still more dimly known first twenty years in London. We have from him no single treatise, as in the cases of Dante and Longinus, no pair of treatises, as in the case of Aristotle, to go upon. But in the four great documents of *The Rambler*, *Rasselas*, the Shakespeare *Preface*, and the *Lives*, we see it—in the two first rigid, peremptory, in the *Preface*, curiously and representatively uncertain, in the last conditioned by differences which allow it somewhat freer play, and at some times making a few concessions, but at others more pugnacious and arbitrary than before.

The critical element in *The Rambler* is necessarily large; but a great deal of it is general and out of our way.[1] Directly concerning us are the papers on the aspects (chiefly formal) of Milton's poetry—especially versification —on which Addison had not spoken, with some smaller papers on lesser subjects. The Miltonic *examen* begins at No. 86. Johnson is as uncompromising as the great Bysshe himself on the nature of English prosody. "The heroick measures of the English language may be properly considered as pure or mixed." They are pure when "the accent rests on every second syllable through the whole line." In other words, "purity" is refused to anything but the strict iambic decasyllable. Nay, he goes further; this is not only "purity" and "the completest harmony possible," but it ought to be "exactly kept in distichs" and in the last line of a (verse) paragraph.

The Rambler on Milton.

Nevertheless, for variety's sake, the "mixed" measure is allowed; "though it always injures the harmony of the line considered by itself," it makes us appreciate the "harmonious" lines better. And we soon perceive that even this exceedingly

---

tery, his religiosity, his strong passions, his tendency to violence in taste and opinions — were all rather Romantic than Classical.

[1] The Allegory on Criticism (daughter of Labour and Truth, who gives up her task to Time, but is temporarily personated by Flattery and Malevolence) in

No. 3 almost speaks itself in the parenthetical description just given. Cf. also 4, on Ancient and Modern Romances; 22, another Allegory on Wit and Learning; 23, on the Contrariety of Criticism; and 36, 37, on "Pastoral Poetry."

grudging, and in strictness illogical, licence is limited merely to substitution of other dissyllabic feet for the pure iamb.   In

> "Thus at their shady lodge arrived, *both stood,*
>   Both turned,"

the rigid Johnson insists on the spondaic character, "the accent is on two syllables together and both strong"; while he would seem to regard "And when," in the line

> "And when we seek as now the gift of sleep,"

as a pyrrhic ("both syllables are weak "). A trochee ("deviation or inversion of accent") is allowed as a "mixture" in the first place, but elsewhere is "remarkably inharmonious," as, for instance, in Cowley's beautiful line,

> "And the soft wings of peace *cover* him round."

The next paper (88) passes, after touching other matters, to "elision," by which he means (evidently not even taking tri-syllabic possibility into consideration) such a case as

> "Wisdom to folly as nourishment to wind."

This licence, he says, is now disused in English poetry; and adds some severe remarks on those who would revive or commend it. He even objects to the redundant ending in heroic poetry.

In the third paper (90) he comes to Pauses; and once more plays the rigour of the game. The English poet, in connecting one line with another, is *never* to make a full pause at less than three syllables from the beginning or end of a verse; and in all lines pause at the fourth or sixth syllable is best. He gives a whole paper to Milton's accommodation of the sound to the sense, and winds up his Miltonic exercitations, after a very considerable interval, with a set critique (139) of *Samson Agonistes,* partly on its general character as an Aristotelian tragedy (he decides that it has a beginning and end, but no middle, poor thing!) and partly on details. These papers show no *animus* against Milton. There are even expressions of admiration for him, which may be called enthusiastic. But they do show that the critic was not in range with his author. Almost every one of his axioms and postulates is questionable.

Of the remaining critical papers in the *Rambler* it is very important to notice No. 121, "On the Dangers of Imitation, and the Impropriety of imitating Spenser." Johnson's

On Spenser.

acuteness was not at fault in distrusting, from his point of view, the consequences of such things as the *Castle of Indolence* or even the *Schoolmistress ;* and he addresses a direct rebuke to "the men of learning and genius" who have introduced the fashion.[1] In so far as his condemnation of "echoes" goes he is undoubtedly not wrong, and he speaks of the idol of Neo-Classicism, Virgil, with an irreverent *parrhesia*[2] which, like many other things in him, shows his true critical power. But on Spenser himself the other idols—the *idola specus* rather than *fori*—blind him. In following his namesake in the condemnation of Spenser's language he is, we may think, wrong ; yet this at least is an arguable point. But in regard to the Spenserian stanza things are different. Johnson calls it "at once difficult and unpleasing ; tiresome to the ear from its uniformity, and to the attention by its length," while he subsequently goes off into the usual error about imitating the Italians. No truce is here possible. That the Spenserian is not easy may be granted at once, but Johnson was certainly scholar enough to anticipate the riposte that, not here only, it is "hard to be good." As for "unpleasing," so much the worse for the ear which is not pleased by the most exquisite harmonic symphony in the long and glorious list of stanza-combinations. As for monotony, it is just as monotonous as flowing water. While as for the Italian parallel, nothing can probably be more to the glory of Spenser than this ; just as nothing can be more different than the pretty, but cloying, rhyme even of Tasso, nay, sometimes even of Ariosto, and the endless unlaboured beauty of Spenser's rhyme-sound.

---

[1] He was no doubt thinking also of Gilbert West, in his *Life* of whom he introduces a *caveat* against West's Imitations of Spenser as "successful" indeed and "amusing," but "only pretty."

[2] "The warmest admirers of the great Mantuan poet can extol him for little more than the skill with which he has . . . united the beauties of the *Iliad* and *Odyssey*," and he adds a longish exposure of the way in which Virgil, determined to imitate at all costs, has put in his borrowed matter without regard to keeping.

It is no valid retort that this is simply a difference of taste. If a man, as some men have done, says that Spenser is pleasing and Dryden and Pope are *not*, then the retort is valid. When the position is taken that *both* rhythms are pleasing, both really poetical, but poetical in a different way, the defender of it may laugh at all assailants.

The criticism of the English historians which immediately follows has an interest chiefly of curiosity, because it was written *On History and Letter-writing.* just at the opening of the great age of the department with which it deals. Prejudices of different kinds would always have prevented Johnson from doing full justice to Robertson, to Hume, and, most of all, to Gibbon; but, as it is, he deals with nobody later than Clarendon, and merely throws back to Raleigh and Knolles. Very much the same drawback attends the criticism on Epistolary writing: for here also it was the lot of Johnson's own contemporaries, in work mostly not written, and hardly in a single case published, at the date of the *Rambler*, to remove the reproach of England. But the paper on Tragi-Comedy (156) is much more important.

For here, as in other places, we see that Johnson, but for the combination of influences above referred to, might have taken *On Tragi-comedy.* high, if not the highest, degrees in a very different school of criticism. He puts the great rule *Nec quarta loqui* into the dustbin, with a nonchalance exhibiting some slight shortness of sight; for the very argument he uses will sweep with this a good many other rules to which he still adheres. "We violate it," he says coolly, "without scruple and without inconvenience." He is equally iconoclastic about the Five Acts, about the Unity of Time, while he blows rather hot and cold about tragi-comedy in the sense of the mixing of tragic and comic scenes. But the close of the paper is the most remarkable, for it is in effect the death-knell of the neo-classic system, sounded by its last really great prophet. "*It ought to be the first endeavour of a writer to distinguish nature from custom, or that which is established because it is right from that which is right only because it is established ; that he may neither violate essential principles by a desire of novelty, nor debar himself from the attainment of beauties within his view by a needless fear of breaking rules which no literary dictator had authority to enact."*

" Oh ! the lands of Milnwood, the bonny lands of Milnwood, that have been in the name of Morton twa hundred years ; they are barking and fleeing, infield and outfield, haugh and holme ! " With this utterance, this single utterance, all the ruling doctrines of sixteenth, seventeenth, and eighteenth century criticism receive notice to quit.[1]

The well-known " Dick Minim " papers in the *Idler* (60, 61) are excellent fun, and perhaps Johnson's chief accomplishment *" Dick* in the direction of humour. The growth of criticism *Minim."* in Dick, his gradual proficiency in all the critical commonplaces of his day (it is to be observed that Johnson, like all true humourists, does not spare himself, and makes one of Minim's *secrets de Polichinelle* a censure of Spenser's stanza), his addiction to Johnson's pet aversion, " suiting the sound to the sense," and his idolatry of Milton, are all capitally done. Indeed, like all good caricatures, the piece is a standing piece to consult for the fashions and creeds which it caricatures. But it neither contains nor suggests any points of critical doctrine that we cannot find elsewhere, and it is only indirectly serious.[2]

The Dissertation upon Poetry of Imlac in *Rasselas* (chap. x.) may be less amusing ; but it is of course much more serious. *Rasselas.* There can be no reasonable doubt that Imlac gives as much of Johnson's self as he chose to put, and could put, in character : 'while it is at least possible that his sentiments are determined in some degree by the menacing appearances of Romanticism. Imlac finds " with wonder that in almost all countries the most ancient poets are reputed the best "; that " early writers are in possession of nature and their successors of art "; that " no man was ever great by imitation "; that he must observe everything and observe for himself, but that he

---

[1] The chief remaining critical *loci* in the *Rambler* are the unlucky strictures in No. 168 on " dun," " knife," and " blanket " in *Macbeth* as " low "; and the remarks on unfriendly criticism in 176.

[2] There are, of course, other passages in the *Idler* touching on Criticism,— 59 on the Causes of Neglect of Books, 68, 69 on Translation, 77 on " Essay Writing," 85 on Compilations. But they contain nothing of exceptional importance.

must do it on the principle of examining, "not the individual, but the species." He is to remark "general properties and large appearances. He does not number the streaks of the tulip or describe the different shapes in the verdure of the forest," but must "exhibit prominent and striking features," neglecting "minuter discriminations." In the same way his criticism of life must be abstracted and generalised; he must be "a being superior to time and place"; must know many languages and sciences; must by incessant practice of style "familiarise to himself every delicacy of speech and grace of harmony."

Surely a high calling and election! yet with some questionable points in it. If the poet must not count the streaks of the tulip, if he must merely generalise and sweep; if he must consult the laziness and dulness of his readers by merely portraying prominent and striking features, characteristics alike obvious to vigilance and carelessness—then even Dryden will not do, for he is too recondite and conceited. Pope alone must bear the bell. Lady Winchelsea's horse in twilight, the best part of a century earlier; Tennyson's ashbuds in the front of March, the best part of a century later, are equally "streaks of the tulip," superfluous if not even bad. Habington's picture of the pitiless northern sunshine on the ice-bound pilot, and Keats's of the perilous seas through the magic casements, must be rejected, as too unfamiliar and individual. The poetic strangeness and height are barred *en bloc*. Convention, familiarity, generalisation—these are the keys to the poetical kingdom of heaven. The tenant of Milnwood has a fresh enfeoffment!

The Shakespeare Preface is a specially interesting document, because of its illustration, not merely of Johnson's native *The* critical vigour, not merely of his imbibed eighteenth-*Shakespeare* century prejudices, but of that peculiar position of *Preface.* compromise and reservation which, as we have said and shall say, is at once the condemnation and the salvation of the English critical position at this time. Of the first there are many instances, though perhaps none in the *Preface* itself quite equal to the famous note on the character of Polonius, which has been generally and justly taken as showing what

a triumph this failure of an edition might have been. Yet
even here there is not a little which follows in the wake of
Dryden's great eulogy, and some scattered observations of
the highest acuteness, more particularly two famous sentences
which, though Johnson's quotation is directed to a minor
matter—Shakespeare's learning—settle beforehand, with the
prophetic tendency of genius, the whole monstrous absurdity
of the Bacon-Shakespeare theory.[1]   The rest, however, is, if not
exactly a zigzag of contradiction, at least the contrasted utterance of two distinct voices. Shakespeare has this and that
merit of nature, of passion ; but " his set speeches are commonly
cold and weak." " What he does best he soon ceases to do."
Johnson, here also, has no superstitious reverence for the
Unities, and even speaks slightly of dramatic rules ; nay, he
suggests " the recall of the principles of the drama to a new
examination," the very examination which Lessing was to give
it.   But he apologises for the period when " *The Death of
Arthur* was the favourite volume," and hints a doubt whether
much of our and his own praise of Shakespeare is not "given
by custom and veneration." " He has corrupted language by
every mode of depravation," yet Johnson echoes Dryden " when
he describes anything you more than see it, you feel it too."
A singular triumph of " depraved language." In short, throughout the piece it is now Johnson himself who is speaking, now
some one with a certain bundle of principles or prejudices
which Johnson chooses to adopt for the time.

It was with these opinions on the formal and substantial
nature of poetry and of criticism that Johnson, late in life, sat
The Lives of down to the *Lives of the Poets*,[2] one of the most
the Poets.   fortunate books in English literature. In very few
cases have task and artist been so happily associated.   For

---

[1] " Jonson, . . . who besides that
he had no imaginable temptation to
falsehood, wrote at a time when the
character and acquisitions of Shakespeare were known to multitudes. His
evidence ought therefore to decide the
controversy, unless some testimony of
equal force could be opposed."

[2] With Johnson, as with others, I do
not specify editions. I must, however,
mention Mr J. H. Millar's issue of the
Lives (London, 1896) for the sake of
the excellent *Introduction. Loci Critici*
contains a selection of remarkable passages from the other works.

almost all his authors, he had biographical knowledge such as no other living man had, and the access to which has long been closed. If, now and then, his criticism was not in touch with his subjects, this was rare: and the fact gave a certain value even to the assertions that result—for *we*, do what we will, cannot see Milton quite as Johnson saw him, and so his view is valuable as a corrective. By far the greater part of these subjects belonged to one school and system of English poetry, a school and system with which the critic was at once thoroughly familiar and thoroughly in sympathy. And, lastly, the form of the work, with its subdivision into a large number of practically independent and not individually burdensome sections, was well suited to coax a man who suffered from constitutional indolence, and who for many years had been relieved from that pressure of necessity which had conquered his indolence occasionally, and only occasionally, earlier. No other man, it is true, has had quite such a chance: but he must indeed have a sublime confidence, both in the strength of his principles and in the competence of his talents, who thinks that, if he had the chance, he could do the task better than Johnson did his.

The work, of course, is by no means equal throughout: and it could not be expected to be. Some was merely old stuff, *Their general merits.* dating from a much less mature period of the writer's genius, and made to serve again. Some was on subjects so trivial that good nature, or simple indolence, or, if any one pleases, an artistic reluctance to break butterflies on so huge a wheel, made the criticisms almost as insignificant as the criticised. Here and there extra-literary prejudice—political-ecclesiastical, as in the case of Milton; partly moral, partly religious, and, it is to be feared, a little personal, as in that of Swift—distorted the presentation. And it is quite possible that a similar distortion, due to the same causes or others, was in the case of Gray intensified by a half-unconscious conviction that Gray's aims and spirit, if not his actual poetical accomplishments, were fatal to the school of poetry to which the critic himself held.

But make allowance for all this, and with how great a thing do the *Lives* still provide us! In that combination of biography and criticism, which is so natural that it is wonderful it should be so late,[1] they are all but the originals, and are still almost the standard. They are full of anecdote, agreeably and crisply told, yet they never descend to mere gossip: their criticism of life is almost always just and sound, grave without being precise, animated by the same melancholy as that of the *Vanity of Human Wishes,* but in milder mood and with touches of brightness. Their criticism of literature is all the more valuable for being the criticism of their time. When we read Johnson's remarks on Milton's minor poems it is foolish to rave, and it is ignoble to sneer. The wise will rejoice in the opportunity to understand. So when Johnson bestows what seems to us extraordinary and unintelligible praise on John Pomfret's *Choice,*[2] he is really praising a moral tract couched in verse not unpleasing in itself, and specially pleasing to his ear. When he speaks less favourably of *Grongar Hill,* he is speaking of a piece of nature-poetry, not arranged on his principle of neglecting the streak of the tulip, and availing itself of those Miltonic licences of prosody which he disapproved. But we shall never find that, when the poetry is of the stamp which he recognises, he makes any mistake about its relative excellence: and we shall find that, in not a few cases, he is able to recognise excellence which belongs to classes and schools not exactly such as he approves. And, lastly, it has to be added that for diffused brilliancy of critical expression, subject to the allowances and conditions just given, the *Lives* are hardly to be excelled in any language. It is not safe to neglect one of them, though no doubt there are some six or seven which, for this reason or that, take precedence of the rest.

The "Cowley" has especial interest, because it is Johnson's

[1] There are blind attempts at it even in antiquity ; but Dryden's Lives of Lucian and Plutarch are, like other things of his elsewhere, the real originals here.

[2] Let me draw special attention to "John." I once, unwittingly or carelessly, called him "Thomas," and I am afraid that I even neglected to correct the error in a second edition of the guilty book. A man who writes "Thomas" for "John," in the case of a minor poet, can, I am aware, possess no virtues, and must expect no pardon. But I shall always henceforth remember to call him "Pomfret, Mr *John.*" "Let this expiate," as was remarked in another case of perhaps not less mortal sin.

only considerable attempt at that very important part of
criticism, the historical summary of the characteristics of a poetical period or school.　And, though far
from faultless, it is so important and so interesting in its kind
that it ranks with his greatest Essays.　Only that singular
impatience of literary history, as such, which characterised the
late Mr Matthew Arnold, and which not infrequently marred
his own critical work, can have prevented him from including,
in his Johnsonian *points de repère*, the Essay which launched,
and endeavoured to make watertight, the famous definition
of the "Metaphysical" School—of the school represented
earlier by Donne, and later by Cowley himself.

The Cowley.

The phrase itself [1] has been both too readily adopted and too
indiscriminately attacked.　Taken with the ordinary meaning
of "metaphysical," it may indeed seem partly meaningless and
partly misleading.　Taken as Johnson meant it, it has a meaning defensible at least from the point of view of the framer, and
very important in critical history.　Johnson (it is too often
forgotten) was a scholar; and he used "metaphysical" in its
proper sense—of that which "comes after" the physical or
natural.　Now, it was, as we have seen, the whole cardinal
principle of his school of criticism that *they* were "following
nature" by *imitating* it.　The main objection to the poetry of
what Dryden calls the "last Age"—what we call, loosely but
conveniently, "Elizabethan" poetry—was that its ideas, and still
more its expressions, went beyond and behind nature, substituted afterthoughts and unreal refinements for fact.　It would
be delightful to the present writer to defend the Metaphysicals
here—but it would not be to the question.

Political and religious prejudice accounts, as has been said,
for much in the *Milton*.　But it will not fully account for the
facts.　The at first sight astonishing, and already
often referred to, criticisms on the minor poems show
a perfectly honest and genuine dislike to the form as well as
to the matter, to the manner as well as to the man.　If Johnson

The Milton.

---

[1] It was of course probably suggested
by Dryden (*Essay on Satire*, "Donne
. . . affects the metaphysics"), but in
Johnson's hands is much altered and
extended.

calls *Lycidas* " harsh," it is because he simply does not hear its
music; he can even call the songs in *Comus* " not very musical
in their numbers." When of the, no doubt unequal but often
splendid, sonnets he can write, " of the best it can only be said
that they are not bad," he gives us the real value of his criticism
immediately afterwards by laying it down that " the fabric of a
sonnet, however adapted to the Italian language, has *never* succeeded in ours." And when he has earlier stated that " all that
short compositions can commonly attain is sweetness and elegance," we see in this the whole thing. Milton is condemned
under statute (though the statute is hopelessly unconstitutional
and unjust) on certain counts; on others his judge, though capable and perfectly honest, does not know the part of the code
which justifies the accused. Johnson is listening for couplet-
music, or for stanzas with regular recurrence of rhyme, for lines
constituted entirely on a dissyllabic, or entirely on a trisyllabic,
basis. He does not find these things: and he has no organ
to judge what he does find.

With the lives of Dryden and Pope we are clear of all difficulties, and the critic is in his element. The poets whom he is
The Dryden criticising occupy the same platform as he does; they
and Pope. have in fact been themselves the architects of that
platform. There is no fear of the initial incompatibilities which,
when aggravated by accident, lead to the apparent enormities of
the *Milton* Essay, and which, even when not so aggravated, condition the usefulness, though they may positively increase the
interest, of the *Cowley*. But there is more than this. In no
instance, perhaps, was Johnson so well in case to apply his
biographical and critical treatment as in regard to Dryden
and Pope. With the latter he had himself been contemporary; and when he first came to London the traditions even
of the former were still fresh, while there were many still living
(Southerne the chief of them) who had known glorious John well.
Further, Johnson's peculiar habits of living, his delight in conversation and society, his excellent memory, and his propensity
to the study of human nature, as well as of letters, furnished
him abundantly with opportunities. Yet, again, his sympathy
with both, on general literary sides, was not unhappily mixed

and tempered by a slight, but not uncharitable or Puritanic, disapproval of their moral characters, by regret at Dryden's desertion of the Anglican Church, and at the half-Romanist, half-freethinking, attitude of Pope to religion.

The result of all this is a pair of the best critical Essays in the English language. Individual expressions will of course renew for us the sense of difference in the point of view. We shall not agree that Dryden " found English poetry brick and left it marble," and we shall be only too apt to take up the challenge, " If Pope be not a poet, where is poetry to be found?" even if we think the implied denial, to which the challenge was a reply, an absurdity. And we may find special interest as well as special difference in the condemnation even of these masters for attempting Pindarics, because Pindarics " want the essential constituent of metrical compositions, the stated recurrence of settled numbers," seeing in it a fresh instance of that Procrustean tyranny of suiting the form to the bed, not the bed to the form, which distinguishes all neo-classic criticism. But these points occur rarely. The criticism, as a whole, is not merely perfectly just on its own scheme, but requires very little allowance on others; nor, in the difficult and dangerous art of comparative censorship, will any example be found much surpassing Johnson's parallel of the two poets.

In the *Milton* and the *Cowley* we find Johnson dealing with schools of poetry which he regards as out of date and imper-*The* Collins fect; in the *Dryden* and the *Pope*, with subjects *and* Gray. which are not to him subjects of any general controversy, but which he can afford to treat almost entirely on their merits. In the *Collins* and the *Gray* we find a new relation between poet and critic—the relation of decided, though not yet wholly declared, innovation on the part of the poets, and of conscious, though not yet quite wide-eyed and irreconcilable, hostility on the part of the critic. The expression of this is further differentiated by the fact that Johnson regarded Collins with the affection of a personal friend, and the generous sympathy of one who, with all his roughness, had a mind as nearly touched by mortal sorrows as that of any sentimentalist; while it is pretty clear, though we have no positive evidence for it, that he reciprocated the personal and political dislike which Gray certainly felt for him.

The result was, in the case of Collins, a criticism rather inadequate than unjust, and not seldom acute in its indication of faults, if somewhat blind to merits; in that of Gray, one which cannot be quite so favourably spoken of, though the censure which has been heaped upon it—notably by Lord Macaulay and Mr Arnold—seems to me very far to surpass its own injustice. Johnson's general summing up—that Gray's " mind had a large grasp; his curiosity [1] was unlimited, and his judgment cultivated; he was likely to love much where he loved at all, but fastidious and hard to please "—is acute, just, and far from ungenerous. That on the Elegy—" The four stanzas beginning, ' Yet even these bones,' are to me original; I have never seen the notions in any other place. Yet he that reads them here persuades himself that he has always felt them. Had Gray written often thus, it had been vain to blame and useless to praise him "—is a magnificent and monumental compliment, said as simply as " Good morning." He is absolutely right when he says that in all Gray's Odes " there is a kind of cumbrous splendour that we wish away," for there never was such an abuser of " poetic diction " (to be a poet) as Gray was. Yet undoubtedly the Essay is not satisfactory; it has not merely, as the *Collins* has, blindness, but, what the *Collins* has not, that obvious *denigration*, that determination to pick holes, which always vitiates a critique, no matter what learning and genius be bestowed on it. And the probable reasons of this are interesting. It has been said that they were possibly personal in part. We know that Gray spoke rudely of Johnson; and there were many reasons why Johnson might rather despise Gray, though he certainly should not have called him " dull."

On the whole, however, I have little doubt—and it is this which gives the essay its real interest for me—that one main reason of Johnson's antipathy to Gray's poetry was the same as that for which we like it. He suspected, if he did not fully perceive, the romantic snake in Gray's classically waving grass.

---

[1] It must be remembered that this word had no unfavourable connotation with Johnson. It meant intelligent and scholarly interest.

And he had on his own grounds good reason for suspecting it. Gray might use Greek and Latin tags almost extravagantly. But he sedulously eschewed the couplet; and, while preferring lyric, he chose lyrical forms which, though Johnson was too much of a scholar to dare to call them irregular, violated his own theories of the prompt and orderly recurrence of rhyme, and the duty of maintaining a length of line as even as possible. The sense of nature, the love of the despised "prospect," was everywhere; even the forbidden "streak of the tulip" might be detected.   And, lastly, Gray had too obvious leanings to classes of subject and literature which lay outside of the consecrated range—early English and French, Welsh, Norse, and the like. It is no real evidence of critical incapacity, but of something quite the reverse, that Johnson should have disliked Gray.   He spied the great Romantic beard under the Pindaric and Horatian muffler—and he did not like it.

On the whole, it may be safely said that, however widely a man may differ from Johnson's critical theory, he will, provided *The critical* that he possesses some real tincture of the critical *greatness of* spirit himself, think more and more highly of the *the Lives* *Lives of the Poets* the more he reads them, and the *and of* *Johnson.* more he compares them with the greater classics of critical literature.   As a book, they have not missed their due meed of praise; as a critical book, one may think that they have. The peculiarity of their position as a body of direct critical appraisement of the poetical work of England for a long period should escape no one.   But the discussion of them, which possesses, and is long likely to possess, prerogative authority as coming from one who was both himself a master of the craft and a master of English, admirable and delightful as it is and always will be, is not, critically speaking, quite satisfactory. Mr Arnold speaks of the Six Lives which he selected in very high terms: but he rather pooh-poohs the others, and, even in regard to the chosen Six, he puts upon himself—and in his amiable, but for all that exceedingly peremptory, way, insists in putting on his readers—a huge pair of blinkers.   We are to regard the late seventeenth and the whole of the eighteenth century as an Age of Prose: and we are to regard Johnson, whether he was speaking of the poets of this age or of others, as the spokesman of an age of prose. Far be it from me to deny that there is an element of truth in this: but it is not the whole truth, and the critic must strive, though he may not boast, to " find the whole."

The whole truth, as it seems to me, about Johnson is that he was very much more than the critic of an age of prose, though he was not (who has been? even Longinus? even Coleridge?)

> " The King who ruled, as he thought fit,
> The universal monarchy of wit "

as regards poetic criticism. He saw far beyond prose, as in those few words of the concluding and reconciling eulogy of Gray which have been quoted above. It is poetry and not prose which has the gift of putting new things so that the man who reads them ingenuously thinks that they are merely a neat statement of what he has always thought. And Johnson was far more than merely a critic of the eighteenth-century Neo-Classic theory, though he was this. A most noteworthy passage in the *Rambler* (No. 156), which I have purposely kept for comment in this place, though it is delivered on the wrong side, shows us, as the great critics always do show us, what a range of sight the writer had. In this he expresses a doubt whether we ought " to judge genius merely by the event," and, applying this to Shakespeare, takes the odd, but for an eighteenth-century critic most tell-tale and interesting, line that if genius succeeds by means which are wrong according to rule, we may think higher of the genius but less highly of the work. It is hardly necessary to point out that this is, though in no way a discreditable, a transparent evasion of the difficulty which is pressing on the defenders of the Rules. " Show me," one may without irreverence retort, " thy genius without thy works; and I will show thee my genius by my works." If Shakespeare shows genius in neglecting the Rules, the inexorable voice of Logic, greater than Fortune, greater than all other things save Fate, will point out that the Rules are evidently not necessary, and, with something like the Lucretian *Te sequar*, will add, " Then for what *are* they necessary?" But Johnson's power is only a little soured and

not at all quenched by this. He has seen what others refused
—perhaps were unable—to see, and what some flatly denied,—
that a process of literary judgment "by the event" is possible, and that its verdicts, in some respects at any rate, cannot
be challenged or reversed. These great critical *aperçus*, though
sometimes delivered half unwillingly or on the wrong side,
establish Johnson's claim to a place not often to be given to
critics; but they do not establish it more certainly than his
surveys of his actual subjects. It was an unfortunate consequence of Mr Arnold's generous impatience of all but "the
chief and principal things," and of his curious dislike to literary
history as such, that he should have swept away the minor
Lives. One may not care for Stepney or Yalden, Duke or
King, much more, or at all more, than he did. But with a
really great member of the craft his admissions and omissions, his paradoxes, his extravagances, his very mistakes
pure and simple, are all critically edifying. How does he
apply his own critical theory? is what we must ask: and,
with Johnson, I think we shall never ask it in vain.

His idea of English poetry was the application to certain
classes of subjects, not rigidly limited to, but mainly arranged
by, the canons of the classical writers—of what seemed to him
and his generation the supreme form of English language and
metre, brought in by Mr Waller and perfected by Mr Pope, yet
not so as to exclude from admiration the *Allegro* of
Milton and the *Elegy* of Gray. We may trace his applications of this, if we have a real love of literature and
a real sense of criticism, nearly as profitably and pleas-
antly in relation to John Pomfret as in relation to Alexander Pope. We may trace his failures (as we are pleased,
quite rightly in a way, to call them), the failures arising from
the inadequacy, not of his genius, but of his scheme, not less
agreeably in relation to Dyer than in relation to Dryden. We
are not less informed by his passing the *Castle of Indolence*
almost *sub silentio* than we are by that at first sight astounding
criticism of *Lycidas*. This Cæsar never does wrong but with
just cause— to use the phrase which was too much for the
equanimity or the intelligence of his great namesake Ben,

in the work of one whom both admired yet could not quite stomach.

Now, this it is which makes the greatness of a critic. That Johnson might have been greater still at other times need not necessarily be denied; though it is at least open to doubt whether any other time would have suited his whole disposition better. But, as he is, he is great. The critics who deserve that name are not those who, like, for instance, Christopher North and Mr Ruskin, are at the mercy of different kinds of caprice—with whom you must be always on the *qui vive* to be certain what particular watchword they have adopted, what special side they are taking. It may even be doubted whether such a critic as Lamb, though infinitely delightful, is exactly "great" because of the singular gaps and arbitrariness of his likes and dislikes. Nay, Hazlitt, one of the greatest critics of the world on the whole, goes near to forfeit his right to the title by the occasional outbursts of almost insane prejudice that cloud his vision. Johnson is quite as prejudiced; but his prejudice is not in the least insane. His critical calculus is perfectly sound on its own postulates and axioms; and you have only to apply checks and correctives (which are easily ascertained, and kept ready) to adjust it to absolute critical truth. And, what is more, he has not merely flourished and vapoured critical abstractions, but has left us a solid reasoned body of critical judgment; he has not judged literature in the exhausted receiver of mere art, and yet has never neglected the artistic criterion; he has kept in constant touch with life, and yet has never descended to mere gossip. We may freely disagree with his judgments, but we can never justly disable his judgment; and this is the real criterion of a great critic.

Johnson is so much the eighteenth-century orthodox critic in quintessence (though, as I have tried to show, in transcendence also) that he will dispense us from saying very much *Minor Criticism: Periodical and other.* more about the rank and file, the ordinary or inferior examples, of the kind. If we were able to devote the whole space of this volume to the subject of the present chapter, there would be no lack of material. Critical exercitations of a kind formed now, of course, a regular part of the work of literature, and a very large part of its hack-work. The *Gentleman's Magazine* devoted much attention to the subject; and for a great part of the century two regular *Reviews*, the *Critical* and the *Monthly*,[1] were recognised organs of literary censorship, and employed some really eminent hands, notably Smollett and Goldsmith. The periodicals which, now in single spies, now (about the middle of the century) in battalions, endeavoured to renew the success of the *Tatler* and *Spectator*, were critical by kind; and dozens, scores, hundreds probably, of separate critical publications, large and small, issued from the press.[2] But, with the rarest exceptions, they must take the *non*-benefit of the old warning—they must merely " be heard by their foreman." Something we must say of Goldsmith; then we may take two contrasted examples, Knox and Scott of Amwell, of the critic in Johnson's last days who inclined undoubtingly to the classical, and of the critic of the same time who had qualms and stirrings of Romanticism, but was hardly yet a heretic. And then, reserving summary, we may close the record.

[1] Johnson's relative estimates of the two (*Boswell*, Globe ed., pp. 186, 364) are well known; as is his apology for the *Critical* Reviewers' habit [he had been one himself] of not reading the books through, as the "duller" *Monthly* fellows were glad to do. Later generations have perhaps contrived to be dull *and* not to read.

[2] For instance, here is one which I have hunted for years—*Essay on the New Species of Writing founded by Fielding, with a word or two on Modern Criticism* (London ? 1751). The better-known *Canons of Criticism* of Thomas Edwards (4th ed., London, 1750) may serve as a specimen of another kind. It is an attack on Warburton's *Shakespeare*, uncommonly shrewd in all senses of the word, but, as Johnson (*Boswell*, Globe ed., p. 87 note) justly enough said, of the gad-fly kind mainly. A curious little book, which I do not remember to have seen cited anywhere, is the *Essay upon Poetry and Painting* of Charles Lamotte (Dublin (*sic*), 1742). La Motte, who was an F.S.A., a D.D., and chaplain to the Duke of Montagu, but who has the rare misfortune of not appearing in the *Dict. Nat. Biog.*, never refers to his French namesake, but quotes Voltaire and Du Bos frequently. He is very anxious for "propriety" in all senses, and seems a little more interested in Painting than in Poetry. As to the latter, he is a good example of the devouring appetite for sense and fact which had seized on the critics of this time (save a few rebels) throughout Europe. The improbabilities of Tasso and of "Camoenus, the Homer and Virgil of the Portuguese," afflict him more, because they amuse him less, than they do in Voltaire's own case, and to any liberty with real or supposed history he is simply Rhadamanthine. "That which jars with probability—that which shocks Sense and Reason—can never be excused in Poetry." Mrs Barbauld and *The Ancient Mariner* sixty years before date: Dennis after Dennis's death !

Of Goldsmith as a critic little need be said, though his pen was not much less prolific in this than in other departments. *Goldsmith.* But the angel is too often absent, and Poor Poll distressingly in evidence. The *Inquiry into the Present State of Polite Learning in Europe* is simply "prodigious." It is admirably written—Macaulay owes something to its style, which he only hardened and brazened. The author apes the fashionable philosophastering of the time, and throws in cheap sciolism like the prince of journalists that he was. It is almost always interesting; it is, where it touches life, not literature, sometimes excellently acute; but there is scarcely a critical dictum in it which is other than ridiculous. So in the *Citizen of the World* the Author's Club is of course delightful; but why should a sneer at Drayton have been put in the mouth of Lien Chi Altangi? And the miscellaneous Essays, including the *Bee*, which contain so much of Goldsmith's best work, are perhaps the best evidences of his nullity here. When one thinks how little it would cost anybody of Goldsmith's genius (to find such an one I confess would cost more) to write a literary parallel to the magnificent *Reverie*, which would be even finer, it is enough to draw iron tears down the critic's cheek. Goldsmith on Taste, Poetry, Metaphor, &c.,[1] is still the Goldsmith of the *Inquiry*. His "Account of the Augustan Age,"[2] though much better, and (unless I mistake) resorted to by some recent critics as a source of criticism different from that mostly prevalent in the nineteenth century, has all the limitations of its own period. And the Essay on Versification,[3] though it contains expressions which, taken by themselves, might seem to show that Goldsmith had actually emancipated himself from the tyranny of the fixed number of syllables, contains others totally irreconcilable with these, supports English hexameters and sapphics,[4] and as a whole forces on us once more the reluctant belief that he simply had no clear ideas, no accurate knowledge, on the subject.

[1] Essays, xii.-xvii.
[2] *The Bee*, viii.
[3] Essay xviii.
[4] It is perhaps only fair to hope that this fancy, as later with Southey and others, was a blind motion for freedom. Yet Goldsmith commits himself to the hemistich theory of decasyllables.

Vicesimus Knox[1] is a useful figure in this critical Transition Period. A scholar and a schoolmaster, he had some of the *Vicesimus* advantages of the first state and some of the defects *Knox.* of the less gracious second, accentuated in both cases by the dying influences of a "classical" tradition which had not the slightest idea that it was moribund. He carries his admiration for Pope to such a point as to assure us somewhere that Pope was a man of exemplary piety and goodness, while Gay was "uncontaminated with the vices of the world," which is really more than somewhat blind, and more than a little kind, even if we admit that it is wrong to call Pope a bad man, and that Gay had only tolerable vices. He thinks, in his Fourteenth Essay on the "Fluctuations of Taste," that the Augustans "arrived at that standard of perfection which," &c.; that the imitators of Ariosto, Spenser, and the smaller poems of Milton are "pleasingly uncouth" [compare Scott, *infra*, on the metrical renaissance of Dyer], depreciates Gray, and dismisses the Elegy as "a confused heap of splendid ideas"; is certain that Milton's sonnets "bear no mark of his genius," and in discussing the versions of "the sensible[2] Sappho" decides that Catullus is much inferior to — Philips! "The Old English Poets [Essay Thirty-Nine] are deservedly forgotten." Chaucer, Gower, Lydgate, and Occleve "seem to have thought that rhyme was poetry, and even this constituent they applied with extreme negligence" — the one charge which is unfair against even Occleve, and which, in reference to Chaucer, is proof of utter ignorance. Patriotism probably made him more favourable to Dunbar, Douglas, and Lyndsay, though he groans over the necessity of a glossary in their case also. In fact, Knox is but a Johnson without the genius. Let it, however, be counted to him for righteousness that he defended classical education, including verse - writing, against its enemies, who even then imagined vain things.

John Scott of Amwell, once praised by good wits, now much forgotten, was a very respectable critic and a poet of "glimmer-

---

[1] *Essays, Moral and Literary*, 2nd ed., London, 1774, 8vo.

[2] This is perhaps the most delightfu'

instance in (English) existence of the change which has come over the meaning of the word.

ings." In fact, I am not at all sure that he does not deserve
Scott of Amwell. to be promoted and postponed to the next chapter, as a representative of the rising, not the falling, tide. His Essays on poetry [1] exhibit in a most interesting way the "know-not-what-to-think-of-it" state of public opinion about the later years of Johnson. He defends *Lycidas* against the Dictator; yet he finds fault with the "daystar" for acting both as a person and an orb of radiance, and admits the "incorrectness" of the poem, without giving us a hint of the nature or authority of "correctness." He boldly attacks the consecrated *Cooper's Hill*, and sets the rival eminence of Grongar against it, pronouncing Dyer "a sublime but strangely neglected poet," yet picking very niggling holes in this poet himself. He often anticipates, and oftener seems to be going to anticipate, Wordsworth, who no doubt owed him a good deal; yet he thinks Pope's famous epigram on Wit "the most concise and just definition of Poetry." In *Grongar Hill* itself he thinks the "admixture of metre [its second, certainly, if not its first great charm] rather displeasing to a nice ear"; and though he defends Gray against Knox, he is altogether yea-nay about *Windsor Forest*, and attacks Thomson's personifications, without remembering that Gray is at least an equal sinner, and without giving the author of the *Seasons*, and still more of the *Castle of Indolence*, any just compensation for his enthusiasm of nature. In fact, Scott is a man walking in twilight, who actually sees the line of dawn, but dares not step out into it. [2]

---

[1] *Critical Essays*, London, 1785, 8vo.

[2] I should like to return to Dennis, in order to notice briefly his comparatively early *Remarks on* Prince Arthur *and* Virgil (title abbreviated), London, 1696. It is, as it stands, of some elaboration; but its author tells us that he "meant" to do things which would have made it an almost complete Poetic from his point of view. It is pervaded with that refrain of "this *ought* to be" and "that *must* have been" to which I have referred in the text; and bristles with purely arbitrary preceptist statements, such as that Criticism cannot be ill-natured because Good Nature in man cannot be contrary to Justice and Reason; that a man must not like what he ought not to like—a doctrine underlying, of course, the whole Neo-classic teaching, and not that only; almost literally cropping up in Wordsworth; and the very formulation, in categorical-imperative, of La Harpe's "monstrous beauty." The book (in which poet and critic are very comfortably and equally yoked together) is full of agreeable things; and may possibly have suggested one of Swift's most exquisite pieces of irony in its contention that Mr Blackmore's Celestial Machines are directly contrary to the Doctrine of the Church of England.

INTERCHAPTER III.

ENGLISH Eighteenth‑Century criticism has a very notable advantage over Seventeenth and Sixteenth. In the earliest of the three, as we saw, criticism exists almost without a critic. Its authorities are either men of something less (to speak kindly) than the first rank as men of letters, or else they devote only a slight and passing attention to the subject. In the Seventeenth this is not quite so, for Dryden is a host in himself. But he is also a host almost *by* himself : a general without an army.

In the Eighteenth the case is far more altered, in regard both to persons and to methods and opportunities of treatment. Addison, Johnson, Pope, are all dictators of literature, whose fame and authority, in the case at least of the first and last, go far beyond their own country—and they are all critics. Moreover, criticism has enormously *multiplied* its appearances and opportunities of appearance : it has, in a manner, become popular. The critical Review — the periodical by means of which it is possible, and becomes easy, to give critical account of the literature, not merely of the past but of the present— becomes common. The critic as such is no longer regarded as a mere pedant ; he at least attempts to take his place as a literary man of the world.

But while this alteration and extension applies to almost all Europe, the contribution of England is specially interesting as working towards a reconstruction as well as a continuation of criticism. In consequence, very mainly, of Dryden's own magnificent championship of Shakespeare and Milton, it was, by the beginning of the eighteenth century, felt in England that these two older writers at any rate had to be reckoned

with; while Chaucer also had the same powerful recommendation, and Spenser had never lost the affection of the fit, though
for a time they might be few. With these four to be somehow or other—by hook or by crook—taken into consideration,
it was impossible for the worst harm to be done; and the
peculiarities of the English character, combined with the more
vigorous condition of English creative literature, helped the
compromise to work. It might have been dangerous if
Johnson had written the *Lives* at the age which was Pope's
when he wrote the *Essay on Criticism;* but this danger also the
Fortune of England—kindest of Goddesses, and most abused in
her kindness, yet justified of Fate !—averted.

Still, as we saw, Neo-Classicism is undoubtedly the accepted
orthodoxy of the time. If that draft confession of Faith, which
has been sketched in a former page, had been laid before an
assembly of the leading men of letters, not many Englishmen
would have refused to accept it. At the same time—until,
towards the later years of the century, the "alarums and
excursions" of the Romantic rising recalled the orthodox to
strictness—a more searching examination would have revealed
serious defections and latitudinarianisms. Pope was perhaps
the most orthodox neo-classic, in criticism as in creation, of
the greater men of letters of the time; but Pope was fond of
Spenser. Addison had never thoroughly cleared his mind up
about criticism; but many things in him point the Romantic
way, and we know that some of the more orthodox thought
him weak and doubtful. And we have seen how the great Dr
Samuel Johnson, though he resisted and recovered himself, was
at least once within appreciable distance of that precipice of
"judging by the event," over which, when a Classic once lets
himself slip, he falls for ever and for ever through the Romantic
void.

But all these things were as the liberalities of a securely
established orthodoxy, estated and endowed, dreading no disturbance, and able to be generous to others—even to indulge
itself a little in licence and peccadillo. Everywhere but
in England the vast majority of men, and even in England
all but a very small minority, had no doubt about the general

principles of the Neo-classic Creed. They still judged by
Rules and Kinds; they still had the notion that you must
generalise, always generalise; they still believed that, in some
way or other, Homer and Virgil — especially Virgil — had
exhausted the secrets of Epic, and almost of poetry; and, above
all, they were entirely unprepared to extend patient and
unbiassed judgment to something acknowledged, and acknowledging itself, to be *new*. On the contrary, they must still be
vindicating even things which they liked, but which appeared
to them to be novel, on the score of their being so very like the
old—as we saw in the case of Blair and *Ossian*.

The Nemesis of this their Correctness, as far as creation is
concerned, in prose to some extent, but still more in verse, has
been described over and over again by a thousand critics and
literary historians. The highest and most poetical poetry they
could not write at all—except when they had, like Collins,
Smart, Cowper, and Blake, a little not merely of *furor poeticus*,
but of actual insanity in their constitution. In their own
chosen way they could at best achieve the really poetical
rhetoric, but at the same time the strictly rhetorical poetry,
of Pope, and, in a lower range, of Akenside. For prose they
had the luck to discover, in the Novel, a Kind which, never
having been to any great extent practised before, was a Kind
practically without rules, and so could make or neglect its
rules for itself. In another, not quite so new, their performance gave striking instance of their limitations. The Periodical
Essay was a thing of almost infinite possibilities: but because
it had happened at first to be written in a certain form by
persons of genius, they turned practice into Kind and Rule
once more, and for nearly the whole century went on imitating
the *Spectator*.

In Criticism itself the effects were not wholly different, though
of course to some extent apparently dissimilar. We have seen
how, during the sixteenth and seventeenth centuries, the necessary and ineluctable set of the critical current towards full
and free "judging of authors" seems to have been resisted by
a sort of unconscious recalcitrance on the part of critics; yet
how they are drawn nearer and nearer to it, and, in Dryden's

case at any rate, achieve admirable results. By the eighteenth, in all countries, the tendency becomes irresistible. The interest in literature, the bent and occupations of men of letters great and small, the new institution of periodicals—all combine to strengthen it: and every kind of critical estimate, from the elaborate literary history to the brief review, begins to be written, and is written, ever more copiously.

This was what criticism wanted; and it could not but do good. Yet the results illustrated, as mere abstract treatises never could have done, the deficiencies of the common critical theory. The writers save themselves, as a rule, from the worst mistakes by simply ignoring that of which they are ignorant. But in regard to the things with which they do deal the inadequacy and the hamper of their theory are sufficiently apparent.

Of course the deficiencies of Eighteenth-century criticism are to be easily matched with other, and sometimes opposite, deficiencies in other times. It takes considerably more pains to get at something like a real appreciation of its subject, something more than a bare reference to schedule, than had been the case, either in ancient times or in the two centuries immediately preceding. It is very much better furnished with a critical theory (whether good or bad does not at the moment matter) than has usually been the case with Criticism from the early years of the nineteenth century to the early years of the twentieth. It is not even intentionally ignorant—its ignorance only proceeds from a mistaken estimate of things as worth or not worth knowing; and there is rarely to be found in it the bland assumption which has been not entirely unknown later, that "I like this," or perhaps rather, "I choose to say I like this," will settle everything. But it combines, in a fashion already perhaps sufficiently illustrated, the awkwardness of dogmatism and of compromise; and it is certainly more exposed to those two terrible questions, "Why?" and "Why Not?" which are the Monkir and Nakir of all critics and all criticism, than the criticism of any other period. It is difficult to see how a critic such as Dennis could give any reasons for admiring Shakespeare at all, save ethical ones; and it is quite

certain that a persistent *Te sequar* with the "Why Not?" will
dispose of almost all the stock eighteenth-century objections
both to Shakespeare and to all other suspected persons. The
anti-Shakespearians had the advantage over their own adversaries of being at least consistent.

The theory not merely of the *authades kallos*, the "head-
strong beauty," but of the "monstrous beauty"—the beauty
which is beautiful but has no business to be so, the miracle-
working power which does work miracles, but is to be forbidden
as Black Magic, because it does not work them according to the
rules—may seem itself so monstrous as to be a patent reduction to the absurd. In fact it acted as such. Yet the logic
of it is undeniable. It had all along been the unspoken
word, but the word that ought to have been spoken, and had
to be spoken some day. Nor need we grudge the admission
that it was in a certain sense better than the practice (which
had been often resorted to before, and which has not seldom
been resorted to since) of denying the beauty altogether, with
the possible result of being, after a time, honestly unable to
see it.

At the same time, the merits of Neo-Classicism deserve
another word or two. The chief perhaps is, that it provided
an *orthodoxy*—and that is never a wholly bad thing. Even if it
is not as really *ortho*dox, as really *right* as its opponents, it has
merits which they can rarely claim. It has no temptations
for the clever fool, who is perhaps on the whole the most pestilent, intellectually, of human beings. It demands a certain
amount of self-abnegation, which is always a good thing. It
does not perhaps really offer any greater temptation to the
merely stupid than does the cheap heterodoxy of other times.
Above all, it directly tends to a certain intellectual calmness—
to an absence of fuss, and worry, and pother, which is certainly
not one of the least characteristics of the Judge. At all times
the wise man would rather be orthodox than not; and at most
times, though not quite at all, the wisest men have been
orthodox, if only because they have recognised that every
opinion has some amount of truth in it, and that this truth,

plus the advantages of orthodoxy just mentioned, is greatest, and should prevail.

This will be recognised by all fair-minded persons as a handsome allowance in any case; it is surely a particularly handsome allowance when the arbiter happens not to be a partisan of the orthodoxy in question. And it is quite sincere. The present writer has emerged from the serious and consecutive examination of " classical " critics, necessary for the writing of this History, with a distinctly higher opinion of them generally, with a higher opinion in most cases in particular, than he held previously on piecemeal and imperfect acquaintance. Yet if we take the true reading of *illud Syrianum*, "Judex damnatur [*capitis*] cum [*in*]nocens [*culpatur vel minime*]," then the case of the criticism with which we have been dealing becomes somewhat parlous. It is all the worse because its worsening is gradual and continuous. The sins of the earliest Renaissance criticism are sins chiefly of neglect, and are not as a rule aggravated by commission; while its merits are very great. We could have done nothing without it: at best we should have had to do for ourselves all that it has done for us. But the bad side of the matter betrays itself in the code-making of the seventeenth century; it is but imperfectly and unsatisfactorily disguised in the compromises of the earlier eighteenth; and it appears in all its deformity in its late eighteenth-century recrudescence, the worst faults of which were seen rather in France than in England, but which were not absent in such men as Knox or Gifford, or even in Johnson sometimes.

And these faults came from the absence of a wide enough collection of instances from the past, and of an elastic and tolerant system of trial and admission for the present and future.

The compiling, in however piecemeal and haphazard a way, of such a collection, and the construction, under whatever similar limitations, of such a system, were the necessary conditions precedent to what is sometimes called "Modern," sometimes "Romantic," Criticism. Both these terms may be much controverted: but the controversies are rather too general for the present volume. We have already seen what its predecessor was, in general, and that in the usual general, gradual, incalculable way, opposition to it, conscious or unconscious, began to grow up at different times and in different places. This opposition was a plant of early though slow and fitful growth in England, but it does not follow that we can put the finger on this and that person as having " begun " the new movement. Such an opinion is always tempting to not too judicious inquirers, and there has been no lack of books on " Romanticism in the Classics," and the like. The fact, of course, simply is that everything human exists essentially or potentially in the men of every time ; and that you may not only find books in the running brooks but (what appears at first more contradictory) dry stones in them : while, on the other hand, founts of water habitually gush from the midst of the driest rock. Indagation of the kind is always treacherous, and has to be conducted with a great deal of circumspection.

It would be difficult to find an author who illustrates this danger and treachery better than the case of Butler (who for that reason has been postponed for treatment here) on Dryden, Rymer, Denham, and the cavalier poet Benlowes. The author of *Hudibras* was born not long after Milton, and nearly twenty years before Dryden, who outlived him by the same space. His great poem did not give much room for critical utterances in literature ; but the *Genuine Remains*[1] are full of it in separate places, both verse and prose. Take these singly, and you may make Butler out to be, not merely a critic, but half a dozen critics. In perhaps the best known of his minor pieces, the *Repartees between Cat and Puss,* he satirises " Heroic " Plays, and is therefore clearly for " the last age," as also in the savage and admirable " On Critics who Judge Modern Plays precisely by the Rules of the Ancients," which has been reasonably, or

---

[1] Published, not entirely, by Thyer of Manchester in 1759 (2 vols.) A handsome reprint of 1827 gives only a few of the prose "Characters": more of these, but not the whole, were given by Mr H. Morley in his *Character - Writing of the Seventeenth* *Century* (London, 1891). The verse remains may be found in Chalmers or in the Aldine (vol. ii., London, 1893), and the whole is now (1910) in the Cambridge edition (1908) of the *Characters and Note-Books.*

certainly, thought to be directed against Rymer's blasphemy of
Beaumont and Fletcher, published two years before Butler's
death.   The satirist's references and illustrations (as in that to
"the laws of good King Howel's days") are sometimes too
Caroline to be quotable; but the force and sweep of his protest is simply glorious.   The *Panegyric on Sir John Denham*
is chiefly personal; but if Butler had been convinced that
Cooper's Hill was the *ne plus ultra* of English poetry he could
hardly have written it: and though the main victim of "To a
Bad Poet" has not been identified,[1] the lines—

> "For so the rhyme be at the verse's end,
>   No matter whither all the rest does tend"—

could scarcely have been written except against the new poetry.
The "Pindaric Ode on Modern Critics" is chiefly directed
against the general critical vice of snarling, and the passages
on critics and poets in the *Miscellaneous Thoughts* follow suit.
But if we had only the verse *Remains* we should be to some
extent justified in taking Butler, if not for a precursor of the
new Romanticism, at any rate for a rather strenuous defender
of the old.

But turn to the *Characters*.   Most of these that deal with
literature are in the general vein which the average seventeenth - century character - writer took from Theophrastus,
though few put so much salt of personal wit into this as Butler.
In "A Small Poet" the earlier pages might be aimed at almost
anybody from Dryden himself (whom Butler, it is said, did not
love) down to Flecknoe.   But there is only one name mentioned in the piece; and that name, which is made the object
of a furious and direct attack, lightened by some of the brightest flashes of Butler's audacious and acrid humour, is the
name of Edward Benlowes.[2]   Now, that Benlowes is a person

---

[1] A blank rhyme indicates "Howard"
—whether Edward or Robert does not
matter.   But another blank requires a
trisyllable to fill it.

[2] Benlowes is a warning to "illustrated poets."   It pleased him to have
his main book (*Theophila, or Love's
Sacrifice :* London, 1652, folio) splen-

didly decorated by Hollar and others;
and the consequence is that copies of it
are very rare, and generally mutilated
when found.   (The present writer included it in the first volume of *Minor
Poets of the Caroline Period* (Oxford.
1905).)

taillable et corvéable à merci et à miséricorde by any critical oppressor, nobody who has read him can deny.   He is as extravagant as Crashaw without so much poetry, and as Cleveland without so much cleverness.   But he is a poet, and a "metaphysical" poet (as Butler was himself in another way), and an example, though a rather awful example, of that "poetic fury" which makes Elizabethan poetry.   Yet Butler is more savage with him than with Denham

The fact is that Butler's criticism is merely the occasional determination of a man of active genius and satiric temper to matters literary.   Absurdities strike him from whatever school they come; and he lashes them unmercifully whensoever and whencesoever they present themselves.   But he has no general creed: he speaks merely to his brief as public prosecutor of the ridiculous, and also as a staunch John Bull.   If he had been writing at the time when his *Remains* were first actually published, it is exceedingly probable that he would have " horsed" Gray as pitilessly as he horses Benlowes; if he had been writing sixty years later still, that he would have been as "savage and Tartarly" to Keats and Shelley, or seventy years later, to Tennyson, as the *Quarterly* itself. This is not criticism: and we must look later and more carefully before we discern any real revolution in literary taste.

It is even very unsafe to attempt to discover much definite and intentional precursorship in Addison, who was born two full generations later than Butler.   There is no need to repeat what has been said of what seems to me misconception as to his use of the word Imagination: nor is this the point which is principally aimed at here.   But the more we examine Addison's critical utterances, whether we agree with Hurd or not that they are "shallow," we shall, I think, be forced to conclude that any depth they may have has nothing to do with Romanticism. Addison likes Milton, no doubt, because he is a sensible man and a good critic, as a general reason.   But when we come to investigate special ones we shall find that he likes him rather because he himself is a Whig, a pupil of Dryden, and a religious man—nay, perhaps even because he really does think that

Milton carries out the classical idea of Epic—than because of Milton's mystery, his "romantic vague," his splendour of diction and verse and imagery. So, too, the admiration of *Chevy Chase* is partly a whim or a joke, partly determined by the fact that at that time the Whigs were the "Jingoes," and that *Chevy Chase* is very pugnacious and very patriotic. Nowhere, from the articles on True and False Wit to the Imagination papers, do we find any real sense of unrest or dissatisfaction with the accepted theory of poetry. There is actually more in Prior, with all his profanation of the *Nut-browne Maid* and his distortions of the Spenserian stanza.

And Dryden himself, Dryden whose method led straight to the Promised Land, and whose utterances show that he occasionally saw it afar off, came too early to feel any very conscious desire of setting out on the pilgrimage of discovery.

But in critical as in other history, readers will rarely find sharp and decided turns, assignable to definite hours and particular men. It is a part of the Neo-Classic error itself to assume some definite goal of critical perfection towards which all things tend, and which, when you have attained it, permits you to take no further trouble except of imitation and repetition. Just as you never know what new literary form the human genius may take, and can therefore never lay down any absolute and final schedule of literary kinds, and of literary perfection within these kinds, so you can never shape the set of the prevalent taste, and you can never do much more than give the boat the full benefit of the current by dexterous rowing and steering. Indeed, as we have seen, the taste in criticism and the taste in creation unite, or diverge, or set dead against each other in a manner quite incalculable, and only interpretable as making somehow for the greater glory of Literature. Somewhere about the time to which we have harked back—the meeting of the seventeenth and eighteenth centuries, or a little later, or much later, as the genius of different countries and persons would have it — a veering of the wind, an eddy of the current, *did* take place. And it is of this and of its consequences we have now to give an account.

CHAPTER V.

THE ENGLISH PRECURSORS OF ROMANTICISM.

THE FIRST GROUP—MEDIÆVAL REACTION—GRAY—PECULIARITY OF HIS
CRITICAL POSITION—THE LETTERS—THE 'OBSERVATIONS' ON ARISTO-
PHANES AND PLATO—THE 'METRUM'—THE LYDGATE NOTES—SHENSTONE
—PERCY—THE WARTONS—JOSEPH'S 'ESSAY ON POPE'—THE 'ADVEN-
TURER' ESSAYS — THOMAS WARTON ON SPENSER — HIS 'HISTORY OF
ENGLISH POETRY'—HURD: HIS COMMENTARY ON ADDISON—THE
HORACE — THE DISSERTATIONS — OTHER WORKS — THE 'LETTERS ON
CHIVALRY AND ROMANCE'—THEIR DOCTRINE—HIS REAL IMPORTANCE
—ALLEGED IMPERFECTIONS OF THE GROUP—STUDIES IN PROSODY—
JOHN MASON: HIS 'POWER OF NUMBERS' IN PROSE AND POETRY—
MITFORD: HIS 'HARMONY OF LANGUAGE'—IMPORTANCE OF PROSODIC
INQUIRY — STERNE AND THE STOP-WATCH — ÆSTHETICS AND THEIR
INFLUENCE — SHAFTESBURY — HUME — EXAMPLES OF HIS CRITICAL
OPINIONS—HIS INCONSISTENCY—BURKE ON THE SUBLIME AND BEAUTI-
FUL — THE SCOTTISH ÆSTHETIC-EMPIRICS: ALISON — THE 'ESSAY ON
TASTE'—ITS CONFUSIONS—AND ARBITRARY ABSURDITIES—AN INTERIM
CONCLUSION ON THE ÆSTHETIC MATTER—THE STUDY OF LITERATURE
—THE STUDY OF SHAKESPEARE — SPENSER — CHAUCER — ELIZABETHAN
MINORS—NOTE: T. HAYWARD—MIDDLE AND OLD ENGLISH—INFLUENCE
OF ENGLISH ABROAD.

WE have already, in the last chapter, said that in England, about
the middle of the eighteenth century, the tables of criticism
turned, and that a company of critics, not large, not as a rule
very great men of letters, began slowly, tentatively, with a
great deal of rawness, and blindness, and even backsliding, to
grope for a catholic and free theory of literature, and especially
of poetry. We are now to examine this group [1] more narrowly
With the not quite certainly to be allowed exception of Gray

---

[1] One celebrated person, much associated with it in some ways, and
referred to in passing above, will not
appear here. Horace Walpole did, for
such a carpet knight, real service in
the general movement; but he was a
literary critic *pour rire* only. His
admiration of Mme. de Sévigné is not
really much more to his credit than his
sapient dictum (to Bentley, Feb. 23,

no one of them could pretend to the first rank in the literature of the time; and most of them (Hurd and Percy were the chief exceptions) did not live to see, even at the extreme verge of life, the advent of the champions who were to carry their principles into practice. But they were the harbingers of the dawn, little as in some cases (perhaps in all) they comprehended the light that faintly and fitfully illuminated them beforehand.

Three of the writers of this class whom it is necessary to name here have been alluded to already; the others were
The first group. Shenstone and the Wartons. As so often happens in similar cases, it is exceedingly difficult to assign exact priority, for mere dates of publication are always misleading; and in this case, from their close juxtaposition, they almost of themselves give the warning that they are not to be trusted. How early, in his indolent industry at Cambridge, Gray had come to a Pisgah-sight of the true course of English poetry; Shenstone, in pottering and maundering at the Leasowes, to glimpses of the same; Percy and Shenstone again to their design, afterwards executed by Percy alone, of publishing the *Reliques;* the Wartons to their revolutionary views of Pope on the one side and Spenser on the other; Hurd to his curious mixture of true and false *aperçus,*—it is really impossible to say. The last-named, judging all his work together, may seem the least likely, early as some of that work is, to have struck out a distinctly original way for himself; but all, no doubt, were really driven, *nolentes volentes,* conscious or unconscious, by the Time-Spirit.

The process which the Spirit employed for effecting this great change was a simple one; indeed, we have almost summed up his inspiration in the oracular admonition,
Mediæval reaction. *Antiquam exquirite matrem.* For more than two hundred years literary criticism had been insolently or ignorantly neglecting this mother, the Middle Age—now with a tacit assumption that this period *ought* to be neglected now with an open and expressed scorn of it. But, as usually

1755) that *A Midsummer Night's Dream* is "forty times more nonsensical than the worst translation of an Italian opera-book." "Notre Dame des Rochers" talked of subjects that interested him in a manner which he could understand: Shakespeare was neither "Gothic" nor modern. So he liked the one and despised the other—uncritically in both cases.

happens, a return had begun to be made just when the opposite progress seemed to have reached its highest point. Dryden himself had "translated" and warmly praised Chaucer; Addison had patronised *Chevy Chase*. But before the death of Pope much larger and more audacious explorations had been attempted. In Scotland—whether consciously stung or not by the disgrace of a century almost barren of literature —Watson the printer [1] and Allan Ramsay [2] had, in 1706–11 and 1724–40, unearthed a good deal of old poetry. In England the anonymous compiler [3] of the *Ballads* of 1723 had done something, and Oldys the antiquary, under the shelter of "Mrs Cooper's" petticoat, had done more with the *Muses' Library* of 1737. These examples [4] were followed out, not without a little cheap contempt from those who would be in the fashion, and knew not that this fashion had received warning. But they *were* followed, and their most remarkable result, in criticism and creation combined, is the work of Gray.

We have not so very many fairer figures in our "fair" herd than Gray, though the fairness may be somewhat like that of

Gray. Crispa,[5] visible chiefly to a lover of criticism itself. His actual critical performance is, in proportion, scantier even than his poetical; and the scantiness may at first sight seem even stranger, since a man can but poetise when he can, but may, if he has the critical faculty, criticise almost when he will and has the opportunity. That opportunity (again at first sight) Gray may seem to have had, as scarcely another man in our whole long history has had it. He had nothing else to do, and was not inclined to do anything else. He had sufficient means, no professional avocations, the knowledge, the circumstances, the *locale*, the wits, the taste, even the velleity—everything but, in the full sense, the will. This indeed he might, in all

[1] *Choice Collection of Scots Poems.* In three Parts. Reprinted in 1 vol. (Glasgow, 1869).

[2] *The Evergreen, The Tea-Table Miscellany.* Reprinted in 4 vols. (Glasgow, 1876).

[3] Said to be Ambrose Philips. If so, the book, despite its uncritical and heterogeneous character, is "Namby-Pamby's" best work by far. There is a reprint, without date (3 vols.), among the very valuable series of such things which were published by Pearson *c.* 1870.

[4] For more of them, see the latter part of this chapter.

[5] Ausonius, Ep. 77.

circumstances and at all times, have lacked, for Mr Arnold showed himself no philosophic student of humanity when he said that at the date of Milton, or at the date of Keats, Gray would have been a different man. His *work* would doubtless have been a different work; but that is another matter. At all times, probably, Gray would have had the same fastidiousness, the same liability to be "put off"; and if his preliminary difficulties had been lightened by the provision, in times nearer our own, of the necessary rough-hewing and first research by others, yet this very provision would probably have prevented him from pursuing what he would have disdainfully regarded as a second-hand business. We may—we must—regret that he never finished that *History of English Poetry* which he hardly began, that he never attempted the half-dozen other things of the kind, which he was better equipped for doing than any man then living, and than all but three or four men who have lived since. But the regret must be tempered by a secret consciousness that on the whole he probably would *not* have done them, let time and chance and circumstance have favoured him never so lavishly.

Yet this very idiosyncrasy of limitation and hamper in him made, in a sense, for criticism; inasmuch as there are two kinds of critical temperament, neither of which *Peculiarity of his critical position.* could be spared. There is the eager, strenuous, almost headlong critical disposition of a Dryden, which races like a conflagration[1] over all the field it can cover; and there is the hesitating, ephectic, intermittent temperament of a Gray, which directs an intense and all-dissolving, but ill-maintained heat at this and that special part of the subject. In what is called, and sometimes is, "originality," this latter temperament is perhaps the more fertile of the two, and Gray has it in an almost astounding measure. Great as was his own reading, a man might, I think, be as well read as himself without discovering any real indebtedness of his, except to a certain general influence of literary study in many times and tongues. He knew indeed, directly or indirectly, most of the other agents in the quiet and gradual revolution which was coming on English poetic and literary taste; but he

---

[1] With acknowledgments to Longinus.

was much in advance of all of them in time. Well as he was read in Italian, he nowhere, I think, cites Gravina, in whom there was something to put him on new tracks; and though he was at least equally well read in French, and does cite Fontenelle, it is not for any of the critical germs which may be discovered in that elusive oracle. The one modern language to which he seems to have paid little or no attention was German,[1] where the half-blind strugglings of the Zürich school might have had some stimulus for him. Whatever he did, alone he did it; and though the volume of his strictly critical observations (not directed to mere common tutorial scholarship) would, if printed consecutively, perhaps not fill twenty—certainly not fifty—pages of this book, its virtue, intrinsic and suggestive, surpasses that of libraries full not merely of Rymers but of (critical) Popes.

From the very first these observations have, to us, no uncertain sound. In a letter to West,[2] when the writer was *The Letters.* about six-and-twenty, we find it stated with equal dogmatism, truth, and independence of authority that "the language of the age is never the language of poetry except among the French, whose verse, where the thought or image does not support it, differs nothing from prose," with a long and valuable citation, illustrating this defence of "poetic diction," and no doubt thereby arousing the wrath of Wordsworth. Less developed, but equally important and equally original, is the subsequent description of our language as not being "a settled thing" like the French. Gray, indeed, makes this with explicit reference only to the revival of archaisms, which he defends; but, as we see from other places as well as by natural deduction, it extends to reasonable neologisms also. In this respect Gray is with all the best original writers, from Chaucer and Langland downwards, but against a respectably mistaken body of critics who would fain not merely introduce the caste system into English, but, like

---

[1] Mr Gosse, I find, agrees with me on this point. It is well known that ignorance of German was almost (Chesterfield, I think, in encouraging his son to the study, says roundly that it was quite) universal among Englishmen in the mid-eighteenth century.

[2] Gray's *Works* (ed. Gosse, 4 vols., London, 1884), ii. p. 106, Letter xliv., dated April, without the year; but the next gives it : 1742.

Sir Boyle Roche, make it hereditary in this caste not to have any children.

This same letter contains some of Gray's best-known criticisms, in his faint praise of *Joseph Andrews* and his warm appreciation of Marivaux and Crébillon. I am not quite certain that, in this last, Gray intended any uncomplimentary comparison, or that he meant anything more than a defence of the novel generally—a defence which itself deserves whatever crown is appropriated to critical merit, inasmuch as the novel had succeeded to the place of Cinderella of Literature. However, both Fielding and Smollett were probably too boisterous for Gray, who could appreciate Sterne better, though he disliked "Tristram's" faults.

But the fact is that it is not in criticisms of his contemporaries, or indeed in definite critical appreciation at all, that Gray's strength lies. For any defects in the former he has, of course, the excuse that his was a day of rather small things in poetry; but, once more, it is not quite certain that circumstances would have much altered the case. We must remember that Mr Arnold also does not come very well out of this test; and indeed, that second variety of the critical temperament which we have defined above is not conducive to enthusiasm.[1] It is, of course, unlucky that Gray's personal affection for Mason directed his most elaborate praises to a tenth-rate object; but it is fair to remember that he does reprehend in Mason faults—such as excessive personification —which were not merely those of his friend, the husband of "dead Maria," but his own. It is a thousand pities that, thanks to Mason himself, we have the similar criticisms of Beattie only in a garbled condition; but they too are sound and sensible, if *very* merciful. The mercy, however, which Gray showed perhaps too plentifully to friends and relations he did not extend to others. That the "frozen grace" of Akenside appealed little to him is less remarkable than his famous pair of judgments on "Joe" Warton and Collins.

[1] Gray has been upbraided with his description (in part at least) of Boswell's Paoli-book as "a dialogue between a green goose and a hero." It does him no discredit; in fact, he might have summarised the whole of Boswell's work, had he lived to see it, as that of a green goose (a thing like him more admirable dead than alive) with a semi-heroic love for heroes.

The coupling itself, moreover, and even the prophecy that "neither will last," are less extraordinary (for the very keenest eyes, when unassisted by "the firm perspective of the past," will err in this way, and Joseph's *Odes* are, as his friend, Dr Johnson, said of the rumps and kidneys, "very pretty little things") than the ascription of "a bad ear" to Collins. This is certainly "a term inexplicable to the Muse." It was written in 1746. Five years later an undated but clearly datable letter to Walpole contains (lxxxiv., ed. cit.) in a notice of Dodsley's *Miscellany*, quite a sheaf of criticisms. That of Tickell—"a poor short-winded imitator of Addison, who had himself not above three or four notes in poetry, sweet enough indeed, like those of a German flute, but such as soon tire and satiate the ear with their frequent return"—is very notable for this glance backward on the great Mr Addison, though it would have been unjust to Tickell if (which does not quite appear) it had been intended to include his fine elegy on Addison himself, and the still finer one on Cadogan.[1] Gray is quite amiable to *The Spleen* and *The Schoolmistress*, and *London;* justly assigns to Dyer (the Dyer of *Grongar Hill*, not of *The Fleece*) "more of poetry in his imagination than almost any of our number," but unjustly calls him "rough and injudicious," and brushes most of the rest away, not too superciliously. A year later (December 1752, to Wharton) he grants to Hall's Satires "fulness of spirit and poetry; as much of the first as Dr Donne, and far more of the latter." In the elaborate "buckwashing" of Mason's *Caractacus* ode, which occupies great part of the very long letter of December 19, 1756, there is a passage of great importance on Epic and Lyric style, which exhibits as well perhaps as anything else the independence, and at the same time the transitional consistency, of Gray's criticism.

He says first (which is true, and which no rigidly orthodox Neo-Classic would or could have admitted): "The true lyric style, with all its flights of fancy ornaments, heightening of expression, and harmony of sound, is in its nature superior to every other style." Then he says that this is just the cause why it could not be borne in a work of great length; then

---

[1] I am well aware that the "parallel-passagers" have tried their jaws on these.

that the epic "therefore assumed graver colours," and only stuck on a diamond borrowed from her sister here and there; then that it is "natural and delightful" to pass from the graver stuff to the diamond, and then that to pass from lyric to epic is to drop from verse to mere prose. All of which seems to argue a curious inequality in clearing the mind from cant. It *is* true, as has been said, that Lyric is the highest style. But surely the reason why this height cannot be kept is the weakness, not of human receptivity but of human productiveness. Give us an *Iliad* at the pitch of the best chorus of the *Agamemnon*, and we will gladly see whether we can bear it or not. Again, if you can pass from the dress to the diamond, why not pass from the diamond to the dress? It is true that in Mason's case the diamonds were paste, and bad paste; but that does not affect the argument. When, in still a later letter (clxii.) to the same "Skroddles"[1] he lays it down that "extreme conciseness of expression, yet pure, perspicuous, and musical is one of the grand beauties of lyric poetry," we must accentuate *one of the*. But there is a bombshell for Neo-Classicism in cvii., still to "Skroddles." "I insist that sense is nothing in poetry, but according to the dress she wears and the scene she appears in."

Gray's attitude to *Ossian* is interesting, but very much what we should have expected. He was bribed by its difference from the styles of which he was weary; but he seems from the very first to have had qualms (to which he did some violence, without quite succeeding, in order to stifle them) as to its genuineness.

No intelligent lover of the classics, whose love is not limited to them, can fail to regret that by very far the larger bulk of Gray's critical *Observations* is directed to Aristophanes and Plato. The annotator is not incompetent, and the annotated are supremely worthy of his labours; but the work was not specially in need of doing, and there have been very large numbers of men as

The Observations on Aristophanes and Plato.

---

[1] After all, he may be forgiven much apparent over-valuation of Mason for this name. Whatever its meaning between the friends, it "speaks" the author of *Elfrida* and *Caractacus*, and the *Monologues* and the *Odes*, and all but those lines of the epitaph on his wife which Gray wrote for him. "To skroddle" should have been naturalised for "to write minor poetry."

well or better qualified to do it. Such things as this—*Aves*, 1114 : "These were plates of brass with which they shaded the heads of statues to guard them from the weather and the birds "—are things which we do not want from a Gray at all. They are the business of that harmless drudge, the lexicographer, in general, of a competent fifth-form master editing the play, in particular. But there was probably at that time not a single man in Europe equally qualified by natural gifts and by study to deliver really critical and comparative opinions on literature, to discuss the history and changes of English, and the like. Nor has there probably at any date been any man better qualified for this, having regard to the conditions of his own time and country. One cannot, then, but feel it annoying that a life, not long but by no means very short, and devoted exclusively to literary leisure, should have resulted, as far as this special vocation of the author is concerned, in nothing more than some eighty small pages of Dissertation devoted to English metres and to the Poems of Lydgate.

Let us, however, rather be thankful for what we have got, and examine it, such as it is, with care.

In the very first words of the *Metrum* it is curious and delightful to see a man, at this early period, cutting right and left at the error of the older editors, who calmly shoved in, or left out, words and syllables to make what they thought correct versification for Chaucer, and at the other error committed by the majority of philologists to-day in holding that Chaucer's syntax, accidence, and orthography were as precise as those of a writer in the school of the French Academy. Even more refreshing are, on the one hand, his knowledge and heed of Puttenham, and, on the other, his correction of Puttenham's doctrine of the fixed Cæsura, his admissions of this in the case of the Alexandrine, and his quiet demonstration that the admission of it in the decasyllable and octosyllable would make havoc of our best poetry. The contrast of this reasonable method and just conclusion, not merely with the ignorant or overbearing dogmatism of Bysshe half a century earlier, but with the perversity, in the face of light and knowledge, of Guest a century later, is as remarkable as anything in the history of English criticism.

The Metrum.

Gray, of course, was fallible. He entangles himself rather on the subject of "Riding Rhyme"; and though he, first (I think) of all English writers, notices the equivalenced dimeter iambics of Spenser's *Oak and Briar*, and compares Milton's octosyllables with them, he goes wrong by saying that this is the *only* English metre in which such a liberty of choice is allowed, and more wrong still in bringing Donne's well-known ruggedness under this head. And he does not allow himself to do more than glance at the Classical-metre craze, his remarks on which would have been very interesting.

His subsequent analysis of "measures," with the chief books or poems in which they are used, is of very great interest, but as it is a mere table it hardly lends itself to comment, though it fills nearly twenty pages. The conclusion, however, is important, and, without undue guessing, gives us fair warrant for inferring that Gray would have had much (and not a favourable much) to say on the contemporary practice he describes if the table had been expanded into a dissertation. And the table itself, with its notes, shows that though his knowledge of Middle English before Chaucer was necessarily limited, yet he knew and had drawn right conclusions from Robert of Gloucester and Robert of Brunne, *The Owl and the Nightingale*, the early English Life of St Margaret, and the *Poema Morale*.[1]

His observations on "the pseudo-Rhythmus" (which odd and misleading term simply means Rhyme), with the shorter appendices on the same subject, present a learned and judicious summary of the facts as then known.

The criticism on John Lydgate which closes Gray's critical *dossier* might have been devoted to a more interesting subject, *The Lydgate Notes.* but they enable us to see what the average quality of the *History* would have been. And they certainly go, in scheme and quality, very far beyond any previous literary history of any country with which I am acquainted. The article (as we may call it) is made up of a

---

[1] As printed in Mr Gosse's edition he is made to say that the *Moral Ode* was written "almost two hundred years *after* Chaucer's time." The sense, however, as well as the use of the word "Semi-Saxon," shows that he meant "before," so that "after" must be a slip, either of his own pen or of the later press.

judicious mixture of biography, account of books (in both cases,
of course, as far as known to the writer only), citation, exposition of points of interest in subject, history, manners, &c.,
criticisms of poetical characteristics in the individual, and now
and then critical *excursus* of a more general kind suggested by
the subject. In one place, indeed, Gray does introduce Homer
in justification of Lydgate : but no one will hesitate to do this
now and then ; and it is quite clear that he does not do it from
any delusion as to a cut-and-dried pattern, or set of patterns,
to which every poem, new or old, was bound to conform.

And to this we have to add certain facts which, if not
critical utterances, speak as few such utterances have done—
the novelty of Gray's original English poetry, and his selection
of Welsh and Scandinavian originals for translation and imitation. These things were themselves unspoken criticism of the
most important kind on the literary habits and tastes of his
country, and of Europe at large. The, to us, almost unintelligible puzzlement of his contemporaries—the "hard as Greek"
of the excellent Garrick, and the bewilderment of the three
lords at York races, establish [1] the first point ; as for the
second, it establishes itself. To these outlying languages and
literatures nobody had paid any attention whatever previously ; [2]
they were now not merely admitted to literary attention, but
actually allowed and invited to exercise the most momentous
influence on the costume, the manners, the standards of those
literatures which had previously alone enjoyed the citizenship
of Parnassus.

Small, therefore, as is the extent of deliberate critical work
which Gray has left us, we may perceive in it nearly all the
notes of reformed, revived, we might almost say reborn, criticism. The two dominants of these have been already dwelt
upon—to wit, the constant appeal to history, and the readiness
to take new matter, whether actually new in time, or new
in the sense of having been hitherto neglected, on its own

[1] See Letter to Wharton, October 7,
1757 (cxxxvi., ii., 340, ed. cit.).

[2] I mean, of course, nobody except
specialists. On the vexed question of
Gray's *direct* knowledge of Norse, on
the priority or contemporaneousness of

Percy's "Five Pieces," and on the subject generally, an interesting treatise,
Mr F. E. Finlay's *Scandinavian Influences on the English Romantic Movement* (Boston, U.S.A., 1903), has appeared since the text was written.

merits ; not indeed with any neglect of the ancients—for Gray
was saturated with "classical" poetry in every possible sense
of the word, with Homer and Virgil, as with Dante and Milton
and Dryden—but purely from the acknowledgment at last of
the plain and obvious truth, "other times, other ways." As a
deduction from these two we note, as hardly anywhere earlier,
a willingness to take literature as it is, and not to prescribe to
it what it should be—in short, a mixture of catholicity with
tolerance, which simply does not exist anywhere before. Lastly,
we may note a special and very particular attention to prosody.
This is a matter of so much importance that we must [1] ourselves bestow presently some special attention upon it, and
may advantageously note some other exercitations of the kind
at the time or shortly afterwards.

Of the rest of the group mentioned above, Shenstone [2] is
the earliest, the most isolated, and the least directly affected

Shenstone. by the mediæval influence. Yet he, too, must have
felt it to have engaged, as we know he did, with
Percy in that enterprise of the *Reliques* which his early death
cut him off from sharing fully. From his pretty generally
known poems no one need have inferred much tendency of
the kind in him : for his Spenserian imitation, *The Schoolmistress*, has as much of burlesque as of discipleship in it.
Nor are indications of the kind extremely plentiful in his
prose works. But the remarkable *Essays on Men and Manners*, which give a much higher notion of Shenstone's power
than his excursions into the rococo, whether versified or hortu-
lary, are full of the new germs. Even here, however, he is,
after the prevailing manner of his century, much more ethical
than literary, and shows deference, if not reverence, to not a
few of its literary idols. The mixed character of his remarks

---

[1] Despite the curious infuriation
which such attention seems to excite
in some minds by no means devoid of
celestial quality. Gradually it will be
seen that current views of prosody are
a sort of "tell-tale" or index of the
state of poetic criticism generally. They
concern us here, however, only at certain moments.

[2] My copy of him is Dodsley's third
edition, in 2 vols., of the *Poems and
Essays* (London, 1768), with the second
edition of the additional volume containing the *Letters* (London, 1769).
These latter are described by Gray in
the less agreeable Graian manner, as
"about nothing but" the Leasowes
"and his own writings, with two or
three neighbouring clergymen who
wrote verses also."

on Pope [1] (which are, however, on the whole very just) may be set down by the Devil's Advocate to the kind of jealousy commonly entertained by the "younger generations who are knocking at the door"; and his objection to the plan of Spenser is neo-classically purblind. But his remarks on Prosody [2] breathe a new spirit, which, a little later, we shall be able to trace in development. His preference for rhymes that are "long" in pronunciation over snip-snaps like "cat" and "not"; his discovery—herald of the great Coleridgean reaction—that "there is a vast beauty in emphasising in the eighth and ninth place a word that is virtually a dactyl"; the way in which he lays stress on harmony of period and music of style as sources of literary pleasure; and above all the fact, that when examining the "dactylic" idea just given, he urges the absurdity of barring trisyllabic feet in *any* place, and declares that a person ignorant of Latin can discern Virgil's harmony,—show us the new principles at work. Perhaps his acutest critical passage is the maxim, "Every good poet includes a critic: the reverse will not hold"; his most Romantic, "The words 'no more' have a singular pathos, reminding us at once of past pleasure and the future exclusion of it." [3]

Shenstone's colleague in the intended, his executor in the actual, scheme of the *Reliques* was allowed by Fate to go very

Percy.

much further in the same path. At no time, perhaps, has Bishop Percy had quite fair play. In his own day his friend Johnson laughed at him, and his enemy

---

[1] Ed. cit., ii. 10–13, 158–161, and elsewhere.

[2] Most of the quotations following are found in two Essays on "Books and Writers," ii. 157–180, 228–239.

[3] ii. 172; ii. 167. The first of these has been echoed, perhaps unconsciously, by more than one great Romantic writer. For the second, compare Regnier's *regret pensif et confus, D'avoir été et n'être plus.* Shenstone's *Letters* (as is implied in the very terms of Gray's sneer) deal with literary subjects freely enough; but their criticism is rarely important, though I have noted a good many places. Some of the most

interesting (p. 58 *sq.*, ed. cit.) concern Spenser, and Shenstone's gradual conversion "from trifling and laughing to being really in love with him." From another (lxii. p. 175) we learn that at any rate when writing, S. was still in the dark about "the distance of the rhymes" in *Lycidas.* There is seen in Letter xc., viii. sq., on "Fables," an intimation (c. iii. p. 321) of the ballad plan with Percy; praise of *The Rambler;* a defence of light poetry as being still poetry, &c. &c. It is almost all interesting as an example of Critical *Education.*

Ritson attacked him with his usual savagery. In ours the publication at last of his famous *Folio Manuscript*[1] has resulted in a good deal of not exactly violent, but strong language as to his timorous and eclectic use of the precious material he had obtained, and his scarcely pardonable tamperings with such things as he did extract. Nobody indeed less one-sided and fanatical than Ritson himself, or less prejudiced than the great lexicographer, could ignore the vastness of the benefit which the *Reliques* actually conferred upon English literature, or the enormous influence which it has directly and indirectly exercised; but there has been a slight tendency to confine Percy's merits to the corners of this acknowledgment.

Yet there is much more, by no means always in the way of mere allowance, to be said for Percy than this. His poetic taste was not perfect: it could not be so. It was unlucky that he had a certain not wholly contemptible faculty for producing as well as for relishing verse, and an itch for exercising this; while he suffered, as everybody did till at least the close of his own life, from failing entirely to comprehend the late and rather decadent principle that you must let ruins alone— that you must not "improve" your original. But a man must either be strangely favoured by the gods, or else have a real genius for the matter, who succeeds, at such a time and in such circumstances, in getting together and publishing such a collection as the *Reliques*. Nor are Percy's dissertations destitute of critical as well as of instinctive merit. Modern scholarship —which has the advantage rather of knowing more than Percy could know than of making a better use of what it does know, and which is much too apt to forget that the scholars of all ages are

> " Priests that slay the slayer
> And shall themselves be slain "—

can find, of course, plenty of errors and shortcomings in the essays on the Minstrels and the Ancient Drama, the metre of *Piers Plowman*, and the Romances; and they are all unnecessarily adulterated with theories and fancies about origin, &c. But this last adulteration has scarcely ceased to be a favourite

[1] By Messrs Hales & Furnivall. 3 vols. and Supplement. (London, 1867– 68.) As for Percy's Scandinavian inquiries, see note above.

"form of competition" among critics; while I am bound to say that the literary sense which is so active and pervading in Percy seems to have deserted our modern philologists only too frequently.

At any rate, whatever may be his errors and whatever his shortcomings, the enormous, the incalculable stimulus and reagency of the *Reliques* is not now matter of dispute; while it is equally undeniable that the poetical material supplied was reinforced by a method of historical and critical inquiry which, again with all faults, could not fail to have effects almost equally momentous on criticism if not quite so momentous on creation.

The two Wartons and Hurd gave still more powerful assistance in this latter department, while Thomas Warton at least supplied a great deal of fresh actual material in his *History*. To none of the three has full justice, as it seems to me, been recently done; while to one of them it seems to me that there has been done very great injustice. The main documents which we have to consider in the case of the two brothers are for Joseph, his *Essay on Pope* (1756–71), and the numerous critical papers in *The Adventurer;* for Thomas, the *Observations on The Faerie Queene* (1754), and of course *The History of English Poetry* (1774–81).

The Wartons.

Warton's *Essay on Pope*[1]—vaguely famous as a daring act of iconoclasm, and really important as a document in the Romantic Revolt—almost literally anticipates the jest of a hundred years later on another document, about "chalking up 'No Popery!' and then running away." It also shows the uncertainty of standpoint which is quite pardonable and indeed inevitable in these early reformers. To us it is exceedingly unlucky that Warton should at page ii. of his Preface ask, "What traces has Donne of pure poetry?" Yet when we come immediately afterwards to the (for the time) bold and very nearly true statement that Boileau is no more poetical than La Bruyère, we see that Warton was thinking only of the satirist, not of the author of *The Anniversaries* and the "Bracelet" poems.

Joseph's Essay on Pope.

---

[1] Vol. i. appeared in 1756, vol. ii. not till 1782—which gap of a quarter of a century is not imperceptible in the work itself, and must be remembered in reading the text.

Further, Warton lays down, *sans phrase* and with no Addisonian limitations, that " a poet must have imagination." He is sure (*we* may feel a little more doubtful) that Young, his dedicatee, would not insist on being called a poet on the strength of his own Satires. And he works himself up to the position that in Pope there is nothing *transcendently* sublime or pathetic, supporting this by a very curious and for its time instructive division of English poets into four classes. The first contains poets of the first rank on the sublime-pathetic-imaginative standard, and is limited to three — Spenser, Shakespeare, and Milton. The second company—headed by Dryden, but including, not a little to our surprise, Fenton—has less of this poetic intensity, but some, and excels in rhetorical and didactic vigour. The third is reserved for those—Butler, Swift, Donne, Dorset, &c.—who, with little poetry, have abundant wit; and the fourth " gulfs " the mere versifiers, among whom we grieve to find Sandys and even Fairfax herded with Pitt and Broome.

There is evidently, both in its rightgoings and its shortcomings, considerable matter in this for discussion, were such discussion in place. But the main heads of it, which alone would be important, must be obvious to every one. In the body of the *Essay*, Warton, as was hinted above, rather "hedges." He maintains his position that Pope was not *transcendently* a poet; and indulges in much detailed and sometimes rather niggling criticism of his work; but readmits him after a fashion to a sort of place in Parnassus, not quite " utmost, last, provincial," but, as far as we can make out, on the fence between Class Two and Class Three. The book, as has also been said, is a real document, showing drift, but also drifting. The Time-Spirit is carrying the man along, but he is carried half-unconsciously.

Warton's *Adventurer* essays are specially interesting. They were written early in 1753–54, some years before the critical period of 1760–65, and two or three before his *Pope* essay; and they were produced at the recommendation, if not under the direct editorship, of Johnson. Further, in the peroratorial remarks which were usual with these artificial periodicals, Warton explains that they were planned with a definite intention

The Adventurer Essays.

not merely to reintroduce Criticism among polite society, but to reinvest her with something more of exactness and scholarship than had been usual since Addison followed the French critics in talking politely about critical subjects. Warton's own exercitations are distinguished by a touch which may be best called " gingerly." He opens (No. 49) with a " Parallel between Ancient and Modern Learning," which is in effect an almost violent attack on French critics, with exceptions for Fénelon, Le Bossu, and Brumoy. Then, taking the hint of Longinus's reference to " the legislator of the Jews," he feigns a fresh discovery of criticisms of the Bible by the author of the Περὶ Ὕψους. He anticipates his examination of Pope by some remarks (No. 63) on that poet from the plagiarism-and-parallel-passage standpoint; upholds the *Odyssey* (Nos. 75, 80, 83) as of equal value with the *Iliad,* and of perhaps greater for youthful students; insinuates some objections to Milton (No. 101); studies *The Tempest* (Nos. 93, 97) and *Lear* (Nos. 113, 116, 122) more or less elaborately.[1] Throughout he appears to be conditioned not merely by the facts glanced at above, by the ethical tendency of these periodicals generally, and by his own profession of schoolmaster, but also by a general transition feeling, a know-not-what-to-think-of-it. Yet his inclination is evidently towards something new—perhaps he does *not* quite know what—and away from something old, which *we* at least can perceive without much difficulty to be the Neo-Classic creed. He would probably by no means abjure that creed if it were presented to him as a test, but he would take it with no small qualifications.

For a combination of earliness, extension, and character no book noticed in this chapter exceeds in interest Thomas Warton's *Observations on Spenser.*[2] To an ordinary reader, who has heard that Warton was one of the great ushers of Romanticism in England, and that Spenser was one of the greatest influences which these ushers

Thomas Warton on Spenser.

---

[1] On this, as on other points in this chapter and the preceding more particularly, as well as elsewhere, a most valuable companion has been supplied, as was noted above, by Mr D. Nichol

Smith's excellent edition of *Eighteenth Century Essays on Shakespeare.* (Glasgow, 1903.)

[2] The full title is *Observations on the Faëric Queene of Spenser* (ed. 1,

applied, the opening of the piece, and not a very few passages later, may seem curiously half-hearted and unsympathetic. Such a reader, from another though closely connected point of view, may be disappointed by the fragmentary and *annotatory* character of the book, its deficiency in *vues d'ensemble*, its apologies, and compromises, and hesitations. But those who have taken a little trouble to inform themselves on the matter, either by their own inquiries or by following the course which has been indicated in this book, will be much better satisfied. They will see that he says what he ought to have said in the concatenation accordingly.

It is impossible to decide how much of yet not discarded orthodoxy, and how much of characteristic eighteenth-century compromise, there is in the opening about "depths of Gothic ignorance and barbarity," "ridiculous and incoherent excursions," "old *Provençal* vein," and the like. Probably there is a good deal of both;[1] there is certainly a good deal which requires both to excuse it. Yet before long Warton fastens a sudden petard on the main gate of the Neo-Classic stronghold by saying : "But it is absurd to think of judging either Ariosto or Spenser by precepts which they did not attend to." Absurd, indeed ! But what becomes of those antecedent laws of poetry, those rules of the kind and so forth, which for more than two hundred years had been accumulating authority ? It is no good for him to go on : "We who live in the days of writing by rule. . . . Critical taste is universally diffused . . ." and so on. The petard goes on fizzing and sparkling at the gate, and will blow it in before long.

In the scattered annotations, which follow for a long time, the attitude of compromise is fairly kept ; and even Neo-Classics, as we have seen, need not necessarily have objected to Warton's demonstration[2] *pièces en main*, that Scaliger "had no notion of simple and genuine beauty " ; while the whole of

London, 1754 ; ed. 2, 1762 (of which is my copy). From Hughes's editions of 1715 to Upton's of 1758 (*after* Warton's first edition) a good deal of attention had been paid to Spenser, if not quite according to knowledge. For a long list of imitations in the eighteenth century see Mr H. A. Beers (*English Romanticism in the Eighteenth Century*, London, 1899, pp. 854–55, note), who copies it from Prof. Phelps.

[1] i. 15, ed. cit.

[2] Ed. cit., i. 96.

his section (iv.) on Spenser's stanza, &c., is full of *lèse-poésie*, and that (vii.) on Spenser's inaccuracies is not much better. But the very next section is an important attack on the plagiarism-and-parallel-passage mania which almost invariably develops itself in bad critics; and the defence of his author's Allegory (§ x.), nay, the plump avowal of him as a Romantic poet, more than atones for some backslidings even here. Above all, the whole book is distinguished by a genuine if not always understanding *love* of the subject; secondly, by an obvious refusal—sometimes vocal, always latent—to accept *a priori* rules of criticism; thirdly, and most valuably of all, by recurrence to contemporary and preceding models as criteria instead of to the ancients alone. Much of the last part of the book is occupied with a sort of first draft in little of the author's subsequent *History;* he is obviously full of knowledge (if sometimes flawed) and of study (if sometimes misdirected) of early English literature. And this is what was wanted. "Nullum numen abest si sit *conscientia*" (putting the verse aside) might almost be the critic's sole motto if it were not that he certainly cannot do without *prudentia* itself. But Prudentia without her sister is almost useless: she can at best give inklings, and murmur, "If you are not conscious of what has actually been done in literature you can never decide what ought and ought not to have been done."

This is what gives the immense, the almost unequalled importance which Warton's *History of English Poetry* [1] should *His* History possess in the eyes of persons who can judge just of English judgment. It has errors: there is no division of Poetry. literature in which it is so unreasonable to expect accuracy as in history, and no division of history to which that good-natured Aristotelian dictum applies so strongly as to literary history. Its method is most certainly defective, and one of its greatest defects is the disproportion in the treatment of authors and subjects. When the author expatiates into

---

[1] Originally issued in the years 1774–78–81. The editions of 1824 and 1840, with additional notes by Price and others, are valuable for matter; and that of Mr W. C. Hazlitt (4 vols., London, 1871), with the assistance of Drs Furnival, Morris, Skeat, and others, *in*valuable. But Warton's own part is necessarily more and more obscured in them.

Dissertation, he may often be justly accused of first getting out of his depth as regards the subject, and then recovering himself by making the treatment shallow.[1]   And I do not know that his individual criticisms betray any very frequent or very extraordinary acuteness of appreciation.   To say of the lovely

"Lenten is come with love to town,"

that it "displays glimmerings of imagination, and exhibits some faint ideas of poetical expression," is surely to be, as Dryden said of Smith and Johnson in *The Rehearsal*, a "cool and insignificant gentleman"; and though it is quite accurate to recognise "much humour and spirit" in *Piers Plowman*, it is a little inadequate and banal.

But this is mere hole-picking at worst, at best the necessary or desirable ballast or set-off to a generous appreciation of Warton's achievement.   If his erudition is not unflawed, its bulk and mass are astonishing in a man of his time; if his method and proportion are defective, this is almost inevitable in the work of a pioneer; and we have seen enough since of critics and historians who make all their geese swans, not to be too hard on one who sometimes talked of peacocks or humming-birds as if they were barndoor fowls or sparrows. The good which the book, with its wealth of quotation as well as of summary, must have done, is something difficult to realise but almost impossible to exaggerate.   Now at least, for England and for English, the missing links were supplied, the hidden origins revealed, the Forbidden Country thrown open to exploration.   It is worth while (though in no unkind spirit) once more to recall Addison's *péché de jeunesse* in his *Account of the English Poets*, in order to contrast it with the picture presented by Warton.   Instead of a millennium of illiteracy and barbarism, with nothing in it worth noticing at all but Chaucer and Spenser——presented, the one as a vulgar and obsolete merryandrew, and the other as half old-wives'-fabulist and half droning preacher——century after century, from at least the thirteenth onward (Warton does not profess to handle Anglo-Saxon) was presented in regular literary development, with abundant examples of complicated literary kinds, and a crowded

[1] *De quo fabula?*

bead-roll of poets, with specimens of their works. Men had before them—for the first time, except in cases of quite extraordinary leisure, opportunities, taste, and energy—the *actual* progress of English prosody and English poetic diction, to set against the orthodox doctrine that one fine day not so very early in the seventeenth century Mr Waller achieved a sort of minor miracle of creation in respect of both. And all these works and persons were accorded serious literary and critical treatment, such as had been hitherto reserved for the classics of old, for the masterpieces of what Callières calls *les trois nations polies* abroad, and for English writers *since* Mr Waller. That Warton did not gush about them was no fault; it was exactly what could have been desired. What was wanted was the entrance of mediæval and Renaissance poetry into full recognition; the making of it *hoffähig;* the reconstitution of literary history so as to place the work of the Middle Period on a level basis, and in a continuous series, with work ancient and modern. And this Warton, to the immortal glory of himself, his University, and his Chair,[1] effected.

The remaining member of the group requires handling with some care. Not much notice has been taken of Bishop Hurd

Hurd.
His Com-
mentary on
Addison.

for a long time past, and some authorities who have given him notice have been far from kind. Their unkindness, I think, comes very near injustice; but Hurd has himself to blame for a good deal of it. As a man he seems to have been, if fairly respectable, not in the least attractive; an early but complete incarnation of the disposition called "donnishness"; a toady in his younger manhood, and an exacter of toadying in his elder. He lived long enough to endanger even his critical fair fame, by representing his admiration for Shakespeare as an aberration, and declaring that he returned to his first love Addison.[2] And his work upon Addison himself (by which, I suppose, he is most commonly known) is of a meticulous and peddling kind for the most part, by no means likely to conciliate the majority of

---

[1] See Appendix.

[2] He is, however, exquisitely characteristic in his description of Addison's own critical work (see the Bohn ed., ii. 383) as "discovering his own good taste, and calculated to improve that of the reader, but otherwise of no great merit."

recent critics.   Most of Hurd's notes deal with mere grammar;
and while nearly all of them forget that writers like Addison
make grammar and are not made by it, some are choice examples of the sheer senseless arbitrariness which makes grammar
itself too often a mere Lordship of Misrule and Abbacy of Unreason.[1]   Yet even here there are good things ; especially
some attempts [2]—very early and till recently with very few
companions in English—to bring out and analyse the rhythmical quality of prose.   But it may be frankly admitted that
if the long-lived Bishop [3] had been a critic only in his
Addisonian commentary, he would hardly have deserved a
reference, and would certainly have deserved no long reference,
here.

His own *Works* [4] are of much higher importance.   The
edition (with commentary, notes, and dissertations) of Horace's
The Horace. *Epistles to the Pisos and to Augustus* is in part of the
class of work to which, in this stage of our history,
we can devote but slight attention, but even that part shows
scholarship, acuteness, and—what is for our purpose almost more
important than either—wide and comparative acquaintance
with critical authorities, from Aristotle and Longinus to Fontenelle and Hume.[5]

The "Critical Dissertations" which follow mark a higher
flight, indeed, as their titles may premonish, they rather dare
that critical inane to which we have more than once referred.
Hurd is here a classicist with tell-tale excursions and divagations.   In his *Idea of Universal Poetry* he will not at first in-

---

[1] *e.g.* iii. 171: "*Men's minds.* Men's,
for the genitive plural of *man*, is not
allowable."

[2] *Vide* ed. cit., ii. 417, and especially
iii. 389–91, a long note of very great
interest. I do not know whether Hurd
had condescended to take a hint from
the humble dissenting Mason (*v. inf.*)

[3] He was born only twenty years
after the death of Dryden, and died
the year before Tennyson was born.

[4] My copy in 10 vols. (London, 1777)
appears to be made up of different editions of the separate books—the fifth of

the *Horace* and *Dialogues*, the third of
the *Cowley.*

[5] These qualities are particularly
shown in a really admirable note, ii.
107–15, on the method and art of
criticism, with special reference to
Longinus, Bouhours, and Addison.
Hurd is, however, once more, and in
more detail, too severe on Addison.
It may be repeated that Lessing pays
very particular attention to Hurd in
the *Hamburgische Dramaturgie*, and
speaks of him with great respect.

clude verse in his definition, nor will he accept the commonplace
but irresistibly cogent argument of universal practice
The Disser- and expectation. Poetry is the only form of com-
tations. position which has pleasure for its end; verse gives
pleasure; therefore poetry must use verse. The fiction or
imitation is the soul of poetry; but style is its body (not
" dress," mark). Hurd even takes the odd and not maintainable but rather original view that the new prose fiction is
a clumsy thing, foolishly sacrificing its proper aids of verse.[1]
He is most neo-classically peremptory as to the laws of Kinds,
which are *not* arbitrary things by any means, nor " to be
varied at pleasure."[2] But the long Second Dissertation *On
the Provinces of the Drama*, which avowedly starts from this
principle, shows, before long, something more than those easements and compromises by which, as we have already said,
eighteenth-century critics often temper the straitness of their
orthodoxy. " It is true," says Hurd,[3] " the laws of the drama,
as formed by Aristotle out of the Greek poets, can of themselves be no rule to us in this matter, because these poets had
given no examples of such intermediate species." It is, indeed, most true; but it will be a little difficult to reconcile it
with the prohibition of multiplying and varying Kinds. The
Third and Fourth Dissertations, filling a volume to themselves,
deal with *Poetical Imitation* and its *Marks*, the hard-worked
word " imitation " being used in its secondary or less honourable
sense.

The Discourses are, in short, of the " parallel passage " kind,
but written in a liberal spirit,[4] showing not merely wide reading but real acuteness, and possessing, in the second instance,
the additional interest of being addressed to " Skroddles "
Mason, who certainly " imitated " in this sense pretty freely.
Even here that *differentia* which saves Hurd appears, as where
he says,[5] " The golden times of the English poetry were undoubtedly the reigns of our two queens," while, as we saw in
the last chapter,[6] Blair was teaching, and for years was to teach,

---

[1] ii. 153.
[2] ii. 154.
[3] ii. 220.
[4] Almost too liberal, as where he
falls foul of Jeremias Holstenius for

saying the plain truth that " but for
the *Argonautics*, there had been no
fourth book of the *Æneis* " (iii. 49).
[5] iii. 153.
[6] P. 197.

his students at Edinburgh, a scheme of literary golden ages in which that of Elizabeth was simply left out.

Still, these three volumes, though they would put Hurd much higher than the Addison Commentary, are not those which give him the position sought to be vindicated for him here.

Neither will his titles be sought by any one in his *Lectures on the Prophecies :* while even that edition of Cowley's *Selected Works* the principle of which Johnson[1] at one time *Other Works.* attacked, while at another he admitted it to more favour, can only be drawn on as a proof that Hurd was superior to mere "correctness" in harking back to this poet.   Nay, the *Moral and Political Dialogues* (which drew from the same redoubtable judge[2] the remark, "I fear he is a Whig still in his heart"), though very well written and interesting in their probable effect on Landor, are not in the main literary.   Literary characters—Waller, Cowley, and others —often figure in them, but only the third, "On the Age of Queen Elizabeth," has something of a literary bent, and this itself would scarcely be noteworthy but for its practically independent appendix, the *Letters on Chivalry and Romance.* Here—not exactly in a nutshell, but in less than one hundred and fifty small pages—lie all Hurd's "proofs," his claims, his titles: and they seem, to me at least, to be very considerable. It is true that even here we must make some deductions. The passages about Chivalry and about the Crusades not merely suffer from necessarily insufficient information, but are *The Letters on Chivalry and Romance.* exposed to the diabolical arrows of that great *advocatus diaboli* Johnson when he said[3] that Hurd was "one of a set of men who account for everything systematically.   For instance, it has been a fashion to wear scarlet breeches; these men would tell you that according to causes and effects no other wear could at the time have been chosen."   This is a most destructive shrapnel to the whole eighteenth century, and by no means to the eighteenth century only; but it is fair to remember that Hurd's Romance was almost as distasteful to Johnson as his Whiggery.   And

---

[1] Boswell, Globe ed., pp. 363, 441.   [3] *Works,* ed. cit., vol. vi., p. 196.
[2] Ibid., p 598.

now there is no need for any further application of the refiner's
fire and the fuller's soap; while on the other hand what remains
of the *Letters* (and it is much) is of altogether astonishing
quality. I know nothing like it outside England, even in
Germany, at its own time; I know nothing like it in England
for more than thirty years after its date; I should be puzzled
to pick out anything superior to the best of it (with the proper
time allowance) since.

At the very opening of the *Letters*, Hurd meets the current
chatter about "monkish barbarism," "old wives' tales," and the
*Their doc-
trine.*
rest, full tilt. "The greatest geniuses," he says,
"of our own and foreign countries, such as Ariosto
and Tasso in Italy, and Spenser and Milton in
England, were seduced by these barbarities of their fore-
fathers; were even charmed by the Gothic Romances. *Was
this caprice and absurdity in them ?   Or may there not be something in the Gothic Romance peculiarly suited to the views of a
genius, and to the ends of poetry ?   And may not the philosophic
moderns have gone too far in their perpetual contempt and
ridicule of it ?"* There is no mistake possible about this; and
if the author afterwards digresses not a little in his "Chivalry"
discussions—if he even falls into the Addisonian track, which he
elsewhere condemns, of comparing classical and romantic methods,
as a kind of apology for the latter, one ought, perhaps, to admit
that it was desirable, perhaps necessary, in his day to do so.
But when he returns to his real subject, the uncompromisingness and the originality of his views are equally evident, and they
gain not a little by being compared with Warton, whose *Observations on the Faërie Queene* had already appeared. After arguing, not without much truth, that both Shakespeare and Milton
are greater when they "use Gothic manners" than when they
employ classical, he comes [1] to Spenser himself, and undertakes
to "criticise the *Faërie Queene* under the idea not of a classical,
but of a Gothic composition." He shows that he knows what
he is about by subjoining that, "if you judge Gothic architecture by Grecian rules, you find nothing but deformity, but
when you examine it by its own the result is quite different."

---

[1] In *Letter VIII.*, ibid., p. 266 *sq.*

A few pages later[1] he lays the axe even more directly to the root of the tree. " The objection to Spenser's method arises from your classic ideas of Unity, which have no place here." There is unity in the *Faërie Queene*, but it is the unity not of action, but of design.[2]   Hurd even reprobates the additional unities which Spenser communicates by the ubiquity of Prince Arthur, and by his allegory.   (He may be thought wrong here, but this does not matter.)   Then he proceeds to compare Spenser with Tasso, who tries to introduce classic unity, and gives the Englishman much the higher place ; and then again he unmasks the whole of his batteries on the French critics.   He points out, most cleverly, that they, after using Tasso to depreciate Ariosto, turned on Tasso himself; and, having dealt dexterous slaps in the face to Davenant, Rymer, and Shaftesbury, he has a very happy passage[3] on Boileau's *clinquant du Tasse*, and the way in which everybody, even Addison, dutifully proceeded to think that Tasso was *clinquant*, and nothing else.   Next he takes the offensive-defensive for " the golden dreams of Ariosto, the celestial visions of Tasso " themselves, champions " the fairy way," and convicts Voltaire out of the mouth of Addison, to whom he had appealed.   And then, warming as he goes on, he pours his broadsides into the very *galère capitaine* of the pirate fleet, the maxim " of following Nature."   " The source of bad criticism, as universally of bad philosophy, is the abuse of terms."[4]   A poet, no doubt, must follow " Nature "; but it is the nature of the poetical world, not of that of science and experience.   Further, there is not only confusion general, but confusion particular.   You must follow the ordinary nature in satire, in epigram, in didactics, *not* in other kinds.   *Incredulus odi* has been absurdly misunderstood.[5]   The " divine dream "[6] is among the noblest of the poet's prerogatives.   " The *Henriade*," for want of it, " will in a short time be no more read than *Gondibert*."[7]   And he winds up a very intelligent account of Chaucer's satire on Romance in *Sir Thopas* by a still more intelligent argument, that it was only the abuse of Romance that Chaucer satirised,

[1] P. 271.   [5] P. 306.

[2] P. 273.   [6] P. 309.

[3] P. 290.   [7] P. 313.

[4] P. 299.

and by an at least plausible criticism of the advent of Good
Sense,   "Stooping with disenchanted wings to earth."

"What," he concludes, "we have gotten is, you will say, a
great deal of good sense; what we have lost is a world of fine
fabling, the illusion of which is so grateful to the charmed
spirit that, in spite of philosophy and fashion, ' Fairy ' Spenser
still ranks highest among the poets; I mean, with all those
who are either come of that house, or have any kindness for it."

And now I should like to ask whether it is just or fair to
say that the work of the man who wrote this thirty-three
years before *Lyrical Ballads* is "vapid and perverted," that it is
"empirical, dull, and preposterous," and, at the best, "not very
useful as criticism"?

On the contrary, I should say that it was not only useful as
criticism, but that it was at the moment, and for the men, the
unum necessarium therein. Why the Time-Spirit
His real im- chose Hurd [1] for his mouthpiece in this instance I
portance.
know no more than those who have used this harsh
language of him; this Spirit, like others, has a singular fashion
of blowing where he lists. But, at any rate, he does not blow
hot and cold here. Scraps and orts of Hurd's doctrine may of
course be found earlier—in Dryden, in Fontenelle, in Addison,
even in Pope; but, though somebody else may know an
original for the whole or the bulk of it, I, at least, do not.
The three propositions—that Goths and Greeks are to be
judged by their own laws and not by each other's; that there
are several unities, and that "unity of *Action*" is not the only
one that affects and justifies even the fable; and that "follow
Nature" is meaningless if not limited, and pestilent heresy as
limited by the prevailing criticism of the day—these three
abide. They may be more necessary and sovereign at one time
than at another, but in themselves they are for all time, and
they were for Hurd's more than for almost any other of which
Time itself leaves record.

Literary currishness and literary cubbishness (an ignoble

[1] Hurd knew Gray (who, characteristically in both ways, described him as
"the last man who wore stiff-topped
gloves") pretty well (see the references
in Mr Gosse's Index). He may have
caught some heat from one who had
plenty, though he concealed it. (*Loci
Critici* contains extracts from Hurd.)

but hardy and vivacious pair of brethren) have not failed almost from the first to growl and gambol over the *Alleged imperfections of the group.* mistakes which——in most cases save that of Gray—— were made by these pioneers. Some of these mistakes they might no doubt have avoided, as he did, by the exercise of a more scholarly care. But it may be doubted whether even Gray was not saved to a great extent from committing himself by the timidity which restrained him from launching out into extensive hypotheses, and the indolence or bashfulness which held him back from extensive publication, or even writing. It was indeed impossible that any man, without almost superhuman energy and industry, and without a quite extraordinary share of learning, means, health, leisure, and long life, should have at that time informed himself with any thoroughness of the contents and chronological disposition of mediæval literature. The documents were, to all but an infinitesimal extent, unpublished; in very few cases had even the slightest critical editing been bestowed on those that were in print; and the others lay in places far distant, and accessible with the utmost difficulty, from each other; for the most part catalogued very insufficiently, or not at all, and necessitating a huge expense of time and personal labour even to ascertain their existence. At the beginning of the twentieth century any one who in these islands cannot find what he wants in a published form could in forty-eight hours obtain from the librarians at the British Museum, the Bodleian, the Cambridge Library, that of Trinity College, Dublin, and that of the Faculty of Advocates in Edinburgh, information on the point whether what he wants is at any of them, and by exerting himself a little beyond the ordinary could visit all the five in less than a week. When the British Museum was first opened, in the middle of the last century, and Gray went to read in it "through the jaws of a whale," it would have taken a week or so to communicate with the librarians; they would probably have had to make tedious researches before they could, if they chose to do so, reply, and when the replies were received, the inquirer would have had to spend the best part of a month or more in exhausting, costly, and not always safe journeys, before he could have got at the books.

There was, therefore, much direct excuse for the incompleteness and inaccuracy of the facts given by Percy, and Warton, and even Hurd; and not a little indirect excuse for the wildness and baselessness of their conjectures on such points as the Origin of Romance and the like. It is scarcely more than thirty or forty years—it is certainly not more than fifty or sixty—since it began to be possible for the student to acquaint himself with the texts, and inexcusable for the teacher not to do so. It is a very much shorter time than the shortest of these since theories, equally baseless and wild with those of these three, have been confidently and even arrogantly put forward about the origin of the Arthurian legends, and since mere linguistic crotchets have been allowed to interfere with the proper historical survey of European literature. The point of importance, the point of value, was that Percy, and Warton, and Hurd, not only to the huge impatience of Johnson, the common friend of the first two, devoted their attention to ballad, and romance, and saga, and mediæval treatise—not only recognised and allowed the principle that in dealing with new literary forms we must use new literary measures—not only in practice, if not in explicit theory, accepted the pleasure of the reader, and the idiosyncrasy of the book, and the "leaden rule" which adapts itself to Art and not Art to itself, as the grounds of criticism, but laid the foundations of that wider study of literary history which is not so much indispensable to literary criticism as it is literary criticism itself.

To this remarkable group of general precursors may be added, for a reason previously given, a couple of pioneers in a particular branch—one contemporary with and *Studies in Prosody.* indeed in most cases anticipating their general work; the other coming level with its latest instances.[1] The fact of them is not contestable, and, as we have seen already, the tyranny of the absolutely syllabic, middle-

---

[1] The original *History of Criticism* contained a passage promising a larger treatment of the special subject of Prosody, if possible, which promise the writer has since been able to carry out. The performances of Mason and Mitford, however, are extremely characteristic of the general trend of "preceptive" criticism at this time, and it seemed unnecessary to omit the account of them. But from this point onwards the handling of infinitely prosodic matters will be for the most part eschewed.

paused, end-stopped couplet coincides exactly with the "prose-and-sense" dynasty in English poetry. We have seen also that most of the precursors, explicitly or incidentally, by theory or by practice, attacked or evaded this tyranny. But not one of them—though Gray's *Metrum* shows what he might have done if in this matter, as in others, he could only have persuaded himself to "speak out"—had the inclination or the courage to tackle the whole subject of the nature and laws of harmony in English composition. The two whom we have mentioned were bolder, and we must give them as much space as is allowable without unduly invading the province of the other History.

In 1749 appeared two pamphlets, on *The Power of Numbers and the Principles of Harmony in Poetic Compositions*, and on *The Power and Harmony of Prosaic Numbers*. No

John Mason: his Power of Numbers *in Prose and Poetry.*

author's name is on either title-page, but they are known to be by a Dissenting minister named John [1] Mason. He seems to have given much attention to the study and teaching of elocution, and he published another pamphlet on that special subject, which attained its fourth edition in 1757.[2]

In his poetical tractate Mason plunges into the subject after a very promising fashion, by posing the question with which he has to deal as "What is the cause and source of that pleasure which, in reading either poetry or prose, we derive not only from the sound and sense of the words, but the order in which they are disposed?" or, as an alternative, "Why a sentence conveying just the same thought, and containing the very same words, should afford the ear a greater pleasure when expressed one way than another, though the difference may perhaps arise only from the transposition of a single word?" One feels, after reading only so far, that De Quincey's well-known phrase, "This is what you can recommend to a friend!" is applicable—that whether the man gives the right answers or not he has fixed at once on the right questions, and has

---

[1] "Skroddles" was *William*.

[2] My copy contains all three bound together. It is interesting, though not surprising, to find that there was no demand for the two original and valuable constituents, and a brisk one for the commonplace third.

acknowledged the right ground of argument. Not "How ought sentences to be arranged?" not "How did A B. C. arrange them or bid them be arranged?" but "How and why do they give the greatest *pleasure* as the result of arrangement?"

So also, in his prose tractate, Mason starts from the position that "numerous" arrangement adds wonderfully to the *pleasure* of the reader. To enter into the details of his working out of the principle in the two respects would be to commit that "digression to another kind" from which we have warned ourselves off. But it is not improper to say that, a hundred and fifty years ago, he had already cleared his mind of all the cant and confusion which to this day beset too many minds in regard to the question of Accent *v.* Quantity, by adopting the sufficient and final principle[1] that "that which *principally fixes and determines* the quantities in English numbers is the accent and emphasis"; that though he is not quite so sharply happy in his definition, he evidently uses "quantity" itself merely as an equivalent for "unit of metrical value"; that he clears away all the hideous and ruinous nonsense about "elision," observing[2] that in

"And many an amorous, many a humorous lay"

there are fourteen syllables instead of ten, and that "the ear finds nothing in it redundant, defective, or disagreeable, but is sensible of a sweetness not ordinarily found in the common iambic verse." Further, he had anticipated[3] Hurd by giving elaborate examples of quantified analysis of prose rhythm. The minutiæ of all this, interesting as they are, are not for us; the point is that here is a man who has not the fear of Bysshe before his eyes, or the fear of anybody; who will not be "connoisseured out of his senses," and whose brain, when his ear tells it that a line is beautiful, proceeds calmly to analyse if possible the cause of the beauty, without troubling itself to ask whether anybody has said that it ought not to exist.[4]

[1] *Power of Numbers*, p. 9.
[2] Ibid., p. 27.
[3] *Prosaic Numbers*, passim.
[4] Mason's very errors are interesting, as where his delight in recovered *rhythm*—in full melody of variety— leads him to something like the old blasphemy of *rhyme* ("one of the lowest ornaments and greatest shackles of modern poesy" (*Power of Numbers*, p. 14).

These inquiries into prosody and rhythm formed no unimportant part of the English criticism of the mid-eighteenth century.[1]   The two different ways in which they were regarded by contemporaries may be easily guessed, but we have documentary evidence of them in an interesting passage of the dedication to John Gilpin[2] of the second edition of the book in which they culminated, and to which we now come.   Mitford's *Inquiry into the Principles of Harmony in Language* represents himself as having paid a visit to Pye, afterwards Laureate ; and, finding him with books of the kind before him, as having expostulated with "a votary of fancy and the Muses" for his "patience with such dull and uninteresting controversy."   Pye, it seems, replied that "the interest in the subject so warmly and extensively taken by English men of letters" had excited his curiosity, which had been gratified by Foster's elucidation of the subject itself.   And Mitford, borrowing the book, soon found his own excited too.[3]

Mitford— his Harmony of Language.

The volume of which this was the genesis, appeared first in 1774.[4]   The second edition, very carefully revised and ex-

[1] Even at this early date Mason was able to quote not a few writers—Pemberton, Manwaring, Malcolm, Gay, who, as well as Geddes, Foster, Galley, and others, had dealt with this subject. In fact, the list of such authors in the eighteenth century is quite long, though few of them are very important. For an excellent reasoned bibliography see Mr T. S. Omond's *English Metrists* (Tunbridge Wells, 1903).   Henry Pemberton, Gresham Professor of Physic, and a man of various ability, published on the to us surprising subject of Glover's *Leonidas*, in 1738, *Observations on Poetry*, which I had hunted in the catalogues for a long time, when Mr Gregory Smith kindly gave me a copy. It shows, as the election of its text may indicate, and as its date would further suggest, no very enthusiastic or imaginative appreciation of the Muse, but is remarkably learned, not merely in the ancients and the modern French-

men, but in Italians like Minturno and Castelvetro.   Pemberton deals with Epic and Dramatic poetry—their rise, dignity, fable, sentiment, character, language, and difference ; with Versification, where his standpoint may be guessed, from his denouncing "the mixture of iambic and trochaic" as a blemish on *L'Allegro* and *Il Penseroso ;* with the Sublime.   He is not an inspiring or inspired writer, but holds some position, both as influential on the Germans, who not seldom quote him, and in the history of Prosody.

[2] Not Cowper's hero, but a son of "Picturesque" Gilpin.   Mitford had been a pupil of Gilpin the elder.

[3] Foster's (John) *Essay on the Different Nature of Accent and Quantity* (second edition, Eton, 1763) is duly before me also, but I must not touch it here.

[4] As *An Essay on the Harmony of Language.*   My friend, Mr T. S.

tended, was not published till 1804. It may appear at first
sight unfortunate, but on reflection will probably be seen to
have been a distinct advantage, that even this second edition
preceded the appearance of any of the capital works of the new
school except the *Lyrical Ballads.* For had it been otherwise,
and had Mitford taken any notice of the new poetry, we should
in all probability have had either the kind of reactionary protest which often comes from pioneers who have been overtaken
and passed, or at best an attempt at awkward adjustment of
two very different points of view. As it is, the book, besides
exhibiting much original talent, belongs to a distinct school
and platform——that of the later but still eighteenth-century
Romantic beginners, while at the same time it represents a
much greater knowledge of old literature, helped by Ellis's
Specimens, by Ritson's work, and other products of the last
years of the century, than had been possible to Shenstone, to
Gray, or even to Warton.

Once more, its detailed tenets and pronouncements, with all
but the general methods by which they are arrived at, belong
to another story. But these general methods, and some special
exemplifications of them, belong to us. Rightly or wrongly,
Mitford sought his explanations of the articulate music of
poetry from the laws of inarticulate music itself. For this
reason, or for another, he was disposed to join the accentual
and not the quantitative school of prosodists, and to express
strong disapproval of the adoption of classical prosodic terms
in regard to English. He is sometimes arbitrary, as when he
lays down[1] " that in English every word has one syllable
always made eminent by accent"; and we have to remember
that he was writing after nearly a hundred years of couplet
verse on Bysshian principles before we can excuse——while we
can never endorse——his statement[2] that " to all who have any
familiarity with English poetry a *regularity* in the disposition
of accents is its most striking characteristic." He is rather

Omond, in the quite invaluable bibliography referred to above, thinks this
" clearer, shorter, more pointed" than
the second. It is at any rate well
to remember that when it appeared,
Johnson had ten years to live, and
Scott, Wordsworth, and Coleridge were
in their nurseries.

[1] *Harmony of Language,* second
edition, p. 51.

[2] Ibid., p. 81.

unsound on the Pause, but lays down the all-important rule that "rhyme is a time-beater" without hesitation.   He admits trisyllabic feet even in what he calls "common time"; but (in consequence of his accentual theories probably) troubles himself with "aberration" of accent (*i.e.*, substitution of trochee for iamb), with redundant or extra-metrical syllables in the middle of the line, and with other epicyclic and cumbrous superfluities. But the most important thing in the whole book—the thing which alone makes it really important to *us*—is that he supports his theories by a regular examination of the whole of English verse as far as he knows it, even back to Anglo-Saxon times, and that in making the examination, he appeals not to this supposed rule or to that accepted principle, but to the *actual* practice of the *actual* poets as interpreted to him by his own ear.

In his errors, therefore (or in what may seem to some his errors), as well as in his felicities, Mitford exhibits himself to the full as an adherent of that changed school of poetical criticism which strives in the first place to master the actual documents, in the second to ascertain, as far as possible and as closely as possible, their chronological relation to each other, and in the third to take them as they are and explain them as well as it may, without any selection of a particular form of a particular metre at a particular time as a norm which had been painfully reached and must on no account be departed from. He shows the same leaning by his constant reference to the ear, not the rule, as the authority.   The first draft of his book was published not only when Johnson was still alive, but long before the *Lives of the Poets* appeared; and it is most interesting to see the different sides from which they attack the prosodic character, say of Milton.   Johnson—it is quite evident from his earlier and more appreciative handling of the subject in the *Rambler*—approaching Milton with the orthodox decasyllabic rules in hand, found lines which most undoubtedly do not accord with those rules, and termed them harsh accordingly. Mitford approaches the lines with nothing but a listening ear, finds them "not harsh and crabbed, but musical as Apollo's lute," and then proceeds to construct, rightly or wrongly, such a rule as will allow and register their music.

The truth is, that these inquirers both builded and pulled down better than they knew. Many persons besides Mitford *Importance of prosodic inquiry.* have begun by thinking controversies about prosody dull and uninteresting, while only too few have allowed themselves to be converted as he did; nor is it common to the present day to find a really intelligent comprehension of the importance of the subject. On the contrary, a kind of petulant indignation is apt to be excited by any criticism of poetry which pursues these "mechanical" lines, as they are called, and the critic has sometimes even to endure the last indignity of being styled a "philologist" for his pains.

Yet nothing is more certain than that these inquiries into prosody were among the chief agencies in the revolution which came over English poetry at the end of the eighteenth century and the beginning of the next. A sort of superstition of the decasyllable, hardened into a fanaticism of fixed pause, rigidly dissyllabic feet and the rest, had grown upon our verse-writers. A large part of the infinite metrical wealth of English was hidden away and locked up under taboo. Inquiries into prosody broke this taboo inevitably; and something much more than mere metrical wealth was sure to be found, and was found, in the treasure-houses thus thrown open.

One expected figure of a different kind may perhaps have been hitherto missed in this part of our gallery. Sterne's well-known *Sterne and the stop-watch.* outburst as to criticism, in the twelfth chapter of the third book of *Tristram Shandy* is far too famous a thing to be passed over with the mere allusion given to it in the last chapter, or with another in this. Nay, it may be said at once, from its fame and from its forcible expression, to have had, and even in a sense still to have, no small place among the Dissolvents of Judgment by Rule. "Looking only at the stop-watch" is one of those admirable and consummate *phrases* which settle themselves once for all in the human memory, and not merely possess—as precisians complain, illegitimately—the force of an argument, but have a property of self-preservation and recurrence at the proper moment in which arguments proper are too often sadly lacking.

Further, it must be admitted that there are few better instances of the combined sprightliness and ingenuity of Sterne's humour. "Befetiched with the bobs and trinkets of criticism" is in reality even happier than the "stop-watch," and of an extraordinary propriety. Though he did "fetch it from the coast of Guinea," nothing was ever less far-fetched or more home-driven. The "nothing of the colouring of Titian" is equally happy in its rebuke of the singular *negativeness*—the attention to what is *not* there, not to what is—of Neo-Classicism; while the outburst, again world-known, as to the "tormenting cant of criticism," and the ingenious and thoroughly English application of this cant itself to the eulogy of the curse of Ernulphus, are all too delightful, and have been too effective for good, not to deserve the heartiest acknowledgment.

At the same time the Devil's Advocate—who is always a critic, if a critic is not always an officer of the devil—may, nay must, point out that Sterne's main object in the passage is not strictly literary. It is assuredly from the sentimental point of view that he attacks the Neo-Classic "fetichism"; the "generous heart" is to "give up the reins of its imagination into the author's hands," to "be pleased he knows not why, and cares not wherefore." To which Criticism, not merely of the Neo-Classic persuasion, can only cry, "Softly! Before the most generous of hearts gives up the reins of imagination (which, by the way, are not entirely under the heart's control) to an author, he must show that he can manage them, he must *take* them, in short. And it is by no means superfluous —it is highly desirable, if not absolutely necessary—to know and care for the wherefore of your pleasing." Nor, wide as was Sterne's reading, and ingenious as are the uses which he makes of it, does it appear that he had any very great interest in literature as such—as being *good*, and not merely odd, or naughty, or out-of-the-way, or conducive to outpourings of heart. He might even, by a very ungenerous person, be described as by no means disinterested in his protests. For certainly his own style of writing had very little chance of being adjudged to keep time according to the classical stop-watch, of satisfying, with its angles and its dimensions, the requirements of the classical scale. So he is rather a "Hal o' the Wynd" in the War of Critical Independence—he fights for his own hand, though he does yeoman's service to the general cause.

From these we may turn—and in fact return—to a group of English writers whose criticism is more directly interconnected. *Æsthetics and their Influence.* In these we may perceive the working of something like a general conception of the philosophical or Æsthetic kind—of theories of Beauty not limited to one kind of Art. This, first distinctly apparent in Descartes, had been more specially cultivated (though there is something of it in Addison) on the Continent than in England—by Baumgarten and Sulzer in Germany, by André in France, and above all by Vico in Italy.[1] But it is as a derivation from Locke, apparent in English, very specially in a contemporary of Addison's who was widely read, and in others later,—Hume, Burke, Adam Smith,[2] Alison, and Gibbon.[2]

There are few writers of whom more different opinions have been held, in regard to their philosophical and literary value, *Shaftesbury.* than is the case with Shaftesbury. His criticism has been less discussed, except from the purely philosophical or the more purely technical æsthetic side; but difference is scarcely less certain here when discussion does take place. It is difficult to put the dependence of that

---

[1] For all these and others see *Hist. Crit.*, ii. 141 *sq.*

[2] On Adam Smith and Gibbon a note must suffice. The former has actually left us nothing important in print concerning the subject, though he is known to have lectured on it, and though to the partisans of "psychological" criticism the *Moral Sentiments* may seem pertinent. His line seems to have been close to those of Hume and Blair, the latter of whom knew and used Smith's Lectures in preparing his own. As for Gibbon, his great work did not give very much opportunity for touching our subject, and he availed himself little of what it did give : though on Byzantine literature generally, and on some individuals—Photius, Sidonius, and others—he acquits himself well enough. His early *Essay on the Study of Literature* is extremely general and quite unimportant.

difference in an uncontentious and non-question-begging manner, because it concerns a fundamental antinomy of the fashion in which this curious author strikes opposite temperaments. To some, every utterance of his seems to carry with it in an undertone something of this sort: "I am not merely a Person of Quality, and a very fine gentleman, but also, look you, a philosopher of the greatest depth, though of the most elegant exterior, and a writer of consummate originality and *agudeza*. If you are sensible people you will pay me the utmost respect; but alas! there are so many vulgar and insensible people about, that very likely you will not." Now this kind of "air" abundantly fascinates some readers, and intrigues others; while, to yet others again, it seems the affectation, most probably of a charlatan, certainly of an intellectual coxcomb, and they are offended accordingly. It is probably unjust (though there is weighty authority for it) to regard Shaftesbury as a charlatan; but he will hardly, except by the fascination aforesaid or by some illegitimate partisanship of religious or philosophical view, escape the charge of being a coxcomb; and his coxcombry appears nowhere more than in his dealings with criticism.[1] From the strictest point of view of our own definition of the art, he would have very little right to entrance here at all, and would have to be pretty unceremoniously treated if he were allowed to take his trial. His concrete critical utterances—his actual appreciations—are almost Rymerical; with a modish superciliousness substituted for pedantic scurrility. "The British Muses," quoth my lord, in his *Advice to an Author*,[2] "may well lie abject and obscure, especially being as yet in their mere infant state. They have scarce hitherto arrived to anything of stateliness or person," and he continues in the usual style with "wretched pun and quibble," "false sublime," "Gothick mode of poetry," "horrid discord of jingling rhyme," &c. He speaks of "that noble satirist Boileau" as "raised from the plain model of the

---

[1] These are to be found almost *passim* in the *Characteristics* (my copy of which is the small 3 vol. ed., *s.l.*, 1749), but chiefly in his *Advice to an Author* (vol. i., ed. cit., p. 105-end) and in the *Third Miscellany* (iii. 92-129).

[2] i. 147.

ancients." Neither family affection, nor even family pride, could have induced him to speak as he speaks of Dryden,[1] if he had had any real literary taste. His sneers at Universities,[2] at "pedantick learning," at "the mean fellowship of bearded boys," deprive him of the one saving grace which Neo-classicism could generally claim. "Had I been a Spanish Cervantes, and with success equal to that comick author had destroyed the reigning taste of Gothick or Moorish Chivalry, I could afterwards contentedly have seen my burlesque itself despised and set aside."[3] Perhaps there is not a more un-happily selected single epithet in the whole range of criticism than "the *cold* Lucretius."[4]

On the other hand, both in the more speciously literary parts of his desultory discourses *de quodam Ashleio*, and outside of them, he has frequent remarks on the Kinds;[5] he is quite copious on Correctness;[6] and there can be no doubt that he deserves his place in this chapter by the fashion in which he endeavours to utilise his favourite *pulchrum* and *honestum* in ref-erence to Criticism, of which he is a declared and (as far as his inveterate affectation and mannerism will let him) an ingeni-ous defender. The main *locus* for this is the Third Miscel-lany, and its central, or rather culminating, passage[7] occurs in the second chapter thereof. The Beautiful is the principle of Literature as well as of Virtue; the sense whereby it is appre-hended is Good Taste; the manner of attaining this taste is by a gradual rejection of the excessive, the extravagant, the vulgar.[8] A vague enough gospel, and not over well justified by the fruits of actual appreciation quoted above;[9] but not perhaps much vaguer, or possessing less justification, than most "metacritic."

The position of Hume in regard to literary criticism has an interest which would be almost peculiar if it were not

Hume.   for something of a parallel in Voltaire. If the literary opinions of the author of the *Enquiry into Human Nature* stood alone they would be almost negligible;

---

[1] iii. 187 *sq.*

[2] i. 224, &c.

[3] iii. 173.

[4] i. 35.

[5] i. 147 *sq.*

[6] i. 157 *sq.*

[7] iii. 125.

[8] i. 163 *sq.*

[9] The lively fashion in which Dr

George Campbell in his *Philosophy of Rhetoric* (*v. sup.*, p. 203) beats up his lordship's quarters, on the score of precious and rococo style, is too much forgotten nowadays.

and if he had worked them into an elaborate treatise, like
that of his clansman Kames, this would probably, if remembered
at all, be remembered as a kind of "awful example." In
their context and from their author, however, we cannot
quite "regard and pass" Hume's critical observations as their
intrinsic merit may seem to suggest that we should do: nay,
in that context and from that author, they constitute a really
valuable document in more than one relation.

It cannot be said that Hume does not invite notice as a
critic; on the contrary, his title of "*Essays: Moral, Political,*[1]
Examples of and Literary" seems positively to challenge it. Yet
his critical his actual literary utterances are rather few, and
opinions. would be almost unimportant but for the considerations just put. He tells us that criticism is difficult;[2] he
applies[2] (as Johnson did, though differently) Fontenelle's remark
about "telling the hours"; he illustrates from Holland the
difference of excellence in commerce and in literature.[3] He condemns—beforehand, and with the vigour and acuteness which
we should expect from him—the idea of Taine, the attempt
to account for the existence of a particular poet at a particular
time and in a particular place.[4] He is shocked at the vanity,
at the rudeness, and at the loose language of the ancients.[5]
He approaches, as Tassoni[6] and Perrault[7] had approached,
one of the grand *cruces* of the whole matter by making his
Sceptic urge that "*beauty* and worth are merely of a relative
nature, and consist of an agreeable sentiment produced by
an object on a particular mind";[8] but he makes no detailed
use or application whatever of this as regards literature.
His Essay on *Simplicity and Refinement in Writing*[9] is psy-
chology rather than criticism, and he uses his terms in a
rather curious manner. At least, I myself find it difficult

---

[1] The literary essays occur almost
wholly in the First part (published in
1742 : my copy is the "new edition"
of the *Essays and Treatises*, 2 vols. :
London and Edinburgh, 1764).

[2] *Essay on Delicacy of Taste*, pp. 5,
7, ed. cit.

[3] *On the Rise and Progress of the*

Arts and Sciences, ibid., p. 125.

[4] Ibid., p. 126.

[5] P. 141 *sq.*

[6] *V. Hist. Crit.*, ii. 327, 417.

[7] *V. Hist. Crit.*, ii. 418.

[8] *The Sceptic*, p. 186.

[9] Pp. 217-222.

to draw up any definitions of these qualities which will make Pope the *ne plus ultra* of justifiable Refinement, and Lucretius that of Simplicity; Virgil and Racine the examples of the happy mean in both; Corneille and Congreve excessive in Refinement, and Sophocles and Terence excessive in Simplicity.[1] The whole is, however, a good rationalising of the "classical" principle; and is especially interesting as noticing, with slight reproof, a tendency to too great "affectation and conceit" both in France and England — faults for which *we* certainly should not indict the mid-eighteenth century. The Essay *On Tragedy* is more purely psychological still. And though *On the Standard of Taste* is less open to this objection, one cannot but see that it is Human Nature, and not Humane Letters, in which Hume is really interesting himself. The vulgar censure on the reference to Bunyan [2] is probably excessive; for it is at least not improbable that Hume had never read a line of *The Pilgrim's Progress*, and was merely using the tinker's name as a kind of type-counter. But this very acceptance of a conventional judgment — acceptance constantly repeated throughout the Essay—is almost startling in context with the *alleszermalmend* tendency of some of its principles. A critic who says [3] that "It is evident that none of the rules of composition are fixed by reasonings *a priori*," is in fact saying "Take away that bauble!" in regard to Neo-classicism altogether; and though in the very same page Hume repeats the orthodox cavils at Ariosto, while admitting his charm on the next, having thus set up the idol again, he proceeds once more to lop it of hands and feet and tumble it off its throne by saying that "if things are found to please, they cannot be faults; let the pleasure which they produce be ever so unexpected and unaccountable." The most dishevelled of Romantics, in the reddest of waistcoats, could say no more.

---

[1] "Refinement" seems here to mean "conceit," "elaborate diction." But the "simplicity" of Lucretius, in any sense in which the quality can be said to be pushed to excess by Sophocles, is very hard to grasp.

[2] P. 257: "Whoever would assert an equality of genius and elegance between Ogilby and Milton, or Bunyan and Addison, would be thought to defend no less an extravagance," &c.

[3] P. 258.

In his remarks upon the qualifications and functions of the critic, Hume's anthropological and psychological mastery is evident enough: but it is at least equally evident that his actual taste in literature was in no sense spontaneous, original, or energetic. In comparing him, say, with Johnson, it is not a little amusing to find his much greater acquiescence in the conventional and traditional judgments. Indeed, towards the end of his Essay[1] Hume anticipates a later expression[2] of a perennial attitude of mind by declaring, "However I may excuse the poet on account of the manners of his age, I never can relish the composition," and by complaining of the want of "humanity and decency so conspicuous" even sometimes in Homer and the Greek tragedies. That David, of all persons, should fail to realise—he did *not* fail to perceive—that the humanity of Homer *was* human and the decency of Sophocles *was* decent, is indeed surprising.

Such things might at first sight not quite dispose one to regret that, as he himself remarks,[3] "the critics who have had some tincture of philosophy" have been "few," for certainly those who have had more tincture of philosophy than Hume himself have been far fewer. But, as is usually the case,[4] it is not the fault of philosophy at all. For some reason, natural disposition, or want of disposition, or even that necessity of clinging to *some* convention which has been remarked in Voltaire himself, evidently made Hume a mere "church-going bell"—pulled by the established vergers, and summoning the faithful to orthodox worship—in most of his literary utterances. Yet, as we have seen, he could not help turning quite a different tune at times, though he himself hardly knew it.

His incon- sistency.

At the close of Burke's *Essay*[5] he expressly declines "to

---

[1] P. 274.

[2] "I must take pleasure in the thing represented before I can take pleasure in the representation," *v. infra* on Peacock himself.

[3] *Essay on Tragedy*, p. 243.

[4] In the larger *History* will be found, preceding the discussion of this part

of the subject, a "Parabasis on Philosophical Criticism" generally.

[5] *A Philosophical Inquiry into the Origin of our Ideas of the Sublime and Beautiful, with an Introductory Discourse concerning Taste:* 1756. I use the Bohn edition of the *Works*, vol. i. pp. 49-181.

consider poetry as it regards the Sublime and Beautiful more *Burke on the* at large"; but this "more" refers to the fact that *Sublime and* his Fifth Part had been given to the Power of *Beautiful.* Words in exciting ideas of the kind. Most of what he says on this head is Lockian discussion of simple and compound, abstract and concrete, &c., and of the connection of words with images, as illustrated by the cases—so interesting in one instance to the English, and in the other to the whole, eighteenth century—of Blacklock the blind poet, and Saunderson the blind mathematician. There is, however, a not unacute contention[1] (against the small critics of that and other times) that the exact analytical composition necessary in a picture is not necessary in a poetic image. But one may doubt whether this notion was not connected in his own mind with the heresy of the "streaks of the tulip."[2] It serves him, however, as a safeguard against the mere "imitation" theory: and it brings (or helps to bring) him very near to a just appreciation of the marvellous power of words as words. His remarks on the grandeur of the phrase "the Angel of the Lord" are as the shadow of a great rock in the weary glare of the *Aufklärung*, and so are those which follow on Milton's "universe of Death." Nor is it a trifling thing that he should have discovered the fact that "very polished languages are generally deficient in Strength."

In the earlier part there are interesting touches, such as that of "*degrading*" the style of the *Æneid* into that of *The Pilgrim's Progress*, which, curiously enough, occurs actually in a defence of a taste for romances of chivalry[3] and of the sea-coast of Bohemia. Part I. sect. xv., on the effects of tragedy, is almost purely ethical. In the parts—the best of the book— which deal directly with the title subjects (Parts II. and III.), an excellent demonstration[4] is made of the utter absurdity of that scheme of physical proportion which we formerly laughed at:[5] but the application, which might seem so

---

[1] *Op. cit.*, p. 175 *sq.* But Burke does not seem to have reached the larger and deeper views of Lessing on this subject.

[2] See above on Johnson.

[3] Of this in turn Blair was perhaps thinking when he wrote the unlucky passage quoted above.

[4] Part III. § iv.

[5] *V. Hist. Crit.*, ii. 417 *sq.*

tempting, to similar arbitrariness in judging of literature,
is not made. Still more remarkable is the scantiness of the
section on "The Beautiful in Sounds"[1] which should have
brought the writer to our proper subject. Yet we can hardly
regret that he says so little of it when we read that astonishing passage[2] in which the great Mr Burke has "observed"
the affections of the body by Love, and has come to the
conclusion that "the head reclines something on one side;
the eyelids are more closed than usual, and the eyes roll gently
with an inclination towards the object; the mouth is a little
opened and the breath drawn slowly with now and then a
low sigh; the whole body is composed, and the hands fall
idly to the sides"—a sketch which I have always wished
to have seen carried into line by the ingenious pencil of
Charles Kirkpatrick Sharpe.[3] A companion portrait of the
human frame under the influence of poetic afflatus, in writer
or in reader, would indeed have been funny, but scarcely
profitable. In fact, the most that can be said for Burke, as
for the generality of these æsthetic writers, is that the specu-
lations recommended and encouraged could not but break
up the mere ice of Neo-classic rule-judgment. They almost
always go directly to the effect, the result, the event, the
pleasure, the trouble, the thrill. That way perhaps lies the
possibility of new error: but that way certainly lies also
the escape from old.

The trinitarian succession of Scottish æsthetic-empirics—
Gerard, Alison, Jeffrey—could not with propriety
be omitted here, but the same propriety would be
violated if great space were given to them. They
connect with, or at least touch, Burke and Smith
on the one hand, Kames on the other: but they are, if rather

*The Scottish
æsthetic-
empirics:
Alison.*

---

[1] III. § xxv.

[2] IV. § xix. i. 160, ed. cit.

[3] In the mood in which he did that
eccentric frontispiece to the Maitland
Club *Sir Bevis of Hampton* (Edinburgh,
1838) at the *abgeschmackt* - ness
of which the late excellent Prof.
Kölbing shuddered when he edited

Arthur and Merlin (Leipzig, 1890,
p. ix.) A picture of *La Belle Dame
sans Merci* in the Royal Academy for
1902 seems to have been actually constructed on Mr Burke's suggestions.
For a very witty and crushing jest of
Schlegel's on *The Sublime and Beautiful*, see *Hist. Crit.*, iii. 400.

more literary than the first two, very much less so than the third. All, in degrees modified perhaps chiefly by the natural tendency to "improve upon" predecessors, are associationists: and all display (though in somewhat decreasing measure as a result of the Time-spirit) that, sometimes amusing but in the end rather tedious, tendency to substitute for actual reasoning long chains of only plausibly connected propositions, varied by more or less ingenious substitutions of definition and equiva-lence, which is characteristic of the eighteenth century. Gerard, the earliest, is the least important:[1] and such notice of Jeffrey as is necessary will come best in connection with his other critical work. Alison, as the central and most im-portant of the three, and as representing a prevailing party for a considerable time, may have some substantive notice here.

The *Essay on Taste*, which was originally published in 1790, and which was sped on its way by Jeffrey's Review (the original *The* Essay form of the reviewer's own essay) in 1811, had *on Taste.* reached its sixth edition in 1825, and was still an authority, though it must by that time have begun to seem not a little old-fashioned, to readers of Coleridge and Hazlitt. It is rather unfortunately "dated" by its style, which—even at

[1] This was not the opinion of some person who has annotated the copy of the *Essay on Taste* (3rd ed., Edin-burgh, 1780: the first appeared in 1758) which belongs to the Uni-versity of Edinburgh, as "wonderfully profound." Other annotators, how-ever, both of this and the *Essay on Genius* (1774)—for the University au-thorities of the past appear to have been somewhat indifferent to the fashion in which students used books —do not agree with him. In plain truth both pieces are rather trying examples of that "saying an infinite deal of nothing" which is so common in philosophical inquiries. "Facility in the conception of an object, if it be moderate, gives us pleasure" (*Taste*, p. 29); "The rudest rocks and moun-tains . . . acquire beauty when skil-fully imitated in painting;" "Where refinement is wanting, taste must be coarse and vulgar" (p. 115). "Perfect criticism requires therefore" (p. 174) "the greatest philosophical acuteness united with the most exquisite per-fection of taste." "The different works of men of genius sometimes differ very much in the degree of their perfec-tion" (*Genius*, p. 236). "Both in genius for the arts and in genius for science Imagination is assisted by Memory." Certainly "here be truths," but a continued course of reading things like them begins before long to inspire a considerable longing for falsehoods. Gerard, however, though habitually dull, is less absurd than Alison, whom he undoubtedly sup-plied with his principle of Associa-tion.

its original date something of a survival—is of the old "elegant" but distinctly artificial type of Blair: and, as has been
hinted already, it abuses the eighteenth-century weakness for
substituting a "combined and permuted" paraphrase of the
proposition for an argument in favour of the fact. There is
a very fair amount of force in its associationist considerations,
though, as with all the devotees of the Association principle
down to Mill, the turning round of the key is too often taken
as equivalent to the opening of the lock. But its main faults,
in more special connection with our subject, are two. The
Its confusions first is a constant confusion of Beauty or Sublimity
with Interest. Alison exhausts himself in proving
that the associations of youth, affection, &c., &c., cause *love* of
the object—a truth no doubt too often neglected by the Neo-
classic tribe, but accepted and expressed by men of intelligence,
from the Lucretian *usus concinnat* down to Maginn's excellent
"Don't let any fool tell you that you will get tired of your
wife; you are much more likely to get quite unreasonably
fond of her." But love and admiration, though closely connected, are not the same thing, and love and interest are still
farther apart. Another confusion of Alison's, very germane
indeed to our subject, is that he constantly mixes up the
beauty of a thing with the beauty of the description of it.

The most interesting point, however, about Alison is his
halting between two opinions as to certain Neo-classic idols.
His individual criticisms of literature are constantly vitiated
by faults of the old arbitrariness, especially as to what is
"low." There is an astonishing lack of critical imagination
in his objections to two Virgilian lines—

> "Adde tot egregias urbes, operumque laborem
>
> .   .   .   .
>
> Septemque una sibi muro circumdedit arces"—

as "cold," "prosaic," "tame," "vulgar," and "spiritless." As
if the image of the busy town after the country beauty were
not the most poetic of contrasts in the first: and as if the City
of the Seven Hills did not justly fire every Roman mind![1]

---

[1] Ed. cit. See a little farther for a
similarly uncritical criticism on the
trahuntque siccas machinæ carinas of
Horace.

These, however, might be due to "the act of God,"—to sheer want of the quality on which the essay is written. A large *and arbitrary absurdities.* part of the second volume exhibits the perils of that Castle Dangerous, the "half-way house," unmistakably and inexcusably. Alison is dealing with the interesting but ticklish subject of human beauty, and, like Burke, is justly sarcastic on the "four noses from chin to breast," "arm and a half from this to that" style of measurement. But he is himself still an abject victim of the type-theory. Beauty must suit the type; and its characteristics must have a fixed qualitative value—blue eyes being expressive of softness, dark complexions of melancholy, and so on. But here he is comparatively sober.[1] Later he indulges in the following: "The form of the Grecian nose is said to be originally beautiful, . . . and in many cases it is undoubtedly so. Apply, however, this beautiful form to the countenance of the Warrior, the Bandit, the Martyr, or to any which is meant to express deep or powerful passion, and the most vulgar spectator would be sensible of dissatisfaction, if not of disgust." Let us at least be thankful that Alison has freed us from being "the most vulgar spectator." Why the Warrior, why the Martyr, why the deep and powerful man, should not have a Grecian nose I fail to conceive: but the incompatibility of a Bandit and a straight profile lands me in profounder abysses of perplexity. The artillery and the blue horse must yield their pride of place: the reason in that instance is, if not exquisite, instantly discernible. But nothing in all Neoclassic arbitrariness from Scaliger to La Harpe seems to me to excel or equal the Censure of the Bandit with the Grecian Nose as a monstrous Bandit, a disgustful object, hateful not merely to the elect but to the very vulgar.[2]

Let us hear the conclusion of this whole æsthetic matter. Any man of rather more than ordinary intelligence—perhaps any man of ordinary intelligence merely—who has been properly educated from his youth up (as all men who show even

[1] Ibid.

[2] The mother of Gwendolen Harleth was wiser. "Oh! my dear, any nose," said she, "will do to be miserable with!" and if so, why not to be preda- tory? The only possible answer of course caps the absurdity. The conventional Bandit is an Italian; the conventional Italian has an aquiline nose: therefore, &c.

a promise of ordinary intelligence should have been) in ancient
and modern philosophy, who knows his Plato, his
Aristotle, and his neo-Platonists, his Scholastics, his
moderns from Bacon and Hobbes and Descartes
downwards, can, if he has the will and the opportunity, compose a theory of æsthetics. That is to say, he
can, out of the natural appetite towards poetry and literary
delight which exists in all but the lowest and most unhappy
souls, and out of that knowledge of concrete examples thereof
which exists more or less in all, excogitate general principles
and hypotheses, and connect them with immediate and particular examples, to such an extent as the Upper Powers permit or the Lower Powers prompt. If he has at the same
time—a happy case of which the most eminent example up
to the present time is Coleridge—a concurrent impulse towards
actual "literary criticism," towards the actual judgment of the
actual concrete examples themselves, this theory *may* more
or less help him, need at any rate do him no great harm. *Mais
cela n'est pas nécessaire*, as was said of another matter ; and
there are cases, many of them in fact, where the attention to
such things has done harm.

An interim conclusion on the æsthetic matter.

For after all, once more Beyle, as he not seldom did, reached
the *flammantia mœnia mundi* when he said, in the character
of his "Tourist" *eidolon*, "En fait de beau chaque homme a sa
demi-aune." Truth is not what each man troweth : but beauty
is to each man what to him seems beautiful. You may better
the seeming :—the fact is at the bottom of all that is valuable
in the endlessly not-valuable chatter about education generally,
and it excuses, to a certain extent, the regularity of Classicism, the selfish "culture" of the Goethean ideal, the extravagances of the ultra-Romantics. But yet

"A God, a God, the severance ruled,"

and you cannot bridge the gulfs that a God has set by any
philosophastering theory.[1]

---

[1] Had all æstheticians approached their subject in the spirit of our English historian of it, much of what I have said would be quite inappli-cable. "The æsthetic theorist," says Mr Bosanquet in his *Preface* (*History*

Yet although all this is, according to my opinion at least, absolutely true ; although literary criticism has not much more to do with æsthetics than architecture has to do with physics and geology—than the art of the wine-taster or the tea-taster has to do with the study of the papillæ of the tongue and the theory of the nervous system generally, or with the botany of the vine and the geology of the vineyard ; although, finally, as we have seen and shall see, the most painful and earnest attention to the science of the beautiful appears to be compatible with an almost total indifference to concrete judgment and enjoyment of the beautiful itself, and even with egregious misjudgment and failure to enjoy,—yet we cannot extrude this other *scienza nuova* altogether, if only because of the almost inextricable entanglement of its results with those of criticism proper.   And it is more specially to be dealt with in this particular place because, beyond all question, the direction of study to these abstract inquiries did contribute to the freeing of criticism from the shackles in which it had lain so long.   Any new way of attention to any subject is likely to lead to the detection of errors in the old : and as the errors of Neo-classicism were peculiarly arbitrary and irrational, the "high *priori* way" did certainly give an opportunity of discovering them from its superior height—the most superfluous groping among preliminaries and foundations gave a chance of unearthing the roots of falsehood.   As in the old comparison Saul found a kingdom when he sought for his father's asses,

---

of Æsthetic : London, 1892), " desires to understand the artist, not in order to interfere with the latter, but in order to satisfy an intellectual interest of his own." With such an attitude I have no quarrel : nor, I should think, need those who take it have any quarrel with mine. I may add that from this point onwards I shall take the liberty of a perpetual silent reference to Mr Bosanquet's treatment of subjects and parts of subjects which seem to me to lie outside of my own plan. I purposely abstained from reading his book until two-thirds of my own were published, and more than two-thirds more of the remainder were written. And I have been amused and pleased, though not surprised, to find that if we had planned the two books together from the first, we could hardly have covered the ground more completely and with less confusion. I cannot, however, help observing that Mr Bosanquet, like almost all æstheticians I know, except Signor Croce, though he does not neglect literature, at least devotes most attention to the plastic arts. This is perhaps a little significant.

so it was at least possible for a man, while he was considering æsthetic abstractions and theories, to have his eyes suddenly opened to the fact that Milton was not merely a fanatic and fantastic, with a tendency to the disgusting, and that Shakespeare was something more than an "abominable" mountebank.[1]

Notice has already been taken of the importance, as it seems to the present writer, of the widened and catholicised study of literature during the earlier eighteenth century. Almost all the "English precursors" have in fact owed part of their position here to their share in this literary "Voyage round the World." Some further exposition and criticism of the way in which the exploration itself worked may be looked for in *Hist. Crit.*, ii., Interchapter vi. Here we may give a little space to some such explorers who, though scarcely worthy of a place among critics proper, did good work in this direction, and to the main lines and subjects on and in regard to which the explorations were conducted. For it cannot be too often repeated that without Literary History, Literary Criticism in the proper sense is impossible; that the defects of the latter have, as a rule, been directly connected with ignorance or imperfect knowledge of the former; and that the ocean of literature almost automatically melts and whelms the icebergs of critical error when they find their way into it.

The most interesting and directly important of the great *The study of* literary countries in regard to this matter is un-*Literature.* doubtedly England. Curiosity in Germany was much more widespread and much more industrious;[2] but in

---

[1] The student who wishes to be thorough on this subject should consult not merely Mr Bosanquet and the "Parabasis" of *Hist. Crit.* mentioned above, but also the work of the Italian critic noticed before, Signor Benedetto Croce, which is now accessible in English. He thinks me "barren in philosophy," and I think him rather superfluous in it; but he has been good enough to compliment my literature, and I think I may say that by aid of that literature I had independently attained some results not very different from the best of his.

[2] The Germans, I believe, have definitely ticketed these explorers as "The Antiquarians."

the first place the notable German explorers are not here[1] our direct concern, and in the second, the width too often with them turned to indiscriminateness, and the industry to an intelligent hodman's work. France, by providing such pioneers as Sainte-Palaye, and by starting the great *Histoire Littéraire*, contributed immensely to the stimulation and equipment of foreign students; but it was some time before this work reacted directly on her own literature. There was less done in Spain, where for a time the adherents of the older literature were, like their ancestors in the Asturias, but a handful driven to bay, instead of as in other countries an insurrectionary multitude gaining more and more ground; and the traditional Dante-and-Petrarch worship of Italy did at this time little real good. Both directly and indirectly — at home and, chiefly in the Shakespeare direction, abroad — England here occupies the chief place.

Her exercises on the subject may be advantageously considered under certain subject-headings: Shakespeare himself, Spenser, Chaucer, minor writers between the Renaissance and the Restoration, Middle English, and Anglo-Saxon. It is not necessary here to bestow special attention on Milton-study, despite its immense influence both at home and abroad, because it was continuous. From Dryden to the present day, Milton has always been with the guests at any feast of English literature, sometimes, it is true, as a sort of skeleton, but much more often as one whom all delight more or less intelligently to honour.

It is not mere fancy which has discerned a certain turning-point of importance to literature, in the fact that between the *The study of* Fourth Folio and the first critical or quasi-critical *Shakespeare.* edition (Rowe's) there intervened (1685-1709) not quite a full quarter of a century. The successive editions of Rowe himself, Pope, Theobald, Hanmer, Warburton, and Johnson not merely have a certain critical interest in themselves, not merely illustrate the progress of criticism in a useful

[1] They and the other Continental pioneers are fully dealt with in the appropriate sections of the larger *History*.

manner, but bring before us, as nothing else could do, the way in which Shakespeare himself was kept before the minds of the three generations of the eighteenth century.[1]

Spenser's fortunes in this way coincided with Shakespeare's to a degree which cannot be quite accidental. The third folio *Spenser.* of the *Faerie Queene* appeared in 1679, and the first critical edition—that of Hughes—in 1715. But the study-stage—not the theatrical, considering a list of adapters which runs from Ravenscroft through Shadwell up to Dryden—had spared Shakespeare the attentions of the Person of Quality.[2] Before Hughes, Spenser had received those of Prior, a person of quality [3] much greater; but Prior had spoilt the stanza, and had travestied the diction almost worse than he did in the case of the *Nut-Browne Maid.* He would not really count in this story at all if his real services in other respects did not show that it was a case of "time and the hour," and if his remarks in the Preface to *Solomon* did not show, very remarkably, a genuine admiration of Spenser himself, and a strong dissatisfaction with the end-stopped couplet. And so of Hughes' edition: yet perhaps the import of the saying may escape careless readers. At first one wonders why a man like Prior should have taken the trouble even to spoil the Spenserian stanza; why an editor like Hughes should have taken the much greater trouble to edit a voluminous poet whose most ordinary words he had to explain, whose stanza he also thought "defective," and whose general composition he denounced as "monstrous" and so forth; why all the imitators [4] should have imitated what most of them at any rate seem to have regarded as chiefly parodiable. Yet one soon perceives that

---

[1] I may once more refer the reader to Mr Nichol Smith's valuable edition of the Prefaces to these. Mrs Montagu's famous *Essay on the Writings and Genius of Shakespeare* (London, 1769, and often reprinted) may expect a separate mention. It is well intentioned but rather feeble, much of it being pure *tu quoque* to Voltaire, and sometimes extremely unjust on Corneille, and even on Æschylus. It is not quite ignorant; but once more *non tali auxilio!*

[2] *V. Hist. Crit.,* ii. 416.

[3] See the *Ode to the Queen,* 1706. Prior inserts a tenth line, and makes the seamless coat an awkwardly cobbled thing of quatrain, quatrain, couplet.

[4] See above, p. 214.

mens agitat molem, that the lump was leavened, that, as in one case at any rate (Shenstone's), is known to be the fact, "those who came to scoff remained to pray." They were dying of thirst, though they did not know how near the fountain was; and though they at first mistook that fountain and even profaned it, the healing virtues conquered them at last.

The same coincidence does not fail wholly even with Chaucer, of whom an edition, little altered from Speght's, appeared in

Chaucer.   1687, while the very ill-inspired but still intentionally critical attempt of Urry came out in 1721, Dryden's wonderful modernisings again coming between. But Chaucer was to wait for Tyrwhitt, more than fifty years later (1775) before he met any full scholarly recognition, and this was natural enough. There had been no real change in English prosody since Spenser, any more than since Shakespeare: and the archaism of the former was after all an archaism not less deliberate, though much better guided by genius, than that of any of his eighteenth-century imitators. To the appreciation of Chaucer's prosody one simple but, till turned, almost insuperable obstacle existed in the valued final *e*, while his language, his subjects, and his thought were separated from modern readers by the great gulf of the Renaissance,—a gulf indeed not difficult to bridge after a fashion, but then unbridged.

Invaluable as the study of Shakespeare was in itself, its value was not limited to this direct gain. Partly to illustrate *Elizabethan* him and partly from a natural extension, his fellow-*minors.* dramatists were resorted to,—indeed Ben Jonson and Beaumont and Fletcher had never lost hold of the acting stage. A few of the greatest, Marlowe especially, were somewhat long in coming to their own; but with others it was different, and the publication of Dodsley's *Old Plays*, at so early a date as 1744, shows with what force the tide was setting in this direction. Reference was made in the last chapter to the very remarkable *Muses' Library* which Oldys began even earlier, though he did not find encouragement enough to go on with it,[1] and the more famous adventure of the *Reliques* was followed up in the latter part of the century by divers explorations of the treasures of the past, notably that of the short-lived Headley.[2]

Nay, about the close of the seventeenth century and the beginning of the eighteenth it looked as if early Middle English *Middle and* and Anglo-Saxon themselves might come in for a *Old English.* share of attention, as a result of the labours of such men as Hearne and Hickes. But the Jacobite antiquary was interested mainly in the historical side of literature, and Hickes, Wanley, and the rest were a little before their time, though that time itself was sure to come. And before it came the all but certain forgeries of Macpherson, the certain forgeries of Chatterton, the sham ballads with which, after Percy's example, Evans and others loaded their productions of the true,

---

[1] To this context perhaps best belongs Thomas Hayward's *British Muse,*[*] *T. Hayward.* an anthology on the lines of Poole and Bysshe, published in 1738 and dedicated to Lady Mary Wortley Montagu. The book has a preface of some length (which is said to be, like the dedication, the work not of the compiler but of Oldys † himself), criticising its predecessors (including Gildon) rather severely, and showing knowledge of English criticism generally; but the point of chief interest about the book is its own interest in, and extensive draughts from, Elizabethan Drama. Not merely "the divine and incomparable" Shakespeare, not merely the still popular sock and buskin of Ben Jonson and of Beaumont and Fletcher, but almost all the others, from Massinger and Middleton down to Goffe and Gomersall, receive attention, although, as he tells us, they were so hard to get that you had to give between three or four pounds for a volume

[*] 3 vols., London.
† It thus connects the book with *The Muses' Library.*

containing some ten plays of Massinger. This is noteworthy; but that his zeal was not according to full knowledge is curiously shown by the contempt with which he speaks, not merely of Bodenham's *Belvedere,* but of Allot's *England's Parnassus,* alleging "the little merit of the obsolete poets from which they were extracted." Now it should be unnecessary to say that Allot drew, almost as largely as his early date permitted him, on "the divine and incomparable" himself, on Spenser, and on others only inferior to these. But this carping at forerunners is too common. If Oldys could write thus, what must have been the ignorance of others?

[2] Even before, at, or about the date of the *Reliques* themselves, a good deal was being done—*e.g.,* Capell's well-known *Prolusions,* which gave as early as 1760 the real *Nut-Browne Maid,* Sackville's *Induction, Edward III.,* and Davies' *Nosce Teipsum,* and the *Miscellaneous Pieces* of 1764, supplying Marston's *Poems* and *The Troublesome Reign of King John.*

all worked (bad as some of the latter might be) for good in the direction of exciting and whetting the literary appetite for things not according to the Gospel of Neo-Classicism.

The study of older Foreign literature was not, till very late in the century, of much importance in England, Gray being once more the chief exception, and its effects on him being, as usual, unproductive, except in the case of Prose. But Cervantes had a great and constant effect especially on and through Fielding, — the theory and practice of the Comic Prose Epic being fatal to Neo-Classic assumptions. Dante, if not much relished, must have been and was sometimes read, and Ariosto and Tasso were favourites with students of "elegant" literature. All these and others could not but work in one way and in ways leading to one goal—little as that goal may have been definitely sought by those who were making for it.

[1] I have seen an ingenious attempt recently made in America by a writer whose work and name I have unfortunately mislaid, to *dis*prove the influence of Spenser - study. I am afraid I cannot regard this as much more than a fresh instance of the temptation to more or less erudite paradox which the system of theses and monographs offers. The author has read meritoriously : but his arguments are of very little validity.

INTERCHAPTER IV.

THE period or stage of English criticism reviewed in the last chapter may seem at first sight extremely confused ; composed as it is of constituents separated from their countrymen, their contemporaries, and in some cases even their fellow-workers, whom we have dealt with formerly. But these constituents have in reality the greatest of all unities, a unity (whether conscious or unconscious does not matter a jot) of *purpose.*

"One port, methought, alike they sought,
One purpose hold where'er they fare."

The port was the Fair Haven of Romanticism, and the purpose was to distinguish "that which is established because it is right, from that which is right because it is established," as Johnson himself formulates it. And now, of course, the horse-leeches of definition will ask me to define Romanticism, and now, also, I shall do nothing of the sort, and borrow from the unimpeachable authority of M. Brunetière[1] my reason for not doing it. What most of the personages of this book sought or helped (sometimes without at all seeking, sometimes in actual antipathy to it) to establish is Romanticism, and Romanticism is what they sought or helped to establish.

In negative and by contrast, as usual, there is, however, no difficulty in arriving at a sort of jury-definition, which is perhaps a good deal better to work to port with than the aspiring

---

[1] *Les définitions ne se posent pas à priori, si ce n'est peut-être en mathématique. En histoire, c'est de l'étude patiente de la réalité qu'elles se dégagent* *insensiblement.* Here a "Classic" states the very principle of the opposite creed.

but rather untrustworthy mast-poles of "Renascence of Wonder" and the like. We have indeed seen, in the whole history of Neo-Classicism, that the curse and the mischief of it lay in the tyranny of the Definition itself. You had no sooner satisfied yourself that Poetry was such and such a thing, that it consisted of such and such narrowly delimited Kinds, that its stamped instruments and sealed patterns were this and that, than you proceeded to apply these propositions inquisitorially, excommunicating or executing delinquents and nonconformists. The principal uniformity, amid the wide diversities, of the new critics was that, without any direct concert, without any formulated anti-creed, they all laboured to remove the bolts and the bars, to antiquate the stipulations, to make the great question of criticism not "What Kind have you elected to try? and have you followed the Rules of it? but "What is this that you have *done?* and is it good?" Yet they never, in any instance, formulated the abolition of restrictions, as, for instance, we find Victor Hugo doing in the Preface to the *Orientales.* They had almost invariably some special mediate or immediate object in view, and so the whole tendency is rather to dissolve what exists than to put anything definite in its place.

The survey of their actual accomplishment, therefore, may be best executed, for the purpose of corresponding with and continuing those formerly given, by first considering more generally the main new critical engines — Æsthetic inquiry and the Study of Literature — which have formed in detail the subjects of the latter part of the last chapter; then by summarising the most significant performances, and indicating, as best may be done, the point to which the stage has brought us.

The advantages and importance of the wider and more abstract æsthetic inquiry in reconstituting or reorganising criticism should be pretty obvious. The worst fault of the later Neo-Classicism, in its corruption, was that it tended to become wholly *irrational*—a mere reference to classification; that even its appeal to Nature, and to Reason herself, had got utterly out of *rapport* with real nature, with true reason. Now the construction of a general theory of the Sublime and

Beautiful—however partial or however chimerical the inquiry
into the appeals of different arts and different divisions of the
same art might be—could not but tend—however indirectly,
however much even against the very will of the inquiry—to
unsettle, and sometimes to shatter, the conventional hypotheses
and theories. "Why?" and "Why not?" must force themselves constantly on such an inquirer; and, as has been said
more than once or twice, "Why?" and "Why not?" are
battering-rams, predestined, automatic, irresistible, to conventional judgments of all sorts. It was, indeed, not impossible
for a person sufficiently stupid, or sufficiently ingenious, to
construct an æsthetic which, somehow or other, should fit
in with the accepted ideas.[1] But what stupid people do does
not count for much in the long-run, despite the proverbial
invincibility of stupidity for the time. And the ingenious
person, unless his perverseness were truly diabolical, must
sometimes hit upon truth which would explode all his
convention.

At the same time Æsthetics have proved, and might by
an observer of sufficient detachment have from the first
been seen to be likely to prove, a very dangerous auxiliary
to Criticism, if not even a Stork for a Log. In the first place,
there was the danger—present in fact from the first, impending from before the very first—of fresh arbitrary rules being
set up in the place of the old ones,—of the old infinitely mischievous question, "Does the poet please *as he ought to please?*"
being juggled into the place of the simple "Does he please?"
No form of abstract inquiry can escape this danger: and that
is why, save in matter of the pure intellect, abstract inquiries
should always be suspected. Form your theory and conduct
your observations of the æsthetic sense, of "the Beautiful," of
the mediate axioms of this or that literary kind, as carefully,
as impartially, with as wide a range and view, as you may—
these perilous generalisations and abstractions will always
bring you sooner or later into contact and conflict with the
royal irresponsibility, or (as some may hold it) the anarchic
individualism, of the human senses, and tastes, and artistic

[1] Père André, in France, probably seemed, to himself or others, to do this.

powers. You will hamper your feet with a network of axioms and definitions; you will burden your back with a whole Italian-image-man's rack-full of types. It is somewhat improbable that you will be a Lessing: yet even a Lessing loses himself in inquiries as to what "*a* jealous woman's" revenge will be, what "*an* ambitious woman's" revenge will be. Shakespeare (for that Shakespeare had very much to do with the whole portraiture of Margaret, from the first gracious and playful scene with Suffolk to the sombre and splendid triumph over Elizabeth Woodville, I at least have no doubt) has shown us in Margaret of Anjou the revenge and the other passions of a woman who is at once ambitious, jealous, the victim perhaps not of actually adulterous but certainly of rather extra-conjugal love, yet loyal to her husband's position if not to himself, a tigress alike to her enemies and to her young, a rival in varying circumstance, an almost dispassionate sibyl reflecting and foretelling the woes of her rivals. You can no more disentangle all these threads, and get the passion of this type and the passion of that separate, than Psyche could have done her task without the ants. Yet, early and crude as is the work, it is all right, it is all there. And Æsthetics are not the ants.

A much more dangerous result of addiction to the æsthetic side of criticism, mainly or exclusively, is that you get by degrees away from the literary matter altogether, and resign yourself to the separation with all the philosophy of Marryat's captain, when he gave orders first that he should be called when the last ship of his convoy was out of sight behind, and then when the first hove in sight again. In the exclusive attraction to the æsthetic, the moral, the dramaturgic side and the like, an absolute break of contact with the literary may come about. This is the case even with Lessing, and much more with others. The "word," the "expression," sinks out of the plane of the critic's purview. His Æsthetics become Anæsthetics, and benumb his literary senses and sensibilities.

The benefits, therefore, of the rise of Æsthetics as a special study were far from unmixed, though the influence of that rise was very great. It is otherwise with the Study of Literature. Here it was all but impossible that extension of consideration—from modern and classical to mediæval, from certain arbitrarily preferred modern languages to others—should fail to do good. Prejudice, the bane of Criticism, received, in the mere and necessary progress of this study, a notice to quit. This notice took various forms and was exhibited and attended to in various ways. But they can be reduced to a few heads with very little difficulty.

The first of these is the attempt to judge the work presented, not according to abstract rules, derived or supposed to be derived from ancient critical authority, nor according to its agreement or disagreement with the famous work of the past. To some extent this revolutionary proceeding was forced upon our students by the very nature of the case—it was one of the inevitable benefits of the extension of study, and especially of the return to mediæval literature. To attempt to justify that literature, as Addison, with more or less seriousness, had done, by showing that its methods were after all not so very different from those of Homer, or even Virgil, was in some cases flatly impossible, in most extremely difficult; while in almost all it carried with it a distinct suspicion of burlesque. There was no need of any *dislike* of the classics; but it must have been and it was felt that mediæval and later literature must be handled *differently*.[1] And so—insensibly no doubt at first—there came into Criticism the sovereign and epoch-making recognition of the "leaden rule"—of the fact that literature comes first and criticism after—that criticism must adjust itself to literature, and not *vice versa*. Very likely not one of the men we are here discussing would have accepted this doctrine *simpliciter*:[2] indeed it is the rarest thing to find it accepted even a century and a half after their time, except in eccentric and extravagant forms. But it lay at the root of all their practice.

Further, that practice, deprived of the crutches and go-carts

---

[1] This is where Hurd is so valuable.

[2] It is doubtful whether Hurd would have accepted it; it is pretty certain that no other English writer, except Hume, quite reached the point of view at which it could have presented itself. And Hume *here* was as reactionary as Voltaire.

of rule and precedent, was perforce obliged to follow the natural
path and play of the feelings and faculties—to ask itself first,
"Do I like this?" then, "How do I like it?" then, "What
qualities are there in it which make me like it?" Again,
these questions may not have formulated themselves quite
clearly to any of our group. Again, it would be hard to name
many critics since who have at once fearlessly and faithfully
kept them before their eyes. But, again also, these were the
questions which, however blindly and stumblingly, they followed as their guiding stars, and these have been the real
questions of criticism ever since.

Postponing the discussion of the relationship of this new
criticism to the old, we may turn to another point of its
differentia. This is that students of mediæval literature
especially were—again perforce and whether they would or
no—driven to make excursions into the region of Literary
History, and, what is more, of Comparative Literary History.
They found themselves face to face with forms—the ballad
and the romance being the chief of them—which were either
not represented at all or represented very scantily and obscurely in classical literature, while they had been entirely
and almost pointedly neglected by classical criticism. They
could not but see that, both in mediæval literature proper
and in modern, there were other forms and subvarieties of
literature, in drama,[1] in poetry, in prose, which differed extremely
from anything in ancient letters. In examining these, with
no help from Aristotle, or Longinus, or Horace, they could
not but pursue the natural method of tracing or endeavouring to trace them to their origins, and in so doing they could
not but become conscious, not merely of the history—so long
interrupted by a mist like that of Mirza's vision—of English
or French or whatsoever literature itself, but also more dimly
of the greater map of European literature, as it spread and
branched from the breaking up of the Roman Empire onwards.

---

[1] Lessing's attempt to confute the
French out of Aristotle's mouth is
thoroughly effective *ad homines,* and
most valuable now and then intrinsically. But it has the drawback of
ignoring the fact that, though much
in Shakespeare is justified by Aristotle, much can only be justified without him, and some must be justified
in the very teeth of the *Poetics.*

And this study of Literary History was in the main, this study of Comparative Literary History was almost absolutely, again a new thing.

Nor were the actual critical results which, either expressly or incidentally, came from the exercitations of these critics, of less importance. The turn of the tide may nowhere be seen so strongly as in Joseph Warton's audacious question whether Pope, the god of the idolatry of the earlier part of the century in England, was a poet, or at least a great poet, at all. This indeed was, like all revolutionary manifestos, an extravagance, yet the extravagance was not only symptomatic but to a great extent healthy. It was probably impossible as a matter of tactics—it would certainly have been unnatural as a matter of history and human nature—to refrain from carrying the war into the enemies' country, from laying siege to the enemies' stronghold. And this was invited by the ignorant and insulting depreciation which had long been, and long continued to be, thrown upon one of the most charming and precious divisions of the literature and thought of the world.

But there were more sober fruits of the revolt. Hurd might indeed have developed further that doctrine of Romantic as independent of Classical Unity, which is one of the most important discoveries or at least pronouncements of any time, which practically established a *modus vivendi* between all rational Neo-classic and all rational Romantic criticism, and which has never yet been worked out as it deserves. But his mere enunciation or suggestion of it is all-important. Percy's *Essay on Alliterative Metre*, despite the comparative narrowness of its basis, is both acute and successful; and with Gray's work, begins a more intelligent devotion to Prosody. Thomas Warton, though often a fanciful and sometimes an insufficiently equipped critic, was a critic both alert and sound. And the bent of almost all of them turned, and turned most beneficially, especially in the case of Warton, to History.

The performance of England here was not so fruitful of great critical personalities, such as Lessing in Germany or as Diderot in France—for her greatest, Johnson, was in intention, though by no means wholly in performance, on the other side.   Nor, though the English Æsthetics were influential abroad[1] as well as at home, can they be ranked very high.   In the other chief branch, however, of that practical operation which has been noticed, the rediscovery and revaluation of the capital of the literature for critical purposes, England takes by far the most important position of all.   The French, except from the anti-quarian side, were still neglecting, and even for the most part despising, their own old treasures: and the Germans, though not neglectful of what they had, had less, and dealt with it in a less thoroughly literary spirit.   But Gray, Percy, Hurd, the Wartons (especially Thomas), and all the painful and meri-torious editors from Theobald to Tyrwhitt, were engaged not merely in clearing away rubbish and bringing treasures to light, but in combating the prejudices, and doing away with the delusions and ignorances, which had led to the neglect and contempt of those treasures themselves.

For once more, it is History which is at the root of the critical—as of almost every other—matter.   To judge you must know,—must not merely know the so-called best that has been thought and done and written (for how are you to know the best till you know the rest?), but take in all, or something of all, that has been written, and done, and thought by the undulating and diverse animal called Man.   His un-dulation and his diversity will play you tricks still, know you never so widely; but the margin of error will be narrower the more widely you know.   The most perfect critical work that we have — that of Aristotle and that of Longinus — is due in its goodness to the thoroughness of the writers' know-ledge of what was open to them; in its occasional badness and lack of perfection to the fact that everything was not open to them to know.

---

[1] In fact, no period, oddly enough, is so free from foreign influence as this. German had not begun to exercise any: what French exercised was chiefly old.

CHAPTER VI.

WORDSWORTH AND COLERIDGE: THEIR COMPANIONS AND ADVERSARIES.

WORDSWORTH AND COLERIDGE — THE FORMER'S PREFACES — THAT TO
'LYRICAL BALLADS,' 1800 — ITS HISTORY — THE ARGUMENT AGAINST
POETIC DICTION, AND EVEN AGAINST METRE—THE APPENDIX: POETIC
DICTION AGAIN — THE MINOR CRITICAL PAPERS — COLERIDGE'S EX-
AMINATION OF WORDSWORTH'S VIEWS—HIS CRITICAL QUALIFICATIONS
—UNUSUAL INTEGRITY OF HIS CRITIQUE — ANALYSIS OF IT — THE
"SUSPENSION OF DISBELIEF" — ATTITUDE TO METRE — EXCURSUS ON
SHAKESPEARE'S 'POEMS' — CHALLENGES WORDSWORTH ON "REAL"
AND "RUSTIC" LIFE — "PROSE" DICTION AND METRE AGAIN — CON-
DEMNATION IN FORM OF WORDSWORTH'S THEORY—THE 'ARGUMENTUM
AD GULIELMUM'—THE STUDY OF HIS POETRY—HIGH MERITS OF THE
EXAMINATION — WORDSWORTH A REBEL TO LONGINUS AND DANTE—
THE 'PREFACE' COMPARED MORE SPECIALLY WITH THE 'DE VULGARI,'
AND DANTE'S PRACTICE WITH WORDSWORTH'S—THE COMPARISON FATAL
TO WORDSWORTH AS A CRITIC — OTHER CRITICAL PLACES IN COLE-
RIDGE—THE REST OF THE 'BIOGRAPHIA'—'THE FRIEND'—'AIDS TO
REFLECTION,' ETC.—THE 'LECTURES ON SHAKESPEARE,' ETC.—THEIR
CHAOTIC CHARACTER AND PRECIOUSNESS—SOME NOTEWORTHY THINGS
IN THEM: GENERAL AND PARTICULAR—COLERIDGE ON OTHER DRA-
MATISTS—THE 'TABLE TALK'—THE 'MISCELLANIES'—THE LECTURE 'ON
STYLE' — THE 'ANIMA POETÆ' — THE 'LETTERS' — THE COLERIDGEAN
POSITION AND QUALITY—HE INTRODUCES ONCE FOR ALL THE CRITERION
OF IMAGINATION, REALISING AND DISREALISING—THE "COMPANIONS"
—SOUTHEY—GENERAL CHARACTERISTICS OF HIS CRITICISM—REVIEWS
—'THE DOCTOR' — ALTOGETHER SOMEWHAT "IMPAR SIBI" — LAMB
—HIS "OCCULTISM" AND ALLEGED INCONSTANCY — THE EARLY
'LETTERS'—THE 'SPECIMENS'—THE GARRICK PLAY NOTES—MISCEL-
LANEOUS ESSAYS—'ELIA'—THE LATER 'LETTERS'—UNIQUENESS OF
LAMB'S CRITICAL STYLE AND THOUGHT—LEIGH HUNT: HIS SOME-
WHAT INFERIOR POSITION — REASONS FOR IT — HIS ATTITUDE TO
DANTE — EXAMPLES FROM 'IMAGINATION AND FANCY' — HAZLITT—

METHOD OF DEALING WITH HIM—HIS SURFACE AND OCCASIONAL
FAULTS: IMPERFECT KNOWLEDGE AND METHOD — EXTRA-LITERARY
PREJUDICE—HIS RADICAL AND USUAL EXCELLENCE—'THE ENGLISH
POETS'—THE 'COMIC WRITERS'—'THE AGE OF ELIZABETH'—'CHAR-
ACTERS OF SHAKESPEARE'—'THE PLAIN SPEAKER'—'THE ROUND
TABLE,' ETC.—'THE SPIRIT OF THE AGE'—'SKETCHES AND ESSAYS'—
'WINTERSLOW'—HAZLITT'S CRITICAL VIRTUE, IN SET PIECES, AND
UNIVERSALLY—BLAKE—HIS CRITICAL POSITION AND DICTA—THE
"NOTES ON REYNOLDS" AND WORDSWORTH—COMMANDING POSITION
OF THESE—SIR WALTER SCOTT COMMONLY UNDERVALUED AS A CRITIC
—INJUSTICE OF THIS—CAMPBELL: HIS 'LECTURES ON POETRY'—HIS
'SPECIMENS'—SHELLEY: HIS 'DEFENCE OF POETRY'—LANDOR—HIS
LACK OF JUDICIAL QUALITY—IN REGULAR CRITICISM—THE CONVERSA-
TIONS—'LOCULUS AUREOLUS'—BUT AGAIN DISAPPOINTING—THE
REVIVAL OF THE POPE QUARRELS—BOWLES—BYRON—THE 'LETTER
TO MURRAY,' ETC.—OTHERS: ISAAC DISRAELI—SIR EGERTON BRYDGES
—'THE RETROSPECTIVE REVIEW'—THE 'BAVIAD' AND 'ANTI-JACOBIN,'
WITH WOLCOT AND MATHIAS—THE INFLUENCE OF THE NEW 'RE-
VIEWS,' ETC.—JEFFREY—HIS LOSS OF PLACE AND ITS CAUSE—HIS
INCONSISTENCY—HIS CRITICISM ON MADAME DE STAËL—ITS LESSON—
HALLAM—HIS ACHIEVEMENT—ITS MERITS AND DEFECTS—IN GENERAL
DISTRIBUTION AND TREATMENT—IN SOME PARTICULAR INSTANCES—
HIS CENTRAL WEAKNESS, AND THE VALUE LEFT BY IT.

THERE are many differences, real and imaginary, partial and
general, parallel and cross, between ancient, and mediæval, and

Wordsworth and Coleridge. modern poetry; but there is one, very striking, of
a kind which specially differentiates ancient and
mediæval (except Dante) from modern.   In the
former class of poets the "critic whom every poet must
contain" was almost entirely silent, or conveyed his criticism
through his verse only.   It would have been of the very
first interest to have an Essay from the hand of Euripides
justifying his decadent and sentimental fashion of drama, or
from that of Lucretius on the theory and practice of didactic
verse: but the lips of neither were unsealed in this direction.
Dante, on the other hand, as we have seen, was prepared and
ready to put the rationale of his own verse, his own beliefs
about poetry, into prose: so at the Renaissance were the
poets of Italy and France; so was Dryden, so was Pope.

In no instance, however, save perhaps that of the Pléiade
and Du Bellay's *Défense et Illustration,* did a protagonist of

the new poetry take the field in prose so early and so aggressively as did Wordsworth in his Preface to the second edition
of *Lyrical Ballads*. In none, without exception, was such an
attack so searchingly criticised and so powerfully seconded,
with corrections of its mistakes, as in the case of the well-
known chapters of the *Biographia Literaria* in which Coleridge
examined Wordsworth's examination. These, it is true, came
later in time, but when the campaign, whereof the first sword
had been drawn in the *Lyrical Ballads*, and the first horn
blown in the Preface of their second edition, though far gone
was not finished, when the final blows, by the hands of Keats
and Shelley, had still to be struck.

The *Preface*, with the little group of other prefaces and
observations which supplements it,[1] provides a bundle of
The former's documents unequalled in interest except by the *De*
Prefaces. *Vulgari Eloquio* in the special class, while, as it
happens, it goes directly against the tenor of that precious
booklet. Wordsworth, there can be no doubt, had been deeply
annoyed by the neglect or the contemptuous reception of the
Lyrical Ballads, to which hardly any one had done justice
except the future Archdeacon Wrangham, while his own
poems in simple language had offended even more than *The*
Ancient Mariner had puzzled. To some extent I do not question that—his part of the scheme being to make the familiar
poetical, just as it was Coleridge's to make the unfamiliar
acceptable, the uncommon common—the refusal of "poetic
diction" which he here advances and defends was a *vera causa*,
a true actuating motive. But there is also, I think, no doubt
that, as so often happens, resentment, and a dogged determination to "spite the fools," made him here represent the
principle as much more deliberately carried out than it actually
was. And the same doggedness was no doubt at the root of
his repetition of this principle in all his subsequent prose

---

[1] It is wisely usual in editions of
Wordsworth to print these together
and consecutively. They are so short,
and accessible in so many different
shapes, that it seems superfluous to
give page-references to any particular
edition. The *Letter to a Friend of*
Robert Burns (1816) (which Mr Rhys
has included in the *Literary Pamphlets*
noticed elsewhere) is less purely literary, but has important passages,
especially that on *Tam o' Shanter*.

observations, though, as has been clear from the first to almost all impartial observers,[1] he never, from *Tintern Abbey* onwards, achieves his highest poetry, and very rarely achieves high poetry at all, without putting that principle in his pocket.

That the actual preface begins with a declaration that he was rather more than satisfied with the reception of his poems,

That to Lyrical Ballads, 1800. and that the appearance of a systematic defence is set down to "request of friends," is of course not in the least surprising, and will only confirm any student of human nature in the certainty that pique was really at the bottom of the matter. As a matter of fact, there is no more typical example of an aggressive-defensive *plaidoyer* in the whole history of literature.

It begins with sufficient boldness and originality (indeed "W. W." was never deficient in either) admitting fully that

Its history. "by writing in verse, an author is supposed to make a formal engagement that he will gratify certain habits of association," and merely urging that these habits have varied remarkably. The principle here is sound enough; it is in effect the same which we have traced in previous "romantic" criticism from Shenstone onwards; but the historical illustrations are unfortunate. They are "the age of Catullus, Terence, and Lucretius" contrasted with that of Statius and Claudian, and "the age of Shakespeare and Beaumont and Fletcher" with that of Donne and Cowley or Dryden and Pope. The *nisus* of the school towards the historic argument, and, at the same time, its imperfect education in literary history, could hardly be better illustrated. For, not to quibble about the linking of Statius and Claudian, the age of Catullus and Lucretius was most certainly *not* the age of Terence; and the English pairs are still more luckless. Donne *and* Cowley, Shakespeare *and* Beaumont and

---

[1] Since this was originally written, there has been a tendency to take up the cudgels for "W. W." I do not think it necessary to add more in consequence: for nothing that has been said has weakened my own opinion in the least, highly as I esteem Professors Raleigh and Bradley, and perhaps others of those who differ with me. Indeed the best of them, I think, are disposed to admit that W. W. said more than he meant, and even to some extent what he did *not* mean.

Fletcher, are bad enough in themselves : but the postponement
of Donne to the twin dramatists, when he was the elder of
Fletcher probably by six or seven years, of Beaumont by
ten or twelve, is rather sad.   However, it is not on history
that Wordsworth bases his attack.

His object, he tells us, was to choose incidents and illustrations from common life; to relate and describe them, as far
The argu- as was possible, in a selection of language really
ment against used by men; and at the same time to throw over
poetic dic- them a certain colouring of imagination, whereby
tion, and
even against ordinary things should be presented to the mind in
metre. an unusual aspect—a long but much less forcible
appendix examining why the life so chosen was not merely
" ordinary," but " rustic and humble."   The kernel of his next
paragraph is the famous statement that all good poetry is " the
spontaneous overflow of powerful feelings," and then, after a
little divagation, he sets to work to show how such a style
as he was using was adapted to be the channel of such an
overflow.   He utterly refuses Personification: he " has taken
as much pains to avoid what is called Poetic Diction as is
ordinarily taken to produce it"; he " has at all times endeavoured to look steadily at the subject with little falsehood of
description "; and he has not only denied himself false poetic
diction, but many expressions in themselves proper and beautiful, which have been foolishly repeated by bad poets till they
became disgusting.   A selected sonnet from Gray [1] is then rather
captiously attacked for the sake of showing (what certainly
few will admit) that, in its only part of value, the language
differs in no respect from that of prose: whence the heretic
goes farther and, first asserting that there is *no* essential
difference between the language of Prose and that of Poetry,
proceeds in a note to object to the opposition of Poetry and
Prose at all, and to the regarding of the former as synonymous
with metrical composition.   Then he asks what a poet *is:*
and answers himself at great length, dwelling on the poet's
philosophical mission, but admitting that it is his business to
give pleasure.   He anticipates the objection, " Why, then, do

---

[1] That on the death of West.

you not write in Prose?" with the rather weak retort, "Why
should I not add the charm of metrical language to what I
have to say?" A little later comes the other famous definition
of poetry as "emotion recollected in tranquillity," with a long
and exceedingly unsuccessful attempt to vindicate some work
of his own from the charge of being ludicrous. And the
Preface ends with two candid but singularly damaging admissions, that there *is* a pleasure confessedly produced by metrical compositions very different from his own, and that, in
order entirely to enjoy the poetry which he is undertaking, it
would be necessary to give up much of what is ordinarily
enjoyed.

There is an appendix specially devoted to "Poetic Diction"
in which Wordsworth develops his objection to this. His

The appendix: Poetic Diction again.

argument is curious, and from his own point of
view rather risky. Early poets wrote from passion,
yet naturally, and so used figurative language: later
ones, without feeling passion, imitated them in the
use of Figures, and so a purely artificial diction was formed.
So also metre was early added, and came to be regarded as a
symbol or promise of poetic diction itself. To which of course
it is only necessary to register the almost fatal demurrer,
"Why, if the early poets used figurative language different
from ordinary, may not later ones do so? or do you mean
that Greek shoemakers of Homer's time said *koruthaiolos* and
dolichoskion?" Again, "How about this curious early 'super-
adding' of metre? Where is your evidence? and supposing
you could produce any, what have you to say to the further
query, 'If the metre was superadded, what could have been
the reason, except that some superaddition was felt to be
wanted?'"

It is proof of the rather prejudiced frame of mind in which
Wordsworth wrote that, in some subsequent criticisms of par-

The Minor Critical Papers.

ticulars, he objects to Cowper's "church-going bell"
as "a strange abuse"—from which we must suppose
that he himself never talked of a "dining-room," for
it is certain that the room no more dines than the bell goes
to church. The later papers on "Poetry as a Study," and

"Poetry as Observation and Description," are also full of interesting matter, though here, as before, their literary history leaves much to desire, and though they are full of examples of the characteristic stubbornness with which Wordsworth clings to his theory. The most remarkable example probably of this stubbornness is the astonishing note to the letter on the last-named subject (addressed to Sir George Beaumont), in which, after attributing to the poet Observation, Sensibility, Reflection, Information, Invention, and Judgment, he adds, with a glance at his enemy, Metre—"As sensibility to harmony of numbers *and the power of producing it* are *invariably* attendants on the faculties above specified, nothing has been said upon those requisites." Perhaps there is no more colossal *petitio principii*, and at the same time no more sublime ignoring of facts, to be found in all literature, than that "invariably."

Interesting, however, as the Preface and its satellites are in themselves, they are far more interesting as the occasion of *Coleridge's examination of Wordsworth's views.* the much longer examination of the main document which forms the centre, and as criticism the most valuable part, of the *Biographia Literaria*[1] of Coleridge, Wordsworth's fellow-worker in these same *Lyrical Ballads.* That Wordsworth was himself not wholly pleased with this criticism of his criticism, we know: and it would have been strange if he had been—nay, if a much less arrogant and egotistical spirit than his had taken it quite kindly. But Coleridge was on this occasion entirely within his right. The examination, though in some parts unsparing enough, was conducted throughout in the most courteous, indeed in the most eulogistic, tone; the critic, especially after the lapse of so many years,[2] could not be denied the right of pointing out the limits of his agreement with a manifesto which, referring as it did to joint work of his and another's, might excusably be supposed to represent his conclusions as well as those of his fellow-worker.

As to his competence for the task, there could even then be little, and can now be no, dispute. Wordsworth himself,

---

[1] I have used, and refer to, the Bohn edition of Coleridge's Prose Works.

[2] 1800-1817. (Recent Wordsworthians, *v. sup.*, prefer rather to belittle Coleridge.)

though he has left some valuable critical dicta, had by no means all, or even very many, of the qualifications of a critic. His intellect, save at his rare moments of highest poetical inspiration, was rather strong than fine or subtle; and it could not, even at those moments, be described as in any degree flexible or wide-ranging. He carried into literature the temperament of the narrowest theological partisan; and would rather that a man were not poetically saved at all, than that he were saved while not following "W. W.'s" own way. His reading, moreover, was far from wide, and his intense self-centredness made him indifferent about extending it: while he judged everything that he did read with reference to himself and his own poetry.

In all these respects, except poetical intensity, Coleridge was his exact opposite. But for a certain uncertainty, a sort *His critical* of Will-o'-the-Wispishness which displays itself *qualifi-* in some of his individual critical estimates—and for *cations.* the too well-known inability to carry out his designs, which is not perhaps identical, or even closely connected, with this uncertainty,—he might be called, he may perhaps even in spite of them be called, one of the very greatest critics of the world. He had read immensely, and much of his reading had been in the philosophy of æsthetics, more in pure literature itself. The play of his intellect—when opium and natural tendency to digression did not drive it devious and muddle it—was marvellously subtle, flexible, and fine. He could take positions not his own with remarkable alacrity; was nothing if not logical, and few things more than historical-literary. Further, such egotisms as came into play in this particular quarrel all made for righteousness in his case, while they were snares to Wordsworth. It may be ungracious, but is not unfair, to say that Wordsworth's contempt for poetic diction, and his belittling of metre, arose very mainly from the fact that, in his case, intense meaning was absolutely required to save his diction from stiffness on the one hand and triviality on the other, while he had no very special metrical gifts. Coleridge, though he certainly had no lack of meaning, and could also write simply enough when he

chose, was a metrist [1] such as we have not more than five or
six even in English poetry, and could colour and harmonise
language in such a way that, at his best, not Shakespeare
himself is his superior, and hardly any one else his equal.
The old, the true, sense of *Cui bono?* comes in here victoriously.
It was certainly to Wordsworth's interest that diction and
metre should be relegated to a low place. Coleridge, though
he had personal reasons for taking their part, could do well
without them, and was not obliged to be their champion.

However all this may be, there is no doubt about the importance of the discussion of Wordsworth's literary theories, in
Unusual in- chaps. xiv. to xxii. of the *Biographia*. Some have
tegrity of held that Coleridge could not write a book; more
his critique. have laid it down that he never did write one.
Certainly the title is to be allowed to the *Biographia* as a
whole only by the most elastic allowance, while large parts
of it are at best episodes, and at worst sheer divagations. But,
if books were not sacred things, it would be possible, and of
no inconsiderable advantage, to sub-title this part of the
book *A Critical Enquiry into the Principles which guided the
Lyrical Ballads, and Mr Wordsworth's Account of Them*, to
print this alone as substantive text,[2] and to arrange what
more is wanted as notes and appendices.

The examination begins with an interesting, and (whether
Epimethean or not) quite probable and very illuminative
Analysis account of the actual plan of the *Ballads*, and the
of it. principle on which the shares were allotted. He
and his friend, he tells us, had, during their neighbourly inter-
course in Somerset, often talked of the two cardinal points
of poetry, the power of exciting the sympathy of the reader
by a faithful adherence to the truth of nature, and the power
of giving the interest of novelty by the modifying colours of
imagination. And he illustrates this finely, by instancing

---

[1] In practice, though not always in
theory: for his famous explanation of
his *Christabel* metre is admitted, even
by an authority who takes such different views of prosody from mine as
Mr Robert Bridges, to be quite wrong.

[2] I have, since this was written, endeavoured to do something of the
kind for a practical purpose (to which
nothing is sacred) in my *Loci Critici*
(London and Boston, Mass., 1903), pp.
303-365.

the sudden charm which accidents of light and shade, of moon-shine or sunset, communicate to familiar objects.

The *Ballads* were to illustrate both kinds: and the poets were to divide the parts generally on the principle of Coleridge *The "suspension of disbelief."* endeavouring to make the unfamiliar credible,[1] and Wordsworth the familiar charming. And with a charity which, I fear, the *Preface* will not bear, he proceeds to represent its contentions as applying *only* to the practical poetical attempt which Wordsworth, in accordance with the plan, was on this occasion making. He admits how-ever, that Wordsworth's expressions are at any rate some-times equivocal, and indicates his own standpoint pretty early and pretty decisively by calling the phrase "language of real life" *unfortunate*. And then he proceeds to state his own view with very frequent glances—and more than glances—at his companion's.

From the first, however, it is obvious that on one of the two cardinal points—the necessity or non-necessity of metre *Attitude to metre.* in poetry—he is, though hardly to be called in two minds, for some reason or other reluctant to speak out his one mind. The revival of this old heresy among such men as Wordsworth, Coleridge, Shelley, is the more to be wondered at, in that their predecessors of the eighteenth century had by no means pronounced on the other side in theory, and that therefore they themselves had no excuse of reaction. No one who, at however many removes, followed or professed to follow the authority of Aristotle, could deny that the subject, not the form, made poetry and poems. But just as the tyranny of a certain poetic diction led Wordsworth and others to strike at all poetic diction, so the tyranny of certain metres seems to have induced them to question the necessity of metre in general. At any rate Coleridge's language, though not his real drift, is hesitating and sometimes almost self-contradictory. He will on the same page grant that "all

---

[1] Or, as he puts it in one of the great critical phrases of the world, "to pro-duce that willing *suspension of dis-belief for the moment* which constitutes poetic faith." It derives of course from Aristotle, but the advance on the original is immense.

compositions to which this charm of metre is superadded, whatever their contents, may be called poems," and yet lay down that a poem is "that species of composition which is opposed to works of science by proposing for its immediate object pleasure, not truth," and (after adding to this a limitation, doubtless intended to take in metre, but nebulous enough to justify Peacock himself,[1]) will once more clear off his own mist by saying that if any one "chooses to call every composition a poem which is rhyme or measure or both, I must leave his opinion uncontroverted."

That he himself saw the muddle is beyond doubt, and the opposite page contains a curious series of *aporiæ* which show the difficulty of applying his own definition.[2] The first (*i.e.*, fourteenth) chapter ends with a soft shower of words, rhetorically pleasing rather than logically cogent, about the poet "bringing the whole soul of man into activity"; "fusing the faculties, each into each, by the synthetic and magical power of imagination," reconciling differences and opposites. "Finally, good sense is the body of poetic genius, fancy its drapery, emotion its life, and imagination the soul." In the fifteenth and sixteenth the author turns with evident relief from the definition of the perhaps indefinable to an illustration of it by discussing *Venus and Adonis*. Here, though it would be pleasant, it would be truancy to follow him.

This study, however, is by no means otiose. It leads him to make a comparison between the poetry of the sixteenth and seventeenth centuries, and that of "the present age," a

---

[1] "And from all other species having this object in common with it, it is discriminated by proposing to itself such delight from the whole as is compatible with a distinct gratification from each component part." This is the dialect of "Cimmerian Lodge" with a vengeance! An attempt to expound it will be found in the abstract of the *Lectures* of 1811 given by J. P. Collier: but it sheds little light. And simpler Estesian definitions elsewhere—"Prose is words in good order: poetry the best words in

the best order," &c.—labour likewise under the common curse that *Poetry* escapes them. What better words in what better order than the Lord's Prayer? Is that poetry?

[2] The extraordinary critical genius of Coleridge can hardly be better shown than by his gloss here on the Petronian enigma, *Præcipitandus est liber spiritus*, to which we have referred so often. The poet—the image is not Coleridge's, but I think it very fairly illustrates his view—*rides* the reader's own genius, and both together attain the goal.

comparison of which not the least notable point is a reference

to the *De Vulgari Eloquio*.[1] Coleridge seems only to have known it in the Italian translation; but it is much that he should have known it at all: and though he does not try to bring out its diametrical opposition to Wordsworth, that opposition must have been, consciously or unconsciously, in his mind. And then he comes back to Wordsworth himself.

He now (chap. xvii.) strikes into a line less complimentary and more corrective than his earlier remarks. It is true, he

says, that much of modern poetic style is false, and that some of the pleasure given by it is false likewise. It is true, further, that W. W. has done good by his sticklings for simplicity. But Coleridge cannot follow him in asserting that "the proper diction for poetry in general consists altogether in language taken from the mouths of men in real life." And he proceeds to show, by arguments so obvious and so convincing that it is unnecessary to recapitulate them, that a doctrine of this kind is neither adequate nor accurate—that Wordsworth's own poems do not bear it out, and (pushing farther) that poetry must be "*dis*realised" (he does not use the word) as much as possible. He proceeds, cautiously and politely, but very decidedly, to set the puerilities and anilities [2] of *The Idiot Boy* and *The Thorn* in a clear light, which must have been extremely disagreeable to the particular author; and goes on to pull W. W.'s arguments, as well as his examples, to shreds and thrums. If you eliminate, he says (and most truly), a rustic's poverty of thought and his "provincialism and grossness," you get nothing different from "the language of any other man of common-sense," so that he will not help you in the least; his speech does not in any degree represent the result of special and direct communing with nature. Nay, "real" in the phrase "real life" is itself a wholly treacherous and

---

[1] This (chap. xvi., not long after the beginning (p. 157, ed. Bohn)) is more important indirectly than directly. It is, in itself, very slight, and merely concerns Dante's jealousy for his mother tongue. But it shows knowledge.

[2] These terms are used with no offensive intention, but in strict reference to the matter of the poems.

equivocal adjective. Nor will you do any good by adding "in a state of excitement."

In the next chapter, the eighteenth, Coleridge carries the fray farther still into the enemy's country, hitting the blot *"Prose" dic-* that though W. W.'s *words* may be quite ordinary, *tion and* their arrangement is not. And after wheeling *metre again.* about in this way, he comes at last to the main attack, which he has so often feinted, on Wordsworth's astounding dictum that "there neither is nor can be any essential difference between the language of prose and metrical composition." After clearing his friend (and patient) from an insinuation of paradox, he becomes a little "metaphysical"— perhaps because he cannot help it, perhaps to give himself courage for the subsequent accusation of "sophistry" which he ventures to bring. Of course, he says, there are phrases which, beautiful in poetry, are quite inappropriate in prose. The question is, "Are there no others which, proper in prose, would be out of place in metrical poetry and *vice versa?*" And he has no doubt about answering this question in the affirmative, urging the origin of metre (for which, as we saw, Wordsworth did not attempt to account), and its effects of use and pleasure. He will not admit the appeal to nursery rhymes; and he confesses (a confession which must have given W. W. dire offence) that he should have liked *Alice Fell* and the others much better in prose.

On the whole, Coleridge still shows too great timidity. He is obviously and incomprehensibly afraid of acknowledging pleasure in the metre itself. But — in this differing more signally from Wordsworth than from Wordsworth's uncompromising opponents—he says, "I write in metre, *because* I am about to use a language different from that of prose." And, though on grounds lower than the highest, he finally plucks up courage to declare that "Metre is the proper form of poetry : and poetry [is] imperfect and defective without metre." 'Twill serve, especially when he brings up in support, triarian fashion, "the instinct of seeking unity by harmonious adjustment," and "the practice of the best poets of all countries and of all ages."

x

It is perhaps an anti-climax, though a very Coleridgean
one, when he proceeds to criticise (very justly) Wordsworth's
Condemna- criticism of Gray, and some passages both of his
tion in form own and others: but we can have no quarrel with
of Words-
worth's him when he ends the chapter, too verbosely indeed,
theory. but unanswerably, with the following conclusion
of the whole matter: "When a poem, or part of a poem, shall
be adduced, which is evidently vicious in the figures and
contexture of its style, yet for the condemnation of which
no reason can be assigned, except that it differs from the
style in which men actually converse,—then and not till then
can I hold this theory to be either plausible or practicable, or
capable of furnishing either such guidance, or precaution, that
might not, more easily and more safely, as well as more naturally, have been deduced in the author's own mind from considerations of grammar, logic, and the truth and nature of
things, confirmed by the authority of works whose fame is
not of one country and of one age."

He has now (chaps. xix., xx.) argued himself into more
confidence than he had shown earlier, and seems disposed
The Argu- to retract his concession that W. W.'s limitations
mentum ad were *not* intended to apply to all poetry. He sees,
Gulielmum. indeed, from the criticism on Gray, and from Wordsworth's references to Milton, that this concession was excessive,
but still he thinks the general notion too monstrous for
Wordsworth to have held. And he swerves, once more, to
point out the especial beauty of beautiful diction and beautiful
metre *added to* fine or just thought, and introduces interesting
but rather superfluous examples of this from all manner of
poets down to Wordsworth himself. These last lead him to
the very just conclusion, "Were there excluded from Mr
W.'s poetic compositions all that a literal adherence to the
theory of his Preface would exclude, two-thirds at least of the
marked beauties of his poetry must be erased."[1] Which indeed
is once more a conclusion of the whole matter.[2]

After an odd, a distinctly amusing, but despite its title a, for

[1] Chap. xx. *sub fin.*, p. 201, ed. cit.
[2] Except, once more, to my friends,
Professors Raleigh, Herford, and Bradley, and some more negligible folk.

our purpose, somewhat irrelevant, excursus on "the present
The study of mode of conducting critical journals,"[1] Coleridge
his poetry. concludes with a pretty long[2] and a very interesting
examination of Wordsworth's poetry. He brings out his
defects, his extraordinary declension from the felicitous to the
undistinguished, his matter-of-factness of various kinds (this
part includes a merciless though most polite censure of *The
Excursion*), his undue preference for dramatic [perhaps we
should say dialogic] form, his prolixity, and his introduction
of thoughts and images too great as well as too low for the
subject. The excellences are high purity and appropriateness
of language; weight and sanity of thoughts and sentiments;
strength; originality and *curiosa felicitas* in single lines and
paragraphs; truth of nature in imagery; meditative pathos;
and, lastly, imagination in the highest and strictest sense of
the word.

In fact this chapter, which forms in itself an essay of the
major scale, is one of the patterns, in English, of a critical study
High merits of poetry. None, I think, had previously exhibited
of the the new criticism so thoroughly, and very few, if
examination. any, have surpassed or equalled it since, although
it may be a little injured on the one hand by its limitation
to a particular text, and by the restrictions which the personal
relations of the critic with his author imposed on Coleridge;
on the other, by his own tendencies to digression, verbosity,

---

[1] Chap. xxi. Personality, partisanship, haphazard, garbling, caricature in selection of instances, are the chief faults that Coleridge finds with both *Edinburgh* and *Quarterly*. The reply is dignified in tone and not unjust; but, like other things of the same kind, it illustrates certain permanent weaknesses of human nature. All the faults, I think, which Coleridge finds with "Blue and Yellow" and "Buff" reviewing might be found with his own critique of Maturin's *Bertram*, printed in this very volume. All these faults are certainly found by every generation of authors with their critics, even when these authors happen to have been copious and constant writers of criticism themselves. Always is the author tempted, like Mr Baxter, to cry, "Ah, but *I* was in the right, and these men are dreadfully in the wrong"; always does he think, like the Archbishop of Granada, that the incriminated part of his sermon is exactly the best part; always, when he bewails the absence of the just and impartial critics of other times, does he forget the wise ejaculation of Mr Rigmarole, "Pretty much like our own, I fancy!" (There is no mental reservation in these remarks.)

[2] Four - and - thirty closely printed pages in the Bohn ed.

and intrusion of philosophical "heads of Charles I." In fact, there is no other critical document known to me which attacks the chief and principal things of poetry proper—poetic language and poetic numbers—in so satisfactory a manner, despite the economy which Coleridge displays on the latter head. Some of the ancient and most of the Renaissance discussions shoot too far and too high, and though the arrows may catch fire and give a brilliant and striking illumination, they hit no visible mark. The discussions of Lessing in the *Laocoön* concern an interesting but after all quite subordinate point of the relation of poetry to other arts; nearly all of those in the *Dramaturgie* deal with a part of literature only, and with one which is not, in absolute necessity or theory, a part of literature at all. But here we have the very *differentia* of poetry, handled as in the Περὶ Ὕψους or the *De Vulgari* itself, but handled in a more full, generally applicable, and philosophically based manner than Dante's prose admitted of, and in a wider range than is allowed by the special purpose of Longinus.

With both these great lights of criticism Coleridge agrees almost as thoroughly as Wordsworth disagrees with them: *Wordsworth a rebel to Longinus and Dante.* and it is proper here to fulfil the promise which was made [1] of a consideration of Wordsworth's work in reference to Dante specially, but with extension to Longinus as well.

The collision of Wordsworth with Longinus appears in the very title of the famous little treatise. Fight as we may about the exact meaning of ὕψος, it must be evident, to poets and pedlars alike, that it never can apply to the "ordinary language of real life"; struggle as Wordsworthians may, they never can establish a *concordat* between the doctrine of the *Preface* and the doctrine of the "beautiful word." But as Longinus was not specifically writing of Poetry, and as in reference to Poetry he was writing from his own point of view only, on a special function or aspect of Poetry and Rhetoric alike, he does not meet the Apostle of the Ordinary full tilt and weapon to weapon. I have said that I do not know whether, when

---

[1] *V. sup.*, pp. 21, 22, also the reference to Prof. Herford's recent article.

Wordsworth wrote the *Preface*, he knew the *De Vulgari* or not. If Coleridge had known it at the time, he probably would have imparted his knowledge in the celebrated Nether Stowey talks: but his own reference, itself not suggestive of a very thorough appreciation, is twenty years later. And as Wordsworth was a perfectly fearless person, and had not a vestige of an idea that any created thing had authority sufficient to overcrow W. W., he would pretty certainly have rebuked this Florentine, and withstood him to his face, if he had known his utterances.

But, on the other hand, Dante himself might almost have been writing with the *Preface* before him (except that had *The* Pre- he done so Wordsworth would probably have face *com-* been at least in Purgatory), considering the direct- *pared more* ness, the almost rude lie - circumstantial of the *specially* *with the* antidote. "Take the ordinary language, especially De Vulgari, of rustic men," says Wordsworth. "Avoid rustic ["silvan"] language altogether," says Dante, "and even of 'urban' words let only the noblest remain in your sieve." "If you have Invention, Judgment, and half a dozen other things," every one of which has been possessed in more or less perfection by most of the great writers of the world whether in prose or poetry, "metrical expertness will follow as a matter of course," says Wordsworth. "You must, after painfully selecting the noblest words and arranging them in the noblest style, further arrange them in the best line that experience and genius combined can give you, and yet further build these lines into the artfullest structure that art has devised," says Dante. "Poetry is spontaneous utterance," says he of Cockermouth. "Poetry, and the language proper for it, is a regular 'panther - quest,' an elaborate and painful toil," says the Florentine.

And their practice is no less opposed than their theory; or rather the relation of the two, to theory and practice taken *and Dante's* together, is the most astonishing contrast to be *practice* found in Poetry. Dante never falsifies his theory for a moment. You cannot find a line, in *Commedia* or *Vita Nuova* or anywhere else, where the "panther-quest" of word, and phrase, and line-formation, and stanza-grouping is not evident; you will be put to it to find one where this quest is not consummately successful. And, in following word and phrase and form, Dante never forgets or starves his meaning. He may be sometimes obscure, but never because there is no meaning to discern through the gloom. He may be sometimes technical; but the technicality is never otherwise than the separable garb of a "strange and high" thought and intention. Matter and form with him admit no divorce: their marriage is not the marriage of two independent entities, but the marriage of soul and body. He has no need of the alternation of emotion and tranquillity, of the paroxysm succeeded by the notebook (or interrupted by it and succeeded by the fair copy), because his emotion and his tranquillity are identical, because the tide of his poetry is the tide "too full for sound or foam," at least for splash or spoondrift. He is methodical down to the counting of syllables in poetic words: and yet who has more poetic madness than he?

The difference in Wordsworth is almost startling; it looks as if it had been "done on purpose." He does obey his *with Words-* theory, does accept the language of ordinary life.[1] *worth's.* But when he does so, as (almost) everybody admits, he is too often not poetical at all—never in touch with the highest poetry.[2] And (which is extremely remarkable and has not, I think, been remarked by Coleridge or by many other critics) even in these poems he has not the full courage of his opinions. In no single instance does he venture on the experiment of discarding the merely "superadded charm" of metre, of which he has such a low opinion. He never in one single instance relies on the sheer power of "spontaneous overflow of powerful feelings" on the impetus of "emotion

---

[1] Yet there are curious lapses even here. Take the extreme example, *Alice Fell*, of whom even her author was half-ashamed as mean and homely. How about "fierce career," and "smitten with a startling sound," and the inversion of "Proud creature was she"?

[2] My friend Prof. Raleigh, in his brilliant and (for that word hath something derogated) really critical study of Wordsworth (London, 1903), is of a different opinion: but I hold my own. And I do not enter into controversy on the point, because I have nothing to add to the text, written before Prof. Raleigh's book appeared.

recollected in tranquillity," *without* metre. In the form of poetry, which he affects to despise, he is even as these publicans.

These are two sufficiently striking points; but they are not so striking as the third. Wordsworth *is* a great poet; he *has* moments of all but the sublimest—for this argument we need certainly not grudge to say of the sublimest—poetry. He can bathe us in the light of setting suns, and introduce us even to that which never was on sea and land;[1] he can give us the full contact, the full ecstasy, the very "kiss of the spouse." But in no single instance, again, does he achieve these moments, except—as Coleridge has pointed out to some extent, and as can be pointed out without shirking or blenching at one "place" of poetry—at the price of utterly forgetting his theory, of flinging it to the tides and the winds, of plunging and exulting in poetic diction and poetic arrangement.

So we can only save Wordsworth the poet — in which salvage there is fortunately not the slightest difficulty—at *The comparison fatal to Wordsworth as a critic.* the expense of Wordsworth the critic. Even in these curious documents of critical suicide there are excellent critical utterances *obiter*, and some even of the propositions in the very argument itself are separately, if not in their context, justifiable. He might, if he could have controlled himself, have made a very valuable exposure, not merely of false poetic diction, but of that extremely and monotonously *mannerised* poetic diction which, though not always bad in its inception and to a certain extent, becomes so by misusage and overusage. He might have developed his polemic against the personification of Gray and others with real advantage. He might have arranged a conspectus of the sins of eighteenth-century poetic diction, which would have been a most valuable pendant to Johnson's array of the extravagances of the Metaphysicals. He might— if he had carried out and corrected that theory of his of the necessity of antecedent "powerful feelings" in the poet—have produced a "Paradox of the Poet" which would have been as true as Diderot's on the Actor, and have had far greater value.

---

[1] I am well acquainted with the glosses on this famous phrase.

But he did none of these things; and what he did do is itself not even a paradox—it is a paralogism.

How much better Coleridge comes out of this affair has already been partly said.   But these concluding chapters[1] *Other criti-* of the *Biographia,* though certainly his capital criti-*cal places in* cal achievement, are very far from being his only *Coleridge.* one.   Indeed, next to his poetical, his critical work is Coleridge's greatest: and with all his everlasting faults of incompleteness, digression, cumbrousness of style,[2] and what not, it gives him a position inferior to no critic, ancient or modern, English or foreign.   But it is scattered all over his books, and it would not be ill done if some one would extract it from the mass and set it together.   In surveying such examples of it as are here most important, we shall take the convenient Bohn edition of Coleridge's Prose, following the contents of its volumes, but supplementing them to no small extent with the very interesting and only recently printed notes which Mr Ernest Coleridge published as *Anima Poetæ,* and with a glance at the *Letters.*

Coleridge himself, at the very beginning of the *Biographia,* has indicated the discussion of the question of Poetic Diction *The rest* as the main point which he had in view; but, with *of the* all its gaps and all its lapses, the whole book is *Biographia.* among the few which constitute the very Bible of Criticism.   The opening, with its famous description of the author's education in the art under the merciless and yet so merciful ferule of Boyer or Bowyer; the reference to Bowles— so little important in himself and on Arnoldian principles, so infinitely important to "*them,*" and so to history and to us, the "us" of every subsequent time; the personal digressions on himself and on Wordsworth and on Southey—are among

---

[1] "Concluding" in strictness they are not; for Coleridge, in one of his whims, chose to transfer *Satyrane's Letters* from *The Friend* to be a sort of *coda* to the *Biographia,* tipped it with the rather brutish sting of the *Critique on Bertram,* and attempted *Versöhnung* with a mystical perora-tion.   But the thing really and logi-cally ends with the words "Betty Foy," *sub fin.,* chap. xxi.

[2] He somewhere sighs for Southey's command of terse crisp sentences, and compares his own to "Surinam toads with young ones sprouting and hang-ing about them as they go."

"the topmost towers of Ilion," the best illustrations of that
"English fashion of criticism" of which, as has been said,
Dryden laid the foundations nearly a century and a half
earlier by uniting theory with elaborate, and plentiful, and
apparently indiscriminate, examples from practice.

One seldom feels inclined to be more angry[1] with Coleridge's habit of "Prommy pas Payy"[2] than in reference to
that introduction to the *Ancient Mariner*—dealing with the
supernatural, and with the difference between Imagination and
Fancy—to which he coolly refers the reader as if it existed,[3]
just before the actual examination of Wordsworth's theories in
the *Biographia*, and after the long digressions, Hartleian,
biographical proper, and what not, which fill the second
division of the book. But that one does well to be angry is
not quite so certain. The discussion would probably have
been the reverse of methodical, and it is very far from unlikely
that everything good in it is actually cast up here, or there,
on the "Rich Strand" of his actual work. To return to that
work,[4] there is little criticism in the extraordinary mingle-
mangle of religion, politics, and philosophy, of "Bell and Ball:
Ball and Bell," Maria Schoening and Dr Price, called

The Friend.   *The Friend*, whichever of its two forms[5] be taken.
At the beginning there are one or two remarks which seem

---

[1] An agreeable American critic, Miss
Agnes Repplier, once remarked that
Coleridge must have been "a very
beatable child." This beatability continued till his death : you can only
worship him in the spirit of the Portuguese sailor towards his saints.

[2] Mrs General Baynes of the Honourable Mrs Boldero in *The Adventures
of Philip*, chap. xx.

[3] Mr Dykes Campbell (whose threading of the maze and piecing of the
ends of Coleridgiana is a standing
marvel) thought, or seemed to think,
that the Introduction grew into the
Biographia itself.

[4] *Satyrane's Letters* themselves contain a good deal of criticism in and out
of the interview with Klopstock (p.

270 *sq.*, ed. cit.), where the credit is
claimed by some for Wordsworth.
The *Critique on Bertram* opens well
on the "Don Juan" story, but the
rest of it is not *muy hermosa cosa*,
combining, as it does, that snarling
and carping tone, against which Coleridge is always and justly protesting,
with more than a suspicion of personal
spite. For *Bertram* had been preferred
to *Zapolya*.

[5] The usually known reprint of the
2nd ed. of 1818 is very different from
the original, published in the extraordinary fashion described by Coleridge himself in the *Biographia*, during
1809-10, and collected in volume form
thereafter. This latter is perhaps the
better worth reading. It is at any rate

to promise matter of our kind, and there is some good Shakespeare comment at p. 299: but that is about all.

Neither should we expect (save on the principle that in Coleridge the unexpected very generally happens) anything

Aids to Reflection, &c. in the *Aids to Reflection* or the *Confessions of an Enquiring Spirit*, though in the first there are some of the usual girds at anonymous reviewing, and the second is important enough for that equivocal if not bastard variety of our kind which has "Biblical" or "Higher" tacked before it. But the three remaining volumes [1] are almost compact of our matter, while there is not a little of it, and of the very best quality, in the *Anima Poetæ*.

The great storehouse next to the *Biographia* is, of course, the *Lectures on Shakespeare* with their satellite fragments,

The Lectures on Shakespeare, &c. unsatisfactory as are the conditions under which we have all these things. There is perhaps no more astounding example of the tricks of self-deception than Coleridge's statement to Allsop that he had "*written*" three volumes of five hundred pages each, containing a complete critical history of the English drama, and "requiring neither addition, omission, nor correction—nothing but mere arrangement." What we actually have of his whole critical work, outside the *Biographia*, consists of perhaps one-third that amount of his own and other people's notes of Lectures, very rarely consecutive at all, requiring constant omission because of repetition, and defying the art of the most ingenious *diaskeuast* to get them into anything like order, and of a smaller but still considerable mass of *Marginalia*, pocket-book entries, and fragments of the most nondescript kinds. And we know from indisputable testimony by persons

a confirmation of the at first sight immoral maxim that you should always buy a book you want, whether you can afford it or not. Thirty years ago it was not common but comparatively cheap; now, alas! it is both uncommon and very dear.

[1] The editor of these, the late Mr Thomas Ashe (author of a poem far too little read—*The Sorrows of Hypsipyle*),

took much pains with them; and if he could have kept back a few flings, would have deserved unqualified thanks. "Never mind God's will" may be a noble counsel, or an unlucky advice to run worse than your head against worse than a stone wall. But it is certainly out of place in very brief and rare notes on a classical author.

who actually heard the *Lectures* which these notes represent, that if we possessed reports *in extenso* by the most accurate and intelligent of reporters, things would be not so very much better, because of Coleridge's incurable habit of apology, digression, anticipation, and repetition. That he found a written lecture an intolerable trammel, and even notes irksome, if he stuck close to them, we can readily believe. Many, if not most, lecturers would agree with him. But it is given to few people, and certainly was not given to him, to speak *extempore* on such subjects in a fashion which will bear printing. And his lectures have, as we have said, only very rarely had even the chance of standing this.

Nevertheless, we are perhaps not in reality so very much worse off. Extreme method in criticism is something of a *Their chaotic character* superstition, and, as we have seen, the greatest critical book of the world, that of Longinus, has, as we possess it, very little of this, and does not appear ever to have had very much. The critic does his best work, not in elaborating theories which will constantly break down or lead him wrong when they come into contact with the myriad-sided elusiveness of Art and Humanity, but in examining individual works or groups of work, and in letting his critical steel strike the fire of mediate axioms and *aperçus* from the flint of these. It does the recipient rather good than harm to have to take the trouble of selecting, co-ordinating, and adjusting such things for himself; at any rate, he escapes entirely the danger of that deadly bondage to a cut-and-dried scheme which was the curse of the Neo-classic system. And there is no critic who provides these examinations and *aperçus* and *axiomata media* more lavishly than Coleridge.[1]

---

[1] The question—a puzzle like other *Quæstiones Estesianæ*—about the exact numbers and dates of Coleridge's Shakespearian courses is not for us. It is enough to say that our extant materials (consisting, in regard to some lectures, of notes and reports from several different sources) chiefly, if not wholly, concern two courses delivered in London (1811-12 and 1818), and one at Bristol, 1813-14. Of the Royal Institution Lectures of 1806-7, on which he relied (throwing them even farther back) to prove his priority to Schlegel, nothing at all, unluckily, is preserved. Indeed Mr Dykes Campbell insisted, and seems to have almost proved, that none at all were delivered till Jan. 1808. And of these we have only Crabb Robinson's brief references.

I remember still, with amusement after many years, the words of, I suppose, a youthful reviewer who, admitting that *and pre-* an author whom he was reviewing had applied the *ciousness.* method of Coleridge as to Shakespeare, &c., with some skill and even some originality, hinted that this method was quite *vieux jeu*, and that modern criticism was taking and to take an entirely different line. And I have been grateful to that reviewer ever since for giving me a mental smile whenever I think of him. That his new critical Evangel —it was the "scientific" gospel of the late M. Hennequin, if "amid the memories long outworn Of many-*volumed eve and morn*" I do not mistake—has itself gone to the dustbin meanwhile does not matter, and is not the cause of the smile. The risibility is in the notion that any great criticism can ever be obsolete. We may, we must, we ought sometimes to differ with Aristotle and Longinus, with Quintilian and Scaliger, with Patrizzi and Castelvetro, with Dryden and Johnson, with Sainte-Beuve and Arnold. But what is good in them —and even what, though not so intrinsically good, is injured only by system and point of view, by time and chance and fatality—remains a possession for ever. "The eternal substance of their greatness" is of the same kind (although it be less generally recognised or relished) as the greatness of creation. *La Mort n'y mord.*

Of such matter Coleridge provides us with abundance everywhere, and perhaps most on Shakespeare. He acknowledges his debts to Lessing, and was perhaps unduly anxious to deny any to the Schlegels; but he has made everything that he may have borrowed his own, and he has wealth untold that is not borrowed at all. He can go wrong like other people. His favourite and constantly repeated denunciation of Johnson's couplet—

> "Let Observation with extensive view
> Survey mankind from China to Peru"—

as "bombast and tautology," as equivalent to "let observation with extensive observation survey mankind extensively," is not only unjust but actually unintelligent,[1] and probably due only to the horror of eighteenth-century personification, intensified in Coleridge by the fact that in his own early poems he had freely indulged therein.

But on the very opposite page [2]—in the very corresponding lines which shut up on this carping when the book is closed— *Some note-* we read, "To the young I would remark that it is *worthy* always unwise to judge of anything by its defects: *things in* the first attempt ought to be to discover its excel- *them :* *general,* lences." I could find nothing better for the motto of this book; I cannot imagine anything better as a corrective of the faults of Neo-classic critics—as a "Take away that bauble!" the stop-watch. Again, observe the admirable separation of poet and dramatist in Lecture vii. of the 1811 course; [3] the remarks (suggested perhaps by Lessing, but in no respect an echo of him) on poetry and painting in the Ninth; [4] and the altogether miraculous "character" of Ariel which follows.[5] The defences of Shakespeare's puns are always consummate [6]— in fact, "Love me, love my pun," should be one of the chief articles of a Shakespearian Proverb-book. In the notes referring (or supposed to refer) to the course of 1818, variations of the *Biographia* (published the year before) were sure to occur and do; one of the most noteworthy being the expansion and application of the idea of "suspension of disbelief." [7] Note, too, the acuteness in the censure [8] (with half-apologies) of the absurd stage-directions which characterised German, and have since characterised Scandinavian, drama.

---

[1] This perhaps should, and can very shortly, be demonstrated:—Observation may be either broad and sweeping, or minute and concentrated; Johnson specifies the former kind in the last half of the first line. Observation may be directed to men, to things, &c.; it is to mankind that he wishes it directed, and he says so in the first half of the second. Further, as this is too abstract, he gives the poetic and imaginative touch by filling in the waste atlas, with "China" and "Peru," with the porcelain and the pigtails, the llamas and the gold associated with mankind in these countries. And in the name of Logic, and Rhetoric and Poetry into the bargain, "Why should he not?"

[2] P. 73, ed. cit. Goethe, of course, was of the same opinion.

[3] P. 89.   [4] P. 138.

[5] P. 139 *sq.*

[6] *E.g.*, p. 152 *sq.*   [7] P. 207.

[8] P. 213.

Of the separate notes on Shakespeare's Plays it is impossible to say much here: and indeed it is not necessary. They are *and par-* to be read—if possible in conjunction with the plays *ticular.* themselves—by everybody: to digest them into a formal treatise would be perhaps impossible, and, as hinted above, would not be a testimonial to their value if it were possible. But their great merit, next to their individual felicity, is the constant cropping up of those *aperçus* of a more general, though not too general, cast which have been noticed.

Coleridge never admires Shakespeare too much; but the Devil's Advocate may perhaps make something of a count *Coleridge* against him that he is often apt to depress others *on other* by a comparison, which is not in the least neces- *dramatists.* sary. On Ben Jonson he is rather inadequate than unjust; but he is certainly unjust to Beaumont and Fletcher, and I almost fear that his injustice, like his more than justice to Massinger, may be set down to extra-literary causes. It is extraordinary that such a critic should have used the language that he uses of Florimel in *The Maid of the Mill.*[1] Her devices to preserve her honour are extravagant: this extravagance, as compared with the perfect *naturalness* of Shakespeare, is the constant note of "the twins"; and if Coleridge had confined himself to bringing it out, there would have been no more to be said. But his remarks are here not merely unjust, they are silly. And yet here, too, we could find the priceless *obiter dicta*, that on words that have made their way despite precisian objection,[2] those on metre[3] almost always, and others.

The motes fly thick for us in the *Table Talk ;* and as they are clearly headed and indexed in the edition referred to, there *The* Table is the less need of additional specification, while Talk. there is, here as everywhere, a good deal of repetition.[4] But one must point in passing to the striking contrast

---

[1] P. 441. [2] P. 412.

[3] *E.g.*, pp. 426, 427.

[4] All men who write for the periodical press must almost necessarily repeat themselves, and Hazlitt (whose work often comes to us directly from the press itself) is not so very much less peccant in this kind than Coleridge. Coleridge's own method exposes the peccadillo ruthlessly. The "Let Observation" criticism occurs several times : the story about the Falls of Lanark and the man who, beginning with "majestic," spoilt it by "very

of Schiller's "material sublime"[1] (and Coleridge was not inclined to undervalue Schiller[2]) with Shakespeare's economy of means; the pertinent, though by no means final, question, "If you take from Virgil his diction and metre, what do you leave him?"[3] the remarks on Spenser's "swan-like movement";[4] a remarkable cluster of literary dicta in the entry for Midsummer-Day 1827 (when H. N. says that his uncle talked "a volume"), to be supplemented by another sheaf on July 12; the contrast of Milton and Shakespeare;[5] the remarks on Rabelais;[6] the wonderfully pregnant one as to the "three silent revolutions in England";[7] those on Latin Literature;[8] on the evolutionary quality of genius;[9] another great *obiter dictum*,[10] that "Great minds are never in the wrong, but in consequence *of being in the right imperfectly*," which is truest of all in criticism itself; yet another,[11] "To please me, a poem must be either music or sense: if it is neither, I confess I cannot interest myself in it"; and, above all, that on Tennyson[12]—one of the *loci classici* of warning to the greatest critics to distrust themselves when they are judging the poetry of the "younger generations." And if we cannot help reproachfully ejaculating "Æschylus!" when he denies[13] sublimity to the Greeks, let us again remember that Æschylus was strangely *occulted* to the whole Neo-classic age, and that it is very much Coleridge's own doing that we of the last two or three generations have re-discovered him.

The few contributions, shortly supplemented from MS., to Southey's *Omniana* give little, but the volume now entitled *The Miscellanies.* *Miscellanies, Æsthetic and Literary*, is very nearly all ours. Much of it, however, is repetition in apparent title, and a good deal of the rest does not quite answer expectations. The general *Essays on the Fine Arts* with which

---

pretty," over and over again. Nor is this repetition merely due to the chaotic state of his publications: it seems to have been a congenital bias, as testified to in his conversation quite early.

[1] P. 15, *ed. cit.*

[2] *V. infra* on *Letters.*

[3] P. 38. [4] P. 45.

[5] P. 74. [6] P. 97.

[7] P. 158. These were, "When the professions fell off from the Church; when literature fell off from the professions; and when the press fell off from literature."

[8] P. 164 *sq.* [9] P. 177.

[10] P. 183. [11] P. 201.

[12] P. 214. [13] P. 174, *v. inf*

it opens (and of which the author, who had lost them, entertained that perhaps rather exaggerated idea which we usually
entertain of lost loves, books, fishes, &c.) possess in abundance
Coleridge's uniquely stimulating quality, but, perhaps in not
much less abundance, his extreme desultoriness and want of
definition, save of the most indefinite character.   The essay on
the *Prometheus* which follows excites (though hardly in the
wary mind, Estesianly "alphabeted," as he would himself say)
great expectations.   But it is scarcely too much to say that
on this—the most purely poetical of all extant Greek dramas,
a miracle of sublimity and humanity mingled, and the twin
pillar, with the *Agamemnon,* of its author's claim to be one of
the greatest poets of the world—Coleridge has not a word to
say that even touches the poetry.   He is philosophico-mytho-
logical from the egg to the apple ; and one is bound to add
that he here shows one of his gravest drawbacks as a critic.
The new fragments, however, of the 1818 lectures are full of
good matter, on Cervantes especially, perhaps a little less
specially on Dante, on Robinson Crusoe very particularly
indeed, on Rabelais and Sterne and Donne: while these are
taken up and multiplied in interest by the "Marginalia," with
which the literary part of the book concludes, and which contain, on Daniel and Chapman and Selden, Browne and Fuller,
Fielding and Junius, some of the best known and nearly of
the best of their author's critical work.   Here also, and here
only, do we find much on Milton, Coleridge's rather numerous
lectures on him having left surprisingly little trace.   He is,
though a fervent admirer, not quite at his happiest.

But the most interesting piece that the book contains is the
Lecture on Style, with its satellite note (a small but sparkling
The Lecture star) on the "Wonderfulness of Prose."[1]   The
On Style. author's definition of his most elusive subject is
indeed not only not satisfying, but (unless you remember his
own dictum about being "right incompletely") demonstrably
and almost astoundingly *un*satisfactory.   "Style is of course
nothing but the art of conveying the meaning appropriately
and with perspicuity."   One feels inclined in one's haste to

[1] Miscellanies, pp. 175-187 *ed. cit.*

say, "That is just what it is *not*"; one must cool down a little before one can modify this to "Style begins exactly where" the art, &c., "leaves off," and one can perhaps never come nearer to an accommodation than "The necessary preliminary to Style, and one essential ingredient of it," is "the art," and so forth.[1] It was no doubt this side of the matter that Coleridge was looking at, and at this he stopped, as far as his general way of looking at the thing went. But the main interest of the piece does not lie here. He bases his definition on, and tries to adjust it to, a survey of English style, which is probably one of the first of the kind ever attempted, after the notion of the Queen Anne men being the crown and flower of English had been given up. And though his history, as was natural, is sometimes shaky, and his conclusions are often to be disputed and even overthrown, the whole is of the highest value, not merely as a *point de repère* historically, but as an introduction to the consideration of Style itself.

But the book of Coleridge which, next to the *Biographia*, is of most importance to the student of his criticism, is perhaps *The* Anima the long-posthumous *Anima Poetæ*. Mr Ernest *Poetæ.* Coleridge, in his preface to the *Anima* itself, says that the *Biographia* is now little read. I hope he is wrong: but if he is right it would explain many things.

This volume—a collection of extracts from Coleridge's pocketbooks—appeared [2] more than sixty years after the poet's death, and the notice taken of it was comparatively small. That it contains passages of ornate prose superior to anything in the previously published writings is interesting, but for our purpose almost irrelevant: it is not so that it gives the fullest and clearest side-lights on Coleridge's criticism that we have. The earliest years (and pages) are not very fertile, though I subjoin some references [3] which will assist the reader in looking them up. But from p. 119 for some fifty pages onward (it is significant that the time of writing, 1805-8, corresponds

---

[1] It is odd, but useful, to remember Coleridge's fancy for stating propositions algebraically. If his definition were true, $a = b$ or even $(a+b)^2 = a^2 + 2ab + b^2$ would be style at its very acme (cf. Addison in *Spec.* 62 on Euclid and Wit).

[2] London, 1895.

[3] Pp. 4, 5, 30, 35, 59, 82, 88.

with Coleridge's absence in Malta, &c., from which we have
little or no published work) the entries are "diamondiferous."
On French poetry (mistaken but so informingly!);[1] on
Cowper;[2] on the absurdity of calling etymology (how much
more philology!) a "science";[3] on the attitude to poetry and
to books;[4] on Leibnitz's "profound sentence" that "men's
intellectual errors consist chiefly in *denying*";[5] on the "instinctive passion in the mind for one word to express one
act of feeling" (Flaubert fifty years before date); on pseudo-
originality,—Coleridge is at his very acme. The *yeast* of criticism—the reagent which, itself created by the contact of the
critical with the creative, re-creates itself in all fit media—has
never been more remarkably represented than here.

And great as are these passages, there are many others
(though not so many in close context) to match them. See
the entry (which I venture to think has been wrongly side-
headed as "A plea for poetic license") at the foot of p. 165
as to the desire of carrying things to a greater height of
pleasure and admiration than they are susceptible of—the
old "wish to write better than you can," the "loss of sight
between this and the other style."[6] See the astonishing anticipation of the best side of Ruskinism in the note on architecture and climate;[7] and that on poetry and prose and on the
"esenoplastic" power;[8] and that on somebody (Byron?) who
was "splendid" everywhere, but nowhere poetical;[9] and that
on scholastic terms;[10] and that on the slow comprehension of
certain (in this case Dantean) poetry.[11] They are all *apices
criticismi*—not easy reading, not for the running man, but
for him who reads them fitly, certain to bear fruit if he reads
them early, to coincide with his own painful and struggling
attainments if he reads them late.

[1] P. 118 *sq.*   [2] P. 121.
[3] P. 123.   [4] Pp. 127-130.
[5] P. 147. Cf. *sup.*, p. 223.
[6] Coleridge quotes neither Quintilian nor Dante, and was probably
not thinking of either. But *we* think
of them.
[7] P. 194.
[8] *I.e.*, "The faculty which makes
many into one"—the creative imagination. This form is much better than
"*esemplastic*," which Coleridge adopts
in the *Biographia*, for there one
stumbles over the second syllable, and
supposes it to be the preposition *ἐν*.
[9] P. 258.   [10] Pp. 274, 275.
[11] P. 293.

Nor must the *Letters*[1] be omitted in any sufficient survey of Coleridge's criticism. That at one early period[2] he apparently thought Schiller more sublime than Milton is not *The* Letters. in the least to his discredit. He was twenty-two; he was, I think, demonstrably in love with *three* ladies[3] at once, and extremely uncertain which of two of them he should marry—a state of mind neither impossible nor unnatural, but likely to lead to considerable practical difficulties, and to upset the judgment very decidedly. His minor critical remarks at this very time on Southey's poems are excellent. That Bowles should be "divine" and Burke "sad stuff"[4] does not matter— we can explain both statements well enough. But how many men of three- or four-and-twenty (or for that matter of three- or four-and-seventy) were there, are there, have there ever been, who could ask, "Why pass an *Act of Uniformity* against poets?"[5] one of the great critical questions of the world, and never, so far as I remember, formulated so pertinently before. It is odd that he should have forgotten (if he knew) Sidney, in his singular and pedantic complaint that to give the name Stella to a woman is "unsexing" it, and his supposition that "Swift is the authority."[6] But another astonishing critical truth is that "Poetry ought not always to have its *highest* relish";[7] and yet another in the contrast[8] of himself with Southey, "I think too much to be a poet; he too little to be a great poet," unjust as the application is in the first half; and yet again on metre itself "*implying* a passion,"[9] a passage worth comparing with, and in some points better than, the *Biographia* (with which compare also pp. 386, 387). Nor these alone, but many others later—the criticism on Wordsworth's

---

[1] Ed. E. H. Coleridge, 2 vols., London, 1895.

[2] i. 97, *ed. cit.*

[3] Miss Mary Evans, Miss Sarah Fricker, and an uncertainly Christian-named Miss Brunton. *More in excelsis Coleridgeano* he, being engaged to No. 2 and desiring to marry No 1, "hoped that he might be cured" by the "exquisite beauty and uncommon accomplishments" of No. 3. See a page or two (89) earlier.

[4] P. 157.

[5] P. 163.

[6] P. 181.

[7] P. 196.

[8] P. 210. This was just after the as yet hollow healing of the first great quarrel in 1796.

[9] P. 384. These passages are most important as showing how *early* Coleridge dissented from Wordsworth.

"Cintra" pamphlet;[1] that on the inadequacy of one style
for all purposes;[2] the remarks on stage illusion,[3]—might be
cited.

When the present writer began his larger task an excellent scholar said, "How will you ever finish that book?
The Coleridgean position and quality. Why, Coleridge himself would take a volume!"
There is something to be said for the hyperbole.
In this and that critic, of the many ages which
a historian has to survey, we may find critical
graces which are not in him; but in all, save two, we shall
find corresponding deficiencies. In all the ancient critics, save
these two, the limitation of the point of view, the hamper
of the scheme, are disastrously felt, nor is either Aristotle or
Longinus quite free from them. In the greatest of the six-
teenth-century Italians these limitations recur, and are repeated in most of those of the seventeenth and eighteenth.
Dante is of the greatest, but he touches the subject very briefly
and from a special side. Dryden is great, but he is not fully
informed, and comes too early for his own point of view.
Fontenelle is very nearly great, but he has the same drawbacks,
and adds to them those of an almost, perhaps a quite, wilful
eccentricity and capriciousness. Lessing is great, but he has
fixed his main attention on the least literary parts of literature;
while Goethe later is great but a great pedant. Hazlitt is
great; but Coleridge was Hazlitt's master, and beside the
master the pupil is insular and parochial in range and reading
if not in spirit. In Sainte-Beuve himself we want a little more
theory; some more enthusiasm; a higher and more inspiriting
choice of subjects. And in Mr Arnold the defects of Fontenelle
reappear without Fontenelle's excuse of chronology.

So, then, there abide these three, Aristotle, Longinus, and
Coleridge. The defects of the modern, as contrasted with the
ancient, man of letters are prominent in Coleridge when we
compare him with these his fellows: and so we cannot quite
say that he is the greatest of the three. But his range is necessarily wider: he takes in, as their date forbade them to take,
all literature in a way which must for centuries to come give

[1] P. 549   [2] P. 557.   [3] P. 663.

him the prerogative. It is astonishing how often, when you have discovered in others of all dates, or (as you may fondly hope) found out for yourself, some critical truth, you will remember that after all Coleridge in his wanderings has found it before, and set it by the wayside for the benefit of those who come after. For all, I believe, of these later days—certainly for all whose mother-tongue is English—Coleridge is the critical author to be turned over by day and by night. Never take him on trust: it is blasphemy to the Spirit of Criticism to do that with any critic. Disagree with him as often as you like, and as you can stand to the guns of your disagreement. But begin with him, continue with him, come back to him after excursions, with a certainty of suggestion, stimulation, correction, edification. *C'est mon métier à moi d'être professeur de littérature*, and I am not going to *parvify* my office. But if anybody disestablished us all (with decent pensions, of course), and applied the proceeds of our Chairs to furnishing the boxes of every one who goes up to the University with a copy of the *Biographia Literaria*, I should decline to be the person chosen to be heard against this revolution, though I should plead for the addition of the *Poetics* and of Longinus.

And if any one is still dissatisfied with particular critical utterances, and even with the middle axioms interspersed among them, let him remember that Coleridge—not *He intro-* Addison, not the Germans, not any other—is the *duces once* *for all the* real introducer into the criticism of poetry of the *criterion of* *Imagination,* realising and disrealising Imagination as a criterion. *realising* Even a hundred years more after his earliest day as *and dis-* *realising.* a critic, the doctrine, though much talked of, is apparently little understood. Even such a critic as the late Mr Traill, while elsewhere[1] admitting that "on poetic *expression*" Coleridge "has spoken the absolutely last word," almost apologised[2] for his putting on a level "lending the charm of imagination to the real" and "lending the force of reality to the imaginary." He confessed that, "from the point

[1] *Coleridge* ("English Men of [2] Ibid., pp. 46, 47. Letters," London, 1884), p. 156.

of view of the highest conception of the poet's office there can
be no comparison "—where indeed I might also " say ditto to Mr
Burke," but in a sense opposite to his.   And if, on such a mind
and such an appreciation as Mr Traill's, this one-sided interpretation of "the *esenoplastic* faculty" had hold, how much
more on others in increasing measure to the present day ?   The
fallacy is due, first, to the hydra-like vivacity of the false idea
of *mimesis*, the notion that it is not re-presentation, re-creation
adding to Nature, but copying her ; and, secondly, to the
Baconian conception of poetry as a *vinum dæmonum*, a poison
with some virtue as a medicine.   What power these errors
have all our history has shown,—all Histories of Criticism
that ever can be written will show if they are written faithfully.   But Coleridge has provided—once for all, if it be not
neglected—the safeguard against this in his definitions of the
two, the co-equal, the co-eternal functions of the exercise
of the poetic Imagination.

In the title of the present chapter I have used the word
"companions" in a double sense—the first and special appli-
The " Com- cation of it being that in which it is technically ap-
panions."   plied to the Companions of the Prophet—to the
early coadjutors of Mahomet in his struggle with the Koreish.
Of these the chief are Southey, Lamb, Leigh Hunt, and Hazlitt,
with perhaps as an even closer ally—though unknowing and
unknown—William Blake.   Then follow companions in the
wider sense—associates in the work, who varied from nearly
complete alliance, as with Scott, to very distant and lukewarm
participation, as in Campbell, and (in literary position) from
the captaincy of Scott again and of Shelley to the more than
respectable full-privateship of the contributors to the *Retrospective Review*.   As for the "Adversaries," they can be more
briefly dealt with, for their work was mostly "wood, hay,
stubble"; but Gifford and Jeffrey at least could not be excluded here, and a few more may deserve notice.   So let the
inquiry proceed in this order.

It may seem at first sight curious, and will perhaps always

remain a little so, that we have no collected examples, nor
Southey. many uncollected but singly substantive pieces, of
strictly critical work, from the most widely read
and the most industrious of the whole literary group of
1800-1830 in England—from a man who, for eleven years
at least, wrote reviews almost wherever he could place them
without hurting his conscience, and who for another five-
and-twenty was a pillar of one of the greatest of critical
periodicals. But Southey's earlier reviewing is for the most
part not merely whelmed in the dust-bins of old magazines,
but, as his son and biographer complains, extremely difficult
to trace even there; and his later was, by choice or by chance
(more I think by the former than by the latter), mainly devoted
to subjects not purely literary. If that great *Bibliotheca
Britannica*[1] (which so nearly existed, and which is a thing
lacking in English to this present day, a hundred years
later) had come actually into existence, it would hardly have
been necessary to look beyond that: as it is, one has the
pleasing but rather laborious and lengthy duty of fishing out
and piecing together critical expressions from *The Doctor* and
other books to some extent, and from the two parallel collections of the *Life and Correspondence*[2] and the *Letters*[3] to
a still greater. The process is necessary for a historian of
criticism, and the results, if hardly new to him, are interesting enough; but they cannot claim any exhibition at all
correspondent to the time taken in arriving at them. Nor
will any such historian, if he be wise, complain, for Southey
is always delightful, except when he is in his most desper-
ately didactic moods: and the Goddess of Dulness only knows
how even the most egregious of her children, unless from
pure ignorance, has managed to fix on him the title of
"dull."

That "a man's criticism is the man himself" is almost truer

---

[1] See *Life and Correspondence*, ii.
316 *sq.* especially, for Coleridge's magnificent "Spanish-Castlery" in connection.

[2] 6 vols., London, 1850.

[3] 4 vols., London, 1856. *The*

Letters to Caroline Bowles (London,
1881) are even fuller proportionately :
and *Omniana*, the *Wesley*, the *Cowper*,
Espriella, the *Colloquies*, with almost
everything, contribute.

than the original bestowal of the phrase; and it is nowhere
truer than with Southey.   That astonishing and
almost godlike *sanity* which distinguished him, in
almost all cases save as regards the *Anti-Jacobin*,
Mr Pitt, the Roman Catholic Church, and my Lord
Byron (who, by the way, lacked it quite as conspicuously in
regard to Southey), is the constant mark of his critical views.
Except his over-valuation of Kirke White,[1] which was undoubtedly due to his amiable and lifelong habit of helping
lame dogs, I cannot, at the moment or on reflection, think
of any critical estimate of his (for that of himself as a poet
is clearly out of the question) which is flagrantly and utterly
wrong; and I can think of hundreds which are triumphantly
right.   In respect of older literature, in particular,[2] his catholicity is free from the promiscuousness of Leigh Hunt, and his
eclecticism from the caprice of Charles Lamb : while, prejudiced
as he can be, I do not remember an instance in which prejudice
blinds or blunts his critical faculty as it does Hazlitt's.   On
all formal points of English poetry he is very nearly impeccable.   He may have learnt his belief in substitution and
equivalence from Coleridge; but it is remarkable that his
defences of it to Wynn[3] are quite early, quite original, and
quite sound, while Coleridge's own account long after, in the
preface to *Christabel*, is vague and rather wofully incorrect.
He knew, of course, far more literary history than any one
of his contemporaries — an incalculable advantage — and he
could, sometimes at least, formulate general critical maxims
well worth the registering.

General character-istics of his Criticism.

---

[1] But see a very curious glimpse of
resipiscence in *Letters*, ii. 171 *sq.*

[2] The projected *Rhadamanthus*, a
periodical on something like the lines
of the later *Retrospective Review*, was
a real loss.

[3] *Letters*, i. 69, and elsewhere, also,
I think—*e.g.*, *Life and Corr.*, iv. 106.
Wynn was evidently a precisian of
Bysshism.   For other noteworthy
critical things in this collection, see
i. 173 (Suggestion of Hist. Novels) ; ii.

91) (Crabbe) ; 214 (Engl. Hexameters);
iii. (the various letters about English Hexameters); iv. 47, Sayers' Poems.
I give but few here, because the *Letters*
have an index.   I wish these and my
other references may prompt and help
some one to examine, at greater length
than would be possible or proper here,
the literary opinions of the best-read
man in England for some fifty years
—1790-1840.

Of his regular critical work, however, which can be traced
in the *Annual* and *Quarterly Reviews* from the list given by
Reviews.   his son at the end of the *Life*, some notice must
be taken, though the very list itself is a tell-tale
in the large predominance of Travels, Histories, and the like,
over pure literature. That he should have made a rule for
himself after he became Laureate not to review poetry (save
in what may be called an eleemosynary manner) is merely
what one would have expected from his unvarying sense of
propriety; but there were large ranges of *belles lettres* to which
this did not apply. The articles which will best repay the
looking up are, in the *Annual*, those on *Gebir*, Godwin's *Chaucer*,
Ritson's *Romances*, Hayley, Froissart, *Sir Tristram*, Ellis's
Specimens, Todd's *Spenser*, and *Ossian;* in the *Quarterly*, those
on Chalmers's *Poets*, Sayers, Hayley again, Camoens, and Lope
de Vega, with some earlier ones on Montgomery (James, not
Robert).[1]

The Doctor also must have its special animadversion, for this
strangely neglected and most delightful book is full of critical
The Doctor.   matter. Its showers of mottoes—star-showers from
the central glowing mass of Southey's enormous and
never "dead" reading—amount almost in themselves to a
critical education for any mind which is fortunate enough to
be exposed to them when young, while the saturation of the
whole book with literature can hardly fail to produce the
same effect. It is lamentable, astonishing, and (the word is
not too strong) rather disgraceful that, except the "Three Bears"
story, the appendix on the Cats, and perhaps the beautiful
early passages on the Doctor's birthplace and family, the
book should be practically unknown. But it by no means
owes its whole critical value to these borrowed and reset

[1] It is unlucky that Guest's *English
Rhythms* came too late in the evening
of his day for him to carry out his
expressed purpose of reviewing it.
He evidently recognised its extraordinary value as a *Thesaurus:* and his summary of the earlier part as "worthless"
is of course not deliberate or final,
though it is a very natural expression
in reference to Guest's astonishing
heresies on Shakespearian and Miltonic prosody. I know no one—not
even Gray—who seems to have had,
before the whole range of English verse
was known, juster notions on the whole
of English prosody. Even his wanderings after hexameters are not fatal.

jewels. The passages of original criticism—direct or slightly "applied"—which it contains are numerous and important. The early accounts of the elder Daniel's library[1] and of Textor's dialogues[2] are valuable ; the passage on "Taste and Pantagruelism"[3] much more so. On Sermons,[4] on Drayton,[5] on the Principles of Criticism,[6] on the famous verse-tournament of the Poitiers Flea,[7] on the Reasons for Anonymity,[8] on Mason[9] (for whom Southey manages to say a good word), on Bowdlerising and Modernising, and (by an easy transition) Spenser[10]—the reader will find nuggets, and sometimes whole pockets, of critical gold, the last-mentioned being one of the richest of all. It is to Southey's immortal honour (an honour not sufficiently paid him by some Blakites) that he recognised and quoted at length[11] the magnificent "Mad Song," which is perhaps Blake's most sustained and unbroken piece of pure poetry. His discussion on Styles[12] is of great value: while the long account[13] of the plays of Langeveldt (Macropedius), and of our kindred English Morality *Everyman*, shows how admirably his more than once projected Literary Histories would have been executed.

Still, I am bound to say that he conveys to my mind the impression of not quite having his soul bound up in the

Altogether somewhat impar sibi.

exercise of his critical function. He was a little too fond of extending his love of books to those which, as Lamb would say, are no books—of giving the children's bread unto dogs. Occasionally, moreover, that want of the highest enthusiasm and sympathy, the highest inspiration, which—after the rather ungracious and ungrateful suggestion of Coleridge—it has been usual to urge against him, and which cannot be wholly disproved, does appear. Some would say that this was due to his enormous reading, and to

---

[1] *The Doctor* (1 vol., London, 1848), p. 18.

[2] P. 34.

[3] P. 42.

[4] P. 65.

[5] P. 86.

[6] P. 99.

[7] P. 194.

[8] P. 245. It is curious, by the way, that Southey bewails the absence in English of any synonym for the Span-ish *desengaño*. That shows that "disillusionment," one of those strictly analogous and justifiable neologisms which he rightly defends, had not then come into use.

[9] P. 315.

[10] P. 379

[11] P. 476.

[12] P. 536.

[13] P. 610.

the penal servitude for life to what was mostly hack-work, which fate and his own matchless sense of duty imposed upon him. I do not think so; but of course if it be said that no one with the more translunary fancies, the nobler gusts, could have so enslaved himself, an authority [1] who takes so high a ground must be allowed his splendid say. Anyhow, and on the whole, we must return to the position that Southey does not hold a very high position among English critics, and that it is easier to give plausible reasons for the fact than entirely to understand it. [2]

In criticising the criticism of Charles Lamb [3] one has to walk warily; for is he not one of the most justly beloved of English writers, and are not lovers apt to love more well than wisely? I shall only say that if any be an "Agnist," I more. Ever since I can remember reading anything (the circumstance would not have seemed trivial to himself), I have read and revelled in, and for nearly fifty years I have possessed in fee, a copy of the original *Elia* of 1823, in the black morocco coat which it put on, at least seven years before Lamb's death, in 1827. I have also read its contents, and all other attainable *Agnalia*, in every edition in which I have come across them, with introductions by "Thaunson and Jaunson," in and on all sorts of shapes and types and papers and bindings. I have never wearied of read-

Lamb.

[1] Such an authority, for instance, as one of the reviewers of this poor book, who decided that "no man of critical genius" would have attempted to write it.

[2] Some readers may like a few out of hundreds of possible references to *Life and Corr.*, which has no Index: i. 85 (Ariosto and Spenser); 122 (Construction); 316-318 (Chapelain, before and after reading); ii. 197 (Greek and Latin taste in poetry); 211, 212 (Modern Ballads); iii. 9 (Archaisms and Neologisms); 140 (the Epistles in *Marmion*); 145 *sq.* (Rhyme, &c.); 205 (the purple patch in *Kehama*); 213, 265 (Advice to E. Elliott); 277 (blank verse); 295 (Spenser); iv. 301, 338

(very interesting, on a prophesied return of "preciousness" and "metaphysical" style in poetry); v. 245 (a never-carried-out plan of continuing Warton); v. 99 (his own method of writing); vi. 93 (To Bowles—reasons for not reviewing poetry).

[3] The editions of Lamb in parts are now fortunately very numerous, and there are even several of the whole, some of which have been begun since the text was written. It is therefore superfluous to give pages, especially as the individual articles are almost always short. But I generally use the late R. H. Shepherd's 1 vol. ed. of the *Works* (London, 1875), and Canon Ainger's of the *Letters* (London, 1888).

ing them; I am sure I never shall weary as long as eye and brain last. That Lamb is one of the most exquisite and delightful of critics, as of writers, is a proposition for which I will go to the stake; but I am not prepared to confess him as one of the very greatest in his critical capacity.

The reasons for this limitation are to be found in two passages of his friend Hazlitt—a ruthless friend enough, but *His "oc-* one who seldom goes wrong in speaking of friend *cultism"* or foe, unless under the plain influence of a prejudice which here had not the slightest reason for existing. The passages (referred to again elsewhere) are that on "the Occult School" in the "Criticism"[1] and one in the "Farewell."[2] The first speaks of those "who discern no beauties but what are concealed from superficial eyes, and overlook all that are obvious to the vulgar part of mankind." "If an author is utterly unreadable they can read him for ever." "They will no more share a book than a mistress with a friend." "Nothing goes down with them but what is caviare to the multitude," &c. The other, in which Lamb is actually named, contrasts his "surfeit of admiration," the antiquation of his favourites after some ten years, with the "continuity of impression" on which Hazlitt prided himself.

I am inclined to think that both these charges—made with what is (for the author) perfect good-humour, and only in the *and alleged* first case slightly exaggerated, as was almost per-*inconstancy.* missible when he was dealing ostensibly with a type not a person—are quite true. One would not indeed have them false; it would be most "miserably wise" economy to exchange Lamb, as he is, for a wilderness of consistent, equitable, catholic mediocrities. As Hazlitt himself admits, *this* "Occult Criticism" does not or need not come from any affectation or love of singularity: indeed, some occult critics "smack of genius and are worth any money." The Lothario part of the indictment, the desertion after enjoyment, is perhaps less easy to authenticate as well as to defend; but I think it existed, and was indeed a necessary consequence of the other tendency. If you love merely or mainly as a

[1] *Table Talk*, pp. 313, 314, *ed. cit. inf.*   [2] *Winterslow*, p. 463, *ed. cit. inf.*

collector, and for rarity,—if not only thus but because others do *not*,—the multiplication of the object or of the taste must necessarily have a disgusting effect. "The bloom is *off* the rye." And I should say that, beyond all reasonable question, there is a distinct character of *eccentricity* in the strict sense, of whim, of will-worship, about many, if not most, of Lamb's preferences. There is no affectation about him; but there is what might be affectation in another man, and has been affectation in many and many another. Take the most famous instances of his criticism—the defence of Congreve and Wycherley, the exaltation of Ford, the saying (productive of endless tribulation to the matter-of-fact) that Heywood is "a prose Shakespeare," the enthusiasm shown towards that rather dull-fantastic play *A Fair Quarrel*, while the magnificence of the same author's *Changeling* was left to Leigh Hunt to find out—these and other things distinctly show the *capriccio*. Lamb, not Hunt, is really the "Ariel of Criticism," and he sometimes pushes tricksiness to a point which would, we fear, have made his testy Highness of Milan rather angry. It was probably in conversation rather than in writing that his fickleness showed itself: we can never conceive Lamb *writing* down anything that he had ever written up. But something of disillusionment must, as has been said, almost necessarily have resulted from the peculiarly whimsical character of his inamoration. Canon Ainger has noted, as the distinguishing features of Lamb's critical power, "width and versatility." One differs with the Master [1] of the Temple unwillingly and *suo periculo*: but neither term seems to me quite appropriate. "Width" implies continuity, and there is little of this in Lamb: "versatility" implies a power of turning to what you will, and Lamb, I think, loved, not as he would but as he could not help it at the time.

But he wants nothing save method and certainty (in response —not even this in touch), and he has critical graces of his *The early* own which make him all but as great as Cole-
Letters. ridge or Hazlitt, and perhaps more delightful than either. In his very earliest critical utterances, in the Letters to Coleridge and Southey especially, much of this delightfulness

[1] Now, as he, alas! became, between pen and press, the *late* Master.

displays itself as well as its two parents—Lamb's unconquer-able originality of thought and feeling, and his unsurpassable quaintness and piquancy of phrase. The critic is, as is in-evitable from his youth, and from the as yet very imperfect reading which he frankly confesses, a little uncertain and in-adequate. His comparative estimates of Coleridge and Southey, Southey and Milton, Southey and Cowper, and of all or most of these poets and others in themselves, exhibit an obviously unregulated compass—a tendency to correct impression rather overmuch, because the first striking off of it has been hasty. But this soon disappears: and though the eccentricity above noted rather increases than lessens with years, the critic's real virtues—those just indicated—appear ever and ever more dis-tinctly and more delightfully.

In a certain sense they never appear to greater advantage than in the brief notes included in the *Specimens of Dramatic Poets* (1808). Everything necessary to excite Lamb's critical excellence united here,—actual merit, private interest (for, though the study of the minor as well as of the major Elizabethans had been progressing steadily, and "Dodsley" had gone through several editions, yet the authors were caviare to the general still); presence of the highest ex-cellence ; and, as we see from the *Letters*, years of familiarity and fondness on the part of the critic.

The Specimens.

The *Notes* themselves pretend to no method, and fulfil their pretence very strictly. Lamb is distinctly inferior to both his great friends and rivals in *grasp*. His appreciation is tan-gential—though in a different sense from that in which Hazlitt applies the word to Coleridge. Lamb is not so much desul-tory or divagatory as apt to touch his subject only at one (sometimes one very small) point. The impact results in a spark of the most ardent heat and glowing light, but neither heat nor light *spreads* much. Sometimes, as is inevitable in this style of criticism, he can be only disappointing: one is inclined to be pettish with him for seeing nothing to notice in the vast and shadowy sweep of *Tamburlaine* save an interesting evidence that Pistol was not merely jesting. Nor is perhaps Barabas "a mere monster brought in with a large painted nose to please the rabble." But you must get out of this mood if you are to enjoy Lamb. How he makes it all up, and more than up, on *Faustus*, and (when he comes to Dekker) on *Old Fortunatus!* "Beware! beware!" is the cry here also, lest we steal too much of his honeydew. Fortunately it has been so widely used, even for the vulgar purpose of sweetening school-editions, that it has become generally accessible. The famous passage on the Witches, which Hazlitt loved to quote, is perhaps as characteristic as any: the Webster and Chapman notices are perhaps critically the best.

Next in order of time come the articles contributed to the *Reflector*, especially the magnificent paper on "The Tragedies of Shakespeare" and their actableness. I may be prejudiced in favour of this, by caring myself infinitely to read the drama, and not caring at all to see it acted; but this objection could not be made to Lamb, who was notoriously a playgoer, and an eager though unfortunate aspirant to the honours of the boards. The piece, of course, shows some traces of the *capriccio*,—especially in the confession of being utterly unable to appreciate "To be or not to be," because of its being "spouted." Shakespeare himself might have taught Lamb better, in a certain passage about age and custom. To learn, to hear, nay, direst curse of all! to *teach* "To be or not to be" leaves it perfect Cleopatra. But Lamb must be Lamb and keep his Lambish mind: and he keeps it here to great purpose. The *Lear* passage, the best known and the most generally admitted as forcible, is not more so than those on the *Tempest* and on *Macbeth*. They all come to that position of the true critic (as I believe it to be), which has been indicated elsewhere, that drama *may* be literature but is not bound to be—that they are different things, and that the points which drama need not have, and perhaps to which it cannot do full justice, are in literature of the greatest importance.

It is natural, though they were written so long afterwards, to take the "Notes on the Garrick Plays" with these other *The Garrick* forerunners and suggesters; nor do I think that so *Play Notes.* much of the "first sprightly running" is lost as has sometimes been thought. How Lamb-like and how pleasant is the phrase on Day's quaint *Parliament of Bees*—"the very air seems replete with humming and buzzing melodies." (Most obvious, of course: only that nobody had *met* it before!) And the imploration to Novello to set the song from Peele's *Arraignment;* and the fine and forcible plea for the minor Elizabethans in the note to *The Two Angry Women of Abingdon* (a play, by the way, every fresh reading of which makes one more thoroughly agree with Lamb). The fewness and slightness of these notes should not be allowed to obscure their quality.

It was seldom that the bee-like nature of Lamb's own genius could settle long on a single flower; and his regular *Miscella-*
neous Essays. "studies" are few, and not always of his very best. The actual state of the paper on *The Excursion*, after its mangling by Gifford, illustrates the wisdom of that editorial counsel, "Always keep a copy," which the contributor (alas! we are all guilty) doth so unwisely neglect; and the two best that we have among the miscellaneous essays are those on Wither and on Defoe's secondary novels. It is difficult to say which is the better: but the singular unlikeness of the two subjects (except that both Wither and Defoe are eminently *homely*) shows what I presume Canon Ainger meant by the "versatility" of the critic's genius. Both are admirable, but most characteristically "promiscuous." The Defoe piece avowedly gives stray notes; but the "Wither," though it has a beginning, has very little middle, and no end at all.

As for *Elia* itself, it is fortunately too well known to need any analysis or much detailed survey. In the first and more *Elia.* famous collection the literary element is rather a saturation than a separable contingent. Except the "Artificial Comedy" paper, there is none with a definitely literary title or ostensible subject: while this itself starts in the closest connection with the preceding paper on Actors, and is dramatic rather than literary. But the "saturation" is unmistakable. As one turns the beloved and hundred-times-read pages, the constant undercurrent of allusion to books and reading strikes one none the less—perhaps indeed the more—for familiarity, whether it is at some depth, as in places, or whether it bubbles up to and over the surface, as in

"Oxford in the Vacation," and the book-borrowing close of
"The Two Races of Men," and that other close of that "New
Year's Eve" which so unnecessarily fluttered Southey's orthodoxy, and not a little of "All Fool's Day"; and in quotations
everywhere. But in the *Last Essays* Lamb exhibits the master-
passion much more openly. The "Detached Thoughts on Books
and Reading" of course lays all concealment aside,—it is a
regular *affiche*, as are also "The Genteel Style in Writing"
and (most of all) "On Some Sonnets of Sir Philip Sidney—
the valiant and triumphant sally against Hazlitt—with not a
little of "Old China" itself. Everywhere there is evident the
abiding, unfailing love of "the book."

And if we recur to the *Letters* we shall find the most
abundant proof of this quality. How admirable are those
The later criticisms[1] of the second edition of *Lyrical Ballads*
Letters. which, because they are not "neat" praise, roused
the poetic irritability, not merely of Wordsworth, whose
views respecting the reception of his own verse were always
Athanasian, but of Coleridge, who had, at any rate, intervals
of self-perception! How sound the judgment of Mrs Barbauld
and of Chapman (a pleasing pair) to Coleridge himself on Oct.
23, 1802![2] How sure the touch of the finger on that absurdity
in Godwin's *Chaucer* which has been so frequently copied since,
"the fondness for filling out the picture by supposing what
Chaucer did and how he felt"![3] The choicest of his observations are naturally those to Coleridge, almost *passim :* but the
vein is so irrepressible that he indulges it even in writing to
Wordsworth, though he knew perfectly well that the most
favourable reception could only be a mild wonder that people
could think or talk of any literature, and especially any poetry,
other than "W. W.'s" own. Even his experiences in 1800
could not prevent him from handling[4] the Poems of 1815 with
the same "irreverent *parrhesia*" which he uses immediately
after[5] also to Southey on *Roderick* as compared with *Kehama*

---

[1] *Letters*, ed. Ainger, i. 162 *sq.*, with
the most amusing additional letter in
the Appendix, p. 328 *sq.*, on the wrath
of Wordsworth and Coleridge.

[2] Ibid., i. 189, 190.
[3] P. 207.
[4] P. 286 *sq.*
[5] P. 290.

and *Madoc.* His famous appreciation of Blake [1] (of whom 'tis pity that he knew no more) is one of the capital examples of pre-established harmony between subject and critic. That he could not, on the other hand, like Shelley, is not unsusceptible of explanations by no means wholly identical, though partly, with those which account for Hazlitt's error. Lamb did not like the word "unearthly" (he somewhere objects to its use) and he did not like the thing unearthliness. The regions where, as Mr Arnold has it, "thin, thin, the pleasant human noises sound," were not his haunt. Now Blake always has a homely domestic everyday side close to his wildest prophetisings,[2] and Shelley has not. On the other hand, how completely does he grasp even Cervantes in the few *obiter dicta* to Southey on Aug. 19, 1825,[3] and how instantly he seizes the "charm one cannot explain" in *Rose Aylmer.*[4] And his very last letter concerns a book, and a book on poetry, Phillips's *Theatrum Poetarum.*

His love was, as we said, "of the book," perhaps, rather than, as in Hazlitt's case, "of literature." The Advocatus *Uniqueness* Diaboli may once more suggest that to Lamb the *of Lamb's* book was a very little too much on a level with *critical style* the tea-pot and the engraving—that he had a shade in excess of the collector's feeling about him. But the Court will not call upon the learned gentleman to say anything more on that head. It is time to acknowledge, without reservations or provisos, the unique quality of "Elia's" critical appreciation. Very much of this quality—if a quality be separable into parts —arises from his extraordinary command of phrase,—the phrase elaborate without affectation, borrowed yet absolutely individual and idiosyncratic, mannered to the *n*th, but never manner- ised, in which, though he might not have attained to it without his great seventeenth-century masters, he stands original and alone. In no critic perhaps—not even in Mr Pater—does style count for so much as in Lamb; in none certainly is it more distinctive, and, while never monotonous, more homogeneous, uniform, instantly recognisable and self-

---

[1] Ibid., ii. 105.
[2] Even as the exquisite figure of Mrs Blake, sitting on the bedside, faces
the sketches of gnashing fiends.
[3] P. 138.   [4] P. 278.

bewrayed. The simulative power—almost as of the leaf-insect and suchlike creatures—with which he could imitate styles, is of course most obvious in the *tour de force* of the Burton counterfeits. But in his best and most characteristic work it is not this which we see, but something much nobler, though closely allied to it. It is not Browne, or Fuller, or Burton, or Glanvill, but something like them, yet different. And though it has more *outré* presentation in some of his miscellaneous writing than in his criticism, yet it is never absent in the most striking pieces of this, and gives them much of their hold on us.

Still, those who, however unnecessarily (for no one surely is going to deny it save in a mood of paradox or of monomania), insist that style must be the body of thought—nay, that this body itself must think (in Donne's phrase), and not merely live, will find no difficulty in claiming Lamb as theirs. Nothing of the kind is more curious than the fact that, strongly marked as are his peculiarities and much as he may himself have imitated, he is not imitable; nobody has ever, except in the minutest shreds—rather actually torn off from his motley than reproducing it—written in Lamb's style save Lamb. And accordingly no one (though not a few have tried) has ever criticised like Lamb. It is very easy to be capricious, fantastic, fastidious—as easy as to wear yellow stockings and go cross-gartered, and as effective. To Lamb's critical attitude there go in the first place that love for the book which has been spoken of; then that faculty of sound, almost common-sense, "taste" which is shown in the early letters to Coleridge and Southey; then the reading of years and decades; and, lastly, the *je ne sais quoi* that "fondoos" the other things, as the old Oxford story has it—a story to be constantly borne in mind by the critic and the historian of criticism.[1] Even the

---

[1] There may be people who do not know this, and those who know it already need not read it. A college cook (I think of Brasenose) was particularly famous for that most excellent dish the *fondue*, but would never tell his recipe. At last some Arthur Pendennis (of the other shop) got round him to this extent: "Why, sir," said he, "you see I takes the eggs, and the butter, and the cheese, you know, and the other things; *and then I just fondoos 'em.*"

other ingredients are not too common, especially in conjunction: the *je ne sais quoi* itself is here, and nowhere else.

Leigh Hunt [1] claims less space from us than either of his friends, Hazlitt and Lamb. This is not because he is an *Leigh Hunt:* inconsiderable critic, for he is by no means this. *his some-* As has been said, he has the immense and sur- *what in-* *ferior posi-* prising credit of having first discovered the great- *tion.* ness of the tragic part of Middleton's *Changeling,* as an individual exploit, and in more general ways he has that, which Macaulay duly recognised in a well-known passage,[2] of being perhaps more *catholic* in his tastes as regards English Literature than any critic up to his time. He has left a very large range of critical performance, which is very rarely without taste, acuteness, and felicity of expression; and he has, as against both the greater critics just named, the very great advantage of possessing a competent knowledge of at least one modern literature [3] besides his own, and some glimmerings of others. He has the further deserts of being almost always readable, of diffusing a pleasant sunny atmosphere, and of doing very much to keep up the literary side of that periodical production which, for good or for evil, was, with the novel, the great literary feature of the nineteenth century. These are not small merits: and while they might seem greater if they were not thrown somewhat into the shade by the superior eminence of Coleridge and Hazlitt, and the superior attractiveness of Lamb, they retain, even in the vicinity of these, claims to full acknowledgment.

A severely critical estimate, however, will discover in Leigh Hunt—perhaps in very close juxtaposition and in a sort of *Reasons* causal relation to these merits themselves—some- *for it.* thing which is not quite so good. Even his catholicity may be set down in part, by the Enemy, to a certain loose facility of liking, an absence of fastidiousness and selection. If Lamb goes too far towards the ends of the Eng-

---

[1] There is no complete ed. of Hunt, and there could not well be one. I shall refer here to the 7 vols. of Messrs Smith & Elder's cheap and uniform reprint of a good deal, and to the pretty American pocket issue of the *Italian Poets.*

[2] At the beginning of the Essay on Restoration Drama.

[3] Italian.

lish literary earth for the objects of his affection, Hunt is
rather too content to find them *in triviis et angiportis*. He does
not exactly "like grossly," but he likes a little promiscuously.
The fault is no very bad one; and it becomes exceedingly
venial—nay, a positive virtue in time and circumstance—when
we compare it with the unreasonable exclusiveness of the
Neo-classic period. But it is a kind of criticism which inclines rather too much to the uncritical.

A further objection may be taken by applying that most
dangerous of all tests, the question "What does he *dis*like?"
His attitude For the twentieth time (probably) let us repeat
to Dante. that in criticism likes and dislikes are free; and
that the man who, however unfortunately, still honestly dislikes what the consensus of good criticism approves, is entitled
to say so, and had much better say so. But he gives his
reasons, descends upon particulars, at his peril. Leigh Hunt,
to do him justice, is not like Mr Rymer—it is not his habit
"no wise to allow." But it is certainly a pity that one of
his exceptions should be Dante, and it is certainly a much
greater pity that among the reasons given for unfavourable
criticism [1] should be because Dante "puts fabulous people with
real among the damned," because Purgatory is such a very
disagreeable idea, and because the whole poem contains "absurdities too obvious nowadays to need remark."

This, however, was merely an exceptional outburst of that
"Liberal" Philistinism and blundering which, it is only fair
to say, had been provoked by plentiful exhibition of the same
qualities on the other side, and which was more particularly
excusable in Leigh Hunt (humanly, if not critically, speaking),
because nobody, not even Hazlitt, had received worse treatment
from that side than himself. But it does something affect his
critical position; for even Hazlitt managed, in some queer
fashion, to distinguish between the prostitute baronet, Sir
Walter Scott, and "the Author of *Waverley*," between that

---

[1] Of course it is not all unfavourable : Leigh Hunt is far too much
of a critic and a lover of poetry for
that. But he is constantly put off
and put out by Dante's "bigotry,"
his "uncharitableness," the "barbarous pedantries" of his age, and the
like.

wicked Mr Burke and the author of the great speeches and
treatises. But the main reasons why Hunt must go with
shorter measure than others, is the combination of abundance
in quantity with a certain want of distinction in quality, which
mars his writings. Not even the largest space here possible
would enable us to go through them all, and we should be
able to select but a few that are of unquestionably distinctive
and characteristic *race*. It is, indeed, rather in his favour
that you may dip almost anywhere into him with the certainty of a wholesome, pleasant, and refreshing critical bath
or draught. He is very rarely untrustworthy; and when
he is, as in the *Dante* case, he tells the fact and its secret
more frankly even than Hazlitt himself. But it would be
unjust to refer to no samples of him, and a few of the
most characteristic shall therefore be given.

Fortunately there is an extremely favourable example of
his criticism which fills a whole book to itself, and is written
Examples from Imagination and Fancy. under something like a general scheme. This is
the volume—modestly sub-titled "Selections," but
containing a very large proportion of comment and
original matter—which he called *Imagination and
Fancy*,[1] and intended to follow up with four others, though
only one, *Wit and Humour*,[2] was ever written. The plan
was begun late (1844); but as we have seen in almost every
instance, a man's critical work very rarely declines with years,
unless he actually approaches dotage: and the book is, on the
whole, not merely the most favourable but the most representatively favourable example of Leigh Hunt's criticism. It opens
by a set Essay on the question "What is Poetry?" from
which, perhaps, any one who knew the author's other work,
but not this, might not expect very much, for Hunt had
not an abstract or philosophical head. He acquits himself,
however, remarkably well. His general definition that Poetry
is "the utterance of a passion for truth, beauty, and power,

---

[1] New ed., *ut sup.*: London, 1883.

[2] This is good, but not so good: and
elsewhere—though critical matter will
be found in all Hunt's collected books
and in all his uncollected periodical
work, from the *Examiner*, "whose very
name is Hunt," and the *Indicator*, and
the *Reflector*, to the *Tatler*, and the
London Journal—we shall never find
him better and seldom so good.

embodying and illustrating its conceptions by imagination and fancy, and modulating its language on the principle of variety in uniformity," is not bad; but these things are never very satisfactory. It will be seen that Hunt, like Coleridge, though with a less "Cimmerian" obscurity of verbiage, "dodges" the frank mention of "metre" or "verse"; but this is not because he is in any way inclined to compromise. On the contrary, he says [1] (taking, and perhaps designedly, the very opposite line to Wordsworth) that he "knows of no very fine versification unaccompanied with fine poetry." But the strength of the "Essay," as of the whole book, is in the abundant and felicitous illustration of the various points of this definition by commented selections from the poets themselves.

That catholicity which has been said to be his main critical virtue will be found (without any of the vice which has been hinted as sometimes accompanying it) in the very list of the authors selected from—Spenser, Marlowe, Shakespeare, Jonson, Beaumont and Fletcher, Middleton, Dekker, and Webster, Milton, Coleridge, Shelley, and Keats: while the less "imaginative" poets are by no means neglected, and in particular Leigh Hunt brings out, often as no one had ever done before, that sheer poetical quality of Dryden to which the critics of 1800-1830 had been as a rule unjust. But the comment (and one cannot say more) is usually worthy of the selection. The fullest division of all is that on Spenser—indeed Leigh Hunt's appreciation of this at once exquisite and magnificent poet is one of the very best we have, and would be the best of all if it had been a little more sensitive to Spenser's "brave*st* translunary things," to the pervading exaltation and sublimation of thought and feeling which purifies the most luscious details, and unites the most straggling divagations in a higher unity. But, short of this, it would be difficult to have a better detailed eulogium, *pièces en main*, of the subject; nor does Hunt fail to make out something of a case against, at least, the exaggeration of Lessing's attack on the *ut pictura poesis* view. But his limitations appear in his complete misunderstanding of Coleridge's exact and pro-

[1] P. 51, *ed. cit.*

found observation that Spenser's descriptions are "not in the true sense of the word *picturesque,* but composed of a wondrous series of images as in dreams." What Coleridge meant, of course, is that sequence rather than strict "composition" is Spenser's secret—that his pageants *dissolve into* one another. But in these finesses Hunt is seldom at his ease. So, again, he blasphemes one of the most beautiful lines of *The Tempest*—

> "The fringed curtains of thine eye advance"—

as "elaborate nothingness, not to say nonsense" [how nothingness can in any case be sense he shall tell us], "pompous," "declamatory," and disapproved of by—Pope !

One really blushes for him. Could he possibly be unaware that when a person is about to look at anything, the natural gesture is to lower the head and thrust it a little forward, raising or depressing the eyelids at the same time? or be insensible to the exquisite profile image of Miranda with the long eyelashes projected against the air? And he was the author of *A Criticism of Female Beauty!* But if he sometimes misunderstands, he seldom misses good things such as (it is true Warton put him on this) the Medea passage of Gower.[1] Ben Jonson made him uncomfortable, which is again a pity; and on Beaumont and Fletcher he is at almost his very worst: but he is sounder than some greater ones on Ford and Massinger, and his great "catch" of De Flores deserves yet a third mention. He is at his very best and pleasantest, too, where most men fail—where they are even often very *un*pleasant—on his contemporaries, Coleridge, and Shelley, and Keats. When you have said such a thing as this[2] of Coleridge, "Of pure poetry, . . . consisting of nothing but its essential self, . . . he was the greatest master of his time," you had better "stand down." Your critical claim is made out: you may damage but can hardly increase it. Yet it is only in the severe court of critical history that one would wish to silence Hunt: for, in truth, nine-tenths of his criticism

---

[1] It is curious what power that dead sorceress has had on almost all her poets.

[2] P. 250, *ed. cit.*

is admirable, and most admirably suited to instruct and encourage the average man. Impressionism and Rulelessness are almost as fairly justified of him, their child, as of any other that I can think of. They scarcely ever lead him wrong in liking; and he mentions what he dislikes so seldom that he has only occasional chances of being wrong there.

But the greatest of the "Cockney critics" (*quelle Cocaigne!*) has yet to come. There is "a company of warm young men," *Hazlitt.* as Dryden has it, who would doubtless disdain the inquiry whether Coleridge or Hazlitt is the greatest of English critics; and it is quite certain that this inquiry might be conducted in a sufficiently futile sense and manner. There are others, less disdainful, who might perhaps be staggered by the acknowledgment *in limine* that it is possible to answer the question either way—nay, for the same person to give both answers, and yet be "not unwelcome back again" as a reasonable disputant. I have myself in my time, I think, committed myself to both propositions; and I am not at all disposed to give up either—for reasons which it will be more proper to give at the end than at the beginning of an examination of Hazlitt himself. That he was a great critic there will probably now be little dispute, though Goethe is said not to have found much good in him; though persons of worship, including Mr Stevenson, have thought him greater as a miscellaneous essayist; and though you may read writings of considerable length upon him in which no attempt is made to bring out his critical character at all.

His critical deliverances are so numerous and so voluminous that the "brick of the house" process, which we have *Method of* frequently found applicable, has in his case to be *dealing* given up, or at least considerably modified—for it *with him.* is too much the principle of the present History to be given up altogether. Fortunately there is no difficulty in the modification. Hazlitt is not, like Coleridge, remarkable for the discovery and enunciation of any one great critical principle, or for the emission (*obiter* or otherwise) of remarkable mediate *dicta*, or for *marginalia* on individual passages or lines, though sometimes he can do the last and sometimes also the second of these things. What he is remarkable for is his extraordinary fertility and felicity, as regards English literature, in judgments, more or less "grasped," of individual authors, books, or pieces. As, by preference, he stops at the passage, and does not descend to the individual line or phrase, so, by preference also,[1] he stops at the individual example of the Kind, and does not ascend to the Kind itself, or at least is not usually very happy in his ascension. But within these limits (and they are wide enough), the fertility and the felicity of his criticism are things which strike one almost dumb with admiration; and this in spite of certain obvious and in their way extremely grave faults.

The most obvious, though by far the least, of these,—indeed one which is displayed with such frankness and in a way so little delusive as to be hardly a fault at all, though it is certainly a drawback,—is a sort of audacious sciolism—acquiescence in ignorance, indifference about "satisfying the examiners"—for half a dozen different names would be required to bring out all the sides of it.

His almost entire ignorance of all literatures but his own gives him no trouble, though it cannot be said that it does *His surface* him no harm. In treating of comic writers, not *and occa-* in English only but generally, he says[2] (with perfect *sional faults:* truth) that Aristophanes and Lucian are two of the *Imperfect* *knowledge* four chief names for comic humour, but that he *and method.* shall say little of them, for he knows little. Would all men were as honest! but one cannot say, "Would all critics were as ignorant!" In his *Lectures on the English Poets* he is transparently, and again quite honestly, ignorant of mostly all the earlier minorities, with some not so minor. He almost prided himself upon not reading anything in the writing period of his life; and he seems to have carried out his principles so conscientiously that, if anything occurred in

---

[1] Preference only, of course: the exceptions are numerous, but not enough to destroy the rule.

[2] References will be made here throughout to the reprints of Hazlitt's literary work in the Bohn Library,

7 vols. This is to *The English Comic Writers*, p. 33. The newer and completer edition of Messrs Waller & Glover had but begun when the text was originally written.

the course of a lecture which was unknown to him, he never made the slightest effort to supply the gap. His insouciance in method was equal to that in regard to material; and when we find [1] Godwin and Mrs Radcliffe included, with no satiric purpose, among "The English Comic Writers," they are introduced so naturally that the absurdity hardly strikes us till some accident wakes us up to it. If inaccuracies in matters of fact are not very common in him, it is because, like a true critic, he pays very little attention to such matters, and is wholly in opinion and appreciation and judgment, and other things where the free spirit is kept straight, if at all, by its own instinct. But he does commit such inaccuracies, and would evidently commit many more if he ran the risk of them oftener.

The last and gravest of his drawbacks has to be mentioned, and though it may be slurred over by political partisanship,

Extra-literary prejudice. those who admire and exalt him in spite of and not because of his politics, are well entitled to call attention to it. To the unpleasantness of Hazlitt's personal temper we have the unchallengeable testimony of his friends Lamb, who was the most charitable, and Hunt, who with all his faults was one of the most good-natured, of mortals. But what we may call his political temper, especially when it was further exasperated by his personal, is something of the equal of which no time leaves record. Whenever this east wind blows, the true but reasonable Hazlittian had better, speaking figuratively, "go to bed till it is over," as John Hall Stevenson is said to have done literally in the case of the literal Eurus. Not only does Hazlitt then cease to be a critic, —he ceases to be a rational being. Sidney and Scott are the main instances of its effect, because Sidney could not have annoyed, and Scott we know did not in any way annoy, Hazlitt personally. Gifford is not in this case, and he was himself so fond of playing at the roughest of bowls that nobody need pity him for the rubbers he met. But Hazlitt's famous *Letter* to him, which some admire, always, I confess, makes me think of the Doll's-dressmaker's father's last fit of the horrors in

[1] Ibid., p. 170 *sq.*, and p. 176 *sq.*

Our Mutual Friend, and of the way in which the luckless "man talent" fought with the police and "laid about him hopelessly, fiercely, staringly, convulsively, foamingly." Fortunately the effect was not so fatal, and I know no other instance in which Hazlitt actually required the strait waistcoat.[1] But he certainly did here: and in a considerable number of instances his prejudices have made him, if not exactly *non compos mentis,* yet certainly *non compos judicii.*

Fortunately, however, the wind does not always blow from this quarter with him, and when it does the symptoms are so

His radical and usual excellence. unmistakable that nobody can be deceived unless he chooses to be, or is so stupid that it really does not matter whether he is deceived or not. Far more usually it is set in a bracing North or fertilising West, not seldom even in the "summer South" itself. And then you get such appreciations, in the best, the most thorough, the most delightful, the most *valuable* sense, as had been seldom seen since Dryden, never before, and in him not frequently. I do not know in what language to look for a parallel wealth. Systematic Hazlitt's criticism very seldom is, and, as hinted above, still seldomer at its best when it attempts system. But then system was not wanted; it had been overdone; the patient required a copious alterative. He received it from Hazlitt as he has—virtue and quantity combined—received it from no one else since: it is a "patent medicine" in everything but the presence of quackery. Roughly speaking, Hazlitt's criticism is of two kinds. The first is very stimulating, very interesting, but, I venture to think, the less valuable of the two. In it Hazlitt at least endeavours to be general, and takes a lesson from Burke in "prodigious variation" on his subject. The most famous, the most laboured, and perhaps the best example is the exordium of the *Lectures on the English Poets,* with its astonishing "amplification" on what poetry in general is and what it is not. A good deal of this is directly Coleridgean. I forget whether this is the lecture which Cole-

---

[1] He is, however, dangerously near requiring it with regard to Scott (see the end of the article on him in *The Spirit of his Age*), and whenever he speaks of the Duke of Wellington.

ridge himself, when he read it, thought that he remembered
"talking at Lamb's"; but we may be quite sure that he had
talked things very like it. Much in the "Shakespeare and
Milton" has the same quality, and may have been partly
derived from the same source: the critical character of Pope [1]
is another instance, and probably more original. For Hazlitt
had not merely learnt the trick from his master but had himself a genius for it; and he adorned these disquisitions with
more *phrase* than Coleridge's recalcitrant pen usually allowed
him, though there seems to have been plenty in his speech.

The Pope passage is specially interesting, because it leads us
to the second and, as it seems to me, the chief and principal
class of Hazlitt's critical deliverances—those in which, without
epideictic intention, without, or with but a moderate portion
of, rhetoric and amplification and phrasemaking, he handles
separate authors and works and pieces. I have said that I
think him here unsurpassed, and perhaps unrivalled, in the
quantity and number of his deliverances, and only surpassed,
if so, in their quality, by the greatest things of the greatest
persons. These deliverances are to be found everywhere in
his extensive critical work, and it is of a survey of some of
them, conditioned in the manner outlined above, that the main
body of any useful historical account of his criticism must consist. The four main places are the Lectures on *The English
Poets* (1818), on *The English Comic Writers* (1819), on *Elizabethan Literature* (1820), and the book on *Characters of Shakespeare* (1817). We may take them in the order mentioned,
though it is not quite chronological, because the chronological
dislocation, in the case of the second pair, is logically and
methodically unavoidable.

How thoroughly this examination of the greater particulars
(as we may call it) was the work which he was born to do is
The English illustrated by the sketches (at the end of the first
Poets. Lecture on *The English Poets* [2]) of *The Pilgrim's Progress, Robinson Crusoe*, the *Decameron*, Homer, the Bible, Dante,
and (O Groves of Blarney!) *Ossian*. Hazlitt's faults (except
prejudice, which is here fortunately silent) are by no means

---

[1] *English Poets*, ed. cit., pp. 92-95. [2] Pp. 18-25.

hidden in them—irrelevance, defect of knowledge, "casualness," and other not so good things. But the *gusto*,[1] the spirit, the inspiriting quality, are present in tenfold measure. Here is a man to whom literature is a real and live thing, and who can make it real and alive to his readers—a man who does not love it or its individual examples "by allowance," but who loves it "with personal love." Even his Richardsonian digression [2]—horrible to the stop-watch man—is alive and real and stimulating with the rest. The Dante passage is a little false perhaps in parts, inadequate, prejudiced, what you will in others. But it is criticism—an act of literary faith and hope and charity too—a substance; something added to, and new-born in, the literary cosmos. He is better (indeed he is here almost at his very best) on Spenser than on Chaucer, but why ? Because he *knew* more about Spenser, because he was plentifully read in sixteenth- and hardly read at all in fourteenth-century literature. And so always: the very plethora of one's notes for comment warning the commentator that he is lost if he indulges rashly. Where Hazlitt is inadequate (as for instance on Dryden) he is more instructive than many men's adequacy could be, and where he is not—on Collins, on the Ballads, and elsewhere—he prepares us for that ineffable and half-reluctant outburst—a very Balaam's blessing—on Coleridge,[3] which stands not higher than this, not lower than that, but as an *A-per-se*, consummate and unique.

In a sense the *Comic Writers* are even better. The general exordium on Wit and Humour belongs to the first class of *The* Comic Hazlitt's critical performances as defined above, Writers. and is one of the cleverest of them; though it may perhaps have the faults of its class, and some of those of its author. That on Comedy—the general part of it—incurs this sentence in a heavier degree; for Aristotle or somebody else seems to have impressed Hazlitt too strongly with the necessary *shadiness* of Comedy, and it is quite clear that of the Romantic variety (which to be sure hardly anybody but Shakespeare

---

[1] This favourite word of his has been adopted by all competent critics as best describing his own manner.

[2] Pp. 19, 20.

[3] The last page of *The English Poets*.

has ever hit off) he had an insufficient idea. He is again inadequate on Jonson; it is indeed in his criticism, because of
its very excellence, that we see—more than anywhere else,
though we see it everywhere—the truth of his master's denunciation of the "criticism which denies." But his lecture
or essay on the capital examples of the comedy which he
really liked—that of the Restoration—is again an apex: and,
as it happens, it is grouped for English students with others—
the morally excellent and intellectually vigorous but rather
purblind onslaught of Collier, the again vigorous but somewhat
Philistine following thereof by Macaulay, the practical confession of Lamb's fantastic and delightful apology, Leigh Hunt's
rather feeble compromise—after a fashion which shows it off to
a marvel. While as to the chapter on the Eighteenth-century
Novel it has, with a worthier subject, an equal supremacy of
treatment. You may differ with much of it, but always agree
to differ: except in that estimate of Lovelace which unfortunately shows us Hazlitt's inability to recognise a *cad* in the
dress and with the manners of a fine gentleman.[1]

The *Lectures on the Age of Elizabeth* (which succeeded the
Comic Writers, as these had succeeded the *Poets*) maintain, if
The Age of they do not even raise, the standard. Perhaps there
Elizabeth. is nothing so fine as the Coleridge passage in individual and concentrated expression; nor any piece of connected criticism so masterly as the chapter on the Novel. But
the level is higher: and nowhere do we find better expression
of that *gusto*—that amorous quest of literary beauty and rapturous enjoyment of it—which has been noted as Hazlitt's
great merit. His faults are here, as always, with him and
with us. Even the faithful Lamb was driven to expostulate[2]
with the wanton and, as it happens, most uncritical belittle-
ment of Sidney,[3] and (though he himself was probably less
influenced by political partisanship or political feeling of any
kind than almost any great writer of whom we know) to

---

[1] It is curious that the critic's
blunder had been anticipated, though
not excused, by the author's. Richardson of course *meant* to make Lovelace
what Hazlitt sees in him: only he
failed.

[2] In the paper on Sir Philip's
Sonnets, noted above.

[3] Lect. vi., p. 201 *sq.*

assign this to its true cause. It is odd [1] that a critic, and a great critic, should contrive to be inadequate both on Browne and on Dryden: and again one cannot but suspect the combination to be due to the fact that both were Royalists. But the King's Head does not always come in: and it is only fair to Hazlitt to say that he is less biassed than Coleridge by the ultra-royalism of Beaumont and Fletcher, and the supposed republicanism of Massinger. And in by far the greater part of the book—nearly the whole of that part of it which deals with the dramatists—there is no disturbance of this kind. The opening, if somewhat discursive, is masterly, and with very few exceptions the lecturer or essayist carries out the admirable motto—in fact and in deed the motto of all real critics—"I have endeavoured to feel what was good, and to give a reason for the faith that was in me when necessary and when in my power." [2] Two of his sentences, in dealing with Beaumont and Fletcher, not merely set the key-note of all good criticism but should open the stop thereof in all fit readers. "It is something worth living for to write or even read such poetry as this, or to know that it has been written." Again, "And so it is something, as our poets themselves wrote, 'far above singing.'" [3]

The *Characters of Shakespeare's Plays* is perhaps not as good as any of these three courses of Lectures; but it should be remembered that it came earlier in time, and that the critic had not "got his hand in." The notes are as a rule nearly as desultory as Coleridge's, with less suggestiveness; there is at least one outburst, in the case of *Henry V.*, of the usual disturbing influence; there is very much more quotation than there need be from Schlegel; and there are other signs of the novitiate. Yet the book contains admirable things, as in the early comparison of Chaucer and Shakespeare, where, though Hazlitt's defective knowledge of Chaucer again appears, there is much else good. Among the *apices* of Shakespearian criticism is the statement that the

Characters of Shake- speare.

[1] But not as unique as odd.
[2] P. 181.
[3] Pp. 115, 126. The elaborate char- acters of Bacon, &c., in this course should be compared with those of Pope, and others earlier.

poet "has no prejudice for or against his characters,"[1] that he makes "no attempt to force an interest: everything is left for time and circumstance to unfold."[2] There is perhaps something inconsistent with this as well as with truth in the observation on *Lear*,[3] that "He is here fairly caught in the web of his own imagination"; but, like most of the greater critics, Hazlitt cares very little for superficial consistency. The characters of Falstaff and Shylock are masterpieces in his *bravura* style, and one need perhaps nowhere seriously quarrel with any critical statement of his except the astonishing one, that *All's Well that Ends Well* is "one of the most *pleasing*" of the plays.

In the remaining volumes the literary articles or passages are only occasional, and are often considerably adulterated with non-literary matter. In *The Plain Speaker*, for instance, the opening paper on "The Prose Style of Poets" holds out almost the highest promise, and gives almost the lowest performance. Hazlitt, as is not so very uncommon with him, seems to have deliberately set himself to take the other side from Coleridge's. That it happens also to be the wrong side matters very little. But even his attack on Coleridge's own prose style (open enough to objection) has nothing very happy in it except the comparison, "To read one of his disquisitions is like hearing the variations to a piece of music without the score." So, too, "On the Conversation of Authors," though intensely interesting, has no critical interest or very little—the chief exception being the passage on Burke's style. Far more important is the glance at the theory of the single word in "On Application to Study,"[4] and in that in "On Envy"[5] on the taste of the Lake School.

Much of *The Plain Speaker* is injured as a treasury of criticism, though improved as a provision of amusement, by The Plain Hazlitt's personal revelations, complaints, agonies; Speaker. but the critical *ethos* of the man was so irrepressible that it will not be refused. There is a curious little piece[6] of critical blasphemy, or at least "dis-*gusto*" (the word is

---

[1] P. 64, ed. cit.   [3] P. 108.   [5] P. 139.
[2] P. 75.   [4] P. 77.   [6] P. 185.

wanted and is fairly choice Italian), in "On the Pleasure of Hating," and, almost throughout the series, the sharp flux and reflux of literary admiration and political rage in respect of Scott is most noteworthy. "On the Qualifications necessary to Success in Life" contains yet another[1] of those passages on Coleridge which are like nothing so much as the half-fond, half-furious, retrospects of a discarded lover on his mistress—which are certainly like nothing else in literature. But "On Reading Old Books" does not belie the promise of its title, and is a complete and satisfactory palinode to the fit of critical headache noted just now. One must not venture to cite from it; it is to be read and re-read, and hardly any single piece, except the immortal "Farewell to Essay-Writing," gives us so much insight into Hazlitt's critical temperament as this. "On People of Sense" contains many critical glances, and, unfortunately, one[2] of those on Shelley which show Hazlitt at his worst. One might think that he who found others so "far above singing" could not miss the similar altitude of the author of *Prometheus Unbound*. But Shelley was a contemporary, something of an acquaintance, a man of some means, a gentleman—so Hazlitt must snarl[3] at him. Let us sigh and pass.

"Antiquity," though on one side only, is almost throughout ours, and therefore not ours: and there is not a little for us in "On Novelty and Familiarity," while "Old English Writers and Speakers" speaks for itself, and is specially interesting for its glances on matters French and its characteristically Hazlittian fling—one I confess with which I have for once no quarrel—that "*'Tis pity She's a Whore* will no more act than Lord Byron and Goethe together could have written it."[4] It puts one in charity for the absurd description,[5] contradicted by

---

[1] P. 278. These passages may remind some of the story of one of George Sand's old lovers pausing before a photograph of her in a shopwindow, and saying to his companion, "Et je l'ai connue *belle!*"

[2] P. 344.

[3] The usual dog-metaphors are no triviality in regard to Hazlitt when he is in this mood. Every one who knows dogs must have noticed the way in which they often snarl, as if they could not help it; the growl and gnash are forced from them.

[4] P. 441.　　[5] P. 449.

his own remarks, of *Redgauntlet* as "the last and almost worst" of Scott's novels, and the prediction (alas! to be falsified) that "Old Sir Walter will last long enough"—in the flesh, not in fame.[1] "Scott, Racine, and Shakespeare" is not unworthy of its title, though it is really on the first and last only. Racine is brought in perfunctorily, and justice is done to him in neither sense.

Table-Talk, one of the greenest pastures of the Hazlittian champaign generally, is among the least literary of the books, and yet so literary enough. "On Genius and Common Sense" contributes its Character of Wordsworth,[2] on whom Hazlitt is always interesting, because of the extraordinary opposition between the men's temperaments. The companion on Shelley,[3] which is supplied by "On Paradox and Commonplace," is hardly less interesting, though, for the reasons above indicated, much less valuable. "On Milton's Sonnets," however, is, as it ought to be, a pure study and an admirable one.[4] "The Aristocracy of Letters" carries its hay high on the horn, yet it is not negligible: and "On Criticism," which follows, really deserves the title, despite its frequent and inevitable flings and runnings-amuck. The good-humoured, though rather "home" description of "the Occult School"[5] (*v. supra* on Lamb) is perfectly just. "On Familiar" Style is also no false promiser, and yet another passage on Coleridge meets us in the paper "On Effeminacy of Character."

Nor is the interesting "omnibus" volume, which takes its general title from *The Round Table*, of the most fertile. The collection of short papers, properly so called, was written earlier (1817) than most of the books hitherto discussed, and therefore has some first drafts or variants of not a little that is in them. In a note of it[6] occurs the

The Round Table, &c.

---

[1] The end-note of this piece coincides curiously with a remark once made to me by a person unusually well acquainted with France but, I feel sure, quite unaware that he was echoing Hazlitt. "The Frenchman has a certain routine of phrases into which his ideas run habitually as into a mould; and you cannot get him out of them."

[2] P. 56. [3] P. 203.

[4] Yet Hazlitt cannot resist a renewed fling at Sidney.

[5] P. 351.

[6] P. 150, ed. cit. I wish that some one, in these excerpting days, would extract and print together *all* Hazlitt's passages on Burke, Scott, and Coleridge.

passage on Burke, which, with that on Scott in the *Spirit of the Age*, is Hazlitt's nearest approach to the sheer *delirium tremens* of the Gifford Letter: but he is not often thus. "The Character of Milton's Eve" is a fine critical paper of its kind, and "takes the taste out" well after the passage on Burke. The long handling of *The Excursion* is very interesting to compare with that in the *English Poets*, as is the earlier "Midsummer Night's Dream" with similar things elsewhere. "Pedantry" and others give something: and though no human being (especially no human being who knows both books) has ever discovered what made Hazlitt call *John Buncle* "the English Rabelais," the paper on Amory's queer novel is a very charming one. "On the Literary Character" does somewhat deceive us: "Commonplace Critics" less so: but to "Poetical Versatility" we must return. Of the remaining contents of the volume, the well-known *Conversations with Northcote* (where the painter plays Hazlitt's idea of an Advocatus Diaboli on Hazlitt) gives less still. But there is a striking passage on Wordsworth,[1] a paradox (surely?) on Tom Paine[2] as "a fine writer" (you might as well call a good getter of coal at the face "a fine sculptor"), an interesting episode[3] on early American nineteenth-century literature; and not a few others, especially the profound self-criticism (for no doubt Northcote had nothing to do with it) on Hazlitt's abstinence from society.[4] In *Characteristics*, one of the few notable collections of the kind in English, CCXC, a most curious and pretty certainly unconscious echo of Aristotle,[5] is our best gleaning; while the 52d "Commonplace," on Byron and Wordsworth, and the 12th and 11th "Trifles light as air," on Fielding and on "modern" critics, play the same part there.

On the other hand, *The Spirit of the Age* (with the exception of some political and philosophical matter) is wholly
The Spirit of the Age. literary; and may rank with the three sets of *Lectures* and the *Characters of Shakespeare* as the main storehouse

---

[1] P. 246. [2] P. 248. written romance than in common his-
[3] P. 317. [4] P. 431. tory."
[5] "We have more faith in a well-

of Hazlitt's criticism. Here, too, there is much repetition, and here, at the end of the Scott article, is the almost insane outburst more than once referred to. But the bulk of the book is at Hazlitt's very best pitch of appreciative grasp. If he is anywhere out of focus, it is in reference to Godwin's novels—the setting of which in any kind of comparison with Scott's (though Hazlitt was critic enough from the first to see that Godwin could by no possibility be the "Author of *Waverley*") is a remarkable instance of the disadvantage of the contemporary, and, to some extent, the sympathiser. But the book certainly goes far to bear out the magnificent eulogy of Hazlitt for which Thackeray[1] took it as text, quite early in his career.

The *Sketches and Essays* are again very rich, where they are rich; and advertise the absence of riches most frankly where *Sketches* they are not. "On Reading New Books"; not a *and Essays.* little of "Merry England"; the whole of "On Taste" and "Why the Heroes of Romances are insipid" speak for themselves, and do not bewray their claim. "Taste," especially, contains[2] one of Hazlitt's own titles to critical supremacy in his fixing on Perdita's primrose description as itself supreme, when "the scale of fancy, passion, and observation of nature *Winterslow.* is raised" high enough. And as for *Winterslow*, its first and its last papers are "things enskied" in criticism, for the one is "My First Acquaintance with Poets," and the last "The Farewell to Essay Writing."

These two last, the sentence on

> "That come before the swallow dares, and take
> The winds of March with beauty";

and (say) the paper referred to a little above on "Poetical Versatility," will serve as texts for some more general remarks *Hazlitt's* on Hazlitt's critical character. We have said at *critical* the beginning of this notice everything that need *virtue,* be said by way of deduction or allowance; we have only hinted at the clear critical "balance to credit" which

---

[1] In 1845, reviewing Horne's very rashly entitled *New Spirit of the Age.* The review will be found in the 13th vol. (1886) of the ordinary ed. of Thackeray's *Works.*

[2] P. 173.

remains; and these essays and passages will help to bring this out.

To take the "Poetic Versatility" first, it is an interesting paper, and with the aid of those "characters" of poets, &c., which have been indicated in the survey just completed, gives the best possible idea of one (and perhaps the most popular) of Hazlitt's forms of critical achievement and influence. In it he eddies round his subject—completing his picture of it by strokes apparently promiscuous in selection, but always tending to body forth the image that presents itself to him, and that he wishes to present to his readers. "Poetry dwells in a perpetual Utopia of its own." It "does not create difficulties where they do not exist, but contrives to get rid of them whether they exist or not." "Its strength is in its wings; its element the air." We "may leave it to Time to take out the stains, seeing it is a thing immortal as itself." Poets "either find things delightful or make them so," &c. &c., some of the etceteras drawing away from the everlasting, and condescending rather lamentably to the particular.

Now there is no need to tell the reader—even the reader of this book, I hope—that this, of these utterances, is a repro- *in set pieces,* duction of Longinus (whom Hazlitt most probably had not read), or that of Coleridge, whom most certainly he had both read and heard.[1] "The man who plants cabbages imitates too": and it is only the foolishest folk of rather foolish times who endeavour to be original, though the wisest of all times always succeed in being so. The point with Hazlitt is that in these circlings round his subject—these puttings of every possible way in which, with or without the help of others, it strikes him—he gives the greatest possible help to others in being struck. One of the blows will almost certainly hit the nail on the head and drive it home into any tolerably susceptible mind: many may, and the others after the first will help to fix it. Of method there may not be very

[1] "Its strength is in its wings" is, in idea, of course, as old as Plato. But the nearest expression of it, the "la lyre est un instrument *ailé*" of Joubert, though by a man more than thirty years Hazlitt's senior, was never, I think, published till ten years after Hazlitt's death.

much—there is rather more here than in most cases; but whether there is method or not, "everything," in the old military phrase, "goes in"; the subject and the reader are carried by assault, mass, variety, repetition of argument, imagery, phrase. Hazlitt will not be refused; he takes towns at a hand-gallop, like Condé at Lerida—and he does not often lose them afterwards.

In this phase of his genius, however, there is perhaps, for some tastes at any rate, a little too much of what has been *and* called *bravura*—too much of the merely epideictic. *universally.* It is not so in the other. Appreciate the appreciation of the *Winter's Tale* passage; still more take to heart (they will go to it without much taking where there is one) the "First Acquaintance with Poets," or still better the marvellous critical swan-song of the "Farewell," and there can be no more doubt about Hazlitt. *Quia multum amavit* is at once his best description and his greatest glory. In all the range of criticism which I have read I can hardly think of any one except Longinus who displays the same faculty of not unreasonable or unreasoned passion for literature; and Longinus, alas! has, as an opportunity for showing this to us, scarcely more than the bulk of one of Hazlitt's longest Essays, of which, long and short, Hazlitt himself has given us, I suppose, a hundred. Nor, as in some others (many, if not most of whom, if I named them, I should name for the sake of honour), is a genuine passion made the mere theme of elaborate and deliberate literary variations. As we have seen, Hazlitt will often leave it expressed in one sentence of ejaculatory and convincing fervour; it seldom appears at greater length than that of a passage, while a whole lecture or essay in the key of rapture is exceedingly rare. Hazlitt is desultory, irrelevant, splenetic, moody, self-contradictory; but he is never merely pleonastic,—there is no mere verbiage, no mere virtuosity, in him.

And the consequence is that this enthusiastic appreciation of letters, which I have, however heretically, taken throughout this book to be really the highest function of criticism, *catches:* that the critical yeast (to plagiarise from ourselves) never fails to work. The order of history, as always, should probably be repeated, and the influence of Coleridge should be felt, as Hazlitt himself felt it, first: it is well to fortify also with Longinus himself, and with Aristotle, and with as many others of the great ones as the student can manage to master. But there is at least a danger, with some perhaps of not the worst minds, of all this remaining cold as the bonfire before the torch is applied. The *silex scintillans* of Hazlitt's rugged heart will seldom fail to give the vivifying spark from its own inward and immortal fire.[1]

There have been times — perhaps they are not quite over — when the admission of William Blake[2] into the category *Blake.* of critics would have been regarded as an absurdity, or a bad jest. Nothing is more certain, however, than that the poet-painter expresses, with a force and directness rather improved by that lack of complete technical sanity which some of his admirers most unwisely and needlessly deny, the opinions of the "Extreme Right," the high-fliers of the Army of Romanticism. He may often be thinking of painting rather than of poetry; but this is sometimes expressedly not the case, and many of his most pointed sayings apply to the one art just as well as to the other— if indeed it would not be still more correct to say that, except

---

[1] Below Hazlitt (who as well as Lamb praised him, though the former *more suo* fell foul of him as well) may be best placed, in the note which is as much as he deserves, that much-written-of "curiosity of literature," the poisoner, connoisseur, and coxcomb, Wainewright. "Janus," however, was too much occupied with pictures, plays, bric-à-brac, Montepulciano, veal-pies in red earthenware dishes, the prize-ring, and other fancies or fopperies, to busy himself directly with literature, save, perhaps, in the curious paper "Janus Weatherbound," which seems to have been *his* "farewell to essay-writing." It is, however, fair to say that, odious as he was in ways not merely moral,

he had something of "a taste" here also. His quotations, which are numerous, are singularly well selected; he admired not merely Fouqué but Shelley long before it was the fashion to do so; and you may pick out of the works, rather probably than certainly his (*Essays and Criticisms*, by T. G. Wainewright, ed. W. C. Hazlitt: London, 1880), stray literary notes not without value.

[2] I use for Blake Gilchrist's *Life and Works* (2nd ed., 2 vols., London, 1880), Mr Swinburne's *William Blake* (London, 1868), Mr Rossetti's Aldine *Poetical Works* (London, 1874), and Messrs Ellis and Yeats's great Blakian Thesaurus (3 vols., London, 1893).

when they concern mere technique, they always apply to both.
His work, despite the attention which it has received from
hands, sometimes of the most eminent, during the last forty
years, has never[1] yet been edited in a fashion making its
chaos cosmic or the threading of its labyrinths easy: and
it may be well to bring together some of the most noteworthy
critical expressions in it. That which has been referred to
in a former passage, "Every man is a judge of pictures who
has not been connoisseured out of his senses,"[2] is in itself
almost a miniature manifesto of the new school of criticism.
For "connoisseurship"—the regular training in the orthodox
system of judgment by rule and line and pattern—is substituted
the impression of the natural man, unconditioned except by
the requirement that it *shall* be impression, and not prejudice.

So, again, that remarkable expression of the Prophet Isaiah[3]
when, as Blake casually mentions, he and Ezekiel "dined
with me"—an occasion on which surely any one
of taste would like to have completed the quartette.
The poet-host tells us that he asked, "Does a firm
persuasion that a thing is so make it so?" and that the
prophet-guest answered, "All poets believe that it does"—
a position from which Neo-Classicism and the reluctance to
"surrender disbelief" are at once crushed, concluded, and
quelled.

His critical position and dicta.

In the remarkable engraved page on Homer and Virgil,[4]
Blake adventures himself (not with such rashness as may
at first seem) against Aristotle (or what he takes for Aristotle),
by laying it down that Unity and Morality belong to philosophy,
not poetry, or at least are secondary in the latter; that goodness and badness are not distinctions of "character" (a saying
in which there is some quibbling but much depth as well);

[1] Save by Mr Sampson for the *Poems* (Oxford, 1905).

[2] Letter to the *Monthly Magazine* of July 1, 1806. "O Englishmen! know that every man ought to be a judge of pictures, and every man is so who has not been connoisseured out of his senses." The whole letter is given

by Mr Swinburne, pp. 62, 63, *op. cit.*

[3] In *The Marriage of Heaven and Hell.* Compare with this Vico's famous doctrine that "the criterion of truth is to have *made* it."

[4] Facsimiled in Ellis and Yeats, vol. iii. Printed as *Sibylline Leaves* in Gil-christ, ii. 178, 180.

that the Classics, not Goths or Monks, "desolate Europe with wars" (a great enough dictum at the junction of the eighteenth and nineteenth centuries); and that "Grecian [wit] is mathematical form," which is only "eternal in the reasoning memory," while Gothic is "living form, that is to say, eternal existence" —perhaps the deepest saying of the whole, though it wants large allowance and intelligent taking.

The "Notes on Reynolds" are naturally full of our stuff.

The "Notes on Reynolds"

"Enthusiastic admiration is the first principle of knowledge." [Sir Joshua had stated just the contrary.] "What has reasoning to do with the art of painting [or, we may safely add, of poetry] ? "

"Knowledge of ideal beauty is not to be acquired; it is born in us."

"One central form . . . being granted, it does not follow that all other forms are deformity. All forms are perfect in the poet's mind, . . . they are from imagination."

"To generalise is to be an idiot. To particularise is the great distinction of merit." [The "streak of the tulip" rehabilitated, and with a vengeance!]

"Invention depends altogether upon execution."

"Passion and expression are beauty itself."

"Ages are all equal: but genius is always above its age."

and Wordsworth.

It is worth while to add to these the very remarkable annotations upon Wordsworth's Prefaces: "I don't know who wrote these: they are very mischievous, and direct contrary to Wordsworth's own practice" [where if Blake had added the words "when he is a poet," he would simply have given the conclusion of the whole matter], with the very shrewd comment that Wordsworth is not so much attacking poetic diction, or defending his own, as "vindicating unpopular poets."

Commanding position of these.

Scanty as this critical budget may seem, its individual items are of extraordinary weight, when we remember that some of them were written before the *Lyrical Ballads* themselves appeared, and all of them by a man of hardly any reading in contemporary literature, and quite out of the circle of Coleridgean influence. It is scarcely, if at all, too much to say that they are almost enough to start, in a fit mind, the whole system of Romantic criticism in its more abstract form, and sometimes even in its particular and concrete applications. All the eighteenth-century Dagons — the beliefs in official connoisseurship, in the unapproachable supremacy of the ancients, in the barbarism and foolishness of Gothic art and literature, in the superiority of the general to the particular, in the necessity of extracting central forms and holding to them, in the supremacy of reason, in the teachableness of poetry, in the virtues of copying, in the superiority of design to execution,— all are tumbled off their pedestals with the most irreverent violence. That the critic's applications in the sister art to Rubens, to Titian, to Reynolds himself, are generally unjust, and not infrequently the result of pure ignorance, does not matter; his own formulas would often correct him quite as thoroughly as those of the classical school. What is important is his discovery and enunciation of these formulas themselves.

For by them, in place of these battered gods of the classical or neo-classical Philistia, are set up Imagination for Reason, Enthusiasm for Good Sense, the Result for the Rule; the execution for the mere conception or even the mere selection of subject; impression for calculation; the heart and the eyes and the pulses and the fancy for the stop-watch and the boxwood measure and the table of specifications. It is not necessary to argue the question whether Blake's own poetical work (we are not concerned with his pictorial) justifies or disconcerts the theories under which it was composed; it may be very strongly suspected, from utterances new as well as old, that approval of the theory and approval of the practice, as well as disapproval in each case, are too intimately bound up with each other to make appeal to either much of an argument. But for our main purpose, which is purely historical, the importance of Blake should, even in these few pages, have been put out of doubt. In no contemporary—not in Coleridge himself — is the counter-creed to that of the Neo-classics formulated with a sharper precision, and withal a greater width of inclusion and sweep.

There are more senses than one (or for the matter of that two) in the famous proverb, "The better is the enemy of the good." And in one of them, though not the commonest, it is eminently true of the criticism of Sir Walter Scott. No one, of course, would give to Scott any such relative rank as a critic as that which is his due either as poet or as novelist; but the extent to which his fame as poet and novelist has obscured his reputation as critic is altogether disproportionate and unfair. It is even doubtful whether some tolerably educated persons ever think of him as a critic at all. For his so-called "Prose Works" (except *Tales of a Grandfather*) are very little read, and as usual the criticism is the least read part of them. Yet it is a very large part—extending, what with the Lives of *Swift* and *Dryden*, the shorter "*Biographies*," the *Chivalry, Romance, and Drama*, and the collection or selection of *Periodical Criticism*, to ten pretty solid volumes, while even this excludes a great amount of critical matter in the notes and Introductions to the *Poems*, the Novels, the *Dryden* and *Swift* themselves, and other by-works of Sir Walter's gigantic industry.

Sir Walter Scott commonly undervalued as a critic.

Mere bulk, however, it may be said, is nothing—indeed it is too often, in work of which posterity is so shy as it is of criticism, a positive misfortune and drawback. What makes the small account taken of Scott as a critic surprising and regrettable is the goodness as well as the bulk of his critical production. Perhaps it may be urged with some justice, in defence of this popular neglect, that his want of attention to style is particularly unfortunate here. He is notoriously a rather "incorrect" writer; and he does not, as many so-called incorrect writers have known how to do, supply the want of academic propriety by irregular brilliances of any kind.

Another charge sometimes brought against him—that he is too good-natured and too indiscriminate in praise—will less hold water;[1] and indeed is much too closely connected with the

---

[1] See in particular his admirable review of Godwin's *Chaucer*, and his just condemnation of the absurd practice—simply wallowed in since by biographers and historians—of bolstering out a book with what the subject *might have* seen, done, thought, or suffered.

popular notion of the critic as a sort of "nigger"-overseer, *Injustice of this.* whose business is to walk about and distribute lashes —a notion which cannot be too often reprobated. As a private critic Scott *was* sometimes too easy-going, but by no means always or often in his professional utterances. And he had what are certainly two of the greatest requirements of the critic, reading and sanity. Sometimes some amiable prepossession (such as the narrower patriotism in his relative estimate of Fielding and Smollett) leads him a little astray; but this is very seldom—far seldomer than is the rule with critics of anything like his range. Here, as elsewhere, he does not much affect the larger and deeper and higher generalisations; but here, as elsewhere, his power of reaching these has been considerably underrated. And the distaste itself saves him—and his readers—from the hasty and floundering failures of those who aim more ambitiously at width, depth, and height. In the methodic grasp and orderly exposition of large and complicated subjects (as in the *Romance* [1] and *Drama* examples) he leaves nothing to desire. Sometimes, in his regular reviews, he condescends too much to the practice of making the review a mere abstract of the book; but I have known readers who complain bitterly of any other mode of proceeding.

Moreover, in two most important divisions of the critic's art Scott has very few superiors. These are the appreciation of particular passages, books, and authors, and the writing of those critical biographies which Dryden first essayed in English, and of which Johnson is the acknowledged master. The Prefaces to the Ballantyne Novels [2] are the best among Scott's good things in this kind on the small scale, as the *Dryden* and the *Swift* are on the great: for evidences of the former excellence the reader has only to open any one of the half-score volumes referred to above. And those golden

---

[1] The two qualities lauded above—knowledge and judgment—are specially noteworthy here, when we compare the article, not merely with the less fully informed work of Hurd, Percy, and Warton (not to say Ritson), but with more recent compositions by persons who had the originals easily at disposal.

[2] They will also be found printed together in the two vols. of *Biographies*, as well as, more recently, and alone, in a vol. of *Everyman's Library* (London, 1910).

qualities of heart which accompanied his genius are illustrated, as well as that genius itself, in his frequent critical writing on other novelists.   The criticism of creators on their fellows is not always pleasant reading, except for those who delight to study the weaknesses of the *verdammte Race*.   Scott criticises great and small among the folk of whom he is the king, from the commonest romancer up to Jane Austen, with equal generosity, acuteness, and technical mastery.   Nor ought we, in this necessarily inadequate sketch, to omit putting in his cap the feather so often to be refused to critics—the feather of catholicity.   Macaulay could not praise the delightful lady, whom both he and Scott did their utmost to celebrate, without throwing out a fling at *Sintram*, as if there were no room for good things of different kinds in the great region of Romance. In Scott's works you may find,[1] literally side by side, and characterised by equal critical sense, the eulogy of *Persuasion* and the eulogy of *Frankenstein*.[2]

Campbell's critical work is chiefly concentrated in two places, one of them accessible with some difficulty, the other only too accessible after a fashion.   The first is the *Lectures on Poetry*, which, after delivering them at the Royal Institution during the great vogue of such things in 1820, he refashioned later for the *New Monthly Magazine* when he was its editor, so that they are only to be had by one of the least agreeeable of all processes, the rummaging *for a purpose* in an old periodical.

Campbell: his Lectures on Poetry.

The accessibility of the other place—the critical matter contributed to the well-known *Specimens of the British Poets*, and to some extent the actual selections themselves —is greater because they are in nearly all the second-hand book-shops, where from sixpence to a shilling a

His Specimens.

---

[1] *Periodical Criticism*, vol. ii.

[2] In connection with Sir Walter, one may pay a note of tribute to the extreme and now too little known critical ability of his "discoverer," J. L. Adolphus, whose *Letters to Heber on the Authorship of Waverley* would come in well as an excursus-subject.   Examining, as he did, certain known works of an at least hypothetically unknown writer, he was bound to give that attention to the *work itself*, which was the great thing necessary ; and he gave it with remarkable ability, craftsmanship, and knowledge of literature.

volume will buy—well bound often and in perfectly good condition—matter which, at any proper ratio of exchange, is worth
a dozen times the money. This worth consists of course mainly
in the matter selected: but the taste which selected it must
figure for no small increment, and the purely critical frame-
work is, to say the least, remarkably worthy of both.
Campbell, a very puzzling person in his poetry, is by no
means a very easily comprehensible or appraisable one in his
critical attitude. In the general arrangement of this he is
distinctly of the older fashion, as the fashions of his time
went. Like his style, though this is a very fair specimen
of the "last Georgian," still in a manner the standard and
staple of the plainer English prose, his opinions are a thought
periwigged and buckrammed. He demurs to the "Romantic
Unity" of Hurd earlier and Schlegel later; and when in his
swashing blow (and a good swashing blow it is of its kind)
on the side of Pope in the weary quarrel, he tries to put
treatment of artificial on a poetical level with treatment of
natural objects, we must demur pretty steadily ourselves.
But, on the other hand, he distinctly champions (and was,
I believe, the first actually so to formulate) the principle that
"in poetry there are many mansions," and, what is more, he
lives up to it. He really and almost adequately appreciates
Chaucer: it is only his prejudice about Unity and the Fable
that prevents him from being a thorough-going Spenserian;
and when we come to the seventeenth century he is quite
surprising. Again, it is true, his *general* creed makes him
declare that the metaphysicians "thought like madmen." But
he is juster to some of them than Hazlitt is; he has the great
credit of having (after a note of Southey's, it is true) re-
introduced readers to the mazy but magical charms of *Pharonnida;* and he admits Godolphin and Stanley, Flatman and
Ayres. If the history of the earlier part of his Introductory
Essay is shaky, it could not have been otherwise in his time;
and it shows that the indolence with which he is so often
charged did not prevent him from making a very good use
of what Warton and Percy, Tyrwhitt and Ritson and Ellis,
had provided.

This indolence, however, is perhaps more evident in the distribution of the criticism, which, if not careless, is exceedingly capricious. Campbell seems at first to have intended to concentrate this criticism proper in the Introduction (to which nearly the whole of the first volume is allotted), and to make the separate prefaces to the selections mainly biographical. But he does not at all keep to this rule; the main *Introduction* itself is, if anything, rather too copious at the beginning, while it is compressed and hurried at the end : not a few of the minor pieces and less prominent poets have no criticism at all; while, in the case of those that have it, it is often extremely difficult to discover the principle of its allotment. Yet, on the whole, Campbell ought never to be neglected by the serious student; for even if his criticism were solely directed from an obsolete standpoint, it would be well to go back to it now and then as a half-way house between those about Johnson and those about Coleridge, while as a matter of fact it has really a very fair dose of universal quality.[1]

There are several critical passages in Shelley's *Letters*, but, as formally preserved, his criticism is limited to the *Defence of Poetry*, which, despite its small bulk, is of extreme interest.[2] It is almost the only return of its times to that extremely abstract consideration of the matter which we found prevalent in the Renaissance, and which in Shelley's case, as in the cases of Fracastoro or of Sidney, is undoubtedly inspired by Plato. It seems to have been immediately prompted by some heresies of Peacock's : but, as was always its author's habit, in prose as well as in verse, he drifts "away, afar" from what apparently was his starting-point, over a measureless ocean of abstract thinking. He endeavours indeed, at first, to echo the old saws about men "imitating natural objects in the youth of the world" and the

Shelley. his Defence of Poetry.

---

[1] Those who will not take the trouble to search the *Specimens* themselves will find copious and admirably selected examples in Jeffrey's article on the book (*Essays*, 1 vol. ed., p. 359 *sq.*), one of the best reviews he ever wrote, but for some superfluous, unjust, and, in the context (*v.* above), specially ungenerous flings at Southey.

[2] This may be found not merely in the edd. of the *Works*, but in Prof. Vaughan's interesting selection of *Literary Criticism* (London, 1896).

like, but he does not in any way keep up the arrangement, and we are almost from the outset in contact with his own ardent imagination—of which quality he at once defines poetry as the expression. Again, the poetic faculty is "the faculty of approximation to the beautiful." Once more we have the proud claim for poetry that poets are not merely the authors of arts, but the inventors of laws, the teachers of religion. They "participate in the eternal, the infinite, and the one." They are not necessarily confined to verse, but they will be wise to use it. A poem is the very image of life, expressed in its eternal truth. "Poetry is something divine," the "centre and circumference of knowledge," the "perfect and consummate surface and bloom of all things," the "record of the best and happiest moments of the happiest and best minds." All which (or all except the crotchet about verse) I for one do most powerfully and potently believe: though if any one says that, as generally with Shelley, one is left stranded, or rather floating, in the vague, denial is not easy. One can only wish oneself, as Poins wished his sister, "no worse fortune."[1]

[1] It is with some misgiving, and after more than one change of mind, that I place Shelley's great poetical twin (or rather tally) in a note only here. The early *Sleep and Poetry* belongs to us as giving Keats's perhaps one-sided but very vigorous and remarkable verse-formulation of the protest against Neo - classicism ; the two prefaces (especially the final one) to *Endymion* have been generally recognised by the competent as perhaps the most astonishingly just judgments which any poet has ever passed on himself : and the *Letters* are full of critical or quasi-critical passages of the highest interest. I myself have a sheaf of them duly noted ; and some persons of distinction whom I know would admit them to the very Golden Book of Criticism. I hope, however, that my own judgment is not too much sicklied o'er with crotchet in holding that Keats's criticism of himself and others is somewhat too spontaneous and automatic, somewhat too much of a mere other phase of his creation, to deserve the name of criticism properly so-called. He speaks of Shakespeare admirably, because he has the same quintessentially English cast of poetry that Shakespeare had. When he speaks of poetry in the abstract, as he does admirably and often, it is this poetry speaking of herself, and therefore speaking truly but not critically. Even in the wonderful remark (vol. v. p. 111., ed. Forman, Glasgow, 1901) on himself and Byron, "He describes what he sees : I describe what I imagine" (where he repeats Philostratus without in the least knowing it), the thing is not criticism : it is self-speaking. And beyond this he seldom goes, and is seldomer happy in his rare excursions. He might have become a critic, as he might have become almost anything good ; but I do not think he was one.

In the course of this History we have seen not infrequent examples of Criticism divorced from Taste—a severance to

Landor.

which the peculiarities of classical and neo-classical censorship lent but too much encouragement. It must be obvious that the general tendency of the criticism which we are calling Modern inclines towards the divorce of Taste from Criticism—to the admission of the monstrous regiment of mere arbitrary enjoyment and liking, not to say mere caprice. But it is curious that our first very distinguished example of this should be found in a person who, both by practice and in theory, had very distinct "classical" tendencies—who, in fact, with the possible exception of Mr Arnold, was the most classical of at least the English writers of the nineteenth century.

Landor's[1] critical shortcomings, however, are the obvious and practically inevitable result of certain well-known

His lack of judicial quality.

peculiarities of temperament, moral rather than intellectual, and principles of life rather than of literature. With him, as with King Lear (whom in more ways and points than one he resembled, though, luckily, with the tragedy infinitely softened and almost smoothed away), the dominant is *impotentia*—the increasing and at last absolute incapacity of the intellect and will to govern the emotions and impulses. Now, as criticism is itself an endless process of correcting impressions—or at least of checking and auditing them till we are sure that they are genuine, co-ordinated, and (with the real if not the apparent consistency) consistent—a man who suffers from this *impotentia* simply cannot be a real critic, though he may occasionally make observations critically sound.

The rule and the exceptions hold good with Landor unfailingly. He was an excellent scholar; his acquaintance with

In regular Criticism.

modern literatures, though much smaller and extremely arbitrary, was not positively small, and his taste, in some directions at least, was delicate and exquisite. But of judicial quality or qualities he had not one single

---

[1] My copy is the eight-volume ed. of 1874-76: but the titles of the various pieces will enable them to be found in others.

trace, and, even putting them out of the question, his intelligence was streaked and flawed by strange veins of positive
silliness. We need not dwell too much on his orthographical
and other whims, which have been shared by some great ones
—the judgments are the things. In the very first paragraph
of his very first regular criticism we find the statement that
the Poems of Bion and Moschus are not only "very different"
from those of Theocritus but "very inferior." Inferior in
what? in bulk certainly: but in what else are the *Adonis*
and the *Bion* itself inferior to anything Theocritean? A
critic should have been warned by his own "different" not
to rush on the "inferior," which is so often fallaciously con-
sequent. I shall not be accused of excessive Virgil-worship,
but what criticism is there in the objection to *me ceperat annus*
as "scarcely Latin" (really! really! Mr Landor, you were
not quite a Pollio!), and in the flat emendation of *mihi coeperat;*
or in the contemptuous treatment of that exquisite piece containing

> ὁ θὴρ δ' ἔβαινε δειλῶς,
> φοβεῖτο γὰρ Κυθήρην,

a phrase which, for simplicity, pictorial effect, and suggestion, is almost worthy of Sappho? Such a sentence as that
of Politian's poems, "one only has any merit," is simply
disabling: mere schoolboy prejudice has evidently blinded
the speaker. Yet it occurs in his best critique, that on
Catullus.

These set criticisms, however, are few, and Landor was
evidently not at ease in them. The literary "Conversations,"
The Conver- it may be said, are the true test. And it is at
sations. least certain that these conversations supply not
a few of those more excellent critical observations which have
been acknowledged and saluted. Especially must we acknowledge and salute one[1] which, though of considerable length,
must be made an exception to the rule of "not quoting."
Nowhere, in ancient or modern place, is the education of the

---

[1] See the opening of "Southey and
Porson." It is, of course, not improved
by the presence of the Landorian
irony, which is an uncertain quality,
too often inclining either to horse-play
or to peevishness : but this is not fatal.

critic outlined with greater firmness and accuracy; and those who, by this or that good fortune, have been put through some such a process, may congratulate themselves on having learnt no vulgar art in no vulgar way.

I would seriously recommend to the employer of our critics, young and old, that he oblige them to pursue a course of study such as this; that, under the superintendence of some *Loculus aureolus.* respectable student from the University, they first read and examine the contents of the book—a thing greatly more useful in criticism than is generally thought; secondly, that they carefully write them down, number them, and range them under their several heads; thirdly, that they mark every beautiful, every faulty, every ambiguous, every uncommon expression. Which being completed, that they inquire what author, ancient or modern, has treated the same subject; that they compare them, first in smaller, afterwards in larger portions, noting every defect in precision and its causes, every excellence and its nature; that they graduate these, fixing *plus* and *minus*, and designating them more accurately and discriminately by means of colours stronger or paler. For instance purple might express grandeur and majesty of thought; scarlet, vigour of expression; pink, liveliness; green, elegant and equable composition; these, however, and others as might best attract their notice and serve their memory. The same process may be used where authors have not written on the same subject, when those who have are wanting or have touched on it but incidentally. Thus Addison and Fontenelle, not very like, may be compared in the graces of style, in the number and degree of just thoughts and lively fancies; thus the dialogues of Cicero with those of Plato, his ethics with those of Aristotle, his orations with those of Demosthenes. It matters not if one be found superior to the other in this thing and inferior in that: the qualities of two authors are explored and understood and their distances laid down, as geographers speak, from accurate survey. The *plus* and *minus* of good and bad and ordinary will have something of a scale to rest upon: and after a time the degrees of the higher parts in intellectual dynamics may be more nearly attained, though never quite exactly.

Yet in close context with this very passage comes an idle *But again disappointing.* "splurt" (evidently half-due to *odium anti-theologicum*) at Coleridge — a thing exactly of the kind which such discipline as has been just recommended should check. And everywhere, especially in the long

Miltonic examen between "Southey and Landor," the effects
of Landor's character appear side by side with a sort of peddling
and niggling censorship which one might have thought not
natural to that character at all, and which perhaps is a
damnosa hereditas from the worse kind of classical scholarship.
Even on Boileau[1] he manages to be unfair; and at his objection to one of Milton's most exquisite and characteristic lines—

"Lancelot and Pelleas and Pellinore"—

one can but cover the face. Caprice, arbitrary legislation,
sometimes positive blindness and deafness,—these are Landor's
critical marks when he quits pure theory, and sometimes when
he does not quit it.

With him we leave the "majorities"—those who, whether
greater or lesser critics, were great either as such or in other
The revival paths of letters. Some smaller, but in some cases
of the Pope not so small, persons remain, with one or two ex-
quarrels. amples—one specially famous—of what we have
called "the Adversaries." And first we must touch (if only in
order to deal with yet another of the majorities themselves,
who has seemed to some to be a critic) on the "Pope a Poet"
quarrel.

We have seen[2] that this quarrel, originally raised by Joseph
Warton, was even by him latterly waged as by one *cauponans*
Bowles. *bellum;* but a lazily and gingerly waged war is
generally a long one, and this instance did not
discredit the rule. Johnson's intervention[3] in it, in his *Life*
of Pope, was sensible and moderate — indeed, with certain
necessary allowances, it is fairly decisive. But Pope, among
his other peculiarities, has had the fate of making foes of his
editors, and this was the case with the Reverend William Lisle
Bowles, who revived the fainting battle,[4] not to any one's
advantage or particular credit, and to his own dire tribulation.
Bowles is one of those not uninteresting people, in all divisions

---

[1] See "Landor and Delille."

[2] *V. sup.*, p. 259.

[3] *V. sup.*, p. 224.

[4] From 1801, when his edition appeared, till well into the 'Twenties. Mr

Rhys (*op. cit. sup.*) has given some
of Bowles's rejoinders to Byron, with
Byron's own *Letter,* mentioned below,
and some references to the battle in
his *Introduction.*

of history, who, absolutely rather null, have not inconsiderable relative importance.   The influence of his early sonnets on Coleridge, and through Coleridge on the whole Romantic revival in England, is well known, and not really surprising.   In the remainder of his long and on the whole blameless life, he committed a great deal of verse which, though not exactly bad, is utterly undistinguished and unimportant.   His theory of poetry, however, though somewhat one-sided, was better than his practice : and it was rather as a result of that dangerous thing Reaction, and from a lack of alertness and catholicity, than from positive heresy, that he fell foul of Pope.   In his edition he laid down, and in the controversy following he defended,[1] certain "invariable principles of Poetry," of which the first and foremost was that images, thoughts, &c., derived from Nature and Passion, are always more sublime and pathetic than those drawn from Art and Manners.   And it was chiefly on this ground that he, of course following his leader Warton, but using newer material and tactics, disabled, partially or wholly, the claims of Pope.   Hereupon arose a hubbub. Campbell in the *Specimens*[2] took a hand ; Byron wrote a *Letter to John Murray*[3] in defence of his favourite, and in ridicule of Bowles ; auxiliaries and adversaries ran up on both sides. Whether Bowles was most happy or unhappy in the turmoil I am unable to say, but he was certainly put in a great state of agitation, and showered Pamphlets with elaborate titles, which one may duly find, with their occasions and rejoinders, in the library of the British Museum.   At last dust settled on the conflict, which, however, is itself not quite settled to the present day, and in fact never can be, because it depends on one of the root-differences of poetical taste.   However, it probably helped the wiser sort to take the *via media*, even such a Romantic as Hazlitt vindicating Pope's possession of "the poetical point of view," and did, for the same sort, a service to the general history of criticism by emphasising the

---

[1] They will be found usefully rearranged by himself in the extract of his answer to Byron given by Mr Rhys (Appendix to vol. ii., *op. cit.*)

[2] i. 262 *sq.*

[3] 1821.   To be found, outside the edd. of the author, in Mr Rhys' book, ii. 162 *sq.*

above-mentioned difference. Bowles himself, if he had been less fussy, less verbose, less given to "duply and quadruply" on small controversial points, and more a man of the world and of humour, might not have made by any means a bad critic. As it was, he was right in the main.

We must, however, I suppose, say something, if only in this connection, of Byron as a critic. I do not think it necessary *Byron.* to say very much; and I shall not, as I could most easily do, concatenate here the innumerable contradictions of critical opinion in his *Letters*, which show that they were mere flashes of the moment, connected not merely by no critical theory but by no critical taste of any consistency, flings, "half-bricks" directed at dog or devil or divinity, according to the mood in which the "noble poet" chose to find himself. Let us confine ourselves to that unquestionably *The* Letter remarkable *Letter to John Murray* on Bowles and to Murray, Pope, which is admittedly his critical diploma-piece. *&c.* There are of course very good things in it. Byron was a genius; and your genius will say genial things now and then, whatsoever subject he happens to be treating. But he cannot in the very least maintain himself at the critical point: he is like the ball in the fountain, mounting now and then gloriously on the summit of the column and catching the rays that it attracts and reflects, much more often lying wallowing in the basin. Never was such critical floundering. He blasphemes at one moment the "invariable principles of poetry," about which the amiable but somewhat ineffectual Bowles prated; he affirms them at the next, by finding in his way, and blindly picking up, the secret of secrets, that the poet who *executes* best is the highest, whatsoever his department; and he makes his affirmation valueless, by saying, almost before we have turned the page, that Lucretius is ruined by his ethics, and Pope saved by them. Even setting ethic against ethic, the proposition is at least disputable: but what on earth has Ethic to do with Execution, except that they both occur in the dictionary under E? There are other excellent things in the letter, and yet others the reverse of excellent; but I have not the least intention here of setting up a balance-sheet

after the manner of Robinson Crusoe, of ranging Byron's undoubtedly true, though not novel, vindication of the human
element as invariably necessary to poetry, against his opinion
of Shelley, and of Keats, and of the English poetry of his
greatest contemporaries generally, as "all Claudian," and
against the implied estimate of Claudian himself. This would
be a confusion like his own, a parallel *ignoratio elenchi*, a
fallacia a fallacioribus. Suffice it to say, that to take him
seriously as a critic is impossible.[1]

Of the work which—sometimes of the inner citizenship of
the critical Rome and at the worst of its "utmost last provincial band"—was done by a great number of
individuals and in no small number of periodicals,
dictionaries, and what not, we cannot speak here
as fully as would be pleasant,—the historian must become
a "reasoned cataloguer" merely, and that by selection. Two
contemporary and characteristic figures are those of Isaac
Disraeli and of Sir Egerton Brydges. Both had the defects
of the antiquarian quality. Rogers, though unamiable, was
probably not unjust when, in acknowledging the likelihood of
Isaac Disraeli's collections enduring, he described him as "a
man with half an intellect." In formation and expression of
opinion, Lord Beaconsfield's father too often wandered from
the silly to the self-evident and back again, like Addison
between his two bottles at the ends of the Holland House
gallery: and his numerous *collectanea* would certainly be more
useful if they were more accurate. But the *Curiosities*, the
Amenities, the *Quarrels*, and all the rest show an ardent love
for literature itself, and a singularly wide knowledge of it:
they are well calculated to inoculate readers, especially young
readers, with both.

Brydges's work, less popular, is of a higher quality. His extensive editing labours were beyond price at his date; in books
like the *Censura Literaria* much knowledge is still readily ac-

Others: Isaac Dis-raeli.

---

[1] It has been suggested to me that
Byron ought to have the benefit, as
well as the disadvantage, of my description of Keats's critical utterances
on the other side, as a phase of his
creation. There is something in this:
but Byron seems to me less *genuine*
even on this showing.

cessible, which can only be picked up elsewhere by enormous
Sir Egerton excursions of reading at large; and his original criti-
Brydges. cal power was much higher than is generally allowed.
Such enthusiastic admiration of Shelley as is displayed in
the notes to his Geneva reprint of the English part of Phillips'
Theatrum Poetarum in 1824,[1] is not often shown by a man of
sixty-two for a style of poetry entirely different from that
to which he has been accustomed. And it shows, not merely
how true a training the study of older literature is for the
appreciation of newer but that there must have been something to train.

Moreover, this first period of enthusiastic exploration did
not merely produce the lectures of Coleridge and Hazlitt,
The Retro- and the unsurpassed essays of Lamb, the hardly
spective surpassed ones of Leigh Hunt. It produced also,
Review. by the combined efforts of a band of somewhat
less distinguished persons, a periodical publication of very
considerable bulk and of almost unique value and interest.
It is not for nothing that while old magazines and reviews
are usually sold for less than the cost of their binding, and
not much more than their value as waste-paper, *The Retrospective Review*[2] still has respectable, though of course not
fantastic, prices affixed to it in the catalogues. It was
started in 1820, under the editorship of Henry Southern,[3]
a diplomatist from the Cantabrigian Trinity, and of the
antiquary afterwards so well known as Sir Harris Nicolas.
Opening with a first volume of extraordinary excellence, it
kept up for seven years and fourteen volumes, on a uniform
principle. The second series, however, which was started
after I know not what breach of continuity,[4] was less for-

[1] The *Censura*, extending to 10 vols.,
but oftenest found incomplete, appeared in 1805-9. The *British Biblio-
grapher, Restituta*, &c., came later.

[2] First Series, 14 vols., 1820-26;
Second, 2 vols., 1827-28. Its con-
tributors included Hartley Coleridge,
Talfourd, and others; while Thomas
Wright wrote largely in a Third, much
later (1854).

[3] Southern afterwards came in contact with Borrow at Madrid. See *The
Bible in Spain* and Dr Knapp's *Life*.

[4] There is none in the dates, but the
title-page is different, the former vig-
nette of a gateway (Trinity? "I cannot tell, I am an Oxford man") dis-
appearing, and being replaced by the
editors' names.

tunate, and extends to two volumes only, though these contain much more matter apiece than the earlier ones. It is not uncommon to find these two volumes, and even some of the first series, wanting in library sets, which librarians should do their best to complete; for though, toward the end, the purely antiquarian matter encroached a very little upon the literary, there is not a volume from first to last which does not contain literary matter of the highest interest and value.[1]

The proud-looked and high-stomached persons who pronounce the best in this kind but shadows, and regard old criticism as being—far more than history in its despised days—"an old almanack," will of course look prouder and exalt their stomachs higher at the use of such terms. So be it. Some day people will perhaps begin to understand generally what criticism is, and what is its importance. Then more—as some do already —will appreciate the interest and the value of this work of Nicolas, Palgrave, Talfourd, Hartley Coleridge, and other good men. It would be perfectly easy to make fun of it. The style may be to modern tastes a little stilted when it is ambitious, and a little jejune when it is not—in both cases after the way of the last Georgian standard prose. Although there is much and real learning, our philologers might doubt-less exalt *their* stomachs over the neglect of their favourite study: and the fetichists of biography might discover that many a Joan is called Jane, and many a March made into February. These drawbacks and defects are more than com-pensated by the general character of the treatment. While not despising bibliography, the writers as a rule do not put it first, like Sir Egerton Brydges: nor do they indulge in the egotistical *pot - pourri* of "Chandos of Sudeley." They have the enormous advantage, in most cases, of coming quite fresh to their work,—of being able to give a real "squeeze" direct from the original brass, with the aid of their own ap-preciation, unmarred and unmingled by reminiscences of this essay and that treatise, by the necessity of combating this or

---

[1] The so-called "*Third* Series" (in 2 vols., 1854) can hardly be considered as really forming part of the original, from which it is separated by a thirty years' interval. But it has (*v. sup.*) some good work in it.

that authority on their subject. They look at that subject
itself, and even when they show traces of a little prejudice—
as in the opposite cases of the man who is rather hard on
Dryden and the man who is, for the nineteenth century,
astonishingly "soft" on Glover—the impression is obviously
genuine and free from forgery.

What is more, these Reviewers give themselves, as a rule,
plenty of room, and supply abundant extracts—things of the
first importance in the case of books, then as a rule to be
found only in the old editions, and in many cases by no means
common now. The scope is wide. The first volume gives,
inter alia, articles on Chamberlayne (one for *Pharonnida* and
one for *Love's Victory*), on Crashaw and Dryden, on Rymer and
Dennis and Heinsius, on Ben Jonson and Cyrano de Bergerac,
on the *Urn Burial*, and on such mere curiosities as *The Voyage
of the Wandering Knight*. The papers throughout on Drama,
from the Mysteries onward, and including separate articles
on the great Elizabethan minors, were, till Pearson's reprints
thirty years ago, the most accessible source of information
on their subjects, and are still specially notable; as are also
the constituents of another interesting series on Spanish
Literature. The *Arcadia* balances Butler's *Remains* in vol. ii.
Vaughan and Defoe, *Imitations of Hudibras*, and that luckless
dramatist and mad but true poet, Lee,[1] have their places in
the Third, where also some one (though he came a little too
early to know the *Chansons de gestes*, and so did not put
"things of Charlemagne" in their right order) has an interesting article on the Italian compilation *La Spagna*. I
should like to continue this sampling throughout the sixteen
volumes, but space commands only a note on the rest in
detail.[2]

---

[1] It is the only adequate thing on
him that I know.

[2] Specially good are, in vol. iv., the
dramatic papers; in v., one on *Witch-
craft;* in vi., those on Coryat and Sir
T. Urquhart; in vii., on Donne and
Ariosto; in ix., on Chaucer (continued later); in x., on *Minor French
Poetry* (Dorat); in xii., on *Latin Plays*
at Cambridge, and one of singular and
wide-reaching merit on the *Roman
Comique;* in xv., an interesting tracing
of Scott's quotations in the novels; in
xvi., an admirable paper on Shadwell.
But there is practically nothing negligible: and good taste, good manners,
good temper, and good learning abound
throughout.

Nor are they afraid of more general discussion. In the above-mentioned article on John Dennis there is a long passage which I do not remember to have seen anywhere extracted, dealing in a singularly temperate and reasonable fashion with the "off-with-his-head" style of criticism put in fashion by the *Edinburgh*; and others will be easily found. But they do not as a rule lay themselves out much for "preceptist" criticism. It is the *other* new style of intelligent and well-willing interpretation to which they incline, and they carry it out with extraordinary ability and success. To supply those who may not have time, opportunity, or perhaps even inclination to read more or less out-of-the way originals with some intelligible and enjoyable knowledge of them at second-hand; to prepare, initiate, and guide those who are able and willing to undertake such reading; to supply those who have actually gone through it with estimates and judgments for comparison and appreciation—these may be said to be their three objects. Some people may, of course, think them trivial objects or unimportant; to me, I confess, they seem to be objects extremely well worth attaining, and here very well attained. The papers in the *Retrospective Review*, be it remembered, anticipated Sainte-Beuve himself (much more such later English and American practitioners as Mr Arnold, who was not born, and Mr Lowell, who was but a yearling when it first appeared) in the production of the full literary *causerie*, the applied and illustrative complement, in regard to individual books, authors, or small subjects, of the literary history proper. When people at last begin to appreciate what literary history means, there will probably be, in every country, a collection of the best essays of this kind arranged from their authors' works conveniently for the use of the student. And when such a collection is made in England, no small part in it will be played by articles taken from the *Retrospective Review*.

For the last subdivision of this chapter we must go a little *The* Baviad backwards. The phenomena of English criticism *and* Anti- in the last decade of the eighteenth century are Jacobin, curious: and they might be used to support such very different theories of the relations of Criticism and Creation, that their most judicious use, perhaps, is to point the moral of the riskiness of *any* such theories. During this decade one great generation was dying off and another even greater was but coming on. Except Boswell's *Life of Johnson*, and Burke's last and best work (which were both entirely of the past, and in the former case, at least, presented a purely personal product), and the *Lyrical Ballads* (which were wholly of the future), with the shadowy work of Blake (hardly of any time or even any place), nothing of extraordinary goodness appeared. But a great deal appeared of a most ordinary and typical badness, and this seems to have excited a peculiar kind of irregular or Cossack criticism to carry on a guerilla war against the hosts of dreary or fantastic dulness. Criticism had at this time little of a standing army: the old *Critical* and *Monthly* Reviews were sinking into dotage (though such a man as Southey wrote in the former), and the new class of comparatively independent censorship, which put money in its purse and carried its head high, was to wait for the *Edinburgh* and the next century. But Hayley and Sir James Bland Burges and the Della Cruscans; but Darwin even, and even Godwin; nay, the very early antics of such men as Coleridge and Southey themselves, with some things in them not so antic perhaps, but seeming to their contemporaries of an antic disposition— were more than critical flesh and blood could stand. The *with Wolcot* spirit which had animated Rivarol[1] on the other *and* side of the Channel came to animate Wolcot (who *Mathias.* had indeed showed it for some time[2]) and his enemy Gifford, and the greater wits of the *Anti-Jacobin*, and even the pedantic and prosaic Mathias.

Now the result of dwelling upon the works of that Pindar who was born not in Bœotia but in Devonshire, and on the ever-beloved and delightful *Poetry of the Anti-Jacobin*, if not also on its prose, would no doubt be far more agreeable to the reader than much of what he actually finds here: and to dwell on them would fall in with some of the writer's oldest and most cherished tastes. Nay, even the *Baviad* and *Mæviad*, out

[1] *Hist. Crit.*, ii. 534.
[2] His best *literary* skit, "Bozzy and Piozzi," deals with the *Tour*, not the *Life.*

of proportion and keeping as is much of their satire, and the *Pursuits of Literature* itself,—despite its tedious ostentation of learning, its endless irrelevance of political and other note-divagation, and its disgusting donnishness without the dignity of the better don,—give, especially in the three first cases, much marrowy matter in the texts, and an abundance of the most exquisite unintentional fooling in the passages cited by the copious notes. Unfortunately so to dwell would be itself out of keeping and proportion here. The things[1] are among the lightest and best examples of the critical *soufflé*, well cheesed and peppered. Or (if the severer muses and their worshippers disdain a metaphor from Cookery, that Cinderella of the Fine Arts) let us say that they exemplify most agreeably the substitution of a sort of critical *banderilla*, sometimes fatal enough in its way, for the Thor's hammer of Dryden and the stiletto of Pope. But they are only symptoms—we have seen things of their kind before, from Aristophanes downwards—and we must merely signal and register them as we pass in this adventure, keeping and recommending them nevertheless for quiet and frequent reading *delectationis causa*. The infallibility and vitality of the *Anti-Jacobin*, in particular, for this purpose, is something really prodigious. The *Rovers* and the *New Morality* and the *Loves of the Triangles* seem to lose none of their virtue during a whole lifetime of the reader, and after a century of their own existence.

There is, however, one point on which we not only may but must draw special attention to them. There can be little doubt that these light velitations of theirs prepared the way and sharpened the taste for a very considerable refashioning and new-modelling of the regular critical-Periodical army which followed so soon. In this new-modelling some of them—Gifford, Canning, Ellis —were most important officers, and there can be no doubt at all that many others transferred, consciously or unconsciously,

The influence of the new Reviews, &c.

---

[1] The earlier *Rolliad* is partly, but less, literary. For more on most of these I may refer to an essay of mine, *Twenty Years of Political Satire*, which originally appeared in *Macmillan's Magazine*, and is reprinted in *Essays in English Literature*, 2nd series, London, 1895.

this lighter way of criticising from verse to prose, or kept it up in verse itself such as *Rejected Addresses*, which in turn handed on the pattern to the *Bon Gaultier Ballads* in the middle, and to much else at the end, of the nineteenth century. Part of the style was of course itself but a resharpening of the weapons of the Scriblerus Club; but these weapons were refurbished brightly, and not a little repointed. The newer critic was at least supposed to remember that he was not to be dull. Unfortunately the personal impertinence which, though not pretty even in the verse-satirist, is by a sort of prescription excusable or at least excused in him, transferred itself to the prose: and the political intolerance became even greater.[1]

It is not the least curious freak of the whirligig of time, as shown working in this history, that not a century ago one of

Jeffrey.

the chief places here would have seemed inevitably due to Francis Jeffrey, while at the present moment perhaps a large majority of readers would be disposed to grudge him more than a paragraph, and be somewhat inclined to skip that.

We cannot "stint his sizings" to that extent. Yet it is also impossible to give him much space, more particularly because

His loss of place and its cause.

his interest has shrunk to, and is very unlikely ever greatly to swell from, that of a kind of representative position. Jeffrey is no mere English La Harpe, as some think: he does not exemplify the Neo-classical "Thorough," the rigour of the Rule, after the fashion which makes that remarkable person so interesting. On the contrary, he is only the last and most noteworthy instance of that mainly Neo-classic inconsistency which we pointed out and on which we dwelt in the last volume. Except that he

---

[1] I do not think it necessary to give Gifford's prose or periodical criticism a separate place. It is by no means easily separable as such; and if separated I fancy there would be very little to say for it, and that what would have to be said against it is better summed up in the words of no less a political sympathiser and personal friend than Scott. A "cankered carle" cannot be a good critic, any more than a mildewed grape can give good wine. But Gifford was not quite so bad as he has seemed to some; and his editorial work, especially on Jonson, deserves almost the highest praise.

looks more backward than forward, Jeffrey often reminds us rather of Marmontel.   He has inherited to the fullest extent the by this time ingrained English belief that canons of criticism which exclude or depreciate Shakespeare and Milton "will never do," as he might have said himself: but he has not merely inherited, he has expanded and supplemented it. He has not the least objection to the new school of students and praisers of those other Elizabethan writers, compared with whom Shakespeare would have seemed to La Harpe almost a regular dramatist, and quite a sane and orderly person. He has a strong admiration for Ford.   He will follow a safe fellow-Whig like Campbell in admiring such an extremely anti-"classical" thing as Chamberlayne's *Pharonnida*.   He uses about Dryden and Pope language not very different from Mr Arnold's, and he is quite enthusiastic (though of course with some funny metrical qualms) about Cowper.

But here (except in reference to a man like Keats, who had been ill-treated by the Tories) he draws the line.   There may *His incon-* have been something political in the attitude which *sistency.* the *Edinburgh* assumed towards the great new school of poetry which arose between 1798 and 1820.   But politics cannot have had everything to do with the matter, and it cannot be an accident that Crabbe is about the only contemporary poet of mark, except Byron, Campbell, and Rogers, whom Jeffrey cordially praises.   Above all, the reasons of his depreciation of poets so different as Scott and Wordsworth, and the things of theirs that he specially blames, are fatal.   There is plenty to be said against Scott as a poet, and plenty to be said against Wordsworth.   *The Lay of the Last Minstrel* is far from faultlessly perfect: but the beauty of its subject, its adaptation of antique matter and manner, and its new versification, are almost beyond praise from the poetical point of view.   It is exactly these three things that Jeffrey most blames.   There are scores and hundreds of things in Wordsworth which are helplessly exposed to the critical arrows : but a man who pronounces the *Daffodils* "stuff" puts himself down once for all, irrevocably, without hope of pardon or of atonement, a person insensible to poetry as such, though there may be kinds and forms of poetry which, from this or that cause, he is able to appreciate.[1]

Once more, as in Leigh Hunt's case (though on the still smaller scale desirable), we can take a "brick of the house" *His criticism* with advantage and without absurdity. Indeed I *on Madame* hardly know anywhere a single Essay which exhibits *de Staël.* a considerable critic so representatively as is done for Jeffrey by his article on Madame de Staël's *De La Littéra-ture*, which appeared in the *Edinburgh* for November 1812 and stands after the Tractate on Beauty in the forefront of his Collected Works.[2] He was in the full maturity of his critical powers; as a woman (for Jeffrey was quite a chivalrous person), and as a kind of foreign and female Whig, his author was sure of favourable treatment; the "philosophic" atmosphere of the book appealed to his education, nationality, and personal sym-pathies; and he had practically most of the knowledge required.[3]

And the article is a very good article,—polite in its mild exposure of Madame de Staël's hasty generalisations, extremely clever and capable in its own survey of literature—Jeffrey was particularly good at these surveys and naturally inclined to them—sensible, competent, in the highest degree readable. It would not be easy, unless we took something of Southey's on the other side, better to illustrate the immense advance made by periodical criticism since the *Edinburgh* itself had shown the way.

Yet there are curious drawbacks and limitations which ex-plain why Jeffrey has not kept, and why he is perhaps not

[1] I know, of course, that even Cole-ridge spoke unadvisedly about these immortal flowers. But he had got a "philosophical" craze at the moment : and he did not call them "stuff."

[2] *Contributions to the Edinburgh Re-view*, London, pp. 36-63 of this the one vol. ed., 1853. The "Beauty" itself requires very little notice. It is an ingenious variation upon Alison, whose book it reviews, praises, and sup-ports, with some unfairness to Gerard.

Selections from Jeffrey will be found in Mr Gates's *Essays of Jeffrey* (Boston, 1894) and Mr Nichol Smith's *Jeffrey's Literary Criticism* (London, 1910).

[3] He makes indeed an awkward slip by linking Machiavel as a contempor-ary with Shakespeare, Bacon, Montaigne, and Galileo ; but it is only recently, if even recently, that literary history has been carefully attended to, and Coleridge himself makes slips quite as bad.

very likely to recover, his pride of place. Part of his idiosyncrasy was a very odd kind of pessimism, which one would rather have expected from a High Tory than from a "blue and yellow," however symbolical these colours may be of fear. To Jeffrey—in the second decade of the new flourishing of English poetry, which had at least eighty good years to run; in the very year of the new birth of the novel; with Goethe still alive and Heine a boy in Germany; with the best men of the great French mid-nineteenth century already born—it seems that "the age of original genius is over." Now, when a man has once made up his mind to this, he is not likely to be very tolerant of attempts on the age's part to convince him that he is wrong. But even his judgments of the past exhibit a curious want of catholicity. The French vein, which is so strong in him, as well as the general eighteenth-century spirit, which is so much stronger, appears in a distinct tendency to set Latin above Greek. He commends the Greeks indeed for their wonderful "rationality and moderation in imaginative work," suggesting, with a mixture of simplicity and shrewdness, that the reason of this is the absence of any models. Having no originals, they did not try to be better than these. His criticism of the two literatures is taken from a very odd angle—or rather from a maze and web of odd angles. "The fate of the Tarquins," he says, "could never have been regarded at Rome as a worthy occasion either of pity or horror." And he does not in the least seem to see—probably he would have indignantly denied —that in saying this he is denying the Romans any *literary* sense at all. In Aristophanes he has nothing to remark but his "extreme coarseness and vulgarity"; and "the immense difference between Thucydides and Tacitus" is adjusted to the advantage of the Roman. He actually seems to prefer Augustan to Greek poetry, and makes the astonishing remark that "there is nothing at all in the whole range of Greek literature like . . . the fourth book of Virgil," having apparently never so much as heard of Apollonius Rhodius.[1]

---

[1] How much of this was got from his author herself I leave to others to decide. "She was very capable of having it happen to her," as Marlborough said of his beaten Dutch general.

That of mediæval literature he says practically nothing is not surprising, but it must be taken into account: and his defence of English Literature against his author, though perfectly good against *her*, is necessarily rather limited by its actual purpose, and suggests somehow that other limitations would have appeared if it had been freed from this.

In short, though we cannot support the conclusion further, the very word "limitation" suggests the name of Jeffrey, in the *Its lesson.* sphere of criticism. He seems to be constantly "pulled up" by some mysterious check-rein, turned back by some half-invisible obstacle. Sometimes — by no means quite always—we can concatenate the limiting causes,— deduce them from something known and anterior, but they are almost always present or impending. As Leigh Hunt is the most catholic of critics, so Jeffrey is almost the most sectarian: the very shibboleths of his sectarianism being arbitrarily combined, and to a great extent peculiar to himself.[1]

Let us conclude the chapter with a figure scarcely less representative of the anti-enthusiast school of critics, and *Hallam.* much more agreeable than either Gifford or Jeffrey. To the English student of literary history and of literary criticism, Henry Hallam must always be a name *clarum et venerabile ;* nor—as has been so often pointed out in these pages, and as unfortunately it seems still so often necessary [2] to point out—need disagreement with a great many

[1] A fuller development of view about Jeffrey as a critic may be found in the present writer's *Essays in English Literature,* First Series, pp. 100-134. Articles of his own specially worth examining are, besides the "Staël," "Cowper," "Ford," "Keats," and "Campbell's *Specimens,*" those on *W. Meister* (very curious and interesting), Richardson, Scott, and Byron (very numerous and full of piquancies), Crabbe, Wordsworth of course (though with as much wisdom as good feeling he kept much of the most offensive matter, both on Wordsworth and Southey, out), and Burns. In regard to the latter I cannot help thinking

that he played the *Advocatus Diaboli* better than either Mr Arnold, Mr Shairp, or my late friend Mr Henley.

[2] The popularity, in late years, of the singularly uncritical words "sympathetic" and "unsympathetic" in describing Criticism, would of itself point to this necessity. It would seem impossible for a large number of persons to "like" otherwise than "grossly" in Dryden's sense, or to imagine that any one else can like delicately, with discrimination, in the old sense "nicely." A "sympathetic" notice or criticism is one which pours unmixed cataracts of what the cooks call oiled butter all over the patient:

of his own critical judgments and belief that—for those who merely swallow such judgments whole—he is not the safest of critical teachers, interfere with such due homage. For Hallam was our first master in English of the true compara-
His achieve- tive-historical study of literature—the study without
ment. which, as one main result of this volume should be to show, all criticism is now unsatisfactory, and the special variety of criticism which has been cultivated for the last century most dangerously delusive. His Introduction to the *Literature of Europe*, with its sketch of mediæval and its fuller treatment of Renaissance and seventeenth-century Literature, is the earliest book of the kind in our language: it is not far from being, to this day, the best book of the kind in any.

A first attempt of its sort (it cannot be said here with too much frankness and conviction) can even less than any
Its merits other book be faultless: and it is almost a suf-
ficient proof of Hallam's greatness that his faults are not greater. Some things, indeed, that seem to me faults may not even seem to be so at all to others. He was aware that he must "pass over or partially touch" some departments of at any rate so-called literature; but his preference or rejection may seem somewhat remarkable. Few will quarrel, at least from my point of view, with the very large space given to mere "scholars," but it is surely strange that a historian should have thought History of secondary importance, while according ample space not only to Philosophy and Theology, but even to Anatomy and Mathematics. A more serious and a more indisputable blemish is the scanty and second-hand character of his account of mediæval literature, which he might almost as well have omitted altogether. It cannot be too peremptorily laid down that second-hand

---

a notice that questions this part of him, rejects that, but gives due value to the gold and the silver and the precious stones, while discarding the hay and the stubble, is "unsympathetic." Many years (many lustres even, alas!) ago, an old friend and colleague of mine, since distinguished in his own country as a critic, M. Paul Stapfer, complained that Englishmen, and still more Englishwomen, had only two critical categories—the "dry" and the "pretty." These were unsatisfactory enough, but I think they were better than "sympathetic" and "unsympathetic" as now often used.

accounts of literature are absolutely devoid of any value whatever:—the best and latest authorities become equally "not evidence" with the stalest and worst. Hallam was *and defects.* aware of this principle to some extent, and he almost states it, though of course in his own more measured way, and with reference to quotation mainly, in his preface. But his first chapter is really nothing but a tissue of references to Herder and Eichhorn, Meiners and Fleury, with original remarks which do not console us. The account of Boethius at the very beginning is a pretty piece of rhetoric, but, as the Germans would say, not in the least "ingoing." It is a horrible heresy to say[1] that "It is sufficient to look at any extracts" from the Dark Ages "to see the justice of this censure," for no collection of extracts will justify the *formation* of any critical opinion whatsoever, though it may support, or at least illustrate, one formed from reading whole works.

Further, in a note of Hallam's[2] I think may be found the origin of Mr Arnold's too exclusive preference for "the best *In general* and principal" things and his disparagement of the *distribution* historic estimate, though I trust that Mr Arnold[3] *and treat-* would not have shared Hallam's contempt, equally *ment.* superfine and superficial, for the "barbarous Latin" of the Dark Ages. Finally, it is difficult to conceive a more inadequate reference to one of the most epoch-making of European poems (which is at the same time in its earlier part one of not the least charming) than the words "A very celebrated poem, the *Roman de la Rose,* had introduced an unfortunate taste for allegory in verse, from which France did not extricate herself for several generations." It is all the worse because nothing in it is positively untrue.

It may be said to be unjust to dwell on what is avowedly a mere overture: but unluckily, when Hallam comes to his subject proper, all trace of second-hand treatment does not disappear. The part played by direct examination becomes

---

[1] P. 5, in the convenient 1-vol. reprint of Messrs Ward and Lock (London: n. d.)

[2] On the same page, ed. cit.
[3] Who loved the Vulgate.

very much larger; and the writer's reading is a matter of just admiration, nor does he ever for one moment pretend to have read what he has not. But he has no scruple in supplementing his reading at second-hand, or even in doubling his own frequently excellent judgments with long quoted passages from writers like Bouterwek. Further, the surprise which has been hinted above as to his admissions and exclusions, and at his relative admissions in point of departments, may perhaps after a time change into a disappointed conviction that his first interest did not lie in literature, as literature, at all; but in politics eccesiastical and civil, juristics, moral and other philosophy, and the like. I am inclined to think that Bacon, Descartes, Hobbes, and Grotius have, between them, more space than is devoted to all Hallam's figures in *belles lettres* from Rabelais to Dryden.

I could support this with a very large number of *pièces* if it were necessary; but a few must suffice, and in those few we *In some* shall find a further count against Hallam arising. *particular* Note, for instance, his indorsement of Meiners' *instances.* complaint that Politian "did not scruple to take words from such writers as Apuleius and Tertullian," an indorsement which in principle runs to the full folly of Ciceronianism, and with which it is well to couple and perpend the round assertion elsewhere that Italian is—even it would seem for Italians—an inferior literary instrument to Latin. Secondly, take the astounding suggestion that the *Epistolæ Obscurorum Virorum* "surely" have "not much intrinsic merit," and the apparent dismissal of them as "a mass of vapid nonsense and bad grammar." As if the very vapidity of the nonsense did not give the savour, and the badness of the grammar were not the charm! Here again another judgment (on the *Satire Menippée*) clinches the inference that Hallam's taste for humour was small. If he is not uncomplimentary, he is strikingly inadequate, on Marot: and in regard to the Pléiade he simply follows the French to do evil, and as elsewhere puts himself under the guidance of—La Harpe! Few "heroic enthusiasts" will read his longer and more appreciative notice of Spenser without perceiving "some want, some coldness" in it; fewer will even expect not to find these privations in that of Donne. But the shortest of his shortcomings are reached in his article on Browne, and in part of that on Shakespeare. In the latter the famous sentence on the Sonnets is not, I think, so unforgivable as the slander on Juliet;[1] in the former one can simply quote in silence of comment. "His style is not flowing, but vigorous; his choice of words not elegant, and even approaching to barbarism in English phrase: yet there is an impressiveness, an air of reflection and serenity, in Browne's writings which redeem many of his faults."[2] The sentence that "*Gondibert* is better worth reading than *The Purple Island*, though it may have less of that which distinguishes a poet from another man"—in other words, that an unpoetical poem is better worth reading than a poetical one—is sufficiently tell-tale. It is not surprising, after it, that Hallam speaks respectfully of Rymer—a point where Macaulay, so often his disciple, fortunately left him.

Something, it has been said, will inevitably emerge from these utterances on a tolerably intelligent consideration. *His central* Hallam has abundant erudition, much judicial qual-*weakness*, ity, a shrewdness which generally guides him more or less right in points of fact; sense; fairness; freedom from caprice—even (except as regards the Middle Ages, and especially mediæval Latin and its ancestors back to the late Silver Age) a certain power of regarding literature impartially. But he has, as is so often done (he alludes to the fact himself somewhere), spoken his own doom in words which he applies (with remarkable injustice as it happens) to Fontenelle. He has

[1] I decline to sully these pages with it: let it go to its own place, buckled neck and heels with Rapin's on Nausicaa.

[2] We could abandon Owen Felltham to him with more equanimity if he did not describe, as "vile English, or properly no English," such words as "nested," "parallel" as a verb, and "uncurtain," all excellent English of the best brand and vintage, formed on the strictest and most idiomatic patents of analogy. There is still far too much criticastry and pedanticulism (here's for them !) of this kind about, and men like Hallam are very mainly responsible for it. Even "obnubilate," to which he also objects, is a perfectly good word, on all-fours with "compensate," which he himself uses in the same context, though less usual. A sovereign of just weight, fineness, and stamp is none the worse for having been little circulated : nor is a word.

" cool good sense, and an incapacity, by natural privation, of feeling the highest excellence in works of taste."

In short, " The Act of God ": and for such acts it is as unreasonable as it is indecent to blame their victims.   But at *and the* the same time we may carry our forbearance to *value left* natural privations too far by accepting blind men *by it.* as guides in precipitous countries, or using as a bloodhound a dog who has no scent.   And therefore it is impossible to assign to Hallam a high place as a critic.   He may be—he is—useful even in this respect as a check and a reminder of the views which once were taken by men of wide information, excellent discipline, literary disposition, and (where it was not seared or paralysed) positive taste; but he will not soon recover any other value.   Even thus he is to a critic that always critically estimable thing a *point de repère*, and in the kindred but not identical function of literary historian, the praise which was given to him at the opening of this notice may be maintained in spite of, and not inconsistently with, anything that has been said meanwhile.[1]

Nay, more, Specialism has made such inroads upon us—has bondaged the land to such hordes of robber-barons—that we may not soon expect again, and may even regard with a tender *desiderium*, the width, the justice, the far-reaching and self-sufficing survey and sovereignty of Hallam.

[1] I can only think of one important blunder that he makes *as a historian*—the statement that Opitz " took Holland for his Parnassus." Now Ronsard (*Hist. Crit.*, ii. 362) was not exactly a Dutchman.

INTERCHAPTER V.

(WITH AN EXCURSUS ON PERIODICAL CRITICISM.)

WE here come to the point antipolar to that reached earlier in this book,[1] where we gave a sketch of the Classic or Neo-classic creed. The challenge to array definitions of Classicism and Romanticism in a tabular form has already[2] been respectfully declined: but that this refusal comes neither from pusillanimity, nor yet from complacency in purblindness, may be best proved by undertaking the much more perilous adventure of an anti-creed to that formerly laid down. Even there we had to interpose the caution that absolute subscription, on the part of all the critics concerned, ought not to be thought of: but here the very essence and quiddity of the situation is that no such agreement is in any way possible. In fact, no single and tolerably homogeneous document could possibly here be drawn up, for there would be minority (or sometimes majority) counter-reports on every article. Even those who resist the extremer developments take large licences upon the old classical position. You have your Jeffrey expressing admiration of a *Pharonnida* which would have seemed to Dennis a monstrous stumbling-block, and to Johnson mere foolishness: while among the extremists themselves, each man is a law unto himself. Still, it is perhaps possible to draw up some articles of the Modern or Romantic Criticism which was reached during this period, and we have already, in the last two books, described at some length the process by which they were reached. These articles will be best

---

[1] P. 94.   [2] *V. Hist. Crit.*, iii. 386.

separated into two batches, the first representing the creed
of centre and extremes at once, the second that of extremes
(left or right) only : and it will be well to mark the difference
from the former statement by giving the articles separately,
and not arranging them in paragraphs.

The more catholic creed is very mainly of a negative and
protesting character, and its articles might run somewhat
thus :—

All periods of literature are to be studied, and all have
lessons for the critic.   "Gothic ignorance" is an ignorant
absurdity.

One period of literature cannot prescribe to another.
Each has its own laws ; and if any general laws are to
be put above these, they must be such as will embrace
them.

Rules are not to be multiplied without necessity :
and such as may be admitted must rather be extracted
from the practice of good poets and prose-writers than
imposed upon it.

"Unity" is not itself uniform, but will vary according to the kind, and sometimes within the kind, itself.

The Kind itself is not to be too rigidly constituted :
and subvarieties in it may constantly arise.

Literature is to be judged "by the event": the
presence of the fig will disprove the presence of the
thistle.

The object of literature is Delight ; its soul is Imagination ; its body is Style.

A man should like what he does like : [1] and his
likings are facts in criticism for him.

To which the extremer men would add these, or some of
them, or something like them :—

Nothing depends upon the subject ; all upon the treatment of the subject.

It is not necessary that a good poet or prose writer

---

[1] See the note above, p. 233, for Dennis's counter-assertion.

should be a good man : though it is a pity that he should not be.   And Literature is not subject to the laws of Morality, though it is to those of Manners.[1]

Good Sense is a good thing, but may be too much regarded : and Nonsense is not necessarily a bad one.

The appeals of the arts are interchangeable : Poetry can do as much with sound as Music, as much with colour as Painting, and perhaps more than either with both.

The first requisite of the critic is that he should be capable of receiving Impressions : the second, that he should be able to express and impart them.

There cannot be Monstrous Beauty : the Beauty itself justifies and regularises.

Once more it has to be stipulated that these articles are not to be regarded as definitely proposed ends and aims, which the critical practice of the period set before itself, and by which it worked. They are, for the most part, piecemeal results and upshots of a long and desultory campaign, often reached as it were incidentally, " windfalls of the Muses," kingdoms found while the finder is seeking his father's (or anybody's) asses. If anything general is to be detected before and beneath them, it is a sort of general feeling of irksomeness at the restraints of Neo-classicism,—a revolt against its perpetual restrictions and taboos.

To recur once more to those egregious *juvenilia* of Addison's, which, though not to be too much pressed as stigmata on his own memory, are a useful caricature of Neo-classicism in regard to English, some lover of English literature feels that there is much more in Chaucer than vulgar jests, now not even fashionably vulgar, and in Spenser than tiresome preaching. He looks about to support his feeling with reasons, and he " finds salvation " in the Romantic sense, more or less fully, more or less systematically, more or less universally. The ways and manners of the finding have been dealt with earlier ; the results

[1] Certain persons would, of course,   them I take no keep.
omit even the provisos here ; but of

of it, in critical form, may deserve some summary and *rationale* here.

In the remarkable group of English critics whom we have called "the companions" of Coleridge, and in Coleridge himself, the contemporary quality, and in some cases the direct suggestion, of that great critic appear unmistakably, while in at least most cases they are free from the chaotic or paralytic incompleteness which he hardly ever, save in the *Biographia*, shook off. They all show, as he does, though in varying degrees, the revolt or reaction from the hidebound failure of the baser kind of Neo-classic to *appreciate*—the effort really to taste, to enjoy, and so to deliver that judgment which without enjoyment is always inadequate. And it would be unjust to regard them as merely the sports and waifs of an irresistibly advancing tide. There *is* something of this in them,—the worst of the something being the uncritical scorn with which they sometimes regarded even the greatest of the departed or departing school—the astonishing injustice of Coleridge himself to Gibbon, and Johnson, and the Queen Anne men; of many of them to Pope; of Hazlitt even to Dryden. But they were not only carried, they swam,—swam strongly and steadily and skilfully for the land that was ahead. Their appreciation is not mere matter of fashion; it is genuine. They are honestly appetent of the milk and honey of the newly opened land of English literature for themselves, and generously eager to impart it, and the taste for it, to others.

But we must not—for these merits, or even for what some may think the still higher one of providing, for almost the first time in any literature, a great bulk of matter which is at once valuable criticism and delightful literature itself—make a refusal of our own critical duty as to their shortcomings, which were neither few nor inconsiderable, and which led directly to the singular decadence of English criticism in the middle third of the nineteenth century. The first and the greatest of these —let us fling it frankly and fairly to any partisan of the older critical dispensation who "expects his evening prey" as our history draws towards its close — was, or at any rate was a result of, the very lawlessness and rulelessness by which they had effected their and our emancipation. True, many of the rules that they threw off were bad and irrational, most perhaps were inadequate, irrelevant, requiring to be applied with all sorts of provisos and easements. But they had at any rate kept criticism methodical, and tolerably certain in its utterances. There had been a Creed; there had been not the slightest difficulty in giving reasons, though they might be doubtful ones, for a faith which, if incomplete and not really catholic, was at any rate formally constituted. With the new men it was different. Coleridge indeed boasted mediate and even higher rules and principles behind his individual judgments. But with the rest it was rather a case of sheer private judgment, of "meeting by yourself in your own house."

Another drawback, dangerous always but intensified in danger by its connection with the former, is that, while most of them were much less intimately acquainted with the classics than the critics of former generations had been, this deficiency was not generally compensated by any of that extensive knowledge of *modern* literature which the ruleless or scantily ruled system of criticism imperatively requires. Nay, they were all, including even Coleridge himself and De Quincey (the two most learned, not only of these but of all English critics), very imperfectly acquainted with *French* literature — which, as a whole, is the best suited to qualify the study of our own, correct it, and preserve it from flaws and corruptions. Leigh Hunt knew little but Italian; and in Italian knew best the things that are of least real importance for the English student. As for Lamb, he was more than a fair Latin scholar; but he seems to have known very little Greek, and not to have had wide reading in the classics, either Greek or Latin, while he betrays hardly the slightest knowledge of, or interest in, any foreign modern literature whatever. Hazlitt's case is worse still, for he evidently knew very little indeed, either of the classics or of foreign modern literature, except a few philosophic writers, here of next to no use. In fact, one cannot help wondering how, knowing so little, he came to judge so well— till the wonder nearly disappears, as we see how much better he would have judged if he had known more. Wilson (to look forward a little as we have done with De Quincey) had some classics: and Lockhart had not only classics, but German and Spanish. But one suspects the former to have known next to nothing of modern literature: and the latter did not use critically that which he knew. Even as regards English itself, the knowledge of all these critics was very gappy and scrappy. They did not, with all their advantages of time, know anything like so much of early English literature (even putting Anglo-Saxon out of the question) as Gray had known nearly a hundred years earlier, and Mitford in their own early days.

Thus, while they had deliberately, and in the main wisely, discarded the rules which at least were supposed deductively to govern *all* literature, they had not furnished themselves with that comparative knowledge of *different* literatures, or at the very least of all the different periods of one literature, which assists literary induction, and to some extent supplies the place of the older rules themselves. They were therefore driven to judge by the inner light alone; and as, fortunately, that inner light, in at least some of them, burnt with the clearest and brightest flame, they judged very well by it. But their system was a dangerous one when it came to be applied, as it inevitably had to be applied, in the majority of cases, when their own torches went out, by the aid of smoky farthing rush-lights in blurred horn lanterns.

Yet, allowing for these drawbacks of commission and of example in the most illiberally liberal manner, there will yet remain to their credit such a sum as hardly any other group[1] in any country—as none in ours certainly—can claim. Here at last, and here almost for the first time, appears that body of pure critical appreciation of the actual work of literature for which we have been waiting so long, which we have missed so sorely in ancient times, and which, in the earlier modern, has been given to us stinted and, what is worse, adulterated, by arbitrary restrictions and preoccupations. In Coleridge, in

[1] The Germans did it rather earlier but not so well: the French almost if not quite as well, and more voluminously, but later.

Hazlitt, in Lamb, in Leigh Hunt even, to name no others, we have real "judging of authors," not—or at any rate not mainly —discussion of kinds, and attempts to lay down principles. They are judges, not jurists, "lawmen," not lawmongers and potterers with codes. Appreciation and enjoyment, with their, in this case necessary, consequences, the communication of enjoyment and appreciation—these are the chief and principal things with them, and these they never fail to provide.

And in English, as in French and German,[1] with whatever diversity of immediate aim, exact starting-point, felicity of method, and perfection of result—all the dominant and representative criticism of this time tends in the direction and obeys the impulse of some form or other of that general creed which we have endeavoured to sketch earlier in this Interchapter, and so contributes to the general progress (straight or circular, who shall say?) of which this book is the history. And when, rather, as usual, by the influence of creative than of critical literature, and by that of Scott and Byron above all, the same purpose was inspired in yet other countries, the results were again the same. The dislike of Rule; the almost instinctive falling back upon mediæval literature as an alterative from classical and (recent) modern; the blending of the Arts; the cultivation of colour- and sound-variety in poetry; the variegation and rhythmical elaboration of prose,—in all these ways, by all these agencies, literary Criticism as well as literary practice was reconstructed. And the end is not even yet.

Some more general remarks on the sub-period must be postponed to the several parts of the Conclusion. But there is one phenomenon which, first appearing somewhat earlier, now becomes what the Germans call *hervorragend*, persistently and almost aggressively prominent. And on this we must say something.

[1] The criticism of neither of these nations produced much effect on English critics, except on Coleridge, during the period surveyed in the last chapter, but it became very influential a little later. Full accounts of it, and of what followed in these two countries and in others, will be found in the larger *History*. (See especially on Goethe, iii. 361-377.)

[1] To enter into all the questions connected with the Periodical here, would be obviously impossible. That it has multiplied criticism itself is a truism ; that it has necessarily
multiplied bad criticism is maintainable ; the question is
whether it has actually multiplied good. I think it has. It is
very difficult to conceive of any other system under which a
man like Sainte-Beuve—not of means, and not well adapted to
any profession—could have given his life practically to the
service of our Muse as he actually did. It is difficult to imagine
any other which would have equally well suited a man like Mr
Arnold, with abundant, and fairly harassing, avocations on the
one hand, and with apparently no great inclination to write
elaborate books on the other. Many officials, professional men,
persons "avocated" (in the real sense) from criticism by this
or that vocation, have been enabled by the system to give us
things sometimes precious, and probably in most times not
likely to have been given at all under the book-and-pamphlet
dispensation. Above all, perhaps, the excuse of the surplusage
which besets the regular treatise has disappeared, while the
blind (or too well-seeing) editor, with his abhorred shears, is
apt to lop excrescences off if they attempt to appear.[2] Although there certainly has been more bad criticism written in
the nineteenth century than in any previous one,—probably
more than in all previous centuries put together,—it is quite
certain that no other period can show so much that is good.
And the change which has resulted in it was needed. The
Bibliothecæ of the late seventeenth century wanted pliancy,
variety, combination of industrial power : the *Reviews* succeeding them were too apt to be mere booksellers' instruments,
while their wretched pay kept many of the best hands from
them, and kept those who were driven to them in undue
dependence. And further, the increasing supply of actual
literature *required* more criticism than could easily be had

---

[1] The rest of this Interchapter may
be taken—as also the Appendix—for
samples of a very much larger body of
"Critical Excursus" which I should
like to give, if I thought that readers
would endure it.

[2] Add some other blessings, as that
the periodical can contradict itself—
which the book sometimes does, but
should not.

under the old system of few periodicals, eked out by independent treatises and pamphlets.

These are not unimportant considerations, but they lie a little outside of—or only touch—the question of the altered quality and increased or decreased goodness of criticism as a whole and in itself. And when we come to discuss this, the question assumes rather a different aspect. The better pay, the increased repute, the greater independence, might be thought likely to attract, and did attract, a better class of writers to the work: but whether this better class was always better fitted for the particular task itself one may sometimes doubt. And there can be no doubt at all that the same attractions must necessarily tempt, and that the increased demand must almost force, a very much larger supply of inferior talent to the said task. Again, this increased demand, if not for critics, for somebody who would undertake to criticise (which is not quite the same thing), coincided with a gradual removal of the not very severe requisitions of competence which had up to this time been imposed upon the aspirant. The Mr Bludyer of the eighteenth century was at least supposed to know his Aristotle and his Longinus, his Horace and his Quintilian, his Boileau and his Le Bossu, his Dryden and his Addison. In the majority of cases he did know them—after a fashion—though he constantly misinterpreted the best of them and put his faith chiefly in the worst. But the Mr Bludyer of the nineteenth has not been supposed to know anything at all of the history and theory of his art. Now, when you at once set up a Liberty Hall, and dispense good things therein freely to all comers, your Liberty Hall is too likely before long to become a Temple of Misrule.

As the older arrangements went to make the critic's trade not merely homely and slighted, but cramped by too many, too strict, and too little comprehended rules and formulas, so the new tended rather to make it a paradise of the ignoramus with a touch of impudence. It has never perhaps been quite sufficiently comprehended, by what may be called the laity, that though, in a way, Blake was perfectly right in saying that every man is a judge of art who is not connoisseured

out of his senses, yet it does not quite follow that every man
without training and without reading, is qualified to deliver
judgment, from the actual bench, on so complicated and treacherous a work of art as a book. You can take in at least great
part of the beauty of a picture at the first glance; and, no
matter what the subject may be, many of the details, with
all the colour and some of the drawing and composition, require
neither previous education nor prolonged and attentive study,
though study and attention will no doubt greatly improve the
comprehension and enjoyment of them. In the case of a book
it is very different. The most rapid and industrious reader
will require some minutes—it may even be some hours—to put
himself in a position to deliver any trustworthy judgment on it
at all: and he must be an exceedingly well-informed one who is
at home with every subject treated in every volume that he has
to review. You have to find out what it is that the author has
endeavoured to do, and then—the most impossible of tasks to
some critics, it would seem—to consider whether he has done
it, and not whether he has or has not done something else which
you wanted him to do. You have to guard against prejudices
innumerable, subtle, Hydra-headed,—prejudices personal and
political, prejudices social and religious, prejudices of style and
of temperament, prejudices arising from school, university,
country, almost every conceivable predicament of man. You
must be able first to grasp, then to take off a total impression,
then to produce that impression in a form suitable for easy
conveyance to the public. One would not perhaps be quite prepared to assert that every one of the hundreds and thousands
who have, under the new dispensation, undertaken the office of
a critic, has been divinely endowed with these gifts before
undertaking that office, or that all of them, even if they took
the trouble to acquire what may be acquired, were likely to
succeed. There remains, of course, the comfortable doctrine
that "practice makes perfect": or, as one of the most agreeable
and acute of modern political satirists, himself an admirable
critic, has ironically put it—

> "That by much engine-driving at intricate junctions
> One learns to drive engines along with the best."

And if this seem small comfort to the suffering author, who thinks that he has had too great a share of the bad criticism and too little of the good, there are two other consolations for him. The one is that under any other system his book would very probably have received no notice at all, which would in some cases (not in all) annoy him worse than blame. If he be of another sort, he may perhaps anticipate the question, all-healing to any *alma* passably *sdegnosa*, "Would you rather *not* have written so, and be praised?"

One very necessary branch of the new criticism, as regarded poetry, the average critic, whether in or out of periodicals, was sadly slow to learn—indeed for the most part he recalcitrated furiously against learning it. This was the proper appreciation of the new effects in verbal painting and verbal music. There had always, of course, been much of this in the great old masters: but there had not been *so* much of it, and the critic had been wont to treat it alternately in a peddling and in a high-sniffing fashion. On the musical side especially, theory had chiefly confined itself to the remarks on "suiting the sound to the sense," in a comparatively infantine fashion,—putting plenty of *ss*'s into a line about a snake or a goose, and plenty of *r*'s into a line about a dog; giving trisyllabic feet in a line that meant swift movement, and clogging it with consonants when effort or tardiness came in. The new poets—Coleridge, Keats, Tennyson,—in increasing degree, changed this simple and rudimentary proceeding into a complicated science of word-illumination and sound-accompaniment, which the new critics perhaps could not see or hear, and at which they were by turns loftily contemptuous and furiously angry. That there was some genuine inability in the matter may appear from looking back to Johnson's well-known and very interesting surprise at Pope's fondness for his couplet—

> "Lo! where Mœotis sleeps, and hardly flows
> The freezing Tanais, through a waste of snows."

This couplet *is* beautiful, though the *homœoteleuton* of "Mœot*is*" and "Tana*is*" is a slight blemish on it. But its beauty arises from such subtle things as the contrast of the metrical rapidity

of "Tănăĭs" and the sluggish progression of its waters, and
from the extremely artful disposition and variation of the
vowel notes, *o, a, ee.*

Even this is not *very* complicated: and it occurs, with Pope
and his clan, once in a thousand or ten thousand lines. *The
Ancient Mariner* and *Kubla Khan* are simply compact of the
colouring symphonies of sound: and the palette becomes
always more intricate, the tone-schemes more various and
more artful, as you journey from the *Eve of St Agnes* to the
Palace of Art, and from the *Dream of Fair Women* to *Rose
Mary*. In the *Palace* especially[1] the series of descriptions
of the pictures pushes both these applications of the two
sister arts towards — almost to — the limits of the possible.
Rossetti alone has since surpassed them. Take, for instance,
the cunning manipulation of the actual quatrain itself to
begin with; the figures and colour of the various designs; and
the sound-accompaniment, to suit these figures and colours,
in such a stanza as—

> "One seemed all dark and red : a tract of sand,
>   And some one pacing there alone,
> Who paced for ever in a glimmering land,
>   Lit with a low large moon."[2]

Now the "values" of this are not really difficult to make
out: they can be thoroughly mastered for himself, without book
or teacher, by an intelligent boy of sixteen or seventeen, who,
having a taste for poetry, has read some—and who happens
to have been born within the nineteenth century. But they
do need intelligent, sympathetic, and to a certain extent submissive, co-operation on the part of the person who is to
enjoy them. The adjustment of the stanza, with its successive
lines of varying capacity and cadence; the fitness of those
lines themselves to receive and express more or less detailed
images, and add, as it were, not merely stroke after stroke, but
plan after plan, to the picture; the monosyllables; the alliteration of the last line, and the crowning effect whereby the

---

[1] It was originally published, remember, before the death of Coleridge,
and well within our present period.

[2] The original form of this, in
1832-33, was less perfect, but the aim
and the principle are there already.

picture is lightened after being displayed in shadow; the trisyllabic foot thrown in by "glimmering," whether you take it in the last or the last but one of the third verse; the atmosphere-accompaniment,—all these things might well be almost invisible and inaudible to a critic brought up on eighteenth-century principles. And if he saw or heard them at all, they might affect him with that singular impatience and disgust at refinement and exquisiteness in pleasure which was affected by ancient philosophers, and which seems to be really genuine in many excellent Englishmen whom the Gods have not made in the very least philosophical. I have never myself understood why it is godliness to gulp and sin to savour; why, if a pleasure be harmless in itself, it becomes harmful in being whetted, and varied, and enhanced by every possible innocent agency. But there are doubtless some people who think it a "poisoning of the dart too apt before to kill." And there are, I strongly suspect, a good many more whose senses are too blunt to taste or feel the refinements, and who receive the attentions of the poetic fairies with as little appreciation, though usually with by no means as much good-humour, as Bottom showed to those of Titania and her meyny.

This, however, is undoubtedly something of a digression, perhaps something too much of it. But it illustrates the perils to which the new reviewers were exposed, and at the same time (which is the excuse for the divagation) the constant opportunity of salvation which reviewing provides.

Nor need much be said of the general quality of the articles in these famous collections. Persons of enterprise have gone "exploring," like Mrs Elton (on or off their donkeys, and with or without their little baskets), into the review-province of *Edinburgh* and *Quarterly*, and have come back saying, more or less wisely, that the land is barren. Some of the more practical of them have brought back specimens of its flora and fauna, its soil and its rocks.[1] It is perhaps more profitable to digest some of the general considerations which have

---

[1] Mr Hall Caine, in his *Cobwebs of Criticism* (London, 1883); Mr E. Stevenson, in a useful and unpre- tentious collection of *Early Reviews* (London, n. d.), &c., &c.

already been stated or indicated than to dwell on particulars.
Not that these particulars are useless or always uninteresting.   It is good to know that *The Monthly Review*, in an article
which could not be called unfriendly, thought *The Ancient
Mariner* "a rhapsody of unintelligible wildness and incoherence" [the whole thing is as clear to *us* as a proposition in
Euclid], with "poetic touches of an exquisite kind."   It is
very interesting, and not at all surprising (especially when
we remember Voltaire), to find the *Edinburgh*, the oracle of
political Whiggery, enunciating the doctrine of Poetical Divine
Right in its article on *Thalaba*.[1]   It is interesting, again, and
almost more instructive, to find the *Quarterly*, in the article
which did *not* kill John Keats, finding fault with that poet
and his master Leigh Hunt, not (as might have been done
plausibly enough) for a flaccid *mollities*, for the *delumbe* and
the *in labris natantia*,[2] but, of all things, for "ruggedness."   If
we have pursued our critical studies aright, we know the
symptoms, we know the diseases.   They are all varieties of
Kainophobia,—the horror and the misunderstanding of the un-
accustomed.

But though it is not original, it is very far from superfluous
to point out that these poor old unjust judges, these Doubters
and Bloodmen of the poetic Mansoul at this crisis of its history, the Giffords, and Jeffreys, and Crokers, were by no means
without their excuses.   The original form of *The Ancient
Mariner* is only less inferior to the later form which most
people know now, than Tennyson's Poems[3] as they appear
in the editions since 1842 are superior to themselves as they
appeared to risk the knout of Wilson and the thumbikins of
Croker.   Southey's unrhymed *vers libres* in *Thalaba* are, when
all is said and done, a mistake: and their arrangement is sometimes as unmusical as the least successful parts of Mr

---

[1] "Poetry has this much at least in
common with religion, that its standards were fixed long ago by certain
inspired writers, whose authority it is
no longer lawful to call in question."
There may seem to be an ironic touch
in this: but the whole article is written to the text.

[2] Critical phrases of Persius.

[3] These texts can be seen partly in
more than one modern book on Tennyson, and wholly in the late Professor
Churton Collins's useful reprint of the
Early Poems (London, 1900).

Arnold's followings of them. Exquisite as are the beauties, intoxicating as is the atmosphere, of *Endymion*, no one nowadays could pronounce it free from faults of taste of more kinds than one, or deny that as, after all, it holds itself out to be a story, the demand for some sort of intelligible narrative procession is not so irrelevant as when it is put to a lyric, in even the widest sense of that word. And the critics were, in every one of these cases, justified of their victims. Coleridge and Tennyson altered into perfection the poems which had been so imperfect. Southey added rhyme and better rhythm in *Kehama;* Keats grew from the incoherence of *Endymion,* and its uncertain taste, to the perfection of *Lamia* and the great *Odes* and the *Eves* of St Agnes and St Mark. " They also serve, who only stand and—*whip.*" But it is better to have a soul above mere whipping.

CHAPTER VII.

BETWEEN COLERIDGE AND ARNOLD.

THE ENGLISH CRITICS OF 1830-60 — WILSON — STRANGE MEDLEY OF HIS CRITICISM—THE 'HOMER' AND THE OTHER LARGER CRITICAL COLLECTIONS—THE 'SPENSER'—THE 'SPECIMENS OF BRITISH CRITICS'—'DIES BOREALES'—FAULTS IN ALL, AND IN THE REPUBLISHED WORK—DE QUINCEY: HIS ANOMALIES AND PERVERSITIES AS A CRITIC, IN REGARD TO ALL LITERATURES—THEIR CAUSES—THE 'RHETORIC' AND THE 'STYLE'—HIS COMPENSATIONS—LOCKHART—DIFFICULTY WITH HIS CRITICISM—THE 'TENNYSON' REVIEW NOT HIS—ON COLERIDGE, BURNS, SCOTT, AND HOOK — HIS GENERAL CRITICAL CHARACTER— HARTLEY COLERIDGE—FORLORN CONDITION OF HIS CRITICISM— ITS QUALITY—DEFECTS AND EXAMPLES—MAGINN—HIS PARODY-CRITICISMS AND MORE SERIOUS EFFORTS — MACAULAY — HIS EXCEPTIONAL COMPETENCE IN SOME WAYS—THE EARLY ARTICLES—HIS DRAWBACKS— THE PRACTICAL CHOKING OF THE GOOD SEED—HIS LITERARY SURVEYS IN THE 'LETTERS'—HIS CONFESSION—THE 'ESSAYS'—SIMILAR DWINDLING IN CARLYLE—THE EARLIER 'ESSAYS'—THE LATER—THE ATTITUDE OF THE 'LATTER-DAY PAMPHLETS'—THE CONCLUSION OF THIS MATTER — THACKERAY — HIS ONE CRITICAL WEAKNESS AND HIS EXCELLENCE—'BLACKWOOD,' IN 1849, ON TENNYSON—GEORGE BRIMLEY— HIS ESSAY ON TENNYSON—HIS OTHER WORK—HIS INTRINSIC AND CHRONOLOGICAL IMPORTANCE — "GYAS AND CLOANTHUS" — MILMAN, CROKER, HAYWARD—SYDNEY SMITH, SENIOR, HELPS — ELWIN, LANCASTER, HANNAY—DALLAS—THE 'POETICS'—'THE GAY SCIENCE'— OTHERS: J. S. MILL.

THERE are few things so difficult to the conscientious writer, and few which he knows will receive so little consideration from the irresponsible reader, as those overlappings on the one hand, and throwings-back on the other, which are incumbent on all literary historians save those who are content to abjure form and method altogether. The constituents of the present chapter give a case in point. Some of them may seem unreasonably torn away from their natural companions in our last chapter dealing with English criticism; some unreasonably kept back from the society of the next. But, once more, things have not been done entirely at the hazard of the orange-peel or the die.

There is, to the present writer at any rate, a distinct colour, or set of colours, appertaining to most of the English criticism *The English* of 1830-1860, and it seems worth while to bring *Critics of* this out by isolating its practitioners to a certain *1830-60.* extent. We shall find these falling under three main divisions—the first containing the latest-writing, and in some cases hardly the least, of the great band of periodical critics, mostly Romantic in tendency, of whom Coleridge is the Generalissimo and Hazlitt the rather mutinous Chief of the Staff. Then come the mighty pair of Carlyle and Macaulay; and then a rear-guard of more or less interesting minors and transition persons. So, first of the first, let us deal with one who, not only to his special partisans and friends, seemed a very prince of critics in his day.

The difficulties of appraising " Christopher North " as a critic are, or should be, well known in general; but it is doubtful *Wilson.* whether many persons have recently cared to put themselves in a position to appreciate them directly. No such revival has come to him as that which has come to Hazlitt: and I have elsewhere given at some length[1] the reasons which make me inclined to fear that no such revival is very likely to come soon. For Wilson accumulated, with a defiance valorous enough but certainly not discreet, provocation after provocation to Nemesis and Oblivion. He is immensely diffuse; he is not more diffuse than he is desultory; and in the greater part of his work he sets his criticism with a habitual strain of extravagant and ephemeral *bravura* which even the most tolerant and catholic may not seldom find uncongenial. But all this, though bad, is followed by things worse — critical incivility of the worst kind, violent

---

[1] In an essay originally published in *Macmillan's Magazine* for July 1886, and reprinted in *Essays in English Literature* (3rd. ed., London, 1896).

political and other partisanship, a prevailing capriciousness
Strange which makes his critical utterances almost valueless,
medley of except as words to the wise; and occasional ac-
his criti- cesses of detraction and vituperation which suggest
cism. either the exasperation of some physical ailment, or
a slight touch of mental aberration. And yet, side by side
with all this, there is an enthusiastic love of literature; a very
wide knowledge of it; a real capacity for judging, wherever
this capacity is allowed to exercise itself; a generosity (as in
the famous palinodes to Leigh Hunt and to Macaulay) which
only makes one regret the more keenly that this generosity
is so Epimethean; and, lastly, a faculty of phrase which,
irregular and uncertain as it is, apt as it is to fall on one
side into bombast and on the other into bathos, is almost
always extraordinary. An anthology of critical passages might
be extracted from Wilson which few critics could hope to
surpass; but the first and probably the last exclamation of
any one who was driven by this to the contexts would be,
"How on earth could such good taste live in company with
a Siamese brother so hopelessly bad!"[1]

Wilson's admirers, from his daughter downwards, have
lamented that the *Homer*—a good thing but not his best—
The Homer was the only one of his longer and more connected
and the critical exercitations that was included[2] in his
other larger
critical collected works, while three others—the *Spenser*,
collections. the *Specimens of British Critics*, and the dialogue
Dies Boreales—were excluded. The reasons of the exclusion
seem obvious enough. At a rough and unprofessional "cast-
off," I should guess each of the two earlier series at about

---

[1] As I am not speaking *enfarin-
hadamente* about Wilson's faults, I
may fairly protest against an exaggeration of them. It is surely unlucky
of Mr Buxton Forman (*Keats's Letters*,
i. 46, ed. 1900) to talk of *Blackwood's
Magazine* having "a monopoly of
frowsy and unsavoury personal gibes"
in "the possession of Christopher
North," when he had himself a few
papers earlier cited Hazlitt's almost

Bedlamite Billingsgate against Southey
in the *Examiner*.

[2] As the 4th vol. of *Essays Critical and
Imaginative* (4 vols., Edinburgh, 1856-
57). It follows Wilson's usual lines
of a running study of the poem and
those who have written about it.
Much of it, as of the essay on the
Agamemnon which follows, is occupied
by a not uninteresting parallel-collec-
tion of translations.

300 of these present pages, and the *Dies* at nearer 400. This would have meant at least another three volumes added to a collection already consisting of twelve. The Devil's Advocate, moreover, would have had other things to urge. Whatever Wilson had gained by age and sobering (and he had gained much), he had lost nothing of his tendency to exuberance and expatiation. After the first paper or two, the whole of the *Spenser* criticism is occupied with an examination of the First Book of the *Faerie Queene* only—the best known part of the poem. The *Specimens of British Critics*—an admirable title which might have served for a most novel, useful, and interesting work—means in fact a very copious examination of Dryden's critical utterances and a rather copious one of those of Pope—so that this *professor* at any rate has not filled this *hiatus*. And the *Dies*, though they have got rid of some of the superabundant animal spirits of the *Noctes*, are (it is necessary to say it) very much duller.

Yet the regretters had some reason. I myself could relinquish without much sorrow, from the matter actually republished, more than as much as would accommodate the *Spenser*, nearly as much as would make room for the *Specimens* also. As for the former, the famous compliment of Hallam [1] (not a person likely, either on his good or his bad side, to be too lenient to Wilson's faults) is at least a strong prerogative vote. Nor does it [2] stand in need of this backing. Wilson spends far too much time in slaying forgotten Satans that never were very Satanic—the silliness of the excellent Hughes, the pedantry of the no less excellent Spence, the half-heartedness, even, of Tom Warton. He does not entirely discard his old horse-play and his old grudges, though we can well pardon him for the fling that "the late Mr Hazlitt" did not think Sidney and Raleigh gentlemen. But he discards them to a very great extent; as well as the old namby-pambiness which sometimes mars his earlier work, when he is sentimental, and which, with him as with Landor,

The Spenser.

---

[1] *Literature of Europe*, chap. **xiv.**, § 82.

[2] It will be found in *Blackwood's*

Magazine, vols. xxxiv., xxxvi., and xxxvii. (Edinburgh, 1833-35).

was a real danger. And the thing is full of admirable things,
—the generous admission that "Campbell's criticism is as
fine and true as his poetry"; the victorious defence of the
Spenserian stanza against those who think it a mere following
of the Italians: a hundred pieces of good exposition and appreciation. While as for mere writing, we have "written fine"
after De Quincey and Wilson himself for some eighty years.
But have we often beaten this: "Thus here are many elegies
in one; but that one [*Daphnaida*] is as much a whole as the
sad sky with all its *misty* stars"?[1]

The *Specimens of British Critics*,[2] ten years later, maintains,
and even with rare exceptions improves, the standard of taste
in the *Spenser*, but its faults of disproportion, irrelevance, and divagation are much greater. The
author himself once insinuates that his work may be
taken for "an irregular history of British Criticism,"
and it certainly might have been made such—"nor so very
irregular neither," as they would have said in the days when
Englishmen were allowed to write English, and grammarians
to prate about grammar. But Wilson cannot resist his propensity to course any hare that starts. As has been said
above, he has the compass of a by no means meagre volume
for dealing ostensibly with no British critics but Dryden and
Pope. If he dealt with them only, and only as critics, there
would not be much fault to find, though we might wish for
a better and fuller planned work. But not a quarter—not,
we might almost venture to say, a tenth—of his space is
occupied with them or with criticism. A very large part is
given to discussion, not merely of Dryden and Pope but of
Churchill as *satirists;* Dryden's plays, rhymed and other,
receive large consideration, his theory of translation almost
a larger, with independent digressions on every poet whom he
translates. Two or three whole papers are devoted to Chaucer,
not merely as Dryden translated him but in all his works, in
his versification, and so forth. I do not wonder that, seeing

The Speci-
mens of
British
Critics.

---

[1] For this is one of the metaphors
which (as Théophile Gautier boasted
of his own, and as so few others can

boast) *se suivent.*

[2] Ibid., vols. lvii., lviii. (1849).

a farrago so utterly non-correspondent to its title, any one should have hesitated to reprint it. But I do know that there is admirable criticism scattered all over it, that if it appeared as *Miscellanies in English Criticism*, or *Critical Quodlibeta*, or something of that sort, it would be worth the while of every one who takes an interest in the subject to read it: and I do think it a pity that it should be practically as if it were not.

Perhaps hardly as much can be said of *Dies Boreales*,[1] which was written when the author's bodily strength was breaking, and which betrays a relapse on senescent methods, with, naturally, no relief of juvenile treatment. The dialogue form is resumed, but "Seward," "Buller," and "Tall-boys" are, as Dryden might have said, "the coolest and most insignificant" fellows, the worst possible substitutes for "Tickler," and the Shepherd, and the wonderful *eidolon* of De Quincey in the *Noctes*. There is no gusto in the descriptions, even of Loch Awe: and among the rare and melancholy flashes of the old genial tomfoolery, the representation of a banquet at which these thin things, these walking gentlemen, sit down with the ghost of Christopher to a banquet of *twenty-five* weighed pounds of food per man, is but ghastly and resurrectionist Rabelaisianism. But if there is not the old exuberance, there is the old pleonasm. Wilson seems unable to settle down to what is his real subject—critical discussion of certain plays of Shakespeare and of *Paradise Lost*. Nor, when the discussions come, are they quite of the first class, though there are good things in them. The theory of a "double time" in Shakespeare—one literal and chronological, which is often very short, and another extended by poetical licence—is ingenious, if somewhat fantastic, and, critically, quite unnecessary. But the main faults of the writer, uncompensated for the most part by his merits, are eminently here.

These faults, to be particularised immediately, result in a lack of directness, method, clean and clear critical grip, which is continuous and pervading. Forty pages could generally be squeezed into fourteen, and not seldom into four, with great gain of critical, no loss of literary,

Dies Boreales.

Faults in all,

---

[1] *Blackwood's Magazine*, vols. lxv.-lxviii. and lxxii. (1849-52).

merit. Now diffuseness, a bad fault everywhere, is an absolutely fatal one in critical literature that wishes to live. It is hard enough for it to gain the ear of posterity anyhow; it is simply impossible when the real gist of the matter is whelmed in oceans of divagation, of skirmishes, courteous or rough-and-tumble, with other critics, of fantastic flourish and fooling. It is no blasphemy to the *Poetics* and the Περὶ Ὕψους themselves to say that to their terseness they owe at least half their immortality.

In the earlier, better known, and more easily accessible work the same merits and defects appear in brighter or darker colours, *and in the republished work.* as the case may be. In once more going through the ten volumes of the *Noctes*,[1] and the *Recreations*, and the *Essays*, I can find nothing more representative than the Wordsworth Essay,[2] the famous onslaught on Tennyson's early Poems,[3] and the eulogy of Macaulay's *Lays*,[4] though I should now add *An Hour's Talk about Poetry* from the *Recreations*.[5] In the first the author tries to be systematic, and fails; in the second he is jovially scornful, not without some acute and generous appreciation; in the third he is enthusiastically appreciative, but not, on the whole, critically satisfactory; in the fourth he compasses English sea and land to find one Great Poem, and finds it only in *Paradise Lost*. Everywhere he is alive and full of life; in most places he is suggestive and stimulating at intervals; nowhere is he critically to be depended upon. Praise and blame; mud and incense; vision and blindness alike lack that interconnection, that "central tiebeam," which Carlyle, in one of the least unsympathetic and most clear-sighted of his criticisms of his contemporaries, denied him. The leaves are not merely—are not indeed at all—Sibylline; for it is impossible to work them into, or to believe that they were ever inspired by, a continuous

---

[1] There is much good as well as bad criticism here; but it is almost inevitable that the goodness should be obscured to too many tastes, and the bad intensified to almost all, by the setting of High Jinks. Yet Wilson, like Shakespeare according to Collier, "could be very serious," and his defence of Croker against Macaulay is far more valid than has usually been allowed.

[2] Essays, i. 387 *sq.*

[3] Ibid., ii. 109 *sq.*

[4] Ibid., iii. 386.   [5] i. 179.

and integral thought or judgment. There is enjoyment on the reader's part, as on the writer's, but it is "casual fruition": there is even reasoning, but it is mostly on detached and literally eccentric issues. A genial chaos: but first of all, and, I fear, last of all, chaotic.

Wilson's neighbour, friend, contributor, and, in a kindly fashion, half-butt, De Quincey[1] is, like Southey, though in *De Quincey:* different measure, condition, and degree, rather *his* puzzling as a critic. He, too, had enormous reading, *anomalies* a keen interest in literature, and a distinctly critical temperament. Moreover, during great part of his long life, he never had any motive for writing on subjects that did not please him : and, even when such a motive existed, he seems to have paid sublimely little attention to it. The critical "places" in his works are in fact very numerous; they meet the reader almost *passim,* and often seem to promise substantive and important contributions to criticism. Nor, as a matter of fact, are they ever quite negligible or often unimportant. They constantly have that stimulating and attractive property which is so valuable, and which seems so often to have been acquired by "the Companions" from contact with the loadstone-rock of Coleridge. Every now and then, as in the well-known "Note on the Knocking at the Gate in *Macbeth,*" De Quincey will display evidence (whether original or suggested) of almost dæmonic subtlety. Very often, indeed, he will display evidence, if not of dæmonic yet of impish and almost fiendish acuteness, as in his grim and (for a fellow artificial-Paradise seeker) rather callous suggestion[2] that Coleridge and Lamb should have put down their loss of cheerfulness in later years not to opium or to gin but to the later years themselves. "Ah, dear Lamb," says the little monster,[3] "but note that the

---

[1] As De Quincey had, for one who was not a novelist, the probably unique honour of four complete editions of his *Works* in his last years and the generation succeeding his death, it is not easy to refer to him. But the last —Professor Masson's of 1890—has the merit of methodical arrangement: and its tenth volume contains most of the *purely* critical things.

[2] In *Coleridge and Opium Eating.*

[3] As it is very dangerous to write about De Quincey, let me observe that this is a phrase of Mr Thackeray's about another person, and implies affection and even admiration.

drunkard was fifty - six years old and the songster twenty-three!"

Yet De Quincey is scarcely—on the whole, and as a whole—to be ranked among the greatest critics. To begin with, his *and per-* unconquerable habit of "rigmarole" is constantly *versities as* leading him astray: and the taste for jaunty per-*a critic,* sonality which he had most unluckily imbibed from Wilson leads him astray still further, and still more gravely and damagingly. In the volume on *The Lake Poets* I do not suppose that there are twenty pages of pure criticism, putting all orts and scraps together. The main really critical part of the essay on Lamb—then a fresh and most tempting subject—is a criticism of——Hazlitt! The extremely interesting subject of "Milton *v.* Southey and Landor" (though the paper does contain good things, and, in particular, some excellent remarks on Metre) is all frittered and whittled off into shavings of quip, and crank, and gibe, and personality. The same is the case with what should have been, and in part is, one of his best critical things, the article on Schlosser's *Literary History of the Eighteenth Century.* The present writer will not be suspected, by friend or foe, of insisting ruthlessly on a too grave and chaste critical manner: but De Quincey here is too much for anything and anybody. "For Heaven's sake, my good man," one may say almost in his own words, "do leave off fooling and come to business." In the very long essay on Bentley he has little or no criticism at all; and here, as well as in the "Cicero," he is too much stung and tormented by his hatred of the drab style of Conyers Middleton to see anything else when he gets near to that curious person, as he must in both. On Keats, without any reason for hostility, he has almost the full inadequacy of his generation, with not much less on Shelley; and when he comes to talk even of Wordsworth's *poetry,* though there was no one living whom he honoured more, he is not very much less unsatisfactory.

Nor are these inadequacies and perversities limited to English. There was a good excuse (more than at one time people used to think under the influence of the fervent Goethe-worship of the mid-nineteenth century) for his famous and

furious attack on *Wilhelm Meister ;* but what are we to think
in regard of a man who (admitting that much has been said
to all and thought of it) coolly "dismisses,"[1] without so
literatures. much as an unfavourable opinion, the lyric and
miscellaneous poetry of one of the greatest lyric poets of
Europe, or the world? He persistently belittles French
literature: and he had, of course, a right to give his judgment.
But, unfortunately, he not only does not give evidence of
knowledge to support his condemnation, but does give negative
evidence of ignorance. That ignorance, as far as contemporary
literature went, seems to have been almost absolute. Even
Chateaubriand (a rhetorician after his own heart) he merely
names in his dealing with French writers in company with
Florian (!), and expressly denies him rhetoric; while the
subject before the seventeenth century seems to have been
equally a blank to him. But he is most wayward and most
uncritical about the classics. He gives himself all the airs
of a profound scholar, and seems really to have been a very
fair one. Yet that "Appraisal of Greek Literature" which
Professor Masson has ruthlessly resuscitated[2] might almost
have been written by the most ignorant of the "Moderns," two
hundred years ago, for its omissions and commissions. He
seems to have been in his most Puckish frame of mind if he
was not serious; if he was, *actum est* (or almost so) with him
as a critic.

The truth seems to be that he had no very deep, wide, or
fervent love of poetry as such. He could appreciate single
lines and phrases,—such as

"Sole sitting by the shores of old romance,"

or

"Beyond the arrows, views, and shouts of men";

but on the whole his curious, and of course strictly "interested," heresy about prose - poetry made him as lukewarm
Their towards poetry pure and simple as it made him
causes. unjust to the plainer prose, such as that of
Middleton, that of Swift, and even (incomprehensible as this

[1] In his "biography" of Goethe. [2] Vol. x., ed. cit. Date, 1838-39.

particular injustice may seem) that of Plato. Yet we should not be sorry for this heresy, because it gave us, independently of the great creative passages of the *Confessions*, the *Suspiria*, and the rest, the critical pieces of the *Rhetoric* and the *Style*. It is somewhat curious that in the midst of an appreciative period we should have to fall back upon "preceptist" work. But it is certainly here that De Quincey, though not without his insuperable faults, becomes of most consequence in the History of Criticism. In fact, he may be said to have been almost the "instaurator"[1] of this preceptist criticism which, since its older arguments had become nearly useless from the disuse of the Neo-classic appreciation upon which they were based, or which was based upon them, very urgently and particularly required such instauration.

The *Rhetoric* in particular, with all its defects, has not been superseded as a preceptist canvas, which the capable teacher

The Rhetoric *and the* Style. can broider and patch into a competent treatise of the ornater English style. Its author's unconquerable waywardness appears in his attempt—based in the most rickety fashion and constantly self-contradictory — to combine the traditional and the popular senses of the word in a definition of Rhetoric as *unconvinced* fine writing,—the deliberate elaboration of mere *tours de force* in contradistinction to genuine and heartfelt Eloquence. But its view is admirably wide—the widest up to its time that can be found anywhere, I think; it is instinct with a crotchety but individual life; and if the defects of the new method appear when we compare it with Rapin or Batteux, the merits thereof appear likewise, and in ample measure. Nor, despite some digression, is there much of the author's too frequent tomfoolery. His erudition, his interest in the subject, and (towards the end) his genuine and alarmed eagerness to contradict Whately's damaging pronouncements as to poetry and prose, keep him out of this. The *Style* is much more question-

---

[1] As such it will prove interesting to compare him with Nisard or Planche, especially the latter. But the comparison will, I fear, bring out that superiority of French criticism at *this* time which, denying it at others, I fully admit. (See the larger *History* for dealings with these.)

able, and has much more ephemeral matter in it—the author rides out all his favourite cock-horses by turns, and will often not bate us a single furlong of the journey to Banbury Cross on them. Moreover, much of it is occupied with often just condemnation of the special vices of ordinary English news-paper-and-book style in the earlier middle nineteenth century —Satans which, though not quite extinct, have given main place to other inhabitants of Pandemonium. But the paper, with the subsidiary pieces on *Language* and *Conversation*, will never lose interest and importance.

No incident in the ruthless duty of the critical historian has given me more trouble, or been carried through with more *His com-* reluctance, than this handling of De Quincey. I *pensations.* have to acknowledge a great, a very early, and a constantly continued indebtedness to him. I could, as was hinted at the beginning of this notice, compile a long and brilliant list of separate instances in which his Old-man-of-the-sea caprices have left him free to give admirable critical pronouncements. His suggestive and *protreptic*[1] quality cannot be overrated. On a philosophical point of criticism he is very rarely wrong, though even here he is too apt to labour the point, as in his deductions in the *Appraisal* from the true and important caution that "sublime" is a defective and delusive word for the subject of Longinus. But he is of those critics, too commonly to be found in the present stage of our inquiry, who are eminently *unsafe*—who require to be constantly sur-rounded with keepers and guards. I do not remember that Mr Matthew Arnold often, or ever, refers to De Quincey. But I cannot help thinking that, in his strictures on the English critics of his earlier time, he must often have had him in mind. He could not have charged him with narrow reading. He could not have charged him with mere insularity, or with flattery of his co-insulars. But he might easily have produced him,—and it would have been very difficult to get him out of the Arnoldian clutches—as a victim of that "eternal enemy of Art, Caprice."

There are few critics of whom we have been less allowed to

---

[1] The objection of some folk to this useful word may be perhaps accounted for by their spelling it "protrept*r*ic."

form a definite and well-grounded opinion, than of one of the most famous of the practitioners of the art in the first half of the nineteenth century. Some, I should

Lockhart.

hope, of the very unjust obloquy which used to rest on Lockhart for his "scorpion" quality has been removed by Mr Lang's *Life:* but of his more than thirty years of criticism not much more is accessible than what was public the day after his death. It is true that this—the main articles of it being the *Scott,* the *Burns,* the *Theodore Hook,* and the earlier *Peter's Letters*[1]—is a very goodly literary baggage indeed, and one which any man of letters might consent to have produced, at the cost of a large curtailment of his *peau de chagrin.* It is true, further, that great part of it puts Lockhart in the forefront of the critical army. But its criticism, like the mousquetaireship of Aramis, is

Difficulty with his criticism.

but of an interim order; and of the great body of anonymous reviewing, wherein at once the sting and the strength of his critical powers must have been revealed, we have but few instances even indirectly authenticated, as he has now been cleared of the famous *Quarterly* review of Tennyson's early work.[2] Eking this further with indications from letters and the like, we shall find in Lockhart a notable though a more accomplished instance of the class of critic to which, on the other side, Jeffrey also belonged. He is differentiated from Jeffrey by a harder, if clearer and stronger, intellect, by more critical system, and, no doubt, by less amiability of temper. He had formed his taste by a deeper and wider education, he possessed a better style, and he had, as his non-critical work shows, far more imagination.

The "Tennyson" paper, though not his own, was published under his editorship, and it represents the school of criticism to which he belongs, very far from at the best, but far also from at the worst. This worst would have been nearly reached by him, if we could

The Tennyson review not his.

---

[1] This book, which often occurs in catalogues at a very moderate price, may be strongly recommended to intelligent book-buyers. *Janus,* another waif, in which he and Wilson collabor-ated, is less interesting.

[2] For this, with the earlier achievement on Keats, has now (1910) been indisputably fathered, in the *Quarterly* itself, on Croker.

believe the earlier "Keats" article in *Blackwood* to be his
—a charge which, fortunately, is also pretty certainly to be
transferred to the heavily laden shoulders of Croker. Undoubtedly Lockhart was capable of indulging in that style
of sneering insolence which, though it is intellectually at a
higher level by far than the other style of hectoring abuse, is
nearly as offensive, and less excusable because it requires and
denotes this very intellectual superiority. But the author of
the Tennyson article displays neither. He is merely polite and
even good-tempered for the most part; and it is constantly
necessary to remember, that if there were beauties which ought
to have drawn his eyes away from the faults, there were, in
the earlier versions of these early poems, faults enough to draw
the eyes of any critic of his stamp away from the beauties.
There were trivial and mawkish things which have disappeared
entirely; flawed things which have been reforged into perfect
ring and temper; things, in the main precious, which were
marred by easily removable disfigurements. From unwilling-
ness to accept the later stages of a movement of which he
had joyfully shared the earlier, Lockhart could not have been
cleared, but Croker can.

In Lockhart's own undoubted work little requires apology.
Quite early, in *Peter's Letters*, he had defended the genius
of Coleridge against his detractors with admirable
On Cole-
ridge, Burns, vigour and sense. He is extraordinarily good on
Scott, and Burns. The abundant critical remarks which he has
Hook. interspersed in the *Life of Scott* itself, afford a wonderful exhibition of sensitiveness and fineness of taste, with
nothing to be set on the other side except the very pardonable
tendency to undervalue and grudge a little in the case of the
non-Scottish novels. But an almost better instance of Lockhart's critical power, on the biographical as well as the literary
side, is to be found in his article on Theodore Hook, with its
remarkable welcome of the new school of Victorian novelists,
which shows that his want of receptivity, as regards new
poetry, did not extend to prose fiction.

On the whole, we have few better examples than Lockhart,
if we have any, of the severer type of critic—of the newer

school, but with a certain tendency towards the older—a little
His general too prone, when his sympathies were not specially
critical enlisted, to think that his subjects would be " nane
character. the waur of a hanging "—a little too quick to ban,
and too slow to bless—but acute, scholarly, logical, wide enough
in range, when his special prejudices did not interfere, and
entitled to some extent to throw the responsibility of those prejudices on the political and literary circumstances of his time.

If the pixies had not doomed Hartley Coleridge [1] to a career
(or an absence of one) so strange and in a manner so sad, there
Hartley would pretty certainly have been a case, not merely of
Coleridge. poetic son succeeding poetic father, against the alleged
impossibility or at least non-occurrence of which succession
he himself mildly protested, but of critical faculty likewise
descending in almost the highest intensity from father to son.
And the not ungracious creatures might plead that, after all,
opportunity was not lacking. During that strange latter half
of his lifetime when he fulfilled, more literally than happily,
the poetic prophecy of Wordsworth in his childhood, he
seems to have had very little other occupation—indoors at
least—besides criticism actual and practical. But, with the
inveterate Coleridgean habit of " marginalling," and the equally
inveterate one of never turning the Marginalia to any solid
account, the results of this practice, save in the case of the
famous copy of Anderson's *Poets* (shabbiest and slovenliest
treasure-house of treasures immortal and priceless!) which
bears his father's and uncle's notes as well as his own, are
mostly Sibylline Leaves *after* the passage of the blast. When
Forlorn con- a man commits his critical thoughts to the narrow
dition of his margins of weekly newspapers *unbound*—indeed, if
criticism. he had them bound, the binder would no doubt have
exterminated them after the fashion of his ruthless race—he
might just as well write on water, and better on sand. Still,
the *disjecta membra* do exist—in the *Biographia Borealis,* or
Northern Worthies, to some extent; in the Essays, collected by

---

[1] *Works,* 7 vols. (London, 1851-52),   *Worthies,* 3. An eighth, of *Fragments,*
ed. Derwent Coleridge; *Poems and*   was promised; but if it ever appeared,
Memoir, 2 vols.; *Essays,* 2; *Northern*   I have not seen it.

the pious, if sometimes a little patronising, care of his brother Derwent, to a much greater; and perhaps in one instance only, the "Massinger and Ford" Introduction, after a fashion in a manner finished. Yet even here the intended critical *coda* is wanting, and the inevitable critical divagation too much present.

But in all this there is also present, after a fashion of which I can remember no other instance, the evidences of a critical genius which not only did not give itself, but which absolutely refused itself, a chance. Hartley Coleridge has never, I think, been the subject of much study: but a more tempting matter for "problem" lovers can hardly exist. Nothing in his *known* history accounts for the refusal. He was admittedly not temperate: but no one has ever pretended that he was the slave of drink to the extent to which his father was the slave of opium; his interest in literature was intense and undying—that every page that he ever wrote shows beyond possibility of doubt; and the fineness of his critical perceptions is equally indubitable. But the extraordinary and, I think, unparalleled intellectual indolence— or rather intellectual paralysis—which beset him, seems to have prevented him not merely from writing, but from that mere reading in which men, too indolent to make any great use of it, constantly indulge as a mere pleasure and pastime. He confesses frankly that he had read very little indeed: and this, though he had been almost all his life within reach of, and for great part of it actually under the same roof with, Southey's hardly equalled library. This ignorance leads him wrong not only on matters of fact, but also on matters of opinion: indeed, he seldom goes wrong, except when he does not know enough about the matter.

Its quality.

Defects

It is unfortunate that we have hardly anything finished from him in the critical way, except the "Massinger and Ford" and the Essays he wrote for *Blackwood*, while these last bear such a strong impress of Wilson's own manner[1]

[1] "The Professor," it is hardly necessary to say, was an early and lifelong friend and neighbour of Hartley, whom he seems to have regarded with particular affection.

that it is impossible not to think them Christopherically
sophisticated. In the *Northern Worthies* he professes not to
meddle with Criticism at all, or to touch it very little. In the
"Marvell," however, the "Bentley," the "Ascham," the
"Mason," the "Roscoe," and the "Congreve," he is better than
his word, and gives some excellent criticism as a seasoning to
the biography. One cannot, indeed, but grudge the time that
and ex- he spends on such worthless stuff as *Elfrida* and
amples. *Caractacus,* but we must remember that in that
generation of transition, the generation of Milman and Talfourd
earlier, of Henry Taylor and others later, the possibility of
reviving the serious drama was a very important subject
indeed. Hartley, whose reverence for his father is as pleasant
as his affection for his mother, evidently thought much of
Remorse and *Zapolya,* and might probably, if he ever could
have got his will to face any hedge, have tried such things
himself. On Congreve he is nearly at his best: and his essay
certainly ought to be included in that unique volume of
variorum critical documents on the Restoration Drama, which
somebody some day may have the sense to edit.

But he would be neither Hartley nor Coleridge if he were
not best in the *Marginalia,* good as the "Massinger and Ford"
introduction is in parts. The "Anderson" notes, and those on
Shakespeare, deserve the most careful reading: and I shall be
much surprised if any competent reader fails to see that the
man who wrote them at least had it in him to have made no
inadequate thirdsman to his father[1] and Hazlitt.

Very few people nowadays, in all probability, think much
of "bright, broken Maginn"[2] as a critic; and of those few
Maginn. some perhaps associate his criticism chiefly with
such examples of it as the article on Grantley
Berkeley, which almost excused the retaliation on its unfor-

---

[1] It is, perhaps, not officious to subjoin a reminder that we have the
curious pleasure of S. T. C.'s notes on
Hartley in the *Biographia Borealis.*
One of these — an objection to the
phrase "prose Shakespeare" for Heywood—is very odd, as apparently showing forgetfulness of the fact that the
phrase is not his eldest son's, but his
oldest friend's.

[2] *Miscellanies, Prose and Verse,* by
William Maginn, ed. R. W. Montagu.
2 vols., London, 1885.

tunate publisher, or the vain attempt to "bluff" out the Keats
matter by ridiculing *Adonais*. Even as to most of his exercitations in this very unlovely department, or rather corruption,
of our art, there is perhaps something to be said for him. He
fights, as a rule, not with Lockhart's dagger of ice-brook
temper, nor with Wilson's smashing bludgeon, but with a kind
of horse-whip, stinging indeed enough, but letting out no
life and breaking no bones at worst and heaviest, at lightest
not much more than switching playfully. Had there,
however, been nothing to plead for him but this, there would
have been no room for him here. But his favourite way of
proceeding in his lighter critical articles, though not invented
by himself (as it was not of course invented even by Canning
and his merry men, from whom Maginn took it), the method
His parody- of parody-criticism[1] is, if not a very high variety,
criticisms and especially not in the least a convincing one,
still one which perhaps deserves a few lines of reference, and
of which he was a really great master.

Still, a mere allusion would suffice for them if they stood
alone, and Maginn's paragraph might be completed by observ-
and more ing that he has repaired the absolutely false state-
serious ment, that "Michael Angelo was a very indifferent
efforts. poet," by the far too true one, that "Any modern
sermon, after the Litany of the Church of England, is an
extreme example of the bathos."[2] But his *Essay on Dr
Farmer's Learning of Shakespeare*,[3] and the much shorter but
still substantial *Lady Macbeth*,[4] are by no means to be omitted
or merely catalogued. These two pieces show that Maginn, if
only he could have kept his hand from the glass, and his pen

---

[1] They are scattered all over the
Memoirs of Morgan O'Doherty, and
often form independent items of the
Miscellanies. The style has borne good
fruit since in Aytoun and Martin's *Bon
Gaultier Ballads* (1845), in Aytoun's
Firmilian (1854), and in the work of
Calverley and Traill (*v. sup.*)

[2] It would have been interesting to
hear Maginn on the Revised Version

"after" the Authorised.

[3] Ed. cit., ii. 1-116. Let me guard
carefully against being supposed myself to speak disrespectfully of Farmer,
whose Essay will be found recently
reprinted in Mr Nichol Smith's collection. Farmer is at least as right
against *his* adversaries as Maginn
against him.

[4] Ibid., pp. 117-144.

from mere gambols or worse, not only might but would have been one of the most considerable of English critics. The goodness, and the various goodness, of both is all the more remarkable because Maginn seems to have owed little or nothing to the influence of Coleridge. Almost the only fault in the first is the hectoring incivility with which Farmer himself is spoken of, and this, as we have seen, is but too old a fault with critics, while it was specially prevalent at this period, and our own is far from guiltless of it. But the sense and learning of the paper are simply admirable: and Maginn's possession of almost the last critical secret is shown by his wise restraint in arguing that Farmer's argument for Shakespeare's ignorance is invalid, without going on, as some would do, and have done, to argue the poet omniscient by learning as well as by genius. As for the *Lady Macbeth*, the sense is reinforced, and the learning (here not necessary) replaced, by taste and subtlety of the most uncommon kind. I do not know a piece of dramatic character - criticism (no, not the thousand - times - praised thing in *Wilhelm Meister*) more unerringly delicate and right. And this man, not, as the cackle goes, by "neglect of genius," by the wicked refusal of patrons to patronise, not by anything of the kind, but by sheer lack of self-command, wasted his time in vulgar journalism at the worst, and with rare exceptions[1] in mere sport-making at the best !

We have been occupied since the beginning of this chapter by men who, save in the case of Hartley Coleridge, were closely connected with the periodical press, and owed almost all their communication with the public to it. We now come to a pair, greater than any of them, who were indeed " contributors," but not contributors mainly.

Another great name is added, by Macaulay, to the long and pleasant list of our examples how "Phibbus car" has, in unexpected and puzzling but always interesting ways, "made or

[1] In prose such as *The Story without a Tail*, and in verse such as *The Pewter Quart*, with at least some others.

marred the " not always " foolish Fates " of critics and criticism.

Macaulay. When we first meet him as a critic of scarcely four-and-twenty, in the articles contributed to *Knight's Quarterly*, we may feel inclined to say that nobody whom we have yet met (except perhaps Southey) can have had at that age a wider range of reading, and nobody at all an apparently keener relish for it. He is, what Southey was not, a competent *His excep-* scholar in the classics; he knows later (if unfortun- *tional com-* ately not quite earlier) English literature extra- *petence in* ordinarily well; he has, what was once common *some ways.* with us, but was in his days getting rare, and has since grown rarer, a pretty thorough knowledge of Italian, and he is certainly not ignorant of French (though perhaps at no time did he thoroughly relish its literature), while he is later to add Spanish and German. But he does not only know, he loves. There is already much personal rhetoric and mannerism especially in the peroration of his review of Mitford's *Greece*, where he reproaches that Tory historian with his neglect of Greek literature. But it is quite evidently sincere. He displayed similar enthusiasm, combined in a manner not banal, in his earlier article on Dante, and he shows wonderful and prophetic knowledge of at least parts of literature in his paper on the Athenian Orators, as well as in the later article on History, belonging to his more recognised literary period. From a candidate of this kind, but just qualified to be a deacon of the Church in years, we may surely expect a *The early* deacon in the craft of criticism before very long, *articles.* particularly when he happens to possess a ready-made style of extraordinarily, and not merely, popular qualities. There are some who would say that this expectation was fully realised: I am afraid I cannot quite agree with them, and it is my business here to show why.

We have said that, even in these early exercitations, Macaulay's characteristics appear strongly: and among not *His draw-* the least strongly appearing are some from which, *backs.* unless a man disengages himself, he shall very hardly become a really great literary critic. The first of these is the well-known and not seriously to be denied tendency, not merely

to "cocksureness," but to a sweeping indulgence in superlatives, a "knock - me - down - these - knaves" gesticulation,
which is the very negation of the critical attitude. Even the
sound, the genuine, the well-deserved literary preferences
above referred to lose not a little by this tone of swaggering sententiousness in their expression; and they lose a
great deal more by the simultaneous appearance of the hopelessly uncritical habit of making the whites more dazzling
by splashing the deepest black alongside of them. The very
eulogy of Dante as a whole seems to Macaulay incomplete
without an elaborate pendant of depreciation of Petrarch,
while "Tasso, Marino, Guarini, and Metastasio" are swept
into a dust-bin of common disdain, and we are told that the
Secchia Rapita, "the best poem of its kind in some respects,"
is "painfully diffuse and languid," qualities which one might
have thought destructive of any "bestness."

It is of less importance—because the fault is so common
as to be almost universal—that the "Mitford" displays very

*The practi-
cal choking
of the good
seed.*

strong political prejudice, which certainly affects,
as it should not do, the literary judgment. Mitford
may have been an irregular and capricious writer,
but the worst vices of the worst Rymer - and -
Dennis criticism appear in the description of him as "bad."
His style could not possibly be so described by a fair critic who
did not set out with the major premiss that whatever is unusual
is bad. And not only here, but even in the purely literary essays,
even at their most enthusiastically literary pitch, we may, I
think, without any unfairness, perceive an undertone, an undercurrent, of preference for the not purely literary sides of the
matter—for literature as it bears on history, politics, manners,
man, instead of for literature in itself and for itself.

With the transference from *Knight's* to the *Edinburgh*, which
was political and partisan-political, or nothing, these seeds of
evil grew and flourished, and to some extent choked the others.
The "Milton," the "Machiavelli," the early and, for a long time,
uncollected "Dryden," serve as very hot-beds for them. All
three are, as the French would say, *jonchés* with superlatives,
arranged side by side in contrast like that of a zebra. The

"Dryden"—a very tempting subject for this kind of work—is not the worst critically; indeed it is perhaps the best. It is, at any rate, far the most really literary, and it may not be unfair to think that this had something to do with the fact that Macaulay did not include it in the collected *Essays*.

The real *locus classicus*, however, for Macaulay's criticism is perhaps to be found, not in his published works at all, but *His literary surveys in the Letters.* in the letters which he wrote to Flower Ellis from Calcutta,[1] taken in connection with their context in Sir George Trevelyan's book, and especially with the remarkable avowal which occurs in a letter, a very little later, to Macvey Napier. Macaulay, as is well known, availed himself of his Indian sojourn to indulge in almost a debauch of reading, especially in pure literature, and especially (again) in the classics. And his reflections to Ellis, a kindred spirit, are of the most interesting kind. He tells his correspondent that he has gone back to Greek literature with a passion quite astonishing to himself. He had been enraptured with Italian, little less pleased with Spanish, but when he went back to Greek he felt as if he had never known before what intellectual enjoyment was. It is impossible to imagine a happier critical *diathesis:* and the individual symptoms confirm it. Admiration of Æschylus is practically a passport for a man claiming poetical taste: admiration of Thucydides holds the same place in prose. And Macaulay puts them both *super æthera.* But it is a tell-tale that his admiration for Thucydides (of whom he says he had formerly not thought much) seems to have been determined by his own recent attention to "historical researches and political affairs." He does full justice to Lucian. He is capital on Niebuhr: a good deal less capital on the Greek Romances; for though Achilles Tatius is not impeccable in taste and exceeding peccable in morality, it is absurd to call his book "detestable trash." Perhaps he is hard on Statius as compared with Lucan: but here taste is free. It is more difficult to excuse him for the remark that St Augustine in his *Confessions* (a book not without interest) "expresses himself in the style of a field-preacher." The

[1] *Life*, p. 309 *sq.*, ed. cit.

present writer is not fond of conventicles, either house or hedge. But if he knew of a field-preacher who preached as St Augustine writes, he fears he might be tempted astray.

And then, after the six months' voyage home in the slow *His con-* *Lord Hungerford* (which must have been six months' *fession.* hard reading, though not penal), comes the great avowal to Macvey Napier, now editor of the *Edinburgh :*—

> You cannot suspect me of any affectation of modesty : and you will therefore believe me that I tell you what I sincerely think, when I say that I am not successful in analysing the effect of works of genius. I have written several things on historical, political, and moral questions of which, on the fullest reconsideration, I am not ashamed, and by which I should be willing to be estimated ; but *I have never written a page of criticism on poetry or the fine arts which I would not burn if I had the power.* Hazlitt used to say of himself, "I am nothing if not critical." The case with me is exactly the reverse ; I have a strong and acute enjoyment of works of the imagination, but I have never habituated myself to dissect them. . . . Trust to my knowledge of myself ; I never in my life was more certain of anything than of what I tell you, and I am sure that Lord Jeffrey will tell you exactly the same.[1]

Such a deliberate judgment on himself by such a man, close on the "age of wisdom,"[2] after fifteen years' constant literary practice, is practically final ; but probably not a few readers of Sir George's book felt, as the present writer did, that it merely confirms an opinion formed by themselves long before they ever read it.

At any rate, in nearly all the best known *Essays* the literary interest dwindles and the social-historic grows. I *The Essays.* do not object, as some do, to the famous "Robert Montgomery." This sort of criticism ought not to be done too often : and no one but a Dennis of the other kind enjoys doing it, except when the criminal's desert is of peculiar richness. But it has to be done sometimes, and it is here done scientifically, without rudeness I think, with as much justice[3] as need be "for the good of the people," and well.

---

[1] *Life*, p. 343 ed. cit.
[2] He was thirty-eight.
[3] One of the *in*justices is curious

from a man of Scottish blood, though every Englishman would commit it, as I own I should have done till very

Still, it is not in the hangman's drudgery, it is in the herald's good office, that Macaulay's critical weakness shows. There are some who, in all good faith and honest indignation, will doubtless cry "What! is there no literary interest in the "Milton" itself or in the "Bunyan"? Certainly there is. But, in the first case, let the Devil's Advocate's devil (it is too easy for his chief) remind us that there is very strong party feeling in both—that no less a person than Mr Matthew Arnold denied criticism to the "Milton"—that the author of the "Bunyan" himself puts in the forefront of his praise of *The Pilgrim's Progress* its "strong *human* interest," and that he goes on to make one of his too frequent uncritical contrasts, and one of his very rare gross blunders of fact, as to the *Faerie Queene.* And, besides, he was still in the green tree, as he was also when he gave the, in part, excellent criticism of the "Byron," where the sweeping general lines of the sketch of the poetry of "correctness" follow those of some inferior but more original surveys of Macaulay's editor Jeffrey. And though there is interesting criticism in the "Boswell," it is pushed to the wall by the (I fear it must be said) ignoble desire to "dust the varlet's jacket," and pay Croker off in the *Edinburgh* for blows received at St Stephen's.[1]

Indeed it would be quite idle to stipulate that anything here said to the detriment of Macaulay's criticism is said relatively, if there were not a sort of doubtless honest folk who seem to think that denying a man the riches of Crœsus means that he is penniless and in debt. Macaulay *was* a critic on his day—a good one for a long time, and perhaps always a great one *in potentia.* But his criticism was slowly edged out by its rivals or choked by its own parasitic plants. It

---

late in my reviewing life. It is the satire on the comparison of a woman's eyes to dew on "a bramble," which of course in England means a *bush,* and in Scotland a *berry.* I wonder whether R. L. S. meant to appease the other poor Robert's *manes* when he wrote the phrase "eyes of gold and bramble-dew," and I should have asked him had Fate permitted.

[1] It may seem whimsical: but I doubt whether any one of a really critical *ethos* would put down, even in his private diary, that a private enemy and a hostile reviewer was "a bad, a very bad man, a scandal to politics and letters." Criticism herself would, I think, condescend to give any of her favourite children's ears an Apollonian twitch.

occupies about a twentieth part (to adopt his own favourite
arithmetical method) of the Essay on Bacon, about one-tenth
of that on Temple.   In the famous piece on "Restoration
Drama" it is the moral and social, not the literary or even
the dramatic, side of the matter that interests Macaulay : and
in dealing with Addison himself, a man who, though not quite
literary or nothing, was certainly literary first of all, the purely
literary handling is entirely subordinated to other parts of
the treatment.   This may be a good thing or it may be a
bad thing: the *tendenz* - critics, and the criticism - of - life
critics, and the others, are quite welcome to take the first view
if they please.   But that it is a *thing;* that Macaulay himself acknowledged it, and that—despite his unsurpassed devotion to literature and his great performance therein—it must
affect our estimate of him, according to the schedules and
specifications of this book, is not, I think, deniable by any
honest inquirer.

A phenomenon by no means wholly dissimilar in kind, but
conditioned as to extent and degree by the differing tempera-
Similar   ments and circumstances of the two men, may be
dwindling seen in the criticism of Macaulay's great contem-
in Carlyle. porary, opposite, and corrective, Carlyle ; [1] and those
who care for such investigations might find it interesting to
compare both with the admitted instances of dwindling literary
interest—not critical but simply enjoying—in cases like that
of Darwin.   But leaving this extension as out of our province,
and returning to our two great men of letters themselves, we
shall find differences enough between them, here as elsewhere,
but a remarkable agreement in the gradual ascendancy obtained by anthropology over (in the old and good sense, not the
modern perversion) philology.   Carlyle had always the more
catholic, as Macaulay had the exacter, sense of literary form ;
but it may be suspected that at no time was the form chiefly
eloquent to either: and in Carlyle's attitude for many years
after the somewhat tardy commencement of his actual critical
career, something ominous may be observed.   It may seem

---

[1] Carlyle was an older man than   original work later.
Macaulay, but he began to publish

strange and impious to some of those who acknowledge no greater debt for mental stimulation to any one than to Carlyle, and who rank him among the greatest in all literature, to find one who joins them in this homage, and perhaps outgoes most of them therein, questioning his position as a critic. Let us therefore examine the matter somewhat carefully.

Carlyle's criticism, like his other qualities, interpenetrates nearly all his work, from *Sartor* to the "Kings of Norway": it appears in the *Life of Schiller*,[1] in *Heroes and Hero-Worship*, in *Past and Present*, in the *Life of Sterling*, while it *fuliginates* itself to share in the general fuliginousness of the *Latter-day Pamphlets*, and is strewn even over the greater biographies and histories of the *Cromwell* and the *Frederick*. We shall, however, lose nothing, and gain much, by confining ourselves mainly to the literary constituents of the great collection of *Essays* in this place. The discussion can be warranted to be well leavened with remembrance of the other work.

Who indeed is more rememberable than Carlyle? Of late years, partly from having read them so much, partly from having so much else to read, I have left parts of these Essays unopened for a long time. Yet, in looking them through for the purpose of this present writing, I have found myself constantly, even in the least familiar and famous parts, able to shut the book and complete clause, sentence, or even to some extent paragraph, like a text, or a collect, or a tag of Horace or Virgil. But in this re-reading it has struck me, even more forcibly than of old, how much Carlyle's strictly critical inclinations, if not his strictly critical faculties, waned as he grew older. In the earlier Essays—those written before and during the momentous period of the Craigenputtock sojourn—there is a great deal of purely or almost purely literary criticism of an excellent kind—sober and vigorous, fresh and well disciplined. There may be, especially in regard to Richter and

[1] Any one anxious really to appreciate Carlyle's *potentia* as a literary critic may be specially commended to this. It was written, of course, not merely before he developed his own style, but before the freer modern criticism had been largely practised by anybody except apart-dwelling stars like Coleridge. But it brands the author as a great critic *if he chose*. He did not wholly choose: and, later, he refused.

Goethe, a slightly exaggerated backing of the German side. But it is hardly more than slightly exaggerated, and the treatment generally is of the most thorough kind compatible with an avowed tendency towards "philosophical" rather than "formal" criticism.   Professor Vaughan was certainly justified in including part of the *Goethe* in his selected specimens of English criticism[1] for its general principles and examples of method.   Nor is Carlyle less to be praised for his discharge of the more definitely practical part of the critic's business. He is thought of generally as "splenetic and rash": but it would be impossible to find anywhere a more good-humoured, and (in parts at least) a more judicial censure than that of William Taylor's preposterous *German Poetry*,[2] or a firmer, completer, and at the same time less excessive condemnation than that of the equally preposterous method of Croker's original *Boswell*.   We may see already that the critic evidently prefers matter to form, and that he is by no means quite catholic even in his fancy for matter.   But he has a right to be this ; and altogether there are few things in English criti-

The earlier cism better worth reading, marking, and learning, *Essays.*   by the novice, than the literary parts of these earlier volumes of *Essays*.[3]   It may be that the channels in which his ink first flowed (especially that rather carefully, not to say primly, banked and paved one of the *Edinburgh*) imposed some restriction on him ; it may be that he found the yet unpublished, or just published, *Sartor* a sufficient "lasher" to draw off the superfluous flood and foam of his fancy.   But the facts are the facts.

And so, too, it is the fact that, later, he draws away from *The later.*   the attitude of purely literary consideration, if he does not, as he sometimes still later does, take up one actually hostile to this.   The interesting "Characteristics"

---

[1] London, 1896.

[2] Not that all Taylor's ideas were preposterous.   He and others of the Norwich School would make a good excursus.   Even the "quotidian and stimulant" theory, of which Carlyle makes such fun, might have a chance

with Carlyle's own "highest aim of a nation."

[3] More especially those on the *Nibelungenlied* and Early German Poetry generally.   These could hardly have been better done.

(as early as 1831) is one of the places most to be recommended
to people who want to know what Carlyle really was, and not
what divers more or less wise or unwise commentators have
said of him. The writer has flings at literary art—especially
conscious literary art — towards the beginning: afterwards
(which is still more significant) he hardly takes any notice of it
at all. In the much better known "Boswell," "Burns," and
"Scott"[1] Essays, his neglect of the purely literary side is again
the more remarkable, because it is not ostentatious. In the
"Diderot," dealing with a subject who was as much a man of
letters first of all (though of very various and *applied* letters)
as perhaps any man in history, he cannot and does not neglect
that subject's literary performance; but the paper is evidence
of the very strongest how little of his real interest is bestowed
upon it. It is of the man Diderot—and of the man Diderot's
relation to, and illumination of, that condition of the French
mind and state of which some good folk have thought that
Carlyle knew nothing—that he is thinking, for this that he
is caring. Later still, he will select for his favourite subjects
people like Mirabeau, who had much better have written no
books at all, or Dr Francia, whose connection with literature
is chiefly limited to the fact of his having written one immortal
sentence. And this sentence, not having myself seen or
wished to see the works of Rengger, I have always suspected
that Carlyle or "Sauerteig" edited for him.[2]

And then things get worse. That invocation of the Devil
The attitude in the *Latter-day Pamphlets*,[3] "to fly away with
of the the poor Fine Arts," is indeed put off on "one of
Latter-day our most distinguished public men." But Carlyle
Pamphlets. avows sympathy with it. He even progresses
from it to the Platonic view that "Fiction" at all "is not

---

[1] As an out-and-out Scottite *and*
Carlylian, I would respectfully depre-
cate hasty judgment of this. It is a
crux ansata, and you may easily get
hold of the wrong handle.

[2] "O people of Paraguay! how long
will you continue idiots?" If a casual
half-breed really thus put politics and

life in a nut-shell, he was certainly
somebody.

[3] The different paging of the different
editions makes it useless to give exact
references. Nor are they wanted: for
the "Contents" and Indices of Carlyle's
works are ideal.

quite a permissible thing" — is "sparingly permissible" at any rate. "Homer" was meant for "history":[1] the arts were not "sent into the world to fib and dance." As for Literature more particularly, "if it continue to be the haven of expatriated spiritualisms," well: but "if it dwindle, as *is probable*, into mere merry-andrewism, windy twaddle, and feats of spiritual legerdemain," there "will be no hope for it." Its "regiment" is "extremely miscellaneous," "more a *canaille* than a regiment," and so forth. The "brave young British man" is adjured to be "rather shy of Literature than otherwise, for the present,"—a counsel which, it is well known, Mr Carlyle repeated in his Edinburgh Rectorial address sixteen years later. Nor did he ever alter the point of view which he had now taken up, either in book, or minor published work, or Letters, or autobiographic jottings, or those *Ana* which still flit on the mouths of men concerning his later years.

A man who speaks thus, and thinks thus, has perforce re-nounced the development of any skill that he may once have

The con-clusion of this matter. had in the analysis of the strands of the tight-rope, or the component drugs of the Cup of Abom-inations. Still less can he be expected to ex-patiate, with the true critic's delight, on the elegance with which the dancer pirouettes over vacancy, or on the iridescent rich-ness of the wine of Circe, as it moveth itself in the chalice. I do not know that—great critic, really, as he had been earlier and always might have been—the loss of his services in this function is much to be regretted. For he did other things which assuredly most merely literary critics could not have done: and not a few good workmen stepped forward, in the last thirty years of his life, to do the work which he thus left undone, not without some flouting and scorning of it. But, once more, the fact is the fact: and his estrangement from the task, like that of Macaulay, undoubtedly had something to do with the general critical poverty of the period of English literature, which was the most fertile and vigorous in the literary life of both.

Another of the very greatest gods of mid-nineteenth century

---

[1] Had he been reading Vico?

literature in England displays the slightly anti-critical turn
Thackeray. of his time still more curiously. It is one of the
oddest and most interesting of the many differences
between the two great masters of English prose fiction in the
mid-nineteenth century that, while there is hardly any critical
view of literature in Dickens, Thackeray is full of such views.[1]
He himself practised criticism early and late; and despite
the characteristic and perhaps very slightly affected depreciation of the business of "reading books and giving judgment
on them," which appears in *Pendennis* and other places, it is
quite clear that he pursued that business for love as well
as for money. Moreover, from first to last,—from his early
and long uncollected "High - Jinkish" exploits in *Fraser* to
the *Roundabout Papers*,—he produced critical work from which
an anthology of the very finest critical quality, and by no
means small in bulk, might be extracted with little pains
and no little pleasure. If he "attains not unto the first
three," it is I think only from the effect of the reaction or
ebb that we note in this chapter, and from a certain deficiency
His one in that catholic sureness which a critic of the
critical highest kind can hardly lack. Nobody is obliged
weakness to like everything good; probably no one *can* like
everything good. But, in case of disliking, the critic must
be able either to give reasons (like those of Longinus in regard
to the *Odyssey*) relatively, if not positively, satisfactory: or
he must frankly admit that his objections are based upon
something extra-literary, and that therefore, in strictness, he
has no literary judgment to give.

Now Thackeray does not do this. He was not, perhaps,
very good at giving reasons at all: and he was specially
affected by that confusion of literary and extra-literary considerations from which all times suffer, but from which his own
time and party—the moderate Liberals of the mid-nineteenth
century in England—suffered more than any time or party
known to us. Practically we have his confession, in the famous
and dramatically paradoxical sentence on Swift, that, though

[1] Since the text was written, full *anepecdota*, have appeared in Messrs
collections of his criticism, with many Macmillan's and the "Oxford" editions.

he is the greatest of the Humourist company, " I say we should
hoot him." The literary critic who has "got salvation" knows
that he must never do this — that whatever his dislike for
the man — Milton, Racine, Swift, Pope, Rousseau, Byron,
Wordsworth (I purposely mix up dislikes which are mine
with those which are not)—he must not allow them to colour
his judgment of the writer. *Gulliver* may be a terrible, humil-
iating, heart-crushing indictment, but nothing can prevent it
from being a glorious book: and so on. Now Thackeray, by
virtue of that quality of his, different sides of which have
been—with equal lack of wisdom perhaps—labelled "cyni-
cism" and "sentimentality," was wont to be very "peccant
in this kind," and it, with some, though less, purely political
or religious prejudice, and a little caprice, undoubtedly flawed
his criticism.

When, however, these outside disturbers kept quiet, as they
very often did, Thackeray's criticism is astonishingly catholic
and his and sound, and sometimes he was able to turn the
excellence. disturbers themselves out. He had a most unhappy
and Philistine dislike of the High Church movement: yet the
passage in *Pendennis* on *The Christian Year* is one of the sacred
places of sympathetic notice. The well-known *locus* in *The New-
comes*, as to the Colonel's horror at the new literary gods, shows
how sound Thackeray's own faith in them was: yet he, least
of all men, could be accused of forsaking the old. He had that
generous appreciation of his own fellow-craftsmen by which
novelists have been honourably distinguished from poets:
though not all poets have been jealous, and though, from
Richardson downwards, there have been very jealous novelists.
If there were more criticism like the famous passage on Dumas
in the *Roundabouts*, like great part of the solid *English
Humourists*, like much elsewhere, our poor Goddess would
not be liable to have her comeliness confounded with the
ugliness of her personators, as is so often the case. And his
is no promiscuous and undiscriminating generosity. He can
"like nicely," and does.

Still, though he has sometimes escaped the disadvantages of
his temperament, he has often succumbed to those of his time;

and what those disadvantages were cannot be better shown than by an instance to which we may now turn.

When, in writing a little book upon Mr Matthew Arnold,[1] the present writer spoke severely of the state of English criticism *Blackwood,* between 1830 and 1860, some protests were made, as *in 1849, on* though the stricture were an instance of that "un- *Tennyson.* fairness to the last generation" which has been frequently noticed, and invariably deprecated and condemned here. I gave, on that occasion, some illustrative instances;[2] I may here add another and very remarkable one, which I had not at that time studied. In April 1849 there appeared in *Blackwood's Magazine* an article of some length on Tennyson's work, which at the time consisted of the revised and consolidated *Poems* of 1842 (still further castigated in the one-volume form, so familiar to the youth of my generation), and of *The Princess.* This article[3] is not in the least uncivil—"Maga" had now outgrown her hoydenish ways: but we do not find the maturer, yet hardly less attractive, graces of the *trentaine.* The writer proclaims himself blind and deaf at every moment. He misses—he positively blasphemes—the beauty of many things that Wilson had frankly welcomed. He selects for praise such second- or third-rate matter as *The Talking Oak. Claribel,* not Tennyson's greatest thing, but the very Tennyson in germ, "leaves as little impression on the living ear as it would on the sleeper beneath." The exquisite *Ode to Memory,* with all its dreamy loveliness, is "an utter failure throughout," it is a "mist" "coloured by no ray of beauty." But the critic is made most unhappy by the song "A spirit haunts the last year's bowers." It is "an odious piece of pedantry." Its admirable harmony, at once as delightful and as true to true English prosody as verse can be, extracts from him the remark, "What metre, Greek or Roman, Russian or Chinese, it was intended to imitate, we have no care to inquire: the man was writing English, and had no justifiable pretence for tortur-

---

[1] Edinburgh, 1899, p. 59.

[2] Ibid., note, p. 10.

[3] It is all the more remarkable that the writer was "not the first comer." He was, I believe, William Smith, the author of *Thorndale* and other books much prized by good judges, a man of great talents, wide reading, and admirable character.

ing our ears with verse like this." The *Lady of Shalott* is
"intolerable," "odious," "irritating," "an annoyance," "a
caprice": anybody who likes it "must be far gone in dilettanteism." Refrains are "melancholy iterations." With a rather
pleasing frankness the critic half confesses that he knows he
ought to like the *Marianas*, but wholly declares that he does
not. He likes the *Lotos-Eaters*, so that he cannot have been
congenitally deprived of *all* the seven senses of Poetry; but he
cannot even form an idea what "the horse with wings kept
down by its heavy rider" means in the *Vision of Sin*, and he
cannot away with the *Palace* and the *Dream*, now purged, let
it be remembered, of their "balloons" and Groves-of-Blarney
stanzas, and in their perfect beauty. "Giving himself away,"
in the fatal fashion of such censors, he does not merely in effect
pronounce them both with rare exceptions "bad and unreadable," but selects the magnificent line—

"Throb through the ribbed stone"—

for special ridicule. "To hear one's own voice throbbing
through the ribbed stone is a startling novelty in acoustics,"
which simply shows, not merely that he had never heard his
own or any other voice singing under a vaulted roof, but that
he had not the mite of imagination necessary for conceiving
the effect. With *The Princess*, as less *pure* poetry—good as
it is—he is less unhappy; but he is not at all comfortable
there.

To do our critic justice, however, though it makes his case
a still more leading one, he is not one of the too common
carpers who string a reasonless "I don't like this" to a tell-
tale "I can't understand that," until they can twist a ball (not
of cowslips) to fling at a poet. He has, or thinks he has, a
theory: and in some respects his theory is not a bad one.
He admits that "the subtle play of imagination" may be "the
most poetical part of a poem," that it may "constitute the difference between poetry and prose," which is good enough. But he
thinks you may have too much of this good thing, that it may
be "too much divorced from those sources of interest which
affect all mankind"; and he thinks, further, that this divorce

has taken place, not merely in Tennyson, but in Keats and in
Shelley. Yet, again, as has been indeed already made evident,
he has not in the least learnt the secret of that prosodic
freedom, slowly broadened down from precedent to precedent of
early Middle English writers, and Chaucer, and the Balladists,
and Spenser, and Shakespeare, and Milton, and Coleridge, which
it is the glory of the nineteenth century to have perfected. And
he detests the new poetic diction, aiming at the utmost reach of
visual as well as musical appeal, which came with this freedom.
His recoil from the "jingling rhythm" throws him with a
shudder against the "resplendent gibberish." In other words,
he is not at focus: he is outside. He can neither see nor hear:
and therefore he cannot judge.

But others' eyes and ears were opening, though slowly, and
with indistinct results, at first.

I hardly know a book more interesting to the real student
of real criticism than George Brimley's *Essays*.[1] That it gives
George Brimley. us, with Matthew Arnold's earliest work, the first
courses of the new temple of English Criticism is
something, but its intrinsic attraction is its chief. The writer
was apparently able to devote his short but not unhappy life,
without let or hindrance other than that of feeble health, to
literature; he was unhampered by any distracting desire to
create; he could judge and enjoy with that almost uncanny
calmness which often results, in happy dispositions, from the
beneficent effect of the *mal physique,* freed from the aggravation
of the *mal moral*.[2] He has idols; but he breaks away from
them, if he does not quite break them. He puts no others
in their places, as Arnold did too often: and, like Dryden
(though they had no other point of resemblance than in both
being admirable critics, and both members of Trinity College,
Cambridge), he never goes wrong without coming right, with
a force and vehemence of leap only intensified by his recoil.
In his best work, what should be the famous, and is, to those

---

[1] My copy is the 2nd ed. Mr W. G.
Clark's preface to the 1st is dated "Ap.
1858," rather less than a year after
Brimley's death.

[2] Cf. Chesterfield's profound remark

to Mme. de Mauconseil, on Christmas
Day 1755: *Il me semble que le mal
physique attendrit autant que le mal
moral endurcit le cœur.*

who know it, the delightful, Essay on Tennyson, we have a thing profitable at once for example, for reproof, and for instruction, as few critical things are.

We find him at the opening a little joined to one idol, that apparently respectable, but infinitely false, god, the belief that the poet must somehow or other deal with modern life.[1] Even from this point of view he will not give up Tennyson, but he apologises for him, and he colours nearly all his remarks on at least the early *Poems* by the apologies. He cannot shake himself quite free. He sees the beauty of *Claribel:* but he will not allow its beauty to be its sole duty. It "is not quite certain what the precise feeling of it is," and "no poem ought to admit of such a doubt." No music of verse, no pictorial power, "will enable a reader to care for such 'creatures of the fancy'" as Margaret or Eleanore, as the Sea Fairies, and many

His Essay on Tennyson.

others. "*If* expression were the highest aim of poetry," *Mariana* would be consummate: but—— ! Mr Tennyson "moved in the centre of the most distinguished young men of the University," "yet his poems present faint evidences of this," strange to say ! *The Miller's Daughter*, and *The Gardener's Daughter*, and *The May Queen* are dwelt on at great length, and with an evident feeling that here is something you can recommend to a practical friend who cannot embrace day-dreams. *Mariana in the South* should "connect itself more clearly with a person brought before the mind"—with a certificate of birth, let us say, and something about her parentage, and the bad man who left her, and the price of beans and garlic in the next village. *The Lady of Shalott* "eliminates all human interest." *Fatima*, justly admired, "has neither beginning, middle, or end." *The Palace of Art* has "no adequate *dramatic* presentation of the mode in which the great law of humanity works out its processes in the soul." [So lyric poets, we understand, are *not* entitled to speak lyrically: but must write drama !] And, greatest shock of all, *The Dream of Fair Women* is

---

[1] This idol had already had notice to quit. The Essay is of 1855, when it originally appeared in *Cambridge Essays*. Matthew Arnold's admirable *Preface* is two years older.

not so much as mentioned. When Brimley wrote it had long shaken off its earlier crudities, — had attained its final symmetry. It was there, entire and perfect, from the exquisite opening, through the matchless blended shiftings of life and literature, woven into one passionate whole, to those last two stanzas which give the motto of Life itself from youth to age, the *raison d'être* of Heaven, the undying sting of Hell, the secret of the peace that grows on the soul through Purgatory. And the critic says nothing about it!

Yet he has justified his instinct—if not quite his cleared vision—from the first. Of *Claribel* itself, of the *Marianas*, of *The Lotos-Eaters*, of the *Palace*, he has given analytic appreciations so enthusiastic, and at the same time so just, so solidly thought, and so delicately phrased, that there is nothing like them in Mr Arnold (who was rather grudging of such things), and nothing superior to them anywhere.

There is a priceless wavering, a soul-saving "suppose it were true?" in that "If" (most virtuous of its kind!), — "*If* expression were the highest aim of poetry," nor do I think it fanciful to see in the blasphemy about music and painting *not* saving "creatures of the fancy," a vain protest against the conviction that they *do*. Where he can get his prejudice and his judgment to run in couples—as in regard to *Locksley Hall*— the car sweeps triumphantly from start to finish, out of all danger from the turning pillar. When he comes to *Maud* (which the folk who had the prejudice, but not the judgment, were blaspheming at the very moment at which he wrote), he turns on them with a vehemence almost inconsistent—but with the blessed inconsistency which is permissible—and lays it down plump and plain, that "it is well not to be frightened out of the enjoyment of fine poetry . . . by such epithets as morbid, hysterical, spasmodic." Most true, and it would be still better to add "beginning," "middle," "end," "not human," the neglect of acquaintance with the most distinguished young men of the university, the absence of dramatic presentation, and the rest of them, to the herd of bogies that should first be left to animate swine, and then be driven into the deep. Once, indeed, afterwards he half relapses, observing that there is "incongruity" in *The Princess*. But his nerves have grown firmer from his long bath of pure poetry, and he agrees to make the best of it.

This "Tennyson" essay is one of a hundred pages, though not very large ones: but the only other piece of length which

His other work. has been preserved, a paper on "Wordsworth" not much shorter than the "Tennyson," is, as was perhaps natural, seeing that it was published immediately after the poet's death, mainly biographical, and so uninteresting: while the remaining contents of the volume are short reviews. The "Wordsworth" starts, however, with reasoned estimates of Byron, Scott, and Shelley, as foils to Wordsworth: and to these, remembering their time,[1] the very middle of the century, we turn with interest. The "Byron" and the "Scott" reward us but moderately: they are in the main "what he ought to have said,"—competent, well-balanced, true enough as far as they go, but showing no very individual grip. The Shelley, a better test, is far more satisfactory in the result. It is quite clear that Brimley sympathised neither with Shelley's religious views, nor with his politics, nor with his morals. He may be thought to be even positively unjust in saying that Shelley's "mind was ill-trained, and not well furnished with facts," for *intellectually* few poets have been better off in this respect. Yet, in spite of all this, he says, "with one exception a more glorious poet has not been given to the English nation," which once more shows how very much sounder he was on the subject of poetry than Arnold, and how little beginnings, and middles, and ends, with all their trumpery, really mattered to him. Among the shorter pieces, the attempts at abstract, or partly abstract, treatment in "Poetry and Criticism" and "The Angel in the House" (only part of which latter is actually devoted to its amiable but rather wool-gathering title-subject) are not conspicuously successful; they are, in fact, trial-essays, by a comparative novice, in an art the secrets of which had been almost lost for nearly a generation. But the attempt in "Poetry and Criticism" to gather up, squeeze out, and give

[1] The "Wordsworth" is some years earlier than the "Tennyson." It ap- peared in *Fraser* during the summer of 1851.

form to the Coleridgean vaguenesses (for that is very much what it comes to), has promise and germ. As for the smaller reviews, Mr Brimley had the good fortune to deal as a reviewer with Carlyle, Thackeray, and Dickens, as well as Bulwer and Kingsley, not to mention such different subjects as the *Noctes Ambrosianæ* and the *Philosophie Positive :* and the merit of coming out, with hardly a stain upon his character, from any one of these (in some cases very high) trials. We may think that he does not always go fully right; but he never goes utterly wrong. And when we think what sorrowful chances have awaited the collision of great books at their first appearance even with by no means little critics, the praise is not small.

Yet a sufficient study of the "Tennyson" essay should have quite prepared the expert reader for these minor successes. *His intrinsic and chronological importance.* Brimley, as we have said, was only partially favoured by time, place, and circumstance, even putting health out of the question. He was heavily handicapped in that respect : and he had no time to work out his critical deliverance fully, and to justify it by abundant critical performance. But he has the root of the matter in him : and it throws out the flower of the matter in that refusal to be "frightened out of the enjoyment of fine poetry by epithets." When a man has once shown himself *ausus contemnere vana* in this way, when he has the initial taste which Brimley everywhere shows, and the institution of learning which he did not lack, it will go hard but he is a good critic *in posse* already, and harder if he is not a good one in such actuality as is allowed him. And this was well seen of George Brimley.

It is one of the penalties, late but heavy, of an attempt to take a kingdom (even one not of Heaven) by storm for the *"Gyas and Cloanthus."* first time, that you have to "refuse" or "mask" not a few of its apparently strong places—and if their strength be more than apparent, the adventurer will not be conqueror. There are in English, as in other nineteenth-century literatures, many persons who addressed themselves more or less seriously to criticism, who obtained more or less name as critics, with whose works every well-read person is more or less acquainted, yet who must be so refused or masked

at the writer's peril of the reader's disappointment or disapproval. Many of them seemed to be pillars of the early
and middle nineteenth-century reviews; from some of them,
no doubt, some institution in criticism has been received by
readers of all the three generations which have passed since
the appearance of the earliest. It may seem intolerable *outre-
cuidance* to put Milman and Croker and Hayward,
Milman, Sydney Smith and Senior and Helps, with others
Croker,
Hayward. not even named, as it were "in the fourpenny box"
of our stall. Yet it is unavoidable, and the stall-keeper must
dare it, not merely—not even mainly—because he has no room
to give them better display. Milman was at least thought
by Byron a formidable enough critic to have the apocryphal
crime of "killing John Keats" assigned to him by hypothesis:
and his merits (not of the bravo kind) are no doubt much
greater than the bad critics who, after Macaulay, depreciate
his style, and the maladroit eulogists of his free thought, who
would make him a sort of nineteenth-century Conyers Middleton,
appear to think. But he has no critical credential, known to
the present writer, that would give him substantive place
here.[1] Croker was neither such a bad man nor such a bad
writer as Macaulay would have had him to be: but the Keats
article is a terrible sin, and the Tennyson one only in part
excusable. Senior, before he became a glorified earwig, or, if
this seem disrespectful, the father of all such as interview, was
a sound, if not very gifted, reviewer, but little more: Hayward, a much cleverer and, above all, much more
Sydney worldly-wise Isaac Disraeli, who made the most of
Smith,
Senior, being "in society" (see Thackeray), talked better
Helps. than he wrote, but still wrote well, especially by
the aid of *l'esprit des autres.* Of Sydney Smith earlier, and
Sir Arthur Helps later, the fairest thing to say in our
present context is, that neither held himself out as a literary
critic at all. Sydney could give admirable accounts of books:
but he nowhere shows, or pretends to, the slightest sense of
literature. Helps, starting[2] a discussion on Fiction,—the very
most interesting and most promising of all literary subjects

[1] He will reappear in the Appendix   of Poetry.
devoted to holders of the Oxford Chair   [2] In *Friends in Council.*

for a man of his time—a subject which was just equipped with material enough at hand, and not yet too much, neither novel to the point of danger nor stale to the point of desperation,— "keeps to the obvious," as one of his own characters acknowledges, in a fashion almost excusing the intrinsically silly reaction from obviousness, which distinguished the last quarter of the nineteenth century, and is now itself obviously stale. The influence of works of fiction is unbounded. The Duke of Marlborough took his history from Shakespeare. Fiction is good as creating sympathy. It is bad as leading us into dreamland. Real life is more real than fiction. Writers of fiction have great responsibility. In shorter formula, " We love our Novel with an N because it is Nice; we hate it because it is sometimes Naughty; we take it to the Osteria [1] of the Obvious, and treat it with an Olio of Obligingness and Objurgation." But Helps, in this very passage, tells us that he prefers life to literature, and no one can be a good critic who, *when he criticises*, does that: though he may be a very bad one, and yet make the other preference.

We must still extend this *numerus* a little in order to do that justice—unjust at the best—which is possible here, and

Elwin, Lancaster, Hannay. which is yet not quite so futile and inadequate as some still more unjust judgments would have it. For the object of this History is to revive and keep before the eye of the reader the names, the critical position, and, if only by touches, the critical personality, of as many of those who have done good service to criticism in the past as may be possible. A little less wilfulness and exclusiveness of personal taste, or rather less opportunity of indulging it, would probably have made of Whitwell Elwin—who survived till the earlier portion of this book was published, but did his critical work long ago — a really great critic. Even as it is, his *Remains* [2] contain some of the best critical essays, not absolutely supreme, to be found among the enormous stores of the nineteenth century, especially on the most *English* Englishmen of letters during the eighteenth, such as Fielding and Johnson. A short life, avocations of business, and perhaps

[1] I have slipped from N to O: but it is only next door.   [2] London, 1902.

the absence of the pressure of professional literary occupation, prevented the work of Henry Lancaster[1] from being much more than a specimen: but his famous essay on Thackeray showed (and not alone) what he could do.   On the other hand, the not always mischievous, though too often galling, yoke of the profession was not wanting to James Hannay.   His literary work was directed into too many paths, some of them too much strewn with the thorns and beset with the briars of journalism. But there are very few books of the kind which unite a certain "popularity" in no invidious sense, and an adaptation for the general reader, with sound and keen criticism, as does his far too little known *Course of English Literature*;[2] while many of his scattered and all but lost essays show admirable insight.

To one remarkable critic, however, who, though a younger man than Mr Arnold, is on the whole of a Præ-Arnoldian type, *Dallas.* and to whom justice, I think, has not usually been done, a little larger space must be given.   I must admit that, having been disgusted at the time of the appearance of *The Gay Science*[3] by what I then thought its extremely silly, and now think its by no means judicious, title, I never read it until quite recently, and then found (of course) that Mr Dallas had said several of my things before me, though usually with a difference.[4]   But I have not the least inclination to say *Pereat:* on the contrary, I should like to revive him.   Fourteen years earlier than the date of his principal book, as a young man fresh from the influence of the Hamiltonian philosophy, and also, I think, imbued with not a little of Ruskinism, he had written a volume of *Poetics*,[5] which, *The* Poetics. though it does not come to very much, is a remarkable book, and a very remarkable one, if we consider its date—a year before Mr Arnold's *Preface*, and when Brimley

[1] *Essays and Reviews*, London, 1876. The other papers—on Macaulay, Carlyle, Ruskin, George Eliot—are good, but not so good, and show that difficulty of the mid-century critic in "sticking to *literature*," which is the theme of this chapter.

[2] London, 1866.

[3] London, 1866.

[4] Of every one of them, however, I can most honestly and conscientiously say that I am sure I did not take it from him; and if we both took it from somebody else (to adopt the comfortable principles of Miss Teresa M'Whirter at the conclusion of *A Legend of the Rhine*), I do not know who the somebody else was.

[5] London, 1852.

and others were only waking up by fits, and starts, and relapses, to the necessity of a new criticism. Not that Dallas is on the right track : but he is on a track very different from that of most English critics since Coleridge. He revives, in an odd way, —odd, at least, till we remember the Philistinism of the First Exhibition period,—the Apologetic for Poetry ; he establishes, rather in the old scholastic manner, the distinction between Poetry the principle and Poesy the embodiment : he talks about the "Law of Activity," the "Law of Harmony," and the like.

There is, for the time, not a little promise in this : and there is much more, as well as some, if not quite enough, perform-

The Gay Science. ance, in the later book. *The Gay Science* (an adaptation, of course, of the Provençal name for Poetry itself) was originally intended to be in four volumes : but the reception of the two first was not such as to encourage the author—who had by this time engaged in journalism, and become a regular writer for *The Times*—to finish it. I cannot agree with the author of the article in the *D. N. B.*, that the cause of its ill-success was its "abstruseness" : for really there is nothing difficult about it. On the contrary, it is, I should say, rather too much in the style of the leading article—facile, but a little "woolly." Its faults seem to lie partly in this, but more in the two facts that, in the first place, the author "embraces more than he can grasp" ; and that, in the second, he has not kept pace with the revival of criticism, though he had in a manner anticipated it. He knows a good deal ; and he not only sees the necessity of comparative criticism, but has a very shrewd notion of the difference between the true and the false Comparisons. Acuteness in perception and neatness in phrase appear pretty constantly : and he certainly makes good preparation for steering himself right, by deciding that Renaissance criticism is too verbal (he evidently did not know the whole of it, but is right so far) ; German too idealist ; Modern generally too much lacking in system. Yet, when he comes to make his own start, he "but yaws neither." He is uncomfortable with Mr Arnold (who, by this time, had published not merely the *Preface* but the *Essays in Criticism*), and finds fault with him, more often wrongly than rightly.

Especially he shows himself quite at a loss to comprehend Sainte-Beuve, whom he, like some later persons, hardly thinks a critic at all.[1] He gets boldly into the "*psycho*logical coach," and books himself, as resolutely as any German, for the City of Abstraction. "The theory of imitation," we are told, "is now utterly exploded"—a remarkable instance of saying nearly the right thing in quite the wrong way. We travel arm-in-arm with "Imagination" and "The Hidden Soul" (which seems to be something like Unconscious Cerebration); we hear even more than from Mr Arnold about the "Play of Thought"; we have chapters on chapters about Pleasure—not the specially poetic pleasure, but pleasure in general. In short, we are here in the presence, not so much of what we have called "meta-critic" as of something that might almost better be called "*pro*critic"—altogether in the vestibule of critical inquiries proper. Of course it is fair to remember the two unwritten or unpublished volumes. But I venture very much to doubt, from a perusal of both his published works, whether Dallas would have ever thoroughly "collected" his method, or have directed it to that actual criticism of actual literature, of which, however (as of most things), there are fragments and essays in his work. The disturbing influences which, as we have seen, acted on so many of his contemporaries or immediate seniors acted differently on him, but they acted: and his literary "ideation" was, I think, too diffuse to make head completely against them. Yet he had real critical talent: and it is a pity that it has not had more adequate recognition.

But it is time to leave this part of the subject, only casting back among the elders, because each of these has "become a name,"—to John Foster,[2] and W. J. Fox,[3] Henry

---

[1] It is important to notice that he is not *hostile*, he is simply puzzled. The great method, which emerges first in Dryden, and which Sainte-Beuve perfected, of "shaking together" different literary examples, is still dark to him in practice, though, as has been said, he had a glimpse of its theory.

[2] Foster's interest in literature—real, but very strongly coloured and conditioned by his moral and religious preoccupations — may be easily appraised by reading his Essays on "A Man Writing his Own Memoirs" and "The Epithet Romantic" in Bohn's Library.

[3] Fox has the credit of "discovering" Browning, but there were personal reasons here. Much more, of course, were there such in A. H.

Rogers,[1] and the first Sir James Stephen, not even naming others of perhaps hardly less fame.   And let us salute the man

Others:
J. S. Mill.

among these elders who, at first sight and frankly, could pronounce *The Lady of Shalott*, "except that the versification is less exquisite [it was much improved later], entitled to a place by the side of *The Ancient Mariner* and *Christabel*," who doubted whether "poetic imagery ever conveyed a more intense conception of a place and its inmate than in *Mariana*," and who justified his right to pronounce on individual poems by the two very remarkable articles on "What is Poetry?" and "The Two Kinds of Poetry." One remembers, with amused ruth, Charles Lamb's friend and his "What a pity that these fine ingenuous youths should grow up to be mere members of Parliament?" as one thinks of the Juvenilia and the Senilia of John Stuart Mill.[2]

Hallam's essay on Tennyson—a rather overrated thing.

[1] Rogers is even "mentioned in despatches"—that is, by Sainte-Beuve.

[2] See his *Early Essays* in Bohn's reprint. The criticism of certain romantic poets of the mid century would make an interesting excursus of the kind which I have indicated as (if it were possible) fit to be included in such a History as this is. Horne's *New Spirit of the Age* (1845), though exhibiting all the singular inadequacies, inequalities, and *inorganicisms* of the author of *Orion*, does not entirely deserve the severe contrast which Thackeray drew between it and its original as given by Hazlitt. Mrs Browning, who took some part in this, has left a substantive critical contribution in *The Greek Christian Poets and the English Poets*, in which again the weaknesses of the writer in poetry are interestingly compensated by weaknesses in criticism, but in which again also, and much more, "the critic whom every poet must [or should] contain" sometimes asserts himself not unsuccessfully. W. C. Roscoe, whose verse is at least interesting, and has been thought something more, is critically not negligible. But perhaps the most interesting document which would have to be treated in such an excursus is Sydney Dobell's *Nature of Poetry*, delivered as a lecture (it must have been something of a choke-pear for the audience) at Edinburgh in 1857. Here the author, though not *nominatim*, directly traverses Matthew Arnold's doctrine in the great Preface (see next chapter), by maintaining that a perfect poem *will be* the exhibition of a perfect mind, and, we may suppose, a less perfect but still defensible poem the exhibition of a less perfect mind—which principle, no doubt, is, in any case, the sole possible justification of *Festus* and of *Balder*. Others (especially Sir Henry Taylor) might be added, but these will probably suffice.

CHAPTER VIII.

ENGLISH CRITICISM FROM 1860-1900.

MATTHEW ARNOLD: ONE OF THE GREATER CRITICS—HIS POSITION DEFINED EARLY—THE 'PREFACE' OF 1853—ANALYSIS OF IT, AND INTERIM SUMMARY OF ITS GIST—CONTRAST WITH DRYDEN—CHAIR-WORK AT OXFORD, AND CONTRIBUTIONS TO PERIODICALS—'ON TRANSLATING HOMER'—"THE GRAND STYLE"—DISCUSSION OF IT—THE STUDY OF CELTIC LITERATURE—ITS ASSUMPTIONS—THE 'ESSAYS': THEIR CASE FOR CRITICISM—THEIR EXAMPLES THEREOF—THE LATEST WORK—THE INTRODUCTION TO WARD'S 'ENGLISH POETS'—"CRITICISM OF LIFE"—POETIC SUBJECT OR POETIC MOMENT—ARNOLD'S ACCOMPLISHMENT AND POSITION AS A CRITIC—THE CARLYLIANS—KINGSLEY—FROUDE—RUSKIN—G. H. LEWES—HIS 'PRINCIPLES OF SUCCESS IN LITERATURE'—HIS 'INNER LIFE OF ART'—BAGEHOT—R. H. HUTTON—HIS EVASIONS OF LITERARY CRITICISM—PATER—HIS FRANK HEDONISM—HIS "POLY-TECHNY" AND HIS STYLE—HIS FORMULATION OF THE NEW CRITICAL ATTITUDE—'THE RENAISSANCE'—OBJECTIONS TO ITS PROCESS—IM-PORTANCE OF 'MARIUS THE EPICUREAN'—'APPRECIATIONS' AND THE "GUARDIAN" ESSAYS—UNIVERSALITY OF HIS METHOD—J. A. SYMONDS—THOMSON ("B. V.")—WILLIAM MINTO—HIS BOOKS ON ENGLISH PROSE AND POETRY—H. D. TRAILL—HIS CRITICAL STRENGTH—ON STERNE AND COLERIDGE—ESSAYS ON FICTION—"THE FUTURE OF HUMOUR"—OTHERS: MANSEL, VENABLES, STEPHEN, LORD HOUGHTON, PATTISON, CHURCH, ETC.—PATMORE—EDMUND GURNEY—'THE POWER OF SOUND'—'TERTIUM QUID.'

IN coming to Mr Matthew Arnold we come again, but for the last time, to one of our chiefs of the greater clans of criticism. *Matthew Arnold: one of the greater critics.* *Vixere fortes post* Mr Arnold; let us hope that *vivunt.* We have heard, more or less vaguely, of new schools of criticism since, in more countries than one or two, and an amiable enthusiasm has declared that the new gospels are real gospels, far truer

and better than any previously known. I am not myself,
by any means, in general agreement — I am often in very
particular disagreement — with Mr Arnold's critical canons,
and (less often) with his individual judgments. But as I
look back over European criticism for the years (approaching
a century) which have passed since his birth, I cannot find
one critic, born since that time, who can be ranked above or
even with him in general critical quality and accomplishment.
And, extending the view further over the vast expanse, from
Aristotle to that birth-date, though I certainly find greater
critics—critics very much greater in originality, greater in
catholicity, perhaps greater in felicity of individual utterance
—I yet find that he is of their race and lineage, free of
their company, one of them, not to be scanted of any sizings
that can be, by however unworthy a manciple, allotted to
them.

It was the way of some of these greater critics in Critical
History, at this or that period of their career, to launch a kind
His position of manifesto or confession, of which their other
defined critical work is but, as it were, the application and
early. amplification: while others have never done this,
but have built up their critical temple, adding wing to wing and
storey to storey, not seldom even deserting or ruining the earlier
constructions. Mr Arnold, in practice as in principle, belonged
to the first class, and he launched his own manifesto about as
early as any man can be capable of forming a critical judgment
which is not a mere adaptation of some one else's, or (a thing
really quite as unoriginal) a flying-in-the-face of some one
else's, or a mere spurt and splash of youthful self-sufficiency.
You can be a bishop and a critic at thirty—not before (by
wise external rule) in the former case; hardly before, according
to laws of nature which man has unwisely omitted to codify
for himself, in the latter. Mr Arnold was a little over thirty
when, collecting such things as he chose to collect out of his
earlier volumes of Poetry, and adding much to them, he
published the collection with a Preface in October 1853. I
doubt whether he ever wrote better, either in sense or in style;

and I am quite sure that, while some of the defects of his criticism, as it was to be, appear quite clearly in the paper, all the pith and moment of that criticism appear in germ and principle likewise.

In the interesting and important "Advertisement" which, eight months later, he prefixed to the second edition of this *The* Preface book, Mr Arnold himself summed up the lessons of *of* 1853.   the *Preface*, which followed it, under two main heads, —the insistence on the importance of the subject—the "great action"; and the further insistence on study of the ancients, with the specified object of correcting the great vice of our modern, and especially English, intellect—that it "is fantastic, and wants sanity." He thus, to some extent, justified the erection of these into his two first and great commandments— the table-headings, if not the full contents, of his creed and law. But, for our purpose, we must analyse the Preface itself rather more closely.

It opens with an account of the reasons which led the author to exclude *Empedocles*, not because the subject was "a Sicilian Greek," but from a consideration of the situation itself. This he condemns in a passage which contains a very great amount of critical truth, which is quite admirably expressed, and which really adds one to the not extensive list of critical axioms of the first class. Even here one may venture to doubt whether the supreme poet will not vindicate his omnipotence in treating *poeticamente*. But if the sentence were so qualified as to warn the poet that he will *hardly* succeed, it would be absolutely invulnerable or impregnable.

But why, he asks, does he dwell on this unimportant and private matter? Because he wishes particularly to disclaim *Analysis* any deference to the objection referred to above as *of it,* to the choice of *ancient* subjects: to which he might have added (as the careful reader of the whole piece will soon perceive), because insistence on the character of the Subject was his critical being's very end and aim. In effect, he uses both these battle-horses in his assault upon the opposite doctrine that the poet must "leave the exhausted past and fix his attention on the present."[1] It is needless to say that over his immediate antagonists he is completely victorious. Whatever the origin of the ignoble and inept fallacy concerned, this particular form of it was part of the special mid-nineteenth century heresy of "progress." But whether he unhorses and "baffles" it in the right way may be another question. *His* way is to dwell once more, and with something already of the famous Arnoldian iteration, on the paramount importance of the "action," on the vanity of the supposition that superior treatment will make up for subjective inferiority. And he then exposes himself dangerously by postulating the superior interest of "Achilles, Prometheus, Clytemnestra, Dido," to the personages of any modern poem, and, perhaps still more dangerously, by selecting as his modern poems *Hermann and Dorothea, Childe Harold, Jocelyn* [! ! !], and *The Excursion.* He may be said here to lose a stirrup at least : but on the whole he certainly establishes the point—too clear to need establishment—that the *date* of an action signifies nothing. While if the further statement that the action itself is all-important is disputable, it is his doctrine and hypothesis.

He is consistent with this doctrine when he goes on to argue that "the Greeks understood it far more clearly than we do"—that "they regarded the whole, we the parts"—that, while they kept the action uppermost, we prefer the expression. Not that they neglected expression—"on the contrary, they were . . . the masters of the *grand style.*" Where they did not indulge in this, where they were bald or trivial, it was merely to let the majesty of the action stand forth without a veil. "Their theory and practice alike, the admirable treatise of Aristotle and the unrivalled works of their poets, exclaim with a thousand tongues, 'All depends upon the subject. Choose a fitting action, penetrate yourself with

---

[1] The immortality of critical error —the impossibility of quelling the Blatant Beast — to which we have alluded more than once, is again illustrated here. One might have thought that Mr Arnold had sufficiently crushed and concluded this fallacy. It has been seen again—in places where it should not have been—in these last few years.

the feeling of its situations; this done, everything else will follow.'"[1]

As a necessary consequence, they were "rigidly exacting" as to construction: *we* believe in "the brilliant things that arise under the poet's pen as he goes along." We refuse to ask for a "total impression": instead of requiring that the poet shall as far as possible efface himself, we even lay it down that "a true allegory of the state of one's own mind in a representative history is perhaps the highest thing one can attempt in the way of poetry." Against this Mr Arnold pronounces *Faust*—though the work of "the greatest poet of modern times, the greatest critic of all times"[2]—defective, because it is something like this. Next he deplores the want of a guide for a young writer, "a voice to prescribe to him the aim he should keep in view"—and, in default of it, insists once more on models.

The foremost of these models for the English writer is, of course, Shakespeare, of whom Mr Arnold speaks with becoming reverence, and of whom he had earned the right to speak by his magnificent sonnet years earlier. But his attitude towards Shakespeare, as a literary Bible, is guarded. Shakespeare chose subjects "than which the world could afford no better"; but his expression was *too* good—too "eminent and unrivalled," too fixing and seductive to the attention, so to draw it away from those other things which were "his excellences *as a poet.*"[3] In leading writers to forget this, Shakespeare has done positive harm, and Keats's *Pot of Basil* is taken as an instance, whence the critic diverges to a long condemnation of this great but erring bard's "difficulty" of language, and returns to the doctrine that he is *not* safe as a model. The ancients are: though even in them there is some-

---

[1] This very generous assumption comes, I feel sure, from the blending of Wordsworth (*v. sup.*, on him) with Aristotle.

[2] Mr Arnold never explicitly retracted this "pyramidal" exaggeration—it was not his way; but nearly the whole of his *French Critic on Goethe*

is a transparent "hedge," a scarcely ambiguous palinode. For Dobell's contention, see note at end of last chapter.

[3] I think Mr Arnold, especially after italicising these words, should really have told us as a WHAT we are to think of the author of Shakespeare's greatest expressions.

thing narrow, something local and temporary. But there is
so much that is not, and that is an antidote to modern banes,
that we cannot too much cling to them as models. These, he
adds at some length, the present age needs morally as much
as artistically. He has himself tried, in the poems he is
issuing, to obey his own doctrines: and he ends with the
famous peroration imploring respect for Art, and pleading for
the observance and preservation of "the wholesome regulative
laws of Poetry," lest they be "condemned and cancelled by
the influence of their eternal enemy, Caprice."

Comment on this, beyond the remarks already made, had
best be postponed till we can consider Mr Arnold's criticism
and interim as a whole. But to one thing we should draw
summary of attention, and that is, that here is a critic who
its gist. knows what he means, and who means something
not, directly, or as a whole, meant, or at least said, by any
earlier critic. That "all depends on the subject" had been
said often enough before: but it had not been said by any
one who had the whole of literature before him, and the
tendency — for half a century distinctly, for a full century
more or less—had been to unsay or gainsay it. Further, the
critic has combined with the older Neo-classic adoration of
the "fable" something perhaps traceable, as hinted above, to
the Wordsworthian horror of poetic diction, a sort of cult of
baldness instead of beauty, and a distrust, if not horror, of
"expression." In fact, though I do not believe that he in the
least knew it, he is taking up a position of direct and, as it
were, designed antagonism to Dryden's, in that remarkable
Contrast preface to *An Evening's Love,* one of those in which
with he comes closest to the Spaniards, where he says
Dryden. plumply "the story is the least part," and declares
that the important part is the workmanship — that *this* is
the *poiesis.* It is hardly possible to state the "dependence" —
in the old duelling sense—of the great quarrel of Poetics, and
almost of Criticism, more clearly than is done in these two
Prefaces by these two great poet-critics of the seventeenth and
the nineteenth centuries in England.

I do not think that there is any published evidence of the

time or of the circumstances at and in which Mr Arnold *Chair-work* began contributing critical articles to periodicals. *at Oxford,* But his appointment (which must have been, at *and con-* *tributions to* any rate to some extent, due to the *Preface* as well *periodicals.* as to the *Poems*) to the Professorship of Poetry at Oxford in 1857 gave him a strong stimulus towards the development of his critical powers in reasoned form; while, shortly afterwards, the remarkable developments of the press, towards the end of the 'Fifties, which began by the institution of *Macmillan's* and the *Cornhill Magazine,* and continued through the establishment of a strongly literary and critical daily newspaper in the *Pall Mall Gazette,* to the multiplication of monthly reviews proper in the *Fortnightly, Contemporary,* and *Nineteenth Century,* supplied him with opportunities of communicating these studies to a public larger than his Oxford audience, and with a profitable and convenient intermediate stage between the lecture and the book. He was, however, always rather scrupulous about permitting his utterances the "third reading": and some of them (notably his Inaugural Address at Oxford) have still to be sought in the catacombs. But the matter of more than a decade's production, by which he chose to stand, is included in the three well-known volumes, *On Translating Homer* and *The Study of Celtic Literature* for the Oxford Lectures, and the famous *Essays in Criticism* for the more miscellaneous work, the last, however, being rounded off and worked up into a whole by its Preface, and by its two opening pieces, *The Function of Criticism in the Present Time* and *The Influence of Academies.*

In these three books the expression of critical attitude, displayed, as we have said, unmistakably in the *Preface* of 1853, is not only developed and varied into something as nearly approaching to a *Summa Criticismi* as was in Mr Arnold's not excessively systematic way, but furnished and illustrated by an extraordinarily interesting and sufficiently diversified body of critical applications in particular. Yet there is no divergence from the lines marked out in the Preface, nor is there to be found any such divergence — if divergence imply the least contradiction or inconsistency—in the work of the last decade of his life, when he had dropped his ill-omened guerilla against dogma and miracles, and had returned to the Muses. He is as much a typical example of a critic consistent in consistency as Dryden is of one consistent in inconsistency: and it naturally requires less intelligence to comprehend him than appears to be the case in the other instance. In fact, he could never be misunderstood in general: though his extreme wilfulness, and his contempt of history, sometimes made him a little bewildering to the plain man in detail.

In discussing the first, and indeed all, of these, it is, of course, important to keep what is suitable for a History of On Trans- Criticism apart from what would be suitable only lating for a monograph on Mr Arnold. Yet the idiosyn- Homer. crasies of the greater critics are as much the subject of such a general history as their more abstract doctrines. We see, then, here something which was not difficult to discern, even in the more frugal and guarded expression of the *Preface,* and which, no doubt, is to some extent fostered and intensified by that freedom from the check of immediate contradiction or criticism which some have unkindly called the dangerous prerogative of preachers and professors. This something is the Arnoldian confidence — that quality which Mr Hutton, perhaps rather kindly, took for "sureness," and which, though strangely different in tone, is not so very different in actual nature from the other "sureness" (with a prefix) of Lord Macaulay. We may think that this confidence is certainly strengthened, and perhaps to some extent caused, by a habit of turning the blind eye on subjects of which the critic does not know very much, and inspecting very cursorily those which he does not much like. But we shall see that, right or wrong, partial or impartial, capricious or systematic as he may be, Mr Arnold applies himself to the actual appreciation of actual literature, and to the giving of reasons for his appreciation, in a way new, delightful, invaluable.

The really important part or feature of the tractate for us "*The grand* is its famous handling of "the Grand Style." He *style.*" had used this phrase, italicising it, in the *Preface* itself, had declared that the ancients were its "unapproached

masters," but he had not said much about it or attempted to
define it.   Here he makes it almost his chief battle-charger—
presenting Homer, Dante, and Milton as the greatest masters
of it, if not the only sure ones, denying any *regular* possession of it to Shakespeare, and going far to deny most other
poets, from Tennyson down to Young, the possession of it at
all.   It was impossible that this enigmatic critical phrase,
applied so provocatively, should not itself draw the fire of
critics.   He could not but reply to this in his "Last Words,"
but he had to make something of a confession and avoidance,
with much sorrow, perhaps not without a very little anger.
For those who asked "What *is* the Grand Style?" mockingly,
he had no answer: they were to "die in their sins."   To others
he vouchsafed the answer that the grand style "arises in poetry
when a noble nature, poetically gifted, treats with simplicity or
severity a serious subject."   Let us, with as much simplicity
and seriousness, but with as little severity as may be, treat
both the expression and the definition.

The expression itself—the origin of which, like that of some
others in our special lexicon, is to be found in the criticism,
Discussion
of it.   not of literature, but of Art in the limited sense,
and which was, I think, first made current in
English by Sir Joshua Reynolds—is of course a vague one,
and we must walk warily among its associations and suggestions.   At one end it suggests, with advantage to itself
and to us honest inquirers, the ὕψος of Longinus.   At the
other, it has perhaps a rather damaging suggestion of the
French *style noble*, and a still more dangerous echo-hint of
"grand*iose*."   And Mr Arnold himself once (*Preface*, ed.
1853, p. xix) uses "grandiose," as, it is true, the Latins and
the French have sometimes done, as equivalent to "grand."
Coming, then, unsatisfied by these vaguenesses, to the definition,
we shall perhaps think it permissible to strike out the first
two members, as in the former case almost self-confessedly, in
the second quite, superfluous.   That the Grand Style in poetry
will only arise when the stylist is poetically gifted scarcely
requires even enunciation: that the nature which produces
the grand style must be *pro tanto* and *pro hac vice* "noble,"

is also sun-clear. Something of the Longinian circularity in one point [1] seems to have infected Mr Arnold here. But with the rest of the definition preliminary and *prima facie* inquiry has no fault to find. Let us take it that the Grand Style in poetry is the treatment of a serious subject with simplicity or severity. Even to this a fresh demurrer arises, which may be partly, but cannot be wholly, overruled. Why this anti-thesis, this mutual exclusion, between "simplicity" and "sever-ity"? "Severe simplicity" is a common, and is generally thought a just, phrase: at any rate, the two things are closely related. We may note this only — adding in Mr Arnold's favour that his special attribution of simplicity to Homer and severity to Milton would seem to indicate that by the latter word he means "gorgeousness *severely restrained.*"

This, with such additional and applied lights as are provided by Mr Arnold's denunciation of *affectation* as fatal to the Grand Style, will give us some idea of what he wished to mean by the phrase. It is, in fact, a fresh formulation of the Class-ical restraint, definiteness, proportion, form, against the Romantic vague, the Romantic fantasy. This had been the lesson of the Preface, given after the preceptist manner. It is now the applied, illustrated, appreciative lesson of the *Lectures.* It is a doctrine like another: and, in its special form and plan, an easily comprehensible reaction from a reaction—in fact, the inevitable ebb after the equally inevitable flow. But when we begin to examine it (especially in comparison with its Longinian original) as a matter of theory, and with its own illustrations as a matter of practice, doubts and difficulties come thick upon us, and we may even feel under a sad necessity of "dying in our sins," just as Mr Carlyle thought that, at a certain period of his career, Ignatius Loyola "ought to have made up his mind to be damned."

To take the last first, it is difficult, on examining Mr Arnold's instances and his comments, in the most impartial and judicial manner possible, to resist the conclusion that his definition only really fits Dante, and that it was originally derived from the study of him. To that fixed star of first

---

[1] As to "Figures" and "Sublimity."

magnitude in poetry it *does* apply as true, as nothing but true, and perhaps even as the whole truth. Nobility, quintessential poetry, simplicity in at least some senses, severity and seriousness in almost all,—who will deny these things to the *Commedia*? But it is very difficult to think that it applies, in anything like the same coequal and coextensive fashion, to either Homer or Milton. There are points in which Homer touches Dante; there are points in which Dante touches Milton; but they are not the same points. It may, further, be very much doubted whether Mr Arnold has not greatly exaggerated both Homer's universal "simplicity" and his universal "seriousness." The ancients were certainly against him on the latter point. While one may feel not so much doubt as certainty that the application of "severity" to Milton —unless it means simply the absence of geniality and humour —is still more rash.

But when we look back to Longinus we shall find at least a hint of a much more serious defect than this. Why this unnecessary asceticism and grudging in the connotation of grandeur? why this tell-tale and self-accusing limitation further to a bare three poets, two of them, indeed, of the very greatest? Mr Arnold himself feels the difficulty presented by Shakespeare so strongly that he has to make, as it were, uncovenanted grand-style mercies for him. But that is only because you have simply to open almost any two pages out of three in Shakespeare, and the grand style smites you in the face, as God's glory smote St Stephen. *We* can afford, which shows our strength, to leave Shakespeare alone. Longinus of old has no such damaging fencing of the table of *his* Grand Style. The Greeks, it is known, thought little of Love as a subject: yet he admitted the sublimity of Sappho. And if he objected to the πλεκτάνην χειμάρροον of Æschylus, it was only because he thought it went too far. How much wiser is it, instead of fixing such arbitrary limits, to recognise that the Grand Style has infinite manifestations; that it may be found in poets who have it seldom as well as in those who have it often; that Herrick has it with

"In this world—the Isle of Dreams";

that Tennyson has it again and again; that Goethe has it in
the final octet of *Faust*; that Heine and Hugo, and hundreds
of others, down to quite minor poets in their one moment of
rapturous union with the Muse, have it. How much wiser to
recognise further that it is not limited to the simple or severe:
whether it is to the serious is another question. For my
part, I will not loose the fragile boat or incur the danger of the
roof,—speaking in a Pickwickian-Horatian manner,—with any
one who denies the grand style to Donne or to Dryden, to
Spenser or to Shelley. The grand is the transcendent: and it
is blasphemy against the Spirit of Poetry to limit the fashions
and the conditions of transcendence.[1]

The other "chair"-book, *The Study of Celtic Literature*, is
tempting in promise, but disappointing in performance. Much
of it is not literary, and when it becomes so, there
are difficulties. In the *Preface* itself, and in the
Homer, Mr Arnold had sometimes been unjust or
unsatisfactory on what he did not know or did not like—
Mediæval literature, the Ballad, &c.,—but his remarks and
his theories had been, in the main, solidly based upon what
he did not know thoroughly and did appreciate—the Classics,
Dante, Milton, Wordsworth. Here not Pallas, I think, but
some anti-Pallas, has "invented a new thing." Whether Mr
Arnold knew directly, and at first-hand, *any* Welsh, Breton,
Cornish, Irish, or Scotch Gaelic, I do not know.[2] He certainly disclaims anything like extensive or accurate knowledge, and it is noticeable that (I think invariably) he
quotes from translations, and only a few well-known translations. Moreover he, with his usual dislike and distrust
of the historic method, fences with, or puts off, the inquiry
what the dates of the *actual* specimens which we possess of
this literature may be. Yet he proceeds to pick out (as if

The Study of Celtic Literature.

---

[1] The present writer has applied the
gist of this argument on the grand
style, in detail, to Milton (*Milton
Memorial Lectures*, 1908), to Shakespeare (*English Association Essays and
Studies*, 1910), and to Dante in a
lecture before the Dante Society some
years ago, which has not yet been
printed.

[2] Those to the manner born or
matriculated in it have generally been
kind to him : but then he has given
them rather considerable bribes.

directly acquainted with the literatures themselves, at dates which make the matter certain) divers characteristics of "melancholy," "natural magic," &c., in Celtic literature, and then, unhesitatingly and without proof of any kind, to assign the presence of these qualities, in writers like Shakespeare and Keats, where we have not the faintest evidence of Celtic *blood*, to Celtic influence.

Now, we may or may not deplore this proceeding; but we must disallow it. It is both curious and instructive that *Its assump-* the neglect of history which accompanied the pre- *tions.* valence of Neo-classicism, and with which, when it was dispelled, Neo-classicism itself faded, should reappear in company with this *neotato*-classicism, this attempt to reconstruct the classic faith, taking in something, but a carefully limited something, of Romanticism. But the fact is certain: and, as has been said, we must disallow the proceeding. Whether melancholy, and natural magic, and the vague do strongly and especially, if not exclusively, appear in Celtic poetry, I do not deny, because I do not know; that Mr Arnold's evidence is not sufficient to establish their special if not exclusive prevalence, I deny, because I do know. That there is melancholy, natural magic, the vague in Shakespeare and in Keats, I admit, because I know; that Mr Arnold has any valid argument showing that their presence is due to Celtic influence, I do not admit, because I know that he has produced none. With bricks of ignorance and mortar of assumption you can build no critical house.

In that central citadel or canon of the subject, *Essays in Criticism*, this contraband element, this theory divorced from *The* Essays: history, makes its appearance but too often: it can *their case* and need only be said, for instance, that Mr Ar- *for Criti-* nold's estimate of the condition of French, and still *cism.* more of German, literature in his own day, as compared with English, will not stand for five minutes the examination of any impartial judge, dates and books in hand. But the divorce is by no means so prominent—indeed most of the constituent essays were, if I mistake not, written before the Celtic Lectures were delivered. The book is so much the best known of Mr Arnold's critical works—except perhaps the Preface to Mr Ward's *Poets*—that no elaborate analysis of it here can be necessary. Its own Preface is defiantly vivacious—and Vivacity, as we are often reminded, is apt to play her sober friend Criticism something like the tricks that Madge Wildfire played to Jeanie Deans. But it contains, in the very last words of its famous epiphonema to Oxford, an admission (in the phrase "this Queen of Romance") that Mr Arnold was anything but a classic *pur sang*. The two first Essays, "The Function of Criticism at the Present Time" and the "Influence of Academies," take up, both in the vivacious and in the sober manner, the main line and strategy of the old *Preface* itself. We may, not merely with generosity but with justice, "write off" the, as has been said, historically false parallels with France and Germany which the writer brings in to support his case. That case itself is perfectly solid and admissible. Those who are qualified to judge — not perhaps a large number — will admit, whether they are for it or against it, that no nonsuit is possible, and perhaps that no final decision for it or against is possible either, except to the satisfaction of mere individual taste and opinion.

The case is, that the remedy for the supposed or supposable deficiencies of English literature is Criticism — that the business of Criticism is to discover the ideas upon which creative literature must rest—that there is not enough "play of mind" in England—that Criticism again is the attempt "to know the best that is known and thought in the world"—that foreign literature is specially valuable, simply because it is likely to give that in which native literature is lacking. These are the doctrines of the First Essay, mingled with much political-social application and not a little banter. The second takes them up and applies them afresh in the direction of extolling the institution of Academies, and contrasting the effects of that influence on French critics and the absence of it in English, very much to the disadvantage of the latter, especially Mr Palgrave. For Mr Arnold had adopted early in his professorial career, and never gave up, the very dubious habit of enforcing his doctrine with "uses" of formally polite but extremely personal application.[1]

Now, this case or bundle of cases is, I have said, quite fairly and justly arguable. Even though I hope that the whole of this volume will have shown and show that Mr Arnold was quite wrong as to the general inferiority of English criticism, he was (as I have, not far back, taken the pains to show also) not quite wrong about the general criticism of his own youth and early manhood—of the criticism which he himself came to reform. Nor was he wrong in thinking that there is, in the uncultivated and unregenerate English mind, a sort of rebelliousness to sound critical principles. Very much of his main contention is perfectly good and sound: nor could he have urged any two things more universally and everlastingly profitable than the charge never to neglect criticism, and the charge always to compare literatures of other countries, literatures of other times, literatures free from the political-religious-social *diathesis* of the actual patient.

It is generally acknowledged that the influence of Sainte-Beuve was an "infortune of Mart" or of Saturn, when it *Their ex-* induced Mr Arnold to take his two first examples *amples* of this comparative study from interesting but un-*thereof.* important people like the Guérins. But except persons determined to cavil, and those of whom the Judicious Poet remarks—

> "For what was there each cared no jot,
> But all were wroth with what was not"—

every one will admit that the rest of the seven—the "Heine," the "Pagan and Mediæval Religious Sentiment," the "Joubert," the "Spinoza," and the "M. Aurelius"—form a pentad of critical excellence, and brilliancy, and instruction, which can nowhere be exceeded. I, at least, should find it hard to match the

---

[1] He has been largely imitated in this, and I cannot help thinking that it is a pity. If a man is definitely and ostensibly "reviewing" another man's work, he has a perfect right, subject to the laws of good manners, to discuss him *quoad hoc*. But illustrations of general discourses by dragging in living persons seem to be forbidden by those laws as they apply in the literary province.

group in any other single volume of criticism. Idle that we
may frequently smile or shake the head—that we must in some
cases politely but peremptorily deny individual propositions!
Unimportant that, perhaps even more by a certain natural
perversity than by the usual and most uncritical tendency to
depress something in order to exalt something else, English
literature is, with special reference to the great generation of
1798-1834, unduly depreciated! These things every man can
correct for himself. How many could make for themselves
instances of comparative, appreciative, loosely but subtly judicial criticism as attractive, as stimulating, as graceful, as varied,
and critically as excellent, being at the same time real examples
of creative literature?

We are fortunately dispensed here from inquiring into the
causes, or judging the results, of that avocation from literature,
The latest or at least literary criticism, which held Mr Arnold
work. for exactly ten years, from 1867 to 1877. Nor
will it be necessary (though it would be pleasant) to discuss
in detail all the contributions of the slightly longer period
which was left him, from his return to his proper task in the
spring of 1877 with the article on M. Scherer's "Milton," to
his sudden and lamented death in the spring of 1888. Just
before that death he had published an article on Shelley,
which (for all the heresy glanced at below) is one of the very
best things he ever did; little less can be said of the Milton-
Scherer paper eleven years earlier, and whenever he touched
literature (which was fairly often) during the interval, he was
almost always at a very high level. A good deal, though not
quite all, of the ebullience of something not quite unlike
flippancy, which had characterised his middle period, had
frothed and bubbled itself away; his general critical views
had matured without altering; and their application to fresh
subjects, if it sometimes (as very notably in the case of Shelley)
brought out their weakness, brought out much more fully
their value and charm. The article on Mr Stopford Brooke's
Primer of English Literature, the prefaces to the selected Lives
of Johnson, to Wordsworth, to Byron, the papers in Mr Ward's
Poets on Gray and Keats (postponing for a moment the more

important Introduction to that work as a whole), the literary part of the *Discourses in America*, and (though I should put this last quartette on a somewhat lower level) those on M. Scherer's Goethe, George Sand, Tolstoi, and Amiel, form a critical baggage, adding no doubt nothing (except in one case) to the critic's general Gospel or theory, but exemplifying his critical practice with delightful variety and charm.

The possible or actual exception, however, and the piece which contains it, require more individual notice. In the *The Intro-* Introduction to Mr Ward's book, Mr Arnold devised *duction to* no one really new thing, but he gathered up and *Ward's* English focussed his lights afresh, and endeavoured to Poets. provide his disciples with an apparently new definition of poetry. He drove first at two wrong estimates thereof, his dislike of the second of which—the "personal" estimate—had been practically proclaimed from the very first, and may be allowed to be to a great extent justified, while his dislike of the first—the "historic" estimate—had always been clear to sharp-eyed students, though it lacked an equal justification. In fact, it is little more than a formulation of Mr Arnold's own impatience with the task—laborious enough, no doubt, and in parts ungrateful—of really mastering poetic, that is to say literary, history. Of course, *mere* age, *mere* priority, confers no interest of itself on anything. But to say —if we may avail ourselves of Gascoigne's instance—that the first discoverable person who compared a girl's lip to a cherry does not acquire, for that now unpermissible comparison, merit and interest, is not wise. To assume, on the other hand, some abstract standard of "high" poetry, below which time and relation will not give or enhance value, is still less wise. Portia, in a context of which Mr Arnold was justly fond, might have taught him that "nothing is good *without respect*," and that *no* "respect" is to be arbitrarily barred.

But even from the sweetest and wisest of doctors he would not, I fear, have taken the lesson. He is set to prove that "*Criticism* we must only pay attention to "the best and *of Life.*" principal things" as of old,—to class and mark these jealously, and to endeavour to discover their qualification.

You must not praise the *Chanson de Roland* or any early
French poetry very highly, but you may praise Homer, Milton,
and Dante without limit. Chaucer, not merely like Dryden
and Pope, but like Burns and Shelley, has not "high seriousness." And poetry is expressly defined as "a criticism of life,
under the conditions fixed for such a criticism by the laws of
poetic truth and poetic beauty."

It is important (though very difficult) to keep undue repetition
out of such a book as this, and we shall therefore, in regard
to "high seriousness," merely refer the reader to what has
been said above on the "grand style." And we shall cut down
criticism of the definition as much as possible, to return to it
presently. The defence of it once made, as "not a definition
but an epigram," certainly lacks seriousness, whether high or
low. The severest strictures made on Mr Arnold's levity
would not have been misplaced had he offered an epigram
here. Nor need we dwell on the perhaps inevitable, but
certainly undeniable, "circularity" of the formula. The
jugulum at which to aim is the use of the word "criticism"
at all. Either the word is employed in some private jargon, or it
has no business here. Mr Arnold's own gloss of the "application of ideas to life," gives it perhaps the doubtful benefit of
the first supposition: but, either in this way or in others,
does it very little good. *All* literature is the application of
ideas to life: and to say that poetry is the application of
ideas to life, under the conditions fixed for poetry, is simply
a vain repetition.

Yet insufficient, and to some moods almost *saugrenu*, as
such a definition may seem at first sight, it is, calmly and
Poetic Sub- critically considered, only a re-forming of the old
ject or Poetic line of battle. Once more, and for the last time
Moment. formally, Mr Arnold is taking the field in favour of
the doctrine of the Poetic *Subject*, as against what we may,
perhaps, make a shift to call the "Doctrine of the Poetic
Moment." It is somewhat surprising that, although this antinomy has been visible throughout the whole long chain of
documents which I have been endeavouring to exhibit in order,
no one, so far as I know, has ever fully brought it out, at

least on the one side. Mr Arnold—like all who agree with him, and all with whom he and they agree, or would have agreed, from Aristotle downwards—demands a subject of distinct and considerable magnitude, a disposition of no small elaborateness, a maintained and intense attitude, which is variously adumbrated by a large number of terms, down to "grand style" and "high seriousness." The others, who have fought (we must confess most irregularly and confusedly as a rule) under the flag which Patrizzi, himself half or wholly unknowing, was the first to fly, go back, or forward, or aside to the *Poetic Moment*—to the sudden transcendence and transfiguration —by "treating poetically," that is to say, by passionate interpretation, in articulate music—of *any* idea or image, *any* sensation or sentiment. They are perfectly ready to admit that he who has these moments most constantly and regularly under his command—he who can co-ordinate and arrange them most skilfully and most pleasingly—is the greatest poet, and that, on the other hand, one or two moments of poetry will hardly make a poet of any but infinitesimal and atomic greatness. But this is the difference of the poets, not of the poetry. Shakespeare is an infinitely great poet, and Langhorne an infinitesimally small one. Yet when Langhorne writes

> "Where longs to fall that rifted spire
>   *As weary of the insulting air*," [1]

he has in the italicised line a "poetic moment" which is, for its poetic quality, as free of the poetic Jerusalem as "We are such stuff," or the dying words of Cleopatra. He has hit "what it was so easy to miss," the passionate expression, in articulate music, unhit before, never to be poetically hit again save by accident, yet never to perish from the world of poetry. It is only a grain of gold ("fish-scale" gold, even, as the mining experts call their nearly impalpable specks), but it is gold: something that you can never degrade to silver, or copper, or pinchbeck.

[1] This pearl of eighteenth century minor poetry occurs in the 7th ("The Wallflower") of its author's *Fables of Flora* (Chalmers, xvi. 447). I think Scott's unequalled combination of memory and taste has used it somewhere as a motto.

To Mr Arnold this doctrine of the Poetic Moment, though he never seems to have quite realised it in its naked enormity (which, indeed, as I have said, has seldom been frankly, as here, unveiled), was from the first the Enemy. He attacked it, as we saw in his *Preface*, when he was young, and he fashions this *Introduction* so as to guard against it in his age. Yet it is curious that in his practice he sometimes goes perilously near to it. On his own showing, I cannot quite see, though I can see it perfectly well on mine, why even such a magnificent line as

"In la sua volontade e nostra pace"

should not only prove Dante's supremacy, but serve as an infallible touchstone for detecting the presence or absence of high poetic quality in other poetry. High poetic quality depends, we have been told, on the selection and arrangement of the subject. Dante, we know accidentally and from outside, *has* that selection and arrangement. But suppose he had not? The line itself can tell us nothing about them.

Nevertheless, as has been said so often, the side which a man may have taken in the everlasting and irreconcilable critical *Arnold's accomplishment and position as a critic.* battle of judges by the arrangement, and judges by the result, hardly affects his place in Criticism as it should be allotted by a final Court of Appeal. How does he express for himself, and how does he promote in others, the intelligent appreciation, the conscious enjoyment of literature? That is the question: and few critics can meet this question more triumphantly than Mr Arnold. Like others, he can but give what he has. If you ask him for a clear, complete, resumed, and reasoned grasp of a man's accomplishment —for a definite placing of him in the literary atlas—he will not have much answer to give you. He does not pretend, and has never pretended, to give any. A certain want of logical and methodical aptitude, which may be suspected, a dislike of reading matter that did not interest him, which is pretty clear, and that dread and distrust of the "historic estimate," which he openly proclaimed, would have made this impossible. But we were warned at the very outset not to go to him for it.

And for acute, sensitive, inspired, and inspiring *remarks* on the man, or the work, or this and that part of work and man—attractively expressed, ingeniously co-ordinated, and redeemed from mere desultoriness by the constant presence of the general critical creed—no critic is his superior.

Nor are these his only " proofs "—his only " pieces in hand." He may be said—imperfectly Romantic, or even anti-Romantic, as he was—to have been the very first critic to urge the importance, the necessity, of that comparative criticism of different literatures, the half-blind working of which had helped to create, if it had not actually created, the Romantic movement. In England he was absolutely the first to do this systematically, and with something like — though not with complete—impartiality. The knowledge of Spanish and Italian poetry and romance, long very common with us, had died down in the first half of the nineteenth century, and had not been much used for critical purposes while it lasted. The *engoue-ment* for French, of the late seventeenth and eighteenth, had reacted itself—in men as different as Coleridge, Landor, and De Quincey—into a depreciation which, if not " violently absurd," as Mr Arnold translates Rémusat's term of *saugrenu* applied to it, was certainly either crassly ignorant or violently unjust. German had, it is true, been exalted on the ruins of the popularity of the three Romance literatures; but it had been worshipped scarcely according to knowledge : and of the whole mediæval literature of Europe there was hardly any general critical appreciation. Mr Arnold himself, in fact, was still too much in the gall of bitterness here. It was imperative, if the Romantic and " result-judging " criticism was not to become a mere wilderness of ill-founded and partial individualisms, that this comparison should be established. It was equally imperative that it should be established, if Mr Arnold's own "*neotato*-classicism," as we have called it, was not to wizen and ossify like Neo-classicism itself. He was its first preacher with us : and there had not, to my knowledge, been any such definite preacher of it abroad, though the practice of Germany had implied and justified it from the first. And he was one of its most accomplished practitioners,—Lessing not being equal to him in charm, and Sainte-Beuve a little his inferior in passion for the best things.

Yet another watch-word of his, sovereign for the time and new in most countries, which he constantly repeated (if, being human, he did not always fully observe it himself), was the caution against confounding literary and non-literary judgment. No one rejected the exaggeration of "Art for Art's sake *only*" more unhesitatingly; but no one oftener repeated the caution against letting the idols of the nation, the sect, the party interfere with the free play of Art herself, and of critical judgment on Art.

His services, therefore, to English Criticism, whether as a "preceptist" or as an actual craftsman, cannot possibly be overestimated. In the first respect he was, if not the absolute reformer,—these things, and all things, reform themselves under the guidance of the Gods and the Destinies, not of men,—the leader in reform, of the slovenly and disorganised condition into which Romantic criticism had fallen. In the second, the things which he had not, as well as those which he had, combined to give him a place among the very first. He had not the sublime and ever new-inspired inconsistency of Dryden. Dryden, in Mr Arnold's place, might have begun by cursing Shelley a little, but would have ended by blessing him all but wholly. He had not the robustness of Johnson; the supreme critical "reason" (as against understanding) of Coleridge; scarcely the exquisite, if fitful, appreciation of Lamb, or the full-blooded and passionate appreciation of Hazlitt. But he had an exacter knowledge than Dryden's; the fineness of his judgment shows finer beside Johnson's bluntness; he could not wool-gather like Coleridge; his range was far wider than Lamb's; his scholarship and his delicacy alike gave him an advantage over Hazlitt. Systematic without being hidebound; well-read (if not exactly learned) without pedantry; delicate and subtle, without weakness or dilettanteism; catholic without eclecticism; enthusiastic without indiscriminateness,—Mr Arnold is one of the best and most precious of teachers on his own side. And when, at those moments which are, but should not be, rare, the Goddess of Criticism descends, like Cambina and her lion-team, into the lists, and with her Nepenthe makes men forget sides and sects in a common love of literature, then he is one of the best and most precious of critics.

Mr Arnold's criticism continued to be fresh and lively, without a touch of senility, or of failure to adapt itself to new conditions, till the day of his death: and when that evil day came, the nineteenth century had little more than a decade to run. On the other hand, though almost all his juniors were more or less affected by him, it cannot be exactly said that he founded any definite school, or started any by reaction from himself. The most remarkable approach to such a school that has been made since was made by Mr Pater, quite fifteen years before Mr Arnold died. No very special necessities of method, therefore, impose themselves upon us in regard to the classification of our remaining subjects in the English division: and we shall be safe in adopting a rough chronological order, taking first three very remarkable persons who—though contemporaries of Arnold—show in criticism as in other literature the influence of Carlyle.

The increasing disinclination to take the standpoint of pure literary criticism which we noticed in the master, and which *The Car-* characterised the second quarter of the century, *lylians.* naturally and inevitably reproduced itself in the three most brilliant of his disciples—Ruskin, Froude, and Kingsley—with interesting variants and developments according to the idiosyncrasy of the individual. There was, indeed, in them something which can hardly be said to have been in Carlyle at all—a weakness which his internal fire burnt out of him. This weakness, formulated most happily by an erratic person of genius whom I have alternately resolved to admit and decided to exclude here—Thomas Love Peacock,—is the principle that you "must take pleasure in the thing represented, before you can derive any from the representation."[1] Incidentally and indirectly, no doubt, *omnes eodem cogimur:* or at least there are very few who escape the suck of the whirlpool. But the declaration and formal acceptance of this principle is compara-

[1] *Gryll Grange*, chap. xiv.

tively modern: and it is one of the worst inheritances of that
Patristic attitude which was referred to long ago.[1] It is indeed
closely connected with the doctrine that "all depends upon the
subject": but the Greeks were too deeply penetrated with
æsthetic feeling to admit it openly, and, from the earliest times,
philosophised on the attraction of *repulsive* subjects. It is
indirectly excluded, likewise, by the stricter kinds of Neo-classic
rule-criticism, which saw nothing to disapprove in such poems
as the *Syphilis.* But it has, like other dubious spirits,
been let loose by "the Anarchy." That you may and should
"like what you like" is open to the twist of its correlative
—that you may *dis*like what *you choose to* dislike.

At any rate, all these three distinguished persons showed
the Carlylian-Peacockian will-worship in their different ways,
to an extent which makes them, as critics, little

Kingsley.

more than extremely interesting curiosities. Kingsley, the least strong, intellectually speaking, of the three,
shows it strongly enough. His saying (reported, I think, by
the late Mr Kegan Paul), when one of his children asked who
and what was Heine, "A bad man, my dear, a bad man," is a
specially interesting blend of the doctrine formulated by
Peacock with the old Platonic-Patristic "the poet-is-a-*good
man*" theory. Heine was not quite "a proper moral man" in
his early years, certainly: though one might have thought that
those later ones in the *Matraszen-Gruft* would have atoned in
the eyes of the sternest inquisitor. But "bad" would have
been a harsh term for him at any time. Still, it emphasises
the speaker's inability to distinguish between morality and
genius, between the man and the work. This inability was
pretty universal with him, and it makes Kingsley's own work
as criticism almost wholly untrustworthy, though often very

---

[1] This attitude was not quite universal. We find an interesting expression of more moderate opinion
from St Basil, the pupil of Libanius,
also the fellow-student of Julian, which
can be introduced here with a reference
to the excellent translation published,
with Plutarch's *How to Read Poetry* (*v.*
sup., i. 140), by Professor Paculford of
the University of Washington ("Yale
Studies," No. xv. : New York, 1902).
The Saint allows the study of the
purer profane literature as a useful
and ornamental *introduction* to higher
things.

interesting and stimulating to readers who have the proper correctives and antidotes ready: it even (which is not so very common a thing) affects his praise nearly as much as his blame. You must be on your guard against it, when he extols *Euphues* and the *Fool of Quality*[1] as much as when he depreciates Shelley.

There was less sentimental and ethical prejudice in Mr Froude than in his brother-in-law, but his political and, in a wide, not to say loose, sense philosophical, prejudices were even stronger, and he drew nearer to Carlyle than did either Kingsley or Ruskin in a certain want of *interest* in literature as literature.[2]

Froude.

We reach, however, as every one will have anticipated, the furthest point of our "eccentric" in Mr Ruskin. His way-wardness is indeed a point which needs no labour-ing, but it is never displayed more incalculably to the unwary, more calculably to those who have the clue in their hands, than in reference to his literary judgments. In-justice would be done to Rapin and Rymer if we did not give some of the enormous paradoxes and paralogisms to which he has committed himself in this way: but the very abundance of them is daunting, and fortunately his work is not so far from the hands of probable readers as the dustbin-catacombs where those poor old dead lie. "Indignation is a poetical feeling if excited by serious injury, but not if entertained on being cheated out of a small sum of money." You may admire the budding of a flower, but not a display of fireworks. Contrast the famous exposure of the "pathetic fallacy" with Scott's supposed freedom from it, and you will find some of the most exquisite *un*reasons in literature. The foam in Kingsley's song must not be "cruel," but the Greta may be "happy," simply because Ruskin does not mind finding fault with Kingsley, but has sworn to find no fault with Scott — perhaps also because he, very justly, likes sea - foam. Squire Western

Mr Ruskin.

---

[1] Not that he is wholly wrong in re-gard to either: while he does allow some of the almost unbelievable ab-surdities of Brooke's eccentric, though far from "unimportant," purpose-novel. But it is evident—and, indeed,

confessed—that he is thinking of the ethical tone and spirit first, midmost, and almost last also.

[2] Not, again, that the *Short Studies* especially can be neglected, even from our point of view.

is not "a character," because Ruskin had determined that only persons "without a *fimetic* taint" can create character, and Fielding had a fimetic taint. And dramatic poetry "despises external circumstance" because Scott did *not* despise external circumstance, and explanation is wanted why he could not write a play. Whether, with the most delicious absurdity, he works out a parallel between a "fictile" Greek vase (which is also, one hears, "of the Madonna") and "fiction," or is very nearly going to worship a locomotive when it makes a nasty noise and convinces him of its diabolism, this same exquisite unreason is always at the helm. It very often, generally indeed, is committed in admiration of the right things; it is always delightful literature itself. But it never has the judicial quality, and therefore it is never Criticism.[1]

That George Henry Lewes had many of the qualities of the critic it would be mere foolish paradox to deny. His *G. H. Lewes.* *Goethe* and his *History* (if not) *of Philosophy* yet "of Philosophers" are sufficient proofs for any one to put in: and of his mastery of that element of criticism which goes to the making of an *impresario* the wonderful success with which he formed and trained his companion, George Eliot, is a still more convincing demonstration. I understand, also, that he had real merits as a dramatic critic. But his chief critical work, *The* *His* Prin- *Principles of Success in Literature*,[2] betrays by its ciples of Success in very title the presence of an element of *vulgarity* in Literature. him, which can indeed scarcely escape notice in other parts of his work, and which is by no means removed or neutralised by the quasi-philosophic tone of the work itself. Much may be forgiven to a man, born in the first quarter of the nineteenth century, when he uses the words "progress," "success," and the like: but not everything. Fame may be the

---

[1] I have purposely taken all these examples from the *Selections*, where they will be easily found.

[2] The Essays comprising this, with their sequel and complement *The Inner Life of Art*, appeared in the *Fortnightly Review* (which Lewes edited) at its beginning in 1865, and have been usefully reprinted by Mr T. S. Knowlson (London, n. d.) I may observe that the cheap and useful collection (the "Scott Library") in which this reprint appears provides a large amount of other valuable critical matter.

last infirmity of noble minds; Success is but the first and last morbid appetite of the vulgar. And, as has been said, Lewes does not fully redeem his title by his text. There is plenty of common-sense and shrewdness. There is plenty of apparent and some real philosophy. Some, no doubt, will delight to be told that there are three Laws of Literature, that "the intellectual form is the Principle of Vision; the moral form the Principle of Sincerity ; and the æsthetic form the Principle of Beauty," and then to have these various eggs tossed and caught, in deft arrangements, for some chapters.

Indeed, there be many truths in the book, and I would most carefully guard against the idea that Lewes knowingly and deliberately recommends a mere tradesman - like view of literature. On the contrary, he strongly protests against it : and writes about Sincerity with every appearance of being sincere.[1] But his view of Imagination is confessedly low, and almost returns to the Addisonian standpoint of " ideas furnished by sight." And when, with a rather rash hiatus, he promises[2] "*for the first time* to expound scientifically the Laws that constitute the Philosophy of Criticism," we listen even less hopefully and even more doubtfully than somebody did when he understood somebody else to say that he had killed the Devil. Lewes is not unsound on the subject of imitation of the classics. He has learnt from Coleridge, or from Wordsworth, or from De Quincey, that style is the *body* not the *dress* of thought : and much that he says about it is extremely shrewd and true. But when he comes to its actual Laws and gives them as Economy, Simplicity, Sequence, Climax, and Variety, the old not at all divine despair comes upon us. All these are well, but they are not Style's crown; they are only and hardly some of the balls and strawberry leaves of that crown. A sentence, or a paragraph, or a page may be economic, simple, sequacious, climacteric, and various, and not be good style. I am not sure that a great piece of style might not be produced to which, except by violence, no one of these epithets—I am sure that many such pieces could be produced to which not all—will apply. Once more the light and holy soul of liter-

---

[1] Chap. iii. p. 47 *sq.*, ed. cit.   [2] Ibid., p. 113.

ature has wings to fly at suspicion of these bonds—and uses them.

Lewes's best critical work by far[1] is to be found in the Essay on *The Inner Life of Art*, where he handles, without *His* Inner ceremony and with crushing force, the strange old *Life of Art.* and new prudery about the connection of verse and poetry, declaring plumply that the one is the form of the other. But it is noticeable that this Essay is in the main merely a catena or chrestomathy of critical extracts, united by some useful review-work. On the whole, even after dismissing or allowing for any undue "nervous impression" created by the unlucky word "Success," it is not very possible to give him, as a critic, a position much higher than one corresponding to the position of Helps. Lewes is a Helps much unconventionalised and cosmopolitanised, not merely in externals. He is not only much more skilled in philosophical terminology, but he really knows more of what philosophy means. He has more, much more, care for literature. But the stamp of the Exhibition of 1851 is upon him also: and it is not for nothing that his favourite and most unreservedly praised models of style are drawn from Macaulay. I have no contempt for Macaulay's style myself: I have ventured in more places than one or two to stigmatise such contempt as entirely uncritical. But the *preference* of this style tells us much in this context, as the *preference* of champagne in another.

The evils of dissipation of energy have been lamented by the grave and precise in all ages: and some have held that *Bagehot.* they are specially discoverable in the most modern times. It is very probable that Criticism may charge to this account the comparatively faint and scanty service done her by one who displayed so much faculty for that service as Walter Bagehot. A man whose vocations and avocations extend (as he himself says in a letter quoted by Mr Hutton) from hunting to banking, and from arranging Christmas festivities to editing the *Economist*, can have but

---

[1] Excepting (largely) the exceptions already made, and also the huge mass of his unreprinted contributions to newspapers. *The Leader*, under his editorship, was a pioneer of improvement in reviewing.

odd moments for literature. Yet this man's odd moments were far from unprofitable. His essay on *Pure, Ornate, and Grotesque Art in Poetry* would deserve a place even in a not voluminous collection of the best and most notable of its kind. The title, of course, indicates Wordsworth, Tennyson, and Browning: and the paper itself may be said to have been one of the earliest frankly to estate and recognise Tennyson—the earliest of importance perhaps to estate and recognise Browning—among the leaders of mid-nineteenth century poetry. As such titles are wont to do, it somewhat overreaches itself, and certainly implies or suggests a confusion as to the meaning of "pure." If pure is to mean "unadorned," Wordsworth is most certainly not at his poetical best when he has most of the quality, but generally at his worst; if it means "sheer," "intense," "quintessential," his best of poetry has certainly no more of it than the best of either of the other two. The classification suggests, and the text confirms, a certain "popularity" in Bagehot's criticism. But it is popular criticism of the very best kind, and certainly not to be despised because it has something of mid-nineteenth century, and Macaulayan, materialism and lack of subtlety. This *derbheit* sometimes led him wrong, as in that very estimate of Gibbon which the same Mr Hutton praises, but oftener it contributed sense and sanity to his criticism. And there are not many better things in criticism than sanity and sense, especially when, as in Bagehot's case, they are combined with humour and with good-humour.[1]

The criticism of a critic just cited, the late Mr R. H. Hutton, affords opportunity for at least a glance at one of the most important general points connected with our subject—the general distaste for pure criticism, and the sort of relief which *l'homme sensuel moyen* seems to feel when the bitter cup is allayed and sweetened by sentimental, or political, or religious, or philosophical, or anthropological, or pantopragmatic adulteration. Mr Hutton's criticism was,

R. H. Hutton.

---

[1] The posthumous *Literary Studies*, and Mr Hutton's essay (*v.* ed. cit. on next paragraph), are the places for studying him. The study may result, without protest from me, in a high opinion of his criticism.

it is believed, by far the most popular of his day; the very respectable newspaper which he directed was once eulogised as "telling you what you *ought to* read, you know"—a phrase which might have awakened in a new Wordsworth thoughts too deep for tears or even for laughter.

The commentary on it is supplied by the two volumes of Mr Hutton's selected and collected *Essays*.[1] These constantly *His evasions* deal with things and persons of the highest import-*of literary* ance in literature; but they abstain with a sort of *criticism.* Pythagorean asceticism from the literary side of them. In his repeated dealings with Carlyle, it is always as a man, as a teacher, as a philosopher, as a politician, as a moralist, that he handles that sage—never directly, or at most rapidly and incidentally, as a writer. On Emerson he is a little more literary, but not much: and on him also he slips away as usual. Even with Poe, whom one might have thought literary or nothing, he contrives to elude us, till his judgment on the Poems suggests that *inability* to judge literature caused his refusal. Dickens, Amiel, Mr Arnold himself—the most widely differing persons and subjects—fail to tempt him into the literary open; and it is a curious text for the sermon for which we have here no room that he most nearly approaches the actual literary criticism of verse, not on Tennyson, not on "Poetry and Pessimism," not on Mr Shairp's *Aspects of Poetry*, but on Lord Houghton. He goes to the ant and is happy: with deans, and bishops, and archbishops, and cardinals he is ready to play their own game. But if Literature, as literature, makes any advances to him, he leaves his garment in her hands and flees for his life.

To assert too positively that Mr Walter Pater was the most important English critic of the last generation of the nineteenth *Pater.* century—that he stands to that generation in a relation resembling those of Coleridge to the first, and Arnold to the latter part of the second—would no doubt cause grumbles. The Kingdom of Criticism has been of old compared to that of Poland, and perhaps there is no closer point of resemblance than the way in which critics, like

[1] 2 vols., London, 1894.

Polacks, cling to the *Nie pozwalam,* to the *liberum veto.* So, respecting this *jus Poloniœ,* let us say that those are fair reasons for advancing Mr Pater to such a position, while admitting that he is somewhat less than either of his fore-runners.

His minority consists certainly not in faculty of expression, wherein he is the superior of both, nor in fineness of apprecia-
His frank tion, in which he is at least the equal of either:
Hedonism. but rather in a certain eclectic and composite character, a want of definite four-square originality, which has been remarkably and increasingly characteristic of the century itself.   In one point, indeed, he is almost entitled to the highest place, but his claim here rests rather on a frank avowal and formulation of what everybody had always more or less admitted, or by denying had admitted the acceptance of it by mankind at large—to wit, the *pleasure*-giving quality of literature.   Even he, however, resolute Hedonist as he was, falters sometimes in this respect — is afraid of the plain doctrine that the test of goodness in literature is simply and solely the spurt of the match when soul of writer touches reader's soul, the light and the warmth that follow.

In two other main peculiarities or properties of his—the, we will not say confusion but, deliberate blending of different
His poly- arts in method and process, and the adoption
techny and (modifying it, of course, by his own genius) of the
his style. doctrine of the "single word,"—he is again more of a transmitter than of a kindler of the torch.   The first proceeding had been set on foot by Lessing in the very act of deprecating and exposing clumsy and blind anticipations of it; the second was probably taken pretty straight from Flaubert.   But in the combination of all three, in the supple-ments of mother-wit, and, above all, in the clothing of the whole with an extraordinarily sympathetic and powerful atmosphere of thought and style—in these things he stands quite alone, and nearly as much so in his formulation of that new critical attitude which we have seen in process of development ever since the Romantic uprising.

The documents of his criticism are to be chiefly sought

in the *Studies in the History of the Renaissance*,[1] in parts of
Marius the Epicurean, and, of course, in the volume

His formu-
lation of the of *Appreciations*, and the little collection of Essays
new critical reprinted from *The Guardian*.[2] The posthumous
attitude.
books are less to be depended on, in consequence
of Mr Pater's very strong tendency to *cuver son vin*—to alter
and digest and retouch. I do not know any place setting forth
that view of criticism which I have myself always held more
clearly than the Preface of the *Studies*. "To feel the virtue of
the poet, or the painter, to disengage it, to set it forth,—these
are the three stages of the critic's duty." The first (Mr Pater
does not say this but we may) is a passion of pleasure, passing
into an action of inquiry; the second is that action consummated;
the third is the interpretation of the result to the world.

He never, I think, carried out his principles better than in
his first book, in regard to *Aucassin et Nicolette*, to Michelangelo,

The Re- to Du Bellay, as well as in parts of the "Pico"
naissance. and "Winckelmann" papers. But the method is
almost equally apparent and equally helpful in the more
purely "fine art" pieces—the "Lionardo," the "Botticelli," the
"Luca della Robbia." In that passage on the three Madonnas
and the Saint Anne of Da Vinci, which I have always regarded as the triumph both of his style and of his method,
the new doctrine (*not* the old) of *ut pictura poesis* comes out
ten thousand strong for all its voluptuous softness. This is
the way to judge Keats and Tennyson as well as Lionardo :
nay, to judge poets of almost entirely different kinds, from
Æschylus through Dante to Shakespeare. Expose mind and
sense to them, like the plate of a camera : assist the reception
of the impression by cunning lenses of comparison, and history,
and hypothesis ; shelter it with a cabinet of remembered reading and corroborative imagination ; develop it by meditation,
and print it off with the light of style :—there you have, in
but a coarse and half-mechanical analogy, the process itself.

[1] I fully expect to be told by some
critic that there is no such book, just
as I once was told that Browning
wrote no such poem as *James Lee*.

[2] Printed by Mr Gosse (London,
1896) privately : but I believe it has
been included in the complete edition.

I fancy that objections to this proceeding take something like the following form: "In the first place, the thing is too *Objections to* effeminate, too patient, too submissive,—it substi-*its process.* tutes a mere voluptuous enjoyment, and a dilettante examination into the causes thereof, for a virile summoning of the artist-culprit before the bar of Reason to give account of his deeds. In the second, it is too facile, too *fainéant*. In the third, it does not give sufficient advantage to the things which we like to call 'great.' The moments of pleasure are too much *atomised:* and though it may be admitted that some yield larger, intenser, more continuous supplies of moment than others, yet this is not sufficient. Lastly [this is probably always *subaud.*, but seldom uttered except by the hotter gospellers], *we* don't believe in these ecstatic moments, analysed and interpreted in tranquillity; we don't feel them, and we don't want to feel them; and you are a nasty hedonist if you do feel them."

Which protest could, no doubt, be amplified, could, with no doubt also, be supported to a certain extent. Nor is it (though he should placard frankly the fact that he agrees in the main with Mr Pater) exactly the business of the present historian to defend it at any length here, inasmuch as he is writing a history, not a "suasory." Let it only be hinted in passing that the exceptions just stated seem inconclusive—that the wanters of a sense cannot plead their want as an argument that no others have it; that the process has certainly given no despicable results; that it has seldom demonstrably failed as disastrously as the antecedent rule-system; and, most of all, that nothing can be falser than the charge of *fainéantise* and dilettanteism. Only as "the last corollary of many of an effort" can this critical skill also be attained and maintained.

At any rate, though, as often happens to a man, he became rather more of a preceptist and less of an impressionist after-*Importance* wards, Mr Pater certainly exemplified this general *of* Marius theory and practice in a very notable manner. the Epi-*Marius* is full of both: it is much more than the curean. *Wilhelm Meister* of the New Criticism. It is this which gives the critical attitude of Flavian, the hero's friend and inspirer, the supposed author of the *Pervigilium*; this, which is the literary function of "Neo-Cyrenaicism" itself— the μονόχρονος ἡδονή, the integral atom, or moment of pleasure, being taken as the unit and reference-integer of literary value; this, which gives the adjustment *ad hoc* of the *Hermotimus*. The theory and the practice take their most solid, permanent, and important form in this most remarkable book, of which I find it hard to believe that the copy, "From the Author," which lies before me, reached me more than twenty years ago. The *Renaissance* holds the first blooms and promises of them; *Appreciations* and the *Guardian Essays* the later applications and developments; but the central gospel is here.

That the opening essays of the two later books happen to contain references to myself is a fact. But I fancy that

Apprecia-tions and the "Guardian" Essays. this will not be the main interest of them to posterity, nor, strange as it may seem, is it their main interest to me.[1] The Essay on *Style* which

opens the larger and more important book, is, I think, on the whole, the most valuable thing yet written on that much-written-about subject. It presents, indeed, as I have hinted, a certain appearance of "hedging," especially in the return to matter as the distinction between "good art" and "great art," which return, as easily rememberable and with a virtuous high sound in it, appears to have greatly comforted some good if not great souls. Certainly a pitcher of gold is in some senses greater than a pitcher of pewter of the same design, especially if you wish to dispose of it to Mr Polonius. A pewter amphora is again in some senses greater than a pewter cyathus. But it does not seem to me that this helps us much. How good, on the other hand, and how complete, is that improvement upon Coleridge's dictum, which makes Style consist in the adequate presentation of the writer's "sense of fact," and the criticism of the documents adduced! How valuable the whole, though we may notice as

---

[1] I have always wondered what made him think that I personally prefer plain to ornate prose. The contrary, if it were of any moment, happens to be the case, though I own I think, as even De Quincey thought, that the ornate styles are not styles of all work.

to the writer's selection of *prose* literature as the representative art of the nineteenth century, that this was *his* art, his in consummate measure, and that verse was not.   Altogether, in short, a great paper,—a "furthest" in certain directions.

There is an interesting tender, or rather pilot-boat, to this Essay in the first of the *Guardian* Reviews on "English Literature," where the texts are the present writer's *Specimens*, Professor's Minto's *English Poets*, Mr Dobson's *Selections from Steele*, and one of Canon Ainger's many bits of yeoman's service to Lamb.   The relation is repeated between the Wordsworth Essay in *Appreciations* and a Wordsworth review among the *Guardian* sheaf : while something not dissimilar, but even more intimate, exists between the "Coleridge" Essay and the introduction to that poet in Mr Ward's well-known book, which Introduction actually forms part of the Essay itself.   In the two former cases, actual passages and phrases from the smaller, earlier, and less important work also appear in the larger and later.   For Mr Pater—as was very well known, when more than forty years ago it was debated in Oxford whether he would ever publish anything at all, and as indeed might have been seen from his very first work, by any one with an eye, but with no personal knowledge—was in no sense a ready writer, and, least of all, anxious to write as he ran, that those who run might read.   There have been critics who, without repeating themselves, and even, perhaps, with some useful additions and variations, could write half a dozen times on the same subject ; and indeed most literary subjects admit of such writing.   But such (we need not say frivolity but) flexibility was not in accordance with Mr Pater's temperament.

There is hardly one of the papers in either book (though some of the *Guardian* pieces are simple, yet quite honest and adequate reviews) that does not display that critical attitude which we have defined above, both directly and in relation to the subjects.   The most interesting and important passages are those which reveal in the critic, or recognise in his authors, this attitude itself—as when we read of Amiel : "In Switzerland it is easy to be pleased with scenery.   But the record of such pleasure becomes really worth while when, as happens with A., we feel that there has been and, with success, an intellectual effort to get at the secret, the precise motive, of this pleasure—to define feeling." Indeed, I really do not know that "to define feeling" is not as good—it is certainly as short—a definition of at least a great part of the business of the critic as you can get. And so again of Lamb: "To feel strongly the charm of an old poet or moralist, . . . and then to interpret that charm, to convey it to others, . . . this is the way of his criticism."

It is certainly the way of Mr Pater's, and it is always good to walk with him in it—better, I venture to think, than to endeavour to follow him in his rarer and never quite successful attempts to lift himself off it, and flutter in the vague. Good, for instance, as is the Essay on "Æsthetic Poetry," it would have been far better if it had contented itself with being, in fact and in name, what it is in its best parts—a review of Mr William Morris.[1] This, however, was written very early, and before he had sent out his spies to the Promised Land in *The Renaissance* (and they had brought back mighty bunches of grapes!), still more before he had reached the Pisgah of *Marius*. Even here though, and naturally still more in the much later paper on Rossetti, he presents us, as he does almost everywhere, with admirable, sometimes with consummate, examples of "defined feeling" about Wordsworth and Coleridge. about Browning and Lamb, about Sir Thomas Browne (one of his most memorable things), about more modern persons—Mr Gosse, M. Fabre, M. Filon. Particularly precious are the three papers on Shakespeare. I have always wished that Mr Pater had given us more of them, as well as others on authors possessing more of what we may call the *positive* quality, than those whom he actually selected. It would, I think, speaking without impertinence, have done him some good: and it would, speaking with certainty, have done us a great deal. One may sometimes think that it was in his case (as in some others, though so few!) almost a pity that he was in a position to write mainly for amusement. But it is not likely that his

[1] Nor do I think the "Postscript" of *Appreciations*, where the writer "Arnoldises" somewhat, one of his best things, good as it is.

sequestered and sensitive genius could ever have done its best
—if it could have done anything at all—at forced draught.
So, as usual, things are probably better as they are.

What, however, is not probable but certain, and what is
here of most importance, is that the Paterian method is co-
Universality extensive in possibility of application with the
of his entire range of criticism—from the long and slow
method. degustation and appreciation of a Dante or a
Shakespeare to the rapidest adequate review of the most
trivial and ephemeral of books. Feel; discover the source of
feeling (or no - feeling, or disgust, as it will often be in the
trivial cases); express the discovery so as to communicate the
feeling : this can be done in every case. And if it cannot be
done by every person, why, that is only equivalent to saying
that it is not precisely possible for everybody to be a critic,
which, again, is a particular case of a general proposition
announced in choice Latin a long time ago, practically anticipated in choicer Greek long before, and no doubt perfectly well
understood by wise persons of all nations and languages at
any time back to the Twenty-third of October B.C. 4004, or
any other date which may be preferred thereto. Besides the
objections before referred to, there may be others—such as
that the critic's powers, even if he possesses them, will become
callous by too much exercise,—an objection refuted by the fact,
so often noticed, that there is hardly an instance of a man
with real critical powers becoming a worse critic as he grew
older, and many a one of his becoming a better. But, at
any rate, this was Mr Pater's way of criticism : this had
already been the way pursued, more or less darkling or in
clear vision, by all modern critics—the way first definitely
formulated, and, perhaps, allowing for bulk of work, most
consistently pursued, by himself. And I have said—perhaps
often enough—that I do not know a better.

Although the relation of "moon" to "sun," so often used
as an image in literary history, will not work with pedantic
J. A. exactness in relation to Mr J. A. Symonds and the
Symonds. critic just mentioned,—for the moon is not many
times more voluminous than the sun, and there are other

difficulties,—it applies to a certain extent. Both were literary
Hedonists; both were strongly influenced by Greek and Italian.
But Mr Symonds's mind, like his style, was very much more
irregular and undisciplined than Mr Pater's (which had almost
something of Neo-classic precision adjusting its Romantic luxuriance), and this want of discipline let him loose[1] into a
loquacity which certainly deserved the Petronian epithet of
enormis, and could sometimes hardly escape the companion one
of *ventosa*. His treatise on *Blank Verse*,[2] interesting as it is,
would give the enemy of the extremer "modern" criticism far
too many occasions to blaspheme by its sheer critical anti-
nomianism: and over all his extensive work, faults of excess
of various kinds swarm. But beauties and merits are there
in ample measure as well as faults: and in the literary parts
of *The Renaissance in Italy* the author has endeavoured to put
some restraint on himself, and has been rewarded for the sacrifice. From some little acquaintance with literary history,
I think I may say that there is no better historical treatment of a foreign literature in English. One can never help
wishing that the author had left half his actual subject un-
touched, and had completed the study of Italian literature.[3]

Not much need be said of the critical production—arrested,
like the poetical, by causes unhappy but well known—of
Thomson James Thomson "the Second," hardly "the Less,"
(*"B. V."*) but most emphatically "the Other." It ought to
have been good: and sometimes (especially under the unexpected and soothing shadow of *Cope's Tobacco Plant*) was so.[4]
Thomson had much of the love, and some of the knowledge,
required; his intellect (when allowed to be so) was clear and
strong; he was, in more ways than one, of the type of those
poets who have made some of the best critics, despite the
alleged prodigiousness of the metamorphosis. But the good

---

[1] Especially in his numerous volumes
of Essays and Studies, under various
names.

[2] London, 1895.

[3] A "pair" for Mr Symonds from
the other University might be found
in the late Mr Frederick Myers, who,

with more philosophical and less artistic tendency, exhibited an equally
flamboyant style.

[4] Its chief monuments or repertories
are *Essays and Phantasies* (London,
1881) and *Poems, Essays, and Frag.
ments* (London, 1892).

seed was choked by many tares of monstrous and fatal growth. The least of these should have been (but perhaps was not) the necessity of working for a living, and not the necessity, but the provoked and accepted doom, of working for it mostly in obscure and unprofitable, not to say disreputable, places, imposed upon a temperament radically nervous, "impotent," in the Latin sense, and unresigned to facts. That temperament itself was a more dangerous obstacle : and the recalcitrance to religion which it was allowed to induce was one more danger-ous still. There are no doubt many instances where rigid orthodoxy has proved baneful, even destructive, to a man's critical powers, or at any rate to his catholic exertion of them : but there are also many in which it has interfered little, if at all. On the other hand, I can hardly think of a case in which religious, and of very few in which political, heterodoxy has not made its partisans more or less hopelessly uncritical on those with whom they disagree. Nor could the peculiar character of Thomson's education and profession fail to react unfavourably on his criticism. It is hard to get rid of some ill effects of schoolmastering in any case ; it must be nearly impossible, in the case of a proud and rather "ill-conditioned" man, who has not enjoyed either full liberal education or gentle breeding, and who is between the upper and nether millstone, as Thomson seems to have been, or at least felt himself, while he was a military schoolmaster. All these irons entered into a critical soul which might have been a fair one and brave : and we see the scars of them, and the cramp of them, too often.[1]

A journalist for one-half of his working life, and a professor —partly—of literature for the other, William Minto executed *William Minto.* in both capacities a good deal of literary work : but his most noteworthy contribution [2] to our subject consisted in the two remarkable manuals of English literary history which, as quite a young man, he drew up.[3] To say

---

[1] On men like Shelley and Blake, of course, Thomson was free from most of his " Satans " : and he speaks well on them.

[2] His *Defoe*, in the *English Men of*

Letters Series, is not to be overlooked.

[3] *Manual of English Prose Litera-ture* (Edinburgh, 1872); *Characteristics of English Poets, from Chaucer to Shirley* (Edinburgh, 1874).

that these manuals were, at the time of their publication, by far the best on the subject would be to say little: for there were hardly any good ones. Their praise can be more of a cheerfully positive, and less of a "rascally, comparative" character. They were both, but especially the *Poets from Chaucer to Shirley*, full of study, insight, originality, and grasp —where the author chose to indulge his genius. Their defects

His books on English Prose and Poetry. were defects which it requires genius indeed, or at least a very considerable share of audacity, to keep out of manuals of the kind. There is, perhaps, too much biography and too much mere abstract of contents—a thing which will never serve the student in lieu of reading, which will sometimes disastrously suggest to him that he need not read, and which must always curtail the space available for really useful guidance and critical illumination to him when he does. In the *Prose* there is something else. The book is constructed as a sort of enlarged *praxis* on a special pedagogic theory of style-teaching, that of the late Professor Bain: and is elaborately scheduled for the illustration of Qualities and Elements of Style, of Kinds of Composition. There is no need to discuss how far the schedule itself is faulty or free from fault; it is unavoidable that rigid adjustment to it—or to any such—shall bring back those faults of the old Rhetoric on which we have already commented,[1] with others more faulty than themselves. For classical literature was very largely, if not wholly, constructed according to such schemes, and might be analysed with an eye on them: English literature had other inceptions and other issues. That Minto's excellent critical qualities do not disappear altogether behind the latticework of schedule-reference speaks not a little for them.

Few writers have lost more by the practice of anonymous journalism than the late Mr Traill. He engaged *H. D. Traill.* in it, and in periodical writing generally, from a period dating back almost to the time of his leaving Oxford,[2] and

---

[1] *V. Hist. Crit.*, vol. i.

[2] I do not know whether he contributed to anything before that remarkable period *The Dark Blue*, which, during its short life in the earliest 'Seventies, had a staff not easily surpassable, and almost reminding one of the earlier English *London Magazine* and of the French *Globe*.

he had to do with it, I believe, till his death, the extraordinary quality of his work recommending him to any and every editor who knew his business. It was impossible, in reading any proof of his, be it on matters political, literary, or miscellaneous, not to think of Thackeray's phrase about George Warrington's articles, as to "the sense, the satire, and the scholarship" which characterised them. In the rather wide knowledge, which circumstances happened to give me, of writers for the press during the last quarter of the nineteenth century, I never knew his equal for combination of the three. For a great many years, however, chance, or choice, or demand, *His critical* directed him chiefly to the most important, as it *strength.* is thought, and the most paying, but the most exhausting and, as far as permanent results go, the most utterly thankless and evanescent division of journalism— political leader-writing, with actual attendance at "the House" during the Session. And this curtailed both his literary press-work and his opportunities of literary book-work. He did, however, a great deal of the former : and the labours of the much-abused but sometimes useful literary resurrection-men, who dig contributions out of their newspaper graves, could hardly be better bestowed than upon him. Fortunately, how-ever, the literary side of his criticism—he was a critic of letters and life alike, born and bred, in prose and in verse, by temper and training, in heart and brain—remains in part of *The New Lucian*, in the admirable monographs on Sterne and Coleridge,[1] and in the collection of Essays[2] issued but a year or two before his death.

In the three last-named volumes especially, his qualities as a critic are patent to any one with eyes. The two mono-*On Sterne* graphs are models of competence and grasp, but *and Cole-* they are almost greater models of the combination *ridge.* of vigour and sanity. Both subjects are of the kind which used to tempt to cant, and which now tempts to paradox. To the first sin Mr Traill had no temptation—

---

[1] Both in the *English Men of Letters.* The *Sterne* appeared in 1882 ; the *Coleridge* in 1884.

[2] *The New Fiction and other Essays on Literary Subjects* (London, 1897).

whatever fault might have been found with him, neither Pecksniffery nor Podsnappery was in the faintest degree his failing. But he might have been thought likely to be tempted, as some very clever men in our day have been, by the desire to fly in the face of the Philistine, and to flout the Family Man. There is no trace of any such beguilement—the moral currency is as little tampered with as it could have been by Johnson or by Southey, while there is no trace of the limitations of the one or of the slight Pharisaism of the other. And yet the literary judgment is entirely unaffected by this moral rectitude: the two do not trespass on each other's provinces by so much as a hair's-breadth.

The title-paper of the collected *Essays*, "The New Fiction," connects itself with several other pieces in the volume, "The *Essays on* Political Novel," "Samuel Richardson," "The Novel *Fiction.* of Manners," and, to some extent, "The Future of Humour." Mr Traill was a particularly good critic of the most characteristic product of the nineteenth century: I doubt whether we have had a better. In poetry he seemed to me to sin a little, in one direction (just as, I know, I seemed to him to sin in the other), by insisting too much, in the antique fashion, on a general unity and purpose. He shows this, I think, here in the paper on "Matthew Arnold," who, indeed, himself could hardly have objected, for they were theoretically much at one on the point. But as to prose fiction he had no illusions, and his criticism of it is consummate. We have not a few instances of onslaughts upon corrupt developments of the art by critics great and small; but I do not think I know one to equal Mr Traill's demolition of the "*grime*-novel" of to-day or yesterday. His highest achievement, however, in a single piece, "*The Future* is undoubtedly "The Future of Humour," which *of Humour.*" transcends mere reviewing, transcends the mere *causerie*, and unites the merits of both with those of the best kind of abstract critical discussion. One may say of it, without hesitation, *Ça restera;* it may be lost in the mass, now and then, but whenever a good critic comes across it he will restore it to its place. It is *about* a day, but not *of* or *for* it: it moves, and has its being, as do all masterpieces of art, small and great,

sub specie æternitatis. If it were not so idle, one could only sigh
at thinking how many a leading article, how much journey-
work in biography, one would give for Traill to be alive again,
and to write such criticism as this.

Others, great and small, we must once more sweep into the
numerus named, or unnamed. Mr Traill himself—for they were

Others:
Mansel,
Venables,
Stephen,
Lord
Houghton,
Pattison,
Church, &c

both of St John's—may be said to have directly
inherited the mantle of Dean Mansel in respect of
critical wit and sense, though the Dean had only
occasionally devoted these qualities, together with
his great philosophical powers, and his admirable
style, to pure literary criticism.[1] Of the immense
critical exercise of Mr George Venables, a little
lacking in flexibility, sympathy, and unction, but excellently
sound and strong, no salvage, I think, has ever been published :
and though a good deal is available from his yoke-fellow, Sir
James Fitzjames Stephen,[2] this latter's tastes—as his father's
had done before, though in a different direction—led him away
from the purer literary criticism. Of three other persons,
eminent in their several ways, more substantive notice may
perhaps have been expected by many, and will certainly be
demanded by some. But Lord Houghton's *Monographs*,[3] admirably written and extremely interesting to read, hardly
present a sufficiently individual kind, or a sufficiently considerable bulk of matter, for a separate paragraph. Mr Mark
Pattison's dealings with Milton and with Pope, as well as
with the great seventeenth-century scholars, may seem more,
and more imperatively, to knock for admission. As far as
scholarship, in almost every sense of the word, is concerned, no
critic can surpass him ; but scholarship, though all but indispensable as the critic's *canvass*, needs much working upon,
and over, to give the finished result. And Pattison's incurable
reticence and recalcitrance—the temperament which requires
the French words *rêche* and *revêche*, if not even *rogue*, to label it—
were rebel to the suppleness and *morigeration* which are required
from all but mere scholastic critics. The happier stars or com-

---

[1] See his *Letters, Lectures, and Re-*
views : London, 1873.

[2] Especially in *Horæ Sabbaticæ.*

[3] London, 1873.

plexion of his near contemporary, Dean Church, enabled him to do some admirable critical work on Dante, on Spenser, and on not a few others, which will be found in the *English Men of Letters*, in Mr Ward's *Poets*, in his own Collected *Essays*, and in separate books. Dr Church combined, with an excellent style, much scholarship and a judgment as sane as it was mild, nor did he allow the natural drift of his mind towards ethical and religious, rather than purely literary, considerations to draw him too much away from the latter.

Mr Coventry Patmore has been extolled to the skies by a coterie. But to the cool outsider his criticism, like his poetry,

Patmore. has somewhat too much the character of "diamondi-ferous rubbish,"—a phrase which, when applied to the poetry itself, did not, I am told, displease him. For though, in *Principle in Art*[1] and *Religio Poetæ*,[2] there may be a few things rich and rare, there is a very large sur-plusage of the *other* constituents of the mixture. The short articles of the first volume consist almost wholly of it, and might have been left in the columns of the daily paper in which they appeared with a great deal of advantage.[3] Indeed those on Keats, Shelley, Blake, and Rossetti, which unfortun-ately follow each other, make a four-in-hand good only for the knacker. Mr Patmore, when he wrote them, was too old to take the benefit of *no*-clergy, to be allowed the use of under-graduate paradox. And as, unfortunately, he was a crafts-fellow, and a craftsfellow not very popular or highly valued with most people, his denigration is all the more awkward. A man who says that *The Burden of Nineveh* " might have been written by Southey " (and I do not undervalue Southey), must have an insensible spot somewhere in his critical body. A man who says that Blake's poetry, " with the exception of four or five pieces and a gleam here and there," is mere drivel, must be suffering from critical hemiplegia. There are better things in the other volume, and its worst faults are excesses of praise,

---

[1] London, 1889.

[2] London, 1893.

[3] I do not mean that they were rub-bish there. Rubbish is only "matter in the wrong place," and what is rubbish in a book need by no means be rubbish in a newspaper.

always less disgusting, though not always less uncritical, than those of blame. But I am not here giving a full examination to Mr Patmore's criticism, I am only indicating why I do not here examine it, as I am perfectly ready to do at any moment in a proper place.

There were, I think, few English writers of the last quarter of the nineteenth century who showed more of the true critical *ethos* than the late Mr Edmund Gurney. I did not know *Edmund Gurney.* Mr Gurney myself, but most of my friends did; a situation in which there is special danger (when the friends are complimentary) of the fate of Aristides for the other person. But the good things which were told me of Mr Gurney I find to be very much more than confirmed by his books, though, of course, I also find plenty to disagree with. The earlier of them, *The Power of Sound*,[1] is in the main musical; and I have generally found (though there are some capital exceptions) that critics of poetry, or of literature generally, who start from much musical knowledge, are profoundly unsatisfactory, inasmuch as they rarely appreciate the radical difference between musical music and poetical music. Even Mitford fails here. But Mr Gurney does not. He was the first, or one of the first, I think, in English to enunciate formally the great truth that "the setting includes a new substance"—meaning not merely the technical music-setting of the composer, but that "sound accompaniment" which, in all poetry more or less, and in English poetry of the nineteenth century especially, gives a bonus, adds a *panache*, to the meaning.

He was right too, I have not the slightest doubt, in laying it down that "metrical rhythm is imposed upon, not latent in, *The Power* speech"; and he went right, where too many scholars *of sound.* of high repute have gone wrong, in seeing that the much-decried English scansion-pronunciation of Latin almost certainly brings out *to an English ear* the effect on a Latin one, better than any conjectured attempt to mimic what might have been the Latin pronunciation itself. I was delighted to find that he, too, had fixed upon Tennyson's "Fair is her cottage" (his is not quite my view, and perhaps we were both guided by a re-

[1] London, 1880.

ported speech of Mr Spedding's) as almost the *ne plus ultra* of "superadded" audible and visual effect combined. And he is well worth reading on certain "illusions" of Lessing's.

The literary part of *The Power of Sound* is, however, if not accidental, incidental mainly: not a few of the papers in the Tertium Quid. second volume of *Tertium Quid*[1] deal with literature pure and simple. They are to some extent injured by the fact that many, if not most of them, are merely strokes, or parries, or *ripostes*, in particular duels or *mélées* on dependences of the moment. And, as I have pointed out in reference to certain famous altercations of the past, these critical squabbles seem to me almost invariably to darken counsel—first, by leading the disputants away from the true points, and secondly, by inducing them to mix in their pleadings all sorts of flimsy, ephemeral, and worthless matter. Not the point, but what Jones or Brown has said about the point, becomes the object of the writer's attention; he wants to score off Brown or Jones, not to score for the truth. So when Mr Gurney contended with the late Mr Hueffer—another literary-musical critic, who did *not*, as Mr Gurney did, escape the dangers of the double employ—when he contributed not so much a *tertium* as a *quartum quid* to the triangular duel of Mr Arnold, Mr Austin, Mr Swinburne about Byron—he did not always say what is still worth reading. And he makes one or two odd blunders, such as that the French are blind to Wordsworth, whereas Wordsworth's influence on Sainte-Beuve, to name nobody else,[2] was very great. But he is always sensible,[3] and he always has that double soundness on the passionate side of poetry and on the peculiar appeal of its form, which is so rare and so distinctive of the good critic.

These qualities should, of course, appear in his essay on the "Appreciation of Poetry";[4] and they do. It is, however, perhaps well to note that, while quite sound on the point that there is a right as well as a wrong comparison, he, like

---

[1] 2 vols., London, 1887.

[2] Such as even Gautier.

[3] This sensibleness, no doubt, ought always to characterise the "Tertium Quid" or "cross-bench" mind. It is equally indubitable that it most commonly does not.

[4] *T. Q.*, vol. ii.

others, hardly escapes the further danger of "confusing the confusion"—of taking what is really the right comparison for what is really the wrong. The comparison which disapproves one thing because it is unlike another is wrong, not the comparison which is used to bring out a fault, though the unlikeness is not assigned as the reason of the fault at all. But I am here slipping from history to doctrine on this particular point. I think Mr Gurney, right in the main, might have been still *righter:* but in general I am sure that he had admirable critical qualities, and I only wish he had chosen, or had been forced, to use them more fully and frequently.[1]

---

[1] I do not take special notice of R. L. Stevenson here, because his criticism, in any formal shape, belongs mainly to the earlier and tentative stage of his work, and never, to my fancy, had much fixity or grip, interesting and stimulating as it is. I ventured to tell him, when I met him first, after the appearance of *The New Arabian Nights* in *London,* that here was Apollo waiting for him, not there: and I hold to the view. Others, such as Mr Henley (with whom also I rowed in that galley—a tight and saucy one, if not exactly a *galère capitaine*), Mr Robert Buchanan, Sir Leslie Stephen, Prof. Bain, have passed away too recently ; and yet others must fall into the *numerus.*

CONCLUSION.

THERE is no need of elaborate summary of the stages of English Criticism as they have been given here. The tale divides itself into three pretty plain parts—the initial stage of Elizabethan Criticism, tentative, hesitating, and scattered; the Neo-Classic period, starting after something of an interval with Dryden and continuing, though by no means without protest, to and almost beyond the beginning of the nineteenth century; and lastly, the season, not entirely unruffled by dissent, of the discrediting of Rules and the more or less free appreciation of Results. We have seen how idle it is to speak with bated breath of a roll and record which contains greater names, like those from Ben Jonson to Pater, and lesser, like those from Gascoigne and Sidney to Gurney and Traill. The record stands, and (when once set forth) can stand by itself, without final flourish of trumpet and waving of flag.

The blunder of belittling English Criticism as it stands is connected with another blunder, that of regarding it as, whether good or bad, mainly unoriginal. Except in so far as the Elizabethans are concerned—and everything must have its "pupillary" state—this is far from being justified. Dryden, it is true, looks and even speaks as if he were largely indebted to the French, but, as has been shown, everything that is good in him is almost wholly original, and when he follows he is almost always wrong. So again with Johnson—his mistakes are traditional, his achievements (and they were neither few nor small) are his own. The indebtedness of Coleridge to the Germans—in the way of general suggestion and of subjection to an atmosphere of stimulating quality at a susceptible time—is probably real, but it goes no further, and, in the sense in which it has sometimes been interpreted, may be said not to exist. From the most original and *germinal* French writer of the eighteenth century—Diderot—it would be difficult to trace any influence on English Criticism till quite recent times, and Diderot himself had owed much of his own attitude to English literature. The influence of Sainte-Beuve on Matthew Arnold was indeed immense—those familiar with the mighty forest of the *Causeries* will find its wood constantly furnishing the Arnoldian arrows. But Mr Arnold's *principles* were not Sainte-Beuvian: they were, as has been said, *neotato*-classic—a novel and rather capricious selection and propagation of Aristotelian doctrine. We may alter the old boast and make it something less modest. Our critical glass is not small, and not a few of us at least have drunk out of it.

But something about the general nature and progress of Criticism itself should perhaps be added.

The difficulty of keeping a steady, achromatic, comparative estimate is not a small one, nor one easily got over. We have seen how, at one time, Criticism has been entirely bewitched by the idea of a Golden Age, when all poets were sacred and all critics gave just judgment: how, at another, a confidence, bland or pert as the case might be, has existed (and exists) that we are much wiser than our fathers. Above all, we have seen repeatedly that constant and most dangerous delusion that the fashion which has just ceased to be fashionable is a specially bad and foolish one, with its concomitant and equally unreasonable but rather less dangerous opposite, that the fashion that *is* in is the foolishest and feeblest of all fashions. Against all other fallacies watch and ward has to be kept.

From these same dangers, however, the very fact of having steadily worked through the history from the beginning, even from so late a one as that of English Criticism proper, yet with a fair retrospect of the past and a clear comprehension of the present, should be something of a safeguard for writer and reader alike. We have seen how justly Mr Rigmarole might

pronounce all times "pretty much like our own" in respect of
the faults and dangers of criticism, though this time might
incline to that danger and that to this.   If one—even one—
lesson has emerged, it must have been that to select the
favourite critical fancy of *any* time as the *unum necessarium*
is fatal—or redeemed only by the completeness with which
such a selection, when faithfully carried out, demonstrates its
own futility.   Yet we have seen also that the criticism of no
time is wholly idle or wholly negligible—that the older periods
and the older men are no "shadows," but almost more real,
because more original, than the newer—that each and all have
lessons, from the times of prim and strictly limited knowledge
to the times of swaggering and nearly unlimited ignorance.

In the last two chapters we have surveyed, in most cases
virtually and in some actually, to the end of the Nineteenth
century, the latest stage or stages of that modified and modern-
ised criticism, the rise of which and its victorious establishment
were traced earlier.   We have seen how—owing partly, no
doubt, to the mere general law of flux and reflux, but partly,
and perhaps mainly, to the enlarged study of literature, and
the breaking down, in connection with this, of the Neo-classic
standards and methods,—judging *a posteriori*, or, as Johnson,
prophesying and protesting, called it, "by the event," came to
take the place of judging *a priori*, or by the rule.   That in many
cases the new critics would not themselves have admitted this
description of their innovations we have not attempted to deny
or disguise: but we have not been able to agree with them.
We have, however, seen also that to satisfy the craving for
generalities and for "pushing ignorance further back," new
preceptist systems, in no small number, and sometimes of great
pretensions and no small complexity, have been advanced, and
that the new subject of "Æsthetics"—in itself little more than
a somewhat disorderly generic name for these systems—has
obtained considerable recognition.   But no one of these has, nor
have all of them together, attained anything like that position
of acknowledgment, "establishment," and authority which was
enjoyed by the Neo-classic faith: and we have seen that some
of the straitest doctrinaires have condescended, while the

general herd of critics have frankly preferred, to judge authors as they found them.

That the results have been in many ways satisfactory, it seems impossible for any one but the extremest of partisans to deny. The last and worst fault of any state, political or other, that of "decreeing injustice by a law," has been almost entirely removed (at least as a general reproach) from the state of Criticism. That a work of art is entitled to be judged on its own merits or demerits, and not according as its specification does or does not happen to be previously entered and approved in an official schedule—this surely cannot but seem a gain to every one not absolutely blinded by prejudice. Nor is it the only point which ought to unite all reasonable suffrages. By the almost necessary working of the new system, the *personnel* of Criticism has been enlarged, improved, strengthened in a most remarkable degree. The old opposition of the poet and the critic has ceased to exist. It is true indeed that, as we have seen, it never existed as an absolute law; but it was a prevailing one, and it deprived criticism of some of its most qualified recruits, or made them, if they joined, inconsistent, now like Dryden, now like Johnson. Nay, Coleridge himself could hardly have been the critic he was under the older dispensation, much less those other poets, of our own and other countries, who have enriched the treasury of a Goddess once thought to be the poet's deadliest foe.

Yet, again, putting the contributions of poets, as poets, on one side, the general literary harvest of the kind has been undoubtedly more abundant, and in its choicer growths more varied, more delightful, even more instructive. A collection of the best critical results of the last century only, and only in English, would certainly yield to no similar book that could be compiled from the records of any other period, even of much greater length. From the early triumphs of Coleridge and Hazlitt, through the whole critical production of Matthew Arnold, to the work of writers unnecessary to enumerate, because all possible enumeration would almost necessarily be an injustice, you might collect—not a volume, not half a dozen, but a small, and not so very small, library, of which you could not merely say "Here be truths," but "Here is reading which any person of ordinary intelligence and education will find nearly, if not quite, as delightful as he can find in any other department of *belles lettres*, except the very highest triumphs of prose and poetic Fiction itself."

Now, the removal of the reproach of injustice, the removal of the reproach of dulness, these are surely good and even great things: while better, and greater still, is the at least possible institution of a new Priesthood of Literature, disinterested, teaching the world really to read, enabling it to understand and enjoy, justifying the God and the Muse to Men.

This is a fair vision; so fair, perhaps, that it may seem to be, like others, made of nothing more solid than "golden air." That would be perhaps excessive, for, as has been pointed out above, the positive gains under this New Dispensation, both of good criticism produced and of good literature freed from arbitrary persecution, have been very great. But, as we foreshadowed in Interchapter III., there is another side to the account, a side not to be ignored. If Buddha and Mr Arnold be right, and if "Fixity" be "a sign of the Law"—then most assuredly Modern Criticism is not merely lawless, but frankly and wilfully antinomian. It is rare to find two critics of competence liking just the same things; it is rarer still to find them liking the same things for the same reason. And so it happens that the catholic ideal which this New Criticism seemed likely to establish is just as far off, and just as frequently neglected or even outraged, as in the old days of strict sectarianism, and without the same excuse. The eighteenth-century critic could render a reason, *pro tanto* valid, for patronising Chaucer, and taking exceptions even to Milton, because neither was like Dryden. But the critic of to-day who belittles Dryden because he is not like Chaucer or Milton is utterly without excuse:—and yet he is to be found, and found in high places. If (as in another case) critics were to be for a single day what they ought to be, the world would no doubt be converted; but there certainly does not appear to be much more chance of this in the one case than in the other.

And so the enemy—who is sometimes a friendly enemy enough — has not the slightest difficulty in blaspheming,— in asking whether the criterion of pleasure does not leave the fatal difficulty: "Yes: but pleasure *to whom ?* "; in demanding some test which the simple can apply; in reproaching "Romantic" critics with faction and will-worship, with inconsistency and anarchy. Nor perhaps is there any better shift than the old Pantagruelian one—to *passer oultre.* There *are* these objections to the modern way of criticism: and probably they can never be got rid of or validly gainsaid. But there is something beyond them, which can be reached in spite of them, and which is worth the reaching.

This something is the comprehensive and catholic possession of literature—all literature and all that is good in all—which has for the first time become possible and legitimate. From Aristotle to La Harpe—even to one of the two Matthew Arnolds—the covenant of criticism was strictly similar to that of the Jewish Law, — it was a perpetual "Thou shalt not do this," or "Thou shalt do this only in such and such a specified way." There might be some reason for all the commandments, and excellent reason for some; but these reasons were never in themselves immortal, and they constantly tended to constitute a mortal and mortifying Letter. The mischief of this has been shown in the larger *History* generally, here as regards English, and there is no need to spend more time on it. Nor is it necessary even to argue that in the region of Art such a Law entirely lacks the justification which it may have in the region of Morals.

But it may fairly be asked, How do you propose to define *any* principles for your New Critic? And the answers are ready, one in Hellenic, one in Hebraic phraseology. The definition shall be couched as the man of understanding would define it: and if any will do the works of the New Criticism he shall know the doctrine thereof. Nor are the works themselves hard to set forth. He must read, and, as far as possible, read everything—that is the first and great commandment. If he omits one period of a literature, even one author of some real, if ever so little, importance in a period, he runs the risk of putting his view of the rest out of focus; if he fails to take at least some account of other literatures as well, his state will be nearly as perilous. Secondly, he must constantly compare books, authors, literatures indeed, to see in what each differs from each, but never in order to dislike one because it is not the other. Thirdly, he must, as far as he possibly can, divest himself of any idea of what a book *ought to be*, until he has seen what it is. In other words, and to revert to the old simile, the plate to which he exposes the object cannot be too carefully prepared and sensitised, so that it may take the exactest possible reflection: but it cannot also be too carefully protected from even the minutest line, shadow, dot, that may affect or predetermine the impression in the very slightest degree.

To carry this out is, of course, difficult; to carry it out in perfection is, no doubt, impossible. But I believe that it can be done in some measure, and could be done, if men would take criticism both seriously and faithfully, better and better —by those, at least, who start with a certain favourable disposition and talent for the exercise, and who submit this disposition to a suitable training in ancient and modern literature. And by such endeavours, some nearer approach to the "Fair Vision" must surely be probable than was even possible by the older system of schedule and precept, under which even a new masterpiece of genius, which somehow or other "forced the consign" and established itself, became a mischief, because it introduced a new prohibitive and exclusive pattern. I have said more than once that, according to the common law of flux and reflux—the Revolution which those may accept who are profoundly sceptical of Evolution—some return, not to the old Neo-classicism, but to some more dogmatic and less æsthetic criticism than we have seen for the last three generations, may be· expected, and that there have been not a few signs of its arrival. But this is a History, not a Prophecy, and sufficient to the day is the evil thereof. Perhaps even the good is not quite so insufficient as the day itself, " chagrined at whatsoe'er *it is*," may be apt to suppose.

"The Whole man idly boasts to find," no doubt. Not many

have even attempted to do it; few who have attempted it have succeeded in that comparatively initial and rudimentary adventure which consists in justly finding the parts. But Criticism is, after all, an attempt, however faulty and failing, however wandering and purblind, to do both the one and the other. No Muse, or handmaid of the Muses (let it be freely confessed) has been less often justified of her children : none has had so many good-for-nothings for sons. Of hardly any have some children had such disgusting, such patent, such intolerable faults. The purblind theorist who mistakes the passport for the person, and who will not admit without passport the veriest angel; the acrid pedant who will allow no one whom he dislikes to write well, and no one at all to write on any subject that he himself has written on, or would like to write on, who dwells on dates and commas, who garbles out and foists in, whose learning may be easily exaggerated but whose taste and judgment cannot be, because they do not exist;—these are the too often justified patterns of the critic to many minds. The whole record of critical result, which we have so laboriously arranged and developed, is a record of mistake and of misdoing, of half-truths and nearly whole errors.

So say they, and so let them say: things have been said less truly. But, once more, all this is no more Criticism itself than the crimes and the faults of men are Humanity in its true and eternal idea. Criticism is the endeavour to find, to know, to love, to recommend, not only the best, but all the good, that has been known and thought and written in the world. If its corruption be specially detestable, its perfection is only the more amiable and consummate. And the record of the quest, while it is not quite the record of the quest for other Eldorados—while it has some gains to yield, some moments of adeption, some instances of those who did not fail—should surely have some interest even for the general: it should more surely have much for those few but not unworthy, faint yet pursuing, who would rather persevere in the search for the unattainable than rust in acquiescence and defeat.

For to him who has once attained, who has once even comprehended, the *ethos* of true criticism, and perhaps to him only, the curse which Mr Browning has put in one of his noblest and most poetic passages does not apply. To him the "one fair, good, wise thing" that he has once grasped remains for ever as he has grasped it—*if* he has grasped it at first. Not twenty, not forty years, make any difference. What has been, has been and remains. If it is not so, if there is palling and blunting, then it is quite certain either that the object was unworthy or that the subject did not really, truly, critically embrace it—that he was following some will-o'-the-wisp of fancy on the one hand, some baffling wind of doctrine on the other, and was not wholly, in brain and soul, under the real inspiration of the Muse. That this adeption and fruition of literature is to a certain extent innate may be true: that it is both idle and flagitious to simulate it if it does not exist, is true. But it can certainly be cultivated where it exists, and it probably in all cases requires cultivation in order that it may be perfect. In any fair state of development it is its own exceeding great reward,—a possession of the most precious that man can have. And the practical value of the Art of Criticism, and of the History of Criticism (which, as in other cases, is merely the exposition of the art in practice), is that it can and does assist this development; that by pointing out past errors it prevents interference with enjoyment; that it shows how to grasp and how to enjoy; that it helps the ear to listen when the horns of Elfland blow.

APPENDIX.

THE OXFORD CHAIR OF POETRY.

THE HOLDERS—EIGHTEENTH CENTURY MINORS—LOWTH—HURDIS—THE RALLY: COPLESTON — CONYBEARE — MILMAN — KEBLE — THE 'OCCASIONAL [ENGLISH] PAPERS'—THE 'PRÆLECTIONS'—GARBETT — CLAUGHTON — DOYLE — SHAIRP— PALGRAVE—"SALUTANTUR VIVI."

(*I have thought this sketch worth giving, partly as an example of the kind of excursus which might be appended, perhaps not without some advantage, and certainly in some numbers, to this History. But I give it also because it illustrates—in a manner which cannot be elsewhere paralleled at all in our own country, and to which I know no Continental parallel—by a continuous and unbroken chain of instances and applications, the course of European as well as English theory, practice, and taste in Criticism, from a period when the Neo-classic creed was still in at least apparently fullest flourishing, through nearly two whole centuries, to what, in the eye of history, is the present moment. The enforced vacation of the Chair after a single decade at most, and its filling by popular election, and not by the choice of an individual or a board, add to its representative character: and the usual publication of at least some of the results, in each case, makes that character almost uniquely discoverable in its continuity, while even the change of vehicles from Latin to English is not without its importance. There is no room here—and it would perhaps be unnecessary in any case—to anticipate the easy labour of summarising its lessons. But I think they may be said to emphasise the warning—frequently given or hinted already—that the result of the altered conditions and laws of criticism is not clear gain. No part of Mr Arnold's best critical work was, I think, done for the Chair; and I should myself be inclined to select, as the best work actually done for it, that of Keble, who represents the combination of the old Classical-Preceptist tradition, with something of the new comparison and free expatiation, as well as very much of the purely appreciative tendency.*)

This Chair—founded by Henry Birkhead, D.C.L., a Trinity man, a Fellow of All Souls, and a member of the Inner Temple—began *The holders.* its operations in 1708, the conditions of its tenure (which have only recently been altered) providing for a first holding of five years, a single renewal for the same period, and a sort of rotation, in the sense that the same college could not supply two successive occupants. The actual incumbents have been: 1708-18, Trapp; 1718-28, Thomas Warton the elder; 1728-38, Spence; 1738-41, John Whitf(i)eld; 1741-51 (the most distinguished name as yet), Lowth; 1751-56, William Hawkins; 1756-66, Thomas Warton the younger; 1766-76, Benjamin Wheeler; 1776-83, Randolph; 1783-93, Holmes; 1793 to 1802, Hurdis. With the nineteenth century a brighter order begins, all but one or two of the Professors having made their mark out of the Chair as well as in it. They were: Copleston, 1802-12; Conybeare, 1812-21; Milman, 1821-31; Keble, 1831-42; Garbett (the dark star of this group, but, as we shall see, not quite lightless), 1842-52; Claughton, 1852-57; Matthew Arnold, 1857-67; Sir Francis Doyle, 1867-77; Principal Shairp, 1877-87; Mr Palgrave, 1887-95; while of living occupants Mr Courthope resigned the Chair after a single tenure; and his successors have undergone a statutory limitation to this term.

Of these, Trapp, Spence, the younger Warton, and Arnold have received notice in the text, which would have been theirs had they never held the Chair. The lucubrations of the first *Eighteenth century minors.* held for some time an honourable place as an accepted handbook on the subject. Spence, profiting by the almost Elysian tolerance of his sensible century, and finding that neither residence nor lecturing was insisted on, seems to have resided very little, and to have lectured hardly or not at all. Tom Warton the younger, whose *History* would have dignified any *cathedra*, appears to have devoted himself during his actual tenure entirely to the classics, and never to have published any of his lectures except one on Theocritus. His father, in the interval between the respectable labours of Trapp and the philosophical silence of Spence, had earned no golden opinions, and though the repeated attacks of Amherst in *Terræ Filius* may have been due partly to political rancour, and partly to that ingenious and unlucky person's incorrigible Ishmaelitism, it seems to have been admitted that the Professor's understanding and erudition lay very open to criticism, and that his elocution and manner were not such as could shield them. Of Whitfield, Hawkins, Wheeler, Randolph, and Holmes, what I have been able to gather may best be set in a note.[1] The first person to make any real figure in and for the Chair

---

[1] Of Whitfield (or Whit*feld*, as some write) I have found nothing but that he wrote some Latin verses on William the Third. The second volume of William Hawkins's *Tracts* (1758) contains, besides a ridiculous tragedy, *Henry and Rosamond*, an *Essay on Drama*, principally occupied by carpings at Mason's *Elfrida*, and some Letters on Pope's Commentary on Homer—both very small critical beer. About Wheeler I find less even than about Whitfield. The piety of his son published—long after date and in our own times—1870—the *Prælections* of John Randolph, a man who, besides holding several other professorships at Oxford, attained to eminence in the Church, and died Bishop of London in 1813. They are very sober and respectable. There is in poetry a *non contemnenda proprietas quod imitando præcipiat;* and the warning, *non aliunde artis suæ rudimenta desumet Criticus nisi ex sanæ Logices præceptis,* might with advantage have been observed oftener than it has been. But Randolph sticks in the bark and the letter. Holmes, a poet after a fashion, a theologian, and what not, seems to have written more freely on anything than on criticism.

was the author of *De Sacra Poesi Hebræorum,* which at once attained not merely an English but a European reputation.

To discuss the Hebrew scholarship of this famous book (which
was first published in 1753, and repeatedly reprinted, revised,
Lowth. translated, attacked, defended) would be wholly out of
place here, even if the writer had not almost wholly forgotten the little Hebrew he learnt at school. It is still, I believe
—even by specialists with no general knowledge of literature—
admitted to have been epoch-making in its insistence on the
parallelism of Hebrew poetry. But to those who take the historical
view of literature and of criticism its place is secure quite apart
from this. Not merely in the Renaissance, but in the Middle and
even the Dark Ages, the matter of the Bible had been used to
parallel and illustrate rhetorical and literary doctrines and rules.
But Lowth was almost the first to treat its poetical forms from
something like the standpoint of sound comparative literary criticism.[1] Now this, as the whole tenor of our book has gone to
contend, was the chief and principal thing that had to be done.
If we have any advantage over the men of old, it is that we (or
some of us) have at last mastered the fact that one literature or
one language cannot *prescribe* anything to another, but that it may
teach much. And this new instance of a literature—unique in
special claims to reverence, unique likewise in the fact that in its
best examples it could owe nothing to those Greeks and Romans
who have so beneficently but so tyrannously influenced all the
modern tongues—was invaluable in its quality and almost incalculable in its moment. That Lowth's exposition resulted directly or
indirectly in not a little maladroit *imitation* of Hebrew poetry was
not his fault; his critical lesson was wholly good.

Hurdis, a person now very much forgotten, had his day of interest
and of something like position. He is not unfrequently quoted by
Hurdis. writers, especially by Southey, of the great period of
1800-1830, which he a little preceded, and he has the
honour—rare for so recent a writer—of a whole article[2] on his
poems in the *Retrospective Review.* As a poet he was mainly an imitator of his friend Cowper—a fact which, with the title of his chief
work, *The Village Curate,* will give intending or declining readers a
sufficiently exact idea of what they are undertaking or relinquishing.
Easy blank verse, abundant and often not infelicitous description,
and unexceptionable though slightly copybook sentiments,[3] form his

---

[1] He complies with the requirements
of method and fashion by dealing *generally* with the End and Usefulness of
Poetry, its Kinds and so forth. But all
this we have had a thousand times.
What we have here specially is a comparison, and a new comparison.

[2] Vol. i. p. 57 *sq.*

[3] Southey, himself a proper moral
man in all conscience, but a sensible
one withal, somewhere remarks, "said
well but not wisely" on Hurdis's

"Give me the steed
Whose generous efforts bore the prize away,
I care not for his grandsire or his dam"

A mild echo of the revolutionary period!

poetic or versifying staple. As a critic I regret to find that my note on him is "Chatter": and I do not know anything of his that makes me, on reflection, think this unjust.

I should be half afraid that the interest which I feel in the next set of Prælections, those of Edward Copleston,—"*the* Provost," as

The rally: Copleston. he anticipated Hawkins in being to Oxford men, even not of his own college of Oriel,—might be set down to that *boulimia* or morbid appetite for critical writings of which I have been accused, if I had not at hand a very potent compurgator. Keble, it is true, was a personal friend of Copleston's. But he was not at all the man to let personal friendship, any more than personal enmity, bias his judgment; and he was admirably qualified to judge. Yet he says deliberately [1] that the book "is by far the most distinct, and the richest in matter, of any which it has fallen to our lot to read on the subject." I cannot myself go quite so far as that, and I doubt whether Keble himself would have gone so far when, twenty years later, he wrote his own exquisite Lectures; but I can go a long way towards it.

The future Provost and Bishop has, indeed, other critical proofs on which to rely,[2]—the famous and excellent "Advice to a Young Reviewer," which I fear is just as much needed, and just as little heeded, as it was a hundred years ago, the admirable smashing of the *Edinburgh's* attack on Oxford, and other matters,—but the *Prælections* [3] are the chief and principal thing. Keble insisted that they ought to be Englished, but I am not so sure. They form one of the *severest* critical treatises with which I am acquainted; and some of the features of this severity would, I think, appear positively uninviting in English dress, while they consistently and perfectly suit the toga and the sandal. But I must explain a little more fully in what this "severity" consists; for the word is ambiguous. I do not mean that Copleston rejects Pleasure as the end of Poetry; for, on the contrary, he writes *Delectare* boldly on his shield, and omits *prodesse* save as an indirect consequence. I do not mean that he is a very Draconic critic of particulars, though he can speak his mind trenchantly enough.[4] Nor do I mean that he is a very abstract writer; for every page is strewn with concrete illustrations, very well selected, and, for the most part, un-hackneyed.

His severity is rather of the ascetic and "methodist" kind; he resembles nothing so much as a preceptist of the school of Hermogenes, who should have discarded triviality, and risen to very nearly the weight and substance of Aristotle. At the very begin-

---

[1] In a review in the *British Critic* (1814), reprinted in *Papers and Reviews*, Oxford and London, 1877.

[2] See the *Remains*, edited by his son. London, 1871.

[3] First published at the end of his tenure in 1813. My copy is the 2nd ed., Oxford, 1828.

[4] See remarks on Trapp, pp. 6 and 7 ed. cit.

ning he makes a statute for himself, to cite no literature but Greek
and Latin, and to use no language but these.   And he never breaks
either rule; for though, on rare occasions, he refers to English writers
—Shakespeare, Milton, Dryden, Burke, Reynolds[1]—it is a reference
only, to books, or poems, or passages, never a citation.   And in the
second place his method is throughout—constant as is his use of the
actual poetic object-lesson—to proceed by general categories, not of
poetic kinds (he shuns that ancient and now well-beaconed quick-
sand[2]) but of qualities, constituents, means.   His whole book, after
a brief definition or apology for not defining, is distributed under
four parts, — Of Imitation, Of the Emotions, Of Imagination
(Phantasia), and Of Judgment, — though he never reached the
fourth,[3] owing to his tenure of the Chair coming to an end.   After
a pretty full discussion of the nature and subject of Imitation, he
makes his link with his next subject by dwelling on the *Imitatio
morum*, and so of the Passions themselves.   In this part a very large
share is given to the subject of *Sententiæ*—"sentiments," as Keble
translates it, though, as I have pointed out formerly,[4] no single translation of the word is at all satisfactory.   The section on Imagination
is very interesting.   Copleston is at a sort of middle stage between
the restricted Addisonian and the wide Philostratean-Shakespearean-
Coleridgean interpretation of the word.   He expressly admits that
other senses besides sight can supply the material of *Phantasia;*
but his examples are mainly drawn from material which *is* furnished
by the sight, and his inclusions of Allegory, Mythology, &c., with
other things, sometimes smack of an insufficient discrimination
between Imagination and Fancy.   Indeed the fact that he is Præ-
Coleridgean helps to give him his interest.

Keble mildly complains that Copleston does not make use of that
doctrine of Association which he himself, writing so early, had
perhaps adopted, not from Coleridge but direct from Hartley.   We
have, in our day, seen this doctrine worked to death and sent to
the knacker's in philosophy generally; but there is no doubt that
it can never be neglected in poetry, being, perhaps, the most universal
(though by no means *the* universal) means of approach to the sources
of the poetic pleasure.   It does not, however, seem to me that
Copleston intended to mount so high, or go so far back : his aim
was, I think, more rhetorical, according to a special fashion, than
metacritical.   But his mediate axioms are numerous and often very
informing : and his illustrations, as has been said, abundant, really
illustrative, and singularly recreative.   He lays most Latin and

---

[1] *V.* pp. 187, 197, 390, 229, 177.
[2] Keble, however, was right in specify-
ing the chief exception—the admirable
prælection on *Epitaphs* (No. 27, p. 340).
[3] This is all the more tantalising in

that his definition of *Judicium* in *Præl.*
2 seems to promise nothing less than an
inquiry into the critical and appreciative faculty as regards Poetry.
[4] *Hist. Crit.*, vol. i.

many Greek poets under contribution; but some of his most effective examples are drawn from a poet whom he does not critically over-value, but who has no doubt been, as a rule, critically undervalued, and for whom he himself evidently had a discriminating affection—that is to say, Claudian.

On the whole, the appearance of a book of this scope and scheme, at the very junction of the centuries and the 'isms, Classic and Romantic, is of singular interest. Until intelligent study of the Higher Rhetoric—reformed, adjusted, and extended—has been re-introduced, such another will not come. But such another might come with very great advantage, and would supply a very important *tertium quid* to the mere Æsthetics and to the sheer Impressionism between which Criticism has too often divided itself.

There is almost as much significance in Copleston's successor, though it is a significance of a different kind. For J. J. Conybeare *Conybeare.* was the first Professor of Poetry to bestow attention on Anglo-Saxon (Warton, even in his *History*, had not gone, with any knowledge, beyond Middle English), and so to complete the survey of all English Literature. Before his appointment he had held, as its first occupant, the chair of Anglo-Saxon itself; and while Professor of Poetry he was a country parson. He died suddenly and comparatively young, and his remarkable *Illustrations of Anglo-Saxon Poetry* [1] were published after his death by his brother, who is actually responsible for a good part of its matter, so that the book is a composite one. It is thus mainly in its general significance—for Conybeare's Prælections as Professor were not, so far as I know, published—that it is valuable for us. But the value thus given is unmistakable. Conybeare's individual judgments and *aperçus* are always interesting, and often acute; but his real importance lies in the fact that he was almost the first—though Mitford, after Ellis, had attempted the thing as an outsider—to move back the focussing-point sufficiently to get *all* English Literature under view. Nothing could serve more effectually to break up the false standing-ground of the eighteenth century.

A curious but perhaps not surprising thing about Milman's Professorship is that it aroused the ire of an undergraduate poet of *Milman.* the rarest though of the most eccentric type—namely, Beddoes. If Milman really did "denounce" *Death's Jest-Book*, [2] it is a pity that his lectures were (so far as I know)

---

[1] London, 1826.

[2] See Beddoes' *Letters* (ed. Gosse, London, 1894), p. 68: "Mr Milman (our poetry professor) has made me quite unfashionable here by denouncing me as one of a 'villainous school.'" These *Letters* are crammed with matter of literary and critical interest.

I was much tempted to give them a place in the text as illustrating the critical opinions of a person in whom great wits and madness were rather blended than allied; in the transition generation—the *mezzanine* floor—of 1800-1830.

never printed, or at least collected, for there might have been more such things of the fatally interesting kind which establishes the rule that Professors should not deal, in their lectures, with contemporary literature. It was certainly unlucky for a man to begin by objecting in one official capacity to *Death's Jest-Book*, and to end by objecting in another to Stevens's Wellington Monument. And that Milman had generally the character of a harsh and donnish critic is obvious, from Byron's well-known suggestion of him as a possible candidate for the authorship of the *Quarterly* article on Keats, though the rhyme of "kill man" may have had something to do with this. If he wrote much literary criticism we have little of it in the volume of *Essays* which his son published, after his death, in 1870. Even on Erasmus—surely a tempting subject—he manages to be as little literary as is possible, and rather less than one might have thought to be; and his much better-known *Histories* are not more so.

Ignorance may sneer, but Knowledge will not even smile, at the dictum that not the least critical genius that ever adorned the Oxford

Keble.

Chair was possessed by John Keble. There is some faint excuse for Ignorance. The actual *Prælections*[1] of the author of *The Christian Year*, being Latin, are not read: his chief English critical works,[2] though collected not so very long ago, were collected too late to catch that flood-tide, in their own sense, which is unfortunately, as a rule, needed to land critical works out of reach of the ordinary ebb. Moreover, there is no question but Keble requires "allowance"; and the allowance which he requires is too often of the kind least freely granted in the present day. If we have anywhere (I hope we have) a man as holy as Keble, and as learned, and as acute, he will hardly express the horror at Scott's occasional use of strong language which Keble expresses.[3] Our historic sense, and our illegitimate advantage of perspective, have at least taught us that to quarrel with Scott again, for not being "Catholic" enough, is almost to quarrel with Moses for not having actually led the children of Israel into Palestine. And no man, as honest as Keble was, would now echo that other accusation against the great magician (whom, remember, Keble almost adored, and of whom he thought far more highly as a poet than many good men do now) of tolerating intemperance; though some might feign it to suit a popular cant.

But in all these respects it is perfectly easy for those who have once schooled themselves to this apparently but not really difficult matter, to make the necessary allowance.[4] And then, even in the

---

[1] *Prælectiones Academicæ Oxonii habitæ annis* 1832-41. Oxford, 1844. 2 vols., but continuously paged.

[2] *Occasional Papers and Reviews,* by John Keble, M.A. Oxford and London,

1877.

[3] *Occ. Pap.,* p. 62.

[4] The place most perilously aleatory is the fling in *Occ. Pap.,* p. 87, at "Mr Leigh Hunt *and his miserable followers.*'

English critical Essays — the "Scott," the "Sacred Poetry," the "Unpublished Letters of Warburton," and the "Copleston"—*verus incessu patet criticus.*

His general attitude to poetic criticism (he meddled little with any other) is extremely interesting.   His classical training impelled

*The Oc-
casional
[English]
Papers.*

him towards the "subject" theory, and the fact that his two great idols in modern English poetry were Scott and Wordsworth was not likely to hold him back.   He has even drifted towards a weir, pretty clearly, one would think, marked "Danger!" by asking whether readers do not feel the attraction of Scott's novels to be as great as, and practically identical with, that of his poems.   But no "classic" could possibly have framed the definition of poetry which he puts at the outset[1] of the Scott Essay as "The indirect expression in words, most appropriately in metrical words, of some overpowering emotion, or ruling taste, or feeling, the direct indulgence whereof is somehow repressed." Everybody will see what this owes to Wordsworth; everybody should see how it is glossed and amplified—in a non-Wordsworthian or an extra-Wordsworthian sense.   We meet the pure critical Keble again, in his enthusiastic adoption of Copleston's preference for "Delight" (putting Instruction politely in the pocket) as the poetic criterion.[2] And his defence of Sacred Poetry, however interested it may seem to be, coming from him, is one of the capital essays of English criticism.   He makes mince-meat of Johnson, and he takes by anticipation a good deal of the brilliancy out of his brilliant successor, Mr Arnold, on this subject.   The passage, short but substantial,[3] on Spenser in this is one of the very best to be found on that critic of critics (as by an easily intelligible play he might be said to be) as well as poet of poets.   Spenser always finds out a bad critic—he tries good ones at their highest.

Still the *Prælections* themselves must, of course, always be Keble's own touchstone, or rather his ground and matter of assay.   And he

*The Præ-
lections.*

comes out well.   The dedication (a model of stately enthusiasm) to Wordsworth as *non solum dulcissimæ poeseos verum etiam divinæ veritatis antistes,* strikes the keynote of the whole.   But it may be surprising to some to find how "broad" Keble is, in spite of his inflexible morality and his uncompromising churchmanship.   He was kept right partly, no doubt, by holding fast as a matter of theory to the "Delight" test—pure and virtuous delight, of course, but still delight, first of all and most of all.   But mere theory would have availed him little without the poetic spirit, which everywhere in him translates itself into the critical, and almost as little without the wide and (whether deliberately so or not) comparative reading of ancient and modern verse

[1] *Occ. Pap.*, p. 6.   [2] Ibid., p. 150.   [3] Ibid., pp. 98-102.

which he displays. His general definition of Poetry here is slightly different from that given above, as was indeed required by his subject and object. He presents it—at once refining and enlarging upon part of the Aristotelian one of Tragedy, and neutralising the *vinum dæmonum* notion at once,—as *subsidium benigni numinis*, the medicinal aid given by God to subdue, soften, and sanctify Passion. But his working out—necessarily, in its main lines, obvious but interesting to contrast with his successor Mr Arnold's undogmatised and secularised application of the same idea—is less interesting to us in itself than the *aperçus* on different poets, ancient and modern, to which it gives rise. Few pages deserve to be skipped by the student: even technical discussion of the *tenuis et arguta* kind, as he modestly calls it, becomes alive under his hand on such subjects as the connection of Poetry and Irony (*Prœl.* v.) But there is a still higher interest in such things as the contrast, in the same Prælection, of the undeviating self-consistency of Spenser in all his work, the bewildering apparent lack of central unity in Shakespeare with its resolution, and the actual inconsistency of Dryden. All the Homeric studies deserve reading, the discussion of the *Odyssey* in *Prœl.* xi. being especially noteworthy, with its culmination in a delightful phrase[1] about Nausicaa which ought to be generally known. Particularly wise and particularly interesting is the treatment of "Imitation" (the lower imitation) in *Prœl.* xvi., where those who are of our mystery will not fail to compare the passage with Vida. How comfortable is it to find a poet-critic, so uncompromising on dignity of subject, who can yet admit, and that with not the faintest grudging, that it "is incredible how mightily the hidden fire is roused by single words or clauses—nay, by the sound of mere syllables, that strike the ear at a happy nick of time."[2] This is almost "the doctrine of the Poetic Moment" itself, though we must not urge it too far, and though it is brought in apropos of the suggestiveness *to poets* of antecedent poetic work. It is still sovereign against a still prevailing heresy. The abundant treatment of Æschylus[3] is also to be carefully noted; for, as we have observed, that mighty poet had been almost neglected during the Neo-classic period.

The second score of Lectures is still technically devoted to the ancients, especially Pindar, the second and third Tragedians, Theocritus, Lucretius, Virgil, and Horace; but references to the moderns, not very rare in the first volume, become still more frequent here, and are sometimes, as those to Spenser and Bunyan in the matter of allegory,[4] and the contrast of Jason and Macduff as bewailing

---

[1] Rapin accused her of "forgetting her modesty." Keble says of her: "Cujus persona nihil usquam aut venustius habet aut pudentius veterum Poesis" (i. 195).

[2] *Prœl. Ac.*, p. 281.

[3] It occupies seven Prælections (xvii.-xxiii.) and some 200 pages.

[4] ii. 415.

their children,[1] very notable. On his narrower subject, the judgment of Sophocles in *Prœl.* xxviii. is singularly weighty ; and I
should like to have heard Mr Matthew Arnold answer on behalf
of his favourite. The comparative tameness, and the want of
variety and range, which some (not all, of course) feel in the
" singer and child of sweet Colonos " are here put with authority
by one whom no one could accuse of *Sturm und Drang* preferences,
or of an undisciplined thirst for novelty. Only on Theocritus,
perhaps, does Morality sit *in banco* with Taste to a rather disastrous
effect, and the fact is curiously explicable. His disapproval of
Scott's strong language, and his want of ecclesiastical-mindedness,
and his lenity to liquor, had not blinded Keble in the least to Scott's
poetry ; he had admitted the charitable and comfortable old plea
of " time, not man," in favour of certain peccadilloes of Shakespeare ; he is, in fact, nowhere squeamish to silliness. But he
cannot pardon Theocritus for the *Oaristys* and such things, simply
because the new Wordsworthian nature-worship in him is wounded
and shocked *insanabiliter.* " Like Aristophanes," he says, " like
Catullus, like Horace, Theocritus betakes himself to the streams
and the woods, not to seek rest for a weary mind, but as provoc-
atives for a lustful one." [2] This new " sin against the Spirit "
is most interesting.

On the other hand, this very nature-worship keeps his balance,
where we might have thought he would lose it, on the subject of
Lucretius. He contrasts the comparative triviality and childishness
of Virgil, agreeable enough as it is, in regard to nature, with the
mystic majesty of his great predecessor. The charges of atheism
and indecency trouble him very little : [3] the intense earnestness,
the lofty delight in clouds and forests and the vague, the likeness
to Æschylus and Dante—all these things he fixes on, and delights
in. I wish he had written more on Dante himself ; what he has [4]
is admirable.

As to Virgil in person, though sensible enough of his merits, he
says things which would have elicited the choicest combinations of
Scaligerian Billingsgate ; and brings out, in a way striking and I
think rather novel, the *permolestum*, the " serious irritation " caused
by the fact that Virgil either could not or would not give Æneas
any character at all, and that you feel sometimes inclined to think
that he never himself had any clear idea what sort of a real man
his hero was. This exaltation of the Character above the Action
is very noteworthy.

[1] ii. 586.

[2] ii. 641. He has a liking for Horace ; but objects to him (not quite unreasonably) as *sordidior quidem* in his
Epicureanism, when you compare him
with Lucretius.

[3] He allows him, as well as Byron
and Shelley, the plea of *vix compos*
in certain respects.

[4] ii. 678 *sq.* and elsewhere.

But, in fact, Keble always is noteworthy, and more. Mere moderns may dismiss him, with or without a reading, as a mill-horse treader of academic rounds. He is nothing so little. He is, in fact, almost the first representative of the Romantic movement who has applied its spirit to the consecrated subjects of study ; and he has shown, unfortunately to too limited a circle, how fresh, how interesting, how inspiring the results of this and of the true comparison of ancient and modern may be.[1] Literary criticism—indeed literature itself as such—was with him, it is true, only a by-work, hardly more than a pastime. But had it been otherwise, he would, I think, twenty years before Arnold, have given us the results of a more thorough scholarship, a reading certainly not less wide, a taste nearly as delicate and catholic, a broader theory, and a much greater freedom from mere crotchet and caprice.

I am not quite so well acquainted with the whole work of Keble's successor Garbett.[2] Elected as he was, by the anti-Tractarian reaction, against the apparently far superior claims of

Garbett.

Isaac Williams, his appointment has generally been regarded as a job ; and I had to divest myself of prejudice in reading him. He has indeed nothing of his predecessor's serene scholarship, and little of his clear and clean taste. His form puts him at a special disadvantage. Instead of Keble's pure and flowing Latinity, you find an awkward dialect, peppered after the fashion of Cicero's letters with Greek words, peppered still more highly with notes of exclamation, and, worst of all, full of words, and clauses, and even whole sentences, in capitals, to the destruction of all repose and dignity. He seems to have simply printed each Prælection as he gave it (the pagings are independent), and then to have batched them together without revision in volume form.[3] But one cannot read far or fairly without perceiving that, either before his election or after it, Garbett had taken the pains to qualify by a serious study of antecedent criticism—a study, it may be added, of which there is hardly any trace in Keble. Garbett devotes especial attention to Longinus and Dryden ; and though I do not (as I have formerly hinted)[4] agree with him in regard to either,[5]

---

[1] I pass, as needless to dwell on at length, the excellence of his style and expression in these lectures. "So acute in remark, so beautiful in language," as Newman says in the letter printed in *Occ. Pap.*, p. xii *sq.*

[2] My only *possession* is *De Re Critica Prælectiones.* Oxford, 1847.

[3] My copy, which is "from the author" to some one unknown, has not a few pen-corrections, apparently in his own hand.

[4] *V. sup.*, p. 112.

[5] It is particularly unfortunate that he has endeavoured to construct a theory of Longinus as a statesman-critic, comparing him with Burke. I have already said that I do not think the identification of the author of the book with Zenobia's prime minister in the least disproved or (with the materials at present at disposal) disprovable: but it certainly is not proved to the point of serving as basis to such a theory.

it is beyond all doubt that he had made a distinct and original attempt to grasp both as critics. He deals with Horace, of course; but it is noteworthy that he has again aimed at a systematic and fresh view, taking Horace as the master of "Art Poetic," and comparing Boileau, &c. He has an abundant discussion of Scaliger, whom he takes as third type and (rightly) as the father of classical French criticism, while Dryden gives him his fourth. He knows the Germans—not merely Lessing and Goethe, but Kant; and whatever the failures in his execution, he can "satisfy the examiners" not merely from the point of view of those who demand acquaintance with the history and literature of the subject, but from that of those who postpone everything to what they think philosophy. He refers to the climatic view of literature,[1] constantly combines historical and literary considerations, and is altogether a "modern." As has been said, I disagree with him more often than I agree; but I do not think there can be any serious denial of the fact that he was worthy of the Chair and of a place here.

The tenure of his successor Claughton, afterwards Bishop, was but for a single term; and he seems to have left little memorial of it except a remarkably elegant Latin address on the appointment of Lord Derby as Chancellor. Elegance, indeed, was Claughton's characteristic as an orator,[2] but I should not imagine that he had much strength or very wide or keen literary knowledge and enthusiasm. Of Mr Arnold we have spoken.

Claughton.

There were foolish folk, not without some excuse of ignorance (if that ever *be* an excuse) for their foolishness, who grumbled or scoffed when he was followed by Sir Francis Doyle. There had been some hopes of Browning, which had been foiled—if by nothing else—by the discovery that an Honorary M.A. degree was not a qualification; and it must be owned that curiosity to see what Browning would do *in* prose *on* poetry was highly legitimate. Moreover, the younger generation was busy with Mr Swinburne and Mr Morris, who had not turned Tennyson and Browning himself out, and they knew little of Sir Francis. Better informed persons, however, reported of him as of an Oxford man of the best old type of "scholar and gentleman," a person of very shrewd wits, of probably greater practical experience than any Professor of Poetry had ever had, and the author of certain things like "The Red Thread of Honour" and "The Private of the Buffs," which,

Doyle.

---

[1] With reference to Schlegel and Madame de Staël.

[2] His sermons have been disrespectfully spoken of; but I think unjustly. I heard them myself in pretty close juxtaposition with those of Pusey and Wilberforce, and even with the, in both senses, rare discourses of Mansel. In vigour and body they were nowhere beside any of these; but they could fairly hold their own in the softer ways of style.

in their own peculiar style and division, were poetry *sans phrase.*
The report was justified by the new Professor's Lectures.[1] They
are frankly exoteric; but they are saved by scholarship from the
charge of ever being popular in the bad sense. They adopt as
frankly, and carry a little farther, that plan of making the lectures,
if not exactly reviews of particular books new and old, at any rate
causeries hung on particular texts and pegs, which the vernacularis-
ation of the Chair had made inevitable, and to which Matthew Arnold
himself had inclined gladly enough. They are, though not in the
least degree slipshod or slovenly, quite conversational in style.
But they deserve, I think, no mean place among the documents of
the Chair. Their easy, well-bred common-sense, kept from being
really Philistine (which epithet Sir Francis good - humouredly
accepted), not merely by their good breeding, but by the aforesaid
scholarship, by natural acuteness, and by an intense unaffected love
for poetry, might not be a good staple. But if the electors could
manage to let it come round again, as an exception, once in a generation or so, it would be well, and better than well.

Of Principal Shairp so many good men have said so many good
things that it is almost unnecessary to add, in this special place

Shairp. and context, the praise (which can be given ungrudgingly)
that he has always, in his critical work, had before him
good intentions and high ideals. Much further addition, I fear,
cannot be made. When I read his question, "Did not Shakespeare
hate and despise Iago and Edmund?"[2] when I remember how
Shakespeare himself put in the mouth of the one—

"I bleed, sir, but not killed";

in the mouth of the other—

"The wheel is come full circle; I am here";

and—

"Yet Edmund was beloved,"

I own I sympathise with an unconventional and unsophisticated
soul who, once reading this same utterance of Mr Shairp's, rose,
strode about the room, and sitting down, ejaculated, "What are
you to do? What are you to say? Where are you to go? when
a Professor of Poetry, uttering such things in Oxford, is not taken
out, and stoned or burnt forthwith, between Balliol and the
Randolph?" And there is an only less dreadful passage[3] of mis-
comprehension on the magnificent close of Tennyson's "Love and

---

[1] First Series (comprising the "Inaugural," with two others on "Provincial Poetry" and *The Dream of
Gerontius*), London, 1869. A second
appeared in 1877.
[2] *Aspects of Poetry* (London, 1881),
p. 30.
[3] Ibid., p. 157.

Duty"—one of the greatest examples of the difficult "*Versöhnung* close," the reconciliation of art, the relapse into peace.

But the lesson of criticism is a lesson of tolerance. A complete and careful perusal of Mr Shairp's *Aspects of Poetry,* and of his other books, will indeed show that the *apices* of criticism, whether historical, or appreciative, or even philosophical, were beyond his climb. He shows that constant necessity or temptation of engaging in comment—eulogistic or controversial—upon the *ephemera critica* of the time, which has been one of the worst results of the change of the lectures from Latin to English. You could not, in the stately old vehicle, do more than occasionally decline upon such a lower level as this. Mr Shairp is always citing and fencing with (or extolling reviewer-fashion) Arnold or Bagehot, Hutton or Myers. *Quotidiana quotidie moriuntur ;* and, though no doubt it saves much trouble to Professors if they can take out of a newspaper or a review, or even a recent book, on their way to Oxford, a text for an hour's sermon, their state *sub specie æternitatis* is far from the more gracious. Oxford is constantly making new statutes now ; I think one forbidding any citation from this Chair of critical or creative literature less than thirty years old would not be bad.

More happy, if not always more critical, were his dealings with things Scottish, where sympathy lifted him out of the peddling, and transformed the parochial. On Burns (even though there must have been searchings of heart there) he could sometimes, though by no means always, speak excellently ; on Scott superexcellently ; on Wordsworth almost as well ; on the Highland poets (if we do not forget our salt-cellar) best of all, because he spoke with knowledge and not as Mr Arnold. His work is always amiable, often admirable : I wish I could say that it is always or often critical.

The great achievement of Mr Shairp's successor, Francis Turner Palgrave, in regard to literary criticism, is an indirect one, and had *Palgrave.* been mostly done years and decades before he was elected to the Chair. Little indeed, though something, was given to the world as the direct result of his professorial work.[1] As an actual critic or reviewer, Palgrave was no doubt distinguished not over-favourably by that tendency to "splash" and *tapage* of manner which he shared with Kinglake and some other writers of the mid-nineteenth century, and which has been recently revived. But his real taste was in a manner warranted by his friendships ; and his friendships must almost have kept him right if he had had less taste. He may have profited largely by these friendships

---

[1] *Landscape in Poetry* (1897) was,   only, collection of lectures.
unless I mistake, the chief, if not the

in the composition of the two parts of that really *Golden Treasury*, which, if it does not achieve the impossible in giving everybody what he wants, all that he wants, and nothing that he does not want, is by general confession the most successful attempt in a quite appallingly difficult kind.   The second part, which has of course been the most criticised, seems to me even more remarkable than the first, as showing an almost complete freedom from one easily besetting sin, the tendency not to relish styles that have come in since the critic "commenced" in criticism.

Salutantur vivi.
Of Mr Courthope and his successors in the Chair we are happily precluded from speaking critically.   May the bar not soon be lifted!

INDEX.

(Dates in the following entries are only given in the case of critical writers actually belonging to the period dealt with in the volume. To economise space, also, the kind of writing practised is only indicated where confusion is possible.)

Account of the English Dramatic Poets, 140, 141.
—— *of the greatest English Poets*, 171, 172.
Addison, Joseph (1672-1719), 152 *note*, 165 *sq.*, 170-181, 196, 236, 243, 247, 251, 265 *sq.*, 299, 305, 337 *note*, 341.
Adolphus, John Leycester (1795-1862), 382 *note*.
Advancement and Reformation of Modern Poetry, 166 *sq.*
—— *of Learning*, 74 *sq.*
Adventurer, The, 260 *sq.*
Advice to an Author, 282.
—— *to a Young Poet*, 185.
Æschylus, 335, 336.
Ainger, Canon, 367 *sq.*
Akenside, 250.
A King and No King, Rymer on, 134.
Alexander, Sir William, Earl of Stirling (1567?-1640), 79, 80.
Alice Fell, 326 *note*.
Alison, Archibald (1757-1839), 288-291, 401 *note*.
All for Love, Preface to, 124.
Anacrisis, 79, 80.
Ancient Mariner, The, 230, 329 *note*.
"Ancients and Moderns," 2, 103, 141, 150 *sq.*, 190.

André, Yves Marc de l'Isle, Père (1675-1764), 303 *note*.
Andromeda, 44.
Anecdotes, Spence's, 187.
An Evening's Love, Preface to, 123.
Anima Poetæ, 328 *sq.*, 337 *sq.*
Annus Mirabilis, Preface to, 115.
Antigone, the, 165.
Anti-Jacobin, The, 396 *sq.*
Antiquity of the English Tongue, The, 185.
Apollo, The British, 146.
Apollonius Rhodius, 133.
Apology of Heroic Poetry, 124.
—— *for Poetry*, 54 *sq.*
—— *for Smectymnuus*, 106.
Appreciations, 501 *sq.*
Arbuthnot, 183 *sq.*
Arcadian Rhetoric, 69 *note*.
Ariosto, 133, 262, 270, 285, 299.
Aristophanes, 34, 362.
Aristotle, 2, 4 *sq.*, 94, 96, 152, 187 and *passim*.
Arnold, Matthew (1822-88), 27-29, 170, 222, 226 *sq.*, 248, 250, 328, 332, 340, 355, 396, 405, 416, 435, 458 *note*, 468-490, 516, 518, 533.
Ars Poetica, see *Epistle to the Pisos*.
Art of English Poesy, Puttenham's, 59 *sq.*
—— *of Poetry*, Bysshe's, 159 *sq.*

Art of Poetry, Gildon's, 162 *sq.*
—— of *Rhetoric*, Wilson's, 31-34.
Ascham, Roger (1515-68), 31-45, 76, 98 *sq.*
Ashe, Thomas (1836-1889), 330 *note.*
Athenian Mercury, The, 146.
—— *Oracle, The*, 146.
—— *Sport*, 146.
Atterbury, Francis, Bishop of Rochester (1672-1732), 182.
Aubignac, F. Hédelin, Abbé d' (1604-76), 103, 109 *note.*
Aurengzebe, Prologue to, 124.

Bacon, 299, 342.
—— Sir Francis, Lord Verulam (1561-1626), 74-79, 89.
Bacon - Shakespeare theory, 90 *note*, 219.
Bagehot, Walter (1826-1877), 495, 496.
Barbauld, Mrs, 230 *note.*
Bartas, Du, 82.
Basil, St, 491 *note.*
Battle of the Books, The, 183.
Baviad and *Mæviad, The*, 396 *sq.*
Beattie, 250.
Beaumont, Sir George, 315.
Beaumont and Fletcher, 118 *sq.*, 133 *sq.*
Beddoes, 530, 531.
Bee, The, 231.
Beers, H. A., 262 *note.*
Behn, Afra, 159.
Bellay, see Du Bellay.
Bembo, Pietro (1470-1547), 188.
Ben, see Jonson.
Bentley, Richard (1662-1742), 132, 140, 141, 183, 184.
Benlowes, Edward (1603-76), 242 *sq.*
Bertram, Coleridge's critique on, 323 *note*, 329 *note.*
Biographia Literaria, 311 *sq.*
Blackwood's Magazine, 455-457. See also De Quincey, Lockhart, Maginn, Wilson.
Blair, Hugh (1718-1800), 195-198, 287 *note*, 290 *note.*
Blake, 131 *note*, 159.
—— William (1757-1827), 342, 346, 354, 376-379.
Blount, Sir Thomas Pope (1649-97), 144, 146.
Boileau, Nicolas B. Despréaux (1636-1711), 103, 129, 130, 188 *sq.*, 240.

Bolton, Edmund (1573 ? - 1633), 70.
Bon Gaultier Ballads, The, 399.
Borrow, George, 393 *note.*
Bosanquet, Mr, 292, 293 *note*, 294 *note.*
Boswell, 207.
Bouhours, Dominique, Abbé (1628-1702), 154.
Bowles, William Lisle (1762-1850), 328, 339, 389-391.
Boyer [Bowyer], 328.
Bradley, Prof., 526, 539.
Bridges, Robert, 317 *note.*
Brimley, George (1819 - 57), 457-461.
British Muse, The, 298 *note.*
Brown, John (1715-66), 209, 210.
Browne, Sir T., 407.
Browning, Mr, 144 *note.*
—— Mrs, 467 *note.*
Bruttezza, Tassoni on, 154, 155.
Brydges, Sir Samuel Egerton (1762-1837), 393, 394.
Buchanan, Robert, 514 *note.*
Buckhurst, see Dorset.
Buffon, Jean Louis Leclerc, Comte de (1707-88), 85.
Bunyan, 285, 287.
Burke, Edmund (1729 - 97), 286-288, 339.
Butler, Samuel (1612-80), 241 *sq.*
Byron, George Gordon, Lord (1788-1824), 338, 344, 390-392.
Bysshe, Edward (*fl. c.* 1700), 159-162.

Cæsar, 35.
Callières, François de (1645-1717), 183.
Camoens, 230 *note.*
Campbell, George (1709 - 96), 203-206.
—— Dykes, 329 *note*, 331 *note.*
—— Thomas (1777-1844), 342, 382-384.
Campion, Thomas (? - 1619), 70-72, 82, 106.
Canning, 398 *sq.*
Canons of Criticism, the, 230 *note.*
Capell, Edward (1713 - 81), 298 *note.*
"Car of Cambridge" — *i.e.*, Carr, Nicholas (1524 - 68), Greek Professor ? 76.

Hobbes, Thomas (1588-1679), 107-111.
Holmes, Robert (1748-1805), 526 note.
Home, Henry, see Kames.
Homer, 286, 474 sq.
Horace, 8, 266 sq.
Horne, Richard Hengist (1803 - 84), 373 note, 467 note.
Houghton, Lord (Milnes, Richard Monckton), (1809-85), 510.
Howard, Edward, 107 note.
—— Henry, see Surrey, Earl of.
—— J., 107 note.
—— Sir Robert (d. 1698 : his birth-date and those of his brothers E. and J. are very uncertain), 116 sq.
Howell's Letters, 111 note.
Hueffer, Mr, 513.
Hughes (editor of Spenser), 296.
Hugo, Victor F. M. (1802-85), 302.
Hume, Alexander, 92 note.
—— David (1711-76), 195, 283-286, 305 note.
Hunt, James Henry Leigh (1784-1869), 112 note, 342, 344, 349, 356-361, 367, 413 sq.
Hurd, Richard (1720-1808), Bishop of Worcester, 202, 246, 265-273, 302, 305 note, 307, 383.
Hurdis, James (1763-1801), 527, 528.
Hutton, Richard Holt (1826-97), 496, 497.

Iago, Rymer on, 135, 136.
Idler, the, 217.
Imagination and Fancy, 358.
"Imagination," Addison on, 176-181.
"Imlac," 217, 218.
Impartial Critic, The, 165.
Indian Emperor, The, Preface to, 122.
Inner Life of Art, The, 495.
Inquiry into the Principles of Harmony in Language, 278, 279.
—— into the Present State of Polite Learning in Europe, 231.

James the First (1566-1625), 60, 61.
Jeffrey, Francis (1773-1850), 342, 384 note, 399-403.
Johnson, Samuel (1709-84), 28, 115, 162, 167, 191, 198, 207, 210-229, 268, 278, 307, 327, 332, 389, 515, 517, 518.
Jonson, Ben (1573-1637), 27, 39, 68,

80-92, 87 note, 88 note, 92 note, 93, 100 sq., 107, 108, 110 sq., 133 sq., 219 note.
Joubert, Joseph (1754-1824), 374 note.
Julius Cæsar, Rymer on, 136.
—— Dennis on, 167.
Juvenal, Dryden's Preface to, 125.

Kames, Henry Home, Lord (1696-1782), 198-203.
Keats, John (1795-1821), 218, 248, 385 note.
Keble, John (1792-1866), 112 note, 531-535.
Ker, W. P., 113 sq.
Kingsley, Charles (1819-75), 44, 491, 492.
Kirke-White, 344.
Klein, Dr David, 81 note.
Knight's Quarterly, 443 sq.
Knox, Vicesimus (1752-1821), 232.

La Casa, 50 note.
La Croze, J. Cornand de [not to be confused with his contemporary, M. Veyssière de la Croze, a learned but fantastic philologist and antiquary], 146 note.
La Harpe, Jean François de (1730-1803), 239, 399, 406.
Lamb, Charles (1775 - 1834), 28, 229, 342, 344, 346-356, 367, 413 sq.
Lamotte, Charles (? - ?), Irish divine and critic, 230 note.
Lancaster, Henry Hill (1829 - 75), 464.
Landor, Walter Savage (1775-1864), 386-389.
Langbaine, Gerard (1656-92), 140, 141, 163.
Langhorne, 182, 486.
Langland, 62 sq.
Latimer, 33.
Latter-Day Pamphlets, 451.
Leibnitz, 338.
Lectures, Coleridge's, 330 sq.
—— on Rhetoric and Belles Lettres, 195 sq.
—— on the Age of Elizabeth, 367, 368.
—— on the English Poets, 362 sq.
Lee, Sidney, 140 note.
L'Estrange, 132, 184.

Carlyle, Thomas (1795-1881), 490 sq.
Castellain, M., 80 note, 87 note.
Castle of Indolence, the, 228.
Catiline, Rymer on, 136.
Catullus, 387.
Caxton, William (1442 ? - 91 ?), 25 note, 28.
Censura Literaria, 392, 393 note.
Cervantes, 283, 299.
Chapelain, Jean (1595 - 1674), 127 note, 133, 154.
Chapman, 82, 124, 127.
Character of Saint Evremond, 125 note.
Characteristics, 282, 283.
Characters of Shakespeare's Plays, 368, 369.
Chaucer, 25, 29 sq., 33, 41 sq., 62 sq., 128, 130, 133, 171, 236, 264, 270, 366, 368, 383.
Cheke, Sir John (1514-57), 31, 34-36.
Chesterfield, Philip Dormer Stanhope (1694-1773), 209 note, 457 note.
Chevy Chase, 56, 176.
Choice, the, 221.
Christopher North. See Wilson, John.
Church, Richard William (1815-90), 511.
Cicero, 204.
Ciceronianus, 76.
Cinna, 119.
Citizen of the World, the, 231.
"Classical Metres," 40 sq.
Claudian, 124, 145, 392.
Claughton, Thomas Legh, Bishop of Rochester (1808-92), 536.
Cleveland, 117, 127, 157.
Cœlius Rhodiginus, 145.
Coleridge, Ernest, 328, 337.
—— Hartley (1796-1849), 393 note, 438-440.
—— Samuel Taylor (1772 - 1834), 28, 85, 292, 310-343, 346, 349, 353, 359, 360, 366, 368, 388, 398, 401 note, 412 sq., 425, 431, 437, 440 note, 442, 489, 494, 501, 515, 518.
Collier, J. P., 319 note.
—— Jeremy (1650 - 1726), 132, 142-144, 166 sq., 184, 367.
Collins (the poet), 223 sq., 251.
Comic Writers, The English, 366, 367.

Comical Gallant, the, 167.
Comus, 223.
Congreve, 143, 349.
Conti, Armand de Bourbon, Prince de (1629-66), 142 note.
Conversations with Drummond, 81 sq.
Conybeare, John Josias (1779-1824), 530.
Cooper's Hill, 233.
Copleston, Edward, Bishop of Llandaff (1776-1849), 528-530.
Corneille, 285.
Courthope, Mr, 182 note, 186 note, 526, 539.
Cowley, Abraham (1618 - 67), 106, 107, 133, 144, 171, 172, 183, 214, 221 sq.
Cowper, 209 note, 314, 338.
Coxe, Leonard, 31 note.
Craik, Sir Henry, 138 note.
Crashaw, Pope on, 186 note.
Creed, attempted summary of the Neo-Classic, 94, 95.
—— The Romantic, 410, 411.
Critical Review, the, 230.
"Criticism of Life," 484 sq.
Croce, Signor Benedetto, 293 note, 294 note.
Croker, John Wilson (1780 - 1857), 437, 447, 462.
Cynthia's Revels, 81 note.

Dallas, Eneas Sweetland (1828-79), 299, 464-466.
Daniel, Samuel (1562-1619), 72-74, 82, 100, 106.
Dante, 21 sq., 43, 109, 112, 113, 145, 299, 320 note, 324-326, 338, 357, 358, 366, 487 sq.
Davenant, Sir William (1606 - 68), 105, 107, 111.
Davideis, 107 note.
De Augmentis, 75 note.
De Interpretatione, the, 7.
Dedication of the Æneis, 125.
—— of the Spanish Friar, 124.
Defence of Poesy, 53 sq.
—— of Poetry, Shelley's, 384, 385.
—— of Rhyme, 72-74.
—— of the Epilogue (to Conquest of Granada), 123.
Defoe, 352.
Denham, 172.

Dennis, John (1657-1734), **127** *note*, 164-170, 233 *note*, 396.

De Quincey, Thomas (**1785 - 1859**), 274, 413, 431-435.

Derby, Lord, 166.

Desmarets de Saint - Sorlin, Jean (1595-1676), 109.

Desportes, Philippe (1546-1601), 106 *note*, 183.

"Despréaux," 183, and see Boileau.

De Vulgari Eloquio, 21, 22 *sq.*, 43, 311, 320, 325, 326.

Diderot, **Denis** (1713-84), 327.

Dies Boreales, 426 *sq.*

Dionysius, 8.

Discourse of English Poesy, 59 *sq.*

—— *on Medals*, 172.

—— *on Music, Painting, and Poetry*, 266 *sq.*

—— *on Satire*, 125.

—— *on the Grounds of Criticism in Tragedy*, 124.

Discoveries, Jonson's, 81 *sq.*

Disraeli, Isaac (1766-1848), 394.

Dissertation on Ossian, 197.

—— *on Phalaris*, 141, 142.

—— *on the Rise of Poetry and Music*, 207.

Dobell, Sydney, 467 *note*.

Doctor, The, 345 *sq.*

Donne, 82, 222.

Dorset, Earl of, 116 *sq.*, 172.

Doyle, Sir Francis Hastings Charles (1810-88), 536, 537.

Drant, Thomas (*d.* 1578 ?), 45 *sq.*

Drayton, 82, 231.

Drummond (of Hawthornden), 81 *sq.*, 139.

Dryden, John (1631-1700), 27, 109, 111-131, 133, 143, 150 *note*, 151, 153, 154, 158 *sq.*, **165**, 171, 172, 182, 187, 205 *note*, 218, 222 *sq.*, 244, 247, 248, 264, 283, 310, 332, 339, 359, 457, 466 *note*, 473, 515.

Du Bartas, 109.

Du Bellay, Joachim (1524-60), 24 *note*, 97, 109, 310.

Dunton, John (1659-1733), 146.

Dyer, Sir Edward, 48.

—— John, 157, 211, 251.

Edinburgh Review, The, 323 *note*, 396, 400.

Edwards, Thomas (1699-1757), 230 *note*.

E. K., 63, 97.

Elements of Criticism, **the**, 198-203.

Elia, 347 *sq.*

Elwin, Whitwell (1816-1900), 463.

Elyot, Sir Thomas, 65 *note*.

English Metrists, 276 *note*.

—— *Parnassus*, the, 159 *note*.

—— *Rhythms*, 345 *note*.

Ephemerides of Phialo, 52 *note*.

Epistle to Augustus, Pope's, 186 *sq.*

—— *to the Pisos*, 3, 8, 13, 14 *sq.*, 22, 65, 93.

Epistles, Ovid's, Dryden's Preface to, 124.

Epistolæ Obscurorum Virorum, 406.

Erasmus, Desiderius (1467 - 1536), 76.

"Esemplastic," ⎫
"Esenoplastic," ⎬ 338.

Essay of Dramatic Poesy, 116-122.

—— *of Heroic Plays*, 123.

—— *on Criticism*, 186 *sq.*

—— *on Genius*, 288 *note*.

—— *on Modern Education*, 185.

—— *on a New Species of Writing*, 230 *note*.

—— *on Pope*, 259.

—— *on Poetry* (Temple's), 141.

—— *on Taste*, Alison's, 288-291.

—— Gerard's, 288 *note*.

—— Jeffrey's, 288, 401 *note*.

—— *on the Genius of Shakespeare*, 167.

—— *on Translated Verse*, 144.

—— *upon Poetry and Painting*, 230 *note*.

Essays, Collier's, 144.

—— *Critical* (Scott's), 233.

—— *in Criticism*, 474 *sq.*

—— *Moral and Literary*, 232.

—— *Moral, Political, and Literary*, 284.

—— *on Men and Manners*, 256.

Estimate of the Manners and Principles of the Times, 209.

Etherege, 196.

Euphuism, 99 *sq.*

Euripides, 310.

Evening's Love, An, Preface to, 123.

Excursion, The, 323.

Fables, Dryden's, Preface to, 126.

Fabricius, Georgius (1515-71), 64.

Faerie Queene, the, 51.

Farmer, Dr, 441.

Felltham, Owen, 407 *note*.

Fielding, 299.

Fingal, 197.

Finlay, F. G., 255 *note*.

Flaubert, Gustave (1821-80), 338, 498.

Flecknoe, 117.

Fletcher, 118 *sq.*

Floriant et Florete, 134 *note*.

Fontenelle, Bernard le Bovier de (1657-1757), 153, 249, 340.

Fool of Quality, The, 492.

Forman, Buxton, 426 *note*.

Foster, John (1731-74), 276.

—— (1770-1843), 466.

Fox, W. J. (1786-1864), 466.

Fraunce, Abraham (*fl. c.* 1590), 69 *note*, 82.

Friend, The, 329.

Froude, James Anthony (1818-94), 492.

Fulgentius, 137.

Fuller, Margaret (1810-50), 288.

"Furor Poeticus," 150, 157.

"Gallo-Classic," the term, 150.

Garbett, James (1802-1879), 535, 536.

—— Rev. J., 112 *note*.

Gascoigne, George (1525?-77), 45 *sq.*, 60, 99, 100, 162.

Gautier, Théophile (1811-72), 428 *note*.

Gay Science, The, 465 *sq.*

Gayley and Scott, Professors, 78 *note*.

Gentleman's Magazine, the, 230.

Gerard, Alexander (1728-95), 289 *note*, 401 *note*.

Gibbon, 281 *note*.

Gifford, William (1756 - 1826), 81 *note*, 342, 352, 363, 396 *sq.*, 399 *note*.

Gildon, Charles (1665-1724), 162, 163.

Gilpin, 276.

Giraldus, Lilius, see Lilius.

Godwin, 353, 363, 373, 380 *note*.

Goethe, Johann Wolfgang von (1749-1832), 112, 292, 333 *note*, 361.

Goldsmith, Oliver (1728-74), 162, 231.

Gondibert, Preface to, 105, 107-111.

Gorboduc, 56, 89, 114.

Gosse, Edmund, 56 *note*, 499 *note*.

Gosson, Stephen (1555-1624), 52-54.

Gower, 29 *sq.*, 62 *sq.*

"Grand style," the, 475 *sq.*

Gravina, 249.

Gray, Thomas (1716-71), 194, 211, 212, 220, 224 *sq.*, 233, 243, 246, 256, 274, 299, 308, 313, 322, 327.

Grongar Hill, 221, 233.

Grosart, Dr, 72 *note*, 79 *note*.

Guarini, Battista (1537-1612), poet, 82.

Guest, Edwin (1800-1880), 345 *note*.

—— Dr, 61, 71.

Gurney, Edmund (1847 - 88), 512-514.

Habington, 218.

Hallam, Arthur Henry (1811 - 37), 466 *note*.

—— Henry (1777 - 1859), 403-408, 427.

Hamelius, Herr, 158 *note*, 165 *note*, 185 *note*.

Hannay, James (1827-73), 464.

Harington, Sir John (1561-1612), 66 *note*, 69, 82.

Harris, James (1709-80), 206-209.

Harvey, Gabriel (1545-1630), 31, 48 *sq.*

Hawes, Stephen (?-1523 ?), 29, 30.

Hawkins, William (1722-1801), 526 *note*.

Hayward, Abraham (1801-94), 462.

—— Thomas (*d.* 1779 ?), 298 *note*.

Hazlitt, William (1778-1830), 28, 112 *note*, 229, 334, 339, 342, 344, 348, 349, 354, 357, 358, 361-376, 383, 390, 413 *sq.*

Heads of an Answer to Rymer, 113 *note*, 137 *note*.

Hédelin, see Aubignac.

Hegel, G. W. F. (1776-1831), 304.

Helps, Sir Arthur (1813-75), 462, 463.

Henley, W. E., 514 *note*.

Hennequin, Emile (1859 - 88), 332.

Henry the Fourth, Dennis on, **167**.

Herford, Prof., 21 *note*, 324.

Hermes, 206.

"Heroic Play," the, 107 *sq.*

"Heroic Poem," the, 107 *sq.*

Heywood, Thomas, 138 *note*, 349.

History of English Poetry (Warton's), 263 *sq.*

—— *of the Rise and Progress of Poetry*, 209.

—— *of the Royal Society*, 138.

Lessing, Gotthold Ephraim (1729-81), 149, 287 *note*, 299, 304, 324, 332, 359, 498.

Letter to a Friend of Robert Burns, 311 *note*.

—— *to a Young Clergyman*, 185.

—— *to John Murray*, 390.

Letters on Chivalry, 202.

—— *on Chivalry and Romance*, 268 *sq.*

—— Pope's, 186.

Lewes, George Henry (1812 - 78), 493-495.

Lilius Gregorius Giraldus (1478-1552), 151.

Lives of the Poets, Heywood's, 138 *note*.

—— Johnson's, 213 *sq.*, 219 *sq.*

—— Winstanley's, 140.

Locke, John (1632-1704), 179 *sq.*, 201, 299.

Lockhart, John Gibson (1794-1854), 414, 432-438.

Lodge, Thomas (1558? - 1625), 53, 54.

London, 514 *note*.

London Magazine, The, 507 *note*.

Longinus, 2, 10 *sq.*, 89, 96, 113, 163, 168.

Lope de Vega Carpio, Felix (1562-1635), 120 *note*.

Love's Labour's Lost, Collier on, 143.

Lowell, James Russell (1819 - 91), 396.

Lowth, Robert Bishop of London (1710-87), 527.

Lucan, 82.

Lucian, 142, 164, 362.

Lucretius, 283, 285, 310.

Lycidas, 223, 233.

Lydgate, 29 *sq.*, 62 *sq.*, 254 *sq.*

—— Gray on, 254, 255.

Lyrical Ballads, Preface to, 311 *sq.*

Macaulay, Thomas B. (1800 - 59), 131 *sq.*, 141 *sq.*, 225, 231, 367, 382, 407, 442-448.

" Machines " and " Machinery," 109 *sq.*, 168.

Macpherson (*Ossian*), 197.

Maginn, William (1793-1842), 290.

Maid of the Mill, the, 334.

Malory, Sir Thomas, 38.

Mansel, Henry Longueville (1820-71), 510.

Marginalia, Coleridge's, 330 *sq.*

Marinism and Marino, 133.

Marius the Epicurean, 499.

Marlowe, 88, 139.

Martinus Scriblerus, 185.

Mason, John (1706-63), 272-275.

—— William, 250 *sq.*

Masson, Prof., 78 *note*, 431 *note*, 433.

Meditation on a Broomstick, 184.

Meres, Francis (1565-1647), 70.

Merry Wives of Windsor, Dennis on, 167.

Mickle, 182.

Mill, John Stuart (1806-73), 467.

Millar, J. H., 219 *note*.

Milman, Henry Hart (1791-1868), 462, 530, 531.

Milnes, see Houghton.

Milton, John (1608-74), 105, 138, 139, 142, 150 *note*, 168 *sq.*, 172, 176 *sq.*, 182, 200, 213 *sq.*, 235, 254, 299, 322, 339, 389, 476 *sq.*

" Minim, Dick," 217.

Minto, William (1845 - 93), 506, 507.

Miscellanies, Dryden's Preface to, 124 *sq.*

—— *Æsthetic and Literary*, 335.

Mitford, William (1744-1827), 47 *note*, 276-279, 444.

Molière, 119 *sq.*

Montagu (Lord Halifax), 172.

—— Mrs (Elizabeth Robinson)(1720-1810), 296 *note*.

Montaigne, Michel de (1533 - 92), 88.

Montgomery, Robert, 493.

Monthly Review, the, 230.

Morley, Prof. H., 45 *note*.

Morte d'Arthur, the, 38.

Mulcaster, Richard (1530 ?-1611), 92 *note*.

Mulgrave, John Sheffield, Earl of, later Duke of Buckinghamshire (1649-1721), 142.

Myers, Frederic William Henry, (1843-1901), 505 *note*.

New World Discovered in the Moon, the, 81 *note*.

Nicolas, Sir N. Harris (1799-1848), 393, 394.

Noctes Ambrosianæ, 425 *sq.*

Notes of Instruction, 45 *sq.*

Observations on Poetry, 276 *note*.
—— on *Spenser*, 261 *sq.*
Of Studies (Bacon's), 75.
Oldys, William (1696-1761), 190, 247, 297, 298 and *note*.
Omniana, 335.
Omond, T. S., 276 *note*.
On Translating Homer, 474 *sq.*
Opitz, 408 *notes*.
Orientales, Preface to the, 278.
Ossian, 59, 197 *sq.*, 299.
Othello, Rymer on, 135.
Ovid, 124.

Paculford, Prof., 491 *note*.
Palgrave, Francis Turner (1824-97), 538, 539.
Paradise Lost, 176 *sq.*
Parallel of Poetry and Painting, 125.
Parnassus, The English, 159 *note*.
Pater, Walter Horatio (1839-94), 497, 504.
Patmore, Coventry K. D. (1823-90), 511, 512.
Patrizzi, Francesco (1529-97) [not to be confused with the Siennese Bp. of Gaeta, in the generation before, who wrote on politics, &c.], anti-Peripatetic philosopher and critic, 23 *sq.*, 151.
Pattison, Mark (1813-84), 510.
Paul, Kegan, 491.
Peacock, Thomas Love (1785-1866), 317 *note*, 384, 490.
Peacham, Henry (1576?-1643?), 70.
Pecock, Reginald (1395-1460), 34.
Pemberton, Henry (1694-1771), 276 *note*.
Pepys, 117 *note*.
Percy, Thomas (1729-1811), Bishop of Dromore, 212, 246, 257-259, 307.
Perceforest, 43.
Peri Bathous, 185.
"Person of Quality," the (who re-wrote Spenser), 154 *note*.
Petrarch, 82.
Petronius, 17, 84 *note*, 319 *note*.
Phalaris, the Pseudo-, 141, 142.
Pharonnida, 383, 400.
Philips, Ambrose (1675?-1749), 247 *note*.
Phillips, Edward (1630-96), 138, 139, 354.
Philological Enquiries, 206 *sq.*

Philosophical Arrangements, 206.
Philosophy of Rhetoric, 203-206.
Philostratus, 385 *note*.
Photius, 13.
Pindar, Peter, see Wolcot.
Pigna, Giovanbattista (*fl. c.* 1550), 38.
Plain Speaker, The, 369, 370.
Plato, 2, 3, 37, 384.
Pléiade, the, 24, 97, 103.
Plutarch, 9, 37.
Poetaster, the, 81.
"Poetic Moment, The," 485 *sq.*
Politian (Angelo Ambrogini, sur-named Poliziano) (1557-94), 142, 188, 387, 406.
Polyeucte, 119.
Pomfret, John, 221, 228.
Pompée, 119.
Poole, Joshua (*fl. c.* 1650), 159 *note*.
Pope, Alexander (1688-1744), 151, 153, 157, 162, 165 *sq.*, 171 *note*, 185-194, 223 *sq.*, 236, 259, 260, 285, 299, 310, 383, 389-392.
Power of Sound, The, 512.
—— *of Numbers, The, in Prose and Poetry*, 273-275.
Prælectiones Academicæ, Garbett's, 112 *note*.
—— Keble's, 112 *note*.
—— Trapp's, 195.
—— See Coplestone, Keble, &c.
Preface to Lyrical Ballads, &c., 310 *sq.*
—— to Mr Arnold's *Poems*, 470 *sq.*
Prior, 152, 161, 162, 296.
Principles of Success in Literature, The, 493 *sq.*
Promos and Cassandra, Preface to, 69 *note*.
Proposal for Correcting the English Tongue, 185.
Pursuits of Literature, The, 397 *sq.*
Puttenham, George, (*fl. c.* 1580), 65-69.
Pye, 276.

Quarterly Review, The, 323 *note*.
Quintilian, 17 *sq.*, 34 *note*, 81 *sq.*, 188, 204, and *passim*, 332, 338 *note*.

Rabelais, François (1495-1553), **33**, 188, 335.

Racine, 285.
Radcliffe, Mrs, 363.
Raleigh, Prof., 312 *note*, 322 *note*, 326 *note*.
Ralph, James (1605 ?-62), 163 *note*.
Rambler, The, 213 *sq*.
Ramsay, Allan, 190, 247.
Randolph, John (1749-1813), Bishop of London, 526 *note*.
Rapin, Rymer's Preface to, 132 *sq*.
Rasselas, 213 *sq*.
Recreations of Christopher North, 425 *sq*.
Rehearsal, The, 152 *note*.
Rejected Addresses, 399.
Relapse, The, Collier on, 196.
Reliques, Percy's, 258 *sq*.
Remarks on Italy, 172.
—— *on the Rape of the Lock*, 168.
Repplier, Miss Agnes, 329 *note*.
Retrospective Review, The, 393, 396.
Reulis and Cautelis, King James's, 59 *sq*.
Reynolds, Sir J., 476.
Rhadamanthus, 344 *note*.
Rhetoric, De Quincey on, 434 *sq*.
Rhys, E., 311 *note*, 389 *note*, 390 *note*.
Richardson, 366, 367.
Rigault, M. H., 128 *note*.
Ritson, 258.
Rival Ladies, Preface to, 114.
Rivarol, 397.
Rogers, Henry (1806-77), 467.
Rolliad, the, 398 *note*.
Rollo (B. and F.'s), Rymer on, 134.
Roman de la Rose, 43 *note*.
Ronsard, Pierre de (1524-85), 24 *note*, 45 *note*, 97, 408 *note*.
Roscoe, W. C., 467 *note*.
Roscommon, W. Dillon, Earl of (1633-85), 144, 172.
Ruskin, John (1819-1900), 338, 492, 493, 496.
Rymer, Thomas (1646-1713), 131-137, 145, 165 *sq*., 241, 357, 407.

Sadolet, 188.
Sainte-Beuve, Charles Augustin (1804-69), 332, 340, 416, 466 *note*.
Sainte-Palaye, 295.
Sallust, Cheke on, 35.
Sand, George, 370 *note*.
Sannazaro, Jacopo (1458-1530), 56, 94.

Satyrane's Letters, 328 *note*, 329 *note*.
Savonarola, Girolamo (1452-98), 56, 94.
Scaliger, Julius Cæsar (1484-1558), 115, 145, 262, 332.
Schelling, Prof., 27 *note*, 83 *note* and *sq*., 87 *note*.
Schiller, Joh. Chr. Friedrich (1759-1805), 335, 339.
Schlegels, the, 331 *note*, 332, **383**.
Schoolmaster, The, 35 *sq*.
School of Abuse, the, 52-54.
Scott, John, of Amwell (1739-83), 232, 233.
—— Sir Walter (1771-1832), 182 *note*, 342, 357, 363, 370, 373, 380-382, 400, 486 *note*, 492, 499.
Sedley, Sir C., 116 *sq*.
Selecta Poemata Italorum, 187 *note*.
Seneca (L. Annæus ?), the tragedian, 166.
Senior, N. W. (1790-1864), 462.
Sévigné, Mme. de, 245 *note*.
Shaftesbury, Anthony Ashley Cooper, Earl of (1671-1713), 281-283.
Shairp, John Campbell (1819-85), 537, 538.
Shakespeare, 60, 82 *sq*., 89 *sq*., 101 *note*, 115, 118 *sq*., 133 *sq*., 139, 149 *note*, 167, 187, 197, 213 *sq*., 218 *sq*., 235, 245 *note*, 294, 295, 296, 299, 304, 330 *sq*., 335, 351 *sq*., 368, **369**, 370, 407, 472 *sq*., 486, 503.
—— Johnson's *Preface to*, 213 *sq*.
—— Pope's *Preface to*, 186, 187.
Shelley, Percy Bysshe (1792-1822), 159, 342, 354, 370, 384, 385, 460.
Shenstone, William (1714-63), 211, 246, 256, 257, 297, 312.
Shepherd's Kalendar, 56.
Sheringham, Robert (1602-78), 132 *note*.
Short View of the Profaneness and Immorality of the English Stage, A, 142-144.
—— *View of Tragedy, A*, 132 *sq*.
Sidney, Sir Philip (1554-86), 54, 59, 82, 99 *sq*., 115, 149, 339, 363, 367.
Silent Woman, The, 120.
Simylus, 86 *note*.
"Skroddles," 252.
Smart, Christopher, 237.
Smeaton, Oliver, 79 *note*.
—— Sydney, 462.

Smeaton, William H. (1808-72), 455, note.

Smith, Prof. Adam, 195, 281 note.

—— Gregory, 27 note, 59 note, 65 note, 70 note, 72 note, 132 note, 159 note, 175 note, 276 note.

—— Nichol, 158 note, 261 note, 296 note, 401 note.

Sophocles, 285, 286.

Southern, Henry (1799-1853), 393.

Southey, Robert (1774-1843), 328 note, 335, 339, 342-347, 353, 354, 382, 527 note.

Specimens, Campbell's, 382.

—— Lamb's, 350.

—— of British Critics, 426 sq.

Spence, Joseph (1698-1768), 153, 171 note, 187, 188, 526.

Spenser, Edmund (1552-99), 48-52, 84 sq., 109, 133, 139, 154, 171-181, 215 sq., 257, 261 sq., 264, 269 sq., 296, 297, 335, 359, 366, 383, 411, 426 sq.

Spenser Redivivus, 154 note.

Spirit of the Age, The, 372, 373.

Sprat, Thomas, Bishop of Rochester (1635-1713), 138, 145, 189.

Staël, A. L. Germaine Necker, Mme. de (1766-1817), 401 sq.

Stanyhurst, 50 note.

Stapfer, M. Paul, 404 note.

Steele, Sir Richard (1672-1729), 181.

Stephen, Sir James (1789-1859), 467.

—— Sir J. Fitzjames (1829-94), 510.

—— Sir Leslie, 514 note.

Sterne, Laurence (1713-68), 88, 279-281, 299.

Stevenson, Robert Louis (1850-94), 361, 447 note, 514 note.

Studies in the History of the Renaissance, 497 sq.

Study of Celtic Literature, The, 474 sq.

Sturm, Johann (1507-89), 36 sq., notes.

Style, Lecture on, Coleridge's, 336 sq.

—— De Quincey on, 434 sq.

Suckling, 196.

Surrey, Earl of (1517 ?-47), 42 sq.

Swift, Jonathan (1667-1745), 182-185, 299, 339.

Swinburne, Mr, 159 note.

Symonds, John Addington (1840-93), 504, 505.

Table Talk, Coleridge's, 334 sq.

—— Hazlitt's, 371.

Tale of a Tub, A, 184.

Talfourd, 393 note.

Tanneguy le Fèvre, 145.

Tasso, Torquato (1544-95), 109, 133, 269.

Tassoni, Alessandro (1565-1635), 154.

Tatler, the, 172 sq., 183.

Taylor (the Water-Poet), 84 note.

—— William, " of Norwich " (1765-1836), 450.

Temora, 197.

Temple, Sir William (1628-99), 141, 171 note, 183.

Tennyson, 218, 235, 437, 455-460.

Terence (Diderot on), 285.

Tertium Quid, 512 sq.

Thackeray, William Makepeace (1811-63), 373, 452-455, 508.

Theatrum Poetarum, 138, 139.

Theobald, 81 note.

Theocritus, 387.

Theophrastus, 7.

Thomson, James (I.), 211, 299.

—— James (II.) (1834-82), 505, 506.

Tickell, 251.

Tory, Geoffrey (1480-1533), 33.

Toxophilus, 36 sq.

Tragedies of the Last Age, the, 132 sq.

Traill, Henry Duff (1842-1900), 341, 342, 507-510.

Trapp, Joseph (1679-1747), 195, 526.

Tristram Shandy, 279.

Tritical Essay, A, 184.

Underhill, Mr, 146 note, 187 note.

Unities, the Three. See especially Scaliger, Dryden, Johnson.

Usefulness of the Stage, the, 166.

Vanbrugh, 143.

Vaughan, Prof., 384 note, 452.

—— Sir W. (1577-1648), 70.

Vauquelin de la Fresnaye, Jean (1535-1607), 79.

Venables, George Stovin (1810-88), 510.

Vico, Giambattista (1668-1744), 377 note, 452 note.

Vida, Marco Girolamo, Bishop of Alba (1480-1546), 86, 188 sq.

Virgil, 153, 215, 338, 387.
—— Dryden's Preface to, 125.
Voltaire, 77, 299, 305 *note*.

Wainewright, Thomas Griffiths (1794-1852), 376 *note*.
Waller, 115 *sq*., 172, 182.
Walpole, Horace, 212, 245 *note*.
Ward, Humphrey, his *English Poets*, 484 *sq*.
Warton, Joseph (1722 - 1800), 246, 259, 261, 389.
—— Thomas, the elder (1688 ?-1745), 62 *note*, 212, 526.
—— Thomas, the younger (1728-90), 246, 261-265, 307, 526.
Watson, James (King's printer in Scotland, 1711-22), 190, 247.
—— Thomas, Bishop of Lincoln, 44.
Webbe, William (*fl. c.* 1580), 61-65.
Webster, John, 70.
Welsted, Leonard (1688-1742), 163, 164.
Wesley, Samuel, 146.
West, Gilbert, 215 *note*.
Whately, 203.
Wheeler, Benjamin, 526.
Whetstone, George (*fl. c.* 1580), 69 *note*.

Whitfield, John, 526.
Wild, 117.
Wilson, John, "Christopher North" (1785-1854), 229, 414, 431, 439.
—— [Sir] Thomas (?-1581), 31-34.
Winchelsea, Lady, 157, 211, 218.
Winstanley, William (1628 ?-90 ?), 139, 140.
Wither, 117, 139, 352.
Wolcot, John, "Peter Pindar" (1738-1819), 396 *sq*.
Wordsworth, William (1770 - 1850), 85, 310-328, 339, 353, 359, 378, 400, 532 *sq*.
Works of the Learned, the, 146 *note*.
Worsfold, Mr, 78 *note*, 170 *sq*.
Wotton, 183.
Wrangham, Archdeacon, 311.
Wright, Thomas (1810 - 77), 393 *note*.
Wyatt, Sir Thomas (1503-42), 42 *sq*.
Wynn, C. W., 344.

Yalden, 228.
Young, 299.

Zoilus, 137.
Zürich School, the, 249.

THE END.

Printed in Great Britain by
WILLIAM BLACKWOOD & SONS LTD.